# LED ZEPPELIN

# LED ZEPPELIN

The Biography

## BOB SPITZ

PENGUIN PRESS   NEW YORK   2021

PENGUIN PRESS
An imprint of Penguin Random House LLC
penguinrandomhouse.com

Page 651 constitutes an extension of this copyright page.

LIBRARY OF CONGRESS CATALOGING-IN-PUBLICATION DATA
Names: Spitz, Bob, author.
Title: Led Zeppelin: the biography / Bob Spitz.
Description: New York: Penguin Press, 2021. |
Includes bibliographical references and index.
Identifiers: LCCN 2020055742 (print) | LCCN 2020055743 (ebook) |
ISBN 9780399562426 (hardcover) | ISBN 9780399562433 (ebook)
Subjects: LCSH: Led Zeppelin (Musical group) |
Rock musicians—England—Biography.
Classification: LCC ML421.L4 S75 2021 (print) |
LCC ML421.L4 (ebook) | DDC 782.42166092/2 [B]—dc23
LC record available at https://lccn.loc.gov/2020055742
LC ebook record available at https://lccn.loc.gov/2020055743

Printed in the United States of America
1   3   5   7   9   10   8   6   4   2

Book design by Daniel Lagin

*for Scott Moyers*

Rock 'n roll will not go on like this. There will be a day of reckoning. It is no longer enough for a band to offer us only greed, bravado, and blatant insincerity and to call that entertainment. There may be some misguided souls who are prepared to buy it now, but there is no future in it.

—Jon Landau, "Led Zeppelin: Nothing Was Delivered"
*The Boston Phoenix*, September 9, 1970

Fuck the sixties, we're going to chart the new decade!

—Jimmy Page

# Contents

Prologue 1

1. A Case of the Blues 13

2. Getting Down to Business 42

3. Reinventing the Wheel 64

4. Front 85

5. The Black Country 107

6. Don't Tread on Me 133

7. Breaking Through the Sound Barrier 164

8. The New Normal 186

9. Into the Distant Past 217

10. Invoking and Being Invocative 243

11. Just Boys Having Fun 270

12. A Law unto Themselves 296

13. The Land of *Mondo Bizarro* 324

14. **Led Zeppelin Was Otherwise Engaged**     344

15. **Flying Too Close to the Sun**     371

16. **Home Away from Home**     395

17. **The Year of Living Dangerously**     422

18. **The Other Side of the Spectrum**     446

19. **Their Own Private Sodom and Gomorrah**     472

20. **A Transition Period**     500

21. **Swan Song**     528

22. **Coda**     554


Acknowledgments     577

Notes     581

Bibliography     645

Photo Credits     651

Index     653

# LED ZEPPELIN

# Prologue

---

## Sunday, January 26, 1969

They had been playing the band throughout the week. Entire sides of the album. FM radio, the underground free-form pipeline, was a godsend. He'd been tuned in to WNEW-FM, New York's preeminent alternative outlet, when it started: "Dazed and Confused," "Communication Breakdown," "You Shook Me," even "Babe, I'm Gonna Leave You," a Joan Baez number that had been hot-wired and jacked. Scott Muni, the station's afternoon deejay, couldn't help himself. He played the grooves off that record. Alison Steele, NEW's Nightbird, programmed it as though it were on a loop.

Led Zeppelin.

The name alone had visceral power. Sure, it was incongruous. A lead zeppelin was the ultimate sick joke, but spelling it "Led" took nerve. It told you everything you needed to know about this band— it was dynamic, irreverent, subversive, *extreme*—primed to rock 'n roll, not a toady to Top 40 populism. Led Zeppelin wasn't gonna hold your hand or take your daddy's T-Bird away. They meant business. This was serious, meaty stuff.

He loved what he'd heard. All that was left was to see them for himself.

As luck would have it, his friend Henry Smith was humping Led Zeppelin's equipment into a club in Boston that weekend. If he could get himself to the gig, Smith had agreed to slip him into the show. But how? He was basically broke. They'd been crashing at his parents' apartment in Yonkers, where his band, Chain Reaction, had been scratching for work. If he was going to get to Boston, he'd have to hitch.

Sunday-afternoon traffic was sparse along the I-95 corridor. The weather hadn't cooperated. An area of low pressure in Oklahoma had been creeping its way eastward, dropping temperatures below the freezing point along the Atlantic coastline. The sky was grim. The forecast predicted a nor'easter would hit Boston later that night or to-morrow morning. With a little luck, he might beat it to the gig.

A ride . . . then another, as the succession of cars plowed up the interstate, stitching a seam from Stamford to Bridgeport to New Haven to Providence and beyond. The songs in his head carried him through dozens of miles. These days, you couldn't take a breath without inhaling a killer. "Jumpin' Jack Flash," "Dock of the Bay," "All Along the Watchtower," "White Room," "Hey Jude," "Heard It Through the Grapevine," "Hurdy Gurdy Man," "Fire." You could feast all day on those babies and never go hungry. But Led Zeppelin had thrown him an emotional curve. Their songs hit him deep. There was something dark and sensual about them, something strangely provocative in their nature. They rolled over him, allowing his imagination to run wild.

Small wonder that they'd erupted via Jimmy Page. He knew all about Page, a guitar virtuoso in the tradition of Clapton, Stills, and Jimmy's itchy alter ego Jeff Beck, with whom Page had served a brief but stormy stretch in the Yardbirds as that seminal band was coming apart at the seams. There was already a heady mystique about Page. He'd contributed uncredited licks to scores of hit records, not least on sessions with The Who, the Kinks, and Them. But Page had taken Led

Zeppelin into another dimension, a province of rock 'n roll that was hard to define. Sometimes it was basic and bluesy, sometimes improvisational, other times a hybrid strain they were calling heavy metal, and all of it seasoned with enough folk, funk, and rockabilly elements to blur the lines. That was a lot to take in for a budding rock 'n roller. Seeing Page and his band would help to put things in perspective.

It was dark by the time he pulled up at the gig, a club called the Tea Party in a converted Unitarian meeting house–cum–synagogue that stood halfway along a solitary street. A hallucinatory gloom had fallen over the South End of Boston, casting East Berkeley Street in a desolate embrace. This was not the Boston of wealthy Brahmins, of culture and entitlement. "It was a tough neighborhood, a place you didn't want to hang out at night," says Don Law, who ran the joint. There was no sign of life in the surrounding tenements, aside from a bodega next door, whose light threw a waxy fluorescence across the pitted sidewalk. In the silhouette it projected, he could make out the outlines of heads, shoulders hunched against the cold, stretching down the street and around the corner. There must have been—what?—a couple hundred people waiting in line to get in. More.

*Where the hell did everyone come from?*

Led Zeppelin was hardly a household name. Until recently, they'd actually been billing themselves as the New Yardbirds. Their debut album had been released only two weeks earlier. Sure, he'd expected the freaks and the diehards, but this turnout was way off the chart. Obviously, word had rumbled out along the jungle drums. It wasn't unheard of. "We'd have a totally unknown British act open on Thursday," Don Law recalls, "and there'd be lines down the street by Saturday." He'd seen it with Jethro Tull, Humble Pie, and Ten Years After, all of whom had played the club during the past few months. Radio helped to a large degree. Boston's FM rock venue, WBCN, was still a novelty, in its infancy. Most of its broadcasts were piped right out of an anteroom at the Tea Party, its jocks a ragtag assortment of ex-college kids from the communications departments at Tufts and Emerson.

Bands would come off the stage and do an on-the-spot interview. FM airplay of any good album had become one of the surefire weapons to launch a new act. With Led Zeppelin, the evidence was right there on the sidewalk.

Getting into the Tea Party for their final performance was going to take some doing. The lines looked daunting; the hitchhiker feared he'd arrived too late. Fortunately, Henry Smith had been on the lookout for him near the door, and the two men disappeared inside before management—or the fire department—could cut off admission.

You could tell from the vibe. An air of expectancy pulsed through the room. The crowd was on top of it. They were ready.

The Tea Party wasn't the most conventional place to showcase a band like this one. It was hard to get past its house-of-worship layout. The stage was a former pulpit with the legend PRAISE YE THE LORD chiseled above the altar; the ballroom floor was pockmarked where pews had been removed; and a huge stained-glass window sported the Star of David. If the music piped over the PA system wasn't exactly liturgical, the psychedelic light show beaming liquid designs from the overhead balcony was downright profane. No service had ever packed in a congregation like the one thronging the hall. The club was legally outfitted to hold seven hundred, but the audience had long ago exceeded that number. The crowd was back to back, belly to belly.

The band had soldiered through a solid three-night warm-up. The Thursday-, Friday-, and Saturday-night shows had gone pretty much as they'd hoped, delivering hard-hitting sets that, as a reviewer noted, "lived up to [their] advance billing as a group of exceptional power and drive." For the most part, Led Zeppelin ran through the highlights of their debut album, slipping in the occasional Yardbirds or Chuck Berry number. Long, discursive solos conjured up improvisational fragments of R&B or blues favorites. Was that "Mockingbird" tucked into "I Can't Quit You Baby"? A few bars of "Duke of Earl"? The familiar riff of "Cat's Squirrel"? Jimmy Page's playing, especially, was loose and luxurious. He felt at home at the Tea Party, having appeared there only nine months earlier during a Yardbirds tour. Then, in June 1968, a few months later, Page and his manager, Peter Grant, had turned up to check out the latest incarnation of another of Grant's acts, the Jeff Beck Group, with a lineup featuring Ronnie Wood and Rod Stewart.

Don Law recalls how Grant arrived before Beck had gone on that day, cradling an acetate as though it were a precious artifact. "This is a new band called the New Yardbirds," he said, as the three men settled in a funky little office at the back of the stage. Listening to the test pressing while Grant and Page exchanged subtle glances, Law knew immediately he had to book the act before a canny competitor snatched them. And Grant talked him into a four-night stand.

He hoped this Sunday-night show on January 26 would give Boston something to talk about.

Law spent a few minutes backstage an hour before showtime that night, chatting with Page, a delicate, almost wraithlike creature who radiated rock-star heat. Law had street cred with Page, owing to his father, also named Don Law, who, in Texas in the mid-1930s, had produced the only known recordings—a mere twenty-nine songs—attributed to blues legend Robert Johnson. Page was as hooked on the influence of Johnson's music as his pals Eric Clapton and Jeff Beck, and he interrogated Law, practically browbeat him, for any unexplored Johnson morsel that would give him more insight into the music. Eavesdropping on their conversation was Zeppelin's feline vocalist, Robert Plant, himself a huge Johnson fan.

"One of the things I picked up from Robert Johnson when I started singing was the liaison between the guitar playing and his voice," Plant noted years later. "It was so sympathetic. It almost seemed as if the guitar was his vocal cords."

Plant was a blues aficionado who had been plumbing arcane Chicago-based anthologies, listening to tracks he could co-opt, since he was fourteen years old. Muddy Waters, Skip James, Son House, Snooks Eaglin—they were all part of Plant's education. Just that Thursday afternoon, a young fan helping the roadies had a tape copy of *King*

*of the Delta Blues Singers Vol. 1,* with a pair of Johnson ballads on it.
Plant considered Robert Johnson the musician "to whom we all owe
more or less our very existence." He strained to overhear Law and
Page's exchange, but there was too much noise, and instead Plant con-
tented himself with sipping his hot tea, prepping his vocal cords, while
his bandmates, bass player John Paul Jones and drummer John Bonham, each clutching a pint of Watney's Red Barrel, stationed themselves across the room, in a huddle with a BCN disc jockey named
J. J. Jackson.

There was a perceptible distance, even an awkwardness, among
the band members that precluded more intimacy. They were still in the
dating phase, still getting to know one another, still developing a camaraderie. They'd only been a unit for slightly more than four months,
assembled by Jimmy Page, the way a cook might choose ingredients
for a recipe. Page and John Paul Jones had known each other as jour-
neymen session players on the London studio circuit; Robert Plant
and John Bonham were mates from the Midlands. Though no one
would admit it, a whiff of the North-South divide lingered in the air.

Their shows had blown hot and cold since they'd landed in the
States at the close of 1968. Debuts in Los Angeles and San Francisco
were star-is-born type affairs. Delirious critics in those cities sized up
Led Zeppelin as phenoms who "were jamming as if they had been
playing together for years" and "ranked in the company of The Who,
Rolling Stones, and the late Cream." The Toronto reviewer said, "Several critics, myself included, had suggested Led Zeppelin just might be
the next so-called supergroup." Jimmy Page felt the lift-off. "After the
San Francisco gig, it was just—bang!" he said.

But often the venues Zeppelin played were ill equipped, the PA
systems Paleolithic, and arrangements sounded about as polished as
high school recitals. In Detroit, in front of an audience of local lumi-
naries like MC5 and the Amboy Dukes, a reviewer in the very first
issue of *Creem* noted, "Each member of the group was on a separate
riff, not at all together. . . . They were playing different things simulta-

neously." It was cringeworthy but forgivable. Growing pains were a common symptom of new bands. Led Zeppelin was no exception. "We got better each day and found ourselves making things up as we went along," Jimmy Page explained not long afterward. The band ached to knock a show out of the park.

A lot depended on the audience. A band draws on the energy in the hall, and the Tea Party was revving up.

When disc jockey Charlie Daniels ambled onstage as the lights came down, the cheers in that old tabernacle sent a chill up the spine of the hitchhiker, posted along the back wall near the door. He took in the scene with a sense of awe. He hoped this band was as good as the hype.

At the back of the hall, a door flung open, and the four musicians marched theatrically through the crowd—"like kings, like conquering heroes parting the masses"—to the front of the stage.

"Here they are," Daniels roared, riding the wave of the buildup. "From England—let's give a warm Boston welcome to *Leddddddd Zeppelin!*"

A sound like a siren cut through the darkness before the spot came up and found Robert Plant contorted, Gumby-like, over the mic, his hand cupped around a harmonica. His bluesy plaint was mimicked by a sinewy guitar line from Jimmy Page's Les Paul as they launched into "The Train Kept a-Rollin'," an old Yardbirds standby, but on steroids and at a pitch that could restore hearing to the deaf. The version, rollicking and capable, served to get the crowd's attention.

Then a wounded-animal cry growled out: "*I . . . I . . . I can't quit you baby. Wooooo-man, I'm gonna put you down a little while.*"

It was the voice of someone who'd experienced despair and heartbreak and had seen the inside of a Southern prison. But somehow it was coming out of the mouth of a skinny, twenty-year-old white guy with hair that would make Goldilocks envious. Plant had stolen the motif out from under generations of immortal Negro minstrels, yet it was more than a cultural appropriation. It was heartfelt. There was a rawness to his delivery that spoke more to the future than to the past, sparked by instrumentation that turned the blues idiom on its head. The playing wasn't indicative of a juke joint so much as a garage. It was loud and aggressive. Page attached jumper cables to the solo break, playing it as if Buddy Guy had gone berserk. His fingers flew up and down the frets as if they were too hot for him to linger on any one for too long. The bass, which John Paul Jones—known as Jonesy by his mates—had cranked as high as his amp could withstand, sent tremors through the crowd. "The vibrations," said an observer in the crowd, "hit your chest with physical force." And the drummer, John Bonham, didn't play the drums—he attacked them "like a runaway freight train." The snare beats were so sharp they sounded like gunfire strafing the room.

By the time Led Zeppelin launched into "Communication Breakdown" a few songs later, the crowd was whipped into a trance state. Heads bouncing, hands jerking, bodies flinging helter-skelter to the beat, the floor of the Tea Party resembled a tribal bacchanal. "You could feel the whole building moving and shaking," recalled an Atlantic Records promotion man looking on that night.

The band was loose, lightheaded from the contact high off the crowd, and the well-rehearsed arrangements had lapsed into free-form jams riddled with improvisation. Rhythms and time patterns changed abruptly. "Dazed and Confused" segued into "Shapes of Things," and Jimmy Page, imitating a hippie Merlin, pulled out a violin bow and sawed it across the strings of his guitar, "getting sound and feedback that was as radical as anyone had heard since [Jimi] Hendrix." A punchy number called "Pat's Delight," featuring an elaborate, five-minute drum solo, saw Bonham, nicknamed Bonzo for good reason, fling away his sticks and play the skins and cymbals with bare hands, egged on by howls of encouragement. The band interrupted its last number, "How Many More Times," to interject pieces of "Smokestack Lightning," "Beck's Bolero," "For Your Love," "The Duke of Earl," and "Over Under Sideways Down" into the mix. "If you don't want to jump, dance, and smile after hearing this, you must be dead," the giddy *Boston Phoenix* critic would marvel.

There was pandemonium at the end of the hour-long set. Led Zeppelin, spent and elated, took several bows and disappeared backstage while the crowd erupted in uncontainable ecstasy. The band celebrated with a round of thirst-quenching Watney's. A chorus of *"More! More! More!"* persisted in the ballroom, picking up steam as each minute passed. It was clear they'd have to go out and play again. But— *what?* They'd exhausted their repertoire. After some deliberation, it was decided they'd play the same set again. What else could they do? It was unheard of. This time they stretched out solos, especially Page's "White Summer" guitar piece that took great aural liberties with the violin bow. And Plant had the temerity to milk Joan Baez's "Babe, I'm Gonna Leave You" for all it was worth in a city that held its hometown sweetheart on the same pedestal as the Madonna. The band gave it everything they had. They looked as though they'd gone through a steam bath. A sweating Page and Bonham had stripped down to their vests, and Plant's tie-dyed T-shirt was soaked through to his chest.

When they'd finished—again—the reaction turned frightening. Applause gave way to stomping and thrashing. "There were kids actually bashing their heads against the stage," a dumbstruck John Paul Jones recalled. The hitchhiker was crying. Crying! "Zeppelin was so fucking heavy," he said, "that I had no other emotional way to react to them."

"You've got to go back," Don Law implored the band after they'd collapsed backstage.

He had to be kidding. No way they were going to play that set again. It was a miracle they'd gotten away with doing it twice, much less had the stamina to pull it off the way they did. That was it, that was the show. Besides, a few nights later they were due in New York, expected to make their debut there at the vaunted Fillmore East. They had to reserve whatever was left in the tank.

After five minutes of unadulterated bedlam, however, they realized it was hopeless. They had to appease the crowd, if for no other reason than to settle them down. Otherwise they were going to rip that place apart.

"It was in such a state that we had to start throwing ideas around," said John Paul Jones, "just thinking of songs that we might all know or that some of us knew a part of, and work it from there."

An hour later, Led Zeppelin had exhausted a full set of cover songs lifted from the set lists of their respective boyhood bands. They just winged them right there onstage, deferring to whichever one of them had a feel for a particular tune. They ripped through a blistering version of "Long Tall Sally"; a couple Eddie Cochran numbers—"Somethin' Else" and "C'mon Everybody"—which Jimmy Page had performed with Red E. Lewis & the Redcaps; a pair of Beatles favorites, "I Saw Her Standing There" and "Please Please Me"; and a Chuck Berry medley of "Roll Over Beethoven" and "Johnny B. Goode" that gave everyone onstage a chance to solo.

As they staggered into the dressing room, Peter Grant, Zeppelin's manager, a behemoth of a man, scooped them into a group grizzly-bear hug, lifting them several inches off their feet. The usually scowling Grant, Jones noticed, "was crying, if you can imagine that," his mouth stretched unnaturally in what the Brits called a nanker. Jimmy Page felt it. He later said that this was *the moment*—the moment he knew they "were actually going to make it." John Paul Jones considered that night at the Tea Party "*the* key Led Zeppelin gig—the one that put everything into focus." After several months of going through the paces—getting to know each other, choosing material, refining a sound, playing a string of gigs in shitty little halls under abysmal circumstances for what amounted to pocket change—months of uncertainty marked by worry and self-doubt, they'd morphed from a wan flock of New Yardbirds into Led Zeppelin, a powerhouse of a rock 'n roll band.

There was no doubting it. Led Zeppelin had played themselves into hero status in Boston, obliging an otherwise jaded critic to admit,

"For four consecutive evenings, they virtually blew an overflow Boston Tea Party crowd clear into the Charles River."

No one realized it more than the hitchhiker. He staggered out into the night. The music was tighter and had a harder edge than anything he'd heard before, played without mercy at a volume that drilled down into the central nervous system. Man, was it loud! He'd never heard six huge Rickenbacker Transonic amps cranking at peak in that small of a space before. The output had whipped people into a frenzy. And the vocalist, Robert Plant, was a revelation. His delivery took the blues to another level, gave it something darker and dirtier than, say, Mick Jagger's foppish theatrics. The hitchhiker had a similar role as front man in his own band, and Plant's magnetism, his flamboyance, had given him ideas. He needed to burnish his image. He'd been thinking of changing his name, for starters. "Steven Tallarico" didn't quite cut it as a rock god; "Steven Tyler" would have more snap. He couldn't wait to get back to his bandmates in Sunapee, New Hampshire, where his parents had a cottage. He wanted to share what he'd seen and heard with his guitarist, Joe Perry. They could do something with "Train Kept a-Rollin'," put their own spin on it, rough it up a bit.

Whatever they decided, it would have to kick ass, because Led Zeppelin had changed the rules of the game. They had done something primal to rock 'n roll. They'd taken its definitive, dynamic beat and supercharged it, turned it inside out, added splenetic distortion, and shot it off in a bold, new direction. The hitchhiker felt it. Hard rock, heavy metal, progressive—fans could call it whatever they liked. Music was about to get a lot more complicated.

## Chapter One

# A CASE OF THE BLUES

## [1]

In the beginning there was the blues. Before jazz, before swing, and long before rock 'n roll, the blues gave voice to African American life in a world of harsh reality. You might be going down to the crossroads to ask the Lord for mercy, making your midnight creep like the backdoor man, or keeping your lamplight trimmed and burning—no matter how it stacked up, brother, you got a case of the blues. You got the blues if you got a woman with the meanest face in town, if you ask for water and your darlin' give you gas-o-line, and if you're fixin' to die. If you got your mojo working, a good twelve-bar blues could cure any number of woes (except, of course, the summertime blues), and in the early 1960s, a generation of postwar British teenagers discovered it was a remedy for the ennui that stifled their very lives.

If the fifties were any indication, they were in for a slog. As a sector of the general public, British teenagers more than deserved to sing the blues. They were a nonentity, classless in a society that prized a stratum of huffy sirs and lords. Teens had no disposable income, zero influence, and little future to look forward to. In most circumstances, they'd wind up in a dead-end job, apprenticed to a factory shop steward, or indentured as a low-level clerk in a lifeless administrative office. Any relief would come from evenings spent in a local pub, getting shit-faced and singing along to moldering World War I–era ditties to blot out the tedium: "Ma, He's Makin' Eyes at Me," "Daddy Wouldn't Buy Me a Bow-Wow," "Knees Up Mother Brown," "K-K-Katy, Show Me the Way to Go Home." God, what a trap! They had to change the tune.

The music being fed to them was an abysmal porridge of torchy music-hall leftovers, orchestral scores, and banal hit-parade crooners that the BBC played with captive indifference. The Beeb's anesthetizing *Two-Way Family Favourites* and *Housewives' Choice*—the only radio programs where popular music was heard—might throw teens a bone by playing one or two numbers by lightweight crooner Tommy Steele or skiffling Lonnie Donegan, and if a deejay felt unusually charitable, a Hank Williams or Roy Acuff classic. The club scene wasn't much hipper. For the most part, it attracted a young crowd that jived to a strain called trad—as in *traditional*—jazz, which was really a rehash of Dixieland played by middle-aged white men, some of whom wore bowler hats.

The Swingin' Sixties were still years off when, in 1960, trad jazz master Chris Barber ceded the closing half hour of his band's residency at London's Marquee Club to an unlikely pair of bluesmen. Alexis Korner and Cyril "Squirrel" Davies were neither Black nor especially world-weary, but their mongrel brand of electrified blues set off sparks among a young, restless audience determined to bust out. They were bored with both the mummery of old-school jazz and the insipid pop of Cliff Richard and Adam Faith. By 1962, Korner, a mediocre guitar player with impeccable taste, and Davies, a hatchet-faced Buckinghamshire bloke who blew the meanest Chicago-style harp, were fronting an outfit they called Blues Incorporated and opened a club to showcase the band in a West London basement directly opposite the Ealing Broadway Tube stop.

The music they played owed its DNA to a concert at St. Pancras Town Hall on October 20, 1958, at which Muddy Waters made his London debut. British audiences were used to a steady cycle of American blues tours featuring folk-blues artists like Big Bill Broonzy, Lonnie Johnson, and Josh White, all of whom accompanied themselves on acoustic guitars. At this show, Muddy had the cheek to plug his Telecaster into an *amp*. What sacrilege! The audience recoiled at his stinging solo lines. It was the first time they'd ever heard electric blues, and to many it "sounded tough, unpolite . . . often very loud." People actually booed, the same way Brits would boo Bob Dylan when he "went electric" in 1966. As Muddy cranked the volume incrementally through "Honey Bee," "Long Distance Call," "I Can't Be Satisfied," and "Louisiana Blues," he set off a depth charge with his urban take on the blues. It put an end to the genteel trad jazz–blues mash-up and, as one historian noted, "reverberate[d] through the annals of rock for the next fifty years."

No doubt about it, four years later its tremors still shook the insides of the Ealing Club. Saturday nights there became life-changing affairs.

The sweaty, foul-smelling joint, "sometimes ankle-deep in condensation," jumped with kids who lived on the fringe, who were curious, who couldn't fit in anywhere else. The blues had become their canon, and Blues Incorporated their unlikely prophet. The night the club opened to a packed house, March 17, 1962, the unit featured a fluid lineup of ex–jazz musicians that included drummer Charlie Watts and Ian Stewart on piano. Sporadically, amateurs would be plucked out of the crowd and invited to sit in. That night, Alexis Korner spotted a slight, pale bottleneck-slide guitarist he knew as Elmo Lewis and called him up to the stage. Lewis had hitchhiked ninety miles from Cheltenham to snag a chance walk on with Blues Incorporated, and now he whipped admirably through the fade-out solo to Elmore James's signature "Dust My Broom." Afterward, Elmo Lewis spotted a friend standing with two gangly teenagers at the back of the club and joined them for a chat.

"Of course, I knew Lewis by his real name, Brian Jones," the friend, David Williams, recalls, "and I introduced him to Mick and Keith, who were both impressed with his performance."

These boys were captivated by the blues—perhaps *obsessed* would be a better word. To find like-minded souls in a vacuum was no small thing. A fantastic amount of musical scuttlebutt got exchanged in the interim. The give-and-take that night went something like this:

"Who are you listening to?"

"I've heard this Memphis Slim record, 'Steppin' Out,' with a fantastic guitar solo on it."

"Who's on guitar?"

"That's Matthew Murphy."

"*Jeeeeez*, Matthew Murphy!"

The new music scene was happening very fast, with Blues Incorporated as its unstable nucleus. Alumni split off to form equally mutable groups. Not long after nineteen-year-old Mick Jagger appeared as the vocalist with the band, "all lips and ears . . . looking like a ventriloquist's dummy," he made off with drummer Charlie Watts. Watts was replaced by Peter "Ginger" Baker, and Jack Bruce stepped in on bass. In the following months John Baldry, Eric Burdon, and Rod Stewart turned up to take their shots at the Ealing Club mic, as did a petrified Eric Clapton, who belted out a credible version of "Roll Over Beethoven," while staring woodenly at the floor. You never knew who was going to turn up. A seminal night featured Brian Jones's buddy Paul Pond, singing the blues in his best Oxbridge accent, years before he resurfaced as Manfred Mann's vocalist, Paul Jones. The club was a cauldron bubbling over with talent.

Saturday nights at the Ealing Club begat Thursday blues nights at the Marquee, a venerable Oxford Street jazz mecca in a cellar below the Academy Cinema that begrudgingly hosted the arrivistes. By the beginning of December 1962, the blues night was pulling in upward of a thousand enthusiasts who chipped away at the Marquee's button-down legacy. Thursday nights soon begat Monday nights, and the Marquee begat the Flamingo, the 100 Club, Studio 51, Eel Pie Island, the Red Lion in Sutton, the Crawdaddy Club in Richmond, the Railway Hotel in Harrow, and the Ricky-Tick in Windsor, as the blues exploded and the scene dug in.

Record albums with obscure material were the purest form of currency. It was nearly impossible to buy a blues album in London at the time. You might stumble over a secondhand specimen in the dusty basement annex of Dobell's Jazz Shop. If one was fortunate enough to unearth a rare gem—say, Howlin' Wolf's 1959 Chess masterpiece, *Moanin' in the Moonlight*, with its scorching rendition of "Smokestack Lightning," or any of the Duke Records imports by Junior Parker, Otis Rush, or Bobby "Blue" Bland—you were *the man*. What a bond it created. "If one person got a record, everybody had it," Dave Williams recalls. The album would be passed around, scrutinized, dissected, interpreted, turned inside out, and analyzed until every last nuance had been picked off its vinyl carcass.

That's what happened when Mick, Keith, and Brian got their hands on a twelve-inch compilation LP called *Bluesville Chicago*, showcasing five of Vee-Jay Records' earthiest artists. It may have been Mick who found it at Dobell's on Charing Cross Road. He haunted that place on Friday afternoons during lunch breaks from classes at the London School of Economics, around the corner. In any case, the album was a gold mine as far as material was concerned, authentic blues that no one else in Britain was doing. With songs like that you could even start a band, which is what the three boys—Jagger, Keith Richards, and Brian Jones—decided. It gave them a solid repertoire to work with, and they immediately rehearsed two Eddie Taylor songs—"Bad Boy" and "Ride 'Em On Down"—as well as "I Wish You Would," "I Ain't Got You," and "Don't Stay Out All Night" courtesy of Billy Boy Arnold.

At the outset, they called themselves the Rollin' Stones, only a trio, months away from a legitimate bass player and drummer. Their first gig, just a jam really, was in the back room of the Grapes, a pub at the bottom of Sutton High Street. Fifteen people turned up, of whom only three actually paid to get in, and they ran down the five songs, along with "Too Much Monkey Business," a Chuck Berry number. Unqualified to headline more substantial gigs, they regularly performed with Alexis Korner's band, playing rudimentary versions of Berry and Bo Diddley B sides.

The Rollin' Stones, perhaps more than anyone, embodied the new sound of the blues. It wasn't anything a young band had played before. They'd taken the Chicago style and given it a churlish British spin. Somehow, both in Mick's punk snarl and the down-and-dirty guitar licks, they locked onto the campy sexual innuendo embedded in the lyrics and laid it bare. The way they played the blues left no doubt what it meant to "look up under the hood and check out the carburetor." "Whatever it was, it was twisted, amplified and warped beyond any hope of familiarity," said Jim McCarty, later the drummer for the Yardbirds, who caught one of the Stones' earliest shows in Richmond, a suburb in the southwest of London. "It was an exhilarating sound, incredibly original." To McCarty, "It was like seeing a band from Mars."

Even with a pared-down ensemble, the Stones made it clear they could not be contained. They worked relentlessly on gentrifying the blues, reinterpreting its sound to accommodate a younger, restless, *whiter* audience. And they weren't alone. Cyril Davies's R&B All-Stars, led by vocalist Long John Baldry with Rod Stewart on harmonica, took over Thursday nights at the Marquee, and John Mayall's Blues Syndicate spread the scene to such venues as Klooks Kleek, Eel Pie Island, and the Fishermen's Arms. For a generation of British teenagers primed to make their mark, the blues had become a state of mind.

A jolt rattled the community in September 1962, when word began circulating that the gods were amassing . . . in Manchester of all places. If the rumors were true, authentic blues artists—not teenage wannabes but high priests of the Mississippi Delta and Chicago's South Side—had agreed to appear for one night at the Free Trade Hall on Sunday, October 21. Word went around "like bloody hellfire," the names mentioned in a reverent hush. *John Lee Hooker. Sonny Terry &*

*Brownie McGhee. T-Bone Walker. Memphis Slim. Willie Dixon.* Together, in person, under one roof. *The American Folk Blues Festival.* As one of the Ealing Club regulars put it: "This was serious shit!"

Indeed. A caravan of disciples from London was organized with the precision of an RAF offensive. A builder's van was hired and a driver, Graham Ackers—the only boy with a driver's license—recruited for the five-hour trip north. Brian Jones, Mick Jagger, and Keith Richards were picked up at a square in London and, with four others, were jammed like sardines into the windowless capsule with nothing more than side benches for seats. Be that as it may, music made up for the pitiful accommodations. Graham Ackers had brought along tape copies of *Swing Low*, a new French release by the Staple Singers, whose last song on side 2 had the refrain "This may be the last time, may be the last time, I don't know." Another passenger, named Mick Sales, was carrying the brand-new album *Howlin' Wolf*, with a rocking chair on the cover, which became the main topic of conversation for a portion of the trip. (Later, when they managed to locate a record player, it was the first time any of the boys heard "Little Red Rooster.") The only person absent from the delegation was nineteen-year-old Jimmy Page, an acolyte on the fringe of that circle, who had a gig that night playing with Neil Christian & the Crusaders and would take the train to Manchester, arriving late Sunday afternoon.

It was a long, edgy drive up the provincial M1, the first time any of the van's passengers had traveled on a motorway. Not all of the logistics had been carefully planned. There was nowhere to stay in Manchester when they arrived Saturday at dusk. The more fortunate crashed at a student flat, Brian Jones sought cover in the YMCA, while Mick and Keith, seriously broke, simply slept in the uninsulated van. Sunday morning was misty and cold. As the first show didn't start until six o'clock, they had to kill most of the day, largely spent walking the streets of the city and lingering over a single dish in a Chinese restaurant. Their conversation, which stretched on for hours, was woefully single-minded.

"Is Hooker going to sound like his record?"

"Are they going to play our favorite songs?"

Mick wondered if the harmonica would be amplified. "You think Shaky Jake Harris will blow directly into the mic?"

Around five o'clock, weary and talked out, they hooked up with Jimmy Page under an arcade of the Free Trade Hall, an Italianate palazzo-style structure in the center of town. Introductions were made to Mick, Keith, and Brian, and a rapport was immediate and deep felt. Jimmy already had the goods. Only nineteen at the time, he'd earned a reputation as a crackerjack guitarist, having played at the Marquee with Blues Incorporated and been a member of two well-known cover bands, Red E. Lewis & the Red Caps and Neil Christian & the Crusaders. Mick, Keith, and Brian were keen to milk his exploits, even though he wasn't part of their world. These were like-minded, kindred spirits, dedicated to music and a life that broke the bounds of convention.

Jimmy wasn't entirely unfamiliar with Brian Jones, whom he regarded as something of a blues prodigy. He'd already checked him out at the Ealing Club during one of Jones's solo sets. "I was struggling with the Elmore James stuff," Jimmy recalled. "Suddenly, it clicked. It was in the tuning. [Brian] was doing it." He'd been looking forward to meeting Brian, though that wasn't his primary objective. "I went because I really wanted to see John Lee Hooker."

The American blues artists were playing two concerts that night, and the boys had tickets for both—cheap seats in the rafters for the first show, but nearly ringside for the second. In between performances, they convened at the bar. Aside from Page, who enjoyed a full dance card of well-paying gigs, most could afford only a half of bitter. The conversation, on the other hand, was priceless.

They marveled at the impressive Memphis Slim, but more for his natty appearance than his florid delivery. The man certainly knew how to wear a suit. He was lithe and loose-limbed, and he looked the epitome of chic with his high-gloss, brilliantined hair, sporting a white Pepé Le Pew streak in the center of his forehead. Slim had rocked Arkansas honky-tonks and dance halls with a set of jump-blues stand-outs that included "Every Day I Have the Blues," "Steppin' Out," and "Rockin' the Blues," but he delivered them in a way that relied more on charm than on a conventional approach to the blues. Be that as it may, the young musicians watched spellbound during his set. They couldn't take their eyes off Slim's upright bass player, a man of prodigious proportions who stood over six foot six and handled the instrument as if it were a child's toy: the legendary Willie Dixon.

More than anyone, Dixon had shaped the sound of Chicago blues. One of Chess Records' irreplaceable cornerstones, he'd arranged and produced the earliest recordings of Otis Rush and Buddy Guy and worked with Howlin' Wolf, Sonny Boy Williamson, Jimmy Witherspoon, Muddy Waters, Chuck Berry, and Bo Diddley—the entire pantheon. Yet it was as a songwriter that Dixon left his indelible stamp. The Dixon songbook was the bible of the blues: "Hoochie Coochie Man," "I Just Want to Make Love to You," "Little Red Rooster," "Spoonful," "You Can't Judge a Book by the Cover," and—perhaps most impressive to the young Jimmy Page—"You Need Love," whose lyric kicks off with *You've got yearnin' and baby I got burnin'.*"

Dixon slapped that bass the way he might have manhandled one of the ring opponents he encountered on his way to the Illinois Golden Gloves Heavyweight Championship in 1937. He was the engine, the rudder, *and* the anchor behind Memphis Slim, and he backed the rest of the acts as each took its turn on the stage.

Mick Jagger and Brian Jones were particularly fixated on Shaky Jake Harris, who "produced a harmonica and blew as hard as he could directly into the microphone." This was the first time they'd ever seen this done. They had heard it was Little Walter's technique, but seeing was believing, and they were thrilled by the explosive sound it produced. They made mental notes for their upcoming gigs. Shaky Jake would leave his imprint on the Stones, but the night's coup de grace came at the hands of T-Bone Walker and John Lee Hooker.

None of the boys had ever witnessed such flamboyant showmanship.

Of course, they'd seen Chuck Berry duck-walking across the screen in *Rock, Rock, Rock!* and *Jazz on a Summer's Day*, but it didn't prepare them for the flash theatrics of T-Bone Walker. He roamed the stage like a gladiator, wielding his guitar as if it were a sword in a Roman coliseum. One observer recalled how "he dropped the guitar between his legs and then swung it up behind his head for a solo." Other times, he lay prone on the lip of the proscenium, facing the audience, and fingered the frets almost by osmosis. In the same way Shaky Jake landed on the young Stones, Jimmy Page never forgot the swashbuckling Walker.

John Lee Hooker, by comparison, was vegetative, the model of restraint—but just as impressive. His driving, boogie-style guitar was so idiosyncratic, mixing tempos and emphases as if they were cocktails, better shaken, not stirred. This was the real thing, the dark Delta blues that Jimmy Page had come to hear. "Boogie Chillun" and "I'm in the Mood" reverberated spiritually through the hall. Through Hooker's abbreviated set, Dave Williams recalls glancing at the men sitting on either side of him—Jimmy Page to his left, Keith Richards to his right. "Their jaws were on their knees," he says. "They were transfixed. They didn't so much as breathe through his set."

After a rousing finale, the boys couldn't contain themselves. They charged the stage while their blues heroes remained by the footlights, somewhat overwhelmed by the unexpected stampede. A squirrelly-faced Mick Jagger nervously thrust his program at his favorite performer—"Please, Mr. Hooker, can I have your autograph?"—as Hooker, looking shell-shocked by the attention, scrawled a signature across the cover. Meanwhile, Brian Jones collared Shaky Jake and cadged a trophy—the performer's harmonica. At the other end of the receiving line, Jimmy Page and Keith Richards managed to shake hands with their idols, but they remained speechless, overawed.

It wasn't until they reassembled in the van for the trip home that the emotional lid came off. The boys were jubilant, ecstatic. The blues had come alive for them. For the past few months, they'd been play-acting as blues artists, serving up what they *thought* the music should sound like. Now here it was, the genuine article, to savor and emulate. It was in their heads; they were drunk on it.

It was late, inching on midnight, by the time the van pulled out of Manchester. After some debate, they'd voted on an all-night drive back to London. Mick was due in class at ten the next morning, Keith needed to report for his job delivering the mail, and Jimmy was booked into a full day of recording sessions that required his early attendance. There was just enough gas left to make the trip, but in fact they could have gotten there on adrenaline alone.

"We were on a big high," Dave Williams recalls. Brian Jones upped the energy by pulling out Shaky Jake's harmonica and blowing a suggestive bluesy vamp. The entire van—even Jimmy Page, not the world's greatest vocalist—burst into song.

> *Bright lights, big city*
> *Gone to my baby's head . . .*

For a hundred miles or so, they worked through a medley of Jimmy Reed songs, segueing into "Big Boss Man," "Baby What You Want Me to Do," and "Shame, Shame, Shame." When they'd exhausted their voices, Brian, who was quite a good mimic, entertained the troops by doing spot-on impressions of their mentors, Alexis Korner and Cyril Davies, keeping the gang in stitches well into the dawn. His send-up of Davies's shuck and jive was particularly savage. "When I's sings a Jimmy Reed song, I's tends to sound like Jimmy Reed," he mugged, providing a mantra the gang recited upon greeting each other throughout the next year.

It was official: Great Britain was infatuated with the blues. By the spring of 1963, the Rolling Stones (no longer merely Rollin')—adding bass player Bill Wyman, Ian Stewart on piano, and drummer Charlie

Watts—had harnessed the power of roots R&B. They'd plundered the grooves of *Jimmy Reed at Carnegie Hall*, Howlin' Wolf's "rocking chair" album, and every Chuck Berry record known to man, investing those songs with a rock 'n roll backbeat, basically reinventing the blues. With a sturdy set of hybrid songs, the Stones eventually gravitated to playing at a makeshift club behind the Station Hotel in Richmond. Not just a gig but a *residency*—and with *fans*. "It was a matter of atmosphere," a local promoter reported. "They seemed in a world of their own as [the Stones] played music that electrified the whole place."

But it was Jimmy Page who was looking beyond the blues. By the summer of 1966, he was fronting the Yardbirds and putting the screws to the British electric blues idiom. The group's blues would become more progressive, less structured, tougher, scrappier; their gigs more unpredictable. But Jimmy Page still wasn't satisfied. The blues had laid the groundwork for a musical upheaval that would draw on innovation, technology, and volume, incredible volume. Page had a clear-eyed idea about the blues; to him, it functioned as a springboard to something bigger and more dynamic. And he knew exactly where he was taking it.

## [2]

Jimmy Page's blues didn't lay claim to either a Mississippi or a Chicago heritage. They originated deep in the Surrey Delta, a place not found on the coordinates of any map.

It seemed inconceivable that the trinity of British guitar gods—Page, Jeff Beck, and Eric Clapton—all hailed from a lush, wooded region in the southeast of England known more for millionaires than for the blues. The county, located on tributaries of the Thames, was part of the booming commuter belt of London. Jimmy's parents—James, a personnel manager in a plastic-coating factory, and Patricia, a dental nurse—moved there, to Epsom, in 1952, when their only child was eight years old.

Epsom was an old market town, with a classic central square flanked by distinctive Georgian-era features: a bank, a church, a town hall. Its best-known site was a redbrick clock tower, rising to seventy feet, which dominated the skyline and served as a hangout for local teenagers who lacked a more suitable place to meet. Throughout its early life, Epsom was rustic and sleepy. Nestled in the lap of unspoiled hills and plains, one could mistake it for Ewell, Guilford, Ashtead, Horsham, or any of the villages clustered nearby. But Epsom got a wake-up call in the latter half of the nineteenth century, when a rich vein of mineral springs transformed the tranquil town into a de rigueur health resort, attracting the upper crusty to its healing waters. The production of Epsom salts—lavish deposits of magnesium sulfate extracted from the waters—furthered the town's reputation as a tony spa, buttressed by five psychiatric hospitals built at the turn of the century. And twice a year, its population more than doubled to fifty thousand for the running of two classic English horse races on Epsom Downs.

The Pages occupied a standard semidetached "two-up, two-down" on Miles Road, a crescent of identical quotidian houses customary to postwar England. These were humble abodes, often lacking indoor toilets, and many, like Jimmy's, backed onto the railroad line to London. Epsom had its share of manors and estates, but Miles Road fell squarely on the wrong side of the tracks. "It was a nondescript street," recalls one of the Pages' neighbors. "There were hardly any cars, because no one could afford to have one, and nothing in the front yards to distinguish any house from the other." However, the back gardens, usually twice the depth of the houses, were precious tracts in those austere years, with almost every square foot devoted to growing vegetables.

Fortunately, there was no scarcity of playmates. The wartime baby boom had visited almost every house on Miles Road. On any given

day, Jimmy could kick a tennis ball around the street or go rollerskat-
ing with his next-door neighbor, Jeff Reese, or with David Housego or
Pete Neal or Dave Williams, all of whom lived on the block. A lot of
the neighborhood boys Jimmy's age were sons of American servicemen stationed in England, so at school they often played baseball instead of cricket.

The Americans also imported their incomparable music. They
owned records—mostly country and western and rockabilly, in addition to a smattering of Chess, Checker, Sun, and esoteric label issues
that straddled the breach between rhythm and blues and nascent
rock 'n roll. Given that the Americans picked up and moved often, many
of those records wound up in secondhand shops, mixed in with jukebox discards—and into the hands of British kids who retrieved them.
Jimmy's mate Dave Williams actively salvaged these rejects by sorting
through endless dusty bins, selecting any records with singers whose
names sounded interesting—*American*. Among them were the long-
forgotten pioneers of recording history, like Texas Tyler, Jackie Lee
Cochran, Wade Hall, Jessie Hill, and Ronnie Self. "So many were
complete and utter junk," Williams recalls, "but every now and then
I'd come up with a Johnny Burnette Trio or a Carl Perkins and rush
right over to Jimmy's to share my discovery."

Jimmy found the music irresistible. "He liked to listen to records on the radio," his mother recalled. The Pages, like most British
families, had a boxy mahogany radiogram in the front room of the
house, and Jimmy worked its Bakelite dials with a safecracker's expertise. Radio Luxembourg, the airwaves' only link to rock 'n roll in the
UK, could be tuned in when the heavens cooperated. Its staticky reception, sounding like it was filtered through a wind tunnel, hinted at
the revolution brewing on the horizon. "You had to stick by the radio
and listen to overseas radio to even hear good rock records," Jimmy
recalled. He never missed a broadcast. On a clear night, with his ear
pressed to the speaker, he might pick up fragments of Fats Domino or
Buddy Holly or LaVern Baker or the Everly Brothers or Elvis. He also

stumbled across disc jockey Alan Freed's fifteen-minute segment on American Forces Network—a potpourri of R&B, rockabilly, pop, and the hard stuff attributed to bad boys like Gene Vincent and Eddie Cochran.

Up until the age of twelve, Jimmy's hands-on musical experience was limited to singing in the choir at St. Barnabas Anglican Church. "He'd have a go on anybody's piano when we went visiting," his mother reminisced. Otherwise, the Pages were indifferent when it came to musical instruments. Of course, there was that cheap Spanish-style guitar that had come with the house. It was nothing more than a neglected ornament in a corner of the living room that no one had bothered to stash in the attic. But . . . a guitar, no less . . . with steel strings . . . ready to play . . . almost. Finding it, Jimmy said, felt "like divine intervention." His curiosity about it coincided with two songs he'd heard on the radio. The first was Elvis Presley's rockabilly masterpiece "Baby, Let's Play House." From its uninhibited, stuttery opening—"*Whoa, baby, baby, baby, baby, baby / Baby, baby, baby, b-b-b-b-b-b-baby, baby, baby*"—Jimmy was hooked. "I heard the acoustic guitar, slap bass, and electric guitar—three instruments and a voice—and they generated so much energy I had to be part of it," he said. It was impossible to ignore. "I wanted to play it. I wanted to know what it was all about."

Almost as alluring, but in an entirely different vein, was "Rock Island Line," Lonnie Donegan's overheated slaughter of the Leadbelly classic, which touched off a mid-1950s musical craze among British teenagers. Called skiffle, after African American slang to describe music provided at rent parties, it mashed up American folk and blues standards in the cornball style of old-timey jug bands. Basically, skiffle enabled working-class kids to assemble backyard combos using conventional homemade instruments—a laundry washboard doubled for percussion, a rope attached to an old tea chest for bass, a comb and tissue paper sandwiched for woodwinds, all anchored by a ukulele or guitar. Calling skiffle a craze was something of an understatement.

Between thirty thousand and fifty thousand skiffle groups got a jump start in Britain, one of them at the hands of twelve-year-old Jimmy Page.

That old Spanish guitar prop came in handy. He convinced an older schoolmate, Rod Wyatt, to help tune the sorry instrument and even show him how to strum a few basic chords. Wyatt could even bash out a version of "Rock Island Line," which impressed Jimmy to no end. It more or less chained him to the guitar until he mastered the damn song. "From the beginning, Jimmy and the guitar were joined at the hip," says Dave Williams, who stopped by regularly to check on his friend's progress. "Once he had those chords down, he basically taught himself how to play."

Jimmy promptly got his hands on a copy of *Play in a Day* by Bert Weedon. It was the bible for future British rock virtuosos like George Harrison, Dave Davies, Keith Richards, Pete Townshend, and Eric Clapton. But playing in a day was an eternity for Jimmy Page. "I was far too impatient," he admitted. Besides, the tutorials were overly simplistic. They didn't match the intricate fingering he heard on records. It was easier for him to play by ear. "You listened to the solo, lifted the tone arm, and put it back down to hear it again." That way, he managed to work out arrangements on his own.

Trouble was, his guitar wasn't cutting it. It was no more than a toy. The strings hovered several inches above the frets and had no give, no resonance. He'd advanced beyond that guitar almost from the moment he picked it up. What he wanted—what he dreamed about— "was something you would see on albums by Gene Vincent and the Blue Caps and Buddy Holly," he said. "Getting a guitar [like that] was like dreaming about a Cadillac." A more respectable guitar, was, for a working-class family, an expensive proposition. His dad wasn't unsympathetic, but there were terms to be met. "Okay," he said, "but you have to do a paper round." Obediently, Jimmy took over the Sunday delivery route in Epsom, going house to house and shouldering a satchel of newspapers filled with weekend supplements that weighed a ton.

"I did a paper round and got a Hofner Senator," he recalled, which was a step up but still no solution. The Senator was a sturdy, maple laminate *f*-hole guitar that tended to vibrate when strummed with any force. Jimmy just couldn't get a decent sound out of it. "After increasing the paper round, I got an electric pick-up for it," he said. But—how to amplify it? Lo and behold, his parents' radiogram had an input on the back panel. "When the sound came through the speakers, I couldn't believe it." It didn't exactly provide Mach 1 thrust, but it served Jimmy's purpose for the time being. What he really needed, however, was an electric guitar.

In the meantime, the Senator gave him enough firepower to cobble together a band. Dave Housego, Jimmy's mate down the street, was recruited for the eponymous James Page Skiffle Group. Housego's father had been a drummer in a wartime dance band and had a kit that he'd handed down to his son. The snare, played with brushes, provided a suitable shuffle accompaniment. From school, Jimmy dredged up a bass fiddle sideman and another guitar player to handle the singing chores. Even at the outset Jimmy knew his limitations. He had no confidence in his voice; the sound he made was nasal and thin. Playing the guitar was enough of a challenge. He decided to leave the singing to others.

But the musical experience was key. "I could get together with my mates," he noted, "and before you knew it, you had the serious spirit of music there." The boys rehearsed in the front room of Jimmy's house, working out arrangements to a universal skiffle set. Once you conquered "Rock Island Line," you were only a hair's breadth away from "John Henry," "Cumberland Gap," "Midnight Special," and a half dozen others. It came together rather quickly. Jimmy's mum was so impressed that, in the spring of 1958 she contacted the producers of the BBC-TV children's staple *All Your Own*, a half-hour show that featured kids demonstrating their talent or discussing their hobbies. As it turned out, they booked the James Page Skiffle Group for an appearance on the Sunday-afternoon broadcast.

In the brief clip that exists of the performance, a well-scrubbed Jimmy Page, decked out in a tidy crewneck sweater, his hair neatly combed in a mock pompadour, leads a quartet capably through a rousing "Mama Don't Allow No Skiffle Round Here" and "Pick a Bale of Cotton." In between the songs, Jimmy endures his first interview, an inane on-camera exchange with the show's host, Huw Wheldon. Do they discuss the music that has just been played? Not a chance. The thirteen-year-old guitarist is interrogated about his career path. Would it be skiffle?

"No," Jimmy deadpans, "I want to do biological research."

*A-ha-ha-ha*—the host is amused and asks him to be specific. "Cancer, if it isn't discovered by then," Jimmy offers. So you'll be studying germs, Wheldon replies, suggesting the limits of his knowledge of the subject. A "quite nervous" Jimmy later admitted that "whatever I said then was probably what I was studying that week."

The James Page Skiffle Group turned out to be a short-lived act. Skiffle provided a platform for playing music, but it was a passing phase. "There was some blues in skiffle music," Jimmy conceded. "You got the songs, but the attitude and playing were not there yet."

The attitude was in rock 'n roll.

Rock 'n roll wasn't an unknown quantity to Jimmy. He was onto it well before skiffle. In early 1956, Dave Williams had come across the road to tell him about a record he'd heard on an American Forces Network broadcast from Germany—"Too Much Monkey Business" by Chuck "Crazy Legs" *Perry*. It wasn't long before they turned up a ten-inch Chuck *Berry* EP with "Maybelline," "Thirty Days (to Come Back Home)," "Wee Wee Hours," and "Together (We Will Always Be)" on it. The discovery was like unearthing the Rosetta Stone. What the hell was he singing about? the boys wondered. The language was completely alien to them. Eventually it dawned on them: *this is all about sex!*

In no time, they got wind of a cinema in Stoneleigh, the next village over from Epsom, that was playing one of the earliest jukebox musicals, *Rock, Rock, Rock!* "It was a crappy film," Dave Williams recalls, "until Chuck Berry and the Johnny Burnette Trio came on—and then it was open mouth time." Burnette and his band motored through "Lonesome Train," which impressed with its riotous energy. Berry's version of "You Can't Catch Me" was a visual tour de force. When he entered the action, duck-walking his guitar across the frame and staring into the camera with a menacing grin, the boys almost came out of their seats. They went back the next day just to see that performance again. Not long afterward, they caught a showing of *The Girl Can't Help It*, another shoddy B movie that was nothing but a pretense for the music. But the *music* . . . If Chuck Berry had whetted their appetites, then Little Richard, Gene Vincent, Fats Domino, and Eddie Cochran provided a three-star dessert. "'Twenty Flight Rock' did a number on our heads," Williams confesses. "The other kids in the theater had no interest in the music. They went to see Jayne Mansfield's tits. But Jimmy and I left there wanting to *be* Eddie Cochran, and we saw that movie over and over again."

Jimmy got a jump on the image makeover. For all intents and purposes, he was a sober kid with a plain-vanilla face, come-hither eyes, and sensuous lips. Once the guitar found a way into his hands, he set about constructing the rest of the package. The black leather trousers, the voluminous pink shirt, and the silver lamé waistcoat were beyond his reach. So was Cochran's Cadillac-size orange Gretsch Signature guitar (at least, for the time being). But Jimmy could suss out how the songs were played. And he could strike the requisite pose. The attitude came naturally.

But it was style and substance more than attitude that captured his imagination. The more Jimmy listened to rock 'n roll, the more he realized that hitmakers like Gene Vincent, Elvis Presley, Dale Hawkins, and Bill Haley were front men, recording artists, not necessarily the engines that drove their songs. The sound Jimmy fell in love with, the real drama on their records, was generated by a corps of unsung guitarists, players who could coax the slinkiest, most seductive sound out of six strings without drawing attention. Names started emerging from the shadows, names that weren't printed on record labels or exalted by disc jockeys—James Burton, Cliff Gallup, Scotty Moore, Joe Maphis, Hubert Sumlin, Johnny Weeks, Matt Murphy. The licks they played lit a fire deep inside Jimmy's imagination. He listened hard, studied them, copied their touch, their expression, teaching himself their techniques as one might a new language.

"Solos which affected me could send a shiver up my spine," he said, "and I'd spend hours, and in some cases days, trying to get them [down]. The first ones were Buddy Holly chord solos, like 'Peggy Sue,' but the next step was definitely James Burton on Ricky Nelson records, which was when it started to get difficult."

"Jimmy was obsessed with James Burton," Dave Williams recalls. "I'd bought these junky Ricky Nelson LPs in secondhand record shops, and I took them around to Jim's. A week later, parts of tracks were scratched away where he'd been playing and replaying the bloody solos. He worked his nuts off mastering them."

Deciphering solos was like solving brainteasers. Jimmy would attempt to solve them like the Allied code breakers at Bletchley Park. "The only way to do that was by listening to the record and moving the needle back to where the solo started again," he explained. "Back and forth you'd go, so it would damage the record itself sometimes."

Williams noted one puzzler that simply stumped Jimmy. "I remember he couldn't get the solo on the instrumental break in 'It's Late.'"

It was a tricky glissando that slid up a few frets and pulled off another string, really bent it, to create a twangy hiccup effect. Remarkably, Rod Wyatt, the schoolmate who'd tuned Jimmy's first guitar, had it all worked out and spent a Saturday morning teaching him the fingering. While Rod was at it, they also tackled the riff on "My Babe," another Burton creation that required some effort. The two boys met regularly at Jimmy's to practice and swap pointers they'd picked up. Over time, they exhausted the James Burton and Cliff Gallup oeuvres.

Jimmy could play those babies blindfolded, according to Wyatt, "That was the style and guitar sound we loved best in those days."

It was fine to listen and learn from records, but Jimmy needed to see it in action. He and Dave Williams took to loitering outside Epsom's Ebbisham Hall on Friday nights. On weekends the town elders, desperate to keep their teenagers off the streets, renamed the drab church facility the Contemporary Club, where the kids could congregate and dance to local groups. "We were too young to get in," Williams recalls, "so Jimmy and I'd sneak around to the fire door and listen to the bands that were playing inside."

Their favorite act was Chris Farlowe and the Thunderbirds. The band was like hundreds of others in England that made their bones playing cover versions of the hits of the day. The Thunderbirds, however, had two aces in the hole that separated them from the pack. Chris Farlowe could really sing. He had a husky, bluesy delivery that could take the shine off a copper penny. His version of "Stormy Monday" was a drop-dead showstopper, as were the Jimmy Reed numbers he belted out. And he was the first of the local crooners to tackle "Just a Dream" and "My Babe," which struck seductive chords with the crowd. He also had Bobby Taylor on guitar.

By local standards, Bobby Taylor was an astonishing virtuoso. "Bobby was so influential," says John Spicer, who later played alongside Jimmy in Neil Christian & the Crusaders. "He had a funky style that was so infectious and really exploded out of his guitar."

"Jimmy idolized Bobby Taylor," Dave Williams recalls. "Once we were able to talk our way into the hall, we'd stand at the back and watch him play solos on any number of amazing Jimmy Reed songs. Jimmy couldn't take his eyes off Bobby."

He'd rush home and try to duplicate the solos from memory, but it required an even better guitar—an actual electric guitar, not some jerry-rigged replica. Jimmy badly wanted a Fender Stratocaster. In the late 1950s, it was still impossible to buy one in England. Sister Rosetta Tharpe had played one during an early tour of the country, but as far as Jimmy knew, only two had been imported into the UK. Cliff Richard had bought one for his sidekick, Hank Marvin, and Bobby Taylor had the other. That was it. Until Fender made them available, British guitarists settled for f-hole archtops or hollowbodies that had been the only option for jazz and dance-band musicians. There were hints, however, that that was about to change. Tony Sheridan, a flashy British rocker who performed with Gene Vincent and Eddie Cochran, had appeared on TV with an approximation of a Fender. It was a Grazioso, a Czech knockoff of a Stratocaster, close enough for Jimmy, who found one at an accordion shop in nearby Surbiton.

Now he was in business.

## [3]

Late in 1958, with a new guitar in tow, Jimmy Page was ready to play his first-ever paying gig. He'd arranged a date at the Epsom Comrades Club, a typical veterans' watering hole southeast of the High Street accustomed to having live music on the weekend. Jimmy had been rehearsing with a small pickup combo—an acoustic guitar player who sang a bit and an older, accomplished pianist. Their set was nothing to marvel at: Cliff Richard's "Move It," which was a staple of every band from Penzance to the Orkneys; "Red River Rock" to show off Jimmy's chops; a couple of Elvis tunes; and a sampling of lightweight pop hits of the day. Be that as it may, Jimmy couldn't wait to play them in front of a live audience.

Dave Williams, who'd been enlisted to hump Jimmy's amp to the gig, had even scrounged up a couple dates, two fifteen-year-old neighborhood girls, Anna and Gillian. "It was a pretty sketchy affair," Anna recalls. "The club was bare bones, a few tables with chairs around them, a bar at one end, and a little dance area. The band wasn't bad. Jimmy seemed to know what he was doing." Halfway through the set, however, things went sideways. The elderly crowd, paying no attention to the music, realized the piano player could play tunes they could waltz to—World War II pub and patriotic songs. And every time he fulfilled a request, someone in the room bought him a pint. Slowly but surely, the pianist got smashed.

This complicated matters. Jimmy and Dave had expectations for the after-gig festivities. Dave's father was conveniently out of town; that left the boys with an empty house for the after-party with their dates. Now the pianist was shit-faced, and someone was going to have to get him home. "Jimmy and I both fancied Anna," Williams recalled. "So we drew straws to see who would take her home. The other guy was responsible for getting the pianist into a taxi." Jimmy lost. Fifty-five years later, Williams is still married to Anna.

But Jimmy Page was just warming up.

He'd been noodling around Surrey with an ad hoc band called the Paramounts. As performers, they didn't have much going for them, limited mostly to playing instrumentals, like "Guitar Boogie Shuffle," "Red River Rock," and the *Peter Gunn* theme, so that Jimmy could shine. Despite that, throughout the summer of 1959, they handled opening-act chores at the Contemporary Club in Epsom. One of the headliners they routinely worked with was Red E. Lewis & the Red Caps, a well-regarded unit on the local club and dance-hall circuit, whose singer had a Gene Vincent fixation and the perfect gruff tenor to deliver rock 'n roll. John Spicer, the bass player, recalls how Jimmy used to hang around their van at the end of gigs. "He'd talk to us as we packed up the gear. He was always interested in what our guitarist, Bobby Oats, was playing and occasionally borrowed Bobby's solid-body guitar to show us what he could do."

Toward the end of the summer, Bobby Oats was accepted into drama school and announced he was leaving the Red Caps. Spicer recalls the dilemma faced by the rest of the band and their manager, Chris Tidmarsh. "We had to come up with another guitar player, and quick," he says. "Chris and Red were both enamored of Jimmy. They said, 'The kid's only fifteen, but he can play, he's fantastic.' It was decided to invite him to a rehearsal in London to see if he fit into the band."

In a room above the Red Lion, a rundown, working-class pub in Shoreditch, the Red Caps put Jimmy through the paces, playing all the highlights from their set. "He knew every single number, all the solos—the James Burton and Cliff Gallup licks—all our routines, everything note-perfect," Spicer says. "I was knocked out. I remember thinking, 'This skinny kid is the best guitarist I've ever heard.'"

It was love at first sight. The rest of the Red Caps made it unanimous. Jimmy Page was invited to be their guitar player on the spot. Only one hurdle remained. "We had to convince his parents to let him come up to London to join a rock 'n roll band."

Although Jimmy believed his parents "were very encouraging," when it came to a full-time gig, James Page Sr. was no pushover. He was rough on his son, not warm or affectionate. Friends say he never called Jimmy by his name. To his father, Jimmy was always Boy, as in "Boy, take out the trash" or "Boy, clean up your room." He expected Jimmy to finish school and pass exams, not run around the home counties with a half-baked rock 'n roll band. But even James Page Sr. was no match for the silver-tongued Chris Tidmarsh. He laid the charm on thick, made it sound as though the band was in the same league as the London Philharmonic. According to Jimmy, "He reassured my parents and said he'd keep a watchful eye on this young lad." Tidmarsh even threw in a cash incentive. "If I promise to pay [Jimmy] £15 a week, would you consider him playing in the group?" Fifteen pounds was nothing to sneeze at; it was more than Mr. Page was making. But—no, still no, the boy had to take his O-level exams and finish school. It was only when Tidmarsh assured him that the gigs would all be weekend dates and he would personally drive young Jimmy home afterward that Mr. Page gave his consent.

The promise of weekend-only gigs lasted about as long as the first weekend. The Red Caps were a working band with a demanding dance card, and pretty soon they leaned on Jimmy's parents to let him take

the train to London after his school day was over in order to fill that
card with weeknight gigs. Reluctantly, and with caveats, Mr. Page gave
in. Most nights, each man made about £2, just enough to get by. When
there were no club dates, Tidmarsh hired function rooms above pubs
in North London or local church halls and promoted their own shows
for 100 percent of the door. They played within a hundred-mile radius
of London almost every night of the week, upholding the promise to
drive Jimmy home afterward, often getting to Epsom at three o'clock
in the morning. It was all Jimmy could do to keep up the routine. He
was burning the candle at both ends.

In fact, he was no longer Jimmy Page but . . . Nelson Storm. For
some unknown reason, the band decided that stage names were more
conducive to the rock 'n roll image. Nelson Storm, the alias Jimmy
picked out for himself, jibed with the drummer, Jimmy "Tornado"
Rook, and played off John Spicer's nom de guerre, Doc Swift. But no
matter what they called themselves, Red E. Lewis & the Red Caps
were a run-of-the-mill cover band, like so many others working the
circuit as the 1950s were drawing to a close.

As history confirms, the chemistry in rock 'n roll bands is an unsteady compound, and Red E. Lewis & the Red Caps were no exception. As their popularity grew, as their ambitions swelled, there were
rumblings from within that Red, whose real name was Billy Stubbs,
had the wrong look to be a pop star. He was a rugged bloke, swarthy,
with a couple of teeth missing in his smile, and about six years older
than his baby-faced sidemen. He could sing, but that was no longer
enough. He wasn't what the tastemakers considered "presentable."
Chris Tidmarsh, the ringleader of the coup, determined they had
taken things as far as they could go with Billy out front. The same went
for their middling drummer. It was time to make personnel changes.

They found their new singer in the 2i's coffee bar, a character who
called himself Smoky Dean, one of his many aliases. Smoky was the
anti–Red E. Lewis: a good-looking guy with slicked-back blond hair
and a buff physique, who stood six feet tall and spoke with a bogus

American accent. "The girls loved him," John Spicer recalls. With Dean straddling the mic, the Red Caps re-formed as the Dean Aces, and for a while all was well. But Smoky Dean had developed other distinctive rock 'n roll idiosyncrasies. He smoked pot and popped pills, which made him unreliable.

"We can't keep going on with Smoky," Tidmarsh explained after a gig at which Smoky was a no-show. It wasn't the first time he'd left them in the lurch, and everyone knew it wouldn't be the last. Jimmy agreed with Chris; it was time for a change. "Why don't you start singing?" he suggested.

That came out of the blue. Nobody knew that Chris Tidmarsh could sing. He'd only ever handled their booking and travel arrangements. He was an impressive guy, a very smooth operator—*presentable*—but singing had never been in the cards. Still, he knew all the band's songs and stage routines. At a rehearsal, he seized the opportunity.

Tidmarsh, it turned out, was smashing, even stylish. The guy had pipes—a lighter voice than Red or Smoky, but nevertheless capable of delivering the band's songs with flair. It seemed a natural fit to work him into the act. But his name—Tidmarsh—had no poetry, no pizzazz. Everyone agreed it had to go. So Chris Tidmarsh became Neil Christian, and the Red Caps/Dean Aces became the Crusaders. Neil Christian & the Crusaders—it had a nice ring to it.

A new name needed a new look. To that end, the band members tromped into the Islington branch of Burton's, an off-the-rack men's store, and got measured for spiffy black shirts and trousers, with matching black-and-white two-toned shoes. And Jimmy got a new guitar—a much-longed-for sunburst Fender Stratocaster, subsidized by the band, that finally allowed him to play with panache. Tidmarsh— make that *Neil Christian*—demanded more than his predecessors in the way of stagecraft; he was a pro and a showman, so he initiated fancy dance routines. From now on during songs, the band would perform the crossover box step—coordinating left legs in front of right, right legs in front of left, while swinging the guitars around at the same time. Jimmy remembers twisting like a contortionist, "arc[ing] over backwards until my head touched the stage." The antics were a crowd-pleaser from the start. And on "One Night," the Elvis Presley song, the pattern was even more elaborate. "We used to build up to a big crescendo," John Spicer recalled. "Jimmy would start his guitar solo in the middle of the song. The drummer would add a heavy beat. It'd be thumping and really *loud* at the end, and we'd all be on the floor, lying on our backs, with Neil Christian slamming his fist on the bloody piano." He was a dynamo onstage. All this time, Neil Christian had been gestating inside Chris Tidmarsh, just waiting for the chance to hatch and bust out. He was "a smart lad, immaculately dressed" and handsome, albeit with a fatal flaw: intense stage fright. For all his self-assurance, his poise and polish, the guy just couldn't face a crowd. He spent long stretches before each show in the bathroom violently throwing up.

Puking aside, Neil Christian & the Crusaders grew in demand on the booming London club circuit. There were churches and dance halls in Barnett, Rumford, and Hatfield, as well as the Contemporary Club in Epsom; all drew a faithful flock of kids across the whole so-cial spectrum who came to dance and unwind. The band was tight, they swung. Their act was practically a carbon copy of Johnny Kidd & the Pirates, whose classic "Shakin' All Over" is that rare commodity—a truly great pre-Beatles British rock 'n roll record. The Pirates were a huge influence on the Crusaders, so much so that Jimmy took the bus to Southfields in South London, where the Pirates' guitarist Mick Green lived, to jam with him and learn his unique rhythmic approach to solos. Jimmy resolved to play *exactly* like the pros. "We did every cover version you could think of," Christian recalled. "[Gene] Vincent, Johnny Burnette, a lot of rhythm and blues. Jimmy loved [Jerry Lee] Lewis and [Chuck] Berry. He could play all that stuff as though you were listening to the record."

Jimmy Page was becoming a local legend in his own right. He got a solo spot in the act to ramp up his rep and a shout-out by Neil on staples like "Rumble" and "Sleep Walk." "Everywhere we played, people always came up to talk to Jim," says John Spicer. "Boys especially made a beeline for the Stratocaster. It was still such a novelty in England. And Jim could make that guitar practically speak." It captivated him for about six months before he was ready to graduate to something more sophisticated. One night, while the Crusaders were playing a multiband gig in Kingston, not far from Epsom, they got wind that Gene Vincent and Eddie Cochran were appearing across town at the Odeon Theatre.

"We managed to arrange our appearance so that we could get out for an hour and a half and go see their show," Spicer recalls. "Eddie came out with the orange Gretsch," the Signature hollowbody, with parallel bracing and double-bound f-holes. "It just bowled us over, Jimmy especially." It was beautiful machine, all right, opulent and shiny like a Cadillac, with a fat, throbbing twang. Cochran wore it belt-high, not on his hip in the usual gunslinger-style. Jimmy, half-delirious, wolf-whistled at it, as one might at a beautiful woman. "I've *got* to have one of those," he announced, and in a week or two, he did.

The Grazioso, the Strat, the Gretsch—it didn't matter what guitar Jimmy played, he handled the instrument intuitively, as though it were a part of his everyday tool kit. You'd hear about eight-year-old prodigies performing Rachmaninoff's Concerto no. 3 in D Minor note-perfect, like the maestro. That was Jimmy Page with the guitar. By the time he was sixteen, he had progressed to the point where he could play the most complicated riffs by ear, not only with proficiency but with finesse. According to Spicer, "Jim was never without a guitar in his hands. He practiced relentlessly, easily several hours every day." When someone asked him specifically how long he worked at it, he said, "Oh, probably six hours a day. When I was at school, probably eight."

After he mastered the James Burton, Ike Turner, and Cliff Gallup playbooks, Jimmy became sidetracked by the explosive barrelhouse gumbo pumped out by Jerry Lee Lewis. "Jerry Lee was his great love in life, his number-one man," Dave Williams recalls. "Jim had all the guitar solos on those Sun records down pat." As a treat, Williams scored them a pair of scarce tickets to see the Killer on one of his UK tour appearances at Fairfield Hall in Croydon. Unfortunately, the day before the show, Williams came down with glandular fever. His girlfriend, Anna, went in his place.

"We had seats in the front row of the balcony," she remembers. "Jim got so excited when Jerry Lee came on. He was standing up on his seat cheering and leaning dangerously over the balcony rail. I hung onto the back of his shirt so that he didn't fall over into the stalls."

Jerry Lee Lewis, Elvis Presley, Chuck Berry, Buddy Holly, Eddie Cochran, Gene Vincent—these were the major exponents, the gurus who inflamed Jimmy Page's aspirations in the years when the music first surfaced. Their hard-driving, untamable sorcery functioned as the secret handshake, Satan's grip, that enabled him to carve out a unique niche for himself and adopt rakish codes of behavior that were novel among Britain's postwar teens. Fifties rock 'n roll was liberating; it aroused and provoked. But as the decade receded, Jerry Lee was blackballed, Elvis had enlisted, Chuck was in jail, Buddy and Eddie were dead, and Gene was broken. The music began to lose its edge to a wave of bobby-soxers and pretty-boy crooners whose records were acceptable to TV audiences and jukeboxes in family-style diners. Danny and the Juniors could insist all they wanted that rock and roll was here to stay, but for Jimmy Page it was too late.

He had come down with a case of the blues.

## Chapter Two

# GETTING DOWN TO BUSINESS

## [1]

Singin' the blues was no common or easy undertaking in Epsom in 1960. It was next to impossible to lay hands on the records that opened up this new world of music. You had to mine for them, much like a prospector, separating the few nuggets from piles of sludge.

Jimmy Page and Dave Williams had few eureka moments. The two friends spent Saturday afternoons at the back of Rodgers', an appliance shop on the High Street adjacent to the clock tower, sifting through stacks of indistinguishable 45s. The names on the labels had no real meaning for them, but as prospectors the boys weren't completely clueless. There were singers you could smell out by name. They learned to eliminate what they referred to as the Bobbys—Bobby Rydell, Bobby Vee, Bobby Darin, the Bobettes. Nothing exciting or important, they decided, could come from such names. The same with the Fours—the Four Aces, the Four Preps, the Four Lads, the Four Freshmen. Those were obvious crooners, teenage pretty boys. No, Jimmy and Dave were searching for something with teeth, with true grit. Occasionally, a conspicuous candidate would jump out of the pack. *Screamin' Jay Hawkins!* Now, there was a name that had promise. When they flipped that record over and read the title—"I Put a Spell on You"—they had to have it. Bo Diddley—they'd take a chance on him, too. But it was just as easy to make a mistake and wind up with a Texas Tyler record that turned out to be country-western. You'd win some, you'd lose some.

To cut their losses, the boys sweet-talked the young woman behind the counter—a pink-haired bombshell named June Cutler—into letting them have a look at the record companies' release sheets so they could scan through the names and underline those they thought might deliver the goods. "Walk Don't Run" . . . "Rumble" . . . "Voo-Doo, VooDoo"—all sounded like they'd pay off. Decca, in particular, owned a subsidiary, London Records, that licensed releases from American independent labels like Chess, Imperial, Atlantic, Dot, Sun, Sue, and Specialty, all of which had fabulous rhythm-and-blues rosters. The boys actually convinced June Cutler to order loads of these titles, without any commitment to buy them. What's more, she let them preview the records in the store's listening booth. That's how they came across "What'd I Say," Ray Charles's 1959 masterpiece that Jimmy delivered to Neil Christian so quickly he practically left skid marks on the floor. And they relented by buying a normally taboo Bobby—Bobby Parker's "Watch Your Step," a transcendent R&B single, which Jimmy adored for its ferocious opening riff and the raw, blistering funk groove it created. In fact, as many have pointed out, Led Zeppelin's "Moby Dick" is actually "Watch Your Step" slowed down a few beats.

Jimmy heard the call loud and clear. "There was this great blues thing going on," he noted, "city blues, Chess style music." *Rhythm and blues.* It was something, he said, that "I was really getting into at the time." R&B was irresistible, exotic, radically different from what he'd been listening to up to now. It had a funky boogie beat, a rich gospel vocal style, and was sexy as hell. Dave Williams supplied him with plenty to listen to, the way a drug dealer might groom an addict. Williams "was a purist," Jimmy realized, an avid blues collector, whose library ran the gamut from B.B. King, Muddy Waters, Jimmy Reed, Elmore James, and Howlin' Wolf to more obscure practitioners like Eddie Taylor, Little Milton, and Jesse Hill. This authentic American blues provided a gritty alternative to the teenage jukebox hits that had been in rotation for the last few years. British kids were getting tired of hearing local bands all play the same set of cover songs over and over and over. The new trend was for bands to make their reputations by finding a tune that no one else was doing and springing it on unsuspecting ears.

Neil Christian & the Crusaders were slow to convert to the new routine. They continued to mine the hits while working in a number of R&B standards, like "Sweet Little Sixteen," "Train Kept a-Rollin'," and "Who Do You Love," but nothing more innovative than that. Even so, the band's popularity continued to grow. Neil Christian was a charismatic performer and the band was tight, and promoters doubled down on booking them.

The schedule in 1960 became untenable for sixteen-year-old Jimmy. The demands of school and performing were brutal, the energy required unsustainable. Ruxley Lane in Ewell, where he attended classes, was a secondary modern school, thus not a feeder into the university system. College had never been in the cards anyway. Jimmy had a pretty good idea his future lay in music. He was already making a pretty good living. At the age of sixteen, "after passing five G.C.E. 'O' level exams"—General Certificate of Education, Ordinary Level— and not taking the academic A levels later, he said, "I left school and went straight into Neil Christian & the Crusaders."

Once Jimmy turned pro, the band could go full tilt. Gigs were plentiful; they could barely keep up the pace. In 1960, it seemed every borough in England had either a town hall or a church assembly where kids danced to live music for as little as three or four shillings. In addition, several club circuits run by promoters had sprung up, which kept the Crusaders more than gainfully employed. The demand was so great, they often played two gigs a night that were nowhere near in proximity. That meant working up a powerful sweat onstage for an hour or two, then jumping into a vehicle and driving fifty or sixty miles at breakneck speeds on dark, twisty back roads to make the next gig in time. These turned into round-the-clock operations. "For instance," John Spicer recalls, "on a Saturday night, we regularly played an out-of-town gig, then made tracks back to London to play what was called an all-nighter at La Discotheque at two a.m. on the Sunday morning."

There was no letup. In between gigs, the Crusaders moonlighted, whether it was serving as the backing band for pop star Eden Kane on his tour of the provinces or opening for Cliff Richard & the Shadows at the Edmonton Regal. No decent-paying job was scorned. They even took a date playing Holloway Prison, a women's correctional facility in a suburb of London, which "was a good show, if you overlooked the obscenities the girls called out—things they'd like to do if they got their hands on us."

"We acquired a good reputation," Jimmy said in retrospect, "but touring was very primitive."

A rickety Ford van quickly became impractical and was replaced by an old London ambulance, a big beast of a vehicle. The band stripped the insides and installed three rows of seats from city bus castoffs, behind which a mountain of gear was piled. At a certain point, as their fortunes grew, they even employed a driver, Don Stewart. A self-styled ladies' man, Don's job description extended to procuring girls from the audience whom Neil Christian had picked out for himself and Jimmy and escorting them backstage after the gig.

You never knew where the next new experience would come from. In late 1960, following a gig at the Harrodian, a social club for the employees of Harrods in the basement of the company's warehouse, the Crusaders were introduced to a young, bearded poet named Royston Ellis, who recited some pseudo-Beat verse he called "rocketry" to guitar accompaniment provided by Jimmy. This was something completely new and interesting. Jimmy recognized the syncopated dynamic between spoken verse and music and was eager to explore the interaction further with Ellis.

"We knew that American jazz musicians had been backing poets during their readings," Jimmy explained. "Jack Kerouac was using piano to accompany his readings. Lawrence Ferlinghetti teamed with Stan Getz to bring poetry and jazz together." Why not poetry and rock 'n roll?

Thus began an alliance between the two men, who performed together, along with a bongo player, at a series of informal and staged events throughout 1961, on the Crusaders' days off. Jimmy composed original moody music to accompany leaden elegies like "Body Parts," "vaguely provocative verse about nipples, thighs, and pubic hair" found in Ellis's anthology, *Jiving to Gyp*. University students and denizens of coffee bars gobbled the stuff up. It was radical. It broke rules, pushed the two art forms into new territory, much in the way rap would forty years later. Ellis and Jimmy even previewed their act at tony venues such as Cambridge University's Heretics Society in March 1961 and later that summer at the Mermaid Theatre in London.

For a year and a half, Jimmy Page, only seventeen, was living the life. Not only were his nights filled with music, but the days as well. Practicing was always at the forefront of his agenda, especially to further his education with the blues. Even when friends visited, he'd have a guitar in his hands, unconsciously fingering along the frets as though he were reading Braille. To sharpen his ear, he bought a tape recorder with two one-and-three-quarter-inch reels that weighed a ton and convinced Dave Williams to smuggle it into the blues shows he haunted. Williams brought back bootlegs to order of a Jimmy Reed gig and a special appearance Muddy Waters and Hubert Sumlin made with a local band. "Jimmy would study those tapes and copy all the nuances," Williams recalls. "When he burrowed deeper into the technical details, his mum bought him a four-track recorder, so he'd put his own guitar bit to songs and get a drum sound on a cardboard box."

Jimmy's main passion became *sound*. "He was always into new noises," Williams explains. After Jimmy heard Chet Atkins's "Trombone," which depended on the guitar's tremolo arm (or whammy bar) to bend the strings for dramatic effect, he had to have one. The same with a foot pedal. "I remember when a record came out and had the first fuzz-box sound," Williams says. "We were sitting in Jimmy's front room, and he said, 'What the fuck is making that sound? Maybe they used an elastic band to vibrate against the frets.' He tried it but couldn't keep the strings in tune." Link Wray's "Rumble" also presented challenges. Jimmy heard that Wray had put pinholes in his amp's speaker to create distortion. For days he debated whether to try to duplicate the sound but decided, "I'm not bloody risking that." It wasn't worth ruining his amp.

He did, however, manage to get his hands on one of the first stereophonic record players in town. It was a Capitol system that came with a demo Jimmy put on to entertain and amaze his friends. The recording was of a man calling a dog. Out of one speaker, the man shouted, "Fido! Fido! C'mon, Fido." The response came from another speaker across the room: "Woof! Woof!" And Fido would track his woofing right across the room.

Creating sounds, Jimmy discovered, was almost as intriguing as playing the guitar. Layering sound was akin to an artist applying paint on top of paint until something entirely new appeared on the canvas. "He was also into overdubbing," says Colin Golding, who played bass for a band called the Presidents and for an early incarnation of the Rolling Stones. "Nobody else was doing it. And frankly, we all thought he was mad." But by using effects, Jimmy realized music wasn't confined; in fact, the possibilities were limitless when it came to tampering with sound.

The seeds of production had been planted in Jimmy Page, and there was an early bloom. Sometime in 1961, Jimmy and Rod Wyatt pooled their resources to record a three-hour session with Chris Farlowe and the Thunderbirds at the primitive R.G. Jones Studios in Morden, Surrey. In an afternoon, with Jimmy directing traffic, they laid down enough work to fill a ten-inch EP that flaunted a broad range of taste and versatility: a respectfully mannered version of Carl Perkins's "Matchbox," with Farlowe scatting over the solo; a hard-charging "Money," the Barrett Strong classic; two instrumentals by his favorite guitarist, Bobby Taylor, including a standout entitled "Fish This Week"; and a Les McCann number whose solo Jimmy wanted to nick.

Jimmy was ecstatic with the result. He played it and played it until the vinyl was practically scratched away, performing a critical postmortem of his work. In the end, he concluded he'd done yeoman's work. The sound he'd teased out, the overall texture, was intuitive and spare. The instruments were clearly distinguishable and separated out distinctly from the vocals. And the mix—well, it wasn't muddy. Not at all a bad first effort sitting in the producer's chair.

It was exhilarating, but the pace was punishing. Between his appearances with Neil Christian & the Crusaders and Royston Ellis and the volume of pick-up engagements, the workload began adding up. There were too many late nights, too many close calls. "All the traveling to one-nighter gigs made me ill," he recalled. "I used to get sick in the van." Small wonder, when you considered the wretched conditions. "We lived out of the back of a van, out of cafes," Neil Christian acknowledged. Jimmy's recollection was every bit as grim. "I remember we were driving to a Liverpool club once and the van broke down and we had to hitchhike. . . . We didn't really have any money, so we ended up sleeping in this little room in the club, in the middle of the desk chairs and the fucking first aid cabinet, and it was really cold." To stay wired, Jimmy embraced the jazz musicians' habit of chewing the tab of Benzedrine inside Vicks nasal inhalers for an added jolt of energy, but it wasn't enough to sustain him.

He was a slightly built, undernourished guy. He wasn't well. "I kept getting glandular fever," he said, using an obsolete term for infectious mononucleosis, which produced fevers, swollen glands, and bouts of persistent fatigue. For weeks on end, he was bedridden, still kipping in the spare, cell-like bedroom at his parents' house. Because of

Neil Christian's commitments, because the show had to go on, Jimmy was often replaced in the Crusaders by Albert Lee, a seminal British guitarist, and occasionally by session player Joe Moretti or Tony Harvey from Vince Taylor & the Playboys.

But it wasn't only the illness that wore Jimmy down. He was bored—bored with playing the same set of songs the same way to the same kind of kids. "The numbers we were doing were really out of character for the audiences that were coming to hear us play," he said. The club scene, moreover, had taken a turn for the worse. "It was just disheartening to go up to, say, Rushton or somewhere like that and find ten people having a punch-up. In the end, it just didn't appear to be going anywhere, so I jacked it in."

He needed a break, a change of scenery. He needed to rethink the direction that the music was taking him. Art college seemed like a good refuge.

## [2]

Art college was a waystation of sorts for a whole host of young, working-class kids who hadn't found their niche in the traditional British educational system—those who were cut out for neither university nor the drudgery of a blue-collar apprenticeship. Art college provided some space, some breathing room, as well as an exemption from the draft. It was a creative place for these outliers, where they were inspired to look at things in new ways, to nurture unconventional interests—and to express themselves. You could dress and act how you liked, you could smoke, you could drink. As future Yardbirds sideman Chris Dreja pointed out, "You didn't have to do a lot of art, but it encouraged you to do a lot of thinking." Art school attracted "hip, young anti-establishment types" who were on the cutting edge of the bohemian scene. John Spicer puts it simply: "It was cool being at art school."

Almost every community had its version. Jimmy enrolled at one close to his home, Sutton Art College. It was relatively easy to get in, nothing more involved than filling out some forms and paying class fees. You didn't have to prove your bona fides or submit a portfolio. The ability to draw came in handy, although Jimmy claimed he was "a terrible draftsman," but he'd always enjoyed painting. Most art college students took what was known as a foundation course, which meant a year studying still life, figure drawing, lettering, etching, sculpture, architecture, and other forms of art, but Sutton was purely art. "It had a very relaxed atmosphere," says Colin Golding, who played guitar with Jimmy. "And during the time you were at art school, somebody would invariably start a band."

Art college was an incubator for rock 'n roll. "There were loads of people playing guitar there," said Keith Richards, a student at Sidcup Art College in London's borough of Bexley. "It was kind of a guitar workshop," a melting pot of technique and influences. There were devotees of the blues, of folk music, of traditional and modern jazz—and, increasingly, of rock 'n roll.

It's mind-boggling to contemplate the front line of guitar wizards who came out of art colleges in the early 1960s. Eric Clapton studied design at Kingston School of Art in Knight's Park, Pete Townshend majored in graphic design at Ealing Art College, Jeff Beck went to the Wimbledon School of Art, John Lennon whiled away his time at the Liverpool College of Art. Ronnie Wood and Phil May played in art school bands. And the experience wasn't limited to guitarists. Michael Des Barres recalls visiting his friend, drummer Mitch Mitchell, who attended the same drama school as Steve Marriott when all three went out one night to see a Black left-handed guitar player from the States debut at the Marquee.

One of the luxuries of art college was its lax regulations. No one took attendance; you came and went as you pleased. If you didn't turn up one morning, there was no fallout, which gave Jimmy Page the freedom to engage in outside musical pursuits. For a while, he joined forces with Cyril Davies in a pickup blues band that played, unrehearsed, during intervals at the Marquee Club on Thursday nights. He also came out of retirement to rejoin Neil Christian & the Crusaders on a session at EMI for their first single, "The Road to Love." In a recollection, Jimmy said, "We didn't play on the tracks. Session musicians did." But, in fact, while producer Norrie Paramor wiped off the Crusaders' bass and drum tracks in favor of professional players, he left Jimmy's guitar intact.

Jimmy's most important pursuit during art school turned out to be life-changing.

In 1962, he recalled, "Glyn [Johns] introduced me to the session world." Johns, another Epsom eighteen-year-old who would go on to become one of his era's most prolific producers of rock 'n roll, was employed as a tape operator at IBC, an independent recording studio in London. They had met years earlier at St. Martin's Parish Church youth club, during a talent night at which Jimmy played guitar. Now Johns manned the board for the studio, which produced everything from small orchestras to Julian Bream guitar concertos to the latest Petula Clark single to the music for the TV show *Wagon Train*. "I was about to do a session for Tony Meehan and Jet Harris, both of whom had left the Shadows," Johns recalls, "and asked Jimmy to play guitar on it."

*Session work*—this was the break Jimmy had been looking for. It was a lift into the big time for a budding musician, the key to a "sort of impenetrable brotherhood," as Jimmy referred to it. Session players worked steadily, the hours weren't ridiculous, and the money was outstanding. Pay was a standard £7.50 a session, and the top players often worked two or three sessions a day. It was a bloody bonanza if you played your cards right.

The gig, however, wasn't a shoo-in. As studio musicians went, Jimmy was young and untested, an obvious risk; most practitioners had paid plenty of dues. Glyn Johns, however, put his neck on the line. "[He] kept telling me that Jimmy Page was a great kid," Tony Meehan recalled. "Glyn said he had the magic and should be given a chance. So, I decided to give him a try."

The Jimmy Page story could have ended right here. The session, as Jimmy envisioned it, didn't go as he'd expected. At the outset, Meehan walked among the players, distributing precise arrangements that he'd written out for the session. Little did he know, Jimmy couldn't read music. The way it seemed to him, "they stuck a row of dots in front of me, which looked like crows on telegraph wires." It might as well have been Greek. Once things got under way, the problem was obvious. "I knew right away that he was faking it," Meehan said.

Meehan could have—*should* have—shown Jimmy the door. Instead, he switched him from lead to rhythm guitar, a duty that only required chording. The result was a single called "Diamonds" that shot to the top of the British charts.

Despite the sight-reading snafu, Jimmy remained undaunted. Session work made perfect sense as an avenue to pursue. He resolved to learn how to read music but had to back off temporarily from accepting more work. "Jimmy rang me and said the art school had found out he was earning money, and he was going to lose his grant," Johns recalled, "so he wasn't going to do any more sessions."

In the meantime, Jimmy continued to paint and practice the guitar at home. The painting was more of an amusement than a commitment. "Jimmy wasn't any kind of an artist," Dave Williams says. "He was just doing little bits of things, like drawing circles." But the guitar was no joke; it was given the highest priority.

There were plenty of musicians attending Sutton Art College, but none who stood up to Jimmy's level of play. Fortunately, word of his virtuosity reached an older student, Annetta Beck. She checked Jimmy out and immediately gave an account to her younger brother, who attended Wimbledon School of Art. "She kept telling me, 'You got to meet this weird, thin guy playing a weird-shaped guitar like yours,'" he recalled. That was all Jeff Beck had to hear. He and his sister hopped on a bus to Epsom, found their way to Miles Road, and knocked on the Pages' door.

One can only imagine Jimmy's reaction to finding Jeff Beck on his doorstep. Jeff was a rangy kid with long, unkempt hair and a guitar that was anything but impressive—a homemade number that was barely functional. It was an odd situation. They paced around for a while, scoping each other out. Who do you listen to? What do you play? The sacred names were uttered: Burton, Moore, Gallup. Jimmy asked Jeff if he knew the solo to "My Babe," a supreme test, and . . . *good lord*, could that boy play! He knocked out a version that gave James Burton a run for his money. Jimmy, for his part, played "Not Fade Away" with all of Buddy's shading. The love match was sealed.

Jeff lived in Wallington, about five minutes from Epsom, which enabled him to hang out at Jimmy's every chance he got. "We would play Ricky Nelson songs like 'My Babe' and 'It's Late' . . . and just [do] a lot of jamming," he recalled. They were like-minded in their approach and degree of dedication. Both boys played at levels years beyond their contemporaries. The jams were like master classes in guitar, but their focus was deeper, more wide-ranging. Invariably, after working out an arrangement, they'd put the song on tape, concocting their own makeshift audio effects. "[Jimmy] used to stick the mic under a cushion on the couch. I used to bash it, and it would make the best bass drum sound you ever heard, said Jeff."

Like Jimmy, Jeff played in a cover band—his was called the Deltones—whose set list bored him. For the most part, the Deltones performed the pop hits of the day, songs by Johnny Tillotson and Fabian, even "The Twist," a horrible number that drove Jeff nuts. It was beneath him, not at all where he was headed. The same went for the Roosters, who offered him a gig replacing Brian Jones on guitar.*

---

* When Jeff Beck snubbed the Roosters, they offered the position to another local lad, Eric Clapton.

Instead, he joined the Tridents, who were more his scene. "They were playing flat-out R&B, like Jimmy Reed stuff," he said, "and we super-charged it all up and made it really rocky."

The blues had become the thinking guitarist's music of choice. Jimmy Page played it almost exclusively now, refining his touch in sub-tle ways in his gigs with Cyril Davies at the Marquee. In early 1963, after one of those Thursday-night intervals, Jimmy was approached by Mike Leander, a young record producer, to play on a session for a group called Carter-Lewis and the Southerners. The "band" was noth-ing more than two songwriters from Birmingham, John Shakespeare and Ken Lewis. "We'd had some modest success getting our material to performers," Shakespeare recalls, "but felt our chances improved if we sung them ourselves." That meant relying on session players to supplement their inadequacies. The date was scheduled at Decca Stu-dios in West Hempstead, one of London's vaunted facilities. Jimmy couldn't resist.

The result—a single entitled "Your Mama's Out of Town"—isn't as important as the chain reaction it inspired. Jimmy's contribution to the session, and the modest effort for which he was paid handsomely, convinced him that he was cut out for this kind of work. He felt com-fortable in the studio; he could play anything they threw at him. He had taught himself how to read music. The fact that he provided *ex-actly* what the producer called for, no questions asked, no fuss, no ego interjected, sealed his reputation as an able-bodied session man. Word traveled quickly along the music-business grapevine. Almost immedi-ately, Jimmy's phone started ringing.

Session musicians were a distinguished group. In Britain, the early sixties functioned as a sort of purgatory between the fading late-fifties rock 'n roll explosion and the revolution that loomed on the horizon. Pop music had taken on a slick, overproduced character that seemed drained of raw energy. Still, the deluge of records being made and the emergence of young, independent record producers demanded an as-sembly line of musicians able to churn out surefire hits targeted for mainstream audiences. Instead of self-contained stylists like Chuck Berry, Little Richard, Buddy Holly, and Jerry Lee Lewis, producers took the lead. They built records around covers of American hits or songs written to order and paired them with singers able to put them across. An entirely new roster of such artists emerged: Frank Ifield, Dave Berry, Petula Clark, Billy Fury, the Bachelors, Mark Wynter, Helen Shapiro, even a teenager from the Midlands named Robert Plant. The session players whose music fortified the records became as important as these artists.

Session crews—the traditional old studio hands—didn't always fit the bill. For years, they were mostly a mash-up of musicians moonlighting from symphony orchestras and old jazz or swing-band cats who were classically trained. The only things the two factions had in common were that they could sight-read arrangements—and they detested rock 'n roll. "The old guard used to sit there reading books until it was time to play," says Dave Berry, one of the emerging teen stars. "They didn't relate to the performers at all." The music of the day, however, demanded young blood. Slowly but surely, pop producers began hiring a select group of sidemen with rock 'n roll chops to augment the old hacks and to add some juice. The young Turks—some referred to themselves as "hooligans"—constituted a small, very exclusive fraternity: Jim Sullivan on guitar, John Baldwin (later known as John Paul Jones) on bass, and either Bobby Graham or Clem Cattini on drums.

Now, often two guitars were needed, which is where Jimmy Page came in. "I was mainly called into sessions as insurance," he acknowledged. Jim Sullivan, a Paul Bunyanesque ex-sideman for Eddie Cochran and Gene Vincent, handled the more exacting lead work. "He had a wonderful fingerpicking style," recalls John Shakespeare, "very nuanced, very precise." Jimmy, who was still learning to read music, brought a rock 'n roll sensibility and was more or less confined to rhythm at the outset. "They had a synchronicity," Dave Berry says. They became colleagues, inseparable, known as Big Jim and Little Jim, booked together on sessions more often than not. "I was more jazz influenced," Sullivan said. "I specialized in country rock—Chet Atkins, Merle Travis, James Burton. . . . Jim had gone along the same way, but was more blues influenced." It was clear they complemented each other's styles.

"Big Jim could play anything, he was a very fluid player," says Glyn Johns. "But he didn't have the energy Jimmy had, or possibly the invention."

Word got around that Jimmy had chops, and perhaps even more important: he was reliable. Time was money in the studio. If strings and brass were booked as accompaniment, ten to fifteen musicians might be on the payroll. Usually three sides were cut in a two-hour session. Producers needed to know you would show up on time and give them exactly what they were looking for. They also wanted "total spontaneity," according to Big Jim Sullivan, "the ability to make things up on the spot." He also recognized that there were trade-offs, personal sacrifices. "You had to be a special breed of person to do sessions, almost insensitive. Some of the producers were assholes." There were artistic temperaments aplenty swirling about. You had to be able to placate the various parties involved without taking sides. Jimmy Page certainly had a thick enough skin. He was self-contained, able to keep an emotional distance from the distractions and flare-ups in the studio.

By mid-1963, Jimmy, now nineteen, was doing all the work he could handle, often as many as three sessions a day: from 10:00 a.m. to 1:00 p.m.; 2:00 p.m. to 5:00 p.m.; and 7:00 p.m. to 10:00 p.m. Drummer Bobby Graham recalled the nerve-racking revolving-door format. "The first session in the morning could be with Tommy Kinsman and his strict-tempo dance orchestra at the Philips studios, then you'd dash across to EMI and it would be a film session or P.J. Proby with a big orchestra, then dash across to Pye in the evening and it would be the Kinks." It ran Jimmy ragged. "You never knew what you were going to do," he lamented. "Sometimes it would be someone you were happy to see, other times it was 'What am I doing here?'"

No matter what, you never complained, otherwise you'd be put "on holiday," a euphemism for suspension, often for as long as two weeks. Money seemed to temper the bellyaches. At the end of the day, a power broker named Charlie Katz handed each session player a little brown envelope with as much as £23 in cash, a king's ransom. If you worked five days a week, like Jimmy Page, you'd struck a rich vein.

The sessions he did were sometimes heady. Highlights included: "I Will" for Billy Fury; Petula Clark's smash hit "Downtown"; Marianne Faithfull's classic "As Tears Go By"; Tom Jones's signature "It's Not Unusual"; The Nashville Teens' "Tobacco Road"; "The Pied Piper" by Crispian St. Peters; the Rolling Stones' demo for "Heart of Stone"; and the theme to *Goldfinger*, sung inimitably by Shirley Bassey. "That was a phenomenal session," Jimmy recalled. "She arrived, took off her coat and went straight in. [Arranger] John Barry counted us in, she sang and at the end, just collapsed on the floor." Graham Nash, the Hollies' extraordinary singer, recalls visiting an early Everly Brothers session in London, where he encountered "a shockingly baby-faced Jimmy Page on guitar and sixteen-year-old Elton John on piano."

"What was stifling," Jimmy said, "was not really knowing what you were going to be doing when you were booked for a session at a particular time. It could be anything from a group to some sort of Muzak type of thing." One time, he pushed through the doors of Olympic Studios, oblivious as usual to whom he'd be working with. "It just happened to be Cliff [Richard] and Hank [Marvin]," he said, barely able to contain his fanboy excitement. "I wasn't on guitar, obviously, but I played harmonica on 'Time Drags By.'" Of course, there were days he pushed through those doors and came face to face with . . . Tubby Hayes, a tenor sax player. No matter who commanded the mic, you had to get up for it.

Jimmy played on hundreds of sessions between 1963 and 1967. His

main assignment had been to back up vocalists, but as the British
music scene began to swell with gifted groups who wrote their own
material, Jimmy's role took a new turn. Suddenly, he found himself
booked for sessions with a new breed of rock 'n roll band, groups who
felt proprietary about playing their own songs. "You'd be there to
strengthen the weak links," he said, "if the drummer wasn't tight
enough or the guitarist not up to scratch."

On July 15, 1964, Glyn Johns sent Jimmy to IBC Studios for a date
under the whip hand of producer Shel Talmy. Talmy was a twenty-
two-year-old American with some engineering experience who had
talked his way into a job at Decca Records by claiming he'd produced the Beach Boys' "Surfin' Safari." "I don't think he had any qual-
ifications at all," says Johns, who'd go on to work often with Talmy, "but
it didn't matter, because he had a great ear and a great sense of feel, to
say nothing of extreme self-confidence. He stepped in with this line of
bullshit that he was the man, and the English labels were as green as
grass, so they bought it without asking questions." Decca, which was
making what Talmy calls "polite, old-fashioned rock 'n roll" records,
lusted after the "American sound" and pressed him to inject a good
dose of it into their acts.

"That meant making my records louder than anybody else's," he
says. He used old valve limiter/compressors to boost dynamic range
and redlined levels to create a garage-band feel. "I'd put guitar on two
channels, pushing one to the point of distortion, the other just simmering under it so it would carry the tune. And I recorded drums
with twelve mics, where the Brits had been using three."

His first major breakthrough was a band called the Creation, a
straight-ahead British rock 'n roll band with a hotshot guitarist, Eddie
Phillips—Talmy calls him "the best unknown guitarist of all time"—
who pushed the instrument into bold new places, including using a violin bow to generate extraordinary sounds. (Kenny Pickett, who was
a roadie on Led Zeppelin's first U.S. tour, briefly served as the group's
vocalist.) Following two quick European number-one hits, Talmy

made an American deal for the Creation with Atlantic Records. "This preceded Cream," Talmy says, "so the Creation would have been Atlantic's first English white rock 'n roll band, but they self-destructed and the deal fell apart."

His follow-up was the Kinks, with another stellar guitarist, Dave Davies. Their first single, a cover of Little Richard's "Long Tall Sally," wasn't the breakout hit they'd hoped for. But Davies's brother Ray had written a barn burner, "You Really Got Me," that Talmy was convinced would change the shape of British rock 'n roll. It was raw and aggressive, with a great, arresting riff—and *loud*. Still, he wasn't convinced the band had the goods to deliver it. "They weren't studio musicians," Talmy is quick to point out. "They were too undisciplined, too loosey-goosey, too used to playing in clubs. They could play adequately but not outstandingly. I couldn't take a chance." Instead, Talmy brought in a quartet of session players, including drummer Bobby Graham and Jimmy Page—"as insurance," he says, "just to play rhythm, because Ray Davies didn't feel he was good enough to handle it."

Even so, Jimmy acknowledged, "Ray didn't really approve of my presence." The new breed of rock 'n roll musician was sensitive about image. Their lack of authority in the studio was a particular sore spot, which the sudden appearance of a session musician only exacerbated. It was like having a relief pitcher come in from the bullpen with the league's best hitter up at the plate.

Despite the awkwardness, that same month Jimmy was called into another Shel Talmy session with a group seemingly capable of playing their own material. "Until The Who came along, no British band was doing rock 'n roll right," Talmy says. "But at the time, I wasn't sure how good of a rhythm player Pete Townshend was, so I brought Jimmy Page in as a backup on The Who's first single, 'I Can't Explain.'"

To his credit, Jimmy admits, "I wasn't really needed." He played the barest of supporting roles on two or three sides. "Just strengthening up riffs, that's all—two guitars doing it instead of one."

Pete Townshend was gracious about it. But later that year, in November 1964, the mood grew downright disagreeable during a session at Decca's studio. Jimmy had been hired to sit in with a self-contained band from Belfast called Them, a pugnacious bunch of characters. He immediately sensed his presence was unwelcome and withdrew into a shell, a condition the band misinterpreted as "a stuck-up prick who thought he was better than the rest of the world." Jimmy understood the awkward situation and wasn't without empathy. "It was very embarrassing," he recalled, "because you noticed that as each number passed, another member of the band would be substituted by a session musician. . . . Talk about daggers!" According to Billy Harrison, Them's guitarist, "There was much grumbling, mostly from me." Harrison harvested a few blistering riffs that needed no reinforcement. Bobby Graham, who sat in on drums, remembered, "Their lead vocalist, Van Morrison, was really hostile." Despite the palpable antagonism, the session produced three monster tracks: "Baby, Please Don't Go," "Gloria," and "Don't Stop Crying Now."

The session's producer, Bert Berns, an American music-business hustler who had cowritten the hits "Twist and Shout," "Tell Him," "Piece of My Heart," and "Hang on Sloopy," effectively held the session's emotions to a simmer, perhaps even giving them a stir once or twice to raise the heat on those tracks. Whatever his intentions were, he recognized Jimmy's flair for spicing up an arrangement and hired him on the spot to add zest to another Berns-penned song, "Here Comes the Night," with a Scottish group, Lulu & the Luvvers.

The demand for Jimmy's services was stronger than ever. He had proved his worth on dozens of recordings that climbed to the top of the UK charts. "There wasn't anyone more reliable—or more creative," Shel Talmy says. Jimmy functioned as the go-to guitarist for almost every producer who sought to capture the zeitgeist that was fast transforming the London music scene. In the few short years between 1963 and 1965, groups like the Beatles, The Who, and the Rolling Stones kicked over the traces of the once-derivative pop genre for a more authentic, original, rougher sound. The Brits were empire-building again. They were reinventing rock 'n roll. Jimmy Page had carved out a niche at its edges, angling to establish exactly where he fit into it.

## [3]

There were hits—and misses.

At the close of 1964, Jimmy found himself booked at EMI's Abbey Road Studios for a demo session with Jackie DeShannon. A bewitching twenty-two-year-old who had been singing professionally in the States since the age of thirteen, DeShannon flourished primarily as a songwriter, partnering with Eddie Cochran's girlfriend, Sharon Sheeley, on early hits for Brenda Lee and the Fleetwoods. Her own singles—"Needles and Pins" and "When You Walk into the Room"—fared modestly but brought her to the attention of the Beatles, whom she supported on their first U.S. tour. Afterward, it was no coincidence that she wound up in London—or that the Beatles' Liverpool mates the Searchers had smash hits covering her singles.

DeShannon, three years older than Jimmy, could accompany herself, but she was no James Burton or Glen Campbell, both of whom had backed her in the past. London hadn't yet developed its own crack crew of eligible guitar greats. Only Jimmy Page's name kept coming up. That was all DeShannon had to hear. "Great, let's have him," she demanded.

They rehearsed a number she'd written called "Don't Turn Your Back on Me," and the two had instant chemistry. They collaborated on writing a number of songs—the first time Jimmy Page ventured down that path—bringing instant success. "Come and Stay with Me," which scored a top-ten hit for Marianne Faithfull, was a steamy little ballad drawn from life. In no time, the two were embarked headlong into a relationship that zigzagged between commerce and romance.

Phase one, which emphasized songwriting, contrived to launch Jimmy as an artist in his own right. That same month, February 1965, he released a single, "She Just Satisfies," on Phillips's Fontana label. A reworking of the Kinks' "Revenge," on which he'd played, it was one of those vanity projects showcasing Jimmy on every instrument except for drums. His ambition was on full display, but an ebullient harmonica flourish between verses wasn't enough to rescue the lukewarm song and mannered delivery that never kicked into a high enough gear. Nor did the flip side, "Keep Moving," a mostly instrumental track with some florid vocal outbursts by Jackie DeShannon that tried too hard to cram every bluesy element into the arrangement until the center fell out. *Record Mirror*'s review summed the disc up neatly: "Furious beat with vocal touches almost vanishing in a welter of amplified backing." Despite the record's disappointing response, there was talk of recording a follow-up, but Jimmy didn't see much point in pursuing it.

Instead, he veered into phase two, which would pay lasting dividends.

Jackie convinced him to accompany her to the States, where the rock 'n roll furnaces were blasting away from coast to coast. In New York City, a preliminary stop, Jimmy kipped with Bert Berns, with whom he'd forged a friendship during the Them sessions. Berns had been a staff producer for Atlantic Records and was in the process of finalizing a deal there for his own independent label, which would be called Bang, after the parent company's principals: Bert Berns, Ahmet Ertegun, Nesuhi Ertegun, and Gerald "Jerry" Wexler. Berns introduced Jimmy to his label partners during sessions for Barbara Lewis and the Strangeloves, a trio of Brill Building songwriters that produced the punk rave-up "I Want Candy." Wexler, as astute a businessman as he was a producer, shrewdly filed away his introduction to Jimmy as a sideman extraordinaire whom Berns intended to use on R&B sessions.

When that didn't pan out, Jimmy flew to Los Angeles—right back into Jackie DeShannon's arms. Los Angeles dazzled Jimmy, as it did so many young British rock 'n rollers who had slogged through rationing and the ennui of postwar England. LA in 1965 was relentlessly sunny and laid-back, with the giddy, buoyant aura of a Beach Boys / Jan and Dean recording and gorgeous young women galore. Music was blaring from every bungalow, beach, and palm grove. "What wasn't to love?" as the Hollies' Graham Nash put it.

Jimmy and Jackie immediately turned on the juice, churning out a portfolio of songs that resulted in important records for P.J. Proby, Esther Phillips, and Dave Berry and album tracks for Marianne Faithfull. They even collaborated musically on "What the World Needs Now Is Love," Jackie's bravura version of the Burt Bacharach / Hal David anthem that shot to the top of the charts. But the output and the relationship couldn't sustain themselves. The kind of songwriting they were doing wasn't exciting enough for a player like Jimmy; it wasn't where the action was, it didn't break new ground. And relations with Jackie got too weird for his taste.

Besides, the music scene in London had begun firing on all cylinders, reshaping rock 'n roll in a way that would ultimately change the world. It was time to go home, to be part of it. It was time for Jimmy Page to get down to business.

## Chapter Three

# REINVENTING THE WHEEL

## [1]

Nothing defined the twin poles of Britain's music revolution quite like the Beatles and the Rolling Stones. The Beatles' records demonstrated all that pop could be, with original melodies and riveting harmonies, while the Stones worked the dark corners of the British electric blues idiom. The two extremes, like all guiding lights, attracted missionaries who steered the direction of music into new and offbeat trajectories. In 1965, a significant crossroads for rock 'n roll, there was a desperate desire for new voices, voices that took on the institutions of pop with a brash disregard for convention.

Astutely, Jimmy Page kept a foot in both camps. On the one hand, he continued his schedule of session work at a breakneck pace, sitting in with Brian Poole & the Tremeloes, First Gear, and Manish Boys, the latter a Shel Talmy production featuring a seventeen-year-old singer named David Jones, who, a few years later, would morph into David Bowie. Other session work leaned heavily on the output of producer Mickie Most.

Most began his career flogging a dated cabaret act, most successfully in South Africa, performing rock 'n roll hits he had no business covering. "He was a ridiculous figure who sang off-key," says Shel Talmy. "But he had ears, he knew how to pick songs." During a tour that took him through Newcastle, Most caught an act appearing at Club a'Gogo and made an impassioned pitch to produce them, a task for which he had no experience. His second effort with them, a somber four-minute single, "The House of the Rising Sun," rocketed Most and the Animals to international fame in 1964. In a little over two years, he produced a string of number-one hits for the Animals, as well as for the Nashville Teens, Brenda Lee, and Herman's Hermits, who clocked six million-selling singles in 1965 alone.

Jimmy Page and bass player/arranger John Paul Jones, both twenty-one, were trusted members of Most's versatile hit-making crew, including two important sessions they did with Donovan—"Sunshine Superman" and "Mellow Yellow"—designed to transform the Scottish singer from his former guise as "a poor man's Bob Dylan" into an eclectic hippie Pied Piper. "They made making records easy for me," Most recalled. In return, Jimmy got an eyeful watching Mickie work the board, learning tricks of the trade, as well as what *not* to do in the studio.

"Mickie had no patience," according to his wife, Chris. "His goal was to make a hit record in three hours and go home." (Most famously he insisted a pop song need take no more than a fleet fifteen minutes to make.) "Mickie," said Chris Dreja, "wanted the backing track at ten, lunch at twelve, overdub vocals by five, and home for dinner." Often, he'd read the newspaper or make phone calls while tape rolled. His respect was reserved for the song—specifically mainstream commercial hits—not necessarily the artist. "All he cared about were singles, and he didn't give a shit about albums." He was therefore regarded as a philistine by many musicians and singers.

With Mickie Most, Jimmy could do his best Clark Kent imitation, playing super-slick guitar on demand by day, then, after the sun set, donning street gear to gig with a pianist named Andy Wren and other down-and-dirty bands at the Marquee. This way, he kept himself in the game, developing solid R&B chops. He became masterful at tweaking solos he played with an array of electronics, taking the blues to another dimension.

The perfect instrument had come into Jimmy's hands while he was touring with Neil Christian. He'd seen it hung like a trophy on the wall of a shop and decided on the spot to trade his Gretsch Chet Atkins for the gleaming black Gibson Les Paul Custom tricked out with three gold-plated humbucker pickups. It was a gorgeous piece of ax, carved out of a solid piece of mahogany, with a wide neck and ebony fingerboard that allowed him to bend strings to his heart's content without skating off the edge. No doubt about it, the Black Beauty, as it became known, was "more responsive to the player's touch." The Les Paul had a punchier, almost guttural sound than the Gretsch, and with a fuzz box Jimmy was using, he could rev the Les Paul into overdrive.

A *fuzz box*? The idea for it had come Jimmy's way a year earlier during a get-together in his parents' front parlor. On a Sunday afternoon, he'd been hanging out with Jeff Beck and a pal named Roger Mayer, whom he'd met at a local youth club. They were analyzing the sounds American artists were getting out of their guitars, trying to figure out what made them so unique. Every time they encountered a particularly innovative tone, either Jimmy or Jeff would say, "I wonder if we can build something to make it sound like that." Something that sounded like a guitarist had stuck his finger in a socket or like his amp was about to blow a fuse. Jimmy knew that Dave Davies had made a small slice in the speaker cone of his amp to pull off the distorted solo in "You Really Got Me" but figured there had to be a more practical way to achieve it.

Roger Mayer immediately perked up. Mayer was an electronics whiz. He'd left school at the age of seventeen to work for the British Admiralty, performing vibration and acoustical analyses that would enable the government to better detect the sounds of submarines. "Jimmy had a Gibson Maestro fuzz tone which the Ventures used on 'The 2000 Pound Bee,' but it sounded mechanical and, quite honestly, boring," Mayer recalls. "He was unhappy with the sustain. So I took apart the Maestro and redesigned the circuit, winding it up with more gain, which increased the sustain." With the new design, Jimmy could hold the note indefinitely or make a completely different sound. Mayer didn't simply want to produce distortion, which caused noise in the signal. His goal was to change the sound of the guitar from a basic electric string instrument into something that was new and exciting. "Once I solved that," Mayer says, "I produced my own version of the fuzz box, and within a matter of months everyone wanted one."

A few years later, Mayer would partner with Jimi Hendrix and Stevie Wonder, two "far-out acoustical visionaries," who helped him understand that the concept of sound was infinite, that there were no limits to what you could do with it. In the meantime, Mayer gave Jimmy Page a tool that enabled him to play dynamic solos using an assortment of tones and basically reinvent the wheel.

It might not have played out that way in lesser hands. The fuzz box provided a new range of interesting sounds, but it was Jimmy's artistry, his imagination, that plied the electronics to express a larger intention. As a lead guitarist, he knew he couldn't practice a solo. He knew he had to be in the zone where the music took him, able to let himself go, much like free-form jazz. There was only so much muscle memory in the hand; the rest, the magic, came from what was in one's head. And Jimmy's head was primed to explore, completely in sync with his instrument. He couldn't really sing, so his guitar took him to places where singers go. He put everything he had into mastering technique, then gave himself over to the magic.

But magic, as conjurers know, is nothing but an illusion. Jimmy needed something more creative, more challenging—more *substantial*—to distract him. Session work had become too much of a grind. The sessions themselves were mechanical affairs. He played whatever was put in front of him for whoever happened to be standing in front of the mic; it required little personal investment. "The whole thing wasn't enjoyable anymore," he admitted. "The work was stifling." It was a paycheck, nothing more. He felt he'd become "a hired hand, a phantom musician." For some time, he'd considered walking away, but the incentive wasn't strong enough. "Until the day I was booked to do a Muzak session, and then it really came down hard as to what it was all about."

While he was mulling options, Andrew Loog Oldham came to his rescue. Oldham was a brash, flamboyant twenty-one-year-old provocateur who had snatched the management of the Rolling Stones from under the nose Giorgio Gomelsky. In 1965, Oldham launched Immediate Records, one of the first independent labels in the UK, and he dangled a staff producer's job to Jimmy.

It was a tantalizing offer. Producing records was a hands-on job; it would give Jimmy creative control over a session, something he'd never had before. But it meant working for Oldham, which was no walk in the park. Jimmy knew Andrew from a session he had played on for Marianne Faithfull's "As Tears Go By" and a few demos for the Stones.

"I know all the crooks," he told an interviewer who asked about his involvement with Oldham. Oldham was known as a hotshot—crafty and opportunistic, not always on the up-and-up. On the other hand, he had a remarkable ear and had his finger on the pulse of the international music business. The new company's manifesto boiled down to its name—*immediate*. There would be no dithering around, no "old farts" controlling the roster, no corporate higher-ups to convince, no budget restrictions. It was *bang, bang, bang*, make those records, get them out, move on. All things considered, the Immediate job was too good to pass up.

Beginning in August 1965, Jimmy produced a series of sessions, beginning with the experimental British band Les Fleurs de Lys, then Chris Farlowe (with Albert Lee on guitar), Small Faces, German chanteuse Nico, Goldie (who later materialized as Genya Ravan with Ten Wheel Drive), and perhaps his most important contribution, John Mayall's Bluesbreakers, with Eric Clapton on guitar.

Jimmy already enjoyed a friendship with Eric. The two had met during one of the Marquee's Thursday-night jams, when Jimmy sat in with Cyril Davies's band, and they'd sporadically bumped into each other at various studios, doing session work. It isn't a stretch to understand their mutual attraction. They were two teenagers who had grown up six miles apart, both art college refugees, both blues aficionados, both prolific, obsessive guitarists, both perfectionists. "I did four tracks altogether with Mayall and Eric," Jimmy recalled—a single of "I'm Your Witchdoctor" backed with "Telephone Blues," and later "Sitting on Top of the World" and "Double Crossing Time," which appeared on a Bluesbreakers album released by Decca.

Immediate proved to be a first-rate apprenticeship. The studio work was creative but challenging—the recording equipment prehistoric by current standards. The tape consoles used either two- or three-track machines that were no more sophisticated than what Jimmy had at home. There were no screens to separate the rhythm section from the drums, so leakage was always an issue. The engineers, especially, lacked imagination.

During the Clapton sessions, the technician proved too conservative for Jimmy's tastes. For the recording of "Witchdoctor," Eric decided to overdub his solo, giving a savage touch of edge to the top end. Accordingly, the levels redlined as if they'd detected radioactivity in the studio, which panicked the engineer. "He'd never heard feedback before," Jimmy recalled. "At one point he screamed out and pulled the faders down on the console." He attempted to scrap the take, calling it unrecordable—*totally unrecordable!*—until Jimmy intervened. "I told him to put the faders up and let me worry about it."

No one, not Shel Talmy, not even Phil Spector, had recorded that kind of a guitar sound before. The lavish use of reverb was daring, game-changing. The way the solo reached for the cosmos provided a stunning jolt of excitement. It took what would otherwise have been a simple musical passage and turned it into spectacle. Page and Clapton had changed the course of how a guitar sounded on record. This was no happy accident. Jimmy had synthesized his years of experience in recording studios with the experimentation he was doing at home and applied it, note by note, to the way he produced records. He laid a steady, confident hand on the controls, advancing the process with effects and electronics. It was like painting with sound. The canvas was still vast and open to possibilities; Jimmy had only scratched the surface.

### [2]

Throughout 1965 and 1966, Jimmy Page drifted from his various day jobs to establish his presence on the flourishing club circuit, where new music was being made. The clubs attracted players much like him who were bumping around the scene, trying to figure out where they fit into the larger picture. On any given night, a spontaneous jam might include Nicky Hopkins, Albert Lee, Jon Lord, Peter Green, Chris Farlowe, Eric Clapton, or Keith Emerson, standout musicians who were the architects of the British rock establishment.

"I'd been going to gigs at Eel Pie [Island], I'd been going to gigs at the Marquee, and I could see it all happen," Jimmy observed.

Still, many of the bands he encountered were too dependent on the past or derivative, merely extracting the essence of true originals like the Beatles and the Rolling Stones. The Stones especially had fused a decidedly edgy, rock 'n roll sensibility to the R&B heard in the clubs, giving the blues an entirely new sound.

Two young musicians—Paul Samwell-Smith and Jim McCarty— had studied the Stones the way Botticelli studied Fra Filippo Lippi, "with awe-stricken disbelief." The Stones managed to interpret all the blues Samwell-Smith and McCarty had been listening to in a way that gave new meaning to it. "It was exactly how we wanted to play the blues," McCarty remembers. "It was the sound we wanted to make."

They'd been experimenting with it in various half-assed configurations, including the Country Gentlemen and the Metropolitan Blues

Quartet. At one point, they were four guitars and a drummer, with a repertoire that hewed to the tried-and-true blues classics already making the rounds. After shaking out the dead weight and reshuffling the lineup, the band that materialized consisted of Samwell-Smith and McCarty, Chris Dreja and Tony "Top" Topham on guitars, and a Brian Jones–lookalike lead singer, Keith Relf, who played a mean harmonica. During a gig at Eel Pie Island opening for the Cyril Davies All-Stars, they came up with a name. "We're the Yardbirds!" they announced from the stage.

"In a matter of weeks, we went from being a warm-up band to being the main attraction," said Chris Dreja. The Yardbirds inherited the Stones' Richmond residency—now called the Crawdaddy Club— and were packing the house with their own brand of electric blues that expressed a less structured, tougher, scrappier sound. They took R&B standards like "Good Morning Little Schoolgirl," "I Wish You Would," and "Got Love If You Want It," and added volume, supercharged tempos, and distortion to the arrangements. Keith Relf treated the harmonica like most bands did a lead guitar, winding out long, asthmatic solos that dueled vigorously with the rhythm section. As Jimmy Page would later note, "The colors were starting to show in the palette."

With the Rolling Stones and the Yardbirds, the cap was off the gusher, supplying a steady flow of dynamic young British electric blues bands. On any weekend night, one could make the rounds of the local clubs and hear the Pretty Things, the Animals, the Graham Bond Organisation, Brian Auger, Mayall's Bluesbreakers, and Georgie Fame and the Blue Flames.

The Yardbirds especially changed up the blues with their signature rave-up instrumental solos. Still, something was missing from the mix. Their lead guitarist, Top Topham, was merely adequate, "a bit stiff." "A nice kid, he really wasn't up to it," Jim McCarty recalls. In any case, Top's parents laid down the law. He was too young, they said, to turn pro with a band. Replacing him was left up to Giorgio

Gomelsky, the Crawdaddy Club's manager, who looked after the Yardbirds' management. According to Gomelsky, it was a no-brainer. "I asked Eric Clapton to join."

Eric Clapton wasn't merely an understudy. He was a player of impeccable taste. There were a few like him who could play unconventional, complex licks, but not with his commitment—nor his touch. The touch was gorgeous. By bending and sustaining notes—a technique he learned by listening to Freddie King records—Clapton could make the guitar sing. When he stepped into the Yardbirds, the result was magical. The band came alive in an extraordinary way.

The Yardbirds, perhaps more than any other band, exemplified the British electric blues idiom. They really dug into the R&B songbook, mining obscure nuggets like John Lee Hooker's "Boom Boom," and "Baby What's Wrong" by Sonny Boy Williamson. They played aggressively, dynamically, by taking beloved blues standards and opening them up—"jamming in the middle," as Clapton described it, "usually with a staccato bass line, which would get louder and louder, rising to a crescendo before coming back down again." So versions of, say, "Good Morning Little Schoolgirl" or "I Wish You Would," which normally ran about two and a half minutes, became six-minute scorchers in the Yardbirds' hands.

Clapton energized the Yardbirds for eighteen months, through a brutal schedule of one-nighters and an unparalleled maiden recording-studio experience. The Yardbirds, like the Stones, were one of the first self-contained British blues bands to snag a major-label record contract. It was their breakout—and ultimately their undoing, as far as Eric Clapton was concerned. "He was obsessed with the blues," Jimmy Page said, "with wanting to sound really authentic." Clapton considered himself a *purist*. "I have to play what I believe is pure and sincere and uncorrupted music," he said. He wasn't interested in making clean-cut, commercial music with Top 40 hit potential, and when the Yardbirds selected the catchy "For Your Love" instead of a purer blues cover like Otis Redding's "Your One and Only Man" for their breakout single, Clapton had had enough. The way he saw it, "I was destroy-ing myself." In mid-February 1965, the week before "For Your Love" was released, he jumped ship.

To replace him, the Yardbirds made a play for Jimmy Page. Jimmy knew the Yardbirds. "He used to come around regularly when we played gigs," Jim McCarty recalls. "It was soon after that that Giorgio asked him to join the band." In fact, Gomelsky, long fed up with Clap-ton's fussy attitude, had approached Page about stepping into the band on an earlier occasion, claiming Eric was taking "a holiday" from per-forming. Page knew bullshit when he heard it; *holiday* was code for sacking. Besides, he and Clapton were friends. Eric was a frequent par-ticipant in the Sunday-afternoon jams at Jimmy's house. "The way [Gomelsky] put it to me, it just seemed really distasteful," Page said, "and I refused."

This time, Jimmy's excuse was his job at Immediate, but he offered a proxy—his good friend Jeff Beck. While the recommendation made sense, first impressions were not exactly inspiring. An audition in March 1965 almost ended before it began. "We were so taken aback by [Jeff's] appearance," Jim McCarty recalled. "His clothes were grease-stained, and he looked like he'd not taken them off for a week. His hair was long, lank, and greasy too." Eric Clapton had been a fash-ion plate, always decked out in the latest threads; Jeff Beck looked more donkey than clotheshorse. None of it mattered, however, when they put him to the test. The band threw everything in their songbook at Beck, who handled each as if he were Superman absorbing enemy bullets. The guy was not of this world. He could play anything—*anything*. And not just the intricate blues arrangements but the rave-ups as well.

Beck was the antithesis of the meticulous Eric Clapton. "Musi-cally, he was so versatile," Jim McCarty recalled. "Jeff looked ready to blow the blues out of the water, and take every other genre with it." Sure, he'd play the blues—but he'd twist it into knots. He'd leave his echo on during a reverent number and drive a stake through the hearts of the purists. Or he'd add fuzz to a hallowed riff. He had no respect. Echo, distortion, jarring his amp, feedback, you never knew what effect he'd come up with next. "He was a great experimenter," said Chris Dreja. "If you wanted a sound like a police siren, Jeff would make it. . . . He was a genius at creating soundscapes."

"We were using feedback all the time," Beck recalled. "You had no choice, because the amplifiers would feed back anyway. It would start whistling and singing, then you found that you could probably handle it and make quite an interesting trumpeting noise with it, and with an echo, all sorts of mysteries started to happen and it would sound really bizarre."

Dreja admits the Yardbirds took Beck for granted. They continued to compare his playing to Eric Clapton's. "They were always talking about Eric this and Eric that," Beck complained. Finally he just said, "Fuck Eric Clapton—you know, *I'm* your guitarist."

Wasn't that the truth! Beck took the Yardbirds to extraordinary new heights. Their blues became bluesier, their gigs more unhinged. He rocked harder, so that audiences who came to see the band became more homogenized, nonpartisan. You want to hear a rustic "I Ain't Done Wrong" or "I'm a King Bee"? Coming right up. But you're also going to hear a red-hot rockabilly "Train Kept a-Rollin'," Johnny Burnette style, which Beck introduced as a Yardbirds staple.

And he had no problem embracing a killer pop song. When it came time to record the Yardbirds' follow-up to "For Your Love," the songwriter Graham Gouldman dredged up another sure shot. "Heart Full of Soul" was made to order. It had an unforgettable riff, an embraceable lyric, and, in what was turning out to be a Yardbirds signature, a weird-sounding instrument. In "For Your Love" it had been a harpsichord; for the new single, they added a sitar. A—*what?* This was before "Norwegian Wood," before George Harrison made the sitar a household item, like the Hoover.

Unfortunately, the classically trained Indian musicians hired to play it couldn't handle the timing of the dominant riff. "They could only play Indian music," says Jim McCarty. "A rock beat completely eluded them." Beck suggested that he give it a try instead. It didn't matter that he'd never seen a sitar, much less played one. He didn't need one, in fact. He came up with an entirely different plan, using his trusty Fender Esquire. "By bending the notes slightly off key, I duplicated the sound of a sitar," he recalled. "I then got the idea to use fuzz to dirty-up the amp." Fortunately for Beck, Jimmy Page was visiting in the studio and happened to have a fuzz box with him. One take with the gear and Beck nailed it, sending the sitar players packing.

Even with Beck now at the helm, the Yardbirds were more determined than ever to keep the blues tradition center stage. They just souped it up another few volts by prevailing upon their lead guitarist to be more innovative, outrageous. Presto: a new species called progressive blues, which Beck epitomized with such barn burners as "Steeled Blues" and "Jeff's Boogie." A nice balance was struck. The Yardbirds could remain faithful to their artsy heritage and still have commercially successful, blues-based pop singles. "Heart Full of Soul" soared straight to the top of the pop charts, as did its successors, "Evil-Hearted You," "Shapes of Things," and "Over Under Sideways Down."

But that formula also sowed discontent.

By mid-1966, following a couple triumphant tours in the States, the Yardbirds were in disarray. Their management was in flux, money disappeared, grievances piled up. Bass player Paul Samwell-Smith was losing interest, lead singer Keith Relf's drinking verged on self-destructive. Something had to give.

Tensions came to a head on June 18, 1966, a little over a year after Jeff Beck joined the Yardbirds. The band was booked to costar with the Hollies at Queens' College for Cambridge University's prestigious May Ball. It was a fancy-dress affair, quite posh, and bathed in tradition, in a setting that rubbed the musicians' working-class sensitivities the wrong way. Keith Relf, for one, felt "uncomfortable playing to the elite of the English establishment," and almost from the moment he arrived he began dipping into the prodigious stash of complimentary liquor laid on by the college's catering service. Meanwhile, Jeff Beck, who drove to the gig in his snazzy Ford Zephyr Six, brought along Jimmy Page for moral support.

"It was a great crowd that night, one of those end-of-term parties, and everyone was fucked up," recalls Graham Nash, who performed with the Hollies. Nash had arrived from London in a Rolls-Royce with Mama Cass Elliot. The two friends were feeling no pain, having fortified themselves on the trip north on rations of gin and weed. It was a high old time backstage when they arrived. Relf was stuporously drunk and looking for camaraderie. To that end, Allan Clarke, the Hollies' lead singer, engaged him in a game of quick draw, in which the two pretend cowboys whipped their pretend guns out of pretend holsters. Alas, the fascination with this wore off quickly. Clarke then dug a broom with a thick handle out of a closet and bragged that he was expert at karate-chopping such objects. "Those broom handles were stronger than hell. They're made out of hickory," according to Nash, who observed the contest with a mixture of amusement and foreboding.

"Do you know about karate?" Clarke asked Relf. Keith said no, so Alan said, "All right, I'll show you how to break things with your hands. You can break that broomstick—and that chair. Let's have a go."

Nash recalled, "Keith took the first swing at it and broke [all the fingers on] his fucking hand, at which point Alan decided he wasn't going to have a go."

By showtime, Relf was drunk, in pain, and generally pissed off at the audience. Miraculously, he managed to pull off a brilliant first set, but when the Yardbirds returned to the stage after an intermission, all bets were off. "Keith decided to have some fun," Jim McCarty recalled, "first slurring his words and forgetting his lyrics, and then spending one entire number . . . just blowing raspberries into the microphone." He berated the crowd, "rolling round the stage, grappling with the mic, blowing his harmonica in all the wrong places." To keep him upright, Chris Dreja said, "we had to literally tie him to the microphone." For extra support, someone stuffed the broken broom handle down the back of his shirt, though it didn't keep him from falling into the drums. The punk performance could have been a blueprint for the Ramones.

Jimmy Page loved every minute of it; it was "just fantastically suitable for the occasion," he thought. "I thought it was a great anarchistic night," he said, "and I went back into the dressing room and said, 'What a brilliant show.'" Not everyone was as giddy as Page. Paul Samwell-Smith—Sam, as he was called—was in a huff, just furious. As the poet said: too much monkey business. The embarrassing scene, for him, was the last straw. "I can't stand this anymore," Sam fumed while packing up. "I'm leaving the group, and if I were you, Keith, I'd do the same." With that, he made an exit, stage left.

On the drive back home, Beck and Page discussed the fate of the Yardbirds. Beck confessed how much he enjoyed playing with the band and mourned Samwell-Smith's imminent departure. Sam's contribution had been enormous; he was a consummate musician, a perfectionist, devoted to the blues. But Beck also saw this as an opportunity to get Jimmy involved.

"Jeff often used to say, 'I wish you could join and we could play together,' and I agreed that it would be good," Jimmy said, "but I never took it seriously, because there was this thing about *five* Yardbirds, and to bring in a sixth would have destroyed that. So my joining was never a real consideration."

But now Beck sensed Page had grown bored navigating the studio treadmill, where he often played on sessions and oversaw productions with little artistic payoff. It was a grind on so many levels. Jimmy had become nothing more than a mechanic, punching the clock. "I began to feel limited," he explained, "not being able to express myself." He felt he was "drying up as a guitarist." Playing with a band would allow him to get back into action, to stretch out, to show off his chops.

Beck wondered aloud how the Yardbirds would fulfill their upcoming gig at the Marquee in London. He knew Jimmy wasn't a bass player, but what the hell—it only had four strings. In the meantime, they'd try to convince Chris Dreja to move to the bass from guitar, where he was marginal, at best, so that Jeff and Jimmy could step out to play dual leads. Wouldn't that just be mind-blowing! Page didn't need any more coaxing: "Yeah, I'll play bass," he volunteered.

The next week, on June 21, he sat in with the Yardbirds during a gig at the Marquee to determine the fit and whether he'd enjoy another go-round with a band.

"I was terrified, having to fill Samwell-Smith's role," Jimmy admitted, "but fortunately it went okay."

Beck, for his part, considered the experiment an absolute calamity. "He couldn't play the bass for toffee," according to Jeff. "He was running all over the neck."

"I tended to play it like a guitar," Jimmy said. "I was just leaping around all over the place with great speed, and I had to stop doing that."

But the *music* . . . Playing those songs onstage was a rejuvenating experience. It was the real thing—the blues—not those cover tunes he'd done with Neil Christian & the Crusaders. With the blues you could stretch out and find a groove that felt right. And the band really cooked. They were all above-average musicians, Keith Relf could sing his ass off, and Jeff Beck—Beck was the wild card. He turned every song into a hair-raising thrill ride that teetered just this side of disaster.

"We needed stability, someone who could keep Jeff in check, while taking us to the next stage of our development," says Jim McCarty.

That night at the Marquee it all seemed to click. It was obvious who could help pull it all together.

It was official: Jimmy Page had joined the Yardbirds.

## [3]

But stability and the Yardbirds were incompatible.

The band had never enjoyed any stretch of internal peace, and their management was another dicey matter. It seemed that Giorgio Gomelsky kept a set of books that had the Yardbirds working for scratch. Despite their hit records and steady bookings, the musicians earned nothing more than a meager weekly wage. "We never saw any money," Jim McCarty says. Even the credit on most of their B sides was attributed to a songwriter billed only as O. Rasputin, an alias for none other than Giorgio Gomelsky. Sacking Giorgio became a foregone conclusion. His successor, however, was another story.

Simon Napier-Bell was a gadabout, a flashy man-about-town who had his fingers in as many pies as Mrs. Lovett. He was a frustrated musician, a film and music editor, an occasional journalist, and a denizen of the nightclub circuit, table-hopping at Annabel's, the Speakeasy, and the Bag O'Nails, where he felt right at home in the lap of Swinging London. Money had never been one of Napier-Bell's shortfalls. He lived near Buckingham Palace, in an apartment twenty-five floors above the Gorringes department store, and didn't shrink from the finer pleasures of life. "We'd see him drive down the King's Road in a Thunderbird convertible, smoking a fat cigar," McCarty recalls. "That image, at the time, was attractive to us."

Napier-Bell wasted no time renegotiating the Yardbirds' contracts with EMI in the UK and Epic Records in America, putting cash money, at long last, into the pockets of the band. He also had a riff in his head that he hummed to Jeff Beck that became the basis for their next hit, "Over Under Sideways Down."

At the outset, Napier-Bell wasn't keen on adding Jimmy Page to the band. "I didn't know much about rock musicians," he confessed, "but I had enough instinct to know it was a crazy idea." He cornered Jeff and expressed his concern that the idea of having two amazing lead guitar players spelled trouble. "But Beck absolutely insisted—and besides, Page would supposedly be playing bass."

With Napier-Bell and Jimmy Page aboard, all seemed peaceful in the Yardbirds camp—at least for a month or two. Jimmy continued to play bass and achieve a degree of harmony with the band, arbitrating wherever he could. Things were always tempestuous with Jeff Beck in the mix. Jeff harbored an eternal frustration. He was temperamental, erratic. If he picked up the slightest vibe that an audience was distracted, or that the rest of the band wasn't in sync with him, he'd walk off, just disappear. Beck acknowledged his prickly nature. "The amp would be crackling or my guitar would be out of tune or Keith Relf would be coughing or sputtering onstage," he explained. Any little distraction might set him off. The Yardbirds sensed they had a head case on their hands. "He did have a discipline [problem] occasionally," Jimmy allowed. "When he's having a shining night, he is fantastic. He plays things of sheer genius—but he's got a funny temperament at times."

Funny—and unpredictable, nerve-racking in fact. Napier-Bell and the Yardbirds attempted to placate Beck as best they could. "To keep me quiet, they said, 'Right, if you promise to play and do what you are told in this band, we'll let you have some studio time . . . and have your own album,'" he recalled.

To that end, Jeff and Jimmy booked a session at IBC Studios for May 16, 1966, and set to work coming up with material. They got together the night before in Epsom, in the Pages' front parlor, the scene of so many of their boyhood jams. Jimmy perched on the arm of a chair and began strumming a dramatic, Spanish-style rhythm, lush A major seventh and E minor seventh chords that gained in intensity and reverberated like an orchestra in the tiny room. "He had a twelve-string [guitar], and it sounded so full, fat and heavy," said Beck, who began to pick out a melody line over the top. Beck interrupted him after more than a few bars of repetition. "Jim," he said, "you've got to break away from the bolero beat—you can't go on like that forever."

*Bolero beat?* Of course! It reminded them of Ravel's orchestration for the legendary ballet. The way they phrased it, with real electricity, had inspired a nifty, unabashed tribute. It pulsed along mightily, picking up speed, but it never resolved. It needed something else, a moment of reckoning—a bridge, maybe, or another passage altogether—to move the piece forward, building to a crescendo.

Beck claims he went home and "worked out the other beat," a rowdy, guitar-driven progression—he called it "the first heavy metal riff ever written—that cuts right through the bolero effect and turns the song inside out, strengthening the power of its epic groove. It created a high-energy interplay that pointed back to the opening motif, allowing the two rhythms, in stylistic contrast, to fight it out in a blistering climax.

Jimmy insists he wrote the opening and the riff. "Keith Relf had a melody on tape, and we used that as a main part of the song," he argued. "Beck's doing the slide bits, and I'm basically playing around the chords." There was never any doubt in Jimmy's mind as to the authorship. Over the years, he stuck to his claim: "Even though he said he wrote it, I wrote it."

Whatever the case, they both agree it was "a momentous recording session." The cast of studio musicians they assembled raised the stakes dramatically. In addition to superduo Page and Beck, session master Nicky Hopkins played piano with The Who's wild man, Keith Moon, on drums. Moon's bandmate, John Entwistle, was booked to play bass, but when he failed to appear, John Paul Jones was recruited at the last minute to take his place. Entwistle may have gotten a case of cold feet. Had Pete Townshend gotten wind of Moon's and Entwistle's participation, all hell would have broken loose. "It was at a point when the [Who] was very close to breaking up," Townshend recalled. Even the usually headstrong Moon was nervous about crossing him. "He got out of the cab at IBC Studios in Langham Place wearing dark glasses and a Russian Cossack hat so that nobody could see him being naughty," Beck noted. Moon insisted they had to get right to it, to play fast; he could only afford three hours on the lam before The Who's roadies put out an APB on him.

"You could feel the excitement in the studio," Beck recalled, "even though we didn't know what we were going to play."

Jimmy and Jeff ran the song down twice, after which the others jumped right in. It needed no rehearsal, no tinkering. "We didn't deliberate, we just played it through," Beck recalled. There was a feeling of total exhilaration. The musicians were burrowed so deep in a groove, it was almost as if they were playing without calculation. Everything clicked neatly into place. The guitars' glissandos burst forth from the blizzard effect and slid artfully across the lines of modulation, whipped along by an overheated salvo of bass and drums—a torrential downpour of sound. "Keith upped the tempo and gave it an extra kick," Jeff said, acknowledging the intermarriage of styles in the mix. "It's a bit of The Who, a bit of the Yardbirds, and a bit of me"— but a completely unique alloy. They locked it down in one or two takes, then hit the sound board, adding layers of overdubs and effects.

"Beck's Bolero," as the piece became known, was a watershed moment for British rock 'n roll. It explored new, subversive possibilities in the form while demonstrating the technical progress being forged in the studio. The resulting track was as heavy and progressive as rock had been played. Its shifting meters, red-hot tempos, and powerful guitar riffs gave a physical tug to the music. It was disturbing—and invigorating. "Beck's Bolero" came before the Beatles' *Revolver*, before *Fresh Cream*, before Jimi Hendrix released "Hey Joe." It had no precedent, nothing to measure its innovation against.

The significance wasn't lost on Simon Napier-Bell, who babysat the "Bolero" session as its producer of record. "Cream was being formed at the same time," he observed. Word had circulated of a so-called supergroup. Yet this gang, Napier-Bell realized, had the makings of something equally special. There was a lot of talent in that studio on May 16. Could they coalesce into a band? It had certainly crossed Jimmy Page's and Jeff Beck's minds. Both would have loved to work with musicians who played at their level of virtuosity. They knew Keith Moon was game. "He told me in a club that he was sick of The Who," Beck recalled. John Entwistle was also intrigued by the prospect. With a little coaxing, he'd join in on bass.

"It was going to be me and Beck on guitars, Moon on drums, maybe Nicky Hopkins on piano," Jimmy fantasized.

Such a band needed an equally talented singer. Entwistle sang, but not with enough star-power, so they began tossing around names. "The first choice was Stevie Winwood," Jimmy recalled. Aside from maybe Paul McCartney, there wasn't a singer in England with a better rock 'n roll voice, but engaging Winwood was wishful thinking. They knew he was happily stationed at keyboards in the Spencer Davis Group, for whom his brother, Muff, played bass.

"Next we thought of Steve Marriott." This choice actually made more sense. Marriott had a similarly soulful voice as Stevie Winwood, but with a rougher edge and less restraint. He was loaded with energy and stage presence, having played the Artful Dodger in the stage production of *Oliver!* when it debuted in 1960 in the West End, and he rocked hard. At the moment, Marriott sang with the Small Faces, but all was not well. The Faces were under contract to Don Arden, an infamous, thuggish manager who, as Glyn Johns recalled, "was well known for threatening violence to get his own way." Arden once dispatched two men to intimidate Johns with a sawed-off shotgun and promise to shoot him and his family if he ever bad-mouthed Arden. The Faces were likewise mistreated by Arden, who refused to pay them what he owed from gigs, so it seemed an opportune time to sound Marriott out.

Marriott was intrigued, if for no other reason than he'd earn some decent money for a change. But word of the approach got back to Arden, and a message was sent: "How would you like to play guitar with broken fingers? You will, if you don't stay away from Stevie."

Arden's point struck a chord. "We just said, 'Let's forget about the whole thing, quick,'" Jimmy recalled.

Nevertheless, the idea lingered. Every once in a while, the musicians revisited their dream of forming a supergroup like Cream. It held such promise. The chaos factor tickled Keith Moon's sense of devilry. "It'd go down like a lead zeppelin," he snickered.

*Lead zeppelin.* Jimmy Page loved the irreverent image. *Lead zeppelin.* He held onto the thought.

## Chapter Four

# FRONT

## [1]

The only band going down like a lead zeppelin was the Yardbirds.

Simon Napier-Bell may not have been their ideal manager, but his instincts were spot-on. Two "genius guitarists," as he referred to them, augured trouble.

Jeff Beck had always envisioned sharing the spotlight with Jimmy Page. "He'd come in on bass," Chris Dreja recalled, "but that was obviously a waste of talent, so I switched to bass and they did dual lead stuff." That had been the goal from the jump. "Jeff was going to be the primary lead guitarist, but we could see the possibility of playing riffs in harmony," Jimmy allowed. "It was a concept no one else was doing."

Chris Dreja had no complaints. He knew he wasn't any kind of flash guitarist. Meanwhile, making space for Jimmy Page fostered its own rewards. "Jimmy had come from a studio set-up where you're punctual and professional," Dreja said, "and he brought all that with him into the band." As soon as Chris felt comfortable with the bass, he'd gladly step aside to let Jimmy take over on guitar.

A couple months, they figured, would do the trick, but with Jeff Beck in the mix, their good plans met with untimely consequences.

On August 5, 1966, just a week after Cream played its debut performance, the Yardbirds kicked off a two-month tour of the States to promote their hit single "Over Under Sideways Down." Jeff Beck had contracted a case of tonsillitis, which put him in a surly mood. After the band made its way through the Midwest into Texas, his petulance became more volatile, destructive. At a small club in New Mexico, things turned lethal. It was a hot night, the temperature up into the triple digits, and Beck's boiling point already dangerously in the red. "Something went wrong during the set, so Jeff just kicked over a stack of amps, and they smashed out through the window," Jim McCarty recalled. The fates were on Beck's side this time. He breathed a sigh of relief at a narrow escape. "The power amp had a fixed cannon socket, so [the cord] wouldn't pull out," he said, "and it was only that which prevented it from hitting a passer-by underneath."

The amps on the tour were invariably crappy, but they weren't the only bane of the Yardbirds' existence. There were girls who lusted after the band and ignited a kind of jealousy that could be dangerous. Their "redneck, shit-kicking" boyfriends threatened violence at every show. "There was a macho contingent in the audience who wanted to kill you straightaway," Beck said. "We never knew if we were going to get home alive."

By the time the Yardbirds rolled into San Francisco, Beck had had enough. For their date at the Carousel Ballroom on August 25, Jeff simply didn't show—later, he claimed to have been too ill—forcing Jimmy and Chris Dreja to switch instruments a month early. "It was really nerve-racking," Jimmy recalled, "because this was at the height of the Yardbirds' concert reputation, and I wasn't exactly ready to roar off on lead guitar." But it was inevitable—and permanent. "So when Jeff recovered, it was two lead guitars from that point on."

*Two lead guitars.* The effect was enormous, sensational, like hearing Isaac Stern and Yehudi Menuhin perform a duet on Bach's Partita no. 2 in D Minor. "It'd take your breath away when they played together," said Henry Smith, who served as roadie for the Yardbirds. "Their styles were different but complementary, and the electricity it generated was fantastic."

The payoff was no accident. "We had talked about playing harmony lines and arranging parts that would be the rock equivalent of a brass or saxophone section from the big-band era," Jimmy said. They'd actually practiced together, playing dual leads but with a free-form feel. "We learned a couple of Freddie King solos note by note, and when we play them in unison it sounds good."

They were exploring new territory. "We rehearsed hard on all sorts of things," Jimmy recalled, "especially introduction riffs to things like 'Over Under Sideways Down,' which we were doing in harmonies. It was the sort of thing that people like Wishbone Ash and Quiver would perfect, that dual lead guitar idea."

Once they took it onstage, the stereo solos became extravaganzas. They were on a frequency that didn't register on normal channels. "There were fucking brainstorms every night!" Beck exclaimed. Jimmy and Jeff pushed each other to innovate, to play harder, to go somewhere they'd never been before. To the untrained ear, it sounded improvisational, impulsive, *rash*—solos took off and soared into the unknown, fishtailing, whipping about like daredevil stunt pilots, as though they'd never find their way home, then suddenly intertwining somewhere in the subtonic universe, where everything existed in perfect harmony. It was a feat of showmanship but evolved into an artistic smackdown. The solos were dares, Jimmy and Jeff staring each other down. *Go ahead. Let's see what you can do.* Chris Dreja, whose thankless job it was to maintain a steady bass line throughout these sorties, characterized the guitarists as "a couple of gunslingers." Jim McCarty, who observed the action from atop his drum kit, said, "It was fascinating to watch, but it was also unhealthy." It was almost as if they were dueling it out. And then it got personal.

"I personally don't think Jimmy ever went out on stage with the intention of trying to blow Jeff off the stage," Dreja said. "But with Jeff, I think, it got to be a 'my-balls-are-bigger-than-yours' sort of thing. . . . He was so much more temperamental than Jimmy."

"On stage," he said, "Jeff was just uncontrollable." There was no rhyme or reason to it. Jimmy added, "Beck would often go off into something else."

Part of the problem was their different styles. Jimmy was a session veteran, where arrangements were polished, tight, and controlled. There was a lot of discipline involved in the way he played guitar, while Jeff played off the top of his head. He was intuitive, perhaps even more inventive than Jimmy, and, as a result, unpredictable. You never knew where he was going to wind up.

As time wore on, there would be a lot of posturing, a lot of one-upmanship. "If Jimmy played something incredible, a look would cross Jeff's face—not exactly a look of appreciation, almost as if he'd been made to look bad—and you could tell he was going to take it to him, to outdo Jimmy any way he could." Jeff wasn't oblivious to the friction. "In the end," he said, "we were just on opposite sides of the stage, glaring at each other and blowing all night."

It should have been exhilarating for the guitarists, but the competition created too much tension. "Every night," as Jim McCarty pointed out, it was "a battle royale." Jimmy enjoyed playing with and against Jeff, but the vibe made it feel as though he was under constant attack. "[It was] like a kettle boiling with a cork stuck in it," he said.

The pressure mounted through two successive tours, one with the Ike & Tina Turner Revue and another with the Stones in September 1966. Some nights were magical, with the guitarists staging a dazzling feat of craft, but more often than not Jeff's ego intruded. In his ongoing quest to outdo Jimmy, he often wound up outdoing himself. Norrie Drummond, reviewing one of the Yardbirds' shows for NME, called out Jeff in particular, saying if he "cut out the gymnastics with his guitar, the group might find some semblance of music."

Something had to give.

For better or worse, Simon Napier-Bell booked the Yardbirds on Dick Clark's Caravan of Stars tour, beginning on October 20, 1966. Clark, the genial host of TV's *American Bandstand* with several hands in related record and concert businesses, was a notorious slave driver when it came to his road shows. He'd package half a dozen acts with records on the charts and tour them through every godforsaken town in America with little regard for comfort or joy—in this case, thirty-three shows in twenty-seven days across sixteen states on a dilapidated, overcrowded Greyhound bus. The routine drove Jeff nuts. "All the American groups on the bus played their guitars non-stop and were always singing," he grumbled. The bill was a mishmash of incompatible attractions: the Yardbirds, Brian Hyland, Sam the Sham & the Pharaohs, Gary Lewis & the Playboys, Distant Cousins, and Bobby Hebb. Often they played two gigs a day in locales that were several hundred miles apart, so that by the time the second show was over, most of the performers were exhausted and on the verge of collapse. Jimmy Page hated the whole operation. "You had to sleep in the luggage racks or the bus seats," he said. "It's just ludicrous to remember how bad it was."

In the Deep South, where the tour began, the audiences were unruly. "People just shouted out all kinds of shit. 'Y'all turn that guitar down!'—and worse," Jim McCarty recalls. "Jeff was unhappy straightaway." The equipment was awful. If he didn't like the way things sounded, he was liable to grab his amp and bolt offstage. He hated the whole setup. It made him "hyper, nervous, insecure." As a result, his playing was erratic: brilliant or inept, a toss-up depending on the gig. "You wake up in the middle of the night, and everything becomes a horror movie very, very quickly," he said. "I wanted to go straight home." He took out his frustration on a succession of amps. On October 29, at the end of his rope, he came offstage at the conclusion of the gig and smashed his beloved Les Paul guitar into a table. "He'd gone fucking crazy!" Jimmy said.

They were back in Texas midway through the tour, and Jeff decided he'd had enough. He had a girlfriend waiting for him in Los Angeles, a bed and destination more appealing than another night on the tour. "Six hours in that thing was enough for me," he said. The band was holed up at the Harlingen airport, waiting to fly halfway across the country, while their road manager was sorting out luggage and ticket itinerary. "I was on this escalator going up to the departure lounge," Jeff recalled. "He was coming down, and called out, 'Hey Jeff, where're you goin'?'" Beck replied he was headed to a shop to buy a magazine and chewing gum. Instead, he got on a plane to LA. "Dumping Jimmy with all the guitar work in mid-tour was a pretty shitty trick," he admitted, "but there was no other way out."

The Yardbirds continued the tour as a four-piece band, and Jimmy Page stepped up superbly. There were nights he seemed to summon Jeff Beck's ghost, playing both leads at once, or at least that was the way he made it sound. Other nights, his solos were so economical they created high drama in what they held back. Either way, the crowds approved wholeheartedly, and he got a taste of what it felt like to command the spotlight in a top-rank band.

"The Yardbirds weren't the biggest thing in America," Robert Plant noted later, "but they were the innovators almost of something that smelled refreshing to the American public."

When the Yardbirds reconvened in LA, where Jeff was billeted with his girlfriend, a powwow was arranged to discuss the band's future. One thing was clear: they neither needed nor wanted to work with Jeff Beck anymore. "They were just totally adamant," Jimmy recalled. Enough was enough. "And when it was over, Beck got up to leave and asked me if I was coming too. I said, 'No, I'm going to stay behind.'"

Jeff never saw that coming. He and Jimmy were mates; they were on the same flight path, the same frequency. The ensuing developments hit Jeff hard. He'd been sacked by his band and deserted by his mate. It finally dawned on him: "I'd burned all my bridges."

# [2]

The Yardbirds also carried on without Simon Napier-Bell. He'd become disinterested in managing the band, and there was no love lost between Jimmy and him. Simon found the guitarist "very difficult to deal with, always narky," a badge that Jimmy wore with pride. More than once he'd served as spokesman for the band, confronting Napier-Bell on the dodgy bookkeeping that left the Yardbirds earning little more than a couple hundred pounds each after their various tours. The whole financial deal didn't add up. He considered Napier-Bell nothing more than "an opportunist" who knew nothing about rock 'n roll, and he was happy to be rid of him.

Though not entirely rid of him. According to Jimmy, "Napier-Bell called up with the news that he was selling his stake in the band to Mickie Most." It was introduced as an unusual comanagement situation. Napier-Bell would operate mostly in the shadows, concentrating on Jeff Beck's solo career, while someone from Most's company, RAK Management, would tend to the Yardbirds. "It was really weird," Jim McCarty recalls. "We went to Most's office in Oxford Street not knowing what to expect, and this enormous guy we'd never seen before told us, 'I'm taking over for Simon.'" The enormous guy's name was Peter Grant.

In truth, Jimmy was already friendly with Peter Grant. "I'd known Peter from way back in the days of Immediate [Records], because our offices were next door to Mickie, and Peter was working for him."

No matter where you were, you couldn't miss Peter Grant. He was larger than life, a Buddha-like figure—six feet, three inches; 250 to 350 pounds, depending on the month—with an outsize personality to match. He commanded attention in any setting, not only by his girth but also by his swagger—he called it *front*—a posture laced with attitude and intimidation that he'd developed over years of working alongside toughs and villains.

Grant's backstory had a gritty, Dickensian flavor. He grew up the illegitimate, fatherless son of a secretary on the mean streets of Battersea, where survival depended on one's ability to defend one's space. He spent his adolescence shuttling in and out of orphanages and boarding schools while his mother struggled mightily to make ends meet. It was at one such residence, Northbrook House, that he first crossed paths with upper-class students, an alien species. The impetus was strong to even the playing field. "There used to be great battles," he boasted, "and we beat them up." Might was the way Grant expressed himself best. He could dominate others with a ferocious stare. *Front!* Sometimes that was all it took, but if violence was required to neutralize a situation, that was also within his power.

In Peter Grant's world, muscle served more use than formal education. Unable to pass Britain's eleven-plus exam, in 1948 he entered Ingram County Secondary School for Boys in Thornton Heath, a seedy district of South London. "Ingram Road, as it was called, was the school for thugs, as opposed to gentlemen," recalls Phil Carson, a student at rival, gentlemanly St. Joseph's, who would become senior vice president of Atlantic Records and Grant's colleague during Atlantic's Led Zeppelin years. "That's one of the early places Peter sharpened his tough-guy image."

But image didn't yield much return in a gloomy technical school. On April 4, 1950, the day before his fifteenth birthday, Grant abandoned school to make his own way in the world. He burned through a series of odd jobs—working the line in a steel-barrel factory, waiting tables, apprenticing with a chef, and delivering messages for Reuters news agency. While working in a hotel kitchen, he was called up for national service, a compulsory two-year stretch, and assigned to the Royal Army Ordnance Corps in Northamptonshire, where he employed his culinary expertise in the company mess hall.

The drift into show business was a bumpy ride. "I was fascinated by the theater," Grant declared in an interview for an unreleased documentary. "It seemed pretty glamorous" to a onetime street kid who got his first taste of vaudeville at age thirteen working part time backstage at the Croydon Empire, sweeping up and ogling the chorus girls. In 1957, newly discharged from the army, he took a job that combined muscle and entertainment at a coffee bar in London.

The 2i's was no mere espresso and latte coffee bar. It served as the launchpad for skiffle and British rock 'n roll, the place where Tommy Steele and Cliff Richard got their starts, and, as such, attained a status that attracted starstruck crowds. To hold them at bay, Peter Grant was posted ominously at the door. He performed the same function, as bouncer, at Murray's Cabaret Club and the Flamingo in Soho, mixing with performers as well as villains like the Kray brothers, whose tentacles stretched into talent management and protection.

While working at the 2i's, Grant forged a friendship with another young guy on the make who operated the coffee bar's espresso and Coke machines and sang whenever the opportunity arose. Michael Hayes, like Peter, was "besotted with show business," and especially James Dean, whom he studied and emulated. Hayes played guitar—though not very well; sang—though not very well; and studied the 2i's performers, hoping to fabricate a workable stage persona. Inadvertently, he stumbled on a winner. He'd been watching American beach-blanket movies and picked up on a new, hip expression: "Oh, baby, you're *the most*." A colleague at the 2i's recalled, "Every new record he heard was 'the most,' every new girl he met was 'the most.'" The Corvette Sting Ray with dual exhausts, not just a hot rod but—*the most*. It struck a chord, and Michael Hayes became Mickie Most. Within weeks, he and a friend, Alex Wharton, formed a singing duo, the Most Brothers, and took their routine on a tour of drinking clubs in the provinces.

"We were kind of like the English Everly Brothers," Most said, "without the harmony or the musical ability."

It was tough to make ends meet for a bouncer and a glorified lounge act. Peter Grant and Mickie Most scrambled to pay the bills, moonlighting in a low-rent form of show business: the wrestling world. Grant worked as a timekeeper at bouts, eventually graduating to an audience shill at the Streatham Regal where he pretended to volunteer to lay his bulk on a plank of wood attached to a rope so that a wrestler—a buff Hungarian dwarf—could pull it with his teeth. One day, when the wrestler failed to appear, Grant took his place, with Mickie Most acting as his cornerman.

For the next eighteen months, Peter Grant was known to wrestling enthusiasts as His Royal Highness Count Bruno Alessio of Milan. He'd emerge into the ring, snarling, in a pair of trunks with a cape thrown over his shoulder, egging on the crowd with gestures and insults. According to Ed Bicknell, who managed Dire Straits and became a confidant of Grant, "Peter only had one surefire move in the ring. He told me, 'I'd simply push over my opponents and fall on them. Those fuckers would never get up.'"

Grant's wrestling prowess was nothing more than an act that he perfected. He decided to pursue theatrics at a higher level. *Acting!* The pretense and exaggeration appealed to him. He began appearing as an extra on TV series like *The Saint* and *The Benny Hill Show*. And from 1958 until 1962, he took bit parts in movies. He played a sailor in *A Night to Remember* and a Macedonian guard in *Cleopatra* opposite—far opposite—Elizabeth Taylor and Richard Burton. His appearance as a bellhop in Stanley Kubrick's adaptation of *Lolita* lasted no more than a discouraging few seconds, exposing his acting career for what it was: a lark. By the time he served as a stand-in for Anthony Quinn in *The Guns of Navarone*, he was looking for other work.

It was a catch-as-catch-can lifestyle. "Nobody had any money," recalled Mickie Most, whose jagged career path paralleled that of Peter Grant. "He was a dreamer, and he hustled."

One sorry hustle tied him to Peter Rachman, a London slumlord notorious for running prostitution in his derelict flats and overcharging immigrants who had no protection under the law. To evict them, he sent brawny henchmen like Grant to hasten their removal by breaking locks, destroying bathrooms, and employing general intimidation.

In his spare time, Grant hired himself out as a driver, shuttling performers of all stripes to and from the airport. His ace in the hole: a Volkswagen Transporter, known as the VW bus, a spacious passenger van with a panorama of airy windows and an enormous luggage compartment. Thanks to a circuit of American army bases in East Anglia that showcased regular entertainment, there was plenty of work for an operator like Peter Grant. One of his fares was an aging song-and-dance man who'd changed his name from Harry Levy to Don Arden. Arden was transitioning from performing to management and promotion, concentrating on the new crop of teenage acts emerging from the States.

Beginning in the fall of 1962, Arden brought Gene Vincent, Little Richard, Bo Diddley, the Everly Brothers, and Sam Cooke to Great Britain and put them on soul-crushing package tours in cinemas and pubs. Arden wound up managing Vincent, who was about as manageable as a category-five tornado. He was an alcoholic with an uncontrollable violent streak who kept a loaded revolver in his carryall, along with knives and whips, and attracted crises the way flame attracted insects. Arden regarded Vincent much like an insect and hired Peter Grant to control him. "Make sure that fucker gets to the shows in one piece," Arden ordered Grant, "and make sure he stays off the whiskey."

This was trial by fire for Peter Grant, who learned very quickly, from no less a bully than Don Arden, that management often required a variable mix of supervision and muscle. There were occasions that necessitated keeping an artist in tow while putting the touch—a robust touch—to reluctant or dishonest promoters. "If you intend to be a manager, you've got to be strong," Ed Bicknell says from experience, "and Peter was not averse to banging heads together." Sometimes more than banging. Later in their association, when Arden was managing the Small Faces and feared Robert Stigwood might lure them away, Arden had Stan Simmons, another extra on *Cleopatra*, and Grant "introduce Stigwood to the view" of the street below his fourth-floor office while being hung by his ankles from the balcony railing. When a singer named Cal Danger billed himself as "Britain's Gene Vincent," Arden and Grant ran his van off the road, pulled out his manager, and roughed him up. Phil Carson, who played bass for Danger, recalls that Grant pushed his way into the van, demanding to know who the other men were seated inside. "'We're in Cal Danger's band,' we said. 'Oh no, you're not. *Fuck off!*' And that was the end of Britain's Gene Vincent."

At some point, Peter Grant retired from the road to become a booking agent for one of Arden's companies, Anglo American Artists, promoting blues performers such as John Lee Hooker, Screamin' Jay Hawkins, Jimmy Reed, and Chuck Berry on double bills with the Animals. With Mickie Most as their producer, Grant became the tour manager of the Animals, who were managed by another rogue, Mike Jeffery. The two friends also collaborated on the Nashville Teens, a pop group from Surrey, with Peter managing and Mickie producing their subsequent hit single "Tobacco Road."

Eventually, Grant's relationship with Don Arden deteriorated over commissions owed from tours with the Animals. In typical fashion, Arden just refused to pay up. That gave Peter the impetus to strike out on his own, joining forces with his pal Mickie Most. In 1964, Most opened an outfit called RAK, an umbrella company for various production, management, and publishing interests he'd launched in a short few years' time. It was unprecedented for a man who seemed to get by more on ambition than on talent. RAK scored unparalleled success, not only with the Animals and the Nashville Teens, but also with Herman's Hermits, Lulu & the Luvvers, and Donovan, whose records Most produced with a seemingly golden touch.

Peter Grant, by comparison, opted for cheap alloys. His first two efforts—a band called the Flintstones and an all-girl group, She Trinity, failed to catch fire. In 1966, however, things turned up. A treacly novelty record, "Winchester Cathedral," had become an overnight sensation with its Rudy Vallee–type parody of an old-timey dance band. Nothing more than a grab bag of session musicians, the New Vaudeville Band was long gone by the time the record was released. To cash in on its hit success, a touring group was hastily assembled for a swing through the United States and managed by Grant.

Grant moved into the RAK offices located in the penthouse of a building at 155 Oxford Street, whose tenants were an assortment of rock 'n roll start-ups. The first floor was Chrysalis Agency, which handled bookings for acts including the Yardbirds and would later flourish in its incarnation as a boutique record label for Jethro Tull, Ten Years After, Supertramp, and Blondie. Island Records, soon to succeed with its roster of eclectic bands like Traffic and Free, was on the floor below RAK, with other music publishers and managers scattered throughout.

Sometime in early 1967, Simon Napier-Bell appeared in the RAK offices to arrange for Mickie Most to produce the Yardbirds' next album. "It was done at Jimmy's insistence," says Jim McCarty. Artistically, it was a preposterous pairing. Most was single-minded about making straight-ahead pop hits, while the Yardbirds continued to explore the esoteric fringes of rock 'n roll. Still, Most's imprimatur might give the Yardbirds the commercial success they craved. It was during this visit that Napier-Bell was overheard whining to the producer about how managing the band was "a bloody nuisance," especially that troublemaker, Jimmy Page.

Grant, who was sitting at an adjacent desk, replied, "Oh, I'd deal with Jimmy, no problem."

That was all Napier-Bell needed to hear. He'd continue handling Jeff Beck's business interests but took the opportunity to unload the Yardbirds onto RAK Management. Without any exchange of formalities aside from a handshake, Peter Grant became their manager.

## [3]

Grant and the Yardbirds seemed made for each other. The band inherited a no-nonsense manager who would protect their interests as
well as their asses, while Grant wound up with a rock 'n roll cash cow.
The Yardbirds had name recognition and enough bookings to last a
lifetime, and with Mickie Most as their producer-in-waiting, the heavens seemed to be in alignment.

Peter Grant's involvement paid off in a promising way. "The first
thing we did with him was a tour of Australia," Jimmy recalled, "and
we found that suddenly there was some money being made after all
this time." A subsequent recording session with Mickie Most, on the
other hand, proved disastrous.

The Yardbirds' labels—Columbia in the UK and Epic in America—
were clamoring for new product. It had been a long stretch since the
band had had an impact on the charts. Their last significant single,
"Happenings Ten Years Time Ago," never cracked the Top 40. And
with a series of tours approaching in the States and Europe, both record companies were eager to capitalize. They wanted hits this time,
not progressive blues, not quirky instrumentation, no over, under, or
sideways. Just *down*—down to business. With Mickie at the controls,
that was more or less guaranteed.

The sessions were booked to begin on March 5, 1967, at Olympic
Studios. The Yardbirds had originally planned to record at Abbey
Road and had even laid down some preliminary tracks there at Christmas with Paul Samwell-Smith producing, but the studio was locked
down in total isolation, with the Beatles recording what would eventually be *Sgt. Pepper's Lonely Hearts Club Band*. As Jim McCarty noted,
"The future was calling," but the Yardbirds were mired in the here
and now.

In fact, not even the Yardbirds. Mickie Most greeted the band
with news that Chris Dreja and Jim McCarty could go home. He was

replacing them with session men who were already in the studio. And he had a parcel of songs written especially for the band by Tin Pan Alley pros, the same characters who cranked 'em out for Herman's Hermits, et al. It didn't matter that they had no relationship to the Yardbirds' sound; they were indisputable *hits*, the kind of homogenous fodder played over the PA system at the supermarket or the airport. As long as the Yardbirds recorded the four *hit* songs he'd prepared in advance—"Little Games," a song that had come in over the transom; "Ha Ha Said the Clown," which had been a hit for Manfred Mann; Harry Nilsson's "Ten Little Indians"; and "Goodnight Sweet Josephine"—they could fill up the rest of the album with their own wanton stuff.

This was the way Mickie worked. He'd done the same thing a few months earlier for a solo album by Jeff Beck. He'd forced Beck to record two cringeworthy singles—"Hi Ho Silver Lining" and "Love Is Blue," the latter a recent Eurovision standout—then turned the rest of the session over to the musicians, while he hopscotched between studios, finishing a Donovan album. Jeff, in the meantime, had put together an exciting band that included Ronnie Wood on bass, Nicky Hopkins on piano, Aynsley Dunbar on drums, and singer Rod Stewart, whose voice Mickie absolutely detested. They even managed to dust off "Beck's Bolero," the track with Jimmy and Keith Moon on it, for the finished product, entitled *Truth*, one of the most important albums of the late 1960s.

The Yardbirds weren't as lucky. Mickie was out of touch with the direction rock 'n roll was taking, paying no attention to advances made by Cream, the Doors, the Byrds, Love, the Beatles' *Revolver*, or the Beach Boys' *Pet Sounds*. Jefferson Airplane's trailblazing *Surrealistic Pillow*, which entered the Top 10 the week before the Yardbirds' session, made no apparent impression on him. Mickie was more focused on finding a follow-up to "These Boots Are Made for Walking" for Nancy Sinatra, his next project.

Jimmy especially was frustrated. For all his artistry, for all his

invention, for all his technical expertise, he was basically taking orders from a hack producer again. "We were conned into those singles," he said in retrospect. "Mickie Most couldn't come to terms with
albums. It was still only singles that were important to him." The producer's whole recording process was anathema to Jimmy. "It was just
so bloody rushed," he continued. "Everything was done in one take."
Jimmy remembered Mickie's theory about guitar solos he'd imparted
years before, on one of the sessions they'd done together. He'd told
Jimmy, "They're something you stick in the middle of the single, where
there isn't any vocal." He didn't believe in working on a track until
everyone was satisfied they'd gotten it right. When Ian Stewart sat in
with the Yardbirds, adding piano to several tracks, Mickie shouted,
"*Next!*" after the first rough take of each. "On half the tracks we didn't
even hear the playbacks," Jimmy complained.

Once Mickie was gone, however, the inmates took over the asylum. Keeping with the band's tradition of creating weird sounds,
Jimmy produced a violin bow and proceeded to draw it across his guitar strings. It was a technique suggested to him by David McCallum
Sr., one of the classically oriented violin session players and father of
*The Man from U.N.C.L.E.*'s Illya Kuryakin. Jimmy told McCallum he
didn't think using a bow would work. "The bridge of the guitar isn't
arched like it is on a violin or cello," Jimmy insisted. But the more he
thought about it, the more intrigued he became. Actually, Eddie Phillips, the Creation's amphibious lead guitarist, had been bowing his
guitar for years, creating wild phantasmagorias of sound, but Jimmy
managed to tame the shrieky, shredding vibrato, giving it breadth and
texture, as a counterpoint to the melodic arrangements. He first used
it dramatically on "Tinker, Tailor, Soldier, Sailor," a number he'd cowritten with Jim McCarty that incorporated tape recordings of the
Staten Island Ferry, locomotives, and fireworks; and "White Summer," an instrumental based on the folk song "She Moves Through
the Fair" that he'd retooled to showcase the technique's disorienting
but mesmerizing effect.

The Yardbirds exploited Mickie's absence to record the dreamy, avant-garde track "Glimpses," a feverish five-minute "tone poem," as Jim McCarty describes it, "all in one key, that we experimented with, using old newsreels, children's voices, chants and bits that Jimmy laid in over the top." The track relied on tape effects that he'd been refining over the years to create overlapping layers of aural color and imagery. It was evidence that he was coming of age technically, embracing the full spectrum of elements that were coming into vogue and would take the recording process forward into the next decade.

Yet for all Jimmy's efforts, the hard-edged groove was not enough to rescue the album *Little Games* from the compromises imposed by Mickie Most. The four fuddy-duddy songs he contributed disrupted any kind of rhythmic flow or coherent sound and left the band's long-time fans scratching their heads. And the fans weren't the only ones baffled by the result. "When I heard 'Goodnight Sweet Josephine,'" Jeff Beck said, "I thought, Thank God I left the Yardbirds."

*Little Games* was a clear indication that the Yardbirds were coming apart. They'd lost their spark, the impulse to evolve. As a band, it appeared as though they were resting on their laurels, no longer relying on their instincts so much as their name. The music had changed and they hadn't changed with it. This reality began to sink in during a relentless schedule of tours. Throughout 1967, Peter Grant kept the band tethered to the road, with performances that stretched from Scandinavia to Japan and France, where the Yardbirds name still had plenty of cachet. In between, they detoured repeatedly to the States, whose thriving circuit of clubs, colleges, and ballrooms remained keen to book them, though no longer at the top of the bill. Everywhere they turned, newer, edgier, more innovative groups were making the kind of music that spoke to the times. It was hard for an old-line blues band to compete with the likes of Steppenwolf, Pink Floyd, the Rascals, The Who, Blood Sweat & Tears, Creedence Clearwater Revival, and Big Brother & the Holding Company.

Back home in London, the calculus had changed. On November 25,

1966, while the Yardbirds were wrapping up another U.S. tour, a seismic shift was felt at the Bag O'Nails, a rock 'n roll hangout on Kingly Street in Soho. Terry Reid, a teenager with an explosive voice who sang with Peter Jay & the Jaywalkers and had toured the States in 1965 with the Yardbirds, Ike & Tina Turner, and the Rolling Stones, was at the bar drinking a Mateus and Coke when he noticed a procession of familiar faces trickling into the empty club. First Brian Jones, then Eric Clapton, John Mayall, Pete Townshend, Jeff Beck, Bill Wyman . . . *What the fu* . . . "Someone tapped me on the shoulder," Reid recalls. "I turned around, and it was Jimi Hendrix, who I knew from the States. I asked him, 'What are you doing here?'"

"Oh, man, I'm going to get up and play," he said. "I'm pretty nervous, man. I haven't really played in London before. Keep your fingers crossed."

Word was out on the left-handed guitar phenom, and the rock cognoscenti kept streaming in. Eric Burdon, Denny Laine, Donovan, Ray Davies . . . *Paul McCartney.*

Reid noticed Jimi patching the club's Hammond organ amp into a stack of Marshalls identical to another stack of Marshalls on the other side of the stage. *Two Marshall stacks* in a small club. Reid remembers thinking, "*Holy shit!* This is going to make an impression."

A few minutes later Jimi ambled onstage while his sidemen, Noel Redding and Mitch Mitchell, slipped behind their instruments. "Hello, everybody," he whispered into the mic, grinning from ear to ear. "My name is Jimi, and I'd like to play a couple of things for you. The first tune I'm gonna play is a little thing I know is close to your heart. It's number one on the charts at the moment, a lovely little rockin' thing."

Reid racked his brain: What was number one on the charts? And what might be close to his heart?

"It's a little thing called . . . 'Wild Thing,'" Jimi purred.

*Wild Thing!* Reid says, "It was the most *hated* song, and the Troggs were the most *hated* group."

Before it had time to sink in, Jimi whipped his hand across the strings of his guitar and made a sound like *whur-onnnnnng*, launching into a straight three-chord change, and the entire room went nuts. "All the guitar gods were sitting right in front of the stage, while Jimi tore through solo after solo, playing with his teeth and shit," Reid recalls. "All the English guitar players saw the future right there. They thought they had it all sewn up, but you never knew what was lurking right around the corner."

Jeff Beck's reaction was indicative of his cronies'. "It was kind of hard to grapple with that fucker," Beck recalled of his first encounter with Hendrix at the Bag O'Nails. "He hit me like an earthquake. I had to think long and hard about what I did next."

Jimmy Page heard the story when he got back from the tour. So much incredible music seemed to be flourishing in London while he was off, plugging away on the road. The Yardbirds had been away from home for so long. It had been two years since they'd performed in the UK; the bottom seemed to have fallen out of their following. They'd become forgettable, passé—relics. To say Jimmy sleepwalked through the next year with the Yardbirds would be less than accurate. Playing gigs with the group still excited him. "What we had going, I was willing to do with them, whatever it was," he volunteered. He did everything in his power to animate the tired, dispirited band, whose individual interests were fracturing. Jimmy could see that Keith Relf and Jim McCarty "just didn't have their hearts in the music." While on the road, they had dipped into LSD and become besotted with the flower power and spiritualism that imbued the San Francisco scene; privately, they'd been writing together, trippy, acoustic songs intended to take their careers in a softer, less progressive direction.

Jimmy had his suspicions about the whole West Coast phenomenon. He loved the Beach Boys and Buffalo Springfield, who were blessed with formidable musicians, but too many of the emerging bands, he felt, weren't up to the task. "I went to see Jefferson Airplane," he recalled, "and they began their set with a bass solo which was absolutely phenomenal . . . and I thought, 'Oh my God, this is going to be just the end of the world when they start!' And then they began playing, and I couldn't believe it. They couldn't keep time, and it was awful." He had the same reaction to the Doors; they just didn't swing.

Relf and McCarty were welcome to go that route, but Jimmy was having none of it. Chris Dreja, who was willing to stay the course, "just didn't seem interested any longer." He had fallen in love with an American woman he'd met and talked about the possibility of moving to the States to pursue a career in photography. Collectively, the Yardbirds had lost their mojo. It was hard for a gung-ho guitarist to motivate such a vagrant group of guys. The inertia was apparent every time the band reassembled onstage. "I used to say, 'Come on, let's make an effort,'" Jimmy recalled, "but it had all gone."

There were still a number of obligations to fulfill—a last U.S. swing through the Midwest and California in June 1968, and an appearance on July 7 at Luton Technical College in the southeast of England. While in America, an offer of $5,000 had come in for the Yardbirds to play the Image Club, a glitzy rock 'n roll venue in Miami Beach. "That was a lot of money," Peter Grant recalled. The band was split on whether or not to accept it, with Relf and McCarty against playing the gig, Page and Dreja in favor. Inevitably, the debate turned contentious. The upshot was harsher still—to disband, to officially dissolve the entity known as the Yardbirds, necessitating that Grant weigh in. "There was a big row in the Holiday Inn. And I drafted out a letter giving Jimmy the rights to the [Yardbirds] name, which they all signed."

The end, when it came, seemed unworthy, lamentable. "I didn't want the Yardbirds to break up," Jimmy recalled, "but in the end it was too much of a headache." He thought there was an outside chance that if the band made it clear they were going to carry on, perhaps Keith Relf and Jim McCarty would change their minds and come back. But he soon realized that was a pipe dream.

Perhaps owning the name would allow Jimmy to reform the band with a new, more dynamic cast. In the meantime, he swung back into the session-playing groove that summer, adding an effusion of fireworks to Joe Cocker's trenchant interpretation of "With a Little Help from My Friends," the Beatles song that launched his career worldwide, as well as a number of other sessions where he could leave his imprint on otherwise anemic tracks. But a return to session work wasn't in Jimmy Page's plans. He'd relished the experience of playing live with a band, the interaction with top-notch musicians, the roar of an audience, the pull of the road.

He explained as much to Peter Grant one afternoon in the summer of 1968, while they were sitting in a traffic jam on Shaftesbury Avenue. Grant was preparing to leave with Jeff Beck on a tour of the States with his band fronted by Rod Stewart to promote the *Truth* album.

"What are you going to do?" Grant asked Jimmy matter-of-factly, not wanting to press too hard. "Do you want to go back to sessions, or what?"

"I've got some ideas," he answered cryptically.

So much was going through his head at the time. Rock 'n roll seemed to be changing faster than ever. Bands were louder, playing harder, getting weirder. Songs were no longer a compact three minutes; American FM radio had given rock artists license to experiment, to explore, by playing entire sides of albums uninterrupted. Inspiration could take a song anywhere you wanted it to go, make any sound you thought was appropriate—or inappropriate. Guitar solos could stretch on . . . *indefinitely*, if that's what a song demanded. For an innovator like Jimmy Page, the potential was intoxicating.

The Yardbirds had hit a musical wall. They'd taken the British blues idiom as far as it could go. Even Cream, which had expanded electric blues with flights of improvisation, was on the verge of calling it a day, with Eric Clapton resolved to pursue his own new horizons. The vanguard was intent on pushing into the unknown.

"When the band folded, I wanted to try something new," Jimmy said. "I just wanted to carry on rocking."

More than rocking. He wanted to cut loose. "I certainly had a good idea of the sort of direction I wanted to go in," he recalled. Ever since the wild session for "Beck's Bolero," he'd been nursing an idea for a new band—*his* band—a band that would give him the freedom to play at the top of his skills. "I knew exactly the style I was after and the sort of musicians I wanted to play with, the sort of powerhouse sound I was really going for." He envisioned a trio—guitar, bass, and drums—"with the fourth member being the singer and using the voice as an instrument," he said. "I knew the material I wanted to do as well. I had a game plan for it."

Jimmy Page had more than enough ideas. It was high time, he decided, to put them into motion.

## Chapter Five

# THE BLACK COUNTRY

## [1]

Voice. It had to start with the voice.

Ever since "Beck's Bolero," Jimmy Page had been obsessed with finding a voice—"a really fiery singer," he said—that could interpret and project the sound that was in his head. The voice had to be powerful, gritty, defiant, a full-throttle juggernaut of fierce conviction able to ride over the roar of the instruments without conceding a decibel. And it had to command center stage. Voice, of course, wasn't enough by itself. A lead singer also needed presence, a presence full of sexual intensity, to look and move the right way, attitude up the wazoo, the ability to convey everything that rock 'n roll entailed. Once Jimmy found the right voice, the rest, he was convinced, would fall into place.

Stevie Winwood epitomized that voice. It contained all the elements and had a center of gravity that drew everything toward it. He was Ray Charles but also Jerry Lee Lewis. A singer like that would allow Jimmy to delve into every style of music—blues, folk, funk, soul, something even harder and more extreme that was tugging at the margins. Winwood had been a free agent for what seemed like the blink of an eye. The Spencer Davis Group had disbanded in 1967, but

by the time Jimmy got serious about putting a band together, only a
year later, Stevie had segued into Traffic, where he was happily en-
sconced. The same went for Steve Marriott, who'd leapfrogged from
Small Faces into a band with guitarist Peter Frampton they were calling Humble Pie.

Undaunted, Jimmy turned his attention to another voice that had
captivated him. "I was mainly going after Terry Reid," he said, "who
had really impressed me during a Yardbirds tour when Jeff was with me
in the band, and we toured with the Stones." Reid, the opening act on
the bill, had the right sound—a booming, soulful, gravel-voiced delivery that had earned him the nickname "Superlungs" and the respect of
important allies like Cream and the Hollies. No less an admirer than
Aretha Franklin had said, "There are only three things happening in
London—the Beatles, the Rolling Stones, and Terry Reid."

Coincidentally, Reid was signed to RAK for production and management. Graham Nash had referred him to Mickie Most, who had
recorded a single with Terry in April 1968 and was in the process of
sorting through material for a follow-up album. In the meantime, Reid
recalls, "I was doing bread-and-butter gigs up and down England and
just waiting to finish up with Cream and go on this big American tour
with the Stones." Peter Grant told Reid that Jimmy wanted to talk to
him and arranged a phone call between them.

"I'd love to give it a shot," Reid told Jimmy after listening to his
proposal, "but I'm just going to pop off and do this tour first."

"No, that won't work." Jimmy was adamant. "I'm putting this
group together now. Either do it or not."

Reid was reluctant. He'd been scuffling on the road for nearly three
years, since he was fifteen, and finally had the chance to score. A tour
with the Stones and the opportunity to do an album with Mickie Most
was too attractive to pass up. Still, he kept Jimmy dangling on the hook.

"If I do it," he proposed, "you'll have to call Keith [Richards] and
tell him I'm not going on tour. And you know Keith—he'll probably
shoot you in the fucking leg."

"Oh-ho, I'm not doing *that!*" Jimmy said, scratching Terry Reid off the list of prospective vocalists.

It was just as well, as far as Peter Grant was concerned. "Terry was controlled by his father, who was a very difficult man," says Carole Brown, Grant's assistant at the time. Reid's father was a successful car salesman, a true wheeler-dealer who had stood up to Don Arden. "Both Peter and Mickie loathed dealing with him."

Before he left with the Stones, Reid did a few small pickup gigs in the provinces, including a date with Tim Rose in Bolton, in the northwest of England. Opening that show was a group called the Band of Joy.

"The lead singer, Robert Plant, was singing along with all the guitar licks, and I thought, 'I'll bet someone like Pagey could keep him busy,'" Reid recalls. "The drummer, a rough lad, was just *crazy*. He was trying to pull somebody's wife, and it all went wrong. A big fight broke out. The husband threw a chair, the drummer ducked, it went through a cantilever window, and the band had to play that gig five times to pay for it."

The next time Reid was in the RAK office, he told Peter Grant, "I've got the rest of Page's band for you."

The trouble was, he had no contact information for either of the individuals. "A lot of people knew them," Reid recalls, "but nobody could find them."

Peter Grant sent a telegram to an address he had been given. It said:

> priority—robert plant. tried phoning you several times.
> please call if you are interested in joining the yardbirds.
> peter grant.

"I thought someone was just taking the mick, so I ignored it." Plant recalled.

Reid sat with Grant one long afternoon, while the manager made phone call after phone call trying to track down the musicians. A couple messages were left at Three Men in a Boat, one of Plant's local pubs in the Midlands. As the day wore on, Reid excused himself to get a train to Cambridge. He left RAK's office building, crossed Oxford Street, and practically walked right into Robert Plant. He'd been in London with a buddy, cutting a demo for a manager named Tony Secunda, whose clients included the Moody Blues and the Move. "I've got something I need to talk to you about," Reid said. "Let's go and have a beer."

The next day, Reid arranged with Plant to speak with Peter Grant, then put in a call to Jimmy Page to give him an update.

"What does the singer look like?" Jimmy asked.

Reid let out a scurrilous laugh. "He looks a fuckin' sight better than you do."

Jimmy hung up on him.

Reid also took it upon himself to speak to the drummer. "Jim's putting this band together, and I think you and Robert would be great for it."

"If you're joking," John Bonham told him, "I'm going to beat the shit out of you."

Jimmy wanted to check out the singer as soon as possible. He called Chris Dreja, who was still mulling whether or not to play bass in the new band, and told him about this discovery.

"I went up to Birmingham with Peter and Jimmy to have a look at Robert Plant," Dreja recalled. On July 20, 1968, Plant was performing at a teachers' training college in Walsall, in the West Midlands, with a rather unimpressive group called Obs-Tweedle. The audience was practically nonexistent, just a handful of kids who were already pretty tanked up on beer, hardly paying attention to the band. Jimmy wasn't wild about the music, either. "The group was doing all of those semi-obscure West Coast kind of numbers," he said, things by Moby Grape, Jefferson Airplane, and Buffalo Springfield. "The band overplayed, and there was a lot of hubbub and flash." But . . . *the singer!* It was impossible to take your eyes off him. He was tall and lanky with skintight jeans and a resplendent halo of hair, which he kept sweeping off his face like a Hollywood ingenue. He moved like an ingenue, too. "He had a distinctive sexual quality," as Jimmy remembered it, almost feline, androgynous in his gestures but in total command of the stage. And . . . *the voice.* At times it sounded like an unrefined Stevie Winwood, earthy and uninhibited, but it also soared into a "primeval wail," which could be unnerving, coming out of the blue as it did. It was the whole package, but it worried Jimmy. "His voice," he said, "was too great to be undiscovered." What was he doing in this godforsaken backwater? Why hadn't he caught on with a top band by now? "I immediately thought there must be something wrong with him personality-wise, or that he had to be impossible to work with."

Afterward, when they were finally introduced, Jimmy explained the seeds of his new venture, and Plant gave Jimmy a demo he'd done with the Band of Joy—three songs: "Hey Joe," "For What It's Worth," and a Cyril Davies number Robert had rewritten as "Adriatic Seaview"— that they'd recorded at IBC Studios in 1967. "We did the whole thing in just a half an hour," recalls Kevyn Gammond, who played soaring Hubert Sumlin–style solos on the session. "The engineer just put mics up and said, 'Okay, play your songs,' so they all went down in one take."

That session might have been slapped together, but the result was as uncompromising as anything Led Zeppelin ever recorded. The brutality of the attack was unmistakable. Robert's delivery was genuinely stirring; it wrung all the tension and excitement out of the material. John Bonham's adrenaline-fueled drumming was like the finale at the end of a fireworks display; it made the earth move. It sounded like no one else. Listening to the scratchy acetate, Jimmy heard the future. This was close to the sound he'd been dreaming about.

Jimmy admitted to Robert that he'd already made a pitch to Terry Reid, whom Robert admired, but said, "You know, I think we should get together. If you're interested, come down and spend some time at my place. We'll go through some sounds and records, see if we've got the same idea, if we're sympathetic, and take it from there." Jimmy wanted to be sure the chemistry was right. "It was obvious he could sing and had a lot of enthusiasm," he recalled, "but I wasn't sure about his potential as a frontman." Jimmy invited Plant to the house he'd bought in Pangbourne, just west of Reading. "Why don't you bring some of your favorite records down?" he said.

Dutifully, Robert went through his precious stack of records and chose a selection to play for Jimmy Page: "Joan Baez's 'Babe, I'm Gonna Leave You' and 'Farewell, Angelina,' Howlin' Wolf's rocking chair album, *5000 Spirits* by the Incredible String Band," he recalled. "And my gatefold Robert Johnson album on Philips, which I bought while I was working at Woolworth's. That was the jewel in the crown." He stuffed them into a satchel and hopped an express train from Birmingham to Reading, where he connected to a commuter train to cover the remaining short distance to Pangbourne.

Jimmy, now twenty-four, lived just down the hill from the station in a 150-year-old Victorian boathouse plunked behind a pub called the Swan. "It's very big, with six bedrooms," he said by way of description. "It has three stories and there are boats downstairs." The interior was decorated with an array of posh art deco and art nouveau artifacts he'd collected as his fortunes rose, along with paintings, books, model trains, and a tank full of tropical fish. The home's focal point was a big stained-glass window that overlooked the River Thames. This was a big change from the cell-like childhood bedroom he'd vacated just two years earlier.

Plant was duly impressed. He was only nineteen, he was broke, living in a spare room above a pub in Wolverhampton, at a standstill career-wise, and this place had all the trappings of rock 'n roll success. Also in residence was a "quite sassy American girlfriend" who took his breath away. Jimmy's hi-fi equipment alone was a pretty swank affair—a mammoth Fisher amplifier with Tannoy speakers, several reel-to-reel tape decks, the kind of setup one expected to see in a full-service recording studio.

It took Jimmy and Robert a while to get comfortable. They were so different in their backgrounds and experience. Robert was unsophisticated, humbled, even awed by his initial brush with the more cosmopolitan, well-traveled, super-successful Jimmy Page. "The way he carried himself was far more cerebral than anything I'd come across before," Robert admitted.

It was music that finally broke the ice. They talked into the night about Elvis, Jerry Lee, Chuck, Buddy, and Eddie, as well as Sonny Boy Williamson, Johnny Burnette, Ben E. King, Otis Clay, and Solomon Burke, whose songs rolled off their tongues. "I looked through his records one day while he was out, and I pulled out a pile to play," Robert recalled. "Somehow or other, they happened to be the same ones that he was going to play when he got back, to play to me to see whether I liked them." Jimmy laid on a full banquet: Muddy Waters's "You Shook Me"; "If I Had a Ribbon Bow," one of Fairport Convention's masterpieces; "She Said Yeah" by Larry Williams; "Justine" by Don and Dewey; and their mutual pick, "Babe, I'm Gonna Leave You." It was clear that they were on the same wavelength.

"His ideas were fresh, and they excited me," Robert said.

Conversation eventually turned to the group Jimmy intended to form. There was already a bass player in place. Chris Dreja had announced his decision not to join, so Jimmy was leaning toward John Paul Jones, his friend from session work with a prodigious list of credits and a reputation for being a musician's musician. They had bumped into each other while working on an album, *No Introduction Necessary*, with newcomer Keith De Groot. "During a break, [John Paul] asked me if I could use a bass player," Jimmy recalled. It was a surprise, but not without precedent. Jones, like Page, suffered from the session man's malaise and ached to play in a band where he could express himself freely. "I was making a fortune [playing sessions]," John Paul recalled, "but I wasn't enjoying it anymore." Nothing concrete was decided at the time, but sometime later his wife, Mo, noticed an article in *Disc* reporting on Jimmy's intention to form a band out of the old Yardbirds. "She prompted me to phone him up," John Paul said, and on July 19, 1968, the day before the Band of Joy performance in Walsall, they made it official.

"Jimmy told me about John Paul Jones," Robert noted, "and I told him about Bonzo. I said I'd never seen another drummer anywhere near as dynamic."

Jimmy had already sounded out other drummers. He'd been interested in B. J. Wilson, whom he had met while playing on the Joe Cocker session, but he was contractually bound to Procol Harum. Clem Cattini, Jimmy's frequent sessionmate, couldn't be torn away from the windfall of steady studio work. "We definitely approached Aynsley Dunbar," Peter Grant said. Dunbar had the right kind of pedigree, having played with John Mayall's Bluesbreakers and the Jeff Beck Group, but he considered the Yardbirds "old news . . . a step backwards, not forwards," and was headed to a gig with Frank Zappa in the States before forming his own band. This drummer friend of Robert's—Bonzo, Plant had called him—Jimmy remembered the incredible sound he'd delivered on the Band of Joy demo. It was enormously attractive to him.

"When I saw what a thrasher Bonzo was," Jimmy said, "I knew he'd be incredible. He was into exactly the same sort of stuff as I was."

Jimmy's excitement was contagious. Robert said, "I hitched back from Oxford and chased after John, got him on the side, and said, 'Mate, you've *got* to join the Yardbirds.'"

The *Yardbirds?* Really? John Bonham wasn't impressed. He had a steady gig with Tim Rose, an American singer-songwriter who'd been part of the American Big Three with Cass Elliot (as opposed to the band from Liverpool with the same name) and now performed almost exclusively in England. Besides, Bonham was being courted by both Joe Cocker and Chris Farlowe. What did he want with a group of has-beens like the Yardbirds?

Jimmy Page wasn't deterred. On July 31, 1968, he popped into a Tim Rose show at the Country Club, a cabaret in West Hempstead.

He'd been around great drummers throughout his professional life, but he wasn't prepared for the sound John Bonham put out. It was enormous, explosive, but a controlled explosion. This guy was unbelievable, the best drummer Jimmy had ever encountered. At one point, John stepped out for a five-minute drum solo, and Jimmy almost came out of his socks. "I'd never seen anyone quite like Bonzo," he recalled. "That was it, it was immediate. I knew that he was going to be perfect."

## [2]

Perfect is a fanciful conceit.

Bands, especially rock 'n roll bands, are a stew of personalities and egos that have to blend in order to jell. A perfect ensemble is a tricky recipe to pull off. One did not have to look further than the Yardbirds to appreciate the pitfalls. A single malcontent or rebel can disrupt a band's chemistry—say, a blues purist or a super-talented head case. Most bands tried to stem the risk by forming with mates or, at least, musicians from the general vicinity. It increased the odds that the stew would coalesce.

Jimmy Page threw caution to the wind by reaching into the deepest, darkest Midlands to complete his band. "He might as easily have gone to Albania," says a native of Birmingham. "The Midlands is a world unto itself."

In England, according to an article in *The Guardian*, ex-Brummies complain that "coming from the Midlands is tantamount to coming from nowhere in particular." It's purgatory—that ill-defined area between the so-called North-South divide, regarded somewhat like the vast, fly-over American Midwest. Folks from the Midlands, where Robert Plant and John Bonham hailed from, saw themselves as *individuals*, neither high-strung, pompous elitists like those in the South nor northern inbred, dry-humored yobs. The Midlands even had a dialect all its own, with a riot of cadences that swooped and varied, producing a lilting, singsong effect. And its own slang, which could drive a listener mad. You went to the dentist if you had a tuff ache. Thirsty? Have a kipper tie. And if you were hungry, yid be off to get yer snap. Of course, *not* getting yer snap could make you a bit yampy, and you might even get a cob on.

Birmingham, or Brum, the key city of the Midlands, had a discernible Brummie accent. But if you crossed the little bridge at Sedgley Bank, a few miles out of town, you were suddenly in the West Midlands, known as the Black Country, Robert Plant's neck of the woods, where the accent became thick and muddy, like molasses. Think Cajun, and you have a pretty good idea of its reedy twang. Brummies like John Bonham referred to Black Country folk as yam-yams for the way they consistently say "you am." Ask them how they were—or "Ow b'ist?"—and they'd respond, "Bay too bah." "You'd need an interpreter or subtitles," says Kevyn Gammond. Across England there was prejudice against both Midlands accents. As snooty Mrs. Elton observed in Jane Austen's *Emma*, "I always say there is something direful in that sound."

Jimmy Page and John Paul Jones might have had trouble communicating with their new bandmates, were it not for the common language of music. London was considered to be the music capital of the UK, but the Midlands, where Robert and John cut their teeth, was a hotbed of rock 'n roll. The Spencer Davis Group, the Moody Blues, and the Move had already made their marks, and the club scene was as vibrant as anyplace on earth. The Brum circuit seemed endless. There was music every night at the Bournbrook Hotel, the Ridgeway Georgian, the Adelphi West Bromwich, the Ritz Kings Heath, the Silver Beat Club, the Crazy E, the Elbow Room, the Carlton Ballroom, the Cedar Club, the Surf Stop . . . *endless*. Pubs like the Swan and the Bull's Head in Yardley had bands three or four nights a week, as did the Black Horse at Northfield, the Selly Park Tavern, and the Morgue under the King's Head. A tradition of all-nighters lit up the Birmingham Town Hall, with the first act going on at 7:30 p.m. and the last unplugging as the sun rose the next morning. "You could actually survive, even make a living, playing music in the Midlands," says Dave Pegg, a Brummie who went on to play bass for Fairport Convention and Jethro Tull. "Everybody had the opportunity to play."

"There were so many bands breaking out of the circuit," recalled Glenn Hughes, who played with Trapeze and later Deep Purple. "That whole Midlands scene was five sets a night, playing whatever was in the charts."

There was less, much less, opportunity in Kidderminster, not far from the Welsh border, where Robert Plant grew up in the early 1950s. Historian Nikolaus Pevsner, in his weighty *The Buildings of England: Worcestershire*, dismissed Kidderminster as a town "uncommonly devoid of visual pleasure and architectural interest." In the postwar years, housing was still mostly primitive, many with a loo situated somewhere in the garden, along with a tin tub where children were bathed. Underneath the rustic surface, however, there was a core of pride that ran deep. Near-full employment boosted morale in Kidderminster, where a profusion of factories spewed an industrial fog so thick you could flick it with the back of your hand. Thriving iron forges churned out the essential train parts that kept the railroads running. "Furnaces everywhere, all open, white molten metal," said Mac Poole, a Black Country drummer, "men with no teeth, wearing leather aprons." And carpet mills droned round the clock, with weavers and dyers shouldering twelve-hour shifts to produce the Wilton and Axminster rugs that were famous worldwide.

Industry boomed, but music came to Kidderminster in time-released doses. In 1956, when Robert was eight years old, skiffle took the town by storm, and an entire generation of postwar babies caught the crest of a wave they would ultimately ride into adolescence. At the Kidderminster Central or the Empire or the Futress or the Grand, all local cinemas that showed cartoons on Saturday mornings, bands like the Seven Valley Skiffle Group and the Downville Saints would play punked-out versions of folk songs in the intermission, and theaters full of eight- and ten-year-olds would dance on their seats.

Robert soon graduated from Lonnie Donegan to Gene Vincent and Eddie Cochran, who rocked the Worcester Gaumont, where he also saw *Love Me Tender* and *Blackboard Jungle*. Trad bands led by Chris Barber and Monty Sunshine appeared at Kidderminster's Town Hall but were upstaged by local lights like Roger LaVern, who played the tinny Farfisa organ riff on the smash hit "Telstar" and a singer named Peter Wynn, who, along with Billy Fury and Marty Wilde, was part of Larry Parnes's famous rock 'n roll heartthrob stable.

Listening to pop music in the Plant residence was akin to a declaration of war. Robert monopolized a red-and-cream Dansette Conquest record player that accommodated discs of every rpm known to man—78, 45, 33 ⅓, even 16 ⅔. He'd gotten it as a present for Christmas in 1960, along with a copy of Johnny Burnette's "Dreamin'," which, in retrospect, his parents probably realized was the beginning of the end. Once he got his hands on that machine, school and everything else took a back seat to rock 'n roll. Plant happened to be bright, a very good student; he was one of the few boys enrolled at the junior school who advanced to Stourbridge Grammar, having passed the eleven-plus exam. However, once he heard *a wop bop-a-loo bop* and *I get-a so lonely baby, I get-a so lonely,* all bets were off. He got that cosmic itch.

"I used to do Elvis impersonations behind the curtains in my living room," he recalled. He too tuned in to Radio Luxembourg whenever the heavens cooperated. When he heard "I Like It Like That" coming over the airwaves, he just had to imitate Chris Kenner's cajoling delivery—over and over and over. It "horrified" his parents. "They cut the plug off the record player and said it was the devil's music," he recalled. They had expectations for him, a good, steady job with a collar and tie. Rock 'n roll, they were convinced, sent their son spiraling down the wrong path, the path to ruin. It got so bad, they considered him "beyond parental control." Music, *Robert's* music, was a constant source of hostilities.

Robert started hanging out in the coffee bars that had sprung up across the West Midlands—the Bongo Hut, the Coventry Jive Caf, even the Worcester Cross Teen Youth Club, all of which had . . . *juke-boxes.* What a way to hear Link Wray's "Rumble" or Duane Eddy's "Forty Miles of Bad Road." And those purely English, primitive Joe Meek productions—"Just Like Eddie" by Heinz, Danny Rivers's "Can't You Hear My Heart," "Be Mine" by Lance Fortune. Those records lit a fire. "I got in with this crew, which upset my parents a bit," Robert said, "and the cleft between Mum and Dad and Robert got a bit wider and wider."

It was about this time, mid-1963, that rock 'n roll, *real* rock 'n roll, came to the Black Country. The fifteen-year-old Plant sat through an all-star bill at the Wolverhampton Gaumont that showcased the Rattles, Mickie Most, Bo Diddley, Little Richard, the Everly Brothers, *and* the Rolling Stones, one after the other in red-hot twenty-minute spots that sent him into a revelatory swoon. "I was sweating with excitement," he recalled years later. R&B acts especially excited him. Robert was already deep into the Miracles and the satin-voiced Smokey Robinson. Now he dug deeper, darker. He steeped himself in the visceral interpretations of Solomon Burke, Patti LaBelle, the Lafayettes, Arthur Alexander, the Jive Five, and their brethren. And deeper. As they had Brian Jones, Mick and Keith, Eric Clapton, and Jimmy Page, the R&B stylists led Plant to explore the roots of blues.

More package tours came through the Black Country, this time caravans full of the blues greats, the heirs to Robert Johnson and Charley Patton—Big Joe Williams, Muddy Waters, Jimmy Witherspoon, Sonny Boy Williamson, Buddy Guy, and Lightnin' Hopkins, who'd hammered bottlecaps into the soles of his shoes and did a boogie shuffle to accompany his snake-bit Texas guitar playing. Robert flew out of that show and into Long's record shop around the corner from Kidderminster Town Hall to buy *Preachin' the Blues*, an anthology that featured Memphis Slim, Jimmy Reed, and John Lee Hooker. Not too long afterward, he ordered *The Blues Volume 1*; *Folk Festival of the Blues*, with Muddy Waters, Howlin' Wolf, and Buddy Guy; and Ray Charles albums, records that took four weeks to arrive.

"I always got a shiver every time I saw Sonny Boy Williamson," Robert said. "Sonny Boy really did it for me, that control that he had, and the tales I've heard about him since. . . . He'd have a really good time, and he was really coarse. He was everything I wanted to be at the age of seventy."

Bands like the Shadows and Johnny Kidd & the Pirates, perhaps even the Yardbirds—bands that had only yesterday meant so much— became unlistenable, "insipid dross," in Robert's opinion.

"All of a sudden," said Dave Pegg, who experienced the same revelation, "you didn't play any of that shit anymore."

"With the blues, you could actually express yourself, rather than just copy," Robert explained. "Only when I began singing blues was I able to use the medium to express what was inside me, my hopes and fears."

Expressing himself was never a problem. He had a voice that sounded like no one else's, with a range that projected from here to there. Shortly after adolescence arrived in earnest, Robert emerged from behind the living room drapes to sing in public, initially playing washboard with the Delta Blues Band, fronted by a mentor, Perry Foster.

"When I was fifteen," Robert said, "I fell immediately under his spell."

Foster came off as "a real white bluesman" who played like Big Joe Williams on an eight-string guitar, one of those battleships favored by jazz cats to facilitate an open, major-thirds tuning that gave the music a funkier sound. With Robert Plant, throughout 1963 and 1964, Foster established a residency at the Seven Stars Blues Club in Stourbridge, fronting a band of rotating musicians, much as Alexis Korner and Cyril Davies had done in London, that attracted a bohemian contingent from the local art college. "We used to wail away on 'Got My Mojo Working,'" Robert recalled. Or Buddy Guy tunes, which brought in the Jamaican crowd from West Brum.

Even so, it wasn't a cozy, brotherly scene. Pubs like the Ivy Bush in Smethwick, on the outskirts of the Black Country, issued an edict to the musicians: "We don't serve blackies in here." And there were posters tacked to poles around the streets: IF YOU WANT A NIGGER FOR A NEIGHBOUR—VOTE LABOUR.

None of this deterred Robert Plant. He continued to mine the influences of rhythm and blues for a tone and fluency that suited his voice. Onstage he oozed confidence and presence. "Robert was on another level, very dynamic," said Bill Bonham, a onetime bandmate. "I'd never seen anything like him." He was unnaturally flexible, able to dance and gyrate; an observer from those days called him "the Rubber Man." But he lacked the right backing to show it off. His first group was a brassy affair called the Tennessee Teens, which echoed The Who and metamorphosed into Listen—which was the Tennessee Teens, only splashier and louder, with a set that included "Hold On, I'm Coming," but powered through a fuzz box. Listen was good enough to attract a professional manager, Mike Dolan, who smartened up the band in "secondhand gangster suits" and scored a few gigs at prestigious clubs in London, where they even cut a single for CBS Records, a cover of the Young Rascals' "You Better Run," with Clem Cattini on drums and Kiki Dee singing backup, that failed to catch.

Those bands gave way to the Crawling King Snakes, which played rock 'n roll with an R&B edge. At the time, the influence of British bands, as opposed to long-established American attractions, was getting heavier in Kidderminster. On Thursday nights throughout the early 1960s, the spartan Town Hall was the unlikely epicenter of the ascendant big beat. Kids would queue all the way down Vicar Street, right through town, for a proper rave-up. Eight hundred overheated teenagers jammed into an auditorium meant to hold half that number. All the great acts came through—the Stones, The Who, the Animals, the Yardbirds. Their impact spurred the emergence of gifted local bands with the goods to stand on their own. In addition to the King Snakes, with Robert at the helm, a local trio from Stourbridge called Chicken Shack caught fire, as did the Shakedown Sound, whose lead singer, Jess Roden, was a stylist in the Stevie Winwood mold. Another Kidderminster band, Clifford T. Ward with the Secrets, even managed to make an album, produced by none other than Jimmy Page.

"We all started to get regular gigs," says Kevyn Gammond, the Shakedown's lead guitar player. "We played in pubs like the Ship & Rainbow in Wolverhampton, making practically nothing, pocket change. A gig in Scotland might bring thirty quid, but it was a four- or five-hour drive and you'd wind up sleeping in the van."

The Crawling King Snakes and the Shakedown covered for each other. "We'd do similar gigs," Gammond recalls, "so if their guitarist, Bruce Oats, didn't make it into the van, they'd knock on the door where I lived and call out, 'Kev!' Because we all had the same repertoire, and all the groups from the Midlands would be on the same bills—Rob and the King Snakes, Jim Capaldi in the Hellions, Dave Mason, Stevie Winwood, Rod Stewart in the Five Dimensions, Noddy Holder in the 'N Betweens, Steve Gibbons in the Uglys, even Bryan Ferry & the Gas Board from Newcastle."

Birmingham was their path to the big time, and nowhere in Birmingham meant more to a nascent rock 'n roll band than landing a thirty-minute set with its £13 payday on the Ma Regan circuit. No one launched more careers than Mary "Ma" Regan, a no-nonsense former schoolteacher and tea-dance impresario whose four ballrooms—the Brum Kavern, the Plaza Old Hill, the Ritz King's Heath, and the Plaza Handsworth—were the Fillmores of their day. The Beatles, the Rolling Stones, the Kinks, The Who, and the Animals all put in appearances there in the early 1960s, and the Brum bands who opened for them took their first steps toward success. The M&Bs, a Ma Regan mainstay sponsored by the Mitchells & Butlers brewery, evolved into the Moody Blues. Denny Laine and the Diplomats played behind practically every headliner. Bev Bevan, the Diplomats drummer at the time, recalled a night in 1963 when they opened for "an absurdly talented thirteen-year-old singer, pianist, and harmonica player who was promoting his USA hit, 'Fingertips.'"

The Crawling King Snakes, with Robert on board, eventually cracked into the Ma Regan circuit on the way up the rock 'n roll food chain. This presented problems for sixteen-year-old Robert Plant, who had landed a position, apprenticing as an accountant, at a little firm in Stourport. A *respectable* job, as his parents regarded it. Working nine to five, however, was a drag on the soul. Nights were late, the scene got headier. After gigs, bands from all over the Midlands would meet up in the Elbow Room or the Cedar Club, places where one could drink after the pubs closed at ten thirty, to exchange war stories. It became impossible to hold down a day job while keeping up this routine.

The decision was an easy one, though nothing Robert's parents would countenance. He quit his job to give his full attention to music. It was indisputable. Nothing could compete with the pull of music, though it caused a serious—irreparable—rift at home. "He'd sleep in the back of the van some nights when his parents locked him out," says Kevyn Gammond, who faced a similar dilemma. Gammond worked days at the local TSB Bank. "Friday nights I'd leave the bank (without locking up, which was my job) in my tailored suit and rush out to do a gig on the back of Robert's Lambretta scooter. After a few weeks of that, the bank manager determined I wasn't cut out to work in a bank."

Robert continued to try on different styles and images, but in 1967, the music was changing fast and so was he. "I never really knew where I wanted to end up," he acknowledged. For a time, he'd flirted with country blues—then a tighter, more urban, Chicago-style take on it. "The first time I heard Fleetwood Mac, they were the very straight blues band that I wanted to be." It was one thing to broaden his musical horizons, but the inconstancy and wavering was digging him into a rut. Nothing quite had the right feel, the right fit.

Instead of playing the field, he started his own band from the ground up. The first incarnation of the Band of Joy mirrored the uncertain direction Robert was feeling. It was a ragtag outfit from the West Brum club scene, where the Jamaican influence was especially strong. They played a little of everything, mostly R&B with a loping ska beat—a medley of Otis Clay songs, something fiery and impassioned by ex–Swan Silvertones member Vernon Garrett, James Carr's "Pouring Water (on a Drowning Man)," and the soul tearjerker "Open the Door to Your Heart," one of the most arresting gems from the slight but brilliant canon of Darrell Banks. These weren't mainstream R&B numbers that were integrated on *Billboard*'s Hot 100 chart. They were gritty, regional hits from regions that didn't cater to sock hops and surf bars. You had to dig to find them on small, independent labels like Revilot, Goldwax, Kent, Gator, and Modern. With a tight set of such pure soul crowd-pleasers, the Band of Joy eked out a nice little groove. Robert attempted to interpret the songs without polishing their edges, but the band's manager, "Pop" Brown, the father of the organ player, found Robert's voice intolerable and sacked him after a few weeks.

Disheartened but not defeated, he bounced back in 1967 with a *second* Band of Joy that he steered in a completely different direction. "All that music from the West Coast [of the U.S.] just went bang," Robert said. "I loved good blues, but all of a sudden I couldn't listen to any old blues anymore and say it's okay." He got blindsided by the profusion of music flooding out of San Francisco and Los Angeles that captured all the energy and enchantment of the hippie counterculture. Three albums, in particular, did a number on his head: *Moby Grape*, the eponymous debut album of the San Francisco band with its catchy, well-structured songs, airtight harmonies, and three red-hot guitarists whose instruments seemed to talk to each other; Love's *Forever*

*Changes*, one of the most influential albums to come out of the sixties, which mashed folk, rock, blues jazz, and flamenco into a kind of mid-tempo psychedelic casserole; and *Buffalo Springfield*, which combined folk and country with rock 'n roll and, along with the Byrds, set the table for Crosby, Stills & Nash, Joni Mitchell, Linda Ronstadt, Poco, Loggins & Messina, and the Eagles. "I thought, this is what an audience wants, this is what I want to listen to."

The songs on those albums grabbed hold of Robert Plant, not only for the music but also for the spirit they conveyed—the essence of flower power, free love, psychedelics, and the besotted optimism of youth. To a teenager from the Black Country, the music was exotic. "There was a romance about it that was so far away from British pop-rock," he recalled. "It had a social conscience and a sense of responsibility." If he was going to play these songs with all the fervor and joy they exuded, he wanted to make sure his bandmates had the same taste in music and were on the same page.

Robert already had his ideal backup band in mind. He got them together one night to discuss it over pints of Ansells Brown Mild in a pub opposite New Street Station in Birmingham. Kevyn Gammond was a lock. He was the best lead guitarist on that scene, and he and Robert had been in each other's wheelhouse for the better part of two years. Attracting Dave Pegg to play bass was something of a coup. Peggy had sealed his status in seminal Brum bands—a hard-rock outfit called the Way of Life, the Exception, and the Uglys with Steve Gibbons.

Finding a decent drummer was more difficult. Pete "Plug" Robinson, who'd played in the first Band of Joy, tended to slow the beat down in the middle of songs and needed too much goading from Robert to recover. No, he needed someone more dynamic, someone who could generate the same level of energy—or more. He remembered a guy in a freaky orange ostrich-skin bomber who had approached him during a gig at the Plaza Ballroom in Oldhill, saying, "Yer all roit, but yer no good without me." Cheeky bastard. He joined the Crawling

King Snakes for a few dates while still working with another band, and the band's sound "moved away from the blue-eyed soul circuit into the underground movement." Peggy had also played with John in Way of Life and knew "there was no better drummer in the Midlands—if anywhere." Unfortunately, the guy had a reputation to live down; he was a certifiable bad boy who "wanted to fight the world." Often there was no separating an unpredictable violent streak from the fury he unleashed on the drums. If only there were some way to harness it, Peggy thought, but he knew there was no controlling John Bonham.

## [3]

There was good reason that everyone called John Bonham "Bonzo." *Green's Dictionary of Slang*, the go-to source, lists *bonzo* as an adjective for "skillful," but also for "eccentric, crazy." Few musicians in the world of rock 'n roll have been as succinctly defined by a nickname.

John Bonham's skill as a drummer was indisputable. "He could have walked into any band in the world and felt comfortable," said Jim Simpson, who'd played with John in a group called Locomotive. Another early group, the Senators, had burned through run-of-the-mill drummers until he sat in and, according to Bill Ford, the bass player, "it was as if someone had stuck rocket fuel in our drinks." The guy was a monster, he kicked out triplets *on his bass drum*.

It was either a colossal mistake or an act of divine inspiration when John's parents gave him a pair of drumsticks when he was just old enough to walk. Everything in his path, inorganic or otherwise, was fair game for those hickory weapons. His younger brother Mick took quite a drubbing until something more percussive came along. The loo or kitchen provided a great source of gear. "I used to play on a bath salt container with wires on the bottom, and on a round coffee tin with a loose wire fixed to it to give it a snare drum effect," John recalled. "Plus, there were always my mum's pots and pans."

A bona fide snare drum kept him occupied for a while, but when he was fifteen, his father bought him a junky secondhand Premier kit on which he got the lay of the land.

There wasn't a lot of opportunity to study drum technique in Redditch, where John Bonham grew up in the early 1950s. The snug Worcestershire enclave, about fifteen miles south of Birmingham, was a bedroom community of the surging Brum sprawl but stingy in providing the means to musical instruction. "I never had any drum lessons," he said. "I just played the way I wanted." John's training was limited to his parents' big-band 78 rpm records, in particular those of Harry James with his red-hot drummer Buddy Rich, and Benny Goodman, whose superstar drummer, Gene Krupa, practically wrote the textbook on swing. There was plenty to glean from listening to those master craftsmen. The beat jumped off those records. To bolster his development, John depended on the radio, especially tuning in to hear Edmundo Ros and his band, whose two-bar Latin rhythm patterns exemplified the rhumba and guaracha drum beats he coveted. "We would sit in front of the 'wireless' every Saturday and listen to Edmundo's show," Mick Bonham recalled.

Everything registered. Gene Krupa, Buddy Rich, also Louie Bellson in Duke Ellington's band, the Jazz Messengers' Art Blakey: "It was from drummers like them that I learned how to develop speed on the bass drum and perform clearly defined solos that hopefully make sense," John explained.

At age fifteen, John's first opportunity to test his chops came in the summer of 1963, when he joined a local band, the Blue Star Trio, that enjoyed a Wednesday-night residency at the Redditch Youth Club. Until that time, the band had relied on the kind of decorous, ballroom-style numbers that prevailed at teenage dances. But everything had changed that year; the influence of the Merseybeat was too strong to ignore, and with John Bonham behind the drums the youth club exploded into a proper rave-up. Rock 'n roll was a strong cup of tea; he delivered it black, strong, no milk or sugar.

John never learned how to play with anything but power. He had what drummers refer to as heavy hands, "a bricklayer vibe," as a fellow musician described it. Every downstroke was delivered as if his life depended on it, with a force that registered in seismic proportions. Part of it could be attributed to might—his enormous strength, meaty hands that operated on their own frequency, excessive, without restraint; and part was his lack of discipline. He was a big kid to begin with, built like a linebacker, all his torque and thrust concentrated from the neck down. Because he'd never been socialized as a musician, because he'd never played in a structured situation under the prerogative of a leader, he played *his way*, which was aggressive, vehement, without regard for anything else.

That was the good news—and the bad news. Rock 'n roll demanded a heavy beat. And it was getting heavier as the months pushed on. The Beatles had changed the sound of pop music with the assistance of their Liverpool and Manchester compatriots, but it was evolving in other ways that delivered more juice. Amps and speakers were getting more powerful, as were sound systems in general, and drummers had to keep up, to compete. John never had a problem in that department. With Terry Webb & the Spiders, the Senators, and Locomotive—bands that succeeded the Blue Star Trio—he raised the heat to complement their sweaty, up-tempo sets. His problem arose with *where* he played, the Birmingham pubs and halls that weren't used to the level of volume he put out.

At the time, Bev Bevan, who played with Denny Laine, was regarded as the loudest drummer in the Midlands. "John used to watch me and the Diplomats at the Wednesbury Youth Center," Bevan recalled. When he was in peak form, the band rose up to meet him. It was instructive how the guitarist who stood next to the drummer absorbed the intensity of the beat and cranked his amp in order to go head to head. The drummer acted as the engine, created the energy that drove the band.

John immediately raised his game, but it came at a price. His

Locomotive bandmate Jim Simpson recalled, "We got banned from several places because of him." A club owner from Kidderminster summed up the situation, saying, "You were very good tonight, Jim, but we're never going to book you again with *that* drummer." Tony Iommi, who played with Rest and would later form Black Sabbath, recalled, "We used to see [John] every other week at this place called the Midland Red Club in Birmingham, and he'd be there one week, and the week after that he wouldn't be there. 'What happened?' 'Oh, he was too loud, we fired him.'"

He was loud, yes—but also "boisterous" and "utterly outrageous." He might strip off his shirt and stand on his drum kit, chest heaving like one of the heavies from the cast of *Demetrius and the Gladiators*, or spark a punch-up if someone happened to look at him the wrong way. His temperament was erratic, a powder keg; you never knew what might touch it off. Trouble was, John Bonham liked to drink, and he could put it away like the best—or the worst—of them. The more he drank, the more unpredictable he became. "You could be sitting there, enjoying a pint or four with him," says a longtime friend, "and the next thing you knew, you'd be on your ass with your nose broken or a tooth missing." Alcohol and Bonham didn't mix. One always had to be vigilant in those situations. It was like stepping on a land mine. Bands dreaded John's volatility. He spun through groups—Pat Wayne & the Beachcombers, the Nicky James Movement, Steve Brett & the Mavericks, and Denny King & the Mayfair Set—in slightly under a year and a half. There are classic stories about how John left bands. "Suddenly the drum kit wouldn't be there," says a Birmingham veteran. "A band would turn up for rehearsal a week or two after forming, and he'd be gone, already playing with another band."

In 1966, just after he'd turned seventeen, John found a bit more stability with a band called Way of Life, which was better suited to his high-spirited style. The music was changing, getting louder, steadily more progressive. "We played Cream-type songs, stuff by Vanilla Fudge, 'So You Want to be a Rock 'n Roll Star' by the Byrds, a couple of Hendrix things like 'Hey Joe' that everybody did," says Dave Pegg, who handled bass chores for the band. "It was a really powerful group, despite the fact we ran everything through a single four-by-twelve speaker in a fifty-watt amplifier."

John immediately put his stamp on their sound. "You guys have got to buy bigger amplifiers," he insisted.

No one had money to spare, least of all John, who had gotten married when he was seventeen and lived with his wife, Pat, in a trailer parked in the garden behind his mother's convenience store. Moreover, the young couple was expecting a child in July. John supplemented the spare change he made from playing music with a series of odd jobs—working part time in a clothing shop, carrying supplies to bricklayers on a building site, and moonlighting as a carpenter at his father's construction business. Gigs didn't provide enough to support a family—at most a skimpy £15 that was split five ways. And the routine was inhuman. You'd have to work six nights a week to come out ahead.

"There were some dreadful trips where we'd go from Birmingham to Bangor on the west coast of Wales, which was a five-hour van ride," recalled Dave Pegg. "Coming back, there were no garages; even if you wanted to buy petrol, it was impossible. So we'd stop and siphon."

There were also nights the pay disappeared altogether. Way of Life was often booked to play at pubs or little clubs that weren't used to the sound they put out. It was ridiculously loud. After the first set, the owner would beg: "Please—*please*—you have to turn it down. I'm getting complaints from the houses next door." But John couldn't play quietly, and they'd be shown the door. One old ballroom, the Top Spot in Ross-on-Wye, had a traffic-light system that started on green, change to amber when the music got louder, and automatically cut the power when it soared into the red. "When we were setting up the gear," Pegg recalls, "Bonzo hit the bass drum and it went straight to red before anything else had been touched. That was the end of our night."

No matter how well they played, Way of Life never got rebooked. They were just too damn loud; club owners fended off too many complaints.

John fared better with the Band of Joy. It suited his take-no-prisoners style of playing. The songs—"White Rabbit," "Hey Joe," "Baby, Please Don't Go," "Bluebird," "Alone Again"—demanded power, and the band didn't shy from volume. "We played with the amps turned up as loud as we could get them," says Paul Lockey, who'd switched from guitar to bass to accommodate Kevyn Gammond. Robert Plant wailed away on a harmonica, eyes closed. John had no trouble keeping pace with the others. "He'd bang away like he was slamming cupboards," Gammond says.

The Band of Joy picked up a nice head of steam. They were making a name for themselves, supporting bands like Georgie Fame and the Blue Flames and the Graham Bond Organization on a tour of Midlands clubs. In London, they'd brought down the house at the Middle Earth, on a bill with Fairport Convention and Ten Years After. It felt like they were going places. That demo they cut at IBC Studios was the perfect calling card to attract a record deal.

They might have gone that route, too, had egos not intruded. At gigs, John began setting up his kit at the front of the stage, forcing Robert and Kevyn into the shadows behind him. During performances, all sorts of maneuvers arose as everyone angled to gain his share of the spotlight. There was always a lot of elbowing for position. The same with billing. "Rob insisted on putting his name out front on our posters," Gammond says. "*Robert Plant* and the Band of Joy." Over the objections of the others. The only time he yielded were those occasions when the band hit a clinic for benzoate as an antidote for the scabies they'd picked up sleeping in cheap B&Bs. "When we parked outside, he'd take a marker and blacken out his name on the poster attached to the back of our van."

These were issues that could be overcome. Still, the money wasn't enough to put food on the table, and John Bonham, ever restless, began looking around.

Sometime in the spring of 1968, he got a call from Tim Rose, who had played a few dates on a bill with the Band of Joy and Terry Reid. Rose needed a drummer and bass player for two upcoming gigs: in Upper Heyford at an American air force base and the RAF Bicester. "I was shocked how Bonzo controlled himself playing behind Tim," says Dave Pegg, who filled in on bass at those shows. "I'm sure it was because of the money, which was quite good."

Better than good. Rose was so impressed with John's playing that he offered him a full-time position on a tour beginning in June 1968 that would pay £40 a week—three times what he was making with the Band of Joy. It was the answer to his problems. A guaranteed salary with a genuine recording artist. He accepted on the spot.

You couldn't argue with security. For the first time, John Bonham was pulling his own weight financially. The work was steady. He was earning a living playing rock 'n roll. The music wasn't all that demanding, the accommodations a cut above the norm. It seemed idyllic. He might even have re-upped for the next Tim Rose tour, had Robert Plant not blown in with this Yardbirds business.

## Chapter Six

# DON'T TREAD ON ME

### [1]

Jimmy Page was running out of patience.

He was *that close* to getting his dream band off the ground. The vocalist and bass player were both squared away, but the damn drummer he wanted was dragging his feet. What was it with this guy Bonham? Tim Rose was small potatoes; he'd be playing clubs for the rest of his career. What Jimmy had in mind was a colossus—a supergroup on the order of Cream, but *not* Cream. Bigger . . . louder, that "powerhouse sound," as he called it . . . more versatile in every respect, with a range of material that defied genre.

"Ultimately, I wanted the group to be a marriage of blues, hard rock, and acoustic music with heavy choruses—a combination that hadn't been explored before, lots of light and shade in the music," he said. He already had a nice little tour, ten bookings in Scandinavia, left over from the Yardbirds, that would kick off on September 7, 1968. Here it was, already the first week in August, and—*no drummer*. Time was running out. They had to put the squeeze on this guy.

Jimmy instructed Peter Grant to nail it down. Unfortunately, the Bonhams had no telephone. Grant claimed he sent "at least thirty telegrams" to John in care of the Three Men in a Boat club in Walsall, where he was playing that week. Finally, Robert Plant was dispatched to John's home in the Midlands to make another pitch. For support, he took along Bill Bonham (no relation to John), who'd played the organ in Obs-Tweedle and was friendly with John and his wife.

"Pat was not happy to see Robert," Bill Bonham recalled, "because John had a good job with Tim Rose."

"Don't you even think about it!" Pat warned her husband. "You're not going off with Planty again. Every time you do anything with him you come back at five in the morning with half a crown."

Robert laid it on thick, but John was complacent; he remained on the fence. "I was doing okay, and I was getting offers," he acknowledged. Word drifted around Birmingham that the Move considered recruiting him. "Joe Cocker was interested, so was Chris Farlowe, and Robert and Jimmy. It was baffling. I had to consider so much. It wasn't just a question of who had the best prospects, but which was going to be the right kind of stuff."

It was time to send in the cavalry. Jimmy and Grant took John to a pub lunch, where Jimmy said they "basically spelled out the whole deal, that it was a once-in-a-lifetime thing." They also sweetened the pitch by offering Bonzo a fixed salary—£25 a gig for anyplace they played in the UK, £50 in Europe, and £100 in America. With the Scandinavian tour already on the books and a U.S. tour in the works, that would guarantee him a hefty chunk of change.

The money was good. He could live with that. What attracted him most, however, was the musical fit. This wasn't going to be Tim Rose songs or Joe Cocker songs but a *band's* songs where he would have an equal voice. He knew Robert was a singer par excellence, Jimmy had real chops, and they assured him that John Paul Jones was a multitalented musician and all-around good guy. "Even if we didn't have any success," John reasoned, "it at least would be a pleasure to play in a good group."

He was in—at least for the time being. He agreed to attend a rehearsal in London on August 12, 1968, and play drums on the tour in Scandinavia. After that—he'd see how he felt. John had been in so many bands that failed to live up to his expectations. If this turned out to be another letdown, he'd pack up his kit and move on.

He'd promised Tim Rose that he'd finish out his tour. There were a few shows left in Middlesbrough in North Yorkshire, but as luck would have it, they overlapped with the Yardbirds' Scandinavia gigs. There was only one solution. In typical John Bonham fashion, he simply didn't show for the Rose dates. He did a runner. A man couldn't be in two places at once.

You couldn't say as much for John Paul Jones. Like Jimmy Page, Jones was a session musician, but an amoeba—he seemed to be able to split himself into parts and be in several places at the same time. The guy was a chameleon. One minute he could be playing bass or keyboards for a philharmonic orchestra, the next minute scratching out an arrangement for Donovan or Cat Stevens. "You name it, I've done it," he said. "I played weddings, I've played bar mitzvahs, I've done Irish weddings, Jewish weddings, Greek weddings, Italian weddings." He had tentacles in every idiom—classical, jazz, pop, and rock. He'd even sat in with the Yardbirds on sessions.

He wasn't even John Paul Jones. He started life in 1946 as John Baldwin in Kent, in the southwestern corner of London, where his parents occasionally dropped anchor when they weren't on the road. Kent was an idyllic place to grow up, the "Garden of England," with its copious orchards and two legendary abbeys, Canterbury and St. Augustine's. But John's upbringing was anything but ideal. His father, Joe, had played piano for the Ambrose Orchestra, a popular big band, featuring vocalists like Vera Lynn and Ann Shelton, that appeared in all the snazzy hotel ballrooms of the day. When the orchestra disbanded in 1947, Joe swapped piano for the British age-old love of variety and went on tour with his wife. "They had a double act," John

Paul recalled, "a musical-comedy thing." He joined them on the stage whenever it suited the act. And for a few years, it was convenient to drag their young son along with them from city to city, town to town, as they toured the provinces.

And then it wasn't. They shipped off John, as he was still called then, to boarding school, where he immersed himself in the three *Rs* of music—reading, writing, and rhythmiticking. He found it so intuitive. His instincts were already well honed. It was in his genes. "My dad bought a record player and let me go out and buy records by Jerry Lee Lewis and the Everly Brothers, Little Richard, Ray Charles," he said. It wasn't Brother Ray's voice that especially spoke to John but *that organ*. The way he played the Hammond B-3 sent a message to somewhere deep inside. Fortunately, John's school had a pipe organ in the chapel that he bent over like the phantom of the opera. What a sound! The way it filled that space sent chills. You could play Poulenc's Organ Concerto in G Minor or Bach's Toccata and Fugue in D Minor but cool it down with a little Jimmy Smith. *The Sermon*, *House Party*, *Home Cookin'*—those albums with the slinky B-3 sound were like catnip to John, who could imitate the single-line passages and the way Jimmy played bass with the foot pedals.

Keyboards were interesting, but so were stringed instruments. "My father had a little ukulele, a little one, and I had that strung up like a bass," he recalled. A Phil Upchurch record, "You Can't Sit Down," drove John into bass-guitar ecstasy; Mingus, Ray Brown, and Scott LaFaro pushed him over the edge. His father wasn't particularly thrilled. "Don't bother with a bass guitar," Joe advised his son. "Take up tenor saxophone. It'll take two years, and the bass guitar will never be heard of again."

The advice went in one ear and out the other. Somehow, John persuaded his father to underwrite a bass, a Dallas Tuxedo solidbody "with a neck like a tree trunk" and an amplifier that "made all kinds of farting noises." Be that as it may, it gave him enough status to join a school band of his own, the Deltas, who played *Light Programme* hits of the day, sneaking in "Shadows, Little Richard, and Jerry Lee Lewis stuff." But Motown spun his head in a different direction, hearing how the bass shaped that trademark sound.

"Motown was a bass player's paradise," John said. "Their bass players were just unbelievable. Some of the Motown records used to end up as sort of concertos for bass guitar." James Jamerson, especially, was a four-string god whose migratory technique on the frets mentored John's education.

The Deltas lathered up a decent reputation, playing private gigs and the U.S. Army base circuit, but by the time John was seventeen he craved a more challenging situation. Everything changed for him in early 1963, when he was seventeen years old. Jet Harris and Tony Meehan, both late of Cliff Richard's Shadows, had a hit single with "Diamonds"—the same record that gave Jimmy Page his first major session—and were putting together a touring band called the Jet Blacks. There was an audition in a pub near the Warren Street Tube station. "John Paul heard about it and showed up," Meehan recalled. "He was just out of school, very young, and a bit nervous. Despite the nerves, he was a good musician and knew his shit. He was cocky, too, in a certain way, and I liked that."

Everything about the Jet Blacks was a huge step up, beginning with the level of musicianship. Harris and Meehan were pros, but there was nothing shabby about their sidemen: John McLaughlin, who would go on to jazz-fusion greatness, on lead guitar and Glenn Hughes the jazz saxophone diva. This was no Brit-pop boy band. They played some of the earliest examples of the progressive rock that would come into vogue years later. Even the gear was progressive. Suddenly, John (still not yet John Paul) found himself cradling a 1961 Fender Jazz bass, a sleek surfboard cutaway polished to a high-gloss sheen. This was the genuine article, a guitar he would play for the next dozen years. The bread wasn't bad, either. He began earning £30 a week, a king's ransom in 1963.

But the Jet Blacks were ahead of their time, and audiences weren't yet ready to absorb sophisticated rock 'n roll. When the band broke up in 1964, John pivoted to keep his place in the music business.

"I wanted to make a solo record, I wanted to be the new Jet Harris," he said.

He hitched his wagon to another rising star—Andrew Loog Oldham, the cheeky rock 'n roll impresario who had started Immediate Records, where Jimmy Page worked. Oldham established John as a musical arranger and allowed him to record as an artist. According to John, "We made a single at Regent Sound called 'Baja,' a Jack Nitzsche surf-type sound," which was released on Pye in early 1964. "It was quite a session. We used a ten-piece orchestra . . . we even had a choir on it later on." The label credited it to "John Paul Jones."

"John Baldwin," for some reason, just didn't cut it. Baldwin was nondescript, much like John's personality. He was cultured and unassuming, more like background music, with the kind of flat, ordinary features that would be hard to pick out of a police lineup. And wry, observant, as opposed to feisty. Something spicier, more character-building, was in order. Andrew Oldham claimed to have cribbed "John Paul Jones" from a poster of the 1959 Warner Bros. movie of the same name, starring Robert Stack as the American Revolutionary War hero. "I just knew that John looked the part," Oldham said, "and that I didn't want my arranger to be named after a piano." That may be so, but Roy Moseley, who managed the Jet Blacks, insisted, "I gave him his name," as a result of Moseley's relationship with Bette Davis, who had an uncredited cameo in the Warner Bros. film. Whatever the case, it stuck. Forever after, John Baldwin was John Paul Jones.

That was the name that suddenly lit up call sheets at sessions in every studio in the city. "I was always in demand because I was one of the only bassists in England that knew how to play a Motown feel convincingly in those days," John Paul recalled. But he was also looking for a more creative role.

"Somebody came up to me and said, 'Can you arrange?'" he recalled. He assured them he could, then rushed out and bought Cecil

Forsyth's classic book, *Orchestration*, in order to teach himself the ropes. Thereafter, he began building a reputation as an arranger, writing charts, which had previously been the bailiwick of ancient, stooped-over notators. "I discovered that musical arranging and general studio directing were much better than just sitting there and being told what to do," he said.

John Paul did a few tracks with Marianne Faithfull and auditioned Nico for Immediate Records, which was churning out sessions one after another (many with Jimmy Page in the producer's role). "I was immediately hired as an arranger by Mickie Most, who I loved working with," Jonesy recalled. Then a tsunami hit: he worked on the Rolling Stones' "She's a Rainbow"; "A Kind of Hush" and "No Milk Today" for Herman's Hermits; "Sunshine Superman," "Hurdy Gurdy Man," and "Mellow Yellow" for Donovan; "Beck's Bolero" and "Hi Ho Silver Lining" with Jimmy Page; "To Sir with Love" for Lulu. The sessions were like revolving-door mysteries; you never knew beforehand which artist would be in the studio. "You walk through that door, and you don't know—it could really be anything," John Paul said. Sessions with Tom Jones, Freddie & the Dreamers, the Everly Brothers, Etta James, Marc Bolan, Shirley Bassey, Wayne Fontana & the Mindbenders, Dusty Springfield, Jimmy Cliff, big bands, philharmonics, TV commercials, *anything*—he did hundreds of sessions.

"It was a twenty-four-hour job, composing the individual scores for horns and strings the night before, handing them out the next day, and knocking out the finished product," John Paul said. "I was arranging fifty or sixty things a month, and it was starting to kill me."

He and Jimmy Page were on the same collision course. The strings were tuned high for them in those years. They encountered each other often, sometimes daily, sometimes *thrice* daily at sessions, and the evidence was in their eyes: they were fried.

"So many sessions were run-of-the-mill, banal, mundane, very boring," John Paul said. "You couldn't wait to get out of them." He and Jimmy had been doing it too long and it wasn't fulfilling or fun anymore. In 1968, both men happened to turn up at Olympic Sound for a passion project—a superstar session called "No Introduction Necessary" with Big Jim Sullivan, Nicky Hopkins, Albert Lee, and Keith De Groot. It was a lark playing with such talented musicians in a band-like situation.

For days afterward, John Paul ruminated at home. He wasn't rushing to accept more session work. He was pacing, contemplating his future, wringing his hands. His wife, Mo, eventually lost patience. "Will you stop moping around the house?" she implored him. "Why don't you join a band or something?"

"There's no bands I want to join," he responded. "What are you talking about?"

She flashed a copy of *Disc.* "Jimmy Page is forming a group. Why don't you give him a ring?"

John Paul called Jimmy to ask about the rumor and offered his services. "If you want a bass player, give me a ring."

According to John Paul, Jimmy said, "I'm going up to the Midlands to see a singer Terry Reid told me about, and we think he knows a drummer. I'll tell you what they're like when I get back.'"

Peter Grant, he learned, was already involved. Their paths had crossed when John Paul toured with the Jet Blacks and Peter was on the road with Gene Vincent and Chuck Berry. Jimmy promised to keep John Paul posted. The next time he heard from him, a rehearsal had been scheduled.

———

Monday, August 12, 1968, was a sweltering summer day. The swampy air felt as thick as porridge, especially in London's Chinatown, whose narrow streets and ancient, squat buildings seemed to press in on the humidity and intensify the heat. Peter Grant had answered an ad in *Melody Maker* for a rehearsal room below a record store at 39 Gerrard Street, which was no bigger than a large closet, making it hotter still.

How the four musicians managed to wedge themselves in there was anyone's guess, what with the wall-to-wall amplifiers and John Bonham's drums. "There was a space for the door, and that was it," John Paul Jones recalled. The equipment was ragged, second-rate, the acoustics terrible. For a brief moment, the whole affair seemed ludicrous, doomed. The Midlands contingent hadn't even met John Paul before. They'd been introduced, somewhat awkwardly, only minutes earlier. There was no time to get comfortable, to bond, to feel each other out. How were they expected to rehearse a set of songs?

"I was absolutely convinced that all that was needed was for us all to get in a room," Jimmy said. He had a sound in his head that he knew would inspire, would make them feel as though they were onto something new and amazing. "It was nothing that they'd ever really played before." But . . . how to start?

"Well, we're all here," he said. "What are we going to play?"

After some shuffling around and shoulder shrugging, Jimmy suggested the old Johnny Burnette standby "Train Kept a-Rollin'" and asked John Paul if he knew it. "It's easy, just G to A."

Without any more discussion, Jimmy counted it out: ". . . two, three, four."

"The room just exploded," John Paul recalled. It was like a dam had broken, with music surging out.

"Far too loud," Jimmy thought, "but so fantastic." All that power! "It just locked together like something that was pretty scary, but had to be." It turned the song's jaunty rockabilly groove into something fierce and feral. And Robert, at his most intense, sold it with his naked cat howl. It kept moving forward, faster, fiercer—and seamless, as though everyone knew his part and how it knit together.

When they'd finished without imploding, everyone broke into laughter.

"Shit!" Jimmy hooted. "What was *that?*"

Robert had an idea. There was nothing pretty about it. In his view, "It was just an unleashing of energy."

"The sound was so great," he thought. "Very, very, very exciting and very challenging. I could feel that something was happening within myself and to everyone else in the room. It felt like we'd just found something that we had to be very careful with . . . or we might lose it."

John Paul was sold as well. "Right, we're on," he knew. "This is it, this is going to work."

Jimmy Page, perhaps more than anyone, was aware of protecting their interests. The sound they had made was *exactly* what he'd fantasized for his band. "It was there immediately," he said. "It was like a thunderbolt, a lightning flash." It was time to close ranks.

The next day, flush with excitement, he gave Peter Grant an account of the rehearsal and expressed concern about contractual liabilities. With RAK's involvement, he feared that Mickie Most would demand to be their producer, which was out of the question as far as Jimmy was concerned. He saw how Mickie had turned the Yardbirds' albums into a repository for his soft-core tunes. It was imperative that he not come anywhere near this band.

There was a hitch: Peter and Mickie had an agreement. The Yardbirds, who were signed to RAK, were managed by Peter and produced by Mickie. The same went for the Jeff Beck Band. There was no way Jimmy would agree to that arrangement. It would not only corrupt the band's sound, it would destroy their credibility. That had been the case with Beck's *Truth* album, with Mickie's insistence they fill the tracks with songs like "Ol' Man River" and "Greensleeves." He'd worked sessions so often with Jimmy and John Paul, it was unlikely that he'd withdraw from producing their new band.

Instead of swapping rights—letting Grant completely control the new Yardbirds band in exchange for giving Mickie all rights to Jeff Beck—as had been reported over the years, Peter's strategy with his partner was more devious. The two men discussed the situation the day following the rehearsal and came to an understanding. Mickie laid it out for his wife, Chris, when he arrived home that evening.

"I've got some terrible news," he told her. "Peter hasn't got long to live. His doctor told him to get his affairs in order. He wants to leave his kids as much money as he can, so I'm giving up my RAK Management shares in Jimmy Page's new band."

Chris Most was aghast. "Are you *mad?*" she said. "I'm heartbroken for Peter, but your deal shouldn't make any difference to him."

"It's okay," Mickie assured her. "We've got enough money."

He decided that it was more important to give his partner, Peter Grant, some peace of mind in the little time he had left.

"Later on," his wife says now, "he knew he'd been conned, but he never spoke about it again. I think he was too embarrassed— embarrassed that Peter put one over on him, but also that Jimmy Page didn't want him involved."

In a way, Mickie was relieved to gradually wash his hands of the partnership. The Kray brothers, Ronnie and Reggie, had begun popping up to the RAK offices on Oxford Street to offer their protection services. Mickie knew them by reputation; they were villains involved in all sorts of local rackets, ranging from threats and assault to murder. It was apparent that Peter had sent them. He knew them from his days tending the door at tatty London clubs, where they hung out. This was one more torment Mickie could live without.

With that about settled, Jimmy and Peter mapped out a strategy they hoped would put this band on the path to stardom. The dates in Sweden and Denmark would give the guys a chance to work on material and get accustomed to playing together, out from under the prying eyes of the UK rock 'n roll media. As soon as they returned, toward the end of September, they'd head into the studio to record an album. To that end, Jimmy called his old Epsom buddy, Glyn Johns, to see if he was interested in working on it.

Johns was surprised to hear from Jimmy. It had been several years since they'd been in touch, and the scope of the project sounded a bit un-Jimmy-like. "He didn't seem to me the sort of bloke who would form a group," Johns says. However, the minute Glyn heard John Paul Jones was involved, he changed his tune. "That guy is a genius bass player and an unbelievable musician. I mean, *fantastic*. I'd worked with him forever. We were pals. This would have to be good."

Glyn was told he had to talk to Peter Grant about any arrangement. "If you want me to do this," Glyn said, "I'm going to end up producing the album, because there won't be anyone else in the studio. So I'm going to want a deal as the producer."

"Go and see Peter Grant," Jimmy repeated.

The two men wasted no time hammering out a deal. "It was clear I'd been hired as a producer," Johns recalls. "My deal was simple, a straightforward percentage deal, and I didn't insist on a contract. It was for Jimmy, and since he and I had grown up together, I figured it was fine." They shook hands on it.

In the meantime, the newly reconstructed Yardbirds fulfilled an obligation that remained on John Paul Jones's books, performing as studio musicians on an album by P. J. Proby. Shortly after that, before they left for Denmark, Robert Plant chose a private moment to approach Peter Grant and take him into his confidence.

"Mr. Grant, I've got a problem," Robert began. "Actually, two— I've been seeing sisters." He explained how he'd met them near his home a few years earlier, a pair of Anglo-Indian beauties. For a time, he had lived with Maureen Wilson while also dating her sister Shirley. "I've got one of them pregnant, but I love them equally. Which one of them do you think I should marry?"

"Oh, for fuck's sake," Grant replied. "I think that would have to be the pregnant one."

It was decided to put off wedding plans until they got back from Scandinavia. The ten dates required the band's utmost concentration, without distractions. Nothing was to interfere with developing a solid set of material and a killer stage act. In addition to the upcoming album plan, Grant was cobbling together a U.S. tour, much like the one he'd just completed for the Jeff Beck Group. It would be a make-it-or-break-it opportunity for these new Yardbirds, so everything had to be airtight by then.

The band's set list came together effortlessly. There were songs that all four musicians knew: "Train Kept a-Rollin'," "I Can't Quit You, Baby," and "You Shook Me" were blues standards that most British bands included in their repertoires. They also rehearsed a haunting version of "Dazed and Confused." It had been a staple of the Yardbirds ever since August 1967, when they appeared on the same bill with its author, singer-songwriter Jake Holmes, at the Village Gate in New York City.

"I loved it immediately," Jim McCarty explains. "It was quite moody and had a great descending bass riff, with plenty of opportunity for Jimmy to improvise." Right after the show, McCarty made a beeline to a Bleecker Street record shop and bought a copy of *The Above Ground Sound of Jake Holmes* so they could put their own stamp on it. Jimmy, with his keening violin bow and the intrepid atmospherics it produced, had adapted "Dazed and Confused" to the degree that he now considered it *his* song—a Jimmy Page original. He also introduced the "self-penned" "How Many More Times," which sounded suspiciously close to Howlin' Wolf's "How Many More Years." And their version of "Babe, I'm Gonna Leave You," with a florid discharge of Robert's vocal pyrotechnics, aimed at obliterating its traditional origins. At least "Communication Breakdown" seemed to be an authentic Jimmy Page number. To round out the set, they updated two covers that Robert Plant had been performing in the Band of Joy and Obs-Tweedle: Garnet Mimms's 1964 soul standout "As Long as I Have You," "I've Got to Move" by Otis Rush, and "Flames," an infectious romp with its penetrating rush of energy, by Elmer Gantry's Velvet Opera.

The New Yardbirds' inaugural shows in the suburbs of Copenhagen had all the awkwardness of a first date. The rented equipment was uncooperative, the band somewhat reticent, the audiences a bit bewildered. *This band doesn't sound or look like the Yardbirds.* There was a degree of uncertainty and indecision onstage.

Their appearance, for one thing, looked oddly mismatched. Jimmy drew attention in an all-white outfit, silky pants, and a matching shirt with an abundance of ruffles that might have turned heads in the court of Louis XIV. Robert, no less flamboyant, was trussed in tight pants and a flowery, puckered shirt whose only nod to modesty was that it knotted at the waist. Their hairstyles, a cascade of shoulder-length waves and curls, had the breadth and heft of cumulus clouds. John Paul and Bonzo dressed more for function with by-now-traditional Beatles haircuts, allowing the front men to stand out.

"In Scandinavia, we were pretty green," Robert recalled. "It was very early days, and we were tiptoeing [around] each other." Jimmy persevered through various hiccups and false starts, admitting, "We were really scared, because we'd only had about fifteen hours to practice together."

That may have been so, but the music came together very quickly. Everything started to jell after four or five appearances. The band started to swing—swing for the fences. The songs took on new, exciting shapes, the musicians began to communicate and trust one another. If Jimmy had any reservations about Robert's ability to carry the load, they were put to rest on September 12 during an outdoor gig at an amusement park in Stockholm. Halfway through their performance, the power blew on his mic, but Jimmy said "you could still hear his voice at the back over the entire group." The guy had an amazing set of pipes, and he was beginning to unwind and command the spotlight.

By the end of the tour, the Yardbirds had gotten their sea legs. They were feeling more confident onstage, beginning to anticipate one another. "The songs began to stretch out," according to Jimmy, "and I thought we were working into a comfortable groove." The shows were more fluid, top to bottom. Peter Grant, who got his first look at the band, agreed. "There was this incredible chemistry," he said. "I can't say that all the notes were correct, but the feeling was there and the magic was there."

There was also a new element woven into their makeup: power—

raw, uncompromising power. These Yardbirds made no concession to volume. The *Stockholm Daily News* reported, "They were so loud it almost hurt."

Jimmy was intrigued by the way modulation affected the mood of songs. The surface gestures in music conveyed the full range of feelings, all of which could be regulated by volume. "I wanted to play hard, heavy rock sounds," he declared. But there was also a part of him that luxuriated in the comfort of traditional folk elements. Loudness was one form of expression, but so was subtlety. "Dynamics," he explained, "whisper to thunder. Sounds that invite you in and intoxicate."

*Sounds that invite you in and intoxicate.* He'd heard stirrings of it in the few gigs they'd played in Scandinavia, the ability to bounce between radically different sounds—moments of carefully calibrated poise and ferocious bursts of intensity. Such were the qualities that emerged during the brief tour. It was time to see if he could capture it on tape.

## [2]

A block of time had been booked at Olympic Sound Studios in Barnes beginning on September 27, 1968, just two weeks after the Yardbirds returned from Sweden. The interval was just long enough for everyone to tie up loose ends at home and catch their breath before recording their debut album—a ridiculous timetable for a group of musicians who had been together for only a little more than three weeks.

A rehearsal at Jimmy's boathouse in Pangbourne was relaxed, unstructured. The concept behind the album was to re-create the band's live act, so it would not require a lot of preparation. Everyone was loose. They had the blues songs down pat. "Dazed and Confused" was a pretty well established part of their repertoire. John Paul Jones recalled, "My contributions were 'Good Times, Bad Times' and 'Your Time Is Gonna Come'"—songs that swung between the extremes, one loaded with demonic energy, the other dulcet and graceful. Jimmy brought in "Black Mountain Side," a tribute to one of his guitar heroes, Bert Jansch, whose innovative "Black Waterside" was evident in every stanza. And they jammed. John Paul discovered a vintage Hohner reed organ in the corner of Jimmy's parlor—not exactly a B-3, but efficient, with enough clout—and piloted it into a full-throttle arrangement of the Band's "Chest Fever," which shook the rafters. Another warm-up, Jimmy's "Tribute to Bert Berns" gave everyone a chance to air it out in a kind of loose, bluesy groove meant to cement a musical bond.

Most times it just felt like a jam—an improvisational jam, the way jazz cats might handle it. "We were all into the idea of opening songs up," Robert explained. "There was a structure, but the structure was prompted and edited according to cues." That meant paying attention to what everyone was playing and anticipating where things might head. It was liberating—but nerve-racking at the same time.

Robert and Bonzo remained a bit overwhelmed. There were remnants of the North-South divide in the air, perhaps more from their perspective than their London counterparts'. They continued to feel somewhat out of their depth. "We'd drive home from rehearsals from Pangbourne," Robert said, "and we started communicating as two guys from the Black Country who had a lot to take in." They were motivated by the need to measure up—"playing with guys who were leagues above and beyond anything we'd played with before." It was musically challenging but stimulating. They were exhilarated. It was encouraging how much they'd risen to the occasion. As a result, their confidence was riding high as they regrouped in the studio the last week in September.

Olympic Sound had started life as an independent four-track operation on Baker Street before moving into bigger, more accommodating digs, a converted cinema in Barnes, in southwest London, with an updated eight-track board. "It was certainly the most versatile room I'd ever worked in," says Glyn Johns, who'd engineered countless ses-

sions in the facility. "The acoustics in there could deal with anything."
He assumed he'd pushed them to the limit on a recent session with the
Stones but was completely unprepared for the output of the Yardbirds. "The minute they started to play, they just blew me out of the
fucking chair," he says. "I was on the bloody floor from the sound that
was coming at me."

He was astonished at how the band was so prepared. They were
ready to play minutes after they'd unpacked their gear. The Stones had
been so loose about showing up on time; Keith was rarely in tip-top
shape. When Johns had recorded the Beatles, they were punctual
but "dicked around" with the songs, rehearsing and rewriting while
the meter was running. Not so with the Yardbirds. "They were fine-
tuned when they arrived, the material was tight, perfectly arranged,"
he recalls.

"The first album was done methodically, with ruthless efficiency,"
according to Jimmy. He had his eye on the clock, inasmuch as he was
personally bankrolling the session. "I knew exactly what I wanted to
do in every respect. I knew where all the guitars were going to go and
how it was going to sound—everything."

Not quite everything. John Bonham's drums were a force unto
themselves. "They made the most astonishing sound," says Glyn Johns,
owing to the "phenomenal way Bonzo tuned them." They'd already
been deemed "unrecordable" by an engineer at Ladbrooke Sound in
Birmingham, and this gave Jimmy and Glyn a problem to cope with.

Jimmy recalled his session days and the way engineers had recorded Bobby Graham, by isolating him in a booth with a mic positioned smack up against his drums. It was the reason they always
sounded tinny on playback. "Essentially, it came down to placement,"
Jimmy said. "I simply moved the mic away to get some ambient sound."
Glyn pitched in by putting Bonzo on a riser and used multiple mics
placed to get a stereo effect, a discovery, he says, that intensified the
drums' sound and forever changed the way they were recorded. The
drums seem to force their way into the mix. Years later, Brad Tolinski,

the editor in chief of *Guitar World*, credited bringing those drums forward as "one of the biggest musical events of the past fifty or sixty years."

John Paul Jones was an instant beneficiary. His bond with Bonzo, as the band's rock-solid rhythm section, was immediate and profound. "It was a lot of fun playing with someone so shit-hot, with such great musicality," he said. But fun was only a fraction of the payoff. Jonesy had found someone who complemented his style of play—someone able to mine the energy in songs to deliver a stirring rhythmic balance. "Lots of people can play fast, but to play slow and groove is one of the hardest things in the world, and we could *both* do it. It was a joy to sit back on a beat like that and just ride."

Their collaboration—and joy—was evident from the outset. Everything the band had rehearsed seemed to come together in a blaze of efficiency.

It took some time before Robert cut loose. His singing was a bit tentative during the first day or two. "I was a little bit intimidated by it all," he acknowledged some time later. "It was like, 'Do I really belong here?'" He sensed he was trying too hard to live up to Jimmy Page's expectations. He was self-conscious about his voice but also unapologetic. In time, he began to relax, to settle in and become more expressive as the music they were making blossomed and impressed on playback. Robert was only twenty, but he'd studied the blues masters, and his voice took on some of their timbre, evoking the 1950s, the 1940s, and before. Jimmy was certainly satisfied. "[Robert] was performing in a very inspired way," he thought, "like everyone else in the band."

"Those guys fed off each other," Glyn Johns recalls. "They just tore through the set of songs, one right after the other. It was so exciting. I'd never heard a band play that way before."

They recorded the entire album in thirty-six hours flat, an astonishing pace, even more astonishing given how thorough they were.

Everyone was satisfied with the outcome. It was tight, aggressive, sensual, dramatic, and powerful, encompassing everything they'd set out to achieve. The album had a fresh sound, but it was more than that. It claimed new musical territory by narrowing the distance between genres, giving the songs a destabilizing spin, and indicating a direction that rock 'n roll was moving toward.

Peter Grant was determined to maintain the band's energy. To keep them sharp and focused, he booked a short UK tour while he scouted local record companies in hopes of securing a label deal. He was convinced that audiences were eager to embrace these new Yardbirds and that the session tapes provided a sure sales vehicle. As it turned out, he was wrong on both counts.

Only a few dozen people turned up to their first gig at Newcastle's Mayfair Ballroom on October 4, 1968, just days after the recording session was finished. Those who showed up expressed a common reaction. *These aren't the Yardbirds.* The same occurred at the Marquee in London, where they played two weeks later to a half-empty club. *No Keith Relf. No "Over Under Sideways Down."* Ed Bicknell happened to be in Peter Grant's office while the manager was on the phone, trying to lure booking agents to the Marquee so they could see the New Yardbirds, as the band was now billing itself. "I could overhear the response, which was uniformly, 'Fuck off!'" Bicknell attended the show, which he said was "terribly exciting but staggeringly loud—the walls in the fucking place were shaking." But the crowd consisted of old Yardbirds fans who expected something different, familiar. Even Bicknell thought the name New Yardbirds "sounded a bit tacky."

A legal snafu forced the issue. A few days later, Grant received a letter from Chris Dreja's lawyer warning them to cease and desist using the Yardbirds name. According to the document, the agreement giving Jimmy the right to use it extended only through the dates in

Scandinavia, which had been booked before the original Yardbirds disbanded. Jimmy, it turned out, didn't *own* the name; he only had the right to use it for the duration of that tour.

That was okay with the guys. They'd never been fond of performing as the Yardbirds. They had their own distinctive identity; their music, after all, had little to do with the Yardbirds. A different name would suit them just fine. Jimmy suggested a few feeble alternatives, like "the Mad Dogs" or "the Whoopie Cushion." Peter reminded him about the business while they were recording "Beck's Bolero"—how Keith Moon thought a group like theirs would go down like a lead zeppelin. Now, *there* was a good name, he said, and Jimmy agreed. *Lead Zeppelin*. But Grant didn't want any confusion with the pronunciation of *lead*, as in "You lead, I'll follow." So he got rid of the *a*. "I was doodling in the office, and it just looked better," he said. *Led Zeppelin*. It was unconventional, cheeky; it had front.

*Led Zeppelin*—exactly.

A new name, however, wasn't a cure for other woes. No matter what they were called, record companies weren't biting. Peter Grant had offered the band to Louie Benjamin, the managing director of Pye Records. "I asked for—the figure was £17,500," Grant recalled, "and he said, 'You've got to be joking.'" It wasn't deemed a good fit for the Polygram roster either. Chris Blackwell, who owned Island Records, was prepared to make an offer. Island had space on the floor below the RAK offices, and one afternoon Peter previewed the album for Chris. "I really liked what I heard," he recalled. Blackwell offered Grant $25,000 per album, a respectable amount, for the world rights excluding the U.S. and Canada, and they shook hands on it, just as Peter had done with Glyn Johns. But U.S. and Canadian rights were the mother lode, where Led Zeppelin stood to cash in—and where Grant was convinced their future lay.

His North American strategy was prompted by a call from Mo Ostin, the head of Warner Bros. Records in Los Angeles. Ostin had heard from Andy "Wipeout" Wickham, a London colleague, that Jimmy Page was forming a new group. All Ostin knew was that Jimmy was a legendary studio guitar player and former member of the Yardbirds—but that was enough to warrant a worldwide deal. "I reached out to the manager, Peter Grant, and told him I wanted to sign them," Ostin recalled.

With tapes in hand, Peter and Jimmy flew to Los Angeles the last week in November 1968, hoping to score a long-term contract, ignoring the fact that Peter already had a handshake deal with Chris Blackwell. They met Ostin for lunch in a booth at Martoni's, a record-industry hangout in the shadow of the Capitol Records Tower, where they hammered out terms agreeable to both parties. Everyone was happy and left the restaurant with the understanding that Led Zeppelin was a Warner Bros. Records artist. According to Ostin, "We were in the process of drafting contracts, and somehow [Jerry] Wexler got wind of the group through his lawyer, Stevens Weiss . . . and he convinced Jerry to go after the group."

Wexler was the master musical partner at Atlantic Records, where Cream had enjoyed their short-lived success. Coincidentally, he was preparing to cut an album with Dusty Springfield in Memphis and was sifting through appropriate material for her. "Twice a week, I would drive out to Jerry's house in Great Neck, where there was peace and quiet, and we would go through songs with Dusty," recalls Jerry Greenberg, who at the time headed Atlantic's promotion department. "Dusty told him that John Paul Jones, her all-time favorite session player, was forming a band with Jimmy Page, and I saw the lightbulb go off in Jerry's head."

He knew that artists were often tuned in to something long before word filtered into the corporate suite. He also remembered meeting Jimmy with Bert Berns and had been impressed with the young guitarist's versatility. Wexler immediately picked up the phone and called Stevens Weiss, who also represented the Young Rascals, Vanilla Fudge, and Dusty and was handling Peter Grant's artists in the States. "I want this band *right now*," Wexler told him. "I don't even have to hear a note of music."

Coincidence was on Atlantic's side. "We arrived on the scene just the right time in America, as Cream had disbanded and Hendrix was into other things," Jimmy concluded. "So many of the good American groups were moving towards softer sounds, which made our heavy rock approach more dramatic. Atlantic Records were looking for a new heavy rock group to boost, and we were it."

His and Grant's subsequent trip to New York coincided with a run on the charts of some of the most celebrated and transformative music in rock 'n roll history. Over the summer of 1968, a series of ground-breaking new albums had been released: Simon & Garfunkel's *Bookends*, *Wheels of Fire* by Cream, Otis Redding's *The Dock of the Bay*, the Band's *Music from Big Pink*, *Cheap Thrills* by Big Brother & the Holding Company, the Small Faces' *Ogdens' Nut Gone Flake*, the Steve Miller Band's *Sailor*, Jimi Hendrix's *Electric Ladyland*, eponymous debuts by Traffic and Spirit, and *Truth* by the Jeff Beck Band. There was also plenty of buzz in the air about the imminent release of the new double Beatles album, the Stones' *Beggars Banquet*, the Kinks' *Village Green Preservation Society*, and Van Morrison's *Astral Weeks*.

Atlantic Records was keen to expand its reputation as the foremost mainstream R&B label into the domain of white rock 'n roll, based on the company's recent success with acts like Buffalo Springfield, Cream, the Rascals, Vanilla Fudge, Iron Butterfly, and the Bee Gees. "The blinking warning light was on about R&B—it was coming to the end of its useful life at that point," says Phil Carson, Atlantic's UK label manager. "They were looking more seriously at British rock bands." It stands to reason that for Jerry Wexler, who had produced "Respect," Aretha Franklin's masterpiece, as well as most of Wilson Pickett's hits and key records for Solomon Burke, King Curtis, Esther Phillips, and the Drifters, acquiring a band like Led Zeppelin was a financial distraction. Musically, Wexler's heart wasn't in it, but he knew not to look a potential windfall in the mouth. He signed acts according to a philosophy he lived by: "Make sure a band has at least one virtuoso musician in it, because virtuosos don't play with good musicians, they only play with *great* musicians." Eric Clapton was a virtuoso, so were Yes's Chris Squire and Buffalo Springfield's Stephen Stills. Wexler put Jimmy Page in the same exalted company.

His meeting with Peter was nothing more than a formality. Wexler made him a sizable offer (more sizable than Mo Ostin's) on the spot for Led Zeppelin "without knowing anything about their actual prospects," he said—an understatement, considering he'd never seen them perform or heard a note of their music. "We signed on the strength of Jimmy's name largely," Peter Grant recalled. The deal Wexler proposed would give the band "a $75,000 advance for the first year and four one-year options." With production costs and incentives added, it was worth about $220,000 overall, an eye-popping sum in 1968.

Jimmy threw a potential monkey wrench into the proceedings. If they were going to sign with the label, he wanted to be on Atlantic, not its sister label, Atco. Atco had been created to give the company a pop image at radio stations, to segregate acts like Bobby Darin, Sonny & Cher, and even Cream from Ray Charles, Ruth Brown, and Solomon Burke. So far, Atco was where all of Atlantic's white groups, aside from the Young Rascals, resided. For Jimmy, it was all about cachet—being the first white UK act on the prestigious red-and-black R&B label. He also demanded complete control of all artistic decisions for Led Zeppelin, including all phases of production, the album cover design, advertising, and image, as well as ownership of the master tapes. He and Peter would also retain all publishing rights to the material under an umbrella company they created called Superhype Music. "And no soundtracks," Grant chipped in at the last minute. "Atlantic couldn't have the rights to any Zeppelin film soundtrack." Incredibly, the record company agreed to everything they asked for.

A few days later, Grant's lawyer, Steve Weiss, called Jerry Wexler with a mouthwatering proposition. For a paltry $35,000 more, Atlantic could acquire world rights to Led Zeppelin, the rights beyond the U.S. and Canadian territories specified in the original deal. Grant's pact with Island and Chris Blackwell wasn't worth the pound of flesh they'd shaken hands with. Wexler, to his credit, took some time to think it over. It would bring Atlantic's initial stake in the group to $110,000, not an inconsiderable sum in 1968. To offset some of the cost, he asked Polydor, Atlantic's UK partner, to chip in $20,000 for the British rights, but got turned down flat. So for $35,000 Atlantic underwrote a deal that would ultimately bring a nine-figure return on its original investment.

Feeling giddy and puffed up with triumph, Peter Grant and Steve Weiss made a crosstown appointment with Clive Davis, the newly appointed president of Columbia Records, and his colleague Dick Asher, who oversaw Columbia's Epic label. Was this a courtesy call—or something more? The Yardbirds, after all, had been signed to Epic in the States. So was Jeff Beck, whose album was firing on all cylinders, and Terry Reid, still under contract to RAK. Word was all over the street about Jimmy Page's new band. It seemed only likely that it, too, would land at Columbia.

"Our contracts specified that we had not only group but individual recording rights, in case the group broke up," Dick Asher recalled. "When we heard that the Yardbirds had split up and Jimmy Page had formed Led Zeppelin, we naturally assumed the rights to Page would go automatically to Columbia."

For Jimmy, signing with either label had never been in the cards. He still had a bad taste in his mouth about a live recording Epic had made with the Yardbirds at the run-down Anderson Theater in New York, their last-ever American gig. Despite the shabby venue, it had been an electrifying performance; the band put everything they had into it for posterity. But Jimmy could tell that "the Epic sound team had no idea how to record us." He was disgusted by their inadequate setup. "They just draped a few mics around. It was pathetic." Fortunately, he'd not been a signatory to the Yardbirds' original contract with Columbia or Epic. By all accounts, he was a free agent.

Peter rather cavalierly dropped that information on Clive Davis, along with the news that he'd already signed Led Zeppelin to Atlantic. "I was surprised, even stunned," Davis recalls. "I really liked the Yardbirds and was proud of our relationship." He took it as a slap in the face.

Peter was no longer concerned about whom he alienated, no matter how influential or powerful. He was confident that Led Zeppelin was something extraordinary, the supergroup of supergroups, and they deserved—he *demanded*—respect. Nothing was going to stand in their way. That meant deploying an extravagance of front, a powerful strain of front that combined attitude with coercion when necessary. Grant was a naturally intimidating man, because of both his size and the strong-arm tactics he'd developed as a bouncer and Don Arden's enforcer. And he was fearless. He had no problem getting in someone's face. "If I'm out at a concert and somebody is gonna do something that's snide to one of my artists," he said, "I'll fucking tread on 'em without thinking about it."

Peter didn't suffer fools gladly. He had a ferocious stare that could freeze someone in place and a backhand able to send them into orbit. "He didn't take shit from anybody," says Phil Carlo, a roadie for Led Zeppelin and later Bad Company, "and you sure didn't want to fuck with him." On the other hand, he was charming, an amusing raconteur, and extremely generous—he'd open his wallet for anyone who needed a handout. But that could turn in the blink of an eye. "He was a lovely guy—but absolutely terrifying," says Michael Des Barres, who encountered him often, much later, during the Swan Song years. In the early days, Atlantic's Phil Carson tended to tread lightly around him. "There was always an underlying tension that he could break your arm if he wanted to—and people knew that when they talked to him." Grant knew from experience that the rock 'n roll business had its share of shady characters—grifters, hangers-on, scoundrels, and worse. From the outset, he began to assemble a team to protect his interests and safeguard his band. "If there were problems that needed sorting out, he'd have people who would sort them."

Their expertise would set an uncompromising tone.

## [3]

Peter Grant—or G, as the band now called him—moved quickly to put key pieces into place, a colorful cast of characters whose unorthodox styles would lend a tough-guy approach to the group's management from then on.

While still in New York, he cemented a partnership with Steve Weiss, the lawyer who had supervised the Atlantic Records deal. Weiss had represented mostly show-business clients in the conservative Madison Avenue firm Steingarten Wideen & Weiss. His top priority in the early sixties was TV talk-show host Jack Paar, but as the culture skewed younger, he refocused his attention solely on pop and rock music clients. Almost overnight, Weiss undertook a makeover of his client list and his image. He grew his hair long and forswore a closetful of Hardy Amies suits for a Carnaby Street wardrobe—still impeccably dressed but in wide-lapel sports coats worn over flowered shirts and ironed bell-bottom jeans. He ditched his late-model Cadillac for a 1957 burgundy-and-tan Rolls-Royce driven by a chauffeur, William, who wore either burgundy or tan uniforms to match the car's finish. Even Jack Paar was sidelined in favor of Herman's Hermits, the Young Rascals, the Yardbirds, Vanilla Fudge, and a handful of similar artists on their way up the charts.

How was Steve Weiss able to move into music so effortlessly? Many attributed it to his business relationship with Vanilla Fudge's manager, Phil Basile, and his entourage. "Phil was a mob guy," says Carmine Appice, Fudge's indefatigable drummer. "His crew was the one in the movie *Goodfellas*. Henry Hill used to come to my house to sell me equipment—Revox tape recorders, color portable TVs, fur coats. 'Carmine, some stuff fell off a truck.' They all worked for Phil—and so did Steve Weiss."

Appice recalls a sit-down with Basile, Weiss, and a few mob heavies who were moving in for a percentage of the bands Steve represented. "They were demanding a ten-percent taste, but somehow they whittled it down to a reasonable one and a half percent, and we had to play for nothing in a big club the mob owned to make up for the difference. Phil and Steve somehow convinced them there was more money to be made going after record companies than bands."

Their deals with bands adhered to a formula—Basile got 25 percent and Weiss took another 5 percent. For Led Zeppelin, Steve Weiss negotiated a similar deal giving him 5 percent across the board, publishing included, with Peter Grant taking 25 percent. Weiss's fee bought more than legal advice. An incident in New York put his leverage in perspective. "During a tour in 1967, the Yardbirds were staying at a hotel in Manhattan, with all of the gear in a truck parked outside," recalls Henry Smith, their roadie at the time and later for Led Zeppelin. "When I woke up the next morning, the truck was gone. Man, I was panicked and called Steve Weiss's office. An hour later, the truck miraculously reappeared with all the gear, nothing missing."

Before Peter left for London, he needed one more piece of the management team: an agent to book concerts. Weiss set up a meeting for him with Frank Barsalona, whose Premier Talent Agency not only represented the top bands but had established a network of young, aggressive promoters whose venues catered specifically to rock 'n roll. Barsalona had begun the agency booking clients who appeared on Dick Clark's package tours—acts like Little Anthony & the Imperials and Mitch Ryder & the Detroit Wheels. In 1966, while he was out of town, one of his co-agents got "suckered" into signing an unknown act called The Who. "And to get them," Barsalona was told, "I had to sign another shit group no one ever heard of called the Cream." Those acts had turned Premier Talent into a powerhouse, and now Led Zeppelin fit nicely into its roster.

Peter was convinced the band would find more acceptance in America than at home in the UK. His extensive experience there, with Chuck Berry, the Animals, Herman's Hermits, the Yardbirds, and Jeff Beck, gave him a solid understanding of the types of cities and venues where a new band could thrive. Seeing was believing, especially a band like Led Zeppelin, who was a great live act. The Yardbirds name still meant something in the States, and Jimmy's growing prestige was a critical factor. Back home it would be more challenging. Audiences in England had been tepid at best where Led Zeppelin was concerned. Local promoters continued to drag their feet when it came to booking the band. "They just wouldn't accept anything new," Jimmy complained. Getting airplay in Britain was next to impossible. The BBC was loath to embrace anything other than mainstream pop music; unconventional or progressive bands were anathema to the old guard that controlled its banal playlists. In the States, John Paul Jones recalled, "FM radio was just beginning to have a huge influence—they weren't afraid to play longer tracks or even whole albums."

Grant came to believe a combination of U.S. exposure and word of mouth might be enough to jump-start the Led Zeppelin express. It became crystal clear to him on December 10, 1968, when the band returned to the Marquee for a final tune-up before regrouping prior to their album's release. He'd been working the phones all afternoon, inviting promoters and the BBC2 to attend the gig, without any luck. Frustrated, Grant left the office and walked the few blocks to Wardour Street, passing just in front of the club. "Fuck me, what's this queue?" he wondered in his inimitable way. "There were about two hundred [people] already lined up. That's when I knew we wouldn't need the media. It was going to be about the fans." And the fans, he sensed, were in the United States.

At Peter's behest, Frank Barsalona booked a U.S. tour for Led Zeppelin, opening for loud-ass bands like Vanilla Fudge and Iron Butterfly—thirty-three shows beginning December 26, 1968, two and a half weeks before their album was slated for release. It'd be a grind, spanning the country from one end to the other, at fees of $1,500, often less, barely subsistence considering the expenses involved. Grant would travel with them in order to handle the business end, but it required an experienced road manager to keep everything—and everyone—on schedule and in line. Peter knew someone up to the task: Richard Cole.

There are few characters in the Led Zeppelin story as colorful as Richard Cole. At the age of twenty-two in 1968, he was already a force of nature. An East London yob, who'd honed his biceps apprenticing as a scaffolder, Cole was as physically striking as Peter Grant. Though not corpulent, he was equally ominous, standing at a solidly built six foot two, with a gold earring and knee-length black leather coat. "We used to call him Mort, because he looked like a mortician," says Carmine Appice, who traveled with Cole on a Vanilla Fudge tour in 1967. And like Grant, he wasn't reluctant to get in someone's face or to throw the first punch. Or the second. "Richard was a tough dude," Appice says, "but a wild guy, a real hell-raiser. Bands loved him."

He'd been around them long enough to stake his claim. In three short years, he'd handled road-managing jobs for The Who, the Searchers, Terry Reid, Jeff Beck, Vanilla Fudge, and Peter Grant's ersatz New Vaudeville Band. Jimmy Page first encountered Richard on a Yardbirds tour of the States, and John Paul Jones had met him during a short-lived stint in the Night Timers, a band he'd played in with guitarist John McLaughlin. Richard's job wasn't limited to getting bands to gigs. "He was a man's man," says Jim McCarty, "our source for dope and girls wherever we went." It was rumored that no matter where you played, "he knew every groupie in town."

"Richard was an act of his own," says Terry Reid. "During a Cream tour of the States I did with him, he disappeared when we got to LA." Freaked out, Reid called Grant, who told him that Richard had gotten sidetracked in San Antonio, where he was presently detained—as in: detained in jail.

"He was disturbing the peace," Peter informed Reid. "You've got to go there and bail him out. They're going to need two thousand U.S. dollars."

"*For disturbing the peace?*" Reid was astonished.

"No," Peter said, "it's only two hundred dollars for disturbing the peace. But he's already won eighteen hundred dollars playing poker with cops at the jail, and they're not going to release him until they've had a chance to win their money back."

Another night, during a gig in Sausalito, Cole got into an egg-throwing fight at one of the city's most exclusive hotels. "That room looked like the inside of an egg," Reid recalls. "It was destroyed and cost us quite a bit of money. When I heard he was going out with Led Zeppelin, I thought, 'Who else would they take?' If you want to get into trouble—take Richard."

Cole wasn't opposed to having a little fun on the road, but with a couple heavyweights like Peter Grant and Steve Weiss in charge, he opted to cool his jets, to play by the rules at first, until he could get the lay of the land.

"Richard," Grant had instructed him by phone the day before Cole was to liaise with the band, "don't let them get into any trouble."

Grant had enough stress worrying how to break it to the band that they'd be leaving for America two days before Christmas, thereby abandoning their families for the holidays. Surprisingly, the backlash was negligible, even from Robert, who only a few weeks earlier had married his girlfriend, Maureen, in a small ceremony that included their families and a few close friends. A Christmas bonus had certainly helped to soothe separation anxieties. Peter awarded each member of Led Zeppelin $3,000 off the top of the Atlantic advance. It was a windfall particularly for the Midlands contingent; John and Robert had never been handed such a lavish amount, and Bonzo immediately blew his share on a Jaguar XK150 roadster.

It was the first time the two twenty-year-olds had ever been out of England. Admittedly there were butterflies—for the veterans as well. A lot was riding on the next few months. Loose ends were tied up, goodbyes were said. Everyone was eager to get the show on the road. The album was finished, the label deal was signed, a capable support staff and road crew were in place. All the boxes had been checked and rechecked. It was time to show the Americans what Led Zeppelin was made of.

## Chapter Seven

# BREAKING THROUGH THE SOUND BARRIER

## [1]

Los Angeles looked exactly as the Beach Boys had promised it would: glorious sunshine from dawn to dusk, palm trees galore, two-tone convertibles cruising the freeways, and California girls-girls-girls who might have stepped out of a Gidget movie. Led Zeppelin—minus John Paul and his wife, Mo, who were spending Christmas with friends in the East—enjoyed a three-day furlough at the fashionably seedy Chateau Marmont, nestled above Sunset Boulevard, to acclimate themselves to the New World before heading out on the road. Jimmy Page had seen it all before, but Robert Plant and John Bonham, both new to the surroundings, could barely keep their eyes in their heads.

"There was all this stuff going on day and night," Robert recalled. The GTOs—Girls Together Outrageously—an early groupie sect of lithe young women who prowled Sunset Strip and slept with rock stars—were holed up in a room down the corridor. Rodney Bingenheimer, a self-styled scene maker who owned a disco on Hollywood Boulevard, prowled the grounds. Famous movie actors lazed by the pool. For lads who'd left gloomy, rainy Great Britain only to land in

Los Angeles where anything seemed to go—well, this was what every English boy dreamed about.

On December 25, 1968, the three band members celebrated Christmas together, gathering for dinner—sad little TV dinners—in one of the hotel bungalows they shared. It was a low-key affair. They suffered serious jet lag. Separation from home and family dampened the holiday spirit, plus there was residual anxiety about playing their first U.S. gig. No one knew how they'd be received. A few shows would give them the lay of the land.

Their debut took place on December 26 at Denver's Auditorium Arena, opening for Spirit and Vanilla Fudge, two bands that were drawing respectable crowds. Led Zeppelin had been a late addition to the bill. Barry Fey, the promoter, was dead set against adding a third band—a complete unknown, for that matter—to a show that was already sold out. Vanilla Fudge's manager, at Steve Weiss's bidding, offered to chip in $750 to cover half of Zeppelin's fee, which ultimately sealed the deal. Fudge's musicians, to their credit, didn't object.

"We knew Jimmy from gigs we'd played with the Yardbirds," says Carmine Appice, the drummer. "We shared the same record label, and in those days, friends helped friends by touring together." They'd also listened to a test pressing of Led Zeppelin's first album and were blown away by what they heard. "We always figured someone would come along who was heavier than us," Appice says, "and Led Zeppelin seemed like they were going to be that band."

Heavier—and louder. The earsplitting roar that Led Zeppelin put out in Denver announced to an unsuspecting audience that rock 'n roll was about to break through the sound barrier. British bands no longer showed up with their trusty Watkins TruVoices or Vox 100 Super Beatles, whose guts were assembled from World War II army surplus. Those amps were as synonymous with early rock 'n roll as Kleenex is with tissue. They were loud enough, but unable to produce heavy, sustained notes, nor were they made to distort. The new sheriff in town was the Marshall JTM-45, and Led Zeppelin had a truckload of them.

Jim Marshall was a relative newcomer to the rock scene. Ostensibly, he was a mechanical engineer who taught drums in a music shop in the Hanwell section of London. Occasionally, in the early 1960s, Pete Townshend had stopped in to complain that the Vox amps Jim sold wouldn't supply the kind of output they desired. Marshall began to experiment and realized that if you overdrove an amplifier to give it more gain, it would produce the sustain and distortion necessary to make these musicians happy. He took a Fender Bassman and cannibalized it—stripping out the amp's American tubes, altering the gain, and replacing its nice, clean sound with a tone that simulated thunder. With a quartet of four-by-twelve speakers in the cabinet, you could play a chord that was heard on the moon. Around 1965, musicians began stacking JTM-45s, daisy-chaining them to raise the stakes exponentially. Terry Reid, recalling one of his earliest encounters, says, "It was so friggin' powerful, it scared the shit out of me."

One can imagine the response of the crowd in Denver. Onstage, Led Zeppelin was surrounded by a phalanx of Marshall stacks, ominous black beasts with blinking red eyes that resembled Darth Vader and sounded like the Titan space missile blasting off overhead. As they launched into their opening number, "Good Times, Bad Times," kids in the front rows literally ducked for cover.

Inexperienced reviewers wrote it off as noise, but Jimmy wasn't about to let them ignore its artistic ingredient. "It's not just noise," he explained. "It's the shape of the noise, the length, breadth, and depth of the noise." He saw loudness as being integral to Led Zeppelin's take on rock 'n roll. But even Jimmy acknowledged that the jolt of power had a residual shock value. "Led Zeppelin was frightening stuff," he said. "There was a real urgency about how we played. Everyone would be getting laid-back, and we'd come on and hit 'em like an express train."

The band's performance was still a work in progress, but with a lot going for it. Robert was a little spooked by the audience, repeatedly introducing the band, stalking around erratically. "I was very uncomfortable on stage and didn't know what to do with myself," he recalled. His arms, especially, felt like foreign objects. Should he wave them, put them on his hips, or fling them out spastically like Joe Cocker? He wasn't sure. Two or three numbers in, he began to unwind, to find a nice groove. The songs and the topflight musicians behind him provided all the confidence building he needed. They tore through "Dazed and Confused" and "Communication Breakdown"—most of the first album, with a sprinkling of Yardbirds hits and rave-up covers to keep things light and loose. Jimmy had plenty of practice in winding up crowds. He unleashed wave upon wave of soaring guitar solos, providing John Paul and Bonzo with the incentive to contribute to the excitement. "Right from the very first live performances there were these stretched-out improvisations," he noted. "There was always that energy, which just seemed to grow and grow."

With no album out and little advance publicity, nobody in the seats knew what to expect. "After the first few gigs, they started to pick up steam," says Carmine Appice, who shared the stage with Led Zeppelin—or "Len Zefflin" as they were billed in Spokane, Washington—on their first five dates. "There were nights I watched them with total awe. You could just tell they were going to break things wide open."

In the meantime, Peter Grant instructed Atlantic's promo department to dispatch test pressings of the Led Zeppelin album to progressive FM stations in the cities where they'd be appearing. He'd always believed that radio was the key to breaking the band. Kids in the States took their cues from a network of hip "underground" deejays who were plugged into the scene. Airplay created buzz in advance of an album's release. Why would they play an unknown band? "Because it was Jimmy Page's new group," says Jerry Greenberg, Atlantic's promotion chief.

The album was all over KMET-FM the first week in January 1969 as the band staggered back into Los Angeles following a terrifying swing through the Pacific Northwest. An unforeseen blizzard had pummeled Washington State, making Led Zeppelin's trip between its cities feel like the cliffhanger in an Arctic disaster movie. Richard Cole, behind the wheel of a Ford LTD, defied a travel ban that had shut down icy Interstate 90, skirting police roadblocks and nearly killing the four musicians in his charge as the car skidded toward the edge of a precipice. The band was so rattled, they could barely pass around the bottle of whiskey intended to calm their nerves. The episode was fraught with significance. It gave them an early indication of Richard's reckless behavior and his determination to keep to the schedule at any cost.

Even sunny Los Angeles wasn't risk-free. Jimmy had come down with a serious case of the flu, and Robert showed enough symptoms to warrant concern. Nevertheless, Led Zeppelin soldiered through— playing half of a four-day stand at the Whisky a Go Go, a converted bank building on the Sunset Strip, where the scene was as important as the music on its small stage. Record companies and critics religiously scouted the club's unheralded acts. Musicians stopped in regularly to check each other out, and a stable of eager young groupies cruised the tables. For a new band, the Whisky was a critical gig—if you played there and created enough heat, word spread through the media-savvy city, practically guaranteeing a breakout. Buffalo Springfield, the Doors, and the Byrds had benefited handsomely from their Whisky debuts. Both bands that played during the first week in January 1969 were virtual unknowns—Led Zeppelin and a group from Arizona fronted by a ghoulish character called Alice Cooper—and when both left Los Angeles, they were not.

In San Francisco, Tom Donahue, generally considered to be the father of free-form radio, had been playing Led Zeppelin's first album endlessly on KMPX before the group hit town on January 9, 1969, Jimmy Page's twenty-fifth birthday.

San Francisco was considered a make-it-or-break-it gig. The Bay Area was one of the world's great rock 'n roll capitals, having launched

Jefferson Airplane, the Grateful Dead, Moby Grape, Janis Joplin, the Steve Miller Band, Blue Cheer, Sly & the Family Stone, and the Beau Brummels, with Santana and Credence Clearwater Revival waiting in the wings. *Rolling Stone* published from a building on Third Street. And a date playing the Fillmore West, the rock 'n roll shrine run by the famously despotic promoter Bill Graham, was comparable to a prodigy's recital at Carnegie Hall. Led Zeppelin had *four* dates at the Fillmore opening for Country Joe & the Fish and Taj Mahal. As Robert Plant recalled, "Peter told us if we didn't crack San Francisco, we'd have to go home."

Competition there was fierce; the city was saturated with great bands. "The audiences were getting [music] three nights a week," Robert acknowledged, "everyone from the Steve Miller Band to the Rascals and Roland Kirk. There was enormous flexibility and choice, and you really had to stand up and be counted for what you were." Even in early 1969, fans were becoming more discriminating, even jaded. John Paul could feel indifference radiating from the crowd at the Fillmore. "When we started the show," he recalled, "there were just a lot of people standing there, thinking, 'Who the hell are you?'" There were also technical problems at the outset. Jimmy had switched from his dependable Telecaster, the guitar Jeff Beck had given him, to a newly acquired Les Paul, and the pickups were glitchy.

Never mind: by the time the first song—"Train Kept a-Rollin'"—had concluded, Led Zeppelin had made believers out of the San Francisco skeptics. The reception was unexpected, delirious. Arrangements came unhinged and gave way to long, drawn-out improvisational riffs, incorporating snatches of "Mockingbird" or "Shake" or even Spirit's "Fresh Garbage" into the set pieces. Each song brought on another rapturous response. The level of play approached Jimmy's vision for it. "There was a real urgency about how we played," he said. The components all seemed to click into place, as a boisterous intimacy with the audience developed.

"Bonzo and I looked at each other during the set and thought,

'Christ, we've got something,'" Robert recalled. "That was the first time we realized Led Zeppelin might mean something."

They weren't alone. The *San Francisco Examiner*, reviewing the show, forgave the band for being "awfully loud" and praised it as "as impressive a new British rock group as we've ever heard." Led Zeppelin got similar enthusiastic press bumps in Boston, New York, and Chicago, where "the audience," according to the *Chicago Tribune*, "absolutely refused to let the four go" at the end of the show, cheering until they reappeared for encores.

The results were a reassuring start. They accomplished much of what they'd set out to do in the United States. They had come a long way in five short months since their genesis as the New Yardbirds in a fusty Chinatown basement. As Led Zeppelin, they'd established themselves as one of the most promising new groups to emerge in 1969 and showed they could hold their own against the American rock 'n roll juggernaut. But they were heading home to a country that had barely taken notice. Their prospects were depressing—a schedule of less-than-impressive one-nighters at regional halls, remote clubs, even a handful of pubs. With no UK album due out until the middle of March, it seemed as if they were starting from scratch.


## [2]


"It was just a joke in England," said Jimmy Page.

Any momentum Led Zeppelin had gained in the States came to a grinding halt once they touched down at Heathrow. Without a record or an effusion of press, they were just another unknown band trying to fight through the weeds. They were still flying high from news that their album had edged into *Billboard*'s Hot 100 chart, debuting at ninety and gradually making its way north. But even its release in the States, on January 12, 1969, hadn't been without mishaps.

The cover posed problems from the start. The band had a built-in, identifiable image in the zeppelin, but applying it raised issues. The designer, George Hardie, who had cut his teeth on Jeff Beck's *Truth* album, mocked up a sleeve depicting a zeppelin emerging from an impressionistic motif of clouds and waves. It wasn't at all what Jimmy had in mind. Instead, he showed Hardie a photograph of the 1937 explosion of the *Hindenburg* over a naval station in New Jersey—*going down like a lead zeppelin*, as Keith Moon had originally envisioned it—and asked him to duplicate it as an illustration. That seemed to everyone like an ideal alternative—that is, until word filtered back to Steve Weiss's office that descendants of Count Ferdinand von Zeppelin, the German industrialist who manufactured the airship, objected to use of the family name. Calling yourself Led Zeppelin was one thing; depicting the *Hindenburg* disaster only added insult to injury. Jimmy and Peter were having none of it, and Weiss buried the complaint, believing, rightly or wrongly, there was no merit to it.

The album's production credit . . . not as easy to resolve. Effectively, Glyn Johns was the producer. He and Peter Grant had negotiated a deal and shaken on it in good faith. Both men were satisfied with the terms, which were pretty standard as far as new bands went. True to his word, Glyn rode herd throughout the session, engineering the board, passing judgment on the band's performance, and delivering the final mix—a mix that he says now, looking back over an extraordinary career, "was one of the best sounding records I've ever made." He wasn't just proud of the production, he believed it would be instrumental in breaking the band. As the album was being pressed, however, Jimmy had a change of heart.

"I put this band together," he reckoned. "I brought them in and directed the whole recording process, I got my own guitar sound." He ordered Grant to renegotiate with Johns.

"Jimmy decided you didn't produce it—he did," Peter told Glyn during a subsequent phone call. As it stood now, he'd get a flat fee for his work as the engineer, but the producer's royalty they'd agreed on was out of the question. In fact, *any* royalty was out of the question. Johns felt blindsided; he was livid.

"I called Grant a cunt," he recalls, "and said, 'Don't ever fucking ring me again.'"

He had good reason to be furious. The album, released in the States on January 12, in the middle of the tour, exceeded all expectations. Johns had known, even when they recorded the album four months earlier, they'd made a record that was "an artistic breakthrough." Its brilliance lay in the balance between the spontaneous interplay of the ensemble and its overall force. Listening to it was thrilling—and challenging. Some songs had a seductive, engaging allure, while others intended to disturb. What sounded like simple mood changes from track to track altered the character of the record drastically, interweaving acoustic-based textures with hard-charging arrangements that blended blues with soul and progressive rock. It was all there, right in the grooves.

The excitement was evident from the top of *Led Zeppelin*. "Good Times, Bad Times" was the kind of song that announced to an unsuspecting listener that this band intended to burn down the house. Everything they'd rehearsed seemed to come together in a blaze of efficiency. John Paul plunked himself down behind the Hammond B-3 and composed the opening riff right there in the studio. "The most stunning thing about that track, of course, is Bonzo's amazing kick drum," Jimmy concluded. "I think everyone was laying bets that Bonzo was using two bass drums, but he only had one."

He always threatened to add a second. "He did in fact bring in a double bass drum for rehearsal, and we played a couple songs with it," John Paul recalled, "but then we hid it when he went for lunch. When he came back, it was gone."

Nevertheless, it sounded as though the guy had five feet working at the same time. Carmine Appice, who watched Bonzo perform the song any number of times, says, "His right foot repeated sixteenth-note triplets with the first triplet left out, putting a backbeat in it, which nobody was doing in those days."

Those palpitations created a rhythmic force field with Jimmy's guitar. For the solo, his Telecaster was wired into an organ's Leslie speaker, whose baffles gave it a fluttery effect, while John Paul's bass functioned as a counterweight that pulled at the center like an undertow. And Robert's voice—it sounded otherworldly, like it was coming out of a pneumatic compressor. A lot of that was due to what session engineers called leakage. Studio A at Olympic was set up for old-style recording, "a big live room" with only a few screens to separate the musicians and the amps. "Robert's voice was extremely powerful," Jimmy said, "and as a result, would [bleed into] some of the other tracks" during the process. Jimmy was loath to clean it up, however, feeling it would destroy the ambience.

If one were bracing for a killer follow-up, something that drew and expanded on the power of the opening number, the transition was unsettling. Jimmy's fetching fingerpicking intro to "Babe, I'm Gonna Leave You" on a Gibson J-200 he had borrowed from Big Jim Sullivan suggested a dip into the homespun folk heritage embraced by Pentangle or Fairport Convention. After all, Joan Baez practically owned the song, delivering it in straightforward operatic fashion on her classic *In Concert* album, which held pride of place in every college student's record collection. Robert approached the song as if he were dead serious about honoring her version—at least through the first verse, at which point the band's scurrilous intentions took over.

Between stanzas, the arrangement fairly exploded in an outburst that stripped away the folksy pretensions to reveal an unhinged instrumental attack—not so much light and shade as fire and brimstone. Robert mowed right over the lyrics, soaring into octaves Joan Baez only dreamed about. His rip-snorting vocal gave the band a sound that struck a raw emotional chord.

The way to underscore their virtuosity was to reinterpret a textbook blues song and to knock it sideways. It seemed like a no-brainer to reimagine "You Shook Me." It was a Willie Dixon song they'd taken off a Muddy Waters Chess EP that Jimmy had dissected note for note in his adolescence. In a larger sense, it was a showstopper for a singer. Robert's delivery injected robust sexual overtones, which gave extra pull to the already steamy interplay with Jimmy's tart little fills.

John Paul Jones admitted this was one area in which he felt out of his depth. "I wasn't used to this style of playing urban blues," he said. "However, Bonzo and I quickly developed a way of playing that allowed us all sorts of improvisational freedom."

Jimmy came up with a dramatic idea for a way to end the song. He remembered an effect he'd convinced Mickie Most to use on the Yardbirds' recording of "Ten Little Indians." It involved turning the tape over and employing echo, then turning it over yet again to make the track sound like it was going backward. He called it backward echo and instructed Glyn Johns to add it to the mix.

"Jimmy, it can't be done," Johns supposedly responded. Jimmy insisted, and they argued back and forth until he says he screamed, "Push the bloody faders up!" at which point the effect worked perfectly. Whether that version of the facts is accurate or further evidence by Jimmy to support his grab of a producer's credit, the effect did justice to the stylish ending.

"Dazed and Confused" was an adaptation of the Jake Holmes song, which Jimmy had heard him sing in New York during a 1967 Yardbirds tour. Jim McCarty recalled their attraction to it for "the way the lyrics hung in isolation above the music" and the "wide open spaces in which Jimmy could frolic," both of which were underscored in Led Zeppelin's interpretation. The song was a free-for-all as far as soloing went. "It was played live in the studio with cues and nods," Jimmy recalled, so that each member of the group got a chance to step out and shine. There were few sounds more memorable than John Paul's walking bass that lumbered along ominously like Lenny in *Of Mice and Men*, with the guitar doubling an octave above it. The accompanying beat Bonzo provided was a feat of tremendous power. And Jimmy contributed "everything but the kitchen sink," as he recalled it—a tone bender for distortion, a wah-wah pedal, and his formidable violin bow, which he sawed across the strings to create "an orchestra of otherworldly textures and sonic dread."

The extended church-organ intro Jonesy played on "Your Time Is Gonna Come"—two Hammond-100 tracks with a layer of vibrato—deceptively gilded the surface of the bitter, mean-spirited lyric that Robert spat out, the accusation *and* reprisal of a scorned lover. Judged against "Good Times, Bad Times" and "Communication Breakdown," the song didn't substitute much in the way of intensity for what it lacked in imagination and charm. Robert's delivery was almost flat, too self-conscious, and it paled against the more delicious bonbons that made side 1 such an irresistible gift. The taunting refrain, nothing more than a vamping of the title, was one of the few times throughout Led Zeppelin's career that the band provided its own background vocals. "The problem was singing them," Jonesy noted, "because neither Jimmy nor I would consider ourselves singers."

"Black Mountain Side," an acoustic guitar showpiece of Jimmy's, provided a kinder, gentler interlude to the potency of heavier rockers. The guitar's steely arpeggios sounded elaborate; his playing seemed effortless, if a bit breathless. The song galloped along as if there were a posse on Jimmy's tail. Be that as it may, he did his best Bert Jansch–John Fahey imitation, weaving themes of traditional folk, bluegrass, elements of raga, and blues in an expansive open-D tuning—the same tuning he'd used on "White Summer" with the Yardbirds—accompanied by an Indian tabla, a pair of small hand drums that sufficed for percussion. "Black Mountain Side" was a nifty little rest stop along the way, but it basically set the table for one of the band's most durable anthems.

"The idea of 'Communication Breakdown,'" according to Jimmy, "was to have a really raw, hard-hitting number." He'd played on dozens of explosive rave-ups during his stint with the Yardbirds, but nothing that came before had alluded to this kind of power. It was physical, enormous. It blasted the album wide open.

The performance, more than anything, defined the sound of Led Zeppelin—rip-roaring, propulsive, feral, uncompromising. It whip-lashed from one chord to another, the drums supplying a merciless tommy-gun effect. The musicians sounded as if they weren't in con-trol of their instruments—a supernatural force had taken over and wired them directly into an atom smasher. The wanton playing un-leashed a swivel-eyed Robert Plant. His singing, or loose approxima-tion thereof, was downright frightening. "I was caught up with the power and excitement of it," he said. "I was floundering in the middle of a very open, free-form extended rock 'n roll thing." He fairly screamed the lyrics, as if he were tied to the stake with flames licking the soles of his feet. By the time he howled the last line of the chorus—*"Having a nervous breakdown / drive me insane"*—a listener was pretty much nod-ding in sympathy.

More than anything, "Communication Breakdown" foreshad-owed the dawn of heavy metal. It's the template for everything that came after in the genre, from Black Sabbath to Iron Maiden to Metal-lica to Mötley Crüe. *Heavy metal.* William Burroughs first used the ex-pression to identify the junkies in his apocalyptic 1961 novel *The Soft Machine,* and in 1968 Steppenwolf gave it a musical shout-out in "Born to Be Wild." Jimmy Page considered *heavy metal* an epithet; he hated to be identified with it. While he conceded that Led Zeppelin was "ba-sically a hard rock group," he called *heavy metal* a "bastard term" and said, "I can't relate that to us because the thing that comes to mind when people say 'heavy metal' is riff-bashing," which he refused to ac-knowledge as a tendency of Led Zeppelin.

Nevertheless, the riff-bashing in "Communication Breakdown"— and again in "How Many More Times"—injected a sustained burst of energy that critic Lester Bangs later described as a "bone-rattling sound," the stimulus that drove a listener to thrash back and forth to the beat.

The album's final two songs were almost anticlimactic by comparison. "I Can't Quit You Baby" was a slow-burning adaptation of the Willie Dixon classic he'd written for Otis Rush, which married what the Stones and the Yardbirds had hot-wired to the blues with an infusion of monster amps and Bonzo's macho beat. If rock 'n roll was an expression of the sex act, Bonzo made the earth move, a feat that tweaked even the weakest songs. As for the sloppy guitar solo, "There are mistakes in it . . . some wrong notes. . . . The timing just seems off," Jimmy admitted.

"How Many More Times," on the other hand, was an extended jam that seemed to go off the rails over its convoluted eight-minute stretch. The song was a pastiche of leftover Yardbirds fragments, with rudiments from Robert's Band of Joy and several identifiable nicks of Howlin' Wolf's "No Place to Go." As a showcase for each band member's improvisational exploits, it was the kind of number that benefited from the drama of live performance as opposed to flying about, this way and that, on a record.

The album contained decidedly more highs than lows. Glyn Johns remembers listening to a test pressing and thinking Led Zeppelin had made "a landmark in rock 'n roll history, taking [the music] to another level altogether." Flushed with excitement, he took the acetate to a preproduction meeting for the Rolling Stones' *Rock and Roll Circus* TV show. "Jimmy's put this band together," he told Mick Jagger during a break. "You've got to listen to this." Mick played a few bars and removed it from the turntable. "He didn't like it at all," Johns recalls. A few nights later, he was leaving Apple, where he'd been working on the *Let It Be* session. "George [Harrison] and I lived in the same direction, and I said, 'On your way home, let's pop around to Olympic. You've got to hear this record Jimmy's done. It's absolutely amazing.'" It was around ten o'clock at night when the two men settled into Studio A, where Johns had made the album. "I got a protection copy of the master that was stored in the basement and played it for George, start to finish. It wasn't that he just didn't get it—he thought it was *awful.*"

Jeff Beck proved eminently more receptive. He'd loved the band when he first saw them perform live back in December 1968 at the Bridge Country Club in Canterbury. "It was just amazing, blew the house down, blew everybody away," he recalled. Peter Grant played the acetate for him later that month at the Americana Hotel in New York when he was delivering the master tapes to Atlantic. For some odd reason, the first cut Jeff heard was "You Shook Me," and he assumed it was an outtake done as a tribute to him, considering it was his band's signature song and the knockout version of it was on *Truth.* He asked Grant, "OK, now where's the album?"

Peter replied, "This is the fucking album, you're listening to it."

Beck was stunned, beside himself. "You're joking," he cried. "We've done that song just three months ago, on *Truth.*"

In fact, John Paul Jones had added organ fills to the track on *Truth* and must have known it was the same song. Jeff found it incredible that John Paul hadn't mentioned it to Jimmy before Led Zeppelin went ahead and recorded its version. Meanwhile, Jeff knew that Jimmy had heard *Truth* long before the Zep session. Peter had given him an advance copy of it, although he disingenuously insisted that Jimmy never actually listened to it. That may have been so, but he'd certainly seen the Jeff Beck Group perform "You Shook Me" innumerable times on their tour of the States.

In his defense, Jimmy insisted, "It was a total freak accident." He considered the two versions as different as day and night. Beck's version playful, bluesy; Zeppelin's sultry and darker. "I didn't know he'd recorded it until our album was already done."

It was a recurrence of the one-upmanship they'd undertaken while playing together in the Yardbirds, a competitive upstaging the two musicians had engaged in since they were teenagers in Surrey. Dueling guitar virtuosos jockeying for the lead in the race to fame. Jeff realized he was fading down the stretch. A more dazzling, more inventive guitar player than Jimmy, he fronted a band that didn't measure up to his brilliance and couldn't go the distance. Led Zeppelin, Jeff knew, was on its way to something special. "It was just a much better package than what I had," he concluded.

A better package, but still no traction in Great Britain. The British press was reluctant to get behind Led Zeppelin, put off, most likely, by news releases of the band's big American record advance. Talking about money was considered crass, not the way things were done in England. "No one likes people who brag about how much they make," says Chris Charlesworth, one of the journalists who covered Led Zeppelin for *Melody Maker*. "It appeared that money was their sole motivation, and it turned the fans and the rock media against them."

"Peter had miscalculated," says Phil Carson, Atlantic's UK general manager. "The country wasn't ready to entertain a business concept called Superhype."

Robert agreed. "The conservatism goes into the music as well," he said at the time. "The musical journalists are still sort of dubious about this sort of music, and they were thinking that it was a flash in the pan, and they didn't think it had any social relevance."

Conservatism, however, had little effect on the rock 'n roll lifestyle. Dave Pegg, who had recently become Fairport Convention's bass player, recalls attending a Led Zeppelin gig on April 8, 1969, at the Cherry Tree, a little pub in Welwyn Garden City, about twenty miles from London. "I got a lift back afterward with Bonzo, who was driving a brand-new gold Jaguar 3.4 saloon," he recalls. "We pulled up at a service station, and there was an identical one at another pump across the way. It was Robert's." Bonzo had also moved his family to a new council flat in Dudley, decked out in incredible style, top to bottom, courtesy of Rackhams, Birmingham's answer to Harrods.

They were savoring their new prosperity. Despite the lukewarm reception in the UK, the album was putting up extraordinary numbers with abundant airplay in the United States. The cap was off the gusher and money was pouring in, with advances mounting for future appearances there. If Led Zeppelin weren't received with open arms at home, they would go to where the love was.

## [3]

The situation in the States wasn't all warm and fuzzy.

On March 15, 1969, *Rolling Stone*, the arbiter of the rock 'n roll scene, published its long-awaited review of the *Led Zeppelin* album. The band's pent-up expectations soon turned bilious as certain words and phrases sank in: "weak, unimaginative songs . . . dull . . . redundant . . . much overdone . . . monotonous . . . avalanche of drums and shouting . . ." There were references to "prissy Robert Plant's howled vocals" and his "shrieks . . . strained and unconvincing shouting." Bonzo was accused of smashing "his cymbals on every beat." And Jimmy, while recognized as "an extraordinarily proficient blues guitarist" was hung out as "a very limited producer." Only John Paul Jones, Led Zeppelin's enigmatic éminence grise, escaped criticism. Individually, the band members felt savaged by the review, but nothing hurt as much as the critic's wholesale appraisal. "In their willingness to waste their considerable talent on unworthy material, the Zeppelin has produced an album which is sadly reminiscent of *Truth*."

That hurt plenty. *Truth* was like the too-perfect cousin you were always measured against, a cousin you secretly despised. "That album haunted Jimmy," says Chris Charlesworth. "It was a masterpiece, a flawed masterpiece, that had beat Zeppelin to the punch by a couple months and was still fresh in everyone's minds. People always compared Zeppelin's first album to *Truth*. And *Truth* was Jeff's, which drove Jimmy mad."

The *Rolling Stone* review was written by John Mendelssohn, a UCLA student who had answered the magazine's famous ad: *Do you want to contribute? Send us something.* His rock gods were The Who, and he'd just fallen in love with the Kinks' new LP, *Village Green Preservation Society,* when the Led Zeppelin album arrived in the mail. "I put it on," he recalls, "and hated every second of it. To my ears, it was so misogynistic and harsh and ugly. Their music, like that of Cream and [Jimi] Hendrix, ceased to be about melody and harmony and became about virtuosity instead. The review didn't begin to convey how much I hated it."

Mendelssohn, a musician who went on to work for Warner Bros. Records, was alarmed by what he saw as the changing musical land-scape. He mistook it for the loss of melody, when in fact it was some-thing more organic and sociological. The generational gap was opening up. Audiences were getting older, reorienting from adolescent girls screaming at heartthrobs to mixed crowds listening to and appreciating the artistry. Vocal attractions like Herman's Hermits, the Tremeloes, the Searchers, and the Hollies were giving way to bands who'd devel-oped their creative skills. The Beatles were no longer the lovable mop tops; the *White Album,* released a few weeks before *Led Zeppelin,* con-tinued to obliterate that image, dispensing with teenage romanticism and defying all musical currents. Rock 'n roll was growing more com-plex. Groups like Pink Floyd, Traffic, the Moody Blues, Yes, and Led Zeppelin saw new, subversive possibilities in the form.

Logical as that seemed, it failed to soothe the sting of the *Roll-ing Stone* review. "It was galling," John Paul Jones admitted, "but at the same time you felt it was a shame that they didn't get it." He felt the review was spiteful, "total damning stuff." There did not seem to be any criteria for the critic's opinion. "If we were crap and they said we were crap, well, fair enough. But we were really good, and we couldn't un-derstand what the agenda was."

Peter Grant had his own agenda. He decided to ignore the rock press entirely. He'd spent plenty of time on the road in the United States with the Animals and Jeff Beck and understood that FM radio, the new force on the scene, connected bands directly to the audience, bypassing the reviewers and critics. These stations, it turned out, had far bigger audiences and more influence than the press did. If kids *heard* Led Zeppelin and *saw* them in concert, it would be all the convincing they'd need, Grant concluded. "That's the way big names are made these days," he said. "Not by press, but by people seeing them and making up their own minds." Led Zeppelin didn't need reviews, good or bad. The album was amassing fans without them.

Jimmy was of the same frame of mind as his manager. "We just couldn't seem to do anything right as far as the critics were concerned," he said. "At which point I think we all just sort of gave up on the idea of ever pleasing them."

Rock critics be damned. They were a different generation than the Zeppelin audience, mostly old men in their midtwenties —and jaded— who saw themselves as tastemakers, aesthetes. "The rock press did not like bands who became famous because of FM radio," says Danny Goldberg, who later handled press for Led Zeppelin and became general manager of their record label. "Their reaction was: 'If we didn't discover them, they're not authentic.' They saw themselves at the center of defining what was good and what was bad, what was cool and what was not cool. And at that moment in time, Led Zeppelin was not cool."

Not to the small fraternity of critics, perhaps, but fans thought otherwise. By the time Led Zeppelin returned to America in the spring of 1969 the album was firmly in the Top 20. Before they left for the States, however, there was one last piece of business to take care of.


Jimmy called a rehearsal at his Pangbourne boathouse the second week of April 1969. He had a riff he'd been banking for almost a year that could be the foundation for something very special. "I suppose my early love for big intros by rockabilly guitarists was an inspiration," he theorized, "but as soon as I developed the riff, I knew it was strong enough to drive the entire song, not just open it." He'd showcased it for the band while they were rehearsing for the first album and everyone agreed it had killer potential—"addictive, like a forbidden thing."

It was simple, all of five notes. But the way Jimmy phrased it gave it the kind of physical tug that was nothing short of convulsive. It throbbed like an erratic heartbeat. By the time the rest of the instruments barged in, two full measures later, the song wasn't just cooking, it was boiling over.

He'd asked Robert to take a crack at the lyrics. Robert wasn't a complete novice in the songwriting department, but his experience was limited. He and Kevyn Gammond had knocked out a throwaway they called "Memory Lane" that the Band of Joy used to play as a way of filling out sets and another number called "The Pill Song." *Oh, the pills we took* . . . "Just atrocious," Gammond recalls. This was different. Jimmy's riff demanded a lyric that stood up to it and grabbed attention right out of the box.

"I just thought, 'Well, what am I going to sing?'" Robert recalled. For inspiration, he referenced his favorite albums. A beloved Muddy Waters LP yielded up "You Need Love," the Willie Dixon blues classic recorded in 1952. *You've got yearnin', and I got burnin'* . . . That had a nice suggestive rhyme scheme to it. And he zeroed in on another tasty line. *Baby way down inside, woman, you need love* . . . That could work as well. It was also reminiscent of the Small Faces' debut album, which Robert had played to death, with "You Need Loving" on it, a souped-up version of Muddy's original, credited to Steve Marriott and Ronnie Lane. Marriott recalled a teenage Robert Plant stationed right in front of the bandstand when the Faces played it at Kidderminster Town Hall. "He used to be at all the Small Faces gigs." In fact, at one of the Faces' shows they did with the Yardbirds, Marriott said, "Jimmy Page asked me what that number was we did. . . . I said, 'It's a Muddy Waters thing.'"

Jimmy wasn't so clear about its origins. "We did, however, take some liberties," he admitted. "And Robert was supposed to change the lyrics," which he did . . . *a little bit.*

*You need coolin'*, he began singing, *baby I'm not foolin.'* In his mind, that was far enough away from Muddy Waters's yearnin'/burnin' narrative so as not to suggest an outright nick. Besides, Robert had something fresh and provocative up his sleeve, a bombshell, actually.

*I'm gonna give you every inch of my love.*

It wasn't especially subtle, but it did the trick and would tap into the primal urges of the teenage boys who were Led Zeppelin's predominant audience at this stage. The moment it captured fired up adolescent fantasies and gave the band an entry into their subconscious. The rest of the lyric "developed in the studio, much of it ad-libbed," Robert recalled, a miscellany of repetitive droning, exclamatory *ooohs*, and whoops of orgasmic joy. "Wherever it comes from, it was all about that riff," Robert said. The riff thrust the song's impact into new territory.

"Addictive," as Jimmy had said, "like a forbidden thing."

Atlantic Records was pleading for another Led Zeppelin album, a follow-up to ride the coattails of the first one before the hoopla died down. This song "sounded strong enough to open our second album," Jimmy thought, "so I wanted to record it first."

On April 19, 1969, a week before their second American tour kicked off, the band trooped into Olympic Sound's Studio A. It was a massive space with a soaring twenty-eight-foot ceiling that was used primarily to record symphony orchestras and film scores. Glyn Johns, still fuming over the screwing he'd taken, was unavailable to engineer the session, so they settled on George Chkiantz, a staff engineer whose credits (*Blind Faith*, Jimi Hendrix's *Axis: Bold as Love*, and the Faces' "Itchykoo Park") were indisputable.

The setup, however, was predetermined. "I had this avant-garde master plan for 'Whole Lotta Love' and could hear the construction coming together in my head," Jimmy said. More than anything, he wanted a strong drumbeat to drive the song, "so that every stroke sounded clear and you could really feel them." He also moved Robert into an isolation booth so his vocals wouldn't bleed into the rhythm tracks. Robert wasn't as unsure of himself this time around. "My confidence was building at that time," he recalled. Since joining the band, he had pushed himself to the front with more authority, both physically and vocally. This song offered him the chance to cut loose and let it all hang out.

They ran it down once to get an overall feel. The song was a monster of thrust and aggression. There was little room to breathe in the interval between verses, with the instruments storming in from every side and Robert gasping and howling away over the top. To give the track expanse, Jimmy had carved out a stretch in the middle to allow an outpouring of discordant sound effects he'd collected on tape to build to apocalyptic proportions. He threw everything available into the mix—a sonic wave sound, explosions, a metal slide with backward echo, assorted traffic noise, Robert feigning the throes of ecstasy, Bonzo's conga obbligato, and the feedback from an electronic gizmo called a theremin that produced an eerie, surreal sound. "It was an oscillator," Jimmy explained. "The closer you get to the aerial, the higher the pitch went." He also monkeyed with his Les Paul Standard. "I detuned it and pulled on the strings for a far-out effect." The rising coil of sound climaxed in an overheated swell before fireworks burst from Jimmy's guitar. The tension it released was tremendous, if not exactly genteel.

"Whole Lotta Love" established a new, exciting standard in rock 'n roll. It was loud, delirious, uncontainable, oozing overheated masculinity, with the kind of unforgettable riff that resonated for the ages. It sounded like all the elements of rock 'n roll distilled to the core of its explosive essence. It not only confirmed Led Zeppelin as a musical force, it signaled they were the torchbearers of heavy metal, whether Jimmy was inclined to wear the badge or not.

## Chapter Eight

# THE NEW NORMAL

## [1]

Led Zeppelin was becoming something else.

As the band bulldozed through tour after tour in 1969, its image evolved as a supergroup of a unique order, playing to besotted audiences and behaving as if rules of civility did not apply.

By the end of May, Led Zeppelin's debut album had achieved gold-record status, lodging on the *Billboard* charts for a solid fourteen weeks, in the company of such standouts as Blood Sweat & Tears, the cast album of *Hair*, Dylan's *Nashville Skyline*, and the death-defying *In-A-Gadda-Da-Vida*. The album's success left no doubt that the band had made its presence felt in the United States. They were a staple of FM radio, bookings were pouring in at spiraling prices, and the press, while still suspicious, had no other choice than to cover the phenomenon. Even square, middle-of-the-road *Life* magazine sent a reporter to follow one of their tours. But the real measure of approval was the audiences. The audiences were out of their heads.

The music took audiences to a place they'd never been before—a place similar to the hysteria-induced level where, years earlier, the Beatles had transported hordes of thirteen-year-old girls. Led Zeppelin's audiences were different, older . . . somewhat. Mostly boys between the ages of fifteen and twenty thronged the area in front of the stage, where Jimmy and Robert, aided by an army of Marshall stacks, whipped them into delirium. As the *Chicago Sun-Times* pointed out in its Led Zeppelin coverage, "Never had loudness been so completely pleasurable. It has the power to vibrate your body and dislocate your nervous system. Fight the sound and you'll have one of the worst headaches on record; move with it and you'll be completely captivated."

Loudness was integral to the music. "Rock 'n roll was meant to be played loud," says Roger Mayer, the electronics guru who invented the fuzz box. In his ongoing work with volume and distortion, he relied on the Fletcher-Munson curves—a set of frequency response curves that human ears use to program the loudness level. "But music doesn't sound loud unless dynamics"—the variation between the loudest and softest levels—"have an impact on it. In the case of emotional reaction, dynamics are more important than loudness."

Led Zeppelin had the dynamics angle all worked out. Playing loud, they knew, distorted an audience's perception. To give the audience an acoustical out-of-body experience, they only had to crank the volume up to twelve. There was nothing clever in that. Adding dynamics—the light-and-shade aspect of Jimmy's blistering guitar solos and his dramatic body language; Robert's roller-coaster vocals from caterwauling highs to warm, sensual lows and peacocky exhibitionism; John Paul's bass pounding out a range of intensities; Bonzo's ability to contrast bursts of great power with more nuanced shuffles—gave an added structure to their performances that incorporated dynamics of loudness without driving the sound over a cliff.

Led Zeppelin's second tour of the United States coincided with Jimmy Page's desire to jump-start a steady pace of recording. "The plan was to capture the energy of the band on the road," he explained, which meant they'd record "on the run between hotel rooms and the GTOs," as Robert Plant put it—in whatever city they happened to be appearing in when the mood struck.

When they touched down in Los Angeles on April 30, 1969, the band went directly from the airport to Mystic Sound, the old Del-Fi studios in Hollywood, where Ritchie Valens had recorded "Come On Let's Go" and "La Bamba" and the Bobby Fuller Four cut "I Fought the Law."

Mystic Sound was a modest four-track studio that just about accommodated Led Zeppelin's gargantuan equipment. With only a baffle placed between the double-stacked Marshall amps to absorb sound, they recorded "The Lemon Song" live—laying down the track with everyone playing together in the same cramped, low-ceilinged room. The song was an adaptation of Howlin' Wolf's "Killing Floor" that they performed regularly in their shows—fairly straightforward blues dominated by Jimmy's scathing riff, a high-flying solo, and nimble, jazz-inflected bass runs from John Paul that underpinned the vocals. Robert rewrote the lyrics, co-opting a line from "She Squeezed My Lemon," a song cut in 1937 by Roosevelt Sykes. Standing in the middle of the studio, using a hand-held microphone, Robert shamelessly belted out, *"Squeeze me, babe, until the juice runs down my leg / The way you squeeze my lemon, I'm gonna fall right out of bed."* It was crude, designed to get a rise out of overeager adolescents.

"When we recorded that it was in L.A.," Robert said, "and it was a time when there was a lot of looning going on—and it was one of those states of mind you get into when everything's rosy and shining. And so a lyric like that comes zooming in." Nevertheless, he acknowledged his role in appropriating key phrases. "It's borrowed admittedly, but why not?" he said. "But 'squeeze my lemon'—I wish I could think of something like that myself."

They also began work on an instrumental, "Pat's Delight," named after Bonzo's wife and featuring an extended drum solo that, during shows, often dragged on—and on and *on*—for fifteen or twenty minutes. The rhythm track was a direct cop of Bobby Parker's "Watch Your Step," which John Lennon marginally rearranged for the Beatles' "I Feel Fine" and had enthralled Jimmy as a teenager in Epsom. He would eventually retitle it "Moby Dick." They worked for hours, trying to get a satisfactory take for Jimmy's solo. Frustration was setting in when the engineer, Chris Huston, finally pulled the plug. "It's not happening," he announced, to some grumbling from the troops. He knew it was futile to indulge accomplished musicians who would arrive at the same conclusion sooner or later. It was better to be up front with them, not waste any more time.

Los Angeles was too distracting for a demanding recording session. The groupie scene at the Chateau Marmont was in full swing when Led Zeppelin arrived, with an eager coterie circling the band. There were always obliging women on the fringes of the music scene who were attracted to the fame and the rock 'n roll energy, but the groupies in Los Angeles were shockingly young. "They were thirteen, fourteen, maybe fifteen tops," says Rodney Bingenheimer, who'd been a publicist at Capitol Records and later a self-styled LA scene maker. "Girls just showed up, they came out of nowhere." To snooty Angelenos, *nowhere* meant the San Fernando Valley, Palos Verdes, or Orange County, suburbs whose starry-eyed denizens were drawn to the city lights. "They were mostly latchkey kids," says Michael Des Barres. "Their fathers were away and their mothers could give a shit." Too young to get into rock 'n roll hangouts like the Whisky a Go Go, the girls prowled the hotels where rock stars congregated, often in bungalows with open doors and easy access.

Led Zeppelin was no strangers to the feast. The guys were a long way from home, and from their wives, whom most of them had married in their teens. Maureen Plant and Pat Bonham were tucked away in the Midlands, Mo Baldwin tended house in Sussex. The guys were in their twenties now. It was open season in LA as far as the band was concerned.

"They all had girlfriends here, temporary girlfriends," says Vanessa Gilbert, who joined the band's entourage when she was "a naive eighteen." Richard Cole made sure the guys always had options. Robert and Bonzo needed no prompting. They indulged in the debauchery from the moment they arrived. Jimmy, who had a longtime American girlfriend named Catherine James, nevertheless allowed Bonzo to dress as a waiter and wheel him, splayed on a room-service cart, into a suite of sybaritic girls.

Once, during Led Zeppelin's stay at the Chateau Marmont, Peter Grant wandered into one of the empty bungalows they'd rented and found a naked young woman tied to the bed by her wrists and ankles. "I said, 'Hello, what are you doing here?' She said, 'I don't know, but guys keep coming in and fucking me.' I said, 'Oh okay, well, have a nice day.'"

No one gave a thought to whether these girls were well below the age of consent. Some were eighteen, some were sixteen, some were fourteen, occasionally younger—mostly no one bothered to ask. "Maybe it was a sign of our immaturity, but after all, we were only twenty or twenty-one ourselves," said Richard Cole, by way of justification, "so a fourteen- or fifteen-year-old wasn't total madness." In any case, he maintained, "they made themselves available to us. We never forced them into doing anything they didn't want to. They were looking for some fun—and so were we."

There was no oversight, no accountability, no inclination to put the brakes on the pursuit. It was a pursuit that would continue to mark Led Zeppelin throughout their career.

Led Zeppelin's music already set a certain lusty tone. What they played and how they worked their audience into a joyous, unrestrained, head-banging mass made them a magnet for kids who wanted to break out and party. Lyrics like *"I'm gonna give you every inch of my love"* and *"Squeeze me, babe, until the juice runs down my leg"* served as come-ons to young, impressionable girls—and boys—who heard messages in the songs that stroked their fantasies. "Sex, in heavy metal's discourse, is sweaty, fun, and without commitments," according to Deena Weinstein, a popular-culture professor at DePaul University in Chicago. The loud, convulsive rhythms uncork the most primal expressions of sexual arousal and empowerment.

For a teenager blasting out of adolescence, Led Zeppelin was the magic elixir, a rampaging hormonal highball of music and acting out.

Acting out had become a highlight of the shows. Robert and Jimmy had mastered the gift of rock 'n roll *dell'arte* in the way they communicated with the audience and with each other under the spotlight. Their kinetic stage presence—the spectacle they created—was often as compelling as the music they made. They used their bodies to great effect to emphasize the feel of the music—striking poses, assertive physical gestures, the lip pouting and pelvis thrusting and hip shaking, the stage prowling and pacing in circles and duck-walking, all of it creating excitement that was liberating, a physical release. It was impossible to attend a Led Zeppelin show without getting lifted out of your seat, feeling the need to move, getting emotionally involved. The band knew how to pace a show in order to build tension and momentum in unsettling ways.

As they toured the mixed bag of halls and arenas from Los Angeles to New York, the energy at their shows grew more feverish and intense. When they jackknifed briefly into Canada for a few pickup dates, a journalist covering one of the shows noted that Led Zeppelin "let loose an earthquake of sound and fury" and that they "blast out with raw, jagged power, enough to bust a new door in your brain." Two sisters at the gig in Seattle—Ann and Nancy Wilson, who were nineteen and fifteen respectively and would materialize later as the hard rockers Heart—"ended up leaving," Ann later said, "because we were so shocked." The music—and everything that went with it— overpowered their senses.

The audiences were in thrall. Sometimes, however, no matter how hard the band worked, the equipment conspired to thwart their best efforts. They were still just traveling catch-as-catch-can with an assortment of rented amplifiers, putting themselves at the mercy of a sorry range of PA systems provided at each of the gigs. Thirty years later,

Robert Plant could recall in excruciating detail a show Led Zeppelin played at the University of Ohio opening for José Feliciano in
May 1969.

"The PA was [nothing more than] a cluster of speakers right up in
the apex of the room," he said. "It was a circular building with the stat-
utory [sic] sixties students sitting around looking suitably astonished
and vacant." It was impossible to squeeze volume out of the creaky
system. There was no way for him to project his voice or to create the
sparks necessary to get a rise out of the crowd. José Feliciano walked
off with the night's biggest hand.

For the most part, though, they were able to swing. The reviews
of their shows were mostly glowing. Every once in a while they hit a
sourpuss who wasn't willing to give them the time of day, no matter
how hard they played or worked the crowd. Such was the case at the
Rose Palace in Pasadena on a bill with Julie Driscoll and Brian Auger
& the Trinity on May 3, 1969. The *Los Angeles Times* hired Led Zeppelin's nemesis, John Mendelssohn, to review the show, and he didn't
back off his *Rolling Stone* slam. The overall affair he called "an exhibition of incredible self-indulgence" and the music "dull, pretentious
versions of blues standards and vapid original material." For good
measure, he zeroed in on Jimmy's "inability to play imaginatively or
even tastefully" and "incoherent howling by lead singer Robert Plant."

Incredibly, John Bonham was spared. He had guzzled a third of a
jeroboam of champagne between the two sets, even cradling the enormous bottle under an arm when the band returned to the stage, drinking liberally from it between songs. Twice during the set, he toppled
off his stool.

Bonzo they could deal with, but the band couldn't make heads or
tails of the review. What was it with this guy Mendelssohn? they wondered. He seemed to be out to get them, a personal vendetta. The review overshadowed the profusion of praise and made the press, in
general, personae non gratae. By the time Led Zeppelin returned to
London in early June, their attitude had hardened. The press wouldn't

be tolerated, and if they persisted in tormenting the band, they'd have an irate Peter Grant to deal with.

"I saw Peter get very, very tough with journalists," says Bill Harry, the founder of *Mersey Beat* and an intimate of the Beatles, who was hired as Led Zeppelin's press officer. "He'd roar at them like a ferocious bear and threaten bodily harm if they wrote negative stuff." Harry's job, in fact, was to shadow the band and to keep the press *away*. "We did very few interviews. They didn't trust the press at all. They'd been dismissed as second-rate too many times."

Only friendly press got access from now on; journalists had to prove their loyalty. And from here on in, no more TV appearances. "They never knew how to get the sound right in a TV studio," Grant declared, "and I realized it wasn't worth the effort."

The resistance in England had started to thaw. Word had filtered back from the States that Led Zeppelin was the real McCoy, that they were taking music in a new, exciting direction, and the media, as well as British fans, jumped on the bandwagon. *Melody Maker* and *New Musical Express*, the two most important music magazines, began following and writing about the group as they went about reintroducing themselves in front of friendlier homeland audiences.

Nothing could have seemed more like an old-home night than their return to Birmingham Town Hall on June 13, 1969. For Robert and Bonzo, especially, it had been the scene of so many boyhood thrills, a place to see their favorite rock 'n roll stars and to dream about one day playing under those lights. Now they'd returned, top of the bill, just as they'd dreamed it. A full house had turned out to cheer them on. Along one wall at the side sat a pair of familiar faces—a couple of guys they used to see regularly in a Hearst Street music shop. Bands would congregate there on Saturday nights, and if you were short a musician to play with, you'd see if anyone local was available to sit in. "Do you know anybody who plays the drums?" "Do you know 'Jeff's Boogie'?" "Can you come and gig with us?" There were always two guys in there who never seemed to have a gig, always the last two left in the music shop, two losers, and now, *blimey*, here they were—Tony and Ozzy—fresh from a new band they were forming called Black Sabbath.

Led Zeppelin pulled out all the stops, just as they would do in Newcastle and Bath. They made converts out of those kids who had been slow to the party. The highlight of the mini UK tour was a gig on June 29, 1969, at the hallowed Royal Albert Hall. The Promenade Concerts, as the concert series was called, had been a staple of London's musical life since 1965, featuring classical or avant-garde performances from some of the most revered cultural icons. The year 1969 broke from tradition, launching the Pop Proms, a seven-day lineup that included not only Led Zeppelin but also Fleetwood Mac, The Who, Chuck Berry, and sundry lesser acts.

The Albert Hall had never experienced anything like Led Zeppelin. When the Beatles appeared there at the BBC's *Swinging Sound* event in 1963, the volume was modulated to suit the facility, the audience polite to a fault. "When Led Zeppelin came on and played at a good ten times the volume of everyone else," wrote a reviewer, "the audience very nearly freaked completely." All hell broke loose. Kids "stormed the stage, danced in the aisles and the boxes, and were screaming so hard the band did three encores." Flowers poured out of the stalls onto the stage, initiating a final jam with Blodwyn Pig, a British blues band that had opened the show.

"You didn't notice that there wasn't a set," John Paul recalled of the evening, "because the music drew you in. And there wasn't much leaping about the stage, because everybody was working hard and concentrating."

Even so, Robert was overcome by the place. He managed to work himself up into a lather and admitted, "I was hanging on for dear life."

*NME* noted that Led Zeppelin scored "a massive personal triumph," not fully realizing how personal the triumph was for some.

"Jimmy was elated," says Carole Brown, who was Peter Grant's assistant. They shared a taxi to their respective homes that Jimmy hailed outside at the curb after the show. "He was flush with pleasure. From what he said, he felt this was a turning point for Led Zeppelin, when they finally earned the respect they'd been denied in London."

He had little time to savor it. Five days later, the band was back in the United States, where they would remain throughout the summer of 1969.

## [2]

There was a Jekyll-Hyde aspect to Led Zeppelin's transatlantic nature. "When we did shows in England, they were always the shows that the press would come to and your family would come to," Jimmy recalled in a reflective moment. At home, the band was on its best behavior. "But when we went out to the States, we didn't give a fuck and became total showoffs."

They would need to pull out all the stops. The summer of '69 was the "festivals summer" in America, with outdoor extravaganzas scheduled in almost every major city. These were generally multiday, mostly open-air events that featured as many as ten to twenty acts and drew crowds of anywhere from 12,000 to 125,000 fans. There were even rumors that the Woodstock Music Festival, in upstate New York in mid-August, would dwarf those numbers with its array of superstars.

Led Zeppelin wasted no time hitting the festival circuit. In just over one week after landing in the States, they played five of these events with the crème de la crème of international rock acts. In Atlanta, they shared the bill with Ten Years After, Joe Cocker, Chicago Transit Authority, Janis Joplin, Blood Sweat & Tears, Spirit, Canned Heat, and Johnny Winter, among others. In Laurel, Maryland, they jammed with Jethro Tull, Jeff Beck, Sly & the Family Stone, the Guess Who, and the Mothers of Invention. Similar casts appeared with them in Newport, Rhode Island, and Philadelphia. By the time they got to New York City, on July 13, a planned day off turned into a busman's holiday with a backstage visit to the Singer Bowl Music Festival in Queens, overlooking the Grand Central Parkway.

Ostensibly, the guys were there to cheer on Vanilla Fudge and Jeff Beck, who were headlining with a number of interesting supporting acts, including Ten Years After. It was a punishingly hot inner-city night, like the inside of a convection oven, and the crowd out front—as well as the one backstage—was feeling inner-city *close*. As Jeff Beck later noted, "Three English groups at the same place has to add up to trouble." Bonzo was warming up to it, working his way through gallons of beer that he'd been knocking back since early afternoon. "John was a good guy," says Carmine Appice, "but when he got drunk, he turned evil."

Halfway through Ten Years After's set, his dark side emerged. From the side of the stage, he chucked a carton of orange juice at Alvin Lee, the band's lead guitarist, landing it, *splat*, on his trademark Gibson ES-335. This didn't sit well with the churlish Lee, who glared murderously at Bonzo hooting in the wings.

Jimmy Page wasn't happy. "Bonzo's got to get a grip on things," he warned Richard Cole.

But Cole knew better than to cross Bonzo when he was tanked up. One wrong word could set off a rampage. Besides, Cole didn't mind egging him on a bit. The outcome, if handled well, was always good for a few laughs.

Bonzo, more than a few sheets to the wind, behaved while Robert, Jonesy, and Jimmy joined the Jeff Beck Group's set and tore through a rip-roaring rendition of "Jailhouse Rock." When vocalist Rod Stewart pivoted into the band's encore, "Rice Pudding," Bonzo turned to roadie Henry "the Horse" Smith, and said, "Horsey, I'm gonna play the drums." Before Smith could grab him, Bonzo made his move to the stage.

He talked Beck's drummer, Tony Newman, into relinquishing his stool and took his place, interrupting the song with a classic burlesque bump-and-grind drum roll. Slowly, the other musicians left the stage.

There were two spotlights, one in each corner of the front of the house, and they were both trained on Bonzo. Goaded on by the crowd, he began to strip—shirt, pants, finally his underpants—wiggling comically in the buff.

According to Smith, who was Bonzo's tech and stationed directly behind him, "Peter Grant and Steve Weiss, at the side of the stage, were yelling 'Get him off the fucking stage!'" But—how? "He was a rock-solid guy and a dead weight," Smith said. "Lifting him was like trying to carry a barrelful of sandbags." Eventually, he locked Bonzo in a full nelson and started walking him backward. Weiss ran over and grabbed the drummer's arms, and the two men dragged him to the bottom of the stage stairs, where a cluster of New York City policemen awaited.

The order had been given to arrest Bonzo for public indecency. Smith, who still had him pinned in his clutches, watched as Grant thrust his hand in his pocket for a wad of cash that was three inches thick. "He licked his thumb and began peeling off hundred-dollar bills until the pile was enough to satisfy the police."

The outcome was somewhat more favorable than the next time Led Zeppelin played the Singer Bowl Festival, later that August, at the old World's Fair grounds in Flushing Meadows Park. Buddy Guy opened the show, and during the Paul Butterfield Blues Band's middle set, Guy and Bonzo polished off a quart of Jack Daniel's. Led Zeppelin came on afterward under a canopy of nighttime stars and launched into their opening number, "Train Kept a-Rollin'." Jimmy delivered the opening riff and waited for the drums to kick in. Bonzo, however, was passed out cold, with his head on the snare.

Peter Grant grabbed one of the roadies by the pants. "Wake 'im up!" he barked.

"How should I wake him up?" Joe Wright asked.

"Push 'im!"

Wright gave Bonzo a less-than-friendly shove. When it failed to produce the necessary response, Grant said, "Hit 'im!"

Wright hiked up his shoulders. "What do you mean—hit him?"

"*Hit 'im!*" Grant demanded.

Jimmy and Jonesy kept the rhythm going while the drama played out in the background.

Wright threw the manager a hangdog look and did as he was ordered. "I slammed Bonzo in the back of the head," he recalls, "and he got up, roaring like a bear."

Unfortunately for Wright, Bonzo threw a cymbal at him, ripping four of the roadie's knuckles. Then the drummer came in on cue without missing a beat.

It didn't last. He eventually passed out again, which pissed off Jimmy. After the show, he and Peter huddled and discussed the possibility of replacing their drummer.

Bonzo's behavior was erratic, often childish, sometimes violent, always unpredictable. Alcohol fueled much of his rowdiness. He was an unquenchable drinker; he'd drink until he dropped. The others could abide it, as long his antics didn't intrude on the band's performance. "You get hammered before the show, buddy, and we're going to have problems," Grant warned him. No one hoped it would come to that. Bonzo was a brilliant drummer, perhaps the best musician of his kind. But he was a walking time bomb.

Led Zeppelin's behavior, in general, was evolving. They were developing an offstage persona that was edging into the realm of supreme indulgence. Ever since their album had turned gold, a sense of extravagance—extravagance awash in decadence—had come over the band. It played out in garish, outrageous, and occasionally freaky ways and unfolded as an integral part of their legend-in-progress. Robert Plant put voice to it quite pithily when, sometime later, he climbed a palm tree at a home in the Hollywood Hills and shouted, "*I am the golden god!*"

The rapturous audiences and the entourages that followed the band conferred godlike status—and Led Zeppelin took it to heart. They danced on tables at posh hotels, trashed their rooms, threw televisions out the windows, ran up room service bills in the thousand-dollar-plus range, ordered fifty drinks at a clip. Money was no object; they were making it hand over fist. At clubs, where an anything-goes ambience prevailed, their drink tabs were always comped, and girls eagerly crawled under the tables to give them blowjobs. They'd lost all perspective when it came to excess.

At times, it got out of hand. Groupies were never in short supply—Richard Cole would pluck girls out of the audience for liaisons backstage—but the scenes got freakier. The one that lives most prominently in Led Zeppelin legend—and perhaps the most lurid—occurred at the end of July 1969, when the band appeared at the Seattle Pop Festival, a three-day affair with the usual lineup of top rock acts.

Led Zeppelin had been on the road with Vanilla Fudge when they checked into the Edgewater Inn, situated on a pier over Elliott Bay. The hotel was famous for offering fishing rods to guests with waterfront rooms, and in fact its most famous guests, the Beatles, were immortalized in a photo showing them fishing from a balcony during a 1964 tour. The spirit of the two bands was unusually high. It was the end of the road for Vanilla Fudge—literally the end of the road—and in Seattle, they were casting fate to the wind.

"We recognized we were done as a band," says Carmine Appice, who was in a lighthearted mood as the festivities there got under way. "We weren't headliners anymore. Things were passing us by. It was the era of great guitar players, and our guy, Vinny [Martell], wasn't one of them. Tim [Bogert] and I had already been in touch with Jeff Beck about forming a new band called Beck, Bogert & Appice as soon as Jeff ditched the guys he was playing with."

The two bands were enjoying a rare day off, lounging about the hotel. Robert and Jimmy drove to the festival site in Woodinville, about twenty-five miles out of town, to check out the Doors, who were playing on a bill with the Youngbloods. They were intrigued by the notoriety swirling around Jim Morrison, who'd recently been arrested in Florida for flashing onstage. Robert, especially, was curious, inasmuch as he'd been compared to Morrison in press coverage and was genuinely flattered. Imagine his disillusionment when a bloated Jim Morrison ambled onstage in a skintight black leather jumpsuit and screamed, *"Fuck you all!"* at the audience. In between songs, which were delivered in a lethargic, indifferent way, he spouted endless pseudopoetic claptrap and nearly toppled off the side of the stage.

"It was really sickening to watch," recalled Robert, who was crushed, doubly so in front of his wife, Maureen, who was visiting from England and had joined him and Jimmy for the show. "The sexual thing had gone. He was just miles above everyone's head."

Meanwhile, back at the hotel, the rest of the entourage idled away the hours in typical rock-star fashion. "We were camped out in John Paul's room smoking some pot, watching the boats go by, and listening to Delaney & Bonnie on Robert's portable record player," Carmine Appice recalls. Their diversion was interrupted when a seventeen-year-old redhead named Jackie knocked on the door. Appice had picked her up the night before, and she'd returned to see if a party was in progress.

Cole and Vanilla Fudge's road manager—a dubious character named Bruce Wayne, who was, naturally, nicknamed Batman—were in the room next door, where they'd been fishing for hours and guzzling champagne. Somewhat miraculously, they'd managed to haul in a catch of mud sharks and red snappers that lay festering in a wastepaper basket half filled with stagnant water. During a break, they grabbed the basket and joined the party in John Paul's room, where Jackie was pretty high from the joints being passed.

"You wanted to party?" they said to her. "Take off your clothes."

"Once she was naked," Appice says, "they started hitting her with the fish, and it left little teeth marks on her back. Things got pretty ugly, pretty intense, so we went out into the hall, where Bonzo and his wife, Pat, joined us, and we watched the action through the door."

The audience grew as others straggled back to the hotel. "In fact, we were invited to bring our wives to take a look," recalled Robert, who had returned from the festival, "but after a while we left because it was all a bit unsavory."

Everyone scattered when the hotel manager appeared to answer a complaint about the noise coming from the room. When he left, not entirely mollified, they reassembled in Carmine's room and ordered room service, until Jackie reappeared wearing nothing but John Paul's robe.

He was furious. "You bloody cunt, get my fucking robe off!" he screamed.

Handing it over, the naked Jackie sat on the bed, ignored and forlorn, while the others finished eating. Sometime thereafter, Cole and Batman resurfaced with their bucket of dead fish.

"Things got weird very fast," Appice recalls. "They grabbed the butter off the cart and rubbed it around her pussy. Then they started screwing her with the nose of the fish, pushing the snappers into her as far as they could, and when they were done, they pissed and shit on her."

If ever there was an example of behavior that was more about dominance than sexuality, this was it. It was a chance to offer up a shocking spectacle to the gang that had gathered to watch.

"Man, it was gross. We were all pretty disgusted," says Appice. Though not disgusted enough to preclude his bandmate from filming it with a video camera, or from describing it in detail to Frank Zappa, whom Vanilla Fudge encountered during a layover at O'Hare the next day. Zappa couldn't resist writing a song about it. "*Lemme tell you the story 'bout the mud shark*," he sang on his live album, *Fillmore East*. "*A succulent young lady! With a taste for the bizarre*."

The landscape was changing, and darkening.

Ellen Sander, who was traveling with Led Zeppelin for her *Life* article, overheard several guys plotting to lure two groupies they deemed undesirable to a motel in Detroit "and pelt them with some cream-filled donuts, then gang bang them." She struggled to make sense of it. She understood the demands of the road—the endless travel, the boredom, the pressure to perform in front of enormous crowds, the mental and physical toll. On this tour alone, Led Zeppelin would travel fourteen thousand miles to play thirteen gigs, all the while attempting to record their next album. "The rock business is volatile, rapid, and dangerous," Sander concluded. She never thought the danger applied to her. But on the last night of the second U.S. tour, at the Fillmore in New York, Sander stopped in the band's dressing room following the show to say goodbye. Bonzo, along with others she couldn't identify, attacked her, ripping her dress down the back. She fought them off, fearing they would rape her, and they might have, had Peter Grant not intervened, hustling her away.

What were the limits of behavior on the road? Where did one draw the line? Was it "just young guys having a good time," as Robert suggested?

"There was a certain amount of hedonism that was involved," Jimmy admitted, and why not? "We were young, and we were growing up."

The summer of '69 and its high points brought everything to a head. More was at stake than ever before. The hotbox conditions were hotter, the big-ass crowds even bigger, the expectations steeper and steeper. And Jimmy drove the guys hard, hustling them into oddball recording studios every chance he got, trying to capture lightning in a bottle.

"It was quite insane, really," he recalled. "We had no time, and we had to write numbers in hotel rooms. We'd put down a rhythm track in London, add the voice in New York, overdub harmonica in Vancouver, and then [go] back to New York to do the mixing."

The recording itinerary was indeed astoundingly peripatetic. At tiny Morgan Studios in North London, with Glyn Johns's brother, Andy, at the board, they'd laid down the tracks for "Thank You," "Livin' Lovin' Maid (She's a Woman)," and "Sugar Mama," the latter of which was eventually abandoned. "Heartbreaker" was recorded in New York, with the rhythm track taped at A&R Studios. Jimmy's solo, however, "was an afterthought," he said. "That whole section was recorded in a different studio"—farther uptown at Atlantic—"and was sort of slotted in the middle." While at Atlantic, he put the finishing touches on "Bring It On Home," which had initially been cut at funky R&D Studios in Vancouver. "Moby Dick" finally came together at Mirror Sound in LA, then back to New York for "Ramble On" at Juggy Sound before heading back to Olympic in London for a session that produced "What Is and What Should Never Be."

"We recorded and overdubbed our way from West Coast to East Coast," Jimmy said, gratified that they were able to pull it off. Miraculously, consistency wasn't a problem, nor was what he called "the attack"—the way they bit into those songs "to get excitement onto a piece of plastic." It was essential to match what was happening onstage—the dynamics, of course, but also the spontaneity and the experience. "Part of the excitement of the album is due to the fact that we were completely energized from the live shows and the touring."

The action had intensified on- and offstage. In August 1969, Led Zeppelin routed back to LA, where they set up headquarters at a new location. The Chateau Marmont left the band too accessible to outside influences. Anyone could simply knock on their bungalow doors, and everyone did. There was little promise of privacy on the premises. More to the point, as the band left a gig in San Bernardino on August 8, the news was aflame with a grisly murder in the Hollywood Hills, just above the Chateau, that had claimed the lives of actress Sharon Tate and her friends. To beef up security, Peter Grant moved the band a few blocks west on Sunset Boulevard to the Continental Hyatt House, a traditional high-rise hotel that catered to the rambunctious rock 'n roll trade.

Security at the Hyatt House was in the eye of the beholder. "It was more like a nightclub than a hotel," said Bebe Buell, a frequent visitor who knew her way around its nooks and crannies. To judge from the scene in the lobby, one might have thought the hotel was hosting the National Conference of Groupies. A swarm of scantily clad teenage girls held court in the lounge, leaving no doubt that this was their turf. They came and went as they pleased, no questions asked, and what pleased them most was a liaison with a musician. Led Zeppelin was catnip to the Hyatt House girls. The band's reputation for frolic preceded them, and the marquee out front—WELCOME LED ZEPPELIN—did little to discourage the ever-expanding crowd.

Within days, the hotel would be forever dubbed the Riot House for the crazy scenes that took place under its roof. "It was the epicenter of rock 'n roll life," according to Michael Des Barres. Led Zeppelin took over the entire ninth floor, where Peter Grant and Jimmy Page had booked themselves into several rooms apiece so they would be difficult to find, even for others in the band. "It was like one big playground," said Danny Goldberg, who lodged there with Led Zeppelin on subsequent tours. "There was an attitude of great anarchy. Bonham would play his records very, very loud at three or four in the morning." If a guest complained, management would move the *guest*. "And so it gave the group a feeling of omnipotence that was unique."

Despite added security, girls could easily make their way to the ninth floor and beyond. Richard Cole maintained a steady flow of what he judged the best-looking and most willing women, with a weeding-out process that was short on civility. If a girl didn't live up to his exacting standards, she'd be dispatched with a curt *"Fuck off!"* or worse. When sex grew tiresome, when boredom set in, one of the guys might heave a television out the window or stage a contest to see who could hit one of the billboards across Sunset Boulevard with a champagne bottle. Broken glass littered the street and pavement out front with frightening regularity. Occasionally, after too much beer, Bonzo would urinate off the balcony, aiming at a convertible idling by the door.

It was anarchy and omnipotence practiced at a heroic level.

Drug dealers—or fans bearing pharmaceutical gifts—also gained easy access to the ninth-floor sanctuary. Weed had always been as essential to tour paraphernalia as a new set of guitar strings, and neither was ever in short supply. But in Los Angeles, where everything was flashier and more excessive, cocaine was emerging as the rock 'n roll drug of choice. A bump of coke took the edge off the grind of a tour.

"How do you alleviate the boredom on the road?" asked Benji Le Fevre, who did sound, among other things, for Led Zeppelin for years. "You start off with a few joints, you get high for a laugh. Then you get into Quaalude and Mandrax. Then cocaine comes along and you feel *fantastic*, because it makes you feel invincible."

Even a golden god felt more alive, ultraconfident, on top of his game. And the sex became more intense. "The bacchanalian quality was a shock and revelation to us young British boys," Michael Des Barres says. Coke dealers earned a free pass to the ninth floor, where the clientele was dedicated and ready cash available. Lots of cash. As Led Zeppelin's stock soared, as their fees and, thus, leverage increased, Peter Grant began demanding payment in cash after the shows. It wasn't unusual to encounter him in a limo to the hotel clutching a hold-all stuffed with fifty- and hundred-dollar bills. He was generous with its disbursement; the guys got whatever they needed. And a portion of that cash now went for cocaine.

The scenes grew more extreme. In *Stairway to Heaven*, Richard Cole's sensationalized account of his years with Led Zeppelin, he describes how, at the Chateau Marmont, he and Bonzo tried and failed to coax a Great Dane into a sexual encounter with a young groupie. By the summer of '69, he'd tweaked the exploit.

Joe Wright recalls, "Richard invited me and Robert to a party in the Hollywood Hills with my buddies from Pacific Gas & Electric," a local blues band of some renown. "He warned us, 'You're gonna see some stuff that might freak you out, so be cool.'" It was a midcentury-modern house nestled among palms with picture-postcard views of the city. They had a few drinks, did a few lines of coke, and hung out around the pool, chatting with the laid-back guests. At a certain point,

Richard steered Joe and Robert toward a bedroom in the back with the curtains drawn. "Whatever you do, just be cool," Richard repeated.

As their eyes adjusted to the darkness, they made out a giant bed—an orgy bed—that could accommodate multiple people. "On it was a beautiful Amazon, like a Las Vegas showgirl, completely naked, stroking the belly of a Great Dane," Wright says. The scene eventually progressed into full-on sexual intercourse while Cole whispered reprimands—"*Ssssh*, don't embarrass us"—to a squeamish Plant and Wright.

The world around Led Zeppelin was becoming something else. They were a long way from home.

## [3]

The U.S. tour ended for Led Zeppelin on the last day of August, without an appearance at Woodstock, the granddaddy of summer festivals. They'd been invited to perform, but Peter Grant took a pass. "I said no to Woodstock because I knew we'd just be another band on the bill." Instead, they finished up playing the Texas International Pop Festival in Dallas and returned home, knowing they'd be back in the States within six weeks' time for the release of their second album.

Jimmy had remained in New York to mix the album, which he did over two days, huddling in A&R Studios with engineer Eddie Kramer, a veteran of Beatles and Jimi Hendrix sessions. There was real concern that recording levels would be problematic, having cut tracks in so many different studios—that the band "may have overstepped the mark," as Jimmy feared—but the two men managed to achieve a uniform balance, working electronic miracles at a relatively primitive console.

When Jimmy got back to London, he found his manager sidetracked with two other bands. Peter Grant had undertaken the direction of Jeff Beck's new group with the remnants of Vanilla Fudge's rhythm section, Tim Bogert and Carmine Appice. They'd tried talking Rod Stewart into staying on for the vocals, but he jumped ship and joined the Faces instead. Stewart issued a farewell warning to Appice. "Don't work with Jeff. He's just going to screw around and mess up your career." But BBA, as the new band was called, reconfigured as a power trio, slapping together an album for Columbia Records. "We had a sold-out tour of the South—ten shows," Appice recalls. "Five shows in, we went to the next gig . . . and Jeff went home. That was the end of BBA."

Grant fared better with the other band, Cartoone, which he signed to a multialbum deal at Atlantic. After the first record tanked, the band's guitarist, Leslie Harvey, told Grant he had another *better* group, Power, with girlfriend Maggie Bell in Scotland. Grant was skeptical but said, "Well, we'll all just have to go up there and see what the story is."

Power had a residency at Burns House in Glasgow, where they were performing when Grant's limo pulled up. "Tom Waterson, the man who ran the club, was a right little asshole and warned us about being pinched by sharpies when he saw Peter and Richard Cole arrive," Bell recalls. Waterson had a contract with the band, paying them a paltry £12.50 a night playing to packed houses.

The band was everything Leslie Harvey had cracked it up to be. They rocked hard, had great songs, and—that *singer!* What a voice!—part Janis Joplin, part Billie Holiday. Maggie Bell was a showstopper, a natural, and Grant was sold. "After the show, Mr. Waterson barricaded us in a back room," Maggie says. "Peter told him, 'You'd better open the door or I'll have to break it down.' He put us in the limousine, took us back to a hotel to talk about plans, and two weeks later we were in London."

Grant renamed the band Stone the Crows and banished them to a basement flat in Earl's Court to rehearse with new sidemen—Jimmy McCulloch, late of Thunderclap Newman, and Fleetwood Mac virtuoso Peter Green, fresh out of rehab and raring to play.

With another North American tour set for Led Zeppelin—nineteen performances in just three weeks' time, beginning on October 17, 1969—there was little attention paid to BBA and Stone the Crows. Zeppelin was breaking wide open, what with a new album due for release and a prestigious kickoff concert at no less than Carnegie Hall in New York.

Carnegie Hall was leery of rock 'n roll bands. It was a storied venue, dating to its opening night in 1891, when the composer of the program's featured symphony, Pyotr Ilyich Tchaikovsky, sat in the audience. The Beatles and the Stones had played there in 1964, with wild, anarchic audiences that ran roughshod through the house. Since then the venue had been placed off limits to anything groovier than, say, Johnny Mathis. Amazingly, Carnegie Hall's board of directors decided that Led Zeppelin's audience was likely to be courteous and civilized.

It was the hottest ticket in New York. A second midnight concert was added to accommodate demand. Right up until showtime, scalpers worked the corner of Fifty-seventh Street and Seventh Avenue, pocketing twice the highest ticket price of $5.50. (It was a different day.) New York's rock cognoscenti vied to attend. A reporter noticed "every musician that happened to be in town standing at the side of the stage during the show." The mainstream and underground press turned out in droves.

Peter Grant was taking no chances when it came to press. Still distrustful and disdainful of reporters, G, as he was now known to insiders, singled out those he considered friendly to Led Zeppelin and whom he could control with perks and favored access. It became a business strategy that was practiced successfully throughout the band's career. There were those in the press who could be bought, so to speak, by being made to feel they were part of Led Zeppelin's trusted entourage. Some, like *Melody Maker*'s Chris Welch, got preferential treatment early on, beginning with the Carnegie Hall show. "Chris was considered *all right*," according to Richard Cole. Welch was flown to New York from London, not by his employer but on Led Zeppelin's dime, and put up in an all-expenses-paid suite at the New York Hilton, with gifts lavished by his benevolent hosts. "Turned out they'd arranged to have some hookers and porn films and whips delivered to my room," he recalled, "but the girls had been stopped by the house detective before they got up to my floor."

Welch didn't disappoint. In an "exclusive report," he delivered a rave—in this case deservedly so. It was one of those New York shows that would become part of the rock 'n roll narrative. *Led Zeppelin at Carnegie Hall*: there are few more incongruous citations. Courtesy and civilized behavior weren't anywhere on the premises. "It was the first time I had ever seen a New York audience, and I couldn't believe how wild and noisy they were," Welch recalled. "They literally went completely mad the moment the band came on."

It was also the first time any of the audience had heard songs like "Whole Lotta Love," "The Lemon Song," and "Heartbreaker"—songs that took electric blues into the heavy-metal sphere. Bonzo stretched his "Moby Dick" solo to an eternal twenty-five minutes, playing the tom-toms with his hands, elbows, and anything else within his grasp, in a tribute to his drum idols, Gene Krupa and Buddy Rich, whose performances at Carnegie Hall had been similar sensations. Three encores at the midnight show put the period at the end of the story. You could almost hear Chuck Berry sing, "Roll over Beethoven—and tell Tchaikovsky the news."

Five days later, when the album dropped, it was almost anticlimactic. Word had flashed from coast to coast that the new songs were something fantastic—something else—and *Led Zeppelin II*, as it was titled by the group, shipped gold, with advance orders of 500,000 units in the United States alone. By the end of the year, it would be the best-selling album in America.

It was a handsome package—a sepia-toned photograph of a Luftwaffe division that navigated the Zeppelins that bombed England during World War I. The four pilots' faces were replaced by those of Messrs.

Page, Plant, Jones, and Bonham. The surrounding pilots were adorned with superimposed headshots of Peter Grant, Richard Cole, blues stylist Blind Willie Johnson, and actress Glynis Johns, the latter a dig at the first album's aggrieved engineer.

Reviews, for the most part, were glowing, especially from the music industry trade magazines that served to spur airplay and point-of-purchase sales. There were a few that took swipes at cosmetics like Robert's "tortured voice and Page's guitar, which at times sounds as disturbing as car tires screaming to a crash." Greil Marcus, then a *Rolling Stone* editor, assigned the magazine's review, somewhat mischievously, to John Mendelssohn, who'd made his contempt for the group well known in his review of their previous album. And there was mutual animosity; Robert Plant had threatened him from the stage in Anaheim, California. This time around, Mendelssohn's voice dripped with sarcasm. "[Marcus] was probably hoping that I'd be amusing," Mendelssohn recalls, contrite-*ish* fifty years later. "As a drummer, I should have enjoyed that album just for Bonham. I listen to it now and think, 'How did I miss how terrific he was?'"

In any event, it increased the band's ire at *Rolling Stone*, if not at critics in general. "Led Zeppelin was very touchy when it came to criticism," says Chris Charlesworth, who covered the band for *Melody Maker*, along with Chris Welch. "With a band like The Who, criticism bounced right off their backs, but Zep had very thin skin, Jimmy most of all. As they got bigger and bigger, their minders got more and more aggressive with us. Especially Peter Grant. We were seriously afraid of him. *Seriously. Afraid.* He still gives Welch and me nightmares."

*New Musical Express*'s Nick Kent was another journalist who toed the manager's line and was granted routine backstage access. "Peter made it abundantly clear he wouldn't be at all happy if anything negative appeared in my write-ups," Kent said.

G's brutishness sharpened in direct proportion to the band's success. It had always been simmering, making snap appearances at salient moments. But his exercise of power reverted to the thuggish

Jimmy Page flashes his new Grazioso, sitting in with the Presidents, 1958. "We thought he was a bit too young to join us." *Left to right:* Jimmy, Tony Busson, Martin Cowtan, Eric Archer

Taking the lead with Red E. Lewis & the Red Caps. *Left to right:* John "Jumbo" Spicer, Red E. Lewis, Jimmy Rook, Jimmy Page

Jimmy, before the dragon suit was finished, with Carter-Lewis and the Southerners, 1964

John Paul Jones in an early publicity shot during his days as a session master

The last incarnation of the Yardbirds. *Left to right*: Jeff Beck, Jim McCarty, Chris Dreja, Jimmy Page, Keith Relf

Jimmy and Jeff Beck tune up backstage at Staples High School, Westport, Connecticut.

Mr. Superlungs, Terry Reid. The lead singer was a plant.

The Band of Joy in a soulful pose, January 1968. *Left to right:* Kevyn Gammond, Robert Plant, John Bonham, Chris Brown, Paul Lockey

The one and only Willie Dixon

Cyril "Squirrel" Davies and Alexis Korner at the Ealing Jazz Club, 1962. That's a teenage Charlie Watts on the drums behind them.

Glyn Johns, denied his Zep producer's credit, managed to eke out a living as producer extraordinaire.

Mickie Most at his Oxford Street desk, in a deluge of Animals and Herman's Hermits 45s

Mickie's desk mate, Peter Grant

The New Yardbirds' first ever gig at the Gladsaxe Teen Club in Copenhagen, September 7, 1968

An early Led Zeppelin publicity photo, 1969

A man and his bow, in the heat of "White Summer"

Christmas dinner at the Chateau Marmont. Bah, humbug! December 1968

The Boston Tea Party, January 1969. Where it changed forever.

The Thames they are a-changin'. Jimmy on the deck of his Pangbourne boathouse.

The man who
kept everything
up in the air,
Richard Cole

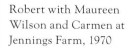

Robert with Maureen
Wilson and Carmen at
Jennings Farm, 1970

Jimmy summons the spirits on the theremin for "Whole Lotta Love."

Robert celebrating the de-pantsing of Phil Carson. The rest of the clothes came off outside the Tokyo Hilton, September 1971.

Ricardo and Jimmy share a parasol at Kyoto Station. G, as always, has their backs, September 1971.

Jimmy with Rodney Bingenheimer and fourteen-year-old Lori Mattix during happier days in Los Angeles, June 1972.

The gang holding court at Rodney's. (Sable Starr leans against Robert; Mick Hinton plays waiter; Lori Mattix mugs next to John Bonham.)

Jimmy with pals Rodney Bingenheimer and Miss Pamela, and Lori hovers in shadow.

Led Zeppelin shows off their new set of wheels.

John Paul Jones provides in-flight entertainment while Ahmet Ertegun and guests look on.

Robert and Ricardo snuggle in the *Starship*'s understated bedroom, June 1973.

ways he'd once learned from the streets. "I don't believe in pussyfooting around if it's my affair," he said with typical candor. Managers, as a rule, were tough characters out of necessity in dealing with shady promoters, shifty lawyers, bootleg merchandisers, and talent poachers. If pushed, a manager had to be able to push back and protect his act. Peter knew how to push—sometimes down a flight of stairs. Often it was the four-finger jab right under the rib cage or a slap across the back of the head with a trademark farewell: "Fuck off, ya cunt." He brought a gangster mentality to the game.

In Detroit, the night after the Carnegie Hall triumph, Led Zeppelin shared the Olympia Stadium stage with Grand Funk Railroad in their hometown. Something about the rival band's performance stuck in Peter's craw, either their cockiness in front of longtime fans, their extended set, or the audience's worshipful approval. Furious, he sought out Terry Knight, Grand Funk Railroad's manager, grabbed him by the neck, and lifted him inches off the ground. "You'll take the group off stage . . . immediately!" Peter roared. Knight obediently pulled the plug. When the bands appeared together two days later, at Public Hall in Cleveland, Terry Knight was nowhere to be seen.

"If somebody had to get trod on, they got trod on."

Such was the punishment that befell fans if they dared to take a verboten picture of Led Zeppelin during a concert. Grant was known to troll through arenas, snatching cameras and demolishing them. Once, in Vancouver, he spotted a fan surreptitiously recording a performance and smashed the apparatus to smithereens, with a bonus shove or two to the solar plexus, only to discover the person was neither a fan nor a bootlegger but an inspector from the Noise Abatement Society checking levels in the arena with a decibel meter. "Four men dragged me upstairs and started to beat me," claimed the inspector, a man named Mac Nelson, who insisted on pressing charges. It took swift intervention on Steve Weiss's part and a packet of cash to get the subsequent warrant for Grant's arrest dismissed.

No matter, it did nothing to ease his inflexible authority over Led

Zeppelin's interests and the demands—*his* demands—on those who dealt with him. The idea was to isolate Led Zeppelin in a protective bubble so they could sow their creativity without outside interference.

Following the release of *Led Zeppelin II*, G demanded that Atlantic Records honor the band's wish that no singles be issued. *No singles?* It was unheard of. Hit singles not only stimulated album sales, they provided a huge windfall to both recording artists and labels. Moreover, they were the engine that drove AM Top 40 radio. It didn't take a genius to pick the obvious hit single from *LZII*. FM radio had already plucked out "Whole Lotta Love," playing it ad nauseum at its five-minute-thirty-five-second length. In record-company parlance: it started to blow up big.

No matter how big, however, Peter Grant put his foot down, reminding Atlantic Records that the band's contract gave them complete control over how the record was released. And not just over albums but over singles. Just in case the label had forgotten, he reminded it again: *no singles*.

Jerry Greenberg, the head of Atlantic's radio promotion department, was understandably frustrated. The big chain of stations he oversaw was begging for a version that conformed to the Top 40 format. "AM radio was not going to play a five-minute cut," Greenberg says. "So I called Peter and said, 'Do me a favor. Ask Jimmy to make an edit so I can get it played on AM stations.'" Grant called back a few minutes later and said, "Jimmy says we're not a singles band. Forget it." And he hung up.

The pressure on Greenberg for a single increased with each passing day. The station manager of KFRC, San Francisco's top AM channel, called him and said, "We can't play that record, but—God, it's number one here in the city. *Do something*, will you?"

Greenberg was caught between two masters. He placed another call to Grant. "*Please*, you've got to give me an edit," he begged. "Or at least let me try one, and I'll send it to you."

Grant explained that it was probably futile but relented somewhat, telling Greenberg he was welcome to give it a shot.

As Jerry recalls, "I'm in our studio, watching the clock. At two forty, they are into the hook." *Need a whole lotta love, need a whole lotta love, need a whole lotta love* . . . "I order a fade and we're out at 3:05."

He cut a dub and sent it to Grant's office with the message: "This is how we can break the band wider in America. I want to press up a few copies, send it to my ten biggest stations, and get it going." After an excruciating few days when he heard nothing from England, Jimmy, to his surprise, gave it his blessing.

A few copies became two thousand, with the short version on one side, the original version on the flip.

"*Boom*, it exploded!" Greenberg recalls. "I mean—*exploded!*"

Grant called him two weeks later and said, "Jimmy wants to know when it's coming on the charts."

"Peter, it can't come on the charts," Greenberg responded. "It's not released as a single."

After a brief interval, only a few minutes at best, Grant called back and said, "Jimmy says it's okay to release it, but you can only put it out in America."

Apparently, Atlantic's office in London did not get the message. The UK label had recently hired Phil Carson to run its operations— the same Phil Carson whom Peter Grant had pulled out of Cal Danger's car and threatened seven years earlier. In the interim, Carson had played bass for the Springfields, a pop trio with Dusty and her brother Tom, and Houston Wells & the Marksmen, an English country band that had supported the Beatles on an early tour of cinemas in Scotland. Carson gave the order to release "Whole Lotta Love" as a single and shipped around four thousand copies. As a result, he was summoned to 155 Oxford Street to explain himself to Peter Grant.

"Peter was not pleasant," Carson recalls.

With Mickie Most looking on, G backed Carson against a wall

and bellowed, "What the *fuck* do you think you are doing? Who the *fuck* do you think you are?"

Carson, no shrinking violet, says, "I told him who the fuck I thought I was, but it didn't seem to matter. He was furious, but I stood my ground, telling him about my strong background in marketing and how I knew what I was talking about."

"You don't fucking know enough," Grant roared.

They both raised their voices, nearly coming to blows, until Carson realized how physically overmatched he was and made a quick exit.

After some transatlantic dickering, Atlantic's president, Ahmet Ertegun, told Carson to "call the fucking record back."

Later, Carson would acknowledge Grant's savvy and call him "a marketing genius" for withdrawing the single in the UK. "Since kids couldn't get a single, they had to buy the album," he concluded, "and *Led Zeppelin II* started selling as if it were a single." They'd approved the single in the United States because there were hundreds of AM radio stations there. In England, at the time, there were only a handful. The BBC was unlikely to play "Whole Lotta Love" no matter how long or short it was. A single just didn't make good business sense.

And business was good, extraordinarily good. The album hit the UK charts in February 1970, where it remained entrenched for ninety-eight weeks, dislodging the Beatles' *Abbey Road* from its stranglehold on the number-one position. By April, *LZII* had sold over three million copies—double platinum—in the United States alone, with the band's take estimated "in excess of $5 million."

A brief tour of Europe, from February 23 to March 12, reintroduced Led Zeppelin to an audience that was starved for a glimpse of the headline-making band. Last time around, they'd played these same venues as the New Yardbirds with rented, barely adequate equipment. This time they took their own Watkins PA, a replica of one The Who used to blow the roof off buildings. Everywhere Led Zeppelin went, "the audience surrendered totally," as the Stockholm papers reported, not just in Sweden but in Helsinki, Vienna, Munich, Hamburg, and Düsseldorf as well.

The only glitch arose in Copenhagen, where the granddaughter of Ferdinand von Zeppelin threatened to sue the band for appropriating the family name. Countess Eva von Zeppelin had been dunning RAK's Oxford Street office with solicitors' letters objecting to the band's name from the time they announced the switch from the New Yard-birds. To safeguard against any complications with their appearance in Denmark, Led Zeppelin appeared as the Nobs instead, named after Claude Nobs, a Swiss promoter close to the band. But graciously, they extended an invitation—more tongue-in-cheek than sincere—to Ms. von Zeppelin to meet them and hopefully reconcile in a local studio where they were doing some recording. Imagine their surprise when she accepted.

The rapprochement turned out to be a pleasurable affair. The lads were on their best behavior, and the dowager was friendly and diplomatic—that is, until she was leaving the studio and spotted a copy of the first album, whose cover depicted her family trademark exploding in flames.

"I had to run and hide," Jimmy recalled. "She just blew her top."

Robert heard her say "she wasn't going to have any 'babbling apes' making money from the family name."

At least the concert—the first and last-ever performance of the Nobs—came off without a hitch, save for a distraction at a postgig press conference held at a local art gallery. "We had a couple of idiot journalists at the reception," said Phil Carson, who accompanied the band, "and they had to be thrown out bodily."

That was the new normal—except that nothing in Led Zeppelin's universe was normal anymore. With the runaway success of the sec-ond album, they had catapulted to superstar status, with all the efflu-via that such a distinction generated. They were idolized but also hounded—by the press, by fans, by groupies, by anyone wanting a piece of the action. Obligations were overwhelming. The record company pressed them to keep their eye on the prize, to continue writing, to keep up the pace, to produce. The pressures of maintaining a grip, to keep surpassing themselves, could not be overstated: the next gig, the next song, the next album. A breather, a good night's sleep, became precious commodities. A chance to reconnect with normalcy, if such a state of being existed for them.

Yes, a breather. They needed to get off the road, off the treadmill. It was time to settle a few personal accounts.

## Chapter Nine

# INTO THE DISTANT PAST

## [1]

A breather, a pause, a break, a time-out—Led Zeppelin knew it for what it was: only a segue into yet another North American tour, their fifth in a year and a half. Peter Grant had already booked it, in fact, a month of back-to-back gigs in the spring of 1970, in arenas of ten-thousand-plus seats. And to up the ante, no opening acts, no intermission. "An Evening with Led Zeppelin," as the dates would be called, meant each night's heavy lifting was all on the band's shoulders.

It was a grind, a blur. The shows were big, long, loud, raucous extravaganzas, the travel exhausting, enervating, inhuman.

"I don't think we can take America again for a while," John Paul said wearily when it was over, in mid-April 1970. "America definitely unhinges you."

There had been so many crazy scenes, so many mishaps. It was ominous from day one, when Jimmy's cherished "Black Beauty," the Gibson Les Paul Custom, disappeared at an airport in Vancouver. "It never came off the conveyor belt," said Henry Smith, whose job it was to retrieve it at baggage claim. But that was only a sample of what lay ahead. "We were driven off the road by rednecks in Austin, Texas,"

Robert recalled. The band's limo was grazed by a bullet on the way to their hotel in Dallas in what was obviously a close call. In Pittsburgh, a brawl broke out, causing them to stop the show until the crowd settled down. Two cops in a bathroom at Raleigh's Dorton Arena were overheard discussing a plan to plant drugs on Led Zeppelin in order to make a bust. Violence erupted outside Miami Beach's Convention Hall when a thousand would-be gate-crashers attempted to storm the doors. And in Memphis, with a coliseum of fans jumping up and down on the seats after a blistering "Whole Lotta Love," a nervous promoter held Robert Plant and Peter Grant at gunpoint until Plant went back onstage to calm down the audience.

This wasn't Norman Rockwell's America. This was post-Altamont and post–Manson murders, a nation divided by the conflict in Vietnam and less than a few weeks away from one of its darkest days, when the National Guard opened fire on a group of college students at Kent State University in Ohio protesting the bombing of Cambodia. The concert landscape had changed to reflect it. Gone were the days of orderly college shows and respectful audiences who came to listen to the lyrics. Arenas, coliseums, and speedways brought out something else in a crowd, where the sound and fury whipped audiences into a frenzy.

"You see so much that is great, but so much that is terrible—the rush, the hassles, the police, you know," Robert said. "In some cities it's so rough that people are scared to come to our concerts."

Bodyguards were hired, especially in the Deep South, where long-haired rock 'n rollers were eyed like varmints and things got itchy. The number of people carrying guns gave Jimmy the creeps. "It's just like being back in the Jesse James era," he observed.

"You'd go into a venue in the South, where kids were up and yelling and screaming and gyrating and out of control—promoters didn't know how to handle it," says Henry Smith. "Their security was limited to off-duty cops who always thought a riot was about to break out, and they were quick to overreact, which led to brute force. This was a whole new ball game for everybody. It was a nerve-racking experience."

No wonder John Paul wanted a break from the States. A different city every night, another hotel room, inedible food, impersonal encounters—"living like an animal for so long." That tour had taken years off of their lives.

Afterward, the bandmates had scattered like pool balls. Jimmy retired to his "baronial life" in the art-and-antique-filled boathouse with a new girlfriend, Charlotte Martin, an arresting French model and ex-lover of Eric Clapton's, to whom he'd been introduced by Roger Daltrey. John Paul moved into a recently acquired manor in Hertfordshire, where his wife and three daughters greeted him like Captain Ahab back from a life-sucking voyage at sea. Bonzo and Pat abandoned their tricked-out council flat for a farmhouse surrounded by fifteen acres of land on the outskirts of Birmingham. And Robert, "fed up with humanity in the big cities," took cover on a working farm he bought for roughly $15,000 in Blakeshall, near Kidderminster, where chickens and goats roamed around a "somewhat derelict farmhouse" and a number of Georgian outbuildings.

Led Zeppelin had earned a dear two months off from the road to recharge and to reconnect with what was important in their lives. Robert, in particular, had a new nine-month-old daughter named Carmen with whom he'd spent less than a few weeks since her birth. He was hardly home a week, however, when he began exchanging calls with Jimmy, who was renovating an estate he had just purchased on the banks of Loch Ness in Scotland. They had ideas for new songs. There was only so much time off one could enjoy before the creative juices started to flow.

Jimmy already had two numbers sketched out—"Immigrant Song" and "Friends"—along with "Since I've Been Loving You," which he called "a work in progress." He'd also been tinkering with "Tangerine," a dreamy song that he'd written years earlier for the Yardbirds under the title "Knowing That I'm Losing You" and which they'd taken an abortive stab at in their final 1968 recording session.

But it wasn't specifically songwriting the two men discussed. "We'd been working solidly and thought it was time to have a holiday, or at least to get some time away from the road," Jimmy said. He and Robert kicked around the idea of a getaway for just the two of them and their families. A proper holiday meant hotels, but neither Jimmy nor Robert could bear the thought of another hotel stay after the countless places they'd holed up in on tour. "Robert suggested going to this cottage in South Wales that he'd once been to with his parents when he was much younger. He was going on about what a beautiful place it was, and I became pretty keen to go there." In truth, Jimmy admitted to Robert, "It would do me a lot of good to get out to the countryside."

South Wales was an annual getaway for the Plant family. Not far from Kidderminster, it was blessed with some of the most breathtaking countryside in the United Kingdom, an abundance of scenic river valleys, ancient forests, the Brecon Beacons, and villages dating to the fourteenth century. As soon as the weather permitted, Robert Plant Sr. celebrated the weekends driving his family south into an exotic kingdom that, to his impressionable teenage son, evoked the setting of a Tolkien fantasy. Misty mountain ranges and turreted castles set the stage for wondrous excursions that stayed with Robert Jr., specifically the family retreat, a remote eighteenth-century cottage called Bron-Yr-Aur (pronounced bron-*rahr*) near the River Dyfi that belonged to friends of his parents.

"It was a fantastic place in the middle of nowhere with no facilities at all," he recalled. There was no road leading to it. The only approach for their Jeep was to traverse a bumpy, mostly barren field. *Primitive* didn't begin to describe the premises. The cottage was a gnarly stone structure on the side of a hill surrounded by sheep that came right up to the door. There was no bathroom, no electricity, interior lighting only from canisters of butane gas.

Jimmy took one look around and thought, "Oh, we're here, we're in nature, we can hear the birds sing, there's not a car sound, there's no airplanes, there's no concert to do. It was just fantastic."

*Fantastic.* The same word had come to both Robert and Jimmy to describe their impressions of the super-rustic Bron-Yr-Aur. Would it provide them with the inspiration, as Robert hoped, "to create a pastoral side of Led Zeppelin?" *Pastoral?* Was that where the Masters of Heavy Metal were headed? Had they forsaken their atomic eruption of sound? With only acoustic guitars and no way to plug in, it was a safe bet any material they came up with would take a softer, gentler approach. "Jimmy was listening to Davy Graham and Bert Jansch and was experimenting with different tunings," Robert recalled, "and I loved John Fahey."

"When I first heard that LP [*Needle of Death* by Bert Jansch], I couldn't believe it," Jimmy said. "It was so far ahead of what anyone else was doing."

It seemed like they were headed somewhere mysterious, into the distant past. Graham, Jansch, and especially Fahey were practitioners of esoteric-sounding versions of traditional roots music that relied on dissonance, layered melodies, and fancy fingerpicking. Jimmy had also been bingeing the Band's monumental album *Music from Big Pink*, with its distinctive rugged "country-soul feeling" and origins in a rural setting. The various influences promised to yield intriguing results.

Settling in, however, proved challenging. Despite the far-flung destination, rock stars needed to be attended to, necessities sorted, so a proper entourage was recruited. Richard Cole begged off chaperone duty, instead sending two roadies—a New Zealander, Clive Coulson, and a nomad calling himself Sandy MacGregor, although that certainly wasn't his name. Maureen, Carmen, and Strider, the family border collie, accompanied Robert, while Jimmy brought Charlotte Martin. Due to the limited sleeping quarters, Robert and Jimmy claimed the two bedrooms, leaving the roadies to carve up the living room couch.

"We collected wood for the open-hearth fire, which heated a range with an oven on either side," recalled Clive Coulson. "We fetched water from a stream and heated it on the hot plates for washing." With no electricity, dinner was lit by candles.

Jimmy swore the trip wasn't designed as a working holiday. "The original plan was to just go [to Wales], hang out, and really appreciate the countryside," he said.

"So, there we were, up in the mountains with one of the very first Sony cassette recorders and a bunch of Eveready batteries," Robert recalled, "just sitting, going, 'Well, what shall we do?'"

It was a rhetorical question. When they went for a leisurely afternoon stroll across the windswept fields, they naturally packed the guitars and tape recorder. After an hour or so, they headed back to the cottage. "It was a tiring walk coming down a ravine, and we stopped and sat down," Jimmy explained. He had an interesting chord pattern he'd been mulling, stimulated by a few hits on a joint they shared. The words started to flow. Robert couldn't contain himself.

"He sang the first verse straight off," Jimmy said.

*"I don't know how I'm gonna tell you / I can't play with you no more . . ."*

Then the next verse—and the next. Before long, the song was intact: "The Boy Next Door," which was eventually retitled "That's the Way."

Over the course of a week, bits and pieces of other songs took shape—"Bron-Yr-Aur Stomp," "I Wanna Be Her Man," "Another Way to Wales," "The Rover," "Poor Tom," and "Friends," the latter fronting a chord riff that sounded suspiciously like the opening of Stephen Stills's exquisite "Carry On," which Jimmy had heard him play at Crosby, Stills & Nash's London debut earlier in the year. Jimmy had written "Friends" following a whopper of a fight he'd had with Charlotte. "I went out on a balcony in my house, and suddenly the whole song spilled out, just like that," he recalled.

Robert composed an ode to his dog: *"Walk down the country lanes, I'll be singin' a song / I'll be callin' your name."*

"Bron-Yr-Aur gave Jimmy and me so much energy," Robert recalled. "Because we were really close to something. We believed. It was absolutely wonderful, and my heart was so light and happy."

Overall, they'd amassed a nice little batch of songs to take back—back to civilization—with them. Was it the basis for a new album? That was definitely in the cards. "When we conceived the initial numbers at Bron-Yr-Aur," Robert said, "we started to see what we wanted this album to do."

It had started taking shape at Bron-Yr-Aur, and by the time they got home, there was no holding back.

## [2]

Jimmy was impatient to record. At the beginning of May 1970, he booked time at Olympic Studios and summoned Robert, John Paul, and Bonzo. But before the first session, Jimmy arranged a meeting in the café just outside of Olympic with his old Epsom buddy Glyn Johns. Johns, by this time, had fortified his rep by engineering heavyweight albums for the Rolling Stones, the Beatles, Joe Cocker, Steve Miller, Traffic, Procol Harum, and Spooky Tooth. And despite all the fetid water under the bridge, he was delighted to see Jimmy, pleased with all the success his friend had racked up.

Jimmy didn't beat around the bush. "What would it take to get you to engineer our next album?" he asked.

"God, you've got more fucking front," Johns laughed. "Why the fuck would I want to do that? I'll tell you what—why don't you pay me for the first one, then we'll talk about it."

Jimmy broached it circumspectly. "Well, what would you want?"

"What do you think I'd fucking want?" Johns said. "I want the same deal I negotiated in the first place."

Jimmy was apoplectic. "Yes, but we're the biggest band in the world now."

"So fucking what!"

"Well, we could get somebody to do it for—*much* less."

Johns stood up and waved Jimmy away. "Well, off you go," he said. And those were the last words they spoke for the better part of a decade.

Led Zeppelin retreated to the studio under the whip hand of twenty-year-old Andy Johns, almost a carbon copy of his celebrated older brother and a talent on the ascent. There was a different mood, a different frame of reference this time around, unhurried, to be sure, also more laid back, less inclined to be quite so riff-conscious.

"We'll be recording for the next two weeks, and we are doing a lot of acoustic stuff as well as the heavier side," Bonzo confided in a *Melody Maker* column.

The band's influences rose to the occasion. "We were into Joni Mitchell a lot and listened to a lot of Fairport Convention as well," recalled John Paul. "There was a lot of music around that was softer." He mentioned Matthews' Southern Comfort and Poco among the groups that would have an impact on the recording session. But there was also desire to go far afield, to refuse to play it safe, to make an album that was unlike anything Led Zeppelin had done or sounded like before. "By then we realized that, again, there were no rules."

Bucking another trend, the songs came together fast. Jimmy and John Paul had always been efficient in the studio, with an eye on the clock, but now Robert and Bonzo picked up the pace.

"As soon as I got a decent sound, off they went," said Andy Johns. "They would bang out two, three tracks a night sometimes, and it'd go by quite quickly."

The first bang emanated from a take they did for "Since I've Been Loving You." This song had been around in one form or another since the Albert Hall concert and had been considered as a cut for *LZII*. In fact, they'd recorded it, but as Jimmy noted, "It didn't come off." They'd been unable to capture "the exact dynamics and the overall tension of it," the dramatic rise and fall inherent to the structure of urban blues. Since then, it had evolved from a straightforward Chicago-style reading to "blues with a rock 'n roll rhythm to the phrasing" that paid its respects to Lee Michaels's kick-ass version of "Stormy Monday," complete with a brutal attack of Hammond organ by John Paul, who pumped its bass pedals as if he were putting out a brush fire with his feet.

"It was meant to push the envelope," Jimmy said. "We were playing in the spirit of the blues, but trying to take it into new dimensions dictated by the mass consciousness of the four players involved."

Perhaps unconsciously—or not—Robert had lifted the opening verse, almost word for word, from a Moby Grape song called "Never" that was on an album in his record collection. Whatever his inspiration, the brute force of the arrangement allowed him to cut loose in a way that squeezed every last ounce of emotion out of the vocal. His voice clung to the melody like honey to a spoon. The tape operator in the control room witnessed how Robert "lived every line." The anguish spilled out of him. It was as if he couldn't contain himself—he had to convince each listener of his sincerity, at the same time begging for understanding.

"I don't know where it came from," Robert recalled of the unhinged burst of passion he injected into the performance. "I don't know whether that was born from the loins of Jimmy or John Paul, but I know that when we reached that point in the song you could get a lump in the throat from being in the middle of it."

Nevertheless, as convincing and dominant as Robert's vocal was, Jimmy pushed him to dig deeper as the song rambled toward the fade. "Let's try the outro chorus again," he suggested. "Improvise a bit more."

A year earlier, a comment like that might have been enough to undermine Robert's confidence, make him doubt his ability to live up to Jimmy's expectations. Not until these sessions was he able to get past the self-doubt, to find his voice, "to calm it down and have the confidence to sing in a different style." It had taken him a while to get over "a lot of insecurity and nerves and the 'I'm a failure' stuff," he said. As a singer, he felt he had finally come into his own.

Later, at another session in a different studio, Jimmy would add a guitar solo infused with earthy, undulating motion that ripped through the song's emotional core, adding another layer of sensuality to its already red-hot atmospherics. As a mood setter for the new album, "Since I've Been Loving You" made a statement about the strength of Led Zeppelin's ability to lift the blues out of the ordinary and into exciting new territory.

At Olympic, they also laid down tracks for "That's the Way" and "Bron-Yr-Aur Stomp," both of which felt inspired by the Incredible String Band, the cutting-edge Scottish folk-rock band. "The places that the String Band were coming from were places that we loved very much," Robert acknowledged. "But because I was a blues shouter and Pagey was out of the Yardbirds, we didn't have that pastoral kick."

Pastoral was one way to describe it. The Incredible String Band "played the kind of music people liked to sit around and have a joint to," said Mike Heron, its rhythm guitarist. In Led Zeppelin's hands, the music turned into the kind people would do a couple lines of cocaine to.

To create that kind of rush, John Paul Jones played the mandolin on "That's the Way," with the main breaks contributed by Jimmy on pedal steel guitar. "I couldn't really play a pedal steel like a pedal-steel player," he said, "but I could play it like me." That meant blowing up the folksy feel with a pedal steel that sounded like it was attached to a whipsaw. After almost four and a half minutes of lush, full-throated guitars, the bass roared in, along with the ball-peen beats from a dulcimer, and the song took off into the jet stream that the pedal steel created for it.

They also worked on another song that built its bones on a furious bass line dispatched by Jonesy at a superhuman pace, exaggerating the rhythm of a human heartbeat recorded at 33⅓ rpm but played back on a 78 rpm turntable. There were no lyrics at the outset, but Robert had what Jimmy referred to as an exotic "sort of 'Bali Ha'i' melody line" that he'd come up with spontaneously in the studio.

The lyrics materialized two weeks later, on June 22, 1970, during a date Led Zeppelin played in Reykjavík, Iceland, as part of a cultural exchange between the two governments. The land of midnight sun and ice and snow provided instant inspiration. Robert said, "It made you think of Vikings and big ships . . . and John Bonham's stomach . . . and bang, there it was—'Immigrant Song.'" The song came together on the spot.

The band's execution of it stands as one of the most arresting and identifiable songs they ever recorded. It opened the album and shockingly so, with a clatter of bass and drums that yielded to a bone-chilling war cry. The rhythm section was unrelenting, practically off its hinges. The vocals were feral. The imagery defied classification. By the time Robert hit the final line—*"For peace and trust can win the day / Despite all your losing"*—he sounded as if he'd been out in the ice and snow too long.

The band decided to showcase "Immigrant Song" at an upcoming gig on June 28. Instead of heading back to America, album unfinished, they remained in the UK to appear at the loftily titled Bath Festival of Blues & Progressive Music, a two-day blowout held in a natural amphitheater not unlike the one that hosted Woodstock, on the fringe of Shepton Mallet, a medieval town in Somerset. The year before, when Led Zeppelin had played the festival, they were practically unknown. This time around, they were booked to headline the closing night, on a star-studded bill that included Jefferson Airplane, Frank Zappa & the Mothers of Invention, the Moody Blues, the Byrds, the Flock, Santana, Dr. John, Country Joe & the Fish, and Hot Tuna.

Everyone knew what was at stake. The jury was still out on Led Zeppelin in England. Their albums sold well, but few fans had been able to see them perform. There had been no large-scale concerts on home soil, a dearth of interviews, and a moratorium on TV appearances.

What's more, the band had developed a reputation as bread heads who ran off to America to make money rather than entertaining the British fans. A chill had set in. They were going to have to prove themselves at the Bath Festival.

"We knew it was an important gig for us," Jimmy said, "so we needed to deliver."

Peter Grant was determined to make the most of the opportunity. "I went down to the site unbeknownst to Freddie Bannister [the promoter] and found out from the [meteorological] office what time the sun was setting." Grant figured that if Led Zeppelin went on at exactly 8:30 p.m., the natural backdrop would be jaw-droppingly spectacular, especially if he had the crew bring the spotlight up on them with the *presto* effect of a Houdini illusion. The crowd would be appropriately wowed.

This wasn't the cozy gathering of a year ago, when twelve thousand fans assembled for the show. Early arrivals had been drifting in all week, sleeping in the field around smoldering campfires. Taking a cue from their Woodstock forebears, thousands of interlopers pulled down the chain-link fences and Bath "suddenly became a free festival" and, to its promoters, "a vision of hell." By the time the first act went on, on Saturday afternoon, the audience was properly wired—and 150,000 strong.

John Bonham was taking no chances. After a late-Saturday-night bacchanal in Birmingham, he set out for Shepton Mallet at three o'clock in the morning in his new, aerodynamically designed Jensen Interceptor with a case of Dom Pérignon champagne, the bulk of which was consumed en route. John Paul hired a helicopter to land him near the site, then caught a ride to the stage on the back of a Hells Angels chopper, while Jimmy and Robert spent most of the day previewing the opening acts.

The size of the crowd staggered them—it would be the largest they'd ever played to. It was mind-blowing, particularly for Robert Plant, who experienced an epiphany. "I remember standing there thinking: I've gone from West Bromwich to this! The whole thing seemed extraordinary to me."

Before their appearance, Led Zeppelin convened in a giant tepee behind the stage to take the edge off and go over their set.

"They were in great spirits," says Chris Charlesworth, who had only recently joined the staff of *Melody Maker* and was on his first assignment, "but you could tell how much was riding on their performance. G more than anyone was pretty wound up, and his anxiety was contagious."

He was watching the clock. The act on before Led Zeppelin was the Flock, a Chicago-based jazz-rock band that featured a lead violin instead of guitar. At 8:20 they were deep into a jam with no sign they'd be winding down anytime in the next five minutes. Freddy Bannister assured Peter they were almost done, but almost wasn't soon enough. Peter wanted them off—*now!*

"Take care of those bastards," he ordered Richard Cole, now rechristened Ricardo by the crew, who in turn summoned roadie Henry Smith.

"He told us to go right down the line and unplug the Flock's guitars, which is exactly what I did," Smith recalls. *In midsong!* "I don't think they realized what was going on, but they knew better than to give us a hard time."

"Hey, we haven't finished yet, man," a Flock roadie protested, however meekly.

"Oh, yes you fuckin' have!" Grant insisted.

Otherwise, it was exactly as G had planned it. The sunset was in full display, with a burst of yellow-orange bleeding across the stage as though someone had colorized a black-and-white movie. Robert, staring out at the sea of humanity, tried the best he could to contain his nerves. "I'd like to say a couple things," he warbled into the mic as the others were tuning up. "We've been playing in America a lot recently, and we really thought, coming back here, we might have a dodgy time."

Dodgy? He needn't have worried. When Led Zeppelin burst into their opening number—the hard-charging "Immigrant Song," albeit unfinished, with lyrics ad-libbed and riddled with gibberish—they took the audience's perception of rock 'n roll to another riotous level. "Crikey!" thought Chris Charlesworth, watching from just in front of the stage, "Those guys blew my mind. I had never heard anything so loud in my life—and my favorite band up to then was The Who." Led Zeppelin played at an earsplitting volume two or three times that of the preceding acts. The crowd was part stunned, part delirious. And then they went wild.

Led Zeppelin played their hearts out for nearly three hours, including five encores that incorporated such crowd-pleasers as Buffalo Springfield's "Mr. Soul," Muddy Waters's "Long Distance Call," Big Joe Williams's "El Paso Blues," Elvis Presley's "I Need Your Love Tonight," Little Richard's "Long Tall Sally," Gene Vincent's "Say Mama," and Chuck Berry's "Johnny B. Goode."

Roy Harper, the esoteric folksinger, who watched from backstage, thought, "There was no way that young people everywhere were not going to be forever attracted to this."

It was a coming-out party. Led Zeppelin left no doubt that they were the stars of the Bath Festival—and the new stars of rock 'n roll in the UK. In fact, a few short months later, *Melody Maker* would make it official, naming them Best Group in its annual Readers Poll, ahead of the Beatles, the Stones, The Who, and Pink Floyd.

For all his careful planning, Peter Grant missed most of the thrilling finale. He'd gotten wind that a couple of guys had crawled under the stage with tape equipment and were in the process of recording the show for what most likely would result in a bootleg. Someone needed to put a stop to it right away. "I couldn't find Freddie Bannister," he said, "so I thought *fuck it*, and went and did it myself." First he threw a bucket of water into the electronics; then he went to work on the perpetrators. "I kicked the shit out of them and all the equipment. I pulled an ax off the wall . . . and did a machete job on the machinery."

These were the new rules of engagement. For the band, it would be *light and shade*—achieving dynamic tones in their music that see-sawed between thematic motifs, as Jimmy intended it. But the manager's guideline—perhaps *decree* would be a better term—was *my way or the highway* coupled with *might makes right*. If anyone failed to toe the line, G would take matters into his own hands without regard for either the law or the consequences.

### [3]

With another U.S. tour scheduled to kick off on August 10, 1970, it became of prime importance to Led Zeppelin to make headway on the new album. Jimmy recalled how productive he and Robert were, writing in isolation at Bron-Yr-Aur, where there was nothing to distract them. Getting away from it all, recording remotely in an atmosphere conducive to relaxing into the music might inspire the band in the same way. "I didn't know exactly how the Band recorded their *Music from Big Pink* album or [Bob Dylan's] *The Basement Tapes*, but the rumor was they were done in a house they had rented."

That suited his sense of sangfroid. "You really do need the facilities where you can take a break for a cup of tea and a wander around the garden," he said. "Instead of walking into a studio, down a flight of steps into fluorescent lights and opening up the big soundproof door and being surrounded by acoustic tiles." To Jimmy, studios had a sterile "hospital atmosphere." They reminded him of those go-go session days. They gave him "studio nerves," put pressure on him to play the solo of a lifetime each time out.

He asked Peter Grant to look into a place in the country that would be adequate for Led Zeppelin to both live and record for a while. Andy Johns suggested they rent Stargroves, Mick Jagger's country manor in Hampshire, a sparsely decorated faux château that came outfitted with the Stones' mobile recording studio.

"How much would that cost?" Jimmy inquired.

Johns had done his homework. "Well, the truck's about £1,000 a week, and Mick's house is about £1,000 a week."

Andy had heard rumors of Jimmy's legendary penny-pinching— he'd famously charged Robert and Bonzo for a beans-and-toast break- fast they shared at Pangbourne in the getting-acquainted days of the band—but he hadn't expected such an emphatic reaction.

"I'm not paying Mick Jagger £1,000 a week for some bloody place!" Jimmy huffed. "I'll find somewhere better than that."

He meant cheaper. Jimmy was known as "Led Wallet" behind his back for a reason. Peter Grant used to joke, "If you want to kill Jimmy, toss a shilling in front of a speeding bus."

G turned it over to Willow Morel, whose Organisation Unlim- ited, staffed by out-of-work actors, "could find you anything you needed," no questions asked. In a matter of days she came up with Headley Grange, an old "dank and spooky" stone manor dating from the late 1700s, straddling several acres in East Hampshire. Peter Grant was familiar with the area. "I'd been evacuated there in the war," he recalled.

"It was very Charles Dickens" to Jimmy's eyes. The place's prove- nance as a Victorian workhouse for the poor and insane, along with orphans and illegitimate children, did nothing to enhance its charm. "It was a pretty austere place," he admitted, "[but] I loved the atmo- sphere of it. The others got a bit spooked." Robert and Bonzo were particularly freaked out, but Jimmy dismissed their whining. It all came down to workability for him. "I knew straightaway that the acoustics would be good."

Jonesy shared his appreciation. "[It] had very large rooms which were very echoey . . . [and] a big stairwell, which was even more echoey." There were hardwood floors and cupboards galore where am- plifiers could be hidden to create a variety of sounds. Musicians could be separated by different rooms or even floors, or stationed outside in the garden. The layout provided for a great ambient recording opportunity—an opportunity, as Jimmy saw it, to do "some amazing hard work—no messing about; a roadie to make beef stew. We eat and sleep and really focus."

Ultimately, Jimmy ponied up for the Stones' mobile recording unit. The "studio," conceived by Ian Stewart with Glyn Johns's engineering input, was little more than an eight-track console wedged into the narrow side of an RV trailer where the kitchen facilities would normally have been situated. "It can get a bit impersonal," Andy Johns acknowledged. "[The] ability to monitor a situation isn't as good as in a proper studio. You end up talking to the band through a closed-circuit camera and a microphone instead of through the studio glass.

That didn't deter Jimmy. "It seemed ideal," he said of the setup. "As soon as we thought of an idea we put it down on tape." The only drawback was keeping the adrenaline in check. "We'd get so excited about an idea that we'd really rush to . . . get it on tape."

There was no holding back. One of the first numbers they worked on was built on a descending riff Jimmy had written, but developed around a drinking song of Bonzo's about hitting the pubs.

"He would just get drunk and start singing things," Jimmy explained. One of Bonzo's standbys went: *"Out on the tiles, I've had a pint of bitter / And I'm feeling better 'cause I'm out on the tiles."* Robert took some liberties with the lyric and turned it into a reedy, ear-piercing, ramblin' song—ramblin' and lovin', aided by a torrential outpour of instrumentation at his back. A song like this was, in Robert's words, "all riffs and rhythm track. I would have to try to weave the vocal in amongst it all, and it was very hard." The runaway tempo became the song's main musical force, letting the instruments gallop into the expanded closing passage that provided the only honorable way out. In its earliest form, it was known as "Bathroom Song," but later adopted Bonzo's phrase as a more suitable title—suitable, but beyond one's grasp.

They also took a poke at a traditional folk song of Leadbelly's called "Gallis Pole." Jimmy got it off "an old Folkways LP by Fred

Gerlach," an intimate of Woody Guthrie and Pete Seeger. It was Jimmy's first stab at playing the banjo, which relied heavily on fingerpicking—"going back to the studio days," he said, a time when he'd developed "a certain amount of technique." He also overdubbed a six-string acoustic, a twelve-string, and electric guitars. John Paul embellished it with a mandolin flourish that provided a sinister counterpoint to the ghoulish lyric.

The change in tempos offered relief in many ways. "There was no conscious desire along the lines of, 'Oh, we've done Heavy, now we should look at Soft,'" said John Paul, reflecting on those sessions and a longer one that followed at Island Studios in London. But after bashing away for several hours, musicians—those who were serious practitioners and played at the top of their craft—got a chance to express themselves in a disarmingly simple but eloquent manner. "The acoustic stuff made Led Zeppelin much more powerful," Robert realized, "not just a hit machine."

Be that as it may, Led Zeppelin's fans expected the hit machine. The new album, titled simply *Led Zeppelin III*, baffled the legions of faithful when it was released in October 1970. And not just the songs but the cover and inner sleeve, with a rotating cardboard wheel that revealed pop-art images of the band, butterflies, chunks of corn, and assorted gewgaws through peepholes die-cut into the mechanism. It was supposed to "reflect the album's bucolic ambience by mimicking an annual crop-rotation calendar," but its critics found the concept silly, "teenybopperish," as Jimmy described it, more suited to a Partridge Family LP.

The songs were an entirely different matter. The songs were a far cry from the character Led Zeppelin had constructed for itself. For many fans, the mixed marriage of rock and folk was too radical a departure, too jarring, too difficult to appreciate. Light and shade was all well and good, but Robert's argument that "there are different moods to our music, just the same as people have different moods," rang hollow. Fans didn't care about moods; they wanted the kind of music they were accustomed to from their favorite rock 'n roll group.

In the band's attempt to puncture the myth of Led Zeppelin, they had emasculated it. There was none of the raw energy of "you need coolin'" or "squeeze my lemon," no attack, no Sturm und Drang. Several reviews accused the band of going *soft*, of losing its backbone. *Q*, the British rock 'n roll monthly, later called the album "a rickety, erratic affair." Critics, even those who had sung Led Zeppelin's praises, found it too contrived, too calculating, too self-indulgent. They mistrusted the band's intentions. The album was said to lack the intensity or edge that had made its two predecessors such inspired affairs. "I, II, III . . . and Zeppelin Weakens" was the banner across the review in *Disc and Music Echo*. *Rolling Stone*, predictably, panned it—Jimmy called it "a definite hatchet job"—as did *Creem* and *Crawdaddy*. *NME* warned that "it remains to be seen how far Zeppelin lovers will go along with what is a pretty drastic change in direction." Of the major music publications, only *Melody Maker*, which two weeks earlier had anointed Led Zeppelin as Best Group in its poll, published an unequivocal rave—"*Zeppelin III* Is Pure Magic"—by Chris Welch, who called *LZIII* "a much better album than *LZII*."

None of the reviews had an effect on album sales. The LP banked advance orders of 700,000 copies and sold briskly throughout the fall and holiday seasons. But Jimmy took it hard. He didn't take criticism well to begin with, and the hammering from the press seriously annoyed him, especially a reference comparing Led Zeppelin's sound to that of Crosby, Stills & Nash. "I got really brought down by it," he said. Unable to put the hard criticism aside, he lashed out, defending the band's position every chance he got.

"We were so far ahead that it was very difficult for reviewers to know what the hell we were doing," he carped in one of several interviews. "They couldn't relate to it. Very rarely could they get the plot of what was going on." In other exchanges, he said the album "went totally over their heads." It was perfectly clear to Jimmy: "The third album was just another evolution."

Evolution—survival of the fittest—was essential to the longevity of a rock 'n roll band. Those, like Vanilla Fudge or Blue Cheer, who persisted in beating their brand to death soon bored even their most loyal fans. Jimmy Page liked to point to the Beatles as master crafts-men able to evolve gracefully from one album to the next. How was it possible that a group could record songs like "Yesterday" and "In My Life," and on the next album dish up head-scratchers like "Taxman" and "Tomorrow Never Knows"—and that was okay with their fans, yet somehow, Led Zeppelin continued to be defined by "Whole Lotta Love"?

As a matter of record, the Beatles were an anomaly. They no lon-ger performed live in concert, so their fans were compelled to listen—carefully—to each new album, interpreting every word, every nuance, enabling them to contemplate how their beloved band had progressed. Led Zeppelin didn't enjoy that kind of artistic license. Contemplation wasn't on the minds of their fans. They craved the visceral experience of Led Zeppelin's explosive sound. The fans came to their live shows to unwind, looking for release, catharsis, not a cerebral exercise in mu-sical evolution.

To his credit, Robert considered *LZIII* "the best album we've ever done—possibly we'll ever do." He said, "It shows we can change. It means there are endless possibilities and directions for us to go in." Likewise, Jimmy never backed down from the music on *Led Zeppelin III.* "I felt a lot better once we started performing it," he said, "because it was proven to be working for the people who came around to see us."

And come they did. In August of 1970, before the album's official release, Led Zeppelin went back to America—the sixth time in two years—to introduce the fans to the new material. The venues were big and so was the paycheck, with the band now commanding a minimum fee of $25,000 a show, a princely sum. The gigs, for the most part, were splashy and didn't skimp on old favorites, but it was a little disconcert-

ing when, at a juncture in the arena and coliseum shows, the four musicians would gravitate to the front of the stage, where they perched
on stools for a brief acoustic set featuring "That's the Way" and "Bron-
Yr-Aur Stomp." It was a noble experiment, but audiences who had just
been treated to barn burners like "Heartbreaker" and "Dazed and
Confused" were noticeably dazed and confused themselves at the sudden shift in tempos. The segment, which lasted about fifteen minutes,
never failed to produce "squirming fans and frustrated musicians."
Jimmy felt the temperature change. "Some places, it's been a bit of a
shock," he allowed. In Detroit, a journalist noted, "Zep had to plug
back in to rescue the evening, which they did with a vengeance." It was
easy when Robert ripped into a song like "Since I've Been Loving You,"
which captured the soulfulness of rhythm and blues so well. The
sound of Jimmy's guitar was astonishing. He bit into his solo with
razor-sharp ferocity to bring the heat quotient back up. And the charged
thunder of "Moby Dick" delivered another layer of excitement.

Bonzo performed his percussive tour de force at a stretch lasting
anywhere from fifteen minutes to half an hour, depending on his
mood. And lately his frame of mind was about as predictable as the
weather. Interviews are filled with testimonials to Bonzo's sweetness,
his boyish charm when he was sober, but on the road, he got homesick. "He was not a guy who was cut out for touring," says Janine Safer,
who later traveled extensively with the band. "He was a homebody.
He missed Pat and his kids. And when he got homesick, he drank. A
lot. And Dr. Jekyll became Mr. Hyde, which did not make for a stable
situation."

Jimmy understood the behavior, which he referred to as schizo-
phrenia. "I'd go abroad on these tours and become totally flamboyant," he said. "Then I'd return home and the coin would flip." He
understood it, but he needed Bonzo to keep it together.

"Bonzo was getting drunk all the time on this tour," says Henry
Smith, who served as the drum tech for most of the shows. In Kansas
City, Missouri, on August 19, Mr. Hyde reared his head. Bonzo had

brooded about his circumstances on the flight west. Only a week into the tour, he was already pining for home, regretting that he'd be gone from the Midlands for another month, angry at himself, unable to cope. He dredged up the memory of the last time Led Zeppelin played Kansas City, not realizing, perhaps, it was a different Kansas City in a different state. That time, the band had played a twin bill—back-to-back shows on the same night. In between the sets, Bonzo got so drunk on champagne that he couldn't play. "He was falling over his drums," Henry Smith recalls. "I was holding his shirt, pulling it up by the scruff of the neck to keep him upright so he could move his arms and hit the drums."

Jimmy glanced at the farcical situation and yelled, *"Play!"* But by that time, Bonzo was out of commission. Instead, Jimmy motioned his head in Smith's direction. *"You play!"*

Smith didn't have a musical bone in his body, so Richard Cole, who was an experienced drummer, pushed Bonzo aside and sat in just long enough to get through the set so the band could get paid.

Bonzo, who became unruly after the gig, spent the night sleeping it off in the Kansas City jail.

That time, he was pretty tanked up in advance but managed to maintain his stamina through the lengthy show. In Tulsa, however, two nights later, Bonzo became enraged when the promoter, nervous about crowd violence, ordered the houselights turned on in the middle of "Heartbreaker," and he had to be held back from charging blindly into the crowd.

Things were getting hairy between the band and Bonzo. After the show, Peter Grant delivered an ultimatum. "You do that again, and this'll be your last tour."

For a while, the warning rang loud in Bonzo's ears, but by the time they rolled into Los Angeles in early September 1970, he'd thrown caution to the wind.

On September 4, Led Zeppelin played a now-legendary gig at the Forum, the home of the Los Angeles Lakers, the pinnacle West Coast showcase for a rock 'n roll band. Enjoying LA, as always, the band was looser than loose, firing up the audience with the usual set of heavy hitters while weaving country and western, R&B, and rockabilly classics into an extended "Whole Lotta Love" medley. For the encore, a particularly raucous version of "Communication Breakdown" included snatches of "Good Times, Bad Times," "For What It's Worth," and "I Saw Her Standing There." They came back to end the evening with a stomping send-up of Fats Domino's "Blueberry Hill."

After the show, still sky-high on adrenaline, the four musicians piled into a limo and headed to the Troubadour in time to catch the late show with Fairport Convention. Once there, Bonzo couldn't stay in his seat. He squeezed through the labyrinth of tables and took over Dave Mattacks's drum kit onstage. Once he was situated, Dave Pegg ceded his bass to John Paul and Robert staked his claim to the mic. Jimmy and Richard Thompson shared the spotlight, providing the kind of fleet-fingered guitar tandem that hadn't been witnessed since the mythic Page-Beck tag team of yore. The new configuration jammed sprightly on half a dozen songs, with extended solos on "Hey Joe" and the Tim Rose standby "Morning Dew." A couple of Elvis numbers were thrown in for good measure.

Afterward, an exuberant Bonzo hugged his old Way of Life bandmate Dave Pegg, admiring how their careers had taken them, two consummate Brummies, down such remarkable paths.

"This bloke has invited us to a new club down the road somewhere," Bonzo told Pegg. "Its grand opening is tomorrow night, and he's staking us to a game of pool and drinks."

Pool . . . drinks. They were magical words for any English band member. Most of Led Zeppelin and Fairport Convention made a beeline to the place on Sunset Boulevard, where a private party was already in full swing. The club's opening headliners, Savoy Brown, were mingling with drummer Aynsley Dunbar, who was in town with his latest group, Blue Whale. Rock 'n roll was blasting over a state-of-the-art PA. In unusually high spirits, the musicians were cautioned to play it cool about their drinking, inasmuch as the club's liquor license didn't take effect until noon the following day, but by two in the morning, as Dave Pegg points out, "we were all seriously over-refreshed."

Bonzo was playing pool with the owner, who decided it was time to close for the night. "I'm worried that all the lights are on," he said, "and if authorities pass by, I'll be fined a fortune before the place even opens."

Bonzo said, "All right. We'll have another game. If I win, we drink for another hour."

Unbeknownst to the owner, Bonzo was a scratch pool player, so of course he won and drank for another hour. Then another hour.

At 4:00 a.m., the owner announced, "Everybody out! A police car has just rolled by. It'll turn around and come back. Everybody out—*now!*"

Someone killed the lights, and a back door flung open for a speedy getaway. Bonzo grabbed Dave Pegg by the sleeve and herded him into a dark corner, behind Savoy Brown's four-by-twelve Marshall stacks. "Just get behind there with me and keep still," he instructed.

The next thing both men knew, they were awakened by sunlight streaming in through the windows. It was ten o'clock in the morning. The club was deserted, and the only thing more appreciable than the eerie silence was their massive hangovers. It took some doing to stagger out of there without setting off any alarms. Fortunately, Bonzo's limo driver had waited at the curb all night, standard operating procedure where John Bonham was concerned.

"I've got to catch a flight at seven thirty to Hawaii," he told Pegg. Led Zeppelin was appearing on the Big Island for two sold-out concerts, and a rehearsal was scheduled for early the following morning. "I'll have time to kill before heading to the airport, so let's meet for a drink or three at lunchtime."

As promised, Bonzo called Pegg around three thirty and arranged to meet him at Barney's Beanery, an old Hollywood actors' dive, now surrendered to the likes of Jim Morrison and Janis Joplin. Sure enough, after a few rounds of beer and tequila, Janis showed up and spotted John Bonham. "She was all over Bonzo," Pegg recalls. "We all got over-refreshed, and by five thirty it was clear that Bonzo had missed his ride to the airport."

Instead, Fairport Convention's road manager appeared and frog-marched Pegg out of the diner, advising him, "You've got to go. You're on at eight o'clock for the first show at the Troubadour."

Bonzo hitched a ride to their hotel, the Tropicana, a rather grotty establishment a short walk from the Troubadour. As they passed the main building on the way to their rooms, Bonzo pushed Pegg into the swimming pool in front of a group of sunbathers that included Andy Warhol and a flock of groupies. Then Bonzo stripped to his under-pants and joined Pegg in the deep end. As they climbed out, two young Texan women appeared with towels and accompanied the men to Pegg's room, where they opened a traveling bag full of grass.

"Do you fellas fancy a smoke?"

Sometime before eight, Dave Pegg chugged a gallon of coffee and made his way to the Troubadour in time to join Fairport for the first of three sets. Halfway through the second set, around eleven fifteen, the sound technician leaned over the stage and said, "Mr. Pegg, there's a call for you from Mr. Bonham."

Apparently, Bonzo was still at the Tropicana, and he sounded quite frantic. "I don't know what happened," he said, "but my clothes are gone, along with my wallet and my ticket to Hawaii. I've missed the plane, and I'm in deep shit."

The next morning, dressed in Pegg's spare clothes, he made his way to LAX, where Fairport Convention's road manager presented him with a ticket to Hawaii that her band had paid for.

The flight got him to Hawaii in time for the shows, but Bonzo was right: he was in deep shit. Peter Grant had had enough of Bonzo's non-sense and was perusing a list of drummers to see who might be available to replace him. If it had been up to G, Led Zeppelin might have gone forward with Carmine Appice, Aynsley Dunbar, or Cozy Powell.

But Jimmy stepped in to give Bonzo another chance. *Another* another chance.

With only a week of shows left on the schedule, including the band's debut appearance at Madison Square Garden in New York City on September 19, Jimmy was laser focused on finishing the tour without distractions or conflict. He wanted to head home after New York with a clear head.

He was ready once again for a breather, a pause, a time out. A new set of songs was looming on the horizon.

## Chapter Ten

# INVOKING AND
# BEING INVOCATIVE

## [1]

*LZIII*, while failing to measure up to their fans' expectations, pushed the band's album sales into prime Beatles territory. An initial shipment of 700,000 units was nothing to sneeze at, and by November 1, 1970, the album had lodged at the number-one spot on *Billboard*'s Top LPs chart. The cool critical reception seemed irrelevant. The controversy about the material and the conflicting reviews only drew more attention to Led Zeppelin.

Once the initial hubbub died down, fans probed the album for its less apparent treasures. "It was a pretty extreme change from our other two [albums]," Jimmy Page acknowledged, "and people needed at least six months to analyze what the hell had gone on." They pondered the effects—the echo tape feedback on "Immigrant Song" and the incandescent sound mix on "Out on the Tiles." They analyzed the lyrics like etymologists trying to make sense of Sanskrit. How to interpret passages like *"You hear her cries of mercy / As the winners toll the bell* and *See my rider right by my side / It's a total disgrace, they set the pace"*? Using headphones, one could make out the muffled studio chat that led into "Friends" or bore into Robert's double-tracked vocal on

"Tangerine" or discern Bonzo's squeaky drum pedal on "Since I've Been Loving You."

But the most perplexing discovery was a few cryptic words etched into the album's plastic run-out between the grooves of the last song on each side and the label, where the catalogue number usually resides. Side 1 featured the inscription "So mote be it"; side 2's maxim read "Do what thou wilt." That gave the conspiracy theorists a mouthful to chew on.

Longtime Jimmy Page disciples already had an inkling. They knew he was a devoted student of the occultist Aleister Crowley, whom Jimmy regarded as "the great misunderstood genius of the twentieth century," and that "Do what thou wilt shall be the whole of the law"—or the Law of Thelema, as it was known to its followers—was the foundation of Crowley's idiosyncratic philosophy. Whether Crowley was a genius or, as many considered, a dangerous crackpot—in any case, not exactly in the Carl Jung department—his influence on Jimmy Page was earnest and profound.

Page had come upon Crowley while still an adolescent. "I read *Magick in Theory and Practice* when I was about eleven," he claimed. The book was a series of essays on alleged magical acts, rituals, and talismans that Crowley, "the prince-priest of the Beast," was commanded to write by a voice claiming to be that of Horus, the Egyptian god of force and fire. It took a few years for Jimmy to process the mumbo jumbo until he could formulate his own worldview from it. He was particularly taken with Crowley's theory of self-liberation. "The thing is to come to terms with one's free will, discover one's place and what one is," Jimmy said, "and from that you can go ahead and do it and not spend your whole life suppressed and frustrated. It's very basically coming to terms with yourself."

Crowley believed there were no restrictions in life, that experimentation of any kind was not only valid but encouraged, no limits should be placed on one's behavior, one should do exactly as one pleased—"there would be nothing which the human imagination can conceive that could not be realized in practice." *Do what thou wilt shall be the whole of the law.* It was a liberating message to an aspiring rock star.

But it was a mixed message. Crowley's fringe writings detailed his experiments with trance states and drugs—hashish, peyote, heroin—the study of the tarot, and omnisexuality. His loopy fascination with human sacrifice, which he articulated in *Magick in Theory and Practice,* described his ideal victim as "a male child of perfect innocence and high intelligence."

Stripped of some of the more outrageous trappings, the main message seemed to be: whatever your desire, whatever your urges, whatever your will—act on it, do what's best for yourself. What was an impressionable adolescent, an only child, to make of this? It was certainly a justification for self-indulgence. Jimmy picked and chose among the menu of Crowley's teachings (forgoing human sacrifice, one assumes). Crowley created the concept of magick, and what is rock 'n roll but magic—transcending the norm? It provided the perfect vehicle for acting out, onstage or offstage. Performances were ripe for androgyny—not just the mannerisms but the clothes, the sequins, and the little antique tops. Getting high never interfered with writing lyrics or executing a fantastic solo. Sexual experimentation was particularly attractive.

"Jimmy was obsessed with the Marquis de Sade and his perversions," says Jim McCarty, who occasionally roomed with Jimmy when the Yardbirds went abroad. "He had a bag of stuff he'd bring on tour—whips, handcuffs, chains, and the like. There was always talk about hiding in the bathroom and looning in on me if I was in the middle of something with a bird in bed." On early tours with Led Zeppelin, there were many sexual encounters with underage girls.

*Do what thou wilt.*

Crowley's influence on Jimmy wasn't limited to behavior. He acquired Crowley's personal deck of tarot cards and ritual robes, as well as an extensive library of the guru's handwritten manuscripts and

autographed first editions. In early 1970, Jimmy had even purchased
Crowley's former residence, Boleskine House, a five-bedroom country estate curtained off by a copse of mature trees on the banks of the
Loch Ness in Scotland. It came furnished with a history of what
Jimmy called "bad vibes . . . suicides, people carted off to mental hospitals." A beheading had supposedly taken place in one of the rooms,
but he knew with certainty that it was built on the site of "a church
that was burned to the ground with the congregation in it."

For all its thankless charm, Jimmy rarely inhabited Boleskine
House. It wasn't a proper place to take Charlotte Martin in the fall of
1970, especially now that she was expecting their first child. But the
Pangbourne boathouse seemed to be under siege by avid Led Zeppelin fans, so Jimmy went house shopping and bought a more remote,
secure pad—Plumpton Place, a sixteenth-century manor surrounded
by a moat, about ten miles north of Brighton on the East Sussex coast.

"He asked me to find black swans for the moat," recalls Carole
Brown, who was Peter Grant's assistant. *Swans*—of course. "I located
a keeper who bred the birds by Royal Assent, and we went on his
waitlist."

He also asked Brown "to walk up to Foyles Bookshop in Charing
Cross Road to find a book of Old English runes"—Rudolf Koch's *Book
of Signs*—"because he had an idea for an album cover."

Ideas for songs had started coming toward the end of the last U.S.
tour. Jimmy, as always, had been sketching out and filing away bits
of riffs that, with input from his mates and enough TLC, would take
more interesting shape once they put aside time to write and rehearse.
Making an album was a democracy, John Paul Jones explained.
"There's really no format, no set ideas," he said. "The group's always
played what comes out, and what comes out goes down. If it sounds
good to everybody, then it's played."

There had been plans to tour England over the holiday season, beginning a month after Led Zeppelin wrapped up their two sold-out shows in New York, but as Bonzo pointed out, "we were drained." Peter Grant suggested they take the rest of the year off. Grant worried that the soft reaction to *LZIII* warranted another album, pronto, to restore the band's two-fisted credibility. The layoff would give Jimmy and Robert plenty of opportunity to write.

In the meantime, Grant decided to take some time off of his own. His weight had ballooned to a stunning twenty-seven stone—roughly 375 pounds—and was contributing to awkward problems he preferred to forgo. His ungainly size now necessitated booking two seats for plane travel—more a personal embarrassment than a matter of cost—and various chairs tended to break under the demands of his bulk. Weight had always been a nuisance to G, but the situation came to a head during the time Led Zeppelin had performed in Hawaii.

"We were in this luxury estate, and there was a VW dune buggy in the driveway," recalled Clive Coulson's wife, Sherry. "It had tipped over, and I could see a man trapped inside—and it was G." It took the roadies considerable time and effort to get it righted while a pinned-down Grant cursed up a storm.

While his band took time off, G booked himself into Enton Hall, a health farm in Sussex where Ian Fleming had shed unwanted pounds and where James Bond visited—the fictional Shrublands in *Thunderball*.

Before checking in, Grant had a last errand that entailed throwing his weight around.

He'd noticed a front-page article in *Melody Maker* that set his blood boiling: "A London record distributor said this week that two new Led Zeppelin albums will shortly be in the shops—both unofficial, illegal bootlegs." The reference was to a double album in the underground pipeline, *Led Zeppelin Live on Blueberry Hill*, recorded in an elaborate pirate fashion "by radio transmitters that picked up the signal . . . in the hall and transmitted it outside to a mobile recording truck" during the band's concerts at the Forum in Los Angeles.

Grant was having none of it. He traced the album's source to the Chancery Lane Record Centre, conveniently located around the corner from the RAK office in London, and staged an unannounced visit with Richard Cole and Mickie Most. As they stepped inside, Richard Cole turned the OPEN sign on the door to CLOSED and sought out the owner, Jeffrey Collins, known around town as "the Bootleg King."

"Have you got the Led Zeppelin album?" Grant inquired.

Collins, who failed to recognize either Peter or Mickie, offered to make him a tape for half the price of the bootleg.

"Peter got hold of this fellow and threw him against the wall," Most remembered, then "went behind the counter and smashed up the tape-copying machine."

As insurance, he "threw the records all over the place and made a bit of a mess," and confiscated the store's stock of *Blueberry Hill* albums. G had always treated bootleggers without mercy. He'd repeatedly warned perpetrators: "I would step on anyone who fucked with my band—personally." The wholesale distribution of these albums had begun to take a sizable bite out of the band's income, a bite estimated "between $150,000 and $200,000," a rather wild exaggeration.

The worst offenders were in Europe. "In Germany, the situation is terrible," Peter huffed. "There were attempts to record us at every venue we played—cables on the end of broomsticks hanging over hall balconies." He was determined "to stamp out the bootleggers," a consequence that he meant to be taken literally.

Led Zeppelin had little or no idea of the details. John Paul and Bonzo had retired to their homes, determined to reap the benefits of the two months off, while Robert and Jimmy went straight back to work. In November 1970, they returned to the little cottage in Wales, Bron-Yr-Aur, to work on songs for the band's next album. There were no wives, children, or pets this time, just two roadies, Henry Smith and Sandy MacGregor, who kept things humming for the ten-day stretch.

It was a relaxed work atmosphere. Without any distractions, Robert and Jimmy wrote during the days, camped out on the living room couch with a couple of guitars at their disposal and the requisite tape recorder. Occasionally, "for inspiration," Robert stepped outside with Henry Smith, "to sit in the grass and smoke some hash." Nights were spent in the nearby village of Machynlleth for dinner and a shower at the Owain Glyndwr Pub, named in honor of the instigator of the Welsh Revolt against Henry IV in 1400. The atmosphere wasn't just relaxed, it was ideal.

It had taken two and a half years for Jimmy and Robert to establish a comfort level, to find themselves, if not on equal footing, at least a few feet closer to appreciating each other's uniqueness. The four-year age difference had been something of an obstacle at first. "He was my senior in every respect," Robert acknowledged, but "by about the eighth song we wrote together, I began to realize that I had something with this guy that was very special. I was no longer just chancing it, so I was feeling better and better all the time."

Jimmy felt it, too. After their initial visit to Bron-Yr-Aur in April, he said, "It was the first time I really came to know Robert. The songs took us into areas that changed the band." Now he recognized the value of their partnership. "We were like a marriage," Jimmy said. "Like Lennon and McCartney."

Not quite, but they were about to embark on their most intricate creative endeavor.


## [2]


Jimmy had been struggling for months with a spellbinding chord progression he'd written at Bron-Yr-Aur on the first visit there, in April— a descending four-measure figure that he continued to work on between tours. He'd been compiling demos for it on a mobile deck installed at his boathouse in Pangbourne, the same deck The Who used to record *Live at Leeds*.

"I'd been fooling around with my acoustic guitar and came up with different sections, which I married together," he said. His concept was for a grand mosaic of song knit together from swatches of dramatic, independent movements. "To have a piece with the sort of naked guitar starting off, and then into a thing that would build up," he fantasized. "Something that would have drums come in at the middle and then build to a huge crescendo. Also, I wanted it to speed up, which is something musicians aren't supposed to do." He wasn't exactly certain how it would progress just yet, but he knew where it was leading—"that there would be this great sort of orgasm at the end."

The song was still pretty sketchy when the entire band assembled at Island Studios in West London in December 1970. The intro was intact, and so were other variable passages, but the overall structure didn't hang together. Nevertheless, the band recorded a ragged instrumental version of it on a reference tape—just drums, acoustic guitar, and John Paul playing electric piano, no bass—and decided to continue work on it in the future. The same with a number called "Four Sticks," which had lost its swing and needed additional work.

One of the problems was the studio itself—it didn't inspire. "A recording studio is an immediate imposition," Robert declared. He, like Jimmy, found it too limiting, not inclusive, not inspiring. Some bands, like the Beatles, could enter the studio with absolutely nothing in the development stage and eventually pull an entire album together with collaborative panache. They felt at home there. But Led Zeppelin was less a single creative entity than a collection of musicians performing distinct roles. If Jimmy and Jonesy were busy working on an arrangement, Bonzo and Robert were left out, and they became bored. It wasn't productive to have them standing around, waiting to play. For Led Zeppelin, studios were fine for putting ideas on tape or refining something that had already been arranged and rehearsed, but when it came to creating the magic, the *je ne sais quoi*, the band thrived in a more informal atmosphere.

John Paul considered the work at Island Studios productive—up to a point. "We've done a good deal, [we've] broken the back of it," he believed at the time. "But rather than waste a lot of studio time thinking of the riffs and the lyrics in the studio, we decided this place in Hampshire was definitely the best place to get the numbers down before we [go back]."

Headley Grange, the manor house in Hampshire where they'd recorded much of *Led Zeppelin III*, for all its grunge, had a nicer feel than the trappings of a studio. "It seemed ideal," Jimmy said, summoning the band to meet him there for a month's stay, beginning just after Christmas 1970. "The idea was to create a comfortable working environment and see what would happen." And with the Stones' mobile unit parked out back, fresh from its sessions for *Sticky Fingers*, Led Zeppelin could "develop material and record it while the idea was still hot."

John Paul knew Headley Grange was ideal in theory, but he wasn't thrilled with going back. He thought the place was grim, a dump. "It was cold and damp," Jones said. "I remember we all ran in when we arrived in a mad scramble to get the driest rooms."

The place was cavernous, with ten rambling bedrooms on the upper floors, so the free-for-all through the rooms felt more like a game of musical chairs. The rest of the place would never make the pages of *Architectural Digest*. "There was stuffing coming out of the couch and springs coming out of the bed," Andy Johns, the engineer, recalled.

"It was so dull," John Paul said, bemoaning the lack of a pool table or even a local pub, "but that really focused your mind on getting the work done."

They rehearsed for a week before the mobile unit was pressed into duty. There were plenty of half-finished songs to mull over and a few that materialized spontaneously. During an early jam to loosen up, they worked on "I'm Gonna Be Her Man" and "Down by the Seaside," the latter of which was begun at Bron-Yr-Aur and assembled imprecisely on the reference tape done at Island Studios. They also tinkered with an early version of "No Quarter," which they'd actually previewed during their September concert at the Forum in LA.

The first serious number they worked on was based on a clever riff that John Paul Jones introduced. The idea for it had come to him some time ago, on a train ride back from visiting Jimmy at his Pangbourne house, where they'd listened to the Muddy Waters album *Electric Mud*. "One track is a long, rambling riff," he said, referring to "Tom Cat," with its fidgety rhythms, "and I really liked the idea of writing something like that—a riff that would be like a linear journey." In other words, the riff "didn't end when you thought it was going to end." He sketched it out on the back of the train ticket using a number-based notation system that his father had taught him, enabling John Paul to remember it when he got back home. The rest of the guys thought it was definitely worth exploring further.

Jimmy was especially taken with it. "I then suggested that we build a song similar in structure to Fleetwood Mac's 'Oh Well,'" he said. "I wanted to create a call-and-response between Robert's vocal and the band."

Trouble was, it was very tricky to pull off. "It was originally all in 3/16 time," John Paul explained, "but no one could keep up with that." A 3/16 time signature was more specific to works by classical composers. A second section he introduced "was actually phrased as three 9/8 bars and one 5/8 bar [played] over the straight 4/4 [time], but nobody else could play it." Even so, they gave it their best shot.

"You know, they just played it, fell about all over the place for about ten minutes in fits of laughter," Robert recalled, "played it again, burst into some more laughter."

Robert played it safe. He chose to begin the vocals a cappella, so as not to get tangled up in the web of wonky time signatures. Throwing his head back, he let loose with a deliciously salty line: *"Hey hey, mama, said the way you move / Gonna make you sweat, gonna make you groove."*

That gave the song a nice kick in the ass. But the rest of it never really "fell into place," like so many of the songs Led Zeppelin recorded. It was a hellish piece to play—stubborn, exacting, but unaccommodating, requiring all of their musical chops, with Bonzo ticking his drumsticks together as a makeshift click track so the others could keep time.

For want of a title to match the inscrutable time signature, they named it simply "Black Dog" after an old Labrador retriever with white whiskers that drifted onto the property and curled up while they played. "It was just a working title that stuck," according to Jimmy.

"Four Sticks" was another song with convulsive cadences played over a loose, rolling riff that gave the band agita. It wasn't exactly four sticks, to begin with. "Bonzo was playing with two sticks," Jimmy recalled, "and the idea was to get this kind of abstract number," something he'd likened to an Indian raga. They tried approaching it in different ways, but "it didn't come off." Bonzo grew especially frustrated.

Jimmy was inclined to call it a day rather than banging their heads against the wall. He knew from experience that frustration crippled the creative process. "If the track isn't happening and it starts creating a psychological barrier, even after an hour or two, then you should stop and do something else," he said. "Go to the pub or a restaurant or something. Or play another song."

*Play another song.* Bonzo was on board with that—without even cueing the band. He simply started banging out the opening drum riff to Little Richard's "Keep a-Knockin'"—"playing this right-handed open hi-hat with a left-handed shuffle," according to Grand Funk's Don Brewer—as a way to expel his vexation. Hitting things always made Bonzo feel better.

To maintain the momentum, Jimmy added a riff he pulled out of his old Chuck Berry–Eddie Cochran bag, which threw the icebreaker into full jam gear. "It actually ground to a halt after about twelve bars, but it was enough to know there was enough of a number there to keep working on it," he said. To get a sense of the structure, everyone trooped into the truck to hear what it sounded like on tape.

Coincidentally, Ian Stewart had showed up that afternoon to make sure the mobile unit was in tip-top shape. Stu, as he was affectionately called, happened to be an incomparable boogie-woogie piano player— "the most intuitive player I ever heard," according to Glyn Johns. There was an old, decrepit upright in the house, so Stu joined the jam, spiraling across the keys with a prodigious left hand and a right hand that walloped out two-octave chords before slicing them into fragments.

Robert, who had no time to craft an appropriate lyric, belted out a line that he felt suited the rhythmic foundation. *"It's been a long time since I rock and rolled."* Vocally, he pulled out all the stops. Robert's full-tilt exuberance made him sound unhinged, and it pulled the others into his manic pace. The song just flowed from there with a unity of attack, and as Jimmy noted, "within fifteen minutes it was virtually complete."

"Rock and Roll"—or "It's Been a Long Time," as it was initially called—was as joyous and uninhibited as anything Led Zeppelin ever recorded. They worked out all the tension that had accrued from their tussle with "Four Sticks" to produce the most spirited and exciting rock song in its most elementary form. At a trim three minutes and forty seconds, it was the kind of riveting performance that would give the fourth album the euphoric thrust it needed.

With such a sweet groove going, the band decided to take advantage of Stu's versatility and segue into another jam. He "just started improvising this amazing lick on [the piano]," as Jimmy recalled, "and the other guys started playing tambourine, hand-claps, and stomping in the hallway." Robert handled the rhythm-guitar chores, with Jimmy busy on mandolin. "It wasn't an intellectual thing, cause we didn't have *time* for that," Robert said. "We just wanted to let it all come flooding out."

The song's structure, while extemporaneous, wasn't original. It was based on Ritchie Valens's doo-wop classic "Ooh My Head," from a posthumously released album; the lyric Robert came up with was an obvious steal. Later, Jimmy and John Paul would overdub a slapping sound to pull back the rhythm track from where it threatened to gallop out of control. It was an expert tweak by two smart session musicians who knew how to salvage a balky execution, but it wasn't enough. It didn't stand out from the pack. The song was ultimately shelved—for the time being, at least—with the working title "Boogie with Stu."

There was a lot of fire and fury in these Headley Grange sessions, but it wasn't all balls-out rock 'n roll. Led Zeppelin enjoyed spiking their repertoire with an acoustic blend of folk and traditional music, and all the snarky reviews about their drift into CSNY land weren't going to steer them off that track. They were intent on keeping a nice balance of sound on the new album, just waiting for the right opportunity to slow down the pace.

Nights were low-key affairs at Headley Grange. Most evenings, after a hearty communal dinner prepared by their cooks, the musicians assembled in the main hall to stay warm, sitting around the fireplace, entertaining themselves with quantities of sharp cider and an assortment of recreational drugs. Richard Cole made sure there was always plenty of weed and hash on hand and the occasional line or two of cocaine. The last time Led Zeppelin was at Headley, Andy Johns had taken a defiant stand on drugs. "If you chaps bring cocaine into this, I will just go home," he'd declared. But working with the Stones on *Sticky Fingers* had brought him up to speed. He must have seen crested buttes of the stuff on that session, so that by the time he reunited with the Led Zeppelin contingent, cocaine was a fixture of his daily diet. "Keith [Richards] led him down that path," his brother, Glyn, says with regret. In any case, there was no resistance from Andy this time around.

"One night I came downstairs and Jonesy's mandolin was lying there," Jimmy recalled. The room was enormous; instruments of all shapes and sizes were scattered about. The other three musicians sat in front of the fireplace, sipping cups of tea. "I'd never played a mandolin before, and I picked it up and started messing around with it." He had a similar experience while working on "Gallows Pole," coming upon John Paul's banjo, picking it up as if it were a foreign object, and giving it a whirl. "I just . . . started moving my fingers around until the chords sounded right, which is the same way I work on compositions when the guitar's in different tunings." His experiment with the mandolin sounded like an old English instrumental—"a dance around the maypole number." Andy Johns slapped a microphone on Jimmy, Robert started singing along, and "The Battle of Evermore" surfaced on the spot.

Robert had no trouble putting lyrics to the melody. "I'd been reading a book of the Scottish border wars just before going to Headley Grange," he said. He drew on some of those graphic battle scenes but also larded the lyrics with imagery from *The Lord of the Rings*, one of his favorite fantasies.

He and Jimmy also dusted off the fragments of another mellow song they'd begun writing in Wales. They'd both listened incessantly to Joni Mitchell's *Blue*, chock full of gauzy treasures like "California," "River," and "A Case of You." That woman was an enchantress, in more ways than one. "She brings tears to my eyes," Jimmy said. For years he had expressed a desire to meet her. Robert, too. "When you're in love with Joni Mitchell, you've really got to write about it now and again," he confessed. In no time, Robert had roughed out the lyrics to "Going to California," a laid-back ballad filled with yearning that affected a distinct Southern California feel: "*Someone told me there's a girl out there, with love in her eyes and flowers in her hair . . .*" The portrait he painted was right on the nose. "It's so simple," he said, "and the lyrics just fell right out of my mouth."

Not as immediate was an electric twelve-bar blues number that paid homage to the early Yardbirds era, when R&B was being reimagined by teenage rebels armed with guitars and amps. Taking a standard like "Smokestack Lightning" or "Bright Lights, Big City" and putting their own souped-up spin on it was the flash point that touched off a revolution—and Led Zeppelin hungrily paid their respects to that tradition. "There are so many classics from way back which we can give a little of ourselves to take them through the years," Robert said. The band prided themselves on foraging a great old song and making it greater—or at least *different*—in this case the 1929 country-blues gem "When the Levee Breaks," by Memphis Minnie and Joe McCoy, which Robert culled from an old album in his collection.

The band had tried "Levee" at Island Studios and "it sounded really labored," according to Jimmy. In fact, it really wasn't at the top of the list to record at Headley Grange. "We'd been working on another song, and there was a lot of leakage from the drums," John Paul recalled, "so we moved them out into the hall where there's a big stairwell."

Actually, it was a new Ludwig drum kit that had been delivered late one afternoon while Led Zeppelin was engaged in an alternate take of "Misty Mountain Hop." To capture the sound in a more vibrant way, they decided take a pub break, giving Andy Johns adequate time to reposition the mics.

"All right," the engineer agreed, "but Bonzo has to stay behind."

Keeping Bonzo from the pub was tantamount to denying a junkie his fix, and he reacted as one might expect. But Andy appealed to his drummer's instincts, explaining that he'd given thought to Bonzo's countless complaints about the sound of his drums and had an idea how to fix it.

Up to this point, the band had been playing in the front room of Headley Grange. Together, they hauled the new drum kit into the palatial entranceway, known as the minstrels hall, with its soaring cathedral ceiling. Andy hung two ambient mics from the staircase, ten feet above, aiming them at Bonzo's setup. A requisite bass drum mic would be superfluous. Echo would make the drums sound like canon fire. When Bonzo listened to a playback in the mobile unit, he was ecstatic. "Whoa! That's it," he shouted. "That's what I've been hearing."

"Jesus," John Paul marveled, "will you listen to that sound!"

The moment Jimmy heard the drums in the hall, he couldn't get over the hugeness of the sound. The only word he could use to describe it was *frightening*. It was that powerful. "Hold on," he said, "let's do 'Levee Breaks.'"

He grabbed his Fender twelve-string guitar that was stepped down in an open G tuning, which made it reverberate in that space almost as mightily as Bonzo's drums. "Jonesy and I came out in the hallway with our headphones and left the amps back in the room," he said, "and banged out the rhythm track to 'When the Levee Breaks' right then and there."

They also tried a version of "Night Flight," a spry, melodic tease that undercut its anti–nuclear arms sentiment with rapturous accompaniment by John Paul on Hammond organ. But like "Down by the Seaside" and "Boogie with Stu," it wasn't given priority and ultimately was shelved.

Jimmy had a more important piece of business that he wanted to get back to. The inspired concept song, still in unrelated sections, that'd been gnawing at him for months was ready for some serious spadework. The action culminated one night early in the stay as he and John Paul were sitting around the fireplace, drinking cider. It was relatively quiet in the house. Robert and Bonzo had gone to the pub, giving the two old session veterans time for contemplation.

As John Paul recalled, "Page had a few things worked out on the guitar. He had these different sections, and he was just playing them through." Jonesy picked up a bass recorder that was on the floor and started accompanying the rundown. Afterward, they worked out the transitions between the sections, knitting them together with keyboard flourishes on an electric piano.

"Both Jimmy and I were quite aware of the way a track should unfold and the various levels it would go through," John Paul said. "I suppose we were both quite influenced by classical music and there's a lot of drama in the classical forms."

The arrangement they composed was fraught with drama—a kind of rock 'n roll *Ring* cycle with its leitmotifs. The simple guitar-recorder duet that introduced the piece was a mood setter in all its fairy-tale frippery, so understated that any further layering to the passage would have destroyed the tranquility. In fact, the way they planned it, an electric guitar wouldn't make an appearance until three minutes into the piece, and the drums, ominous in their staggered punch, a minute and a quarter later. Until then, the melody almost tiptoed in its approach to an intersection where one might expect renegade musicians to jump from the sidelines in an attempt to pick up the beat. Somehow, restraint persisted.

Sharp strums across the guitar strings after five minutes shattered the illusion they had created and acted like a fanfare to announce the song's next stage—something trenchant and harder. The transition opened up, at which point Jimmy's guitar solo burst from out of nowhere with the kind of fury reminiscent of "Communication Breakdown" and lashed away, picking up speed, as though goading the others to keep up. The runaway riff surged and swelled, gaining intensity, extending the fireworks, until a few razor-edged shrieks at the height of the coloratura—"a hysterical trill," Jimmy called it—drew the song to an unexpected climax.

Calling it "Götterdämmerung" would have been almost an injustice. It was "*hammer* of the gods," one of Robert's mumbled asides from "Immigrant Song," come to life. Jimmy and John Paul had the whole lollapalooza mapped out in an hour or two, with intervals marked where the others would engage.

The following night, the same creative show prevailed, only the dramatis personae had changed. John Paul escorted Bonzo to dinner at the Speakeasy in London, while Robert took his seat in front of the fireplace.

"I was sitting with Jimmy, and I was feeling really, really tranquil," he recalled. Tranquil for a time—he'd been reading *The Magic Arts in Celtic Britain* by Lewis Spence—but an undertow of anxiety pulled him away as Jimmy played him the opening chords. Something changed inside. "I was holding a pencil and paper, and for some reason I was in a very bad mood. Then, all of a sudden, my hand was writing out the words: *'There's a lady who's sure all that glitters is gold / And she's buying a stairway to heaven.'*"

Huh? *Stairway to heaven?*

"I just sat there and looked at the words, and then I almost leapt out of my seat."

Robert felt "as if I were being guided to write down what I did." The lyric's main theme came quickly, but it wasn't until the next afternoon, while the band was running down the song, that the rest of the words fell into place. "While we were doing it, Robert was penciling down lyrics," Jimmy said. "He must have written three quarters of the lyrics on the spot."

No one minded that they were rather cryptic. There were words that have no meaning, spirits that cry for leaving, pipers that lead to reason, bustles in the hedgerow, rings of smoke, and shadows taller than our soul.

"Nobody's quite sure what 'stairway to heaven' means," John Paul mused, "but it seems to fit."

Robert attempted a brief interpretation. "The lyrics were a cynical thing about a woman getting everything she wanted all the time without giving anything back." At other times, he expanded the premise, adding, "It's like she can have anything forever, so long as she doesn't have to think about it." The lyrics, to Robert, sounded "almost medieval." That stood to reason, inasmuch as his influences were drawn from the Spence book. But forever after, "Stairway to Heaven" would confound most listeners.

The arrangement was organic for the most part. As John Paul explained it, "Somebody would start something and somebody would follow, and it would turn into something else. You would sit down and work out what sections you've got and you'd put them together. It was all very easy, very relaxed."

Relaxed—but incomplete. It needed a controlled environment where the engineer could manage effects, like ambience and echo, necessary to dramatize each of the sections properly. "We really couldn't have done the acoustic guitar and drums at Headley," Jimmy concluded. "We needed a nice big studio."

At the end of January 1971, Led Zeppelin went back to Island Studios to finish what they had started. There were fourteen songs in various stages of development, enough for a double album. Songs that either were too elusive or had stalled at Headley Grange suddenly began to come together. "Four Sticks," for instance.

"I couldn't get that to work until we tried to record it a few times," Jimmy said. He seriously considered abandoning the song altogether. The time signature seemed too difficult for Bonzo to handle—a rhythmic pattern that swung inconsistently between five- and six-beat measures. They decided to take a day off from struggling with it to give them a little perspective. That night, Bonzo went to a show in order to blow off some steam. Instead, it had the opposite effect.

"He had been to see Ginger Baker's Airforce, and he came in and was really hyped about it," Jimmy recalled.

Baker was one of Bonzo's idols, but seeing him take center stage at the Royal Albert Hall, strutting and showboating with reinforcement from two extra drummers, had touched a competitive nerve. Settling down behind his kit, Bonzo primed his performance with a can of Double Diamond pale ale and picked up his sticks—not the usual two, but *four*, two in each hand.

"We did it again," Jimmy said, "and it was magic, one take. The whole thing had suddenly been made."

Jimmy added several guitar tracks to "Black Dog." He was looking to give the song a more aggressive snarl by triple-tracking each riff. "I wanted a totally different tone color," he said, "so I ran my guitar through a Leslie [speaker] and mic-ed that in the usual way." They also polished "When the Levee Breaks," adding slide guitar riffs and backward echo, with a hypnotic harmonica solo contributed by Robert.

"The Battle of Evermore" needed another element, but—*what?* The song, which Robert described as a "playlet," begged for a vocal foil—a town crier, so to speak—to play against his bluesy delivery. He and Jimmy huddled and came up with a possible solution. Jimmy suggested they bring in his old art-school mate Sandy Denny, who had recently bowed out of Fairport Convention. There was no argument from Robert, who considered Denny his "favorite singer out of all the British girls." Besides, they were already studio friends, her voice and his having intertwined so harmoniously on "Gallows Pole." On "Evermore," they reprised their ensemble singing with a lovely call-and-response that polished off the song.

Things were moving at a brisk, businesslike pace, and Andy Johns was enjoying the experience. With Led Zeppelin, "there was never a struggle to get a decent groove," he said. These musicians were pros, he thought, not prima donnas. "With the Stones, sometimes you would sit there for days and days and days, just trying to get a basic track." Led Zeppelin worked fast, no fragile egos intruded, there was no hand-wringing, no one-upmanship, thanks in no small part to Jimmy Page, "who had his hands on the reins."

For better or worse, Led Zeppelin remained Jimmy's band. "Even in rehearsals, Jim was always in charge," says Phil Carlo. "Peter made sure of that. Whatever Jimmy did, G thought was great, as opposed to Robert, whom he called 'that cunt.'" John Paul, Robert, and Bonzo felt secure in their roles, but they deferred to Jimmy. Even John Paul, who brought as much expertise to the equation. He, like the others, recognized that Jimmy had the name—and the ambition. In the studio, Jimmy rose to the occasion. He rode the board as capably as any top-ranked engineer or producer, with the determination to replicate any sound that was in his head. And he was headstrong, sure of himself.

The confidence allowed him to tackle a beast like "Stairway to Heaven," whose inventive but ungovernable construction begged a game hand and an open mind. There were so many moving parts, a labyrinth of circuitry. It required a ringmaster to put it all together.

The rhythm track, rerecorded in the studio, laid the song's groundwork and acted as a guide. It required nothing more than a basic setup—Jimmy on guitar, John Paul on electric piano and Moog bass, and John Bonham on drums. Afterward, listening to the playback, Bonzo delivered the verdict. "Sounds wonderful," he said triumphantly. "That's it, then."

Jimmy wasn't so sure. He sat staring at the tape deck, contemplating the situation, reluctant to give it his seal of approval.

Bonzo was ready to move on but picked up on Jimmy's indecision. "What's wrong?" he wanted to know. "Is this the take or isn't it?"

Jimmy equivocated. "It's all right," he conceded, but the perfectionist in him prevailed. "I think we've got a better take inside us."

For some reason, Bonzo took it personally. He grabbed his sticks, stormed out of the control room, and posted himself behind his kit, seething.

"When he finally comes in [on the take]," said the tape operator, Richard Digby Smith, "he beat the crap out of his drums, and all the meters are going into the red."

It was a better performance all around, sharper, more exciting. Jimmy had been right. After hearing the playback, Bonzo grudgingly admitted as much.

The ethereal intro synthesized easily enough once they turned their focus to it. John Paul multitracked the recorders over the melody line, which Jimmy, surrounded by baffles, fingerpicked on an acoustic guitar. For two studio pros, it was a morning's work. There were no charts, as in the old days, but enough intuition and experience to make quick work of it. After that was locked, Jimmy added a twelve-string rhythm figure before picking up his trusty "Dragon" Telecaster, the one Jeff Beck had given him, to lay in the solo.

"I had the first phase worked out, and a link here and there," Jimmy recalled, "but on the whole that solo was improvised."

They'd first tried it at Headley Grange, working on it for three or four hours without getting a decent take. In the studio, instead of playing to the rhythm track with headphones, Andy set Jimmy up in front of giant Tannoy monitors to simulate the feel of a live band. The earsplitting playback blasted at him in much the same way a fan heard it, sitting in front of the PA system at an outsize arena.

According to Digby Smith, "He just leaned up against the speakers with his ear virtually pressed against them and rattled out that solo."

Jimmy played it three times, layering on harmonies, just building them up . . . and *up* . . . and *up* . . . until the piece had nowhere else to go.

Except that it still needed a vocal. Robert was sitting at the back of the control room, a yellow pad balanced on his knees, minding his own business.

Andy Johns gave him a friendly nudge. "Robert, it's your turn to sing," he said.

"Really?" he responded without looking up, continuing to furiously scribble away. "Well, I'm not finished with the lyrics. Can you play it again?"

After another playback, Robert was ready to go—and he nailed the vocal in two takes.

Led Zeppelin had completed a new album—their fourth in a little more than two years, an astonishing output, considering the seemingly endless, soul-sucking tours that encroached between records. But this one felt different. Everyone agreed. This one felt special, more organic and collaborative. They'd taken their time making it under unbeatable conditions, with an abundance of material to work from— the best of the bunch, whittled down from fourteen to eight. Seven killer songs, and just maybe one masterpiece.

*Led Zeppelin IV*? Not if Jimmy had anything to do with it. That would give the demon press too much ammunition to continue its remorseless target practice with the band. No, if Jimmy had his way— and Jimmy usually got his way—this album's title would stupefy the critics and the suits alike, it would beat them at their own game. He had the perfect title for it.

It would be called nothing.

# [3]

Not quite nothing. There would be hints as to what the album *might* be called if someone were to put a title on it—which was not happening.

The cover was given over to a painting of a wizened little character in a bowler hat with a faggot of branches strapped to his back, who looked as though he'd stepped out of a Marcel Pagnol novel. Robert had unearthed it in "a real dingy second-hand shop" in Reading during one of the trips he and Jimmy made to Headley Grange. Jimmy haunted antique shops. He'd developed into an avid collector of twentieth-century decorative arts—art deco, art nouveau, arts and crafts, modernist, Favrile glass, Biedermeier, and ceramics—and he couldn't pass a gallery without making a pit stop. He'd discovered gems, real treasures, in bric-a-brac places all over the world. But this place—this place was a dump, and the prize was Robert's.

Sure, why not put this painting on the cover to give those pundits something to think about? It was to be hung on a wall of peeling wallpaper. On the back was a photo of a Midlands high-rise, the contrast of which, according to Jimmy, represented "the old being knocked down, the new buildings going up." But nothing was to be explained or identified. Spelling it out, he said, "would make the whole thing disappointing on that level of your own personal adventure into the music." Jimmy had other ideas along the same lines. In a ballsy, defiant contrivance, the band's name wouldn't appear on the LP cover—they'd remain anonymous—maybe just a symbol that stood for their name, as Prince would do twenty years later—nor would any record company information appear, just . . . nothing. It would be mysterious and confounding. All of it intrigued and amused the four musicians, but they knew it would be a hard sell to Atlantic Records. Was it "pretty bold," as a fellow musician proclaimed—or professional suicide?

And what of the inside of the gatefold? More intrigue or artifice, a little chicanery at the suits' expense? One side of the panel conveyed an arcane pencil illustration entitled *View in Half or Varying Light* depicting a sinister-looking, hooded figure atop a mountain, holding a lantern and gazing down the slope at the figure of a younger man on bended knee, his arms flung out in supplication. Supposedly, it was drawn by a friend of Jimmy's named Barrington Coleby, although people close to the band suspect it was one of Jimmy's art-college projects. In any case, he acknowledged, "It actually comes from the idea from the Tarot card of the Hermit." For Jimmy, the Hermit was "basically an illustration of a seeker aspiring to the light of truth . . . a symbol of self-reliance and wisdom."

The opposite side of the gatefold displayed the "title" of the album. Eventually, the band decided that it would be represented by four glyphs—or runes, figures used for written language before the introduction of the Latin alphabet—each designating one of the musicians. "We wanted to demonstrate that it was the music that made Zeppelin popular," Jimmy said. "It had nothing to do with our name or image." He produced his copy of Koch's *The Book of Signs*, the one he'd had Carole Brown buy for him some months earlier, and encouraged the guys to have a look.

"Each of us decided to . . . choose a metaphorical-type symbol [that] somehow would represent each of us individually," Robert said, "be it a state of mind, an opinion, or something we felt strongly about, or whatever."

Robert decided to design his own—a feather in a circle, "drawn," he claimed, "from sacred symbols of the ancient Mu civilization," which he mistook as history from reading the fictional boyhood adventure *The Lost Continent of Mu* by Colonel James Churchward. All sorts of interpretations have been ascribed to the symbol. According to Jimmy, "it represents courage to Red Indian tribes." The Churchward book associated it with Maat, the Egyptian goddess of truth and justice. And sometimes, to paraphrase Freud, a feather in a circle is just a feather in a circle.

John Paul and Bonzo selected their signs from Jimmy's book. John Paul's—a circle overlaid with three intersecting almond shapes—"was said to represent a person who is both competent and confident." At least, that was how Jimmy explained it. But the Koch book classified it as an emblem meant to ward off evil spells. John Paul didn't care much either way. As with most group decisions, he went along with the flow, intent on not making waves, happy just to play music and create in the studio.

John Bonham's sign was three circles, what Robert regarded as being "the trilogy—man, woman, and child," but what others saw clearly as the Ballantine beer logo.

Only Jimmy failed to explain his symbol. He was cagey when asked the meaning of the character that read as "ZoSo." He insisted it wasn't a word, wasn't meant to be pronounced. "It's just a doodle," he said, somewhat disingenuously. And when pressed, he drilled down into obfuscation: "My symbol was about invoking and being invocative, and that's all I'm going to say about it."

A cottage industry grew up around the interpretation of Jimmy's stylized sign, with armchair sleuths weighing in on everything from its similarity to Zos, the magical name of Austin Osman Spare, an occultist whose satanic and sexual obsessions rivaled those of Aleister Crowley, to "a graven image of energy, a frozen imprint of physical desire that has a material life of its own." In fact, the ZoSo symbol had appeared in texts as early as 1557, when a mathematician, Girolamo Cardano, used it in a manuscript entitled *De rerum varietate* to represent Saturn, the planet that rules Capricorn, which is Jimmy Page's astrological sign. He did nothing to discourage that interpretation when, for several months in 1971, Jimmy performed in a pair of velvet trousers embroidered with the signs for Capricorn, Scorpio (his ascendant), and Cancer (his moon sign).

Intended meanings, interpretations, and mumbo jumbo aside, the four symbols ⚙ ⚛ ⊗ ① looked handsome as well as mysterious when lined up together on the album sleeve. And for good measure, a fifth symbol, three triangles with their points all touching, was added to identify Sandy Denny.

"There was a lot of opposition from Atlantic about it being untitled," Robert recalled.

That was putting it mildly. "The record company was in shock and horror," says Phil Carson, who recalls sitting in "countless meetings" in an attempt to change the band's minds.

"I had to go in personally and argue with the record company about it," Jimmy recalled. He and Peter Grant waved their contract and stood their ground despite demands from Atlantic's attorney, Mike Mayer, that Led Zeppelin come to their senses, or at the very least allow Atlantic to sticker the album's shrink-wrapping with the band's name. At some point, Grant made it clear that they wouldn't deliver the master tapes until they had Atlantic's assurance that the cover would be printed exactly as they intended it. He promised Ahmet Ertegun that "the fans were going to find it, with or without a title on it," and Ertegun reluctantly agreed. Nevertheless, Atlantic put the company's salesmen on high alert.

Nick Maria, the local rep in northern New Jersey, recalls not batting an eye when the album arrived. "It didn't matter what was on that cover," he says. "Everyone knew what it was. FM radio was playing it. Besides, it was revolutionary at the time."

Trailerloads were coming in from the distributor. Usually, rack jobbers, as the wholesalers were known, took four or five copies of each new album—say, the new Fifth Dimension or Johnny Rivers LPs—for each of the outlets they served. "With Led Zeppelin," Maria recalls, "we were taking thousands and thousands."

Led Zeppelin had moved out of the communal bins that mingled Jethro Tull, Creedence, Yes, Nilsson, and Humble Pie albums. They were no longer simply a hit bestselling rock band. There were plenty of those average Joes working the trenches. No, they were now in the rarefied upper reaches, where the muses and deities resided. That much was clear to everyone associated with the music business. With this new album, Led Zeppelin had become a phenomenon.

## Chapter Eleven

# JUST BOYS HAVING FUN

## [1]

Even a phenomenon needed a dose of reality.

John Lennon could chant, "*Give me money, that's what I want,*" and the Mothers of Invention could claim, *We're Only in It for the Money,* but flaunting fat box-office grosses and hefty sales figures didn't sit well with folks in England.

Peter Grant had had it up to here with press complaints that painted his band as a bunch of money-grubbing toffs. "*Melody Maker* and all that lot were saying Zep were getting too big for their boots with their U.S. tours," he grumbled. Grant figured it would shut the critics up and be a public-relations coup if the band played select dates in small, intimate venues that didn't involve big paydays. Better yet, they'd play for free.

It would have been impossible to stage Led Zeppelin on the top of a London building, as the Beatles had done, but there were other locales that might do the trick. Two places attracted G's attention: the Waterloo Station and the Kennington Oval at the Surrey County Cricket Club in South London. Both required permits, which the authorities were loath to grant, and despite the argument that Led Zeppelin would appear unannounced, the applications were rejected.

As an alternative, the band was talked into undertaking a short tour of UK clubs so that they could ostensibly reconnect with their roots. Not only would ticket prices match the 1968 prices, but so would the price of drinks at the bar. It would serve to kill two birds with one stone. The band would get the "money monkey" off their back and at the same time keep their swing in a groove until the new album was released in front of a big U.S. summer tour.

The plan had been to have ⚙ ▲ ⊛ ⦸ in stores by late March 1971. On February 9, Jimmy and Andy Johns flew to Los Angles and spent a week mixing the album at Sunset Sound, with its state-of-the-art monitors. To an occultist like Jimmy, the earthquake that greeted their arrival should have been an omen. It turned out the monitors in the studio were as shaky and unpredictable as the tremors that rattled the foundation of their hotel, where, fortunately, no one was injured. If only the mix had fared as well.

"[Jimmy] brought the tapes back and they sounded terrible," Robert said. The sound they'd heard over the monitors in the LA studio wasn't true to what was transferred to tape, and when they listened to the playback at Olympic Sound in London, it was a mess, muddy and flat. There was no high end, no treble frequencies. The album had to be completely remixed.

Consequently, the release of ⚙ ▲ ⊛ ⦸ had to be postponed, which pleased no one, neither the band nor the record company. G had already booked a series of dates they were calling the Back to the Clubs tour beginning March 5, followed by gigs throughout Europe. Worst-case scenario, Led Zeppelin would play a massive summer tour in the States without new product in the stores, a situation that would cost them millions of dollars.

As it was, the Back to the Clubs tour was already a loss leader. The idea was to charge promoters and fans the same amount as when the band first toured as the New Yardbirds in 1968. "We're going to restrict prices to twelve bob [shillings] a ticket," Grant announced with uncharacteristic benevolence.

Jimmy attempted to justify the band's motivation, saying, "The audiences were becoming bigger and bigger but moving further and further away. They became specks on the horizon and we were losing contact with people—those people who were responsible for lifting us off the ground in the early days."

It was a noble sentiment but undercut with headaches. Plenty of fans would inevitably be turned away due to space restrictions in clubs—and so would the press. "If they expect red-carpet treatment," Jimmy warned, "then my advice is don't bother to come. We're not playing for the sole benefit of the press or the critics who we all know review most of the shows from the beer tent or the bar!"

Sound was going to be another challenge; an arena-compatible PA might blow out the walls, to say nothing of a few eardrums. But Jimmy chose to look at the upside. "The only major difference," he said, "is not having to worry about someone leveling a gun at your head as they do in the U.S., so there is less emphasis on security."

Apparently, he hadn't seen the itinerary. The tour was set to open in Belfast, where someone leveling a gun at your head was no laughing matter. Rory Gallagher had famously played there on New Year's Day while bombs were exploding outside the hall. Rock 'n roll bands had avoided playing in Ireland during the rampant sectarian violence that had stretched on for years. Jimmy fretted about going. "The situation's gotten very bloody over there," he said, but Grant had thrown caution to the wind. "It was frightening as all-get-out," says Henry Smith, who drove one of the equipment vans through war-torn streets patrolled by self-styled militias. "I wasn't used to people walking around with machine guns."

Richard Cole was uncommonly nervous. "Just hours before our concert in Belfast, there was a confrontation between police and demonstrators about a mile from Ulster Hall, where the band would be performing," he claimed. According to reports, "a petrol tanker was hijacked, a youth was shot dead, and fire bombs were hurled."

The gig, however, supplied a priceless measure of peace, a word not commonly used to describe a Led Zeppelin concert. The band shook that Victorian hall with the kind of firepower heard throughout the city, but without any tragic effect. Hearing "Immigrant Song," "Heartbreaker," and a particularly trenchant "Dazed and Confused" served as a balm to the so-called Troubles. But the sixth song in the set spun things in an extraordinary direction.

Jimmy strapped on a new, strange-looking guitar, a beast of an instrument with two necks, like Janus, the god of beginnings and endings, and picked out a riff that marked the first-ever performance of "Stairway to Heaven." For a while it had stumped Jimmy how to reproduce the song onstage. In the studio, he'd begun the intro with his Harmony acoustic guitar, switched to a Fender electric twelve-string for the section that preceded the entry of drums, and played the solo with his Telecaster. There was no way to go through such a hectic instrument change onstage. But he remembered seeing Earl Hooker, Sonny Boy Williamson's guitarist, play a twin-necked model that offered a perfect solution—if only Jimmy could get his hands on one. Unfortunately, Gibson no longer produced them, so he ordered a custom model made of cherry with mahogany necks that weighed in at a lissome thirteen pounds.

Fans watched openmouthed as he used the bottom six strings for the intro and the first verse, then switched to the twelve-string on top, before going back to the six-string for the solo and the twelve-string for the fade. It was a feat of musical prestidigitation, even for a magus like Jimmy Page.

In spite of the stirring milestone, Led Zeppelin was relieved to get out of Belfast. After the last notes were played, they bolted in a limousine heading to Dublin, chugging bottles of Jack Daniel's to soothe their nerves. By the time they covered the hundred-mile distance, it was well after midnight. Appreciable tension between Robert and

John had been brewing all evening. Earlier, following a fifteen-minute drum solo, Robert had made a spectacle of offering Bonzo a banana, which earned him a murderous glare. It was payback of sorts for a nickname that had stuck to Robert like discarded gum. Peter had dubbed him "Percy," which Bonzo took pleasure in calling him every chance he got. The party line was that the name referred to Percy Thrower, a beloved but fuddy-duddy horticulturist who hosted the long-running TV show *Gardeners' World* in the UK, where gardening was a form of religion. In truth, however, it was based on a recent film about a guy who had a transplanted penis that he named Percy. The nickname stuck—and Robert hated it.

Bonzo enjoyed winding him up. There were plenty of Percy taunts and put-downs, like "All you've got to do is stand out there and look good. We'll take care of the music!"

Chris Welch, who was covering the tour for *Melody Maker*, recalled, "I quaked in my hotel bedroom as I heard the row blazing." A few minutes later, there was furious pounding on Grant's door.

"Peter, I've done something terrible," Bonzo cried. "I've hit Robert!"

G was an ex-wrestler, not a referee. "Shut up and go to bed," he roared.

Bonzo should have taken him up on it. Instead, pretty well looped on scotch, he strode into the hotel kitchen and picked a fight with the chef, who was in no mood for such nonsense. When he came at Bonzo with a carving knife, Richard Cole—now called Ricardo by one and all—decked Bonzo, breaking his nose "for his own safety."

The Back to the Clubs tour was off to an auspicious start.

———

The gigs were designed to bring Led Zeppelin closer to their audiences, but not everyone enjoyed the experience. "Once you've played in the big places, these small clubs are murder," Jimmy complained.

The facilities were pretty grim and the sound systems, minuscule by Zep standards, overloaded with feedback during the sets. "In a place like the Marquee, which held three hundred people comfortably, the sound was too loud for anyone too appreciate it," recalls Chris Charlesworth. Robert couldn't stalk the stages, which felt as big as a postage stamp. He compared it to being confined in a straitjacket, and audiences felt pretty much the same way.

On March 24, 1971, the day after the Marquee performance, which officially ended the Back to the Clubs tour, Charlotte Martin gave birth to a daughter, whom she and Jimmy named Scarlet Lilith Eleida Page. There wasn't much time allotted to parenting before Jimmy barricaded himself in the studio, at Olympic again, in an attempt to salvage the ⚙ ⚓ ⊛ ① mix. No matter how hard he worked, the album still didn't live up to his expectations; there were too many technical "hang-ups" for his ear. He remained dissatisfied—dispirited. "We just didn't have time to sit down and get a balance on things," he said. "My senses have been battered to a pulp. I've lived with it for so long. I can't hear it anymore."

Atlantic Records was losing its patience. The company was pressing for new product, especially with Led Zeppelin on the road, performing. The way it stacked up now, the album would be delayed until the fall of 1971, *after* the next big American tour.

In the meantime, the band went back on the road, playing a handful of European arenas to sharpen and integrate the new material. It was important to learn how still-unreleased songs like "Gallows Pole," "Misty Mountain Hop," "Four Sticks," "Black Dog," and "Stairway" went over in live performances. For the most part, the shows were instructive, the material well received. In Denmark, the audiences were enthusiastic, even ecstatic. But in Italy, everything went to hell.

On July 5, 1971, Led Zeppelin headlined the government-sponsored Cantagiro Cantamondo Festival in Milan, with nine opening acts, all of them Italian. There was an air of foreboding even before they arrived. Peter Grant recalled a four-month Italian tour he'd done in the fifties with Wee Willie Harris, Britain's so-called wild man of rock 'n roll, and "knew what a dodgy place it could be." To allay his fears, he'd "demanded all the money up front and got the air tickets back in advance," just in case Led Zeppelin had to make a hasty getaway.

The signs were unpromising as the band's van approached the Velodromo Vigorelli, an oval-shaped football stadium, where the Beatles had performed in 1965. "We could see the riot police," Jimmy said. Soldiers, too. There were scores of them, well armed, in full battle dress. It looked like the casting call for one of the Italian gladiator spectacles. "If all concerts were as well-secured as this one," Ricardo remarked, "I'd feel a lot more comfortable."

His reassurance was premature. The crowd grew impatient sitting in the heat through the endless parade of twee Italian bands. They'd come to see Led Zeppelin, and as the collective restlessness rose in pitch, the cops moved in, taking up positions on a catwalk that ringed the stadium.

The situation intensified when Led Zeppelin finally took the stage. After several numbers, Jimmy noticed "smoke at the far end of the arena." At the promoter's request, Robert continually implored fans to stop lighting fires. "Then we suddenly twigged that it wasn't smoke from fires—it was bloody tear gas that the police were firing into the crowd."

The band's eyes stung, but they continued to play until a beer bottle sailed out of the crowd and struck Bonzo's drum roadie, Mick Hinton, on the forehead. Almost simultaneously, someone lofted a cannister of tear gas that exploded in front of the stage.

"Blow this!" Jimmy yelled to his bandmates. "Let's cut it really short."

Before they could scramble to safety, a full-scale storm erupted, with "thirty or forty cannisters of tear gas all going at once." The crowd charged the stage with the cops close on their heels. It was everyone for himself.

"Everyone was running," Robert recalled. "We split and ran down a passage under the cycle arena—and then they tear-gassed the passage."

G, whose weight became a factor, was unable to run fast and had Ricardo and the wounded Mick Hinton acting as defensive linebackers, blocking for him as they muscled through the smoke-filled tunnel. But—where to go? No one could see.

"It was just pandemonium," Jimmy said, "and nowhere was immune from this blasted tear gas."

Eventually, the band and roadies made their way into a dressing room. "I barricaded the door with a medicine cabinet and got everybody to put wet towels around their heads," Robert explained. Almost futilely, a nurse attended to them with some oxygen. "Then they broke the windows and popped a couple of cannisters [of tear gas] in from the street."

It seemed an eternity until police arrived to escort the entourage out of the stadium.

The plane ride back to London was especially somber. There was very little conversation, but one thing was on everyone's mind. In a month, Led Zeppelin was due to kick off a lengthy schedule of American concerts, followed by tours of Japan and the English provinces. Forty-three gigs, right up to the end of the year.

No one was saying it, but everyone was thinking: How long could they keep up this crazy pace?

## [2]

Touring had become a slog. Due largely to Led Zeppelin's skyrocketing popularity, disturbances occurred routinely throughout the summer dates they played in America in 1971. Shows sold out quickly, often leaving throngs of disgruntled fans no choice but to try to force their way into arenas. Concerts had to be stopped to avoid riots, and the length of performances, often two and a half to three hours, taxed Robert's vocal cords as never before.

Japan offered a welcome respite. On September 23, 1971, Led Zeppelin opened at the Budokan, Tokyo's hallowed premier martial-arts venue, where music had once been taboo. "It was such a shock to go out there and play to Japanese audiences," Jimmy said. Instead of passing bottles of Jack Daniel's and joints or lobbing cherry bombs, standing on their seats and flinging themselves off balconies, the Japanese behaved in a way the band had never been treated before—with *respect*. No one left their seats, even to stand up, and at the end of each song, polite applause rippled through the arena, but only for a brief, prescribed time. No one screamed *"Mooore!"* or *"We loooove you!"* or *"Play 'Whole Lotta Loooove!'"* What a revelation. "It was so quiet, it was sort of eerie," Jimmy said.

Most of the action took place backstage. After finishing their pre-arranged set, Led Zeppelin regrouped in the wings to decide what they might do for an encore. But Robert, who had been singing for three straight hours, demurred. "I can't do any more," he squawked. "I've got no voice."

Bonzo gave him a spot of Midlands snark. "It never mattered before," he said. "You're no good anyway. Just go out there and look good."

Robert threw the first punch—and missed. Bonzo's fist connected, however, forcing Robert to muddle through "Communication Breakdown" with a fat lip.

"It was just boys having fun," says Phil Carson, the head of Atlantic's European affairs, who was along to keep an eye on the label's cash cow. "There were no drugs yet to speak of. Just a lot of drink, a *lot* of drink—and a lot of high jinks."

"For example, there was a night when one of us got our clothes tossed out the window and that person took advantage of the opportunity to run around on the rooftops of Japan naked," Jimmy recalled.

"Then there was a public phone that disappeared off the streets and was found outside our doorway with all sorts of money in it."

Bonzo, especially, was in rare form. He embarrassed his Japanese host in one of Tokyo's ritziest restaurants by demanding that a waiter bring him a tankard full of sake instead of the traditional thimbles in which it was served. Later that same night, at Byblos, the city's hot, membership-only disco, an over-refreshed Bonzo urinated from the balcony onto a deejay whose music he disdained. And even later, his display of fall-down-drunkenness on the curb outside of the Tokyo Hilton was eyed with shame by the hotel's genteel management.

The tour moved on to Hiroshima, for a charity benefit for victims of the atomic bomb. To Bonzo's credit, there was a moratorium on childish behavior. But on the overnight train to Osaka, he drank himself silly again, and while Jimmy and his Japanese girlfriend were in the dining car, Bonzo found her handbag and shit in it. His little stunt, along with a food fight, started a chain reaction of bedlam on the crowded passenger train that sprang from Peter Grant to Ricardo, Percy, and Led Zeppelin's mortified Japanese host.

Things calmed down a bit once they arrived in Osaka, and their performance, in the city's renowned concert hall, benefited. One of the band's trademarks was incorporating classic rock 'n roll hits into their extended medleys. In Osaka, during "Whole Lotta Love," they dug deep into their song bag to include the Beatles' "Please Please Me" and "From Me to You," along with licks from Jimi Hendrix's "Third Stone from the Sun." "Communication Breakdown" brought out two Cliff Richards & the Shadows numbers—"D in Love" and "Bachelor Boy"—before segueing into Chuck Berry's "Down the Road Apiece" and "Maybelline." For encores, they played "C'mon Everybody" and "Hi-Heel Sneakers," two standbys from Jimmy's Neil Christian days.

It was a joyous affair for the audience and the band, and spilled over into the following night's show, featuring a thirty-one-minute "Whole Lotta Love" medley that incorporated Elvis's "I Gotta Know" into the mix, as well as "Twist and Shout" and "Fortune Teller."

Both Osaka concerts were resounding successes, and the band celebrated into the early-morning hours. Following an excursion to a nightclub, it was Phil Carson who bore the brunt of the horseplay. "During dessert, they started to relieve me of my clothes," he recalls, "and I realized that I didn't want to have to fight four guys, so I took everything off myself except for my shoes, which they let me keep." As soon as everyone got up to go, Carson snatched the tablecloth and wrapped it around his body in order to get to the waiting taxi without too much embarrassment.

As they arrived at the Hilton, Robert graciously allowed Carson to enter first through the revolving door. "Except he got hold of one end of the tablecloth," Phil says, "and I was propelled into the lobby at six in the morning stark naked aside from my shoes." In Japan at six in the morning, the lobby was filled with businessmen heading to work. Ignoring the pop-eyed stares, Carson sashayed calmly to the front desk, asked for his room key, and walked nonchalantly to the elevator.

Upstairs, Bonzo and Richard were engaged in another unruly caper. They'd gotten their hands on a couple of samurai swords and were swinging away at each other in what might have been a scene out of Yojimbo. It was a miracle that neither man sustained injury, but they slashed and destroyed everything in the suite.

Afterward, they had a go at John Paul, who was out cold in an adjoining room. "Jonesy was sleeping on a tatami mat," Phil Carson recalls. "So they picked him up on the mat and placed it in the elevator, where it went up and down all night long. The Japanese were too polite to wake him up. Instead, the hotel management put a portable screen around him and left him to sleep."

"Night after night after night, we had all this stuff going on," Jimmy said, "and we got away with murder."

It wasn't entirely an acquittal. Richard Cole maintained he was called into the Hilton administrative office, where the manager informed him that Led Zeppelin was barred from ever staying at the hotel again. "But even lectures by hotel managers didn't have any effect on our behavior," he claimed.

It was something darker and more destructive that affected their behavior.

"At this point, cocaine started to intervene," said Phil Carson. "It very definitely changed the makeup of the band. And it did everything that cocaine does—it made people paranoid and reclusive and nasty. And that's how it all started."

———

The first sign of trouble came while the band was in Japan. During a layover in Hong Kong between gigs, Richard was charged with scoring some coke, which the guys snorted in a restaurant kitchen—and which turned out to be heroin, much to their alarm. Then, in Perth, Australia, in February 1972, the police ransacked their hotel rooms looking for narcotics, which, as luck would have it, had been stashed elsewhere. But by the time the summer tour got under way, "drugs," as Jimmy said, "were an integral part of the whole thing, right from the beginning, right to the end."

Richard—Ricardo—always made sure there were plenty on hand. "Drugs for the band were often given to me by fans, by friends," he said, "who would knock on my hotel room door, hand me a bagful of cocaine or marijuana, and say something like, 'We have a present for you.'" But if fans or friends were somehow unavailing, Ricardo had his own trusted sources who always delivered.

Cocaine took the edge off of being on the road—the extreme lows and the supreme highs. "Led Zeppelin was a musician's dream," Jimmy explained. "It was euphoric, and you can't just switch off the adrenalin. For us, the way to wind it down was to go off and party. And before you know where you are, you've missed a night's sleep. Then two weeks later, you've missed a few nights sleep, because you're having such a good time."

Instant gratification—it was the doctrine of a band made up of mostly working-class Brits who, practically overnight, had ascended to aristocracy. "There was a new aristocracy called rock 'n roll," says Michael Des Barres, himself the son of a ruined marquis, "and you got the best table if you were Bill Wyman, but not if you were a lord or prince."

Led Zeppelin were more like young gods. The success of ⚡⚡⚡⚡ launched them into the rock 'n roll pantheon, where their wishes were only commands away. The album had flown off store shelves in record numbers, despite the usual swamp of lukewarm reviews. It became a mainstay of the U.S. Top 40 for the next three years, led by an insatiable craving for "Stairway to Heaven."

Atlantic Records pleaded—*begged*—for permission to edit "Stairway" for a single, despite Jimmy's avowal that there would be no "messing around with that song." The label pointed to its success with the Stones' *Sticky Fingers* LP, released a few months earlier, which boasted two million-selling singles, "Brown Sugar" and "Wild Horses." But—nothing doing. Jimmy was adamant. "'Stairway' was never, ever, *ever* going to be released as a single." Nothing—neither public pressure nor money—could change his mind. "The whole thing was we wanted people to hear it in the context of the album," he said.

Jerry Greenberg, head of Atlantic's promotion department, was beside himself. "AM radio was insisting on a 'Stairway' single," he recalls. "It was nuts. I reminded Jimmy that I'd done that edit on 'Whole Lotta Love,' but he wouldn't budge. I did my own edit anyway, a five-minute version, but they wouldn't let me distribute it. Peter told me that if people wanted to hear the song, they had to buy the album." G used Atlantic's own argument about the Rolling Stones to make his point. Despite their two hit singles, ⚡⚡⚡⚡ was outselling *Sticky Fingers* by two to one.

No, Led Zeppelin was calling their own shots from now on. Grant had the record company over a barrel, and he was about to do the same thing to the concert business.

From the beginning, the band's gigs were booked by Premier Talent Agency in New York. The deals were standard across the board for all top rock 'n roll acts. Led Zeppelin was given a guarantee for each performance—say, $25,000 to play Madison Square Garden—and after the promoter recouped that amount and his expenses, he and the artist split the remaining net income on a sixty-forty percentage basis. It was an equitable deal because the promoter assumed the risk; he put up the money for the band's guarantee, the cost of renting the arena, and the advertising. But during a chat Peter had with Ahmet Ertegun, the Atlantic Records chief suggested that Led Zeppelin's drawing power was a force unto itself. If G called a local radio station to announce the dates of Led Zeppelin's next tour, tickets would sell out instantly.

Sure, just cut out the middleman, in this case the promoter. Grant had an allergy to promoters that dated to his road-managing days for Don Arden's acts. He felt the promoters ripped everybody off. "On a tour with, say, Little Richard," he recalled, "the promoters were making more money than the acts were. That always went against my grain."

Steve Weiss had encountered similar problems with his client Jimi Hendrix. Bill Graham prided himself on offering Jimi only a ridiculously low flat fee and threw him an insulting $1,500 bonus if he sold out. So Weiss decided to self-promote Jimi's gigs. "We hired a promoter and paid him a small percentage for promoting the concert," he recalled. Grant got extra excited when Weiss told him how The Who had been circumventing the sixty-forty split with promoters.

"We'd been doing ten-percent deals in Europe," says Bill Curbishley, The Who's manager. "I wasn't asking promoters for sell-out guarantees, which meant they didn't have to put up their own money, so we split the box office ninety-ten after expenses. And on that tour The Who made a huge amount more."

Weiss knew that an arrangement like that only worked for the top acts, "because if you guessed wrong, the artists wouldn't make as much or might even *lose* money." He figured that if it had worked for The Who in Europe, then why not try it with Led Zeppelin on their summer American tour in 1972?

G was beside himself. "Fuck those promoters!" he said. "I'm not giving them forty percent when we're the ones selling tickets."

It was easier said than done. Frank Barsalona, the head of Premier Talent and the reputed "most powerful man in the music business," wouldn't hear of it. He'd put most of the young rock promoters in business and constantly fed them acts to keep their venues booked. The sixty-forty split was the way he did business so that everyone got a fair piece of the pie. Now Peter Grant wanted a bigger piece, and Barsalona put his foot dow: not seventy-thirty, not eighty-twenty, certainly not ninety-ten. He demanded the split remain sixty-forty, and no one crossed Frank Barsalona.

Mickie Most, who still shared an office with Peter, overheard his argument on the phone. "You don't have to promote Led Zeppelin," G argued. "Just announce on the radio that they're playing at Madison Square [Garden], and an hour later there won't be a ticket to be had."

As far as he was concerned, Barsalona and Premier Talent were expendable. To test the waters, Peter ordered Tony Mandich, Atlantic's West Coast artist relations manager, to call a radio station with the dates of Led Zeppelin's next tour and information that tickets would go on sale the following Monday at 10:00 a.m. "By eleven o'clock or noon, we got a phone call from the Forum that they'd sold out," Mandich recalled. The same thing happened after a second show was announced.

That was all the proof Grant needed. From now on, he'd see to booking Led Zeppelin himself—or with someone else willing to work using the ninety-ten split—and the promoters, he believed, would all go along with it. What other choice did they have? Let them gripe. They'd still wind up pocketing plenty of money, but it would be on his terms: *take it or leave it.*

"We never liked it," says Don Law, who promoted concerts in the

Boston arenas, "but we understood what Grant was up to. If you have the hottest band in the world, you wind up setting the terms."

As G had figured, the promoters all rolled over. He'd have done the same thing were he in their shoes. "I'd take ten percent of Led Zeppelin," he bragged. "That's a lot of money for no risk."

Premier Talent washed its hands of Led Zeppelin, and with the aid of Concerts West, a new power broker on the scene, the entire summer North American tour was conducted on a ninety-ten split. Thanks to the sold-out, arena-size crowds, fantastic sums of money flowed into the band's coffers, and mostly in cash; G didn't accept promoters' checks. It wasn't so much a lack of trust as it was avoiding a heavy tax bite. Why leave a paper trail? He merely stuffed the cash into a travel bag and carried it from town to town—hundreds of thousands of dollars, *millions*. Whatever anyone needed—pocket money, equipment, drugs—a fistful of bills was tendered.

As the money increased, so did the length of the shows, often running in the three-hour-plus vicinity. There were so many favorites to play: "Heartbreaker," "Rock and Roll," "Dazed and Confused," and of course "Stairway." The "Whole Lotta Love" medley and "Moby Dick" took up an hour between them. And Jimmy's solos were stretching out as marathon showstoppers. There were times Robert wondered if he'd ever find his way back into a song. When he did, he'd slyly drop in a few bars of his own favorites, like "Hello, Mary Lou," "Money Honey," "Heartbreak Hotel," "It's Your Thing," "Everybody Needs Somebody to Love," even Simon & Garfunkel's "59th Street Bridge Song (Feelin' Groovy)." Loose—everyone was feeling loose.

This was a tour for showcasing much of ▩ ▩ ▩ ▩, but there were new songs that managed to wiggle their way into the set. Led Zeppelin introduced a smattering of songs in various stages of development—"The Ocean," "Dancing Days," "The Crunge," and "Over the Hills and Far Away." Unbeknownst to most of the fans, since early in the year, the musicians had been working on another new album.

## [3]

Jimmy had complained that recording ⚡︎⚜︎⊛①︎ was an uphill slog. "It was probably more painful to get this one out than childbirth," he said facetiously, and like many mothers who agonized through the ordeal, he was prepared to do it all over again. "My main goal . . . was just to keep rolling," he said.

Back in February 1972, Led Zeppelin spent a week rehearsing at Ilsington Farmhouse in Dorset, a setting for Thomas Hardy's *Tess of the d'Urbervilles*. It was owned by Arthur Brown, the singer who'd had the 1968 smash hit "Fire," and came with a built-in studio called Jabberwocky. Andy Johns had been replaced as engineer by Eddie Kramer, the whip hand of so many Jimi Hendrix sessions and wingman on *LZII*, who had flown over from the States to oversee the proceedings.

Returning to Headley Grange wasn't an option. The place was too tatty, too drafty to warrant another stay for young gods. Why skimp on accommodations with so much disposable income? The £1,000 weekly rent at Stargroves, Mick Jagger's country estate in Hampshire where *Sticky Fingers* had been recorded, now seemed reasonable, and Led Zeppelin moved there in May 1972, with Jimmy installing himself in Mick's posh bedroom.

Jimmy came prepared. He'd been recording "bits of taped ideas" in the home studio of his new Plumpton manor and was eager to see them expand and ripen into songs. So much depended on the creative input he received from John Paul, whose versatility often took Jimmy's fragments in unexpected directions. The same with Robert's words. In fact, the first thing they worked on at Stargroves was earmarked as an instrumental—Jimmy had even titled it "The Overture" as an intended lead-in to another song—that was retooled to stand on its own once Robert began putting words to it and figured out how to decrease the meter halfway in, so that it fit.

As an overture, it had sweep. It established an album prologue of sorts, filled with fanfare-like elements and grand drama, fitful syncopation, and nifty guitar flourishes that foreshadowed what lay ahead. It built with great urgency, full of pulsating bass, until Robert weighed in, and then the sudden shift in tone, a kind of woozy, hallucinatory digression, contradicted everything that came before and dragged it down as the charged energy drifted into pathos. The two passages seemed disconnected, patched together like an awkward blind date. Robert polished off the lyrics in one sitting, hitting on a much-preferable title when he sang the run-on lines, *"California sunlight, sweet Calcutta rain / Honolulu star bright—the song remains the same."*

The song might have worked better had it remained the curtain raiser to Jimmy's ballad with the working title "Slush," a tune born in his home studio that arrived practically intact. If "The Song Remains the Same" was inspired as an overture, this was the symphony he intended it to precede. Unlike the full-frontal attack of its predecessor, the poignancy of "Rain Song"—Led Zeppelin's first straightforward ballad, written with a nod to George Harrison's "Something"—was bathed in the warmth of lush orchestration and the right amount of understated grace.

Jimmy set the tone with a restrained, almost effortless twelve-string guitar introduction that provided immediate fluency. By the time Robert tiptoed in a few bars later, if only briefly, the inherent suppleness of the piece crystallized, allowing the guitar to introduce a new melodic theme that gave the song a fuller shape. The moment it settled in, John Paul amplified it with the string section of a Mellotron and a contrasting piano figure to build scale and emotion. Here were the two former session masters employing their most inventive skills, commenting on each other's riffs, returning to earlier themes, expressing them with new shades and voicings. When Robert reappeared, almost four minutes into the piece, he did so delicately at first, as though careful not to intrude, until the music invited him to turn it loose, to liberate the swelling accompaniment with a string of ad-libs and asides. Still, "Rain Song" never soared, never sought to become anything more than a gorgeously orchestrated ballad. After almost seven minutes, the vocals faded and the instrumentation began peeling away—first the piano, then the drums, and finally the Mellotron—before Jimmy's detuned acoustic guitar returned the song to its humble origins.

"Rain Song" was a departure for Led Zeppelin. Musically, it was epic, in the mode of "Stairway to Heaven" but without "Stairway's" colorful imagery and savage guitar solos. The song's reserved tone and orchestral pretensions called to mind the Moody Blues' *Days of Future Passed* more than, say, the sonic experimentation of Pink Floyd's soon-to-be-released *Dark Side of the Moon*. It bore none of the familiar Led Zeppelin attributes; it certainly wasn't riff-laden or metal. Would the fans accept it? No one knew nor cared. The band was determined to explore other sides of its personality.

"It's time that people heard something about us other than that we were eating women and throwing the bones out the window," Robert said.

They were leaving those honors to Black Sabbath, Deep Purple, and Sir Lord Baltimore, bands dependent wholly on distorted guitar riffs and brute force. Led Zeppelin hadn't entirely given up those impulses. They thrived playing all-out rockers. "The rock 'n roll is in all four of us, and on stage that's what comes through," Jimmy explained. But their objectives were constantly shifting.

"There is no place we wouldn't try and joyfully go," Robert said.

The joy was on particular display in two songs that emerged from the Stargroves sessions. "D'Yer Mak'er" owed its lineage to the band's attraction to ska and Caribbean music. Robert, especially, was influenced early by reggae.

"There were Jamaicans all over West Brum where we lived," says Kevyn Gammond, the guitarist from the Band of Joy who graduated to playing in Jimmy Cliff's band. "Growing up, Rob and I used to listen to their music in coffee bars like the Casa and the Ivy Bush. We bought their records on West Indian labels like Trojan. We cut our teeth in their clubs in Huddersfield and Smethwick and played to Black Jamaican audiences at the Ridgeway Georgian. 'D'Yer Mak'er' comes right out of those days."

Jimmy saw the song as "a cross between reggae and a Fifties number—'Poor Little Fool,' Ben E. King's things, stuff like that." But the result was more of a lark than an homage. (Jimmy referred to it as "just a giggle . . . a send-up.") The track itself was blistering, spurred by Bonzo's ferocious drum punctuation recorded in the house's glassed-in conservatory to make it sound "like bombs going off," as Eddie Kramer noted. Robert's vocal mimicked the heavily accented beat—"*Oh, oh, oh, oh, oh, oh / You don't have to go, oh, oh, oh, oh*"—but instead of digging into the rock-steady undertones, the band offered only a derivative calypso beat and ignored the idiom's stinging political commentary completely. The song's buoyancy caught the sly Jamaican feel, but it lacked conviction; it wasn't persuasive enough to succeed.

"The Crunge," on the other hand, just tried too damn hard. It set out to imitate the driving, funk-infested rhythms of so many James Brown rave-ups. Even a discriminating listener might have mistakenly assumed that Jimmy Nolen, Bootsy Collins, and Clyde Stubblefield contributed the signature backing track. It was all there—the chicken-scratch guitar, the hiccuping bass, the corn-popping drum pattern. But . . . the *vocals*! Robert explained how the original idea was for him and Bonzo to trash-talk in a barely understandable Black Country patois. That would have put a distinctive stamp on the song. Instead, Robert chose to prattle in a cringeworthy James Brown dialect, an impersonation that bordered on caricature.

Jimmy even nursed the idea of portraying the crunge as a dance, in the tradition of the boogaloo or the funky chicken, and to diagram the steps for it on the album sleeve.

Too many giggles, too many send-ups.

The band grew more serious in its approach to a song held over from the Bron-Yr-Aur period called "Many, Many Times." It suggested the pastoral Welsh countryside with a traditional folk-style intro that signaled a return to the spare, acoustic musings of *LZIII*. Robert supported the homespun flavor by singing over Jimmy's arpeggios with an awkward, amorous expression of vulnerability.

*"Hey lady, you got the love I need / Maybe, more than enough."*

The effect was disarming but a smokescreen. A few bars later, sturdy strumming redirected the musical flow, building steadily until the rhythm section leaped in whole hog—power chords, a pulsating bass, cascading drums, the works—demolishing all sentimentality. "The rhythm section on that is exceptional," Jonesy declared. "There's a lot of very, very tight, exciting moments." The song began to rock with significant muscle. In accordance, Robert's delivery veered into the upper atmosphere and gave the whole thing contour as he leaped contemplatively from line to line. *"Many have I loved, and many times been bitten / Many times I've gazed upon the open road."* The lyrics revealed Robert at his most introspective. An uncompromising guitar solo completed the quintessential Led Zeppelin touch.

Reassuringly, they had not given up the stance that, at heart, they were a rock 'n roll band. All their sessions were structured to allow for improvisational jams that often laid the groundwork for inventive new songs. At Stargroves, they polished off "Dancing Days," an uninhibited rocker that juxtaposed strains of Indian influence with a gutsy, combustive guitar riff that tethered the choppy tempos and kept the structure in check. They also laid down versions of "The Rover" and "The Ocean," both full-fledged riff rockers that hearkened back to "Whole Lotta Love" and "Communication Breakdown." "Black Country Woman," necessitating more work at a later date, was recorded outside on the lawn.

Stargroves was made for capturing ambient sound. Eddie Kramer recalled how they utilized every aspect of the house and grounds. "I remember putting a Fender amp in the fireplace and putting a mic in there," he said. "Jonesy's bass was in another room. Everybody's gear was in a different room." The house had expanse—but little warmth.

Jimmy wasn't satisfied with the sound they were getting, and Robert agreed.

"The sound in the place wasn't as good, recording-wise, as we'd got in . . . Headley Grange," he said.

They'd put a lot of very good work on tape, but rather than fighting the limited acoustics, they decided to pack it in and head to Olympic Sound.

There wasn't enough time, however, to finish the album, their fifth, in order for its release to coincide with their June 1972 tour in the U.S. Several songs still had to be recorded, too many guitar lines needed massaging with overdubs and effects. And Robert disappeared for a while, going home when Maureen gave birth to a son they named Karac, after a legendary Welsh general. By the time he returned, the tour was set to begin.


With so much more money at stake, the theme of the tour was Bigger and Better. "Everything would be sorted, so that the only thing Led Zeppelin had to worry about was playing music," according to Phil Carlo. Creature comforts made sense to reduce the demands of travel. Crowded commercial flights seemed counterproductive, so Peter Grant leased a nine-seat Dassault Fan Jet Falcon 20 to give the band privacy and freedom while schlepping from city to city. Cases of chilled champagne—and not just any champagne, but Dom Pérignon—accompanied each leg of the tour. Idling limousines awaited them outside the arenas. Private security replaced overaggressive police forces at gigs. And there was cocaine—they referred to it as "Charlie" or "Peruvian marching powder"—mounds of cocaine.

"Everybody was now doing it," recalls Phil Carson, "but the worst examples were Peter, Jimmy, and John Bonham."

Grant loved cocaine and had developed quite an appetite for it. He attributed his taste for it to a prescription following a tooth extraction, but taste turned to insatiable hunger after an incident on May 2,

1972. He had gone to Wales to see Stone the Crows play at Swansea University's graduation ball. The band remained one of his pet projects, owing in no small part to its soulful singer, Maggie Bell, and her charismatic boyfriend, guitarist Leslie Harvey. The Crows were readying their fourth album, and G wanted to touch base before leaving for America with Led Zeppelin. It was an impressive crowd, not only students but a full array of dignitaries. Les Harvey grabbed the mic to announce the first song and was thrown three feet into the air. When he hit the stage, he was dead, electrocuted by a wire that had been left ungrounded.

"Peter went to pieces," Maggie Bell recalls. "He broke down crying and found a way to numb the sorrow"—she makes snorting sounds to illustrate her point—"that we all felt over Les's death."

From that point on, coke became an essential part of Grant's wardrobe; he was never without a large plastic bag of it, "perhaps a kilo," says a stagehand. And he was generous in dispensing it. If you were part of the entourage, even for a short visit, you were invited to have a snort or two, and not just a line but something that resembled a garden hose. He proclaimed himself "the Bionic Hooter," assuring everyone that cocaine wasn't addictive.

But Pete Townshend, someone well versed on the subject, knew otherwise. "Whether you snort it or mainline it or take it in your mouth," said Townshend, who'd managed to wean himself off a steady diet, "it's addictive, and much more than just psychologically addictive. It's slower to get to you, but it gets you in the end."

There was no end in sight for Led Zeppelin. In fact, their coke adventures were just picking up steam.

The tour's Bigger and Better aspect had other drawbacks. The all-arena itinerary put the band at an even greater remove from the audience. Places like Cobo Arena in Detroit, the Spectrum in Philadelphia, the Montreal Forum, and especially Nassau Coliseum on Long Island were hellholes in which to hear a rock band. No matter how much money an act invested in a quality PA system—and Led Zeppelin's was state of the art—music reverberated in those concrete monsters, sounding more like a busy construction site than a concert hall. There was no intimacy, no way to appreciate the experience. And no matter how large the venue, it wasn't large enough to satisfy demand. Scalpers did land-office business in the shadows outside, demanding five or ten times the face value of tickets. At Nassau Coliseum it was reported they got as much as $200 for $8.50 seats in the nosebleed sections.

And bigger was relative when it came to recognition by the press. Night in, night out, Led Zeppelin played their hearts out, but the reviews didn't reflect the crowds' reactions. They got trashed by critics in *The Gazette* (Montreal), *The Washington Post*, *The Bulletin* (Philadelphia), *Newsday* (New York), and *The Seattle Times*. No review was as harsh, however, as the one filed by the *Los Angeles Times*'s Robert Hilburn for the June 25, 1972, performance at the Forum. Hilburn, never a Led Zeppelin fan but usually reasonable in his appraisals, considered the band so derivative that he found it "still hard to take them seriously." In his opinion, their set was "as tedious as ever (largely because their songs are so trivial in every way excepting occasional violent, high-volume outbursts)." It befuddled him that "the audience again seemed delighted."

Part of the backlash was due to scheduling. Only two nights earlier, the Rolling Stones had played the same Forum to great acclaim. Led Zeppelin had been caught in the Stones' vapor trail right across the United States. Everywhere they went, everyone they talked to could only gush about the Stones. What *was* it with that band, John Bonham wanted to know? "It's the Stones this, the Stones that," he griped. "It made us feel we were flogging our guts out, and for all the notice we've been given we might as well have been playing in Ceylon." The Stones continued to overshadow Led Zeppelin despite the fact that their latest album—*Exile on Main Street*, a double album to boot—had no hits on it, other than "Tumbling Dice."

Musically, Robert said, "they were a long way from where we were going."

It steamed Jimmy that the press treated Mick Jagger like royalty while barely mentioning him. "Who wants to know that Led Zeppelin broke an attendance record at such-and-such a place when Mick Jagger's hanging around with Truman Capote?" he complained.

What eluded him was that the Stones were *personalities*. They courted the press, whereas Led Zeppelin had shunned it. Their former press officer, Bill Harry, had made it clear his job was to keep the press *away*, and Harry's successor, BP "Beep" Fallon, would be more of a court jester than someone who had a relationship with serious journalists. Jimmy shunned most interviews, and when he did grant one, he was enigmatic or dismissive. The Stones were a publicity machine; they mixed comfortably with their fans. Keith Richards and Ronnie Wood never passed up photo requests from kids on the street or refused unsolicited handshakes. If a strange kid had reached out a hand to touch Jimmy or Robert, Richard Cole would have broken it.

There was satisfaction in knowing that Led Zeppelin's albums outsold the Stones'—and not by an insignificant margin. Jimmy was regarded as one of the best rock 'n roll guitarists of all time. Still, the Stones tour dominated the summer newspapers and trades. That damn band made Led Zeppelin insecure, and instead of keeping it to themselves, they brooded and bellyached. Reviewers were "so authoritative," Jimmy said. Many were "twits." The press didn't understand music; critics had it in for them. "They were too busy being messed up with all their preconceived ideas of what they expected to hear and outraged because there wasn't heavier rock or outraged because there wasn't enough—they didn't know what to write." It was galling.

Instead of sitting for interviews and raising their image on days off, Led Zeppelin retreated into the studio. In New York, they booked time at Electric Lady to continue work on the new LP with in-house engineer Eddie Kramer. Kramer was happier to have them on his turf. Working at Stargroves, while productive, had tested his concentration. "There were all sorts of scenes with Bonzo bursting in the room in the middle of the night," he said. And Robert had "bagged" the young woman who'd accompanied Eddie to England. At Electric Lady, it was all business. They recorded "Houses of the Holy," which, as it turned out, would not make the album cut, polished "No Quarter," left over from Headley Grange, and mixed almost everything from the Stargroves sessions. It was productive and pretty much wrapped things up. All the album needed was a name and a cover.

Once again, it was time to go to war.

## Chapter Twelve

# A LAW UNTO THEMSELVES

## [1]

Rock stars coveted spectacular trappings—the flashiest guitar, the loudest amp, the prettiest chick, the poshest house. Frankly, they were all easy to come by. More elusive, and definitely higher up on the chest-thumping scale, was an outlandish, drop-dead, eye-grabbing album cover.

Album covers had become fashionably hip, a way to flex muscle in the mine-is-bigger-than-yours competition. They stood for so much where sales were concerned. Before MTV, before *Saturday Night Live*, before Spotify, and before YouTube, a band's visual media exposure was limited to two or three decent music papers and a handful of sorry-ass TV shows. Bands who traded in being aloof and enigmatic (and bands who refused to release singles—like Led Zeppelin and Pink Floyd) got incalculable mileage from a sensational album cover. Interesting imagery delivered mystery, and mystery delivered sales. Led Zeppelin had made that clear with the triumph of ⚝ ⚶ ⊛ ⓘ.

Edgy cover art was a relatively new phenomenon. For years, record companies had kept tight creative control over the jackets. By and large, labels demanded they be illustrated by a photograph of the band, usually poorly shot in a studio setting, with the name of the act and the album in standard block lettering. Visiting a label's art department in London, one would encounter elderly men—men who'd serviced the great symphony orchestras and opera stars, men who despised rock 'n roll—wearing white lab coats and white gloves, just slapping text on jacket mock-ups. The early Beatles, Stones, and Yardbirds albums are perfect examples.

Peter Blake had changed that landscape. His cover for *Sgt. Pepper's Lonely Hearts Club Band* raised album jackets to an art form. *Sgt. Pepper's* unleashed a deluge of extraordinary covers—Andy Warhol's pop-art banana on the Velvet Underground and Nico's 1967 debut, the surrealist art on Miles Davis's *Bitches Brew*, and Blind Faith's controversial cover photo featuring a topless eleven-year-old girl holding a gold-plated model airplane. Perhaps more notable was Warhol's zipper cover for *Sticky Fingers*, perfectly expressing the Rolling Stones' image, as well as the music on the record itself.

Album design was one more aspect of the recording process that artists jockeyed to control. Fortunately for Led Zeppelin, that control was embedded in their contract with Atlantic, giving Jimmy Page the luxury to have the company meet his demands. Of course, labels never gave in without a fight. Jimmy had already gotten a preview of Atlantic's stubborn resolve in the conflict over ⚭ ⚮ ⊛ ⓘ. That was a resounding artistic *and* commercial success, and the game plan for the next release was to outdo it in every way.

Jimmy had his eye on an album cover by Wishbone Ash called *Argus* that depicted the back of a helmeted warrior gazing out at a misty mountainside. It had been designed by a studio called Hipgnosis, and he liked the sound of that too. The edgy studio, as it turned out, was the brainchild of two former Royal College of Art students, Storm Thorgerson and Aubrey Powell, who had subsisted since graduation by designing book covers and photographing centerfolds for men's magazines.

"We happened to be sharing a flat with Syd Barrett, when he was going out of his mind from too much LSD and Pink Floyd was falling apart," Powell recalls. "The Floyd had a meeting at our apartment, and during the course of it someone said, 'We have to have a new album cover, and we don't want the same old shit that the record company insists on.' David Gilmour immediately turned to Roger Waters and said, 'Why don't we give the guys a chance?'" Thorgerson and Powell did a mock-up—a gauzy image based on a Marvel Comics Doctor Strange story—and it became the cover for Pink Floyd's A *Saucerful of Secrets*, only the second cover (the first being *Sgt. Pepper's*) that EMI sanctioned from an independent design studio.

It was Hipgnosis's big break and opened the door for their offbeat craftsmanship, designing covers for the Pretty Things, Marc Bolan, and the Rolling Stones, each job earning them a princely $45.

Jimmy called Hipgnosis and said, "I wonder if you'd have a go coming up with some ideas for a Led Zeppelin cover?" He didn't give them much to go on—the album didn't have a title and there was no music they could listen to. "You know the kind of image Led Zeppelin has. I'm sure you've read about us. Meet us in three weeks."

On schedule, Powell and Thorgerson trooped up to RAK's grubby little office on Oxford Street. The entire band showed up, with everyone sitting cross-legged on the floor for the presentation, illustrated by several sketches on bits of cardboard. Powell opened by asking them if they'd read *Childhood's End* by Arthur C. Clarke. Robert, Jimmy, and John Paul had, and there was a mushroom of approval from Peter Grant, who observed from a distance.

Powell said, "We have an idea about going to Giant's Causeway in Northern Ireland and photographing a naked family running up some rocks, being spearheaded by a silver surfer figure, also naked, as if they were heading into outer space from the end of the earth."

It saluted the conclusion of *Childhood's End*, in which all the children of Earth suffer an explosion and are taken up into the heavens. There was some vague mumbo jumbo about the people climbing up rocks symbolizing Led Zeppelin's trying to attain the unattainable, which appealed to Jimmy in particular.

"It's a sort of dawn and dusk, this feeling of expectancy," he mused sometime later, "the children crawling to the top and what there they're going to find—bags of pollution and shit probably."

Robert loved the mythology surrounding the causeway, a stretch of underwater land that joined Scotland with Northern Ireland on which giants supposedly walked to get from one coast to the other.

The second idea was even wilder. The Hipgnosis duo explained their desire to visit the plain of Nazca in Peru, a World Heritage site, where enormous symbols that can be seen only from the air—spiders and strange animal shapes several kilometers wide—are gouged out of the earth. "It'd be interesting to go there and bulldoze the ZoSo logo," Thorgerson proposed. Hearing that, Jimmy percolated with excitement.

They had been kicking both ideas around for several hours without coming to a decision, when Peter Grant heaved himself up and interrupted. "Right, that's enough," he said to Powell and Thorgerson. "We've got other things to discuss. You decide what to do, whichever idea you feel is best." Money was no object. "Whatever it costs, *just don't fuck up.*"

Led Zeppelin was headed back to Japan for a second tour in October 1972, followed by several gigs in Switzerland as a warm-up to a longer string of European dates. They'd be back in London in six weeks and expected to see a finished cover.

*Just don't fuck up.* Coming from a heavy like G, it gave Powell and Thorgerson night sweats.

By process of elimination, the designers chose the causeway locale as being the least likely to get them into trouble. With free rein (and Led Zeppelin's money), their imaginations ran wild. They sought to create a *Lord of the Flies* atmosphere with children who looked otherworldly. For their template they used *The Midwich Cuckoos*, a science-fiction novel about children who all looked identical. A casting call went out for a young blond girl and boy, and soon enough an agency came through with two experienced ad models, seven-year-old Samantha Gates and her five-year-old brother Stefan. Three adults would round out the cast.

Powell met with the Gates children's parents and assured them there would be no frontal nudity, just from behind. But, he told them, it would be cold and miserable in Northern Ireland in October. The parents were completely okay with it. "It would *not* be okay today," Powell acknowledges.

Nor would it have been wise to take such a company to Northern Ireland at the height of the Troubles. "When our team arrived in Belfast," Powell says, alluding to his wife, the kids, their mother, the makeup artist, and the chaperones, "the car rental company warned me, 'You are not insured to drive in Northern Ireland. If you get stopped at roadblocks, always have your identification papers handy, and never go anywhere within twenty miles of Belfast, where carjackings are routine."

Fortunately, the causeway was deserted. The schedule was to get up at four o'clock in the morning, have the kids and adults made up, and get to the rocks for daybreak. Powell and Thorgerson imagined they'd photograph a gorgeous sunrise bursting over the rocks and the sea, but it poured nonstop for the five days they were there. Tom Smith, who would go on to be the makeup artist on *Raiders of the Lost Ark*, had planned to cover the children in gold paint, coating the Silver Surfer figure in silver paint, with only a skullcap for his wardrobe. But they ran out of gold paint early in the shoot and resorted to spray-painting the kids with automotive paint, to which their mother only reluctantly agreed. The contact sheets betrayed rain in the puddles between the rocks. The three adult models were deemed superfluous and sidelined. Armed border guards arrived to express displeasure with the crew's careless movements around the area. It was like revisiting the ten plagues, a woeful turn of events.

*Just don't fuck up.*

Desperation set in. The only way around the problems was to shoot everything in black-and-white, photograph the children multiple times, then blow up the images, cutting them together to form a collage, hand-tinting it so that it looked like a science-fiction fantasy. The process was tactile and time-consuming. The images had to be sanded so that they were paper-thin in order to create the collage, and the hand-tinting, done on a torpedo boat in the Thames, proved harrowing, a six-week process. Hipgnosis missed Grant's deadline.

G was pitiless. "Where's the fucking artwork?" He gave them an ultimatum. "I'll be arriving at St. Pancras Station tomorrow afternoon at four o'clock. Pick me and Jimmy up and show us the artwork." The *or else* was implicit.

The next day, Powell collected Grant and Jimmy outside St. Pancras and was told to drive them across town to Victoria Station. G deposited himself in the passenger seat of Powell's Mini Cooper, which Powell drove without changing out of second gear, due to Peter's girth being lodged firmly against the shift.

At Victoria, it took Powell and Jimmy a few minutes to free G from the seat, which caused great laughter. It was five o'clock, in the midst of rush hour, and as Powell popped the trunk to exhibit the artwork, a crowd of commuters gathered round. Grant held it up. "It's fucking incredible!" he declared. The inside gatefold was a photograph of Dunluce Castle, a sixteenth-century fortress just down the road from the Giant's Causeway. "*That's* the front cover," Jimmy decided. "I love it."

Powell was adamant. "*No,* Jimmy. The other photo is better," and the crowd broke into applause, endorsing his argument.

What held up release of the album, now entitled *Houses of the Holy,* was the printing of the cover. Powell—now affectionately nicknamed Po by the band—was sent to oversee the presses in New York. The four-color process there was prehistoric. This was before the days of sophisticated ink-jet printing, and reproducing the multitude of subtle colors on the hand-tinted cover was complicated, ticklish. The record-company plants that manufactured the covers were used to printing photographs of Frank Sinatra and were not always diligent in their handiwork.

"The first load of colors that came off were appalling," Po recalls.

Jimmy took one look at the result and agreed. "The sky started to look like an advert for Max Factor lipstick," he said, "and the children looked as if they'd turned purple from the cold."

Po stopped the presses and demanded they regenerate the covers from scratch based on the original artwork. But such an undertaking would delay the album further, possibly precluding it from being available in time for a massive U.S. tour. Peter Grant, Steve Weiss, even Ahmet Ertegun expressed displeasure—extreme displeasure— about incurring a delay. It could put a lot of income at stake, multimillions of dollars. Admirably, perhaps suicidally, Po stood his ground. "You would not be happy," he assured the men he described as "sharp people," heavy hitters.

Ahmet Ertegun, to his credit, ordered that the covers be scrapped at enormous expense and insisted they be reprinted overnight. It was a bottom-line business decision; sales of the first four Led Zeppelin albums accounted for a quarter of the annual sales of the entire Atlantic catalog. The cover rerun wasn't perfect but satisfied the situation—just not *every* situation. Once promotional albums were distributed, an uproar arose from radio stations in the American Midwest. *The children's naked bottoms!* This was sinful, an affront to moral decency. Bible-thumpers intended to have the album banned. "So we had to put a white band around the center of the cover that said 'Led Zeppelin' on it to hide the kids," Po said. "Truthfully, I thought it added to the mystery."

Indeed, *Houses of the Holy* mystified critics and fans alike when it was released on March 28, 1973. It had all the ambition of 𝄞 △ ⊕ ① but none of its pluck. The meandering crosscurrents of the music stopped some listeners cold as it hopped from rock to folk to reggae to funk, then doubled back to cover psychedelic and thrash. But there were qualitative obstacles as well. Robert's voice on "The Song Remains the Same," buried in the mix, sounded too distant and impersonal, not easily embraced. Although it would explode like a time bomb on stage, "The Rain Song" squandered the power of "Stairway to Heaven" and lacked the fire of "The Battle of Evermore." The former "Many, Many Times"—now entitled "Over the Hills and Far Away"—was sharp and feverish, a true highlight, as was "No Quarter" for its textural brevity, but "The Crunge" and "D'Yer Mak'er" floundered in cheeky contrivance.

"Maybe you could attack 'The Crunge' and 'D'Yer Mak'er' for being a bit self-indulgent," Jimmy conceded, "but they're just a giggle. They're just two send-ups."

"There was a lot of imagination on that record," Robert said in retrospect. "I prefer it much more than the fourth album. I think it's much more varied and it has a flippance [sic] which showed up again later."

It took more than a cursory listen to appreciate the album's breadth. There were incisive pleasures embedded in its crevices that held the melodic fabric together, but the something-for-everybody aspect disrupted the flow of the record so that it wasn't instantly *comfortable*. It wasn't an obvious Led Zeppelin album; a first listen yielded a collective *huh?* Criticism was predictably withering. *Rolling Stone* dismissed it as "a limp blimp . . . one of the dullest and most confusing albums." *Music World* called it "a clunker." *Disc and Music Echo* faulted it for being "strangely sluggish" and "inconsistent." The review in *Phonograph Record* began, "It's time to bring out the Sominex again." The critics' constant din was becoming insufferable. There were the usual suck-ups in *Melody Maker* and *NME*—*NME* found the barefaced cheek to call *Houses of the Holy* "an album of the highest quality possible"—that offered flattery instead of constructive criticism. Perhaps the most accurate evaluation, in *Let It Rock*, stated, "Unlike the previous Zep albums, this one takes a few listenings to assimilate."

"People still have this preconceived notion of what to expect," Jimmy accurately observed. "How they should approach our albums is to forget they ever heard of a band called Led Zeppelin, forget about what they expect to hear and just listen to what's on that particular record. That's all we ask, but we don't get it."

The fans were impatient when it came to letting an album open and breathe like a fine wine, unwilling to bear with a band's creative exploration. Change and evolution? Not from Led Zeppelin, brother. They wanted instant gratification, reassurance that Led Zeppelin was the heaviest, headbangingest, mainlining band on record, *this* record and the next one and the next after that. It was the reason that after five years and forty-three songs, the first shout-out from the audience that cut through every live performance was: "'*Whole Lotta Love!*' '*Whole Lotta Love!*'"

The mystery was no longer working. It was time to bring in the cavalry.

## [2]

Led Zeppelin wanted recognition.

That seemed absurd coming from a band considered the number-one rock act in the world. But in April of 1973, they were still smarting over being overshadowed by the Stones on their last American tour and fuming at the attacks on *Houses of the Holy*. They wanted star treatment.

Led Zeppelin wanted to be loved.

Their fans loved them, but they wanted warmth and affection from the mainstream rock press—*Creem*, *Crawdaddy*, and the iniquitous *Rolling Stone*, where Zep were looked upon as bottom-feeders and deemed uncool.

Led Zeppelin wanted to be cool.

They needed to change their image, to do a makeover of sorts, tucking in their shirttails while preserving a strain of the devilish DNA from their bad-boy bloodlines. BP Fallon, last seen masterminding Marc Bolan's rise from elfin folkie to glam rock pinup for girls in training bras, wasn't up to the job. His PR beat was confined mainly to England, where his twinkle-toed, elfin game was tolerated by the rock press. He boasted that he was "the entertainment manager." He dressed glam—feathers, fur, and glitter. In the States that approach was viewed as toxic. No, Led Zeppelin needed a heavyhitter, and Steve Weiss, who dealt in heavyhitters, legitimate or otherwise, knew just such a guy.

Weiss went to the top of the PR food chain, contacting Lee Solters, the godfather of press agents. The firm Solters/Sabinson/Roskin represented just about every show-business colossus—Frank Sinatra, Barbra Streisand, a majority of the Broadway shows, Caesars Palace in Las Vegas, and Ringling Bros. and Barnum & Bailey Circus. How Led Zeppelin fit into their roster was anyone's guess, but Weiss wanted PR muscle and Solters was about as muscular as it got. Lee was old school—the prototypical paunchy, broad-shouldered, wavy-haired, thick-glasses, Jewish Hollywood tough guy—a workaholic who ate lunch at his desk and stayed there well into the night.

Solters had just hired a twenty-two-year-old college dropout and failed journalist named Danny Goldberg to shore up his pop music department. Goldberg had street cred, he'd worked for Bob Dylan's and Janis Joplin's manager, Albert Grossman, and he loved rock 'n roll, the real thing, not the pretty-boy acts in Solter's Rolodex. Danny's turf was the late-night Greenwich Village club scene, with backstage access to the Fillmore East and, more important, the tastemakers at Max's Kansas City.

Solters had popped his head into Goldberg's cubicle and said, "Led Zeppelin—do we want them?"

That was a tough call. Danny's tastes ran to Hendrix, Cream, Dylan, the Stones, the Dead, Tim Hardin. He was definitely not a Led Zeppelin fan. To him, "Led Zeppelin was not only not cool, they were uncool." It would blow his authenticity sky high.

Nevertheless, he wanted them. "Yeah, of course, they're big," he told Solters, who knew zip about the rock 'n roll world.

Danny explained they had a very mixed reputation. They were known for being unpleasant to journalists, and he laid out their exploits in dealing with Ellen Sander, the *Life* magazine reporter who had had her dress ripped away by John Bonham. They'd never get mileage from any of the sixties music critics. "We'll be walking into a negative attitude with the rock press," he cautioned Solters.

Didn't matter. It was money in the bank.

Solters and Goldberg agreed to make their pitch on April 1, 1973, in Paris, where Led Zeppelin was appearing at the Palais des Sport. The band was holding court at Hotel George V, where throwing TV sets and furniture out the window would have gotten them a swift French boot. Everyone was on his best behavior. To keep the band entertained, high-class prostitutes were hired and a private sex show was arranged so they could watch two women making love to each other. Peter Grant, like a pasha, conducted business in his suite.

"Tell Peter what you told me," Solters instructed Danny Goldberg.

Danny swallowed hard. He'd heard plenty of stories about Grant's snarly reputation, how he'd just as soon flick someone away with the back of his hand as deal with a pest. He certainly looked the part, a huge, fierce hombre in a Fu Manchu mustache and beard, an undisguised comb-over, blue jeans big enough to reupholster a sofa, with flashy turquoise rings on his fingers and silk scarves draped around his neck.

What the hell, Danny thought—he'd give it to Peter straight. "Look, the band has a reputation of being barbarians," he said.

G stared at him stone-faced, not giving much away . . . and then he grinned, a big Colgate smile. "Yes, but we're *mild* barbarians," he said, laying on extreme charm.

*Mild barbarians.* It worked for Danny Goldberg. Lee Solters loved it; it was an angle, he told Danny, that would play in the press.

The next day Danny met with the mild barbarians, preparing himself to be treated the way they manhandled most journalists. Instead, they reached out to him and asked thoughtful questions, especially Robert, who made it seem as if it had been his idea to hire a publicist. Fame, Robert felt, *real* fame still eluded Led Zeppelin. He lamented that his father didn't understand how successful he was. And it continued to bum him out that the Stones had gotten more press on their last tour. The *covers* of magazines. With Truman Capote. *The Stones!* Those wankers weren't worthy of Led Zeppelin's groupie castoffs.

Jimmy also bad-mouthed the critics, more so about the bad album reviews than about the Stones. He still had it out for John Mendelssohn. Mendelssohn had poisoned the well for rock journalists, as far as Jimmy cared. And even house pet Chris Welch was now on Jimmy's shit list for a tepid *Houses of the Holy* review in *Melody Maker*.

Peter introduced what he called "the barbarians thing," unconvinced that it was bad for their reputation.

"Look, we were very young when we first started," Robert admitted. "We're over all of that now."

Danny took him at his word. It was solid—and it wasn't.

There wasn't time to ease into a proper press campaign. Led Zeppelin was due to arrive in America for a three-month summer tour on May 1, 1973. And it wouldn't be another version of Bigger and Better. They were going for Epic—playing stadiums the size of small cities in order to break all attendance records. In fact, the show itself would be equally grandiose. They'd given almost as much thought to the production as they had to the music—*dramatic* changes, no longer just four blokes in jeans and T-shirts standing in front of Marshall stacks and a few beams of spotlight. There was going to be *staging* and *wardrobe* and *special effects*, with a director named Ian Knight to coordinate the whole extravaganza.

The last week in April, the band and production crew moved into Shepperton Studios, where *Dr. Strangelove* and *Oliver* had been filmed and where Peter Grant had done stand-in work in *The Guns of Nava-rone*. A sound stage was the perfect place to run through "the new bits and pieces," as Jimmy referred to "No Quarter" and "The Ocean," while ironing out the atmospherics. A large-scale production was nothing to take superficially. There was an igloo's worth of dry ice, exploding cannon fire, a couple of mirrored balls that rotated overhead, strobes, and a refraction mechanism—an eight-foot convex disc covered with broken glass that would be positioned to the right of Bonzo. "When you put the spotlights on all of this," Robert explained, "it should be like being in the middle of a diamond."

Lighting itself was going to be a spectacle. Showco, a production company out of Texas, had built a lighting apparatus on a hydraulic ram. "It was a big box," explained Benji Le Fevre, a new addition to Led Zeppelin's road crew, "and you pushed a button and out came a pod with eight or ten power lamps on it." Their intensity befit the name "Super Troopers." In addition, there would be three scaffolding towers onstage with follow spots so Robert's hair would be lit to emulate the Second Coming and another follow spot to match the beats of Jimmy's violin bow.

The output of sound was designed to be heard in the next county. "The idea was to put up as many speakers as you could with as many amplifiers as you could, and turn it all up to *eleven*," Le Fevre said. The tour also had the very first Eventide Digital Delay device, which added a clean echo to Robert's voice and fed it back into itself to make his voice soar. They could now digitally set two delay times so that his single voice would be three—and even feed it back onto itself so that it would be six or twelve, producing a veritable Robert Plant chorus. This way, it could duplicate how he sounded on records, which excited him and got him more fully involved.

Jimmy wasn't inclined to play second fiddle. Now that Robert was getting star treatment, Jimmy sought to fortify his share of the turf. He intended to be able to play his guitar *backward*. In the recording studio, he simply reversed the tape and *ssssssswt*, instant backward guitar. But live, it was impossible to play a note before it had been played. To get around that, he developed with his Echoplex tape-delay effect a system whereby he would play and record something, then it would play back in a loop so that he could play against it—not quite backward, but mesmerizing nevertheless. It would definitely stand up to Robert's high profile.

Such a spectacle required comparable attire, custom-made clothing to give the musicians pizzazz. "We decided that the denim trip had been there for too long," Robert said.

"Sparkly clothes became available," John Paul added.

Jimmy chose a matador-style jacket stitched with hummingbirds along either lapel. He also had a stunning white linen suit with red poppies on the front and *ZoSo* stitched on the back to stand out against whatever guitar he draped sash-like across his chest. Robert picked out a series of hand-dyed vests, usually open to reveal his décolletage, with a long silk scarf knotted at his neck and tight pants that bordered on the obscene.

"I got a silly jacket with pom-poms," said John Paul, hardly the fashionista, "because the people who made Page's dragon suit came by with a vanload of clothes, and we all just went, 'Oh, *that* looks fun." Another of his jackets had oversize hearts sewn onto the sleeves. It would never make the cover of *GQ*.

What Led Zeppelin did make was the Sunday edition of the *New York Daily News*, which had the largest circulation of any newspaper in the U.S. Danny Goldberg used every last drop of goodwill he had with the *News*'s Lillian Roxon, the doyenne of rock journalists, to have her cover the band's arrival at JFK. "Please don't ask me to see this fucking group," she pleaded. She had zero interest in their music. "But this is a news article," Danny assured her, and in the end she let him spoon-feed her the story. He also managed to corral *Disc & Music Echo's* New York correspondent, Lisa Robinson, to accompany the band to Atlanta, where they were set to open the tour on May 3.

So began the practice of co-opting rock writers. With a mandate

to court the press and an unlimited budget to do it, the way to ensure good copy was to make writers feel like they were part of the Led
Zeppelin entourage, give them VIP access, and make sure they were
well taken care of. It was relatively easy to take care of a journalist,
most of whom made hardly enough to cover their rent. The band
picked up the cost of their plane tickets, provided them with hotel
suites, plied them with liquor and food and in some cases cocaine and
prostitutes, gave them front-row seats to the shows and backstage
passes for afterward. A quid pro quo was understood—they'd basically write puff pieces.

The show in Atlanta would be a bellwether. It was meant to change
the course of everything—Led Zeppelin's place in the rock pantheon
and their image with the press. An epic required epic strategies. Whatever it took. Cost was no factor. The stairway to heaven wasn't always
paved with the best intentions.

## [3]

Atlanta Stadium was enormous, more than fifty thousand seats, which
had challenged no less than the Beatles in 1965. Playing music to a
crowd of that size conjured Ben-Hur in the Roman Colosseum. It was
surreal, there was an element of gladiatorial bloodlust involved. The
stage alone deserved a zip code—it was eighty feet by thirty-five feet,
comparable to the dimensions used to put on a three-ring circus—
with thirty-three technicians covering its expanse. Concrete crash
barriers ten feet high lined a tract in front of the stage to hold back the
crowd like a seawall. The entire setup was larger than life, and when
Led Zeppelin took to the stage—a half hour late, not bad considering
their track record—two sixteen-by-twenty-four-foot screens on either
side of the stage assured the capacity crowd that life-size images of
Jimmy, Robert, Jonesy, and Bonzo would loom over the stadium.

Robert was a bit nervous appearing in front of such a multitude.

Looking out over the vast sweep of humanity, he flashed on a show
Led Zeppelin had done in January in Aberystwyth, Wales, near the
Bron-Yr-Aur cottage. "It was a very well-meant gesture on the part of
Jimmy and me, intended to drag Bonzo and John Paul up there and
give something back to the mountains and the people," he recalled.
"We felt quite warm vibes about the place and, so, when we set up our
last tour we said, 'Wouldn't it be a gas if we did Aberystwyth?' Like a
nostalgic thing." They'd played a tiny hall that held about eight hundred people—"bearded, pipe-smoking folk," as Robert recalled them,
who were "just aghast." They couldn't have been less interested and
talked through the show. "I remember Bonzo bashing away and giving me one of those looks that said, 'This was a fookin' good idea,
wern it?'"

The Atlanta crowd splashed cold water on that memory. Everything about Atlanta was otherworldly. It took Robert a few minutes
to get his sea legs. But the *sound!* As soon as they launched into "Rock
and Roll," that place shook so hard it might have come loose from its
moorings. Bonzo had a new Ludwig Vistalite drum kit that replicated
the artillery fire at the Battle of Pickett's Mill. It sent out as many
shock waves as it did the backbeat. The light show made eyes spiral,
smoke bombs rattled skeletal cages. The production was something to
see—and feel.

A gust of dry ice clouded the floor of the stage during the first few
notes of "No Quarter," allowing Jimmy and Robert to emerge from
the mist like Arthurian knights. Danny Goldberg, who was standing
in the wings, recalled watching "a teenage boy's jaw literally drop at
the sight of a laser beam hitting the mirror ball as Robert sang the last
line of 'Stairway to Heaven.'"

The next morning, during breakfast at the Atlanta Hilton, the four
musicians gathered around a copy of *The Atlanta Constitution*, whose
front page was dominated by three photos of the concert. A headline
proclaimed, STADIUM ROCKS: LED ZEPPELIN PLAYS TO 50,000. It was coverage they'd never gotten before; things were looking up.

Peter Grant was far from satisfied. He got into Danny Goldberg's face and said, "This is Atlanta. We've got to get somebody to say that it's the biggest thing that happened here since the premiere of *Gone with the Wind*."

"Do *you* want to say it?" Goldberg asked. It seemed to him such an irrational request.

"No, no—somebody important has to say it," G insisted. "Just make sure it fucking happens."

Panicked, not wanting to incur Peter's wrath, Danny told Lisa Robinson that the mayor of Atlanta, Sam Massell, had said it. "I'm pretty sure she knew I was lying," Danny says, "but she dutifully led with it in her column. The mayor's office never complained. No one there ever noticed it, but Peter saw it, and it established a trust that I was listening to him."

The next night, in Tampa, Led Zeppelin broke the Beatles' record for a single performance—at New York's Shea Stadium in August 1964—drawing a crowd of 56,443, a fact picked up by the two major wire services and republished in newspapers across the United States. A festive atmosphere was palpable. As *The Tampa Times* reported, "The majority of the crowd had arrived at the stadium by 3 p.m. in the afternoon to secure coveted positions on the field." Frisbees flew back and forth across the bleachers, and giddy fans were tossed high into the air on tautly held blankets. But in Tampa, the band found it harder to connect. Gusty winds prohibited putting up the video screens, making intimacy almost impossible to achieve. The excitement was lost on a lot of fans at the back. Robert could feel it; the backbenchers were left to pick up on the vibe as best they could. The crew tried to make up for the remoteness by resorting to gimmickry. During the "Whole Lotta Love" medley, two crates of white doves were released from the stage, turning the stadium into a cheering, worshipful mass. By the finale, "Communication Breakdown," the entire crowd was on its feet.

The tour adopted its own surge of momentum. Jacksonville, Tuscaloosa, Mobile, New Orleans, Houston, Dallas, and right across the American Southwest, with the Led Zeppelin engine chugging at full throttle, a remarkable driving force. Immense crowds—*immense*. Shows lasting an average of three hours *without a break*. Unimaginable wads of cash jammed into Peter Grant's bulging red holdall. At 90 percent of the net receipts, there was often several hundred thousand dollars at a clip resting between G's legs on plane flights.

*Disc's* Lisa Robinson, now part of the band's entourage, churned out the kind of copy that might have come from a PR factory's assembly line. "I had heard that on a good night Led Zeppelin is magic, is Rock 'n Roll," she wrote after the Jacksonville gig. "This has GOT to be what Rock 'n Roll was all about; what it was meant to be." In New Orleans, she heaped praise on Jimmy, noting that "his guitar-playing is so consistently great. Perhaps he only hears the differences each night; to us mortals it just sounds SO bloody GREAT."

Local, honest-to-goodness critics were less effusive. The *St. Louis Post-Dispatch* considered the Led Zeppelin show an "unusual, maddening performance." It was too big, too loud, too *too*. The *Mobile Press-Register* reviewer decided "the band just isn't inventive enough, or varied enough, to warrant three hours." The Dallas critic had a bone to pick about the group's identity, that Led Zeppelin "has become a showcase for individual stars . . . and that rock music may have lost something in the process," while his colleague in San Antonio dismissed the concert as "a show one could take or leave."

But critics be damned. Led Zeppelin's fans, the ultimate judges of showmanship, critics whose opinions were registered in ticket and record sales, expressed general agreement that the band delivered everything they had hoped for—the staging, the theatrics, the enthusiasm, the *music*. The audiences were totally involved, from "the thunderous opening notes of 'Rock and Roll' blasting through 33,000 watts of amplification" to the high-octane encore, "Communication Breakdown," often played well after midnight. The excitement in those arenas never let up. The experience, for most kids, was unforgettable.

At the end of May, Led Zeppelin took over the ninth and eleventh floors of the Continental Hyatt House, their home away from home on Sunset Boulevard in Los Angeles. It served as their base for two sold-out shows at the Forum, as well as bookend gigs in San Diego and San Francisco. The band couldn't wait to get to LA. There were plenty of sensual pleasures to be gleaned on the road, but nothing compared to the hedonism of California.

"L.A. in particular was like Sodom and Gomorrah," Jimmy said. "You just ate it up and drank it down."

He'd been indoctrinated with the city's charms by Jackie DeShannon in 1964, and from that time on he'd indulged himself freely. He pushed the boundaries of what was acceptable behavior and what he was entitled to by virtue of his place in the pantheon. To a disciple of Aleister Crowley, there was no such thing as excess. *Do what thou wilt shall be the whole of the law.* Nothing, no desire or fantasy, should be denied, no matter how extravagant, immoderate, wicked, or plain offensive. Drugs, sex, pain, degradation, you name it. Women? Sure, whatever you wanted. They were there to feed the egos and urges. And they were disposable.

In LA, Led Zeppelin were a law unto themselves. "It was the feeling of 'We can do absolutely anything,'" Jimmy said. "There were no rules." Besides, where the girls were concerned, he'd famously said, "Everyone knows what they come for."

The Hyatt House was crawling with women—*young girls*—when Led Zeppelin arrived. Rodney Bingenheimer, who owned Rodney's English Disco, put the word out when the band hit town. "He was like the Pied Piper or Mercury, the guy who led all these rich debutantes from Pacific Palisades and grubby Valley girls to the front door of the hotel," says Michael Des Barres. "There would always be a phalanx of beautiful Porsches driven by teenage girls behind Rodney, who sat regally in the back of a Cadillac."

Richard Cole would scope out the prettiest candidates—he knew each musician's tastes, his proclivities—and make sure the girls had access to the restricted floors, where private security patrolled the corridors. The coke dealers also got a pass. "Management made it all run smoothly," Des Barres says. "The elevator guys were getting their cocks sucked. They were in on the game."

When it came to frolicking in LA, Jimmy Page had his hands full. Since Led Zeppelin's performance at the Whisky in 1969, he'd had an ongoing relationship with Pamela Miller, a doe-eyed, twenty-one-year-old "muse" (a gussied-up term for groupie) from Reseda, California, whom everyone referred to as Miss Pamela or Miss P, depending on the degree of intimacy. She and Jimmy weren't exclusive. Jimmy, of course, had Charlotte Martin and his daughter stashed at home in England. Another girlfriend, Catherine James, drifted in and out of his life. And Miss Pamela had her share of rock-star lovers, among them Jim Morrison, Noel Redding, Chris Hillman, and Mick Jagger. But Miss P had been through the wars with Jimmy Page, from giving him extensive notes on the band's albums to accompanying him on a buying trip of Crowley artifacts to entertaining his "wicked sexual side" and fascination with a suitcase full of whips, chains, and handcuffs.

"Pamela *loved* Jimmy," says Michael Des Barres, who later, for a short time, became her husband. "He was the love of her life to a great degree. Jimmy desperately wanted to connect, and Pamela is the person to connect to because she is so guileless, with an open heart. She has great style and is a great therapist, who happens to be really sexy. She adores music and has great musical knowledge. She brought out in Jimmy what he really needed."

But the bedrock of girlfriends, like LA's tectonic plates, was shifting, realigning. Jimmy was tiring of Miss P. Now twenty-four, she had, he felt, outlived her shelf life. There were more desirable—younger—muses in the pipeline, and Jimmy had his eye on a successor.

Beep Fallon had shown him a picture of several "models" who'd appeared in a rag called *Star* that made the rounds at Rodney's British Disco. There was a layout in the June 1973 issue entitled "Your Very Own Superfox" that was basically an excuse to publish photos that sexualized underage girls. Some of the copy, for want of a better word, expressed the publication's underlying intention. "It is written that the time must come for a girl to move forward and up from the ranks of the shy, blushing Teenybopper, and to express herself as a brave new woman in a brave new world."

During an earlier LA visit when Beep was in town with a band called Silverhead, a few of these girls wound up in his hotel room at the Hyatt House. Two, in particular, caught his fancy: Sabel Shields, a fifteen-year-old from Palos Verdes who was known throughout the club scene as Sable Starr, and Lori Mattix, a friend of hers who had just turned fourteen.

Lori recalls, "We were cutting school, very much part of the scene, hanging out at the Mainman house," a crash pad headed by David Bowie's manager, Tony Defries, where a party was in full swing twenty-four hours a day. "*Star* had dressed us up to look like groupies. Sable really was one; she was the original groupie, an iconic, legendary character who had lost her virginity to David Bowie when she was twelve and was dating Jim Osterberg—Iggy Pop."

Michael Des Barres, the vocalist for the band Silverhead, who had accompanied the two girls to Beep's room, says, "Sable's morality was something out of Hieronymus Bosch. She was capable of anything."

"She was after Jimmy [Page]," says Lori, who also claimed to have lost her virginity to David Bowie a year earlier in the singer's suite at the Beverly Hilton after being braced with champagne and ganja.

Beep decided to photograph the girls but became infatuated with Lori. "Oh my God, Jimmy's going to love you!" he exclaimed.

He intended to share Lori's picture with Jimmy, along with an offer to introduce them. He saw nothing improper about the transaction. "Why would I not photograph her?" Beep offered in his defense. "The thing about groupies that's misunderstood is that it was all consensual. The girls were the predators, not the bands."

In any case, he showed Jimmy the photos while Led Zeppelin was performing in Texas. As Beep had figured, there was instant attraction. Lori was tall, darkly Italianate, and very pretty, with a suggestive allure that was well beyond her years. "She's magnificent," Jimmy cooed. "Give me her phone number."

Later that night, Lori's phone rang. "Hi, this is Jimmy Page. I'm going to meet you when I'm in LA."

Figuring it was a crank call, she hung up on him.

The competition was fierce in LA. There were girls at the Hyatt, at Rodney's, at the Whisky, and at the Roxy. There were girls backstage, in the bathrooms, and under the beds. Girls "outrageously gorgeous, draped over one another, rubbing against one another, caressing each other in their seductive dance," ratcheting up the heat. "They came out of the woodwork," says Vanessa Gilbert, an eighteen-year-old recent high-school graduate at the time, who was part of Led Zeppelin's SoCal entourage.

Gilbert and her friend, Gyl Corrigan-Devlin, were living at the Chateau Marmont, earning their keep by doing drug runs to Mexico. "I happened to drive by the Hyatt House and [the marquee] said WELCOME LED ZEPPELIN. Gyl was in Mexico on a run and instructed me to call Richard Cole, whom she knew, so we could see the guys when she returned. They got us our own room key, an expense tab, took us to Trader Vic's with them, and the Roxy, where they pushed all the tables together to accommodate all the girls. You always felt like you were at a happening with Led Zeppelin. The energy was high, the music was loud, the girls were game, and the drugs were pure."

Occasionally, to scope out the youngest girls on tap, they'd head to Rodney's, where Watneys Red Barrel and Bass ale were imported to enhance the British disco vibe. "Rodney's was amazing," recalls Lori, a denizen of the club, "prepubescent teenagers dressed up like groupies, glam rock, the best music, no age limit."

"It was a glitter cathedral, like *Clockwork Orange*," says Rodney Bingenheimer, its master of ceremonies. "We had a mirrored dance floor and strobe lights. Every kind of girl you could imagine. The kids wore vintage stuff they bought at Granny Takes a Trip and Berman's

Costumes, and four-inch platforms from Ed Slattern's. They dressed 'beyond' because people wanted to look at themselves in the mirrors. And the girls wanted to be noticed by the rock stars. We'd get a call in advance that Led Zeppelin was coming. We'd clear the VIP section, have the beer ready, tell the girls—the Rodnettes—to be ready for anything."

If you were Led Zeppelin, you had the pick of the litter—mostly junior high school girls from the Valley, Palos Verdes, or Orange County. "These guys were party animals, beyond party animals," Bingenheimer said. "The wild guy, of course, was Bonham. Robert was a little crazy. John Paul Jones never participated. And Page just observed."

Jimmy was a voyeur. He found the action interesting to watch and occasionally encouraged it with commentary. But he liked his privacy; he rarely made the first move. "If you went to a disco or a club with him, he wouldn't go up to girls," Danny Goldberg recalled. "He would want the road manager or someone else to get them to come over. A 'Jimmy wants to meet you' kind of thing."

That's how it happened during a pool party on the roof of the Hyatt House. It was a rowdy, high-spirited affair. Lots of young girls in bikinis—and less. Jimmy, who did not know how to swim, steered clear of the action as one nubile lass after the next got thrown into the deep end. His radar zeroed in on Lori Mattix, the fourteen-year-old, whom he recognized from Beep's photos. He let it be known to her that she was on his radar.

That same night, there was a caravan to Rodney's—the band, a stable of young girls, many of whom had been at the rooftop pool party, and the usual cordon of minders to keep gawkers away. Jimmy showed up with Miss Pamela but took Lori aside long enough to whisper, "I told you I was going to be with you."

"Please," she implored him, "you're going to get me in trouble with my friends."

She had been warned by Sable Starr to keep her hands off Jimmy.

His relationship with Miss P was rumored to be on the rocks, and Sable intended to move in on him postbreakup. It wasn't a gentle warning. Sable had said, "If you go near Jimmy, I'll kill you," and Lori took her at her word.

No one knew that better than Rodney Bingenheimer. He'd seen a lot go down that put him on his guard. "The girls would scratch your eyes out if you crossed their path," he said.

The action soon moved from Rodney's to the Rainbow Bar & Grill, where the crowd was slightly older, the music harder, less glam. Following several rounds of drinks and lines of coke, Richard Cole and Peter Grant grabbed Lori in the parking lot outside the club and hustled her into a waiting limo. "If you move, we'll have your fucking head," she was told. Richard jumped in next to her and told the driver to take off.

"Where are you taking me?" she cried. She was fourteen and frightened. These men meant business. It felt to her like she "was being kidnapped."

At the Hyatt, she was escorted up to Led Zeppelin's ninth-floor stronghold and marched down the corridor into a candlelit anteroom to one of the suites. A man sitting there in a wide-brimmed hat and holding a cane looked up at her in a slow reveal.

"I told you I'm going to have you," Jimmy Page said.

He was a man of his word. "He just swept me off my feet and made me fall madly in love with him," Lori says. "He was the rock-god prince to me, a magical, mystical person who was really convincing. I know he fell in love with me because of my innocence. He was twenty-nine; I was fourteen. It was no secret he liked young girls."

The age difference was an obvious concern for Jimmy. In 1973, scrutiny of such matters was pretty loose, but dating a girl who was in the eighth grade pushed the limits. "He had the respect enough to call on my mother," Lori says. "He didn't want to get in trouble because I was underage. He worried she might have him thrown in jail."

There was little chance of that. Lori's mother, who ran the concession stand at Chasen's restaurant, understood the byways of Hollywood. She'd even accompanied her daughter and Sable Starr on their first visit to the upper floors of the Hyatt House, when Silverhead was the main babe attraction. She knew the score. "My mom knew that I wasn't a virgin," Lori says. But Jimmy Page was another matter. He was the big score. "She knew he was a huge rock star. He sent me flowers and limousines. She said, 'Well, Priscilla's with Elvis . . . Lori's with Jimmy Page.'"

Lori knew he lived with Charlotte Martin and their daughter in England. But he assured her, "She's not in tune with me or what my needs are. There is no romance left."

For the most part, they kept a low profile, confining their swooning to Jimmy's suite. As it happened, he'd hurt his left hand—his chording hand—reaching through a wire fence to sign autographs for fans when the band arrived at LAX. It was his finger, a bad sprain, causing Led Zeppelin to reschedule their May 30 concert at the Forum. Fortunately, the band traveled with its own doctor, who gave Jimmy a vitamin B-12 shot and a supply of Dilaudid, a powerful opioid guaranteed to dull the pain (and just about everything else). The Dilaudid got him through their follow-up Forum performance on May 31, which coincided with Bonzo's twenty-fifth birthday.

Bonzo hadn't been on his best birthday behavior. The night before, he'd attended a press party for Jo Jo Gunne, an Asylum Records band from LA, at the Encore Theater in the Valley. While everyone gathered to watch campy films, Bonzo wandered into the lobby, where the theater manager was keeping an eye on an exhibit of artwork. John removed one of the framed pictures and asked the manager how much it was worth. When he was told $150, Bonzo broke the artwork over the manager's head and threw enough bills at him to cover the cost.

A similar incident occurred at a movie premiere the band attended, where "Bonzo got *really* drunk." Richard Creamer, a noted rock photographer, was taking pictures of the guests for an LA magazine when Bonzo grabbed him. "What the *fuck* are you doing?" he demanded. According to a bystander, "He took a picture off the wall and slammed it over Richard's head."

There was another incident, at the Hyatt House, when Bonzo and Ricardo grabbed a friend of Rodney Bingenheimer's and dangled him upside down over the balcony, eleven stories in the air.

Bonzo seemed determined to live up to a nickname bestowed upon him by Benoit Gautier, Atlantic's exec in France. *La Bête*—the Beast— he'd called Bonzo following an episode at a concert in Nantes when, dissatisfied by the catering, he ran amok backstage and demolished three trailers with a mallet. Gautier was already at his wit's end. On the way to Nantes from Lyon, Bonzo, who was pretty well plastered, had commandeered Gautier's Volvo sedan and driven recklessly along the A6, barely avoiding oncoming traffic. Later, with police in hot pursuit of the car, Bonzo and the roadies pried off the trunk bonnet, the sunroof, and all four doors before kicking in the dashboard—for which they were eventually arrested.

It seemed prudent to give John a wide berth on his birthday, when copious amounts of alcohol would be consumed. He was in full party mode from the time he got up. The drinking started early in the day, leading to several well-placed punches thrown at Mick Hinton, Bonzo's drum tech.

"He treated Mick badly, in general," says Benji Le Fevre, "but when alcohol was involved, it was worse than usual." Drinking and driving? That wasn't really a concern when it was done *inside* the Hyatt House. Richard surprised Bonzo with a new Honda motorcycle, and the two men tear-assed up and down the eleventh-floor hallway, shredding the carpet and leaving bumper marks on the walls. When the motorcycle's novelty wore off, a number of televisions and sundry furniture went flying over of the balcony, wreaking havoc on the street below.

*A law unto themselves.*

Robert couldn't resist marking the milestone at the Forum show. "He's twenty-one [sic] today," he announced, pointing to Bonzo seated behind his kit, "and a bastard all his life."

Bonzo took it well. "He was easy to get along with when he was soberish," says Vanessa Gilbert, who accompanied him to a party in his honor following the show. "He could be a teddy bear, but there were times you needed to run for the hills."

The Hollywood Hills were exactly where they ran to celebrate, at the home of the general manager of KROQ, LA's premier FM rock station. It was a lovely house with kids' toys scattered in the yard and a VCR—a rather new, novel appliance—playing a continuous loop of *Deep Throat*. The door was open to a ground-floor playroom, and as guests arrived they could see no less a grandee than George Harrison in there, sitting on a little rocking horse. Mostly, everyone gathered around the pool. Champagne flowed freely, there were platters of shellfish, punch bowls abounded with cocaine. "There was a beautiful birthday cake," Gilbert recalls, "three tiers."

As everyone sang and Bonzo prepared to cut the cake, George Harrison ran over, lifted off the top tier, and crowned the birthday boy with it, which touched off a full-scale food fight. Harrison took the second tier between the shoulder blades. To clean the cake off, Bonzo tossed George into the pool before going on a rampage. Rodney Bingenheimer went in next, furious that his Nikon was still around his neck. Beep Fallon got dunked, despite the expensive velvet suit he was wearing. Vanessa Gilbert was allowed to remove her mink coat before taking a header. One by one, everyone got baptized, except for Jimmy Page. The party line was that Jimmy was spared due to his inability to swim and instead allowed to walk into the shallow end up to his waist, but in actuality he was holding the drugs.

Not to be outdone, Peter Grant intended to drive a car into the pool. He got behind the wheel of one of the band's rented Cadillacs but was foiled by nature. "It got wedged between two palm trees," he explained.

Watching the debauchery from the top of an overhanging palm tree was Robert Plant, who had shimmied up there for a bird's-eye view. He was extremely high, both in altitude and in spirit, feeling no pain, and amazed at—well, *everything*. What a life! He was the lead singer of the most successful rock 'n roll band in the world. He had all the money he'd ever need, a loving family back home, unlimited girls on the road. He was surrounded and acknowledged by admirers of every stripe. Every need, every whim taken care of. Not a care in the world. The city of Los Angeles stretched out before him like a magic carpet.

In a moment of rapture, he threw his hands out and screamed to the mortals below: *"I am the golden god!"*

**Chapter Thirteen**

---

# THE LAND OF
# *MONDO BIZARRO*

## [1]

Even golden gods required rest. Robert Plant's voice was stretched thin from weeks of punishment and Jimmy Page's injured finger remained slow to mend. As a matter of necessity, Led Zeppelin took off the month of June 1973 for a time-out and a chance to recharge before resuming the summer tour. Jimmy chalked it up to part of a band's balancing act. "There was the intensity and energy and creativity that was going on," he explained. "The rest of the time was preparation or recovery."

Recovery was vital. It was the difference between normalcy and insanity. Being on the road, passing as rock stars, wasn't all it was cracked up to be. On the surface, it appeared utterly glamorous. "Everything is done for you," John Paul said. "All you have to do is turn up in a reasonably fit state to play." It always seemed that simple at the beginning of a tour. The limos, suites, food, and booze—the royal treatment—were all irresistible perks. There were few professions that offered such a luxurious lifestyle. But as the tour wore on, the grind extracted a toll that was debilitating, physically and mentally. The wear and tear on the body was progressive, intense. Fatigue set in fast, isolation, boredom. It was easy to catch a cold hopping from one air-conditioned chamber to the next. Easy to find fault with your mates. Easy to resent the fans, the routine, even the music. *If I have to sing "Stairway to Heaven" one more time . . .* Easy to resent the whole damn situation.

*Recovery was vital.*

Led Zeppelin scattered as soon as the last concert at LA's Forum had ended. It was a disappointing performance, sluggish, and it seemed to many as if the band was going through the motions. The tour had been more demanding than expected, the wages of fame—astonishing fame—particularly steep, exhausting. The guys were spent.

Robert Plant and John Bonham withdrew to their newly pur-chased retreats—Plant to a sheep farm in Wales near the coast and Bonham to a spread in Worcestershire where he tended a herd of Hereford cattle. Both men welcomed the interval to reconnect with their families and less glitzy surroundings. John Paul Jones was taken into custody by his wife and daughters, while Jimmy Page returned to Plumpton Place, which he shared, however superficially, with Char-lotte Martin and their daughter.

During this period, Jimmy's fascination with the occult became a preoccupation. He stepped up his pursuit of Aleister Crowley memo-rabilia. He already owned the occultist's robes, hats, canes, annotated manuscripts, diaries, tarot cards, signed folios, anything he could get his hands on. In January 1973, he'd even attempted to acquire what could have become the most precious artifact in his collection.

Aubrey Powell was on his way to Cairo to photograph the pyra-mids for the *Dark Side of the Moon* album cover. "Jimmy called me and said, 'As long as Pink Floyd is paying your airfare, could you go by the Egyptian Museum and ask them about the Stele of Revelation?' Po re-calls. "'I'd be very interested to get hold of it.'"

*The Stele of Revelation?* Po had no idea what he was talking about. Digging around, he discovered it was a wood engraving dating to 680 BC, created as an offering for the tomb of a Montu priest. It was covered in hieroglyphics representing text from the Book of the Dead. Crowley had maintained that the stele depicted the three chief gods of Thelema, his so-called spiritual philosophy. Jimmy salivated at the prospect of getting his hands on it.

Po called the director of the museum, an Egyptian scholar, and was invited to his office. "It was just after the Yom Kippur War, and the place was locked and sandbagged. Nobody had been there in months," he recalls. He showed the man a picture of the stele that Jimmy had given him. "I have a client who is interested in purchasing it," he told him. It was as though he had asked to buy the Shroud of Turin. The stele was one of the country's most precious relics, *revered*, not for sale, not for anything. He was, however, willing to show it to Po, and the two men set off into one of the museum's spooky subterranean vaults, an exploit right out of *Raiders of the Lost Ark*.

"There was no electricity," Po said. "We had a couple of torches and we walked for miles. Dark tunnels, cobwebs everywhere, a rather scary experience." They finally encountered the stele lying in a dust-covered box, thrown in among other, lesser relics. In the end, Jimmy paid $2,000 for a plaster cast of it.

Money was no object to the members of Led Zeppelin. The summer tour was due to net them $4.5 million, much of it in cash, and God knows how much more from merchandise that went unreported, to say nothing of album sales. Peter Grant bragged to the *Financial Times* that the band would earn $30 million in 1973, a good portion of it off the books.

With so much residual income, no indulgence, no creature comfort was deemed too costly to augment the experience of touring. Every facet of being on the road was about to get an upgrade. For starters, the musicians were given more authority over the provisions in their hotel suites. An order came down from high command. From now on, in whatever room they slept, Jimmy was to have flowers, fresh fruit (stipulating grapes and green apples), bottled water, an electric kettle, champagne on ice, fresh orange juice, the curtains pulled and candles lit, and a stereo tuned to the hip local FM station.

"This time, I'm going to get some Afghani hangings and my rooms are going to look like, well, like mosques," he told Lisa Robinson. "You get loads of carpets and lay them on top of each other and have everything candlelit."

Robert seconded those perks and added Earl Grey tea and limited his fruit selection to grapes and lemons. John Paul added a piano to the growing list, and Bonzo ordered plenty of beer, champagne, and a sheepskin rug. And God help any retainer who failed to meet those conditions.

Danny Marcus, Atlantic Records' artist relations rep based in the Midwest, was directed to have a stereo in every room that Led Zeppelin booked at the Ambassador Hotel in Chicago, the band's first stop. "And no boom boxes—*components*," Marcus says. "I also had the best sources for pot and monogrammed [rolling] papers. In those days, the British were smoking hash and tobacco, which was wretched, so I introduced them to the romance of top-notch weed."

Marcus called himself "the enabler—the director of health, education, and welfare." If balloons needed to be filled with water so they could be launched from a high hotel window, he was the guy to handle it. If opium was requested by a rock star, he could find some. If there was a party in the vicinity, he'd score invitations. "My job was to satisfy Led Zeppelin," he says, "so that Atlantic never got a call from them."

If it meant sacrificing his body or personal possessions—so be it. On one of the first legs of the tour, Marcus joined Led Zeppelin on their personal plane and was confronted almost immediately by Bonzo in Beast mode. "I went to shake his hand," Marcus recalls, "but he found my nipple and pinched it as hard as he could, something he enjoyed doing to people. Then he took off my glasses and stomped on them." Marcus didn't flinch; he had a second pair to get him through the trip. But two nights later, when he saw Bonzo homing in on him, Marcus whipped off his glasses, threw them on the floor, and stomped on them himself.

Security was also enhanced. Rumors always circulated about crazed-fan weirdos, but there was credible evidence that someone was determined to do harm to Jimmy Page. "Actually, it was a lot more serious than I thought," Jimmy explained. "It was a real Manson situation, and he was sending out waves of this absurd paranoia which a friend of mine got mixed up with." There were also bags full of cash to worry about. Few precautions were taken where money was concerned.

Out of necessity, Peter Grant hired Ogden Security, a Boston-based firm that deployed ex-cop Bill Dautrich to coordinate the band's safety and protection. He flew ahead to each city on the tour to coordinate local police efforts, an army of bodyguards, and security at the various arenas, stadiums, and hotels. In addition, each of the musicians got a personal assistant to shadow him and attend to any need.

But the pièce de résistance awaited the band in Chicago. Peter Grant had expressed his displeasure with the private plane they'd been using, the nine-seat Fan Jet Falcon that transported them from city to city. The band members loved the luxury it provided, but there was a downside. "On that small plane, you were too in a cocoon," G said. "They had to sit opposite each other all the time, and of course there were rows. Somebody might get chinned by one of the others, having punch-ups between themselves. Bonzo and Robert were famous for that."

There was also a fear factor. The Falcon didn't do well in turbulence. On its last flight, from San Francisco to Los Angeles, the plane had gotten tossed around in an air pocket and everyone's hearts had caught in their throats. G in particular went bat shit. "I've had it with these little fucking planes!" he cried. "This is the last time we fly them." He ordered Richard Cole to find something more substantial for the second leg of the tour.

More substantial was never a problem. Richard heard about a Boeing 720B kitted out for rock 'n roll bands that was co-owned by teen singing star Bobby Sherman and his manager, Ward Sylvester. Steve Weiss and Mark London, Peter's Stone the Crows partner, checked it out at Newark Airport and arranged to rent it for the remainder of the tour at a cost of $30,000, about $10,000 a week. The plane—christened the *Starship*—was beyond deluxe. It was a forty-seater, furnished with a thirty-foot couch and revolving armchairs, several closed-circuit TVs, an artificial fireplace, and a bar with a built-in organ. "There was a bedroom in the back that became Peter's," says Danny Goldberg, "and he sometimes had sex in there with one woman or another." An unlimited menu of food was available—steak, shrimp, caviar, anything anyone's heart desired. Ricardo stocked the hold with several cases each of vintage Dom Pérignon, Jack Daniel's, and Singha beer. Two flight attendants—eighteen-year-old Susie and twenty-two-year-old Bianca—drew the line at sexual favors but catered to every other whim.

"The idea was for Zeppelin to base themselves in major cities and just fly out to gigs in nearby towns," says Phil Carson, a frequent passenger aboard the *Starship*. "So if we were located at the Ambassador in Chicago, we'd commute to St. Louis, Milwaukee, Minneapolis, or Detroit without having to change hotels." They could do the entire Midwest from Chicago. They'd be picked up at the hotel at 5:30 p.m., arrive at the airport by 6:00, be in the air by 6:45, land by 8:00, play the gig, and be back in their beds in time to sleep. The convenience was undeniable. "Our feet never really touched the ground," Jimmy said. Upon landing in any city, the band was conveyed directly from the plane to limos that were driven onto the tarmac so that no one had to set foot in an airport lounge. Luggage was transferred on the spot, which ensured that their drugs wouldn't be compromised.

On off nights, Jimmy arranged flights to Los Angeles in order to liaise with Lori Mattix, who was forbidden on board the *Starship* by Peter Grant over concerns about transporting a minor across state lines.

Otherwise, the *Starship* allowed for a bona fide entourage to accompany Led Zeppelin, which turned the plane into an airborne party. In addition to the band, Peter, Richard, and Steve Weiss, a flight's manifest might include Danny Goldberg and any journalist he was wooing, the local Atlantic rep, occasionally Phil Carson or Beep Fallon, a few handpicked women over the age of sixteen (but sometimes younger), and an assortment of friends, colleagues, and freeloaders. Vanessa Gilbert and Gyl Corrigan-Devlin, who had connections to the best drugs, were summoned to Chicago from LA to function as den mothers to the band. And folksinger Roy Harper now traveled everywhere with them as the band's guest, a tribute to the esteem, deserved or otherwise, in which he was held by Robert and Jimmy.

This was the outfit that arrived in Chicago on July 6, 1973, for two opening shows at Chicago Stadium. Led Zeppelin was eager to be back in front of an audience, and they wasted no time launching into the meat of their show. The fans couldn't argue with the unapologetic fury of "Rock and Roll," "Celebration Day," "Bring It On Home," and "Black Dog." It was an uncompromising reentry but managed to incite a faction of the crowd to overturn chairs, launch firecrackers, and raise all sorts of miscellaneous hell. Robert had to stop the show at several junctures and wait for order to be restored. "What's with that," he complained to a reporter from the *Chicago Tribune*, "people wearing beads and punching each other in the face!"

But this was Chicago, home of Chess Records and the Chicago blues, both of which contained vital components of Led Zeppelin's DNA. They loved the Windy City. For some unexplained reason, Chicago had been bypassed on the 1970 and 1972 tours, so they set aside ample time to reacquaint themselves with the city. Jimmy saluted the location by the selection of albums in his room, in particular Otis Spann's *Memorial* LP, with Otis Rush on guitar, which spun prominently on his turntable. There were few sounds more identified with the West Side brand of Chicago blues than Spann's barrelhouse piano.

Rush remained one of Jimmy's favorite stylists, with his version of "I Can't Quit You Baby" an extraordinary influence.

Danny Marcus dropped into Robert's room to discover which records he was listening to. "It was strange, because I didn't see the stereo," says Marcus, who could have sworn it had been there at check-in. "Robert marched me into the bathroom, and there it was, under a foot of water in the tub. Apparently, he'd been expecting studio-quality equipment, and this was his way of reviewing the components."

Marcus intended to make it up to him by introducing the band to Chicago's nightlife. He recalls, "I took the guys to see Bobby 'Blue' Bland at the Burning Spear," a storied blues club on State Street that played host to the likes of Little Milton, Junior Parker, and the Kings— B. B., Albert, and Freddie. "I brought Bobby over to meet Robert, who he called Led, because he thought his name was Led Zeppelin." That didn't stop Robert from getting up and jamming with Bland and Otis Clay, one of the city's great R&B vocalists, with Bonzo sitting in on drums.

Chicago proved an exceptional warm-up to the tour, with both shows received warmly by fans and critics alike. But Chicago was a notoriously tough town; there were places where one had to watch one's back. During Bonzo's drum solo, Benji Le Fevre took a bathroom time-out and was mugged by two hooligans determined to swipe his all-access pass. By the time he crawled back to the mix tower, Benji was covered in blood. Peter Grant escorted him into an ambulance and directed it to the hospital. "This isn't necessary, G," Benji protested. "The siren isn't even on." Peter pulled a wad of cash out of his pocket and thrust a couple bills through the ambulance window. "Oh, driver," he said, "here's a hundred bucks. Put the siren on."

G could be caring and solicitous, especially to anyone in his employ, but since returning from the June hiatus, he'd developed a monster cocaine habit that wired him tighter than a sailor's knot. "Peter was sure that cocaine wasn't additive," says Phil Carson. "The cost didn't mean anything to him. He had so much cash at his disposal."

Cocaine was prevalent in the rock 'n roll scene but ubiquitous on the *Starship*. "Definitely the Zeppelin crowd was coked all the time," says Danny Goldberg. That was especially true when it came to Peter, whose appetite for anything was notorious to begin with. "Orgasmic," was how a friend described his habit. Peter wouldn't even wait to chop his coke into lines. He'd thrust a long car key into a bag and snort directly from his stash. Other times he simply put his nose in the bag. "He seemed to have the constitution of an ox," said one onlooker.

"The amount of cocaine was insane," says Benji Le Fevre, "there was so much of it—and never enough."

Jimmy was already pursuing a bigger high with a better payoff. In Milwaukee, three nights later, someone left a line of coke on one of the dressers in a hotel room. Not to let a perfectly good gift go to waste, it was shared by a resourceful group. "It turned out someone had put heroin in with the coke, and we were all absolutely ill," said Gyl Corrigan-Devlin. "Jimmy was really the only one who wasn't [ill], and it was obvious to me that the line had been a gift for *him*."

Contrary to what every musician believes (or needs to believe), drugs had an impact on the way they played. Most nights Led Zeppelin performed brilliantly, but there were nights when they veered out of control. "Jimmy's guitar playing got sloppy," says Benji Le Fevre, who monitored the music through headphones at the soundboard. Nor was Robert always in exceptional voice; music critics who were enlightened fans of the band and well versed in the songs noted how he was unable to reach many of the high notes and defaulted to a lower register. And performances routinely started late, often thirty minutes but sometimes as much as an hour or more, and the young, inebriated crowds could get ugly. In Boston and again in Pittsburgh, delayed starts led to clashes with police.

The fans, however, gave Led Zeppelin a pass. The band delivered an eruptive surge of high-energy music and stellar theatrics that obliterated any recognition of glitches. Three hours of mostly solid, sustained rock 'n roll by virtuoso musicians was a rare and exceptional treat. The interplay between the musicians was contagious. There was a lot of acrobatic movement on stage—mugging, prancing, high-stepping, duck-walking. Jimmy and Bonzo were especially snuggly, often playing into each other's faces.

"I think we always start off *shaky*, and it's at the end when the whole thing builds," Jimmy explained. "We build up the—I don't know what you might call it—the ESP aspects of it when you do start jamming and entering areas which are open to free-form. . . . A lot of that is just off the cuff. And that's where everybody's really working."

The band made sure to include highlights from each of their five albums. No matter that they were bored churning out "Whole Lotta Love" and "Stairway to Heaven." They made every effort to play the fan favorites as though for the first time. And the effects—the dry ice, the massive light show, and the dazzling overhead screen—delivered an assault on the senses. The audiences weren't just ecstatic, they let themselves be overcome, whipped into a frenzy. As one reviewer noted, "Led Zeppelin doesn't give concerts; they perform physical transformations."

On July 17, 1973, the entourage landed in Seattle and checked in to the Edgewater Hotel, scene of the legendary mud shark affair. There must have been something in the Edgewater's air ducts that drove rock 'n rollers to anarchy. Ahmet Ertegun threw a party for the band in the hotel's banquet room, which the guys decided to bail on. The real party was in Bonzo's room, where Peter, sprawled across a king-size bed and chugging from a quart bottle of ouzo, conducted the action as if it were a three-ring circus.

"The freaks had come out of the woodwork," recalls one of the guests. "It was like a Fellini slow-motion debauchery, filled with ugly chicks in hot pants and green-painted fingernails." Bonzo pulled back the shower curtain with a flourish to reveal a bathtub full of near-dead mud sharks flapping around. He and Richard Cole had reeled in about thirty of the unfortunate creatures. The stench was incredible. "He intended to rub those fish over the girls in hot pants, which depended on what level freak they were—a full-on 'rub the fish on me' freak or 'just pour ouzo on my head.'"

The gig that night at the Coliseum served merely as an intermission to the hijinks. After the show, back at the hotel, Robert and Bonzo rifled through the luggage belonging to Vanessa Gilbert and paraded about in her clothes and high heels. From time to time, depending on the circumstances, they, along with John Paul, enjoyed larking about in drag. Robert's stage outfits alone provided ample flouncy apparel—gauzy shirts studded in rhinestones, midriff-baring blouses, and shirtwaists.

John Paul, however, had other mischief on his mind that night. While the Midlands lads were cavorting in the corridors, he'd crept into Bonzo's deserted room with a suitcase full of tools. With the precision of a master craftsman, he began undoing everything that was bolted to the floor—the ugly orange couch, the TV, the dresser, the lamps, even the mattress and bed—and sent all of it sailing over the balcony into the sea. When Bonzo returned, there was nothing left in the room.

The next morning at checkout, the desk manager congratulated Peter Grant on Led Zeppelin's restraint—only trashing a single room. "Rod Stewart's gang destroyed five," he revealed, before going down the list of other visiting bands that had done greater damage. "But the Methodist Church trashed *ten* rooms!" Grant was impressed by the young Christians' handiwork. "Apparently the Methodists didn't just throw out the TV sets and fridges—even the carpets went," he said.

"The guy was so frustrated about not being able to just go bonkers in a room himself," Peter said. G famously led the desk manager up to a vacated suite and offered him the experience of trashing it himself. "Here you are." He peeled off $670 in cash and folded it into the manager's palm. "Have this room on Led Zeppelin." Roughly another

$1,000 covered John Paul's vandalism. Peter was used to it. Hotel rooms on tour were collateral damage. But the cost to Led Zeppelin was about to soar.

## [2]

On July 14, 1973, just prior to a concert in Buffalo, New York, Peter Grant phoned Joe Massot, a filmmaker on the fringes of the artistic mainstream, and asked him to join the tour in Boston on July 20 to begin shooting sequences for a Led Zeppelin movie. This had been on the band's drawing board for some time—as a logical phase of their overall career strategy—but relegated to a back burner due to various scheduling obstacles. For some unexplained reason, G decided the time was right. They'd filmed parts of the illustrious Albert Hall concert in 1970, but the footage was dark and grainy, basically unusable. "By 1973, we had moved on so far in such a short time that we felt the Albert Hall footage was passé in every respect," Jimmy said. "We looked and dressed differently, and the whole communicative quality of the music had been improved." If Led Zeppelin was going to allow a film to be made, it had to be a first-class affair, subject to their creative control and approval at every stage of the process.

Joe Massot was an unconventional choice to handle the job. His CV was slim in the filmmaking department. He'd done a few short films about pre-Castro Cuba and assisted George Harrison in providing the soundtrack to the 1968 film *Wonderwall*, a messy psychedelic romp starring Jane Birkin. He'd also written a forgettable art-house western based on *Siddhartha* called *Zachariah*, with Don Johnson and various rock 'n roll cameos that had slipped through the cracks. That was about it. But Massot had badgered Peter for years about undertaking a Led Zeppelin documentary and had become friends with Charlotte Martin and Jimmy Page. He did a number on Jimmy, who was impressed by Massot's proposed structure for such a film—interweaving live concert footage with dreamlike reenactment sequences featuring each of the band members, as opposed to talking-head interviews.

Peter gave him five days to assemble a crew and to meet the band at Boston Garden. They could begin filming the five concerts remaining on the tour, starting with the Baltimore show on July 23. Money and irritating studio production overlords wouldn't interfere. Led Zeppelin intended to finance the entire enterprise themselves.

If Massot had any illusions that the venture would go smoothly, they were snuffed out in Boston. He took the opportunity to tag along with Peter Grant in order to get a feel for what Led Zeppelin's backstage life was like. That night, the crowd out front was especially rowdy, ignoring Robert's pleas throughout the show to settle down. A handful of overenthusiastic fans eventually pushed through the barriers in front of the stage, prompting the manager to organize a hasty getaway.

The band charged out the back of the Garden into the employee parking lot. Most of the limo drivers had taken off at the first sign of violence. G ordered the one remaining driver out of his Cadillac. "You call your boss and tell him this car is now mine," he declared, handing over his gold American Express card while the band clambered over one another, squeezing into the back seat. Peter took over the chauffeuring himself. "He drove like a maniac," recalled a member of the film crew, who stared in disbelief, "right through a fire hydrant which exploded. He bumped over the gutter and onto the main road," flooring it all the way to the hotel.

The next installment, at the Baltimore Civic Center, was no less bumpy. Mickie Most and Steve Weiss showed up to keep G company as he led Joe Massot on a stroll through the arena. As chance would have it, they encountered a rogue entrepreneur doing brisk business selling posters of the band. The film crew's camera captured Peter at his most monstrous. The confrontation was a terrifying big-screen scene.

The stage manager, Larry Vaughan, who worked for Concerts East, was brought before Grant to answer for the offense. The pirate poster seller sat quivering in the corner. Peter lurched out of his chair and swooped down on the man, like Mothra about to devour his prey.

"Don't fucking talk to him," Peter growled at Vaughan, "it's *my* bloody act!"

"I don't know how this guy got in the building," Vaughan said, and turned to exchange a word with Steve Weiss.

Peter was indignant. "Talk to *me*! I'm the manager of the group. You had people inside the building selling posters, and you didn't know anything about it."

It didn't matter what Vaughan said or how diplomatically he handled the situation; Peter was out to eviscerate the poor guy.

"How much kickback are you getting?" G demanded, even though he knew that wasn't the case. This was a star turn, and he was ready for his close-up.

It was all leading up to a point where Peter could lord over the man and call him a "silly cunt," one of his trusty rebukes, displaying the kind of rage that turned grown men into Jell-O.

For the live concert footage, everything depended on the three consecutive shows Led Zeppelin played at Madison Square Garden in New York. It was the perfect venue to capture the magic, an intimate crowd of eighteen thousand as opposed to the masses at monolithic stadiums. The Garden had history, it was a landmark, a New York institution. "For me," Robert Plant maintained, "Madison Square Garden was a seminal moment."

The entourage that arrived in New York was massive and defied reason. Since Pittsburgh, folks had been joining the tour the way a snowball rolling downhill picks up detritus. The *Starship* added a team of journalists from *Playboy* and various insignificant publications,

Ahmet Ertegun, half a dozen groupies of disparate stripes, Iggy Pop, who had come in from LA, and sundry hangers-on. Of the latter, Roy Harper had just about worn out his welcome. In LA, he'd spent a lot of time at Led Zeppelin's expense frolicking with a groupie from Phoenix who made love potions and cast spells. "When I think that I was sixteen, and he must have been thirty"—Harper was thirty-two—"it's kind of like, 'Wow!'" she exclaimed. Since then, Harper's sole function on the tour had been to stand at the side of the stage and shake a toy stuffed monkey on a stick at Jimmy while he performed. The crew was not amused.

Headquarters in New York was the Drake Hotel on Park Avenue at Fifty-sixth Street. The place had a regal, old-world charm, but it might have been Grand Central Station for all the foot traffic in and out of the suites. The parade was nonstop—friends, well-wishers, old girlfriends, record-company reps, deejays, promoters, drug dealers, guitar salesmen. *Enough!* Led Zeppelin was exhausted and craved peace and quiet, but there was no rest for the weary. Jimmy especially was a shadow of himself. He looked haggard, wraith-like. Drugs had begun to take a toll. The pace was killing him. He claimed he hadn't slept in five days.

"We're all terribly worn out," he admitted. "I went past the point of no return physically quite a while back, but now I've gone past the mental point too, I think. I've only kept going by functioning automatically."

It was essential they pull it together for the three Garden shows. They were proof to G that his scheme to cut out the middlemen was on the money—90 percent of the money. "We announced the dates via Scott Muni's radio show, and [they were] instantly sold out," he said. No other promotional costs were incurred. "It was the demand from the street and the fans."

The shows served as the only opportunity for the film team to get exciting concert footage. They'd shot 16mm footage in Pittsburgh and Baltimore, but those were dry runs to allow the film crew to work out camera strategy on such short notice. No attention was paid to continuity—that is, making sure songs on different nights were played in the same key and that the band members wore the same clothes, to make it seem like a single take once editors got their hands on it. In New York, everyone was going for broke—three nights, plenty of opportunity to cover all angles of a Led Zeppelin concert, and a big step up in quality to 35mm film stock.

Good plan, lousy execution. For some unknown reason, John Paul Jones missed the memo about continuity and wore different clothes on the successive nights. "I would ask if we were filming tonight but be told that nothing was going to be filmed," he said, "so I'd think, 'Not to worry, I'll save the shirt I wore the previous night for the next filming.' Then I'd get on stage and see cameras all ready to roll." It would be a nightmare in the editing room. His outfits would never match up. Perhaps worse was the decision about the film stock. "They started filming on 35mm film, but on four hundred-foot rolls, which only gave [them] about three-and-a-half minutes," according to one of the crew. "During reel changes, the cameramen were missing so much material." It would be impossible to sync and sequence during the edit.

In the end, there were too many distractions. Richard Cole claimed that on the second night, while John Bonham was in the throes of his interminable "Moby Dick" solo, Ricardo had arranged for a teenage girl to give the other band members blowjobs in the dressing room. This hearkened back to Led Zeppelin's first appearance at the Garden in September 1970. "I went to the locker room while the band was onstage," recalls Henry Smith, their primary roadie during the early tours. "There was a policeman's hat sitting on a bench, with his belt and gun right next to it. Richard and Peter were practically pissing themselves with laughter. They had a groupie giving the cop a blowjob in the stall. Richard organized scenes like that on a regular basis."

As far as scenes went, the third night at the Garden was the pièce de résistance. Just prior to the beginning of the show, word drifted to those backstage that the safe-deposit box behind the desk in the Drake Hotel, where the band had secured cash and other valuables, had been rifled. A little over $200,000 was missing. In the best show-must-go-on tradition, the band soldiered through as details were emerging from various sources.

Upon check-in, Richard Cole and Steve Weiss had placed stacks of hundred-dollar bills, along with everyone's passports and a few credit cards, in the box for safekeeping. The cash was mostly for incidentals—for the film crew's expenses, spontaneous purchases like antiques for Jimmy or a car for Bonzo, or as Ricardo noted, "in case we wanted to buy a guitar in the middle of the night, or a bit of blow." As a matter of fact, Jimmy had called him around three in the morning on the second night in New York and requested $800—in some retellings it was $600, even $8,000—for a Les Paul that a fan was offering him. Cole went to the box and swore that all the money had been there at that time. When he returned the next morning, only the passports remained.

The Drake turned into a major crime scene. New York City police and the FBI moved in to investigate, but so did the paparazzi. To safeguard the band's privacy, the musicians were stashed in an apartment on East Eighty-sixth Street belonging to Shelley Kaye, Steve Weiss's assistant, until things cooled down. Meanwhile, Richard Cole, the FBI's primary suspect, combed the band's rooms, scrubbing them of drugs. There was plenty for him to worry about. At the same time that law enforcement arrived, so did a shady character who called one of the suites and got Vanessa Gilbert on the phone.

"Hey, I've got some stuff for Zeppelin," he said. "Stuff," code for drugs. A few minutes later he was in Gilbert's room, the gigantic corner suite Peter had awarded her, unpacking a briefcase with an assortment of powders. "Here's the good stuff, and here's the great stuff." Although she'd never seen brown cocaine before, she chose the great stuff, which she snorted to assess.

A heroin bust would have been fatal to Led Zeppelin. Ricardo was already in enough hot water. No one else had access to the strongbox at the Drake; he had the only key. It certainly looked to the cops like an inside job. He was interrogated and fingerprinted. Cole also said that he had taken and passed a lie detector test. Nevertheless, he remained a primary suspect, as did a bellman who, according to Phil Carson, "was watched by the FBI for years."

There have been many theories about the theft, which was never solved. Questions remained about all the cash floating around, unaccounted for, doled out for arbitrary purposes, often to avoid paying income tax. The British rate for the kind of money Led Zeppelin made was 90 percent, and no less an aggrieved tax drudge than Peter Grant alluded to his "false-bottomed suitcases" stuffed with cash being smuggled into Great Britain to avoid the levy. Maybe that's what happened to the safe-deposit-box stash. No less than five sources close to the band told this author that Grant had admitted spiriting the Drake money away. Michael Des Barres, who later recorded for Led Zeppelin's record label, says, "Peter told me that Richard did it. It was a tax thing. He said, 'Why would you let all that money go to these other cunts?'"

The band didn't seem too put out by the theft. "Jimmy and I just laughed about it," Robert said cavalierly. He thought it "somehow made sense." In the scheme of things, a loss of $200,000 was pocket change to Led Zeppelin, but it sure didn't look that way to the outside world. The New York dailies converged to try to make their own sense of the theft. When a *New York Post* photographer arrived at the Drake, G grabbed his camera and smashed it, doing a bit of damage to its owner's face as well. For that, Peter was promptly arrested and tossed into a cell at 100 Center Street, the nerve center of the New York City criminal court system.

Steve Weiss leaped into action. He placed a call to a young attorney a couple years out of the DA's office named Jeff Hoffman. "I was in a new private practice," Hoffman recalls, "and when we opened the firm, we took whatever walked in the door. And what walked in the door were drug dealers from Harlem." Among his principal clients were Frank Lucas, the heroin kingpin who was later immortalized in *American Gangster* by Denzel Washington, and "the money people between organized crime and the wannabes." The latest addition to his client roster, Peter Grant, was in fine company.

"Do whatever you have to, but get him out of jail," Weiss instructed. "He has a plane to catch."

An hour later, Hoffman encountered Peter in a night-court holding cell. "He was off the wall, a monstrous guy stalking around the cell," Hoffman remembers. "He growled at me: '*Get me out of here!*'"

Before G's arraignment, one of the court personnel pointed out the *Post* photographer to Hoffman. They huddled outside and agreed to a reasonable settlement, which allowed the case to be dismissed on the spot. But the young lawyer knew a tall story when he heard one when Peter told him about the Drake robbery. Hoffman, who was savvy when it came to clients who dealt strictly in cash, concluded, "It had all the markings of an inside job."

The robbery, the publicity, the nonstop travel, the breakneck schedule, the vast sums of money, the death threats and security, the drugs, the rumors, the push-pull, push-pull, push-pull, *the Led Zeppelin phenomenon*—the whole thing was becoming too much to handle. The band was knackered. The guys were in a daze.

"I was just totally and completely spaced out," Jimmy admitted. "There was an enormous amount of adrenaline that we were building up on stage, and just taking it offstage into the land of *mondo bizarro*." Drugs had become a pacemaker—drugs to stay awake, drugs to fall asleep, and drugs for in between, when it was essential that the pace stayed nice and groovy. "And part of the condition of drug taking," he said, "is that you start thinking you're invincible." He recalled a recent episode when circumstances veered toward disaster. "I remember one night climbing out of a nine-story window in New York and sitting on one of those air-conditioning units, just looking out over the city."

Peter promised them a sabbatical from live appearances, not just a token break but a year, more if necessary. Time off was a good start, but the overriding issue was larger than that. Perhaps a reevaluation was due. Overdue. The band's five-year deal with Atlantic Records was ending. Jimmy was physically sick, Jonesy was disillusioned, Robert had missed seeing his son's first steps, and Bonzo was Bonzo. It was time for a reset.

"Nothing's preconceived right now," Robert explained upon returning to the United Kingdom. The band, he said, was coming to different decisions and conclusions. "We'll work a bit and then we'll take a break. That's the way it works—that's Led Zeppelin right now."

## Chapter Fourteen

# LED ZEPPELIN WAS OTHERWISE ENGAGED

### [1]

The aftermath of a tour was always unsettling. Rejoining the family, sleeping in your own bed, tuning to a new, slower pace, the peace and quiet, the sanity—all of it necessitated a major readjustment. When the screaming ceased, when the retainers departed, when the music faded, the return to normalcy had a sobering and disorienting effect. Star treatment was limited to extra helpings at the table. Wives took over a dignified groupie role. Even at the pub, a golden god got no more of an oblation than a friendly nod or a deferential pint. What a welcome relief!

It was time to take stock of home and hearth. In Jimmy's case, that meant finding a residence in London, closer to his business interests. He'd only recently acquired a driver's license, and despite owning a gorgeous Bentley, he never drove anywhere. To get from Plumpton Place to a studio in the city, he depended on hitching a ride with Ricardo or on public transit. "Jimmy would hop on a train and come up to Victoria Station, then get a bus to the office," says one of the staff. But in the last year, his face had become too familiar. He started getting hassled by fans. A home in London made more sense, and not just any home but Tower House in Holland Park, considered by many to be "the most beautiful residence in London."

Tower House was a veritable redbrick fortress built in 1881 by architect William Burges in the French Gothic revival style. It was opulent in every detail, from its eponymous turret poking up above the tree line to its exotic interior rooms, adorned with intaglios and marquetry inlays of astrological signs, mythical creatures, and pagan symbols. The place was fantastic in every sense of the word. It was a residence that befit an eccentric personality, and that Jimmy bought it from no less a flamboyant character than actor Richard Harris is no coincidence. The house was also conveniently located a short walk from Holland Street in Kensington, where Jimmy was in the process of opening a bookshop, the Equinox, dedicated to the occult and all things Crowley.

Not to be outdone, Peter Grant purchased his own estate called Horselunges, a sixteenth-century Elizabethan manor house surrounded by a moat near Eastbourne, in leafy Sussex. "It was a very spooky place," says Carole Brown, G's longtime assistant, who spent the first night in the house with Peter and his family. "There were suits of armor and stuffed hunters' trophies and a portrait of a former owner whose eyes seemed to follow you everywhere." The kitchen staff told Brown that the house was haunted by a dog that had jumped out of a window, and sure enough, that first night Grant's wife, Gloria, swore she heard a dog scratching at her bedroom door. Horselunges became a repository for Peter's enormous collection of art nouveau—Tiffany lamps, Mistinguett posters, and a bed that had belonged to Sarah Bernhardt. Grant chose the house much for its location, convenient to Gatwick Airport.

The Horselunges housewarming party was an unforgettable affair, Grant style. "The catering team were dressed in Elizabethan clothing and served traditional mead," Carole Brown recalls. Gloria "Glo"

Grant, Peter's wife, was especially vivacious, though she turned a re-proachful eye on Richard Cole, who remained upstairs throughout the evening, inhaling poppers of amyl nitrate.

Peter also needed a new base of operations. During Led Zeppelin's tour in the States, he'd notified Mickie Most that their twelve-year partnership on Oxford Street was at an end. There was too little over-lap; it had outlived its usefulness. Most decried the breakup and or-dered Carole Brown out of the office while a search team looked for another headquarters. "Jimmy and Peter were considering purchasing Hammer House, where they made the Hammer horror movies, for their offices," she says. In the end, Mark London, Peter's partner in Stone the Crowes, found a much more suitable space on the King's Road in Chelsea, a two-floor suite above the Royal British Legion Hall and directly across from the World's End pub. The rent was a ridicu-lous £19 a week.

"Peter particularly liked it," says Ed Bicknell, "because of a fire es-cape that led from the first floor, where he had his office, onto an alley in the rear." He liked to say, "The perfect office was any building with two staircases." It allowed him to slip out the back to avoid an unwel-come visitor, be it an artist, an underworld rival, or the law. Carole Brown recalls such an instance when a genial folksinger named Duster Bennett dropped in unexpectedly one afternoon. "He'd been pursu-ing Peter, who wasn't keen to get involved," she says. "Duster sat in the reception until eight or nine o'clock, waiting for Peter to finish his calls. When I finally knocked and opened his door, there was no one there and the fire escape was wide open."

Peter Grant wasn't a natural office-bound soul. Before Carole Brown handled his day-to-day calendar, he was assisted by an Irish woman named Irene, who complained that he'd lock himself in the office and be "unavailable" for days on end. The only way she could communicate with him was to slip messages under the door.

In any case, the King's Road office was a refuge away from the hus-tle of 155 Oxford Street. The only other occupant was a ground-floor council of mostly older women who met there once a year to organize the sale of poppies honoring Remembrance Day's fallen heroes. Otherwise, the building was devoted entirely to Peter Grant Ltd. Grant's private sanctum was furnished with a brown leather sofa and a stunning old barge door coated in resin and converted into a coffee table. A gaudy chandelier lit a gallery of Gerald Scarfe illustrations that decorated the walls. The focal point, however, was a large, plush carpet with a red wine stain on it, the victim of one of Led Zeppelin's mishaps at a hotel in California. When told that the band would be held responsible for the damage, Peter responded, "If you're going to charge me for the carpet, you'd better roll it up and ship it to England."

The first order of business in the King's Road office was renegotiating Led Zeppelin's contract with Atlantic Records, which was expiring on October 28, 1973. The initial five-year period had flown by with the kind of payoffs that gamblers dream about. "The band was thirty percent of Atlantic's turnover," Phil Carson says. Both parties were eager to re-up.

The initial plan was to send Steve Weiss in to negotiate the new deal, but his relationship with the label had frayed at the edges. He had a running fight with Atlantic to get his acts paid and employed Jeff Hoffman, the lawyer who defended Peter Grant during the Drake fracas, to put the squeeze on Ahmet Ertegun. "From time to time, I would threaten him with a RICO* lawsuit," Hoffman recalls, "and Ahmet would always relent and pay up."

Instead, Peter Grant and Ahmet hammered out the terms in an all-night session that tried both moguls' patience. Ahmet's initial solution was to give Led Zeppelin a five-year extension on the original deal. They'd both profited handsomely—more than handsomely. Why tinker with a winning formula? Peter was having none of it. He'd brokered that deal for an unknown band that had transformed itself

---

* The Racketeer Influenced and Corrupt Organizations Act, a U.S. federal law enacted in 1970, designed to combat organized crime.

into a financial gold mine. He wanted a new deal structured to reflect
the band's stature, something not just more respectable but crowned
with laurel. Led Zeppelin wanted a label deal—their *own* label—like
the ones that Ahmet had given to David Geffen and Elliot Roberts for
Asylum Records and to the Rolling Stones. Zeppelin wanted not only
their own label but the freedom to run it with autonomy in every aspect other than marketing and distribution, crumbs they'd leave to
Atlantic. It was unfair, Grant argued, to compare it to the Stones deal.
That was basically a vanity label with one act on it. Grant assured
Ahmet that Led Zeppelin intended to sign a full slate of new artists
and to promote the hell out of them. In fact, they were already compiling a list of potential acts, including one built around Free's former
guitarist Paul Rodgers; another around Maggie Bell, the vocalist from
Stone the Crows; and the omnipresent Roy Harper.

There were other alternatives. "I had great ambitions as a label boss
because I really wanted to promote good music," Robert said. "Jimmy
and I were in a position to buy both Sun Records and Chess. They were
for sale and we took it to the other guys and said we can take these labels and reintroduce them into mainstream popular music."

Ahmet got wind of this and relented. He agreed to the terms Peter
demanded, which ultimately torpedoed the Sun and Chess court-
ships. "The deal was a great one for the band," says Phil Carson, who
consulted on the negotiations. Most attractive was the new royalty
rate. The standard deal Atlantic offered bands was a percentage on
90 percent of sales, less 15 percent for what was referred to as "free
goods"—albums for promotional purposes. Led Zeppelin was awarded
18 percent on 90 percent, which was extremely generous. They also
got an allowance for their office overhead and for expenses.

The label would operate out of Peter's King's Road office in London and Steve Weiss's law office in New York, a warren of rooms in
the *Newsweek* building on Madison Avenue. The band asked Phil Carson, whom they affectionately called Phyllis, to handle the label's day-
to-day operations, an offer he was tempted to accept until Ahmet

Ertegun intervened. According to Carson, "Ahmet said, 'Are you *nuts?* You've got this great career at Atlantic.'" Carson had signed AC/DC and brought in Richard Branson's new Virgin Records venture, and he re-signed Yes after Atlantic had mistakenly let the band depart. A healthy promotion and raise convinced Carson to reconsider and remain where he was.

In addition to finding a suitable label head, there was plenty of work that went into launching the start-up, not only staffing two offices but coming up with a name that would pop. "Led Zeppelin Records" didn't cut it; they felt it would overshadow other acts on the label. A number of names were proposed—"Slag" and "Slut" were two that were rejected for obvious reasons. Something more appropriate was a harder nut to crack.

In the meantime, there was important work to be done on the film they'd begun in New York City. The band knew those performances left a lot to be desired. There'd been too much tumult, too many distractions, the end-of-the-tour blahs, no magic, to say nothing of the robbery. The three nights at Madison Square Garden would never make a Led Zeppelin highlight reel. Collectively, Jimmy referred to them as "an honest sort of mediocre night." The trouble was, mediocre didn't cut it in the editing room. The footage was spotty, the soundtrack wasn't syncing up. There was no complete take of "Whole Lotta Love"! Jimmy castigated the film crew—director Joe Massot, Ernest Day, who'd been behind the camera for *Lawrence of Arabia*, and Bob Freeman, who had shot the resplendent cover for *Meet the Beatles* (*With the Beatles* in the UK)—whom he blamed for being "really out of it." Filming additional concerts was out of the question. Considering it had already cost the band $85,000, the strategy turned to salvaging what was already in the can.

Joe Massot reverted to his original concept: interspersing fantasy sequences into the concert footage, fictional reenactments that would portray each of the band members in a representative way. It was a means of beefing up the sparse coverage and producing something unconventional, artistic, something outside the traditional concert film fattened by the usual self-serving interviews.

Led Zeppelin was game. During October 1973, Massot took a small crew on the road to shoot the vignettes. "It was weird," he said. "I'd go to each one's home, he'd show me around, we'd talk about the film, and two days later we'd be making it." The whole thing was fly-by-the-seat-of-one's-pants filmmaking.

John Paul was flummoxed by it. "I'm suddenly told that a film crew was coming down to my house to shoot a sequence," he said, "and what was I going to do?"

He thought quick. He'd just finished watching a Disney TV mini-series, *The Scarecrow of Romney Marsh*, in which a country priest named Dr. Syn leads a band of marauders against the king's press gangs that are enslaving young men into the Royal Navy. Disney refused to license the rights to the main character, so John Paul simply fashioned his own version in which, according to Joe Massot, "one man and a bunch of masked riders terrify villagers, rape women, and act horribly," after which the man returns home, removes his mask, and reads *Bedknobs and Broomsticks* to his adoring wife and children.

If it was meant as an allegory for Led Zeppelin, no one was saying so. John Paul found the whole episode embarrassing—his acting, especially, but nothing more so than his appearance. After the U.S. tour, he'd cut his long hair in a style that was more army recruit than rock star. For the purposes of continuity, he was forced to wear a cheesy Sir Lancelot page-boy wig, giving his scenes of pillaging a kooky, high-camp effect.

Robert's sequence was just as awkward. Filmed on the beaches of Cardigan Bay in Wales, he envisioned himself as a dashing Arthurian knight, as evinced by mincing, studly poses in a flowing white cape, on a quest to rescue a fair maiden, who, Robert was overheard to say, returned the favor in ways characteristic of Led Zeppelin's extramarital pursuits. In a series of far-fetched sketches, Robert scaled the walls of Raglan Castle, brandished a sword, and fenced to the finish with a raggedy lout. The duel ended when the hero hurled the cad over the castle wall into the moat below. One thing was clear: Robert Plant had nothing on Errol Flynn. Throughout the scenes, he repeatedly strayed out of character and had trouble keeping a straight face. Even the score, a mash-up of "The Rain Song" and "The Song Remains the Same," lent the action a florid artificiality.

Bonzo, to his credit, decided to play it straight. "The camera people came down to my place for a week, and if I was going out somewhere they'd . . . just follow me about," he said. To no less an oratorio than "Moby Dick," Bonzo was filmed in his natural habitat—playing pool at the Conservative Club, having a pint at his local pub, tootling about in a horse and cart with his wife, Pat, drag racing along country lanes in a newly acquired Model T Ford and at Santa Pod Raceway in a nitrogen-fueled AA Dragster, showing off his herd of steer, and bumping around Old Hyde Farm, his estate in Worcestershire.

Peter Grant had already been represented fairly accurately in the scene of him verbally berating a promoter at the Baltimore gig. But just in case his character warranted further definition, he appeared in a skit with his henchman, Richard Cole, in which the two villains were typecast as . . . villains, dressed in Roaring Twenties garb, tear-assing around in a 1928 Pierce-Arrow and dispensing mob justice with machine guns. No doubt the scene gave the creeps to a whole host of viewers who, at one time or another, had been roughed up by the pair.

Jimmy, typically, insisted he be filmed last and on the night of a full moon. A few days before Christmas 1973, he met Joe Massot's crew at Boleskine House, the former Crowley residence near Loch Ness. "Jimmy felt he had something to say about time and the passage of time," Massot recalled. "There's a mountain out back of his house in Scotland, so he decided that he would climb it and act out a very symbolical tale about a young man fighting his way to the top to meet with the old man of the mountain at the summit, Father Time." Both characters, of course, were played by Jimmy Page.

"They created several different faces that showed me as I might look at various ages of life," Jimmy explained. "Then they joined all those shots of the different faces together." It was an honest attempt to express a larger idea. "What I was trying to say was that enlightenment can be achieved at any point in time; it just depends on when you want to access it."

Massot now had plenty of film in the can, some of it intriguing, most of it a mishmash that needed to be assembled into a coherent theme. The concert footage was spotty, the fantasy stuff mostly cringeworthy. And Peter Grant was breathing down his back. Something told G he'd bought a pig in a poke. A lot of time and money had been invested in the project. (Peter had begun referring to it as "the most expensive home movie ever made.") A rough cut might provide a measure of comfort, a kind of road map to determine where everything was headed, but that would require a few months' time in the editing room, pushing the ETA into the spring of 1974.

By that time, Led Zeppelin was otherwise engaged.

## [2]

The itch began in late October 1973. Led Zeppelin had been off the road for a good long month, without a word of complaint from any of its four principals. No one was about to torpedo a good thing. But a month without music—away from playing—was harder to reconcile. A tingle developed under the skin, and with it came the need to scratch that itch.

Jimmy, ever itchy, gathered the troops. He was already looking down the road at another album. It was high time to put some things down on tape, so he sent word: everyone was expected to meet at Headley Grange at the end of the month for a stretch of recording. He'd arranged for a sound truck—an Airstream RV belonging to the Faces' Ronnie Lane that had been converted into a mobile unit with a sixteen-track board—and a hot young engineer, Ron Nevison, who had just finished working with The Who on *Quadrophenia*.

Headley Grange was key to the sound in Jimmy's head, a return to the expansive, echo-filled chamber that had captured such knockout rockers as "Celebration Day," "Black Dog," and "Rock and Roll." "Most of the album will get back to something people think we've been drifting away from: straightforward rock 'n roll," he avowed.

Be that as it may, the Grange was uneasy about renting to Led Zeppelin again. During their last visit, Bonzo, in a drunken rampage, had driven a Range Rover back and forth across the lawn and garden, and the owners refused to book the place until reparations were made.

Another unexpected problem: John Paul Jones never showed. "He turned up at my house one afternoon and told me he'd had enough," Peter Grant recalled. This was an alarming piece of news. No one had seen this coming. G asked Jonesy what he intended to do if he left the band and got a typically droll answer. "He said he was going to be the choirmaster at Winchester Cathedral."

"I'd had enough of touring," John Paul revealed. "There was a lot of pressure on my family, what with being away so long." His young daughters were growing up without their father. And truthfully, he'd never counted on the gig lasting as long as it had. "I thought the band would be fun for a few years, and I needed to do something musically free and fun and liberating—but then I'd get back to the more serious career in the studio. I didn't want to harm the group, but I didn't want my family to fall apart either."

He made a convincing case. Grant was a family man; he understood the drawbacks of the rock 'n roll life. His wife, Gloria, was making similar noises about his constant absences. On the other hand, Led Zeppelin was a multimillion-dollar enterprise. Everyone's livelihoods depended on it. Jonesy needed to get his priorities straight.

"Have you told anyone else?" G asked him.

John Paul shook his head. "No, I came straight to you."

"Well, you're going to be *not too well*," G said, meaning that he would report John Paul's absence as a temporary illness. "Take some time off and think about it."

Even the band wasn't told about Jonesy's disenchantment. He was ill, he had some personal issues—that was all they needed to know. He wouldn't be coming to Headley Grange for the time being. Instead, "the band spent a week or so just running down songs," according to Ron Nevison. "They were doing Elvis covers and stuff like that."

"We began as always, playing around and fooling about for two days," Robert recalled, "playing anything we want, like standards or our own material or anything that comes to us, and slowly but surely we develop a feel that takes us on to the new material."

One night, as a down-and-dirty trio, a loose jam produced versions of "Baby, I Don't Care," "Jailhouse Rock," "One Night," and "Don't Be Cruel," before segueing into the Drifters' "Money Honey" and the old garage-band standby "Summertime Blues." But amusing themselves like that eventually wore thin. Without John Paul they were just spinning their wheels. All three men had better things to do with their time. They decided to break camp and head home.

That presented problems for Ron Nevison. "I'd made a commitment to Pete Townshend to start the *Tommy* film in late January," he recalled, "and because of Jonesy not appearing for a week, I had to ask to leave the [Led Zeppelin] project."

The band went nuts. They gave Nevison a real bollicking, blaming him for running out and ruining their recording session. Bonzo predictably got nasty, Nevison said, "screaming at me, 'You mother-fucker, fuck you, you fucking . . .'"

Considering Ron was on the payroll, G insisted that he remain at Headley Grange throughout November. To cover any losses, it was arranged that Paul Rodgers's new band—one of the first acts signed to Led Zeppelin's new label—would move in and use the time booked at the Grange to lay down some tracks, with Nevison as engineer. That session proved more productive than anyone had anticipated. "We'd been rehearsing like mad," Rodgers recalled, "and we went in and recorded the entire album—banged it all down in one." Boz Burrell, the bass player, marveled at their productivity. "We did eleven tracks in nine days," he said. The band decided to name itself after one of its songs—Bad Company.

L ed Zeppelin took the Christmas holidays off. When the band re-convened at Headley Grange right after the new year, they were a quartet again. No one asked about Jonesy's "illness," and it was never discussed again. He was refreshed and ready to pick up where they'd left off. "Eventually," Peter Grant concluded, "I think he just decided he was doing something he really loved."

Another topic that got glossed over was Robert Plant's voice—it sounded throaty, gravelly. Unbeknownst to the others, he'd had an operation on his vocal cords and hadn't been able to speak for three weeks. He could sing, but not up to his usual octave-piercing output.

Jimmy's enthusiasm made up for any obstacles they encountered. He'd been a busy man and came loaded with riffs that he'd mined over the holidays in his home studio at Plumpton Place. There were bits and pieces of what would eventually become "In the Light," "Ten Years Gone," and "The Wanton Song." He also had a demo that he'd recorded with Bonzo. "He started the drums, and I did the riff and overdubs," Jimmy recalled. It was just that, a shuffle and riff, but it was seductive, moody—Robert described it as a *shoom shoom* tempo—a sturdy foundation to build on.

It was fortunate that Bonzo had found a groove. He'd arrived with Robert, driving a new souped-up BMW and carrying a bag that con-tained fifteen hundred doses of Mandrax, a powerful sedative that rose to fame under its other brand name, Quaalude.

Benji Le Fevre, who'd been recruited to cook for the band, advised Bonzo to stash the pills somewhere safe, away from prying eyes. "A little later, he said to me, 'Come and look,'" Le Fevre recalls. "He'd taped them to the inside of his tom-tom—forgetting, of course, that it was a Perspex [plexiglass] kit, so we could all see it."

When Robert heard that laid-back *shoom shoom* riff, he was suspicious. "Mandrax?" he posited. "No." It had a livelier, more exotic-sounding spirit—"the feel of foreign lands . . . a touch of the east," he concluded, that conjured up his recent holiday in southern Morocco, where he'd tinkered with some lyrics that might be of use. It also reminded him of a trip to India he'd taken with Jimmy in 1971, and imagery from the two recollections—the Himalayas and desert sands—gave him inspiration to work with.

"I wrote the first verse before we had any music," Robert recalled of the visit to Morocco. He was driving into the Sahara Desert, bumping down a dusty track, no sign of humanity for miles, other than the chance Bedouin on a camel who waved at Robert in a nonchalant way. "I just started to write a poem: *'Let the sun beat down upon my face, and the stars to fill my dreams / I am a traveler of both time and space. . . .'*"

He recalled driving into the surrounding hills and feeling the eyes of people watching, as if he "were going through a no-man's land between the borders, where all the Bhutan warriors sit with their horses and muskets, waiting for the tourists." He thought of the Sufi trance musicians of Joujouka, and jotted down: *"To sit with the elders of a gentler race the world has seldom seen. . . ."*

What it all boiled down to was "Kashmir."

"Kashmir" was epic, among the most accomplished songs Led Zeppelin ever recorded. "I had a long piece of music I'd been working on," Jimmy recalled, "and just on the tail end of it I had that riff, that cascade with the brass parts." Another riff, he said, "was going round, just going round and catching up with itself." He could hardly wait to get to Headley Grange to see how the two figures resolved.

From the opening chord sequence, a repetitive drone filled with trepidation and mystery, it sounded like a processional arriving from a far-off kingdom. As the pattern plodded ahead, guided by Robert's timeless narrative, an orchestral fanfare leaped from the trenches, ambushing the moody Moorish theme and disrupting its forward flow. "I wondered whether the two parts could go on top of each other, and it worked!" Jimmy exulted. The rhythmic ground shifted, the two tempos pulling against each other like cultural adversaries defending their borders. It was an exciting tapestry of overlapping musical textures that, like its geographical origins, emphasized the distance the band had traveled. Only experienced musicians could have arrived at this destination.

Later, Jimmy would overdub strings and horns with session players from a Pakistani orchestra based in London which, in his estimation, brought the song "even more to life" and rounded out the arrangement's "ominous . . . particular quality."

The band knew with "Kashmir" they'd created something haunting, special. "I knew what 'Kashmir' was before we'd even recorded it," Jimmy gloated. Robert eventually considered it "the definitive Led Zeppelin song." To him, "Stairway to Heaven" was a trifle, whereas "Kashmir" evoked a time and place that had left its imprint, and he could convey it with conviction. Jimmy played a rough mix for Phil Carlo, the former Zeppelin roadie now working with Bad Company, and told him, "This is the best thing I've ever written." And John Bonham was so excited about the song's outcome, he called Peter Grant, breathlessly imploring him, "'Kashmir'—Come down! Come down! Get in the Porsche and get down here!"

"Kashmir" was a breakthrough. It set the bar high and raised the energy level a few notches, which primed the band to pick up the beat. There was a definite summoning back to the British electric-blues era, when the Yardbirds and Rolling Stones built their sounds on the backs of Mississippi Delta and Chicago mentors. The appropriation was never more evident than in "Custard Pie," a discernibly Led Zeppelin interpretation of a twelve-bar blues. There were plenty of throwback references in the crevices, namely Blind Boy Fuller's 1939 rendition of "I Want Some of Your Pie" and its 1947 heir, "Custard Pie Blues," by Sonny Terry and Brownie McGhee. Robert's lyrics were a near steal of "Drop Down Mama," the Sleepy John Estes classic, with a little of Bukka White's "Shake 'Em On Down" thrown in for good measure.

But the arrangement was all Led Zeppelin. It highlighted the twin poles of the genre—the heritage it was rooted in and the direction in which they were taking it. The distorted vitriol of the guitar solo that stormed in, underscored by a scorching rhythm section, announced that the blues was entering another dimension.

The drumming was especially vicious. The kit had been set up in the entryway of Headley Grange, at the foot of the stairwell, where it had done its thunderous spadework on "When the Levee Breaks" the year before.

"When I got there, I put mics all around the drums," Ron Nevison reported, "but Bonham told me not to use them, to take them down." He assured Bonzo they were there "just in case," but Bonzo was adamant. "No, *not* just in case—*take them down!*" He remembered how Andy Johns had managed to capture the snap and whomp with just two solitary mics and that overmicing muddied the sound.

They'd used the same setup for "The Rover" back at Stargroves (although the song dates back to 1970 at Bron-Yr-Aur), with the benefit of Jimmy's rollicking opening riff that spilled over into a high-strung, inebriated groove. "The Rover" is often referred to as the younger brother of "Whole Lotta Love," but the groove is looser, funkier, and it doesn't peddle a hodgepodge of sound effects and psychedelia swirling around the midsection to fatten the track. If anything held the song in check, it was Robert's tortured vocal cords, which sounded forced into labor, straining for a foothold, much like Rod Stewart in the Jeff Beck Group.

Be that as it may, "Custard Pie" and "The Rover"—the opening numbers on what would be the next album—signaled a blatant return to form for Led Zeppelin, the form that earned them kudos for the highest-energy rock 'n roll since Jerry Lee Lewis bashed out "Whole Lotta Shakin' Going On." These interpretations of American blues incorporated the furious kineticism of garage-band pugnacity with fresh, inventive licks.

The energy was high at Headley Grange. The guys were stoked.

They worked long hours each day, laying down tracks for eight new songs, with ample time set aside for R&R. "There was a lot of camaraderie at that point," says Benji Le Fevre, "four young men really enjoying themselves." The atmosphere was laid-back and loose. They met for breakfast at a greasy-spoon diner on the A3 each morning, then sat around the living-room fireplace with an array of instruments at their feet, exchanging ideas.

"Some artists like to sit down and plan an album," Robert explained. "We just can't do that. Our music is more an impromptu thing. It falls out of your head and onto the floor, and you pick it up and it bounces. That's how it works."

And sometimes a little extra was needed to stimulate inspiration. "There were quite a lot of drugs coming through the door," Benji recalls. At times, Headley Grange was better provisioned than a pharmacy. There was hashish, Quaaludes, acid, heroin, and enough cocaine to light up a small city. "You'd just work and break for dinner, and then 'Charlie' would turn up," Ron Nevison said.

Nevison wasn't used to working under the auspices of cocaine. His experience with The Who had hewed to a different refreshment and timetable. "When I worked with Pete [Townshend] on *Quadrophenia*, he would start drinking a bottle of cognac at noon, and when it was empty was when we finished, around ten at night." Cocaine wasn't set to a standard clock. "With Zeppelin . . . they were waking me up at four o'clock in the morning and we weren't getting anything done." Wired to the teeth, convinced it was time to record, they tinkered futilely until passing out. To save his sanity, Ron moved out of Headley Grange to a guesthouse down the road and began locking the remote studio at midnight.

That, of course, didn't sit well with the band. Nevison was already on thin ice with them. He'd made it clear he was leaving soon to work on the *Tommy* movie. And in general they considered him "a bit of a pompous ass." When he'd turned up in January, it was behind the wheel of a flashy Bentley that raised eyebrows as the ride for a young engineer. Bonzo got pissed at him one day, snuck into the kitchen, and shoved a baking potato into the exhaust pipe of the car. In a scene more suited to an Our Gang comedy, the guys hid behind a tree waiting for Ron to drive off and split their sides laughing when they heard the inevitable *bang!*

Jimmy's irritation with Nevison was more consequential. In the studio, Ron felt the need to get creative, to impress, whereas Jimmy simply wanted him to press "record." Other times, Ron's concentration seemed too nonchalant, so that Jimmy took to calling him Ron Nevermind. For the time being, there was détente, but a growing feeling ensued that he wouldn't be missed when he moved on.

In the meantime, the rich vein of creativity continued to yield songs. "'Ten Years Gone' was originally going to be an instrumental," Jimmy explained. "It has a certain feeling to it, a melancholy feeling, and the theme the lyrics took was exactly along the lines I had been thinking as I had been putting it together." He and Robert had developed a nice synchronicity in their collaboration. "There's a certain amount of discussion, but usually it's just there naturally. I'm sure I could write down on a piece of paper how I visualized a piece of music before Robert writes the lyrics, and they would match up."

"Ten Years Gone" played right into their wheelhouse. "I demoed it at home, the guitars . . . everything," Jimmy said. "I really was quite passionate about getting that one together." He'd envisioned it as an instrumental, propelled by an expansive overlay of fluid guitar passages, but at Headley Grange, the song blossomed into something more. At the top, Jimmy laid down a rolling, reverb-laden groove that was both melancholy in mood and exotic in texture. For more than a minute, the sound that enveloped the main theme was spellbinding. The chords created a soothing whirlpool effect, building to a crescendo of anticipation.

When Robert finally broke into the extended curtain-raiser, there was a sense of inevitability. Alas, he sounded miles away, lethargic.

The dreamy imagery he contributed was as discursive as the musical texture: "*Then, as it was, then again it will be / And though the course may change sometimes, rivers always reach the sea.*" But when John Paul and Bonzo staged their long-overdue entrance, the song began to gain momentum. A gyrating guitar solo halfway through served to drive Robert into an earthy R&B groove, swinging "Ten Years Gone" back and forth between deliverance and a more wistful pace.

The songs' intricate construction grew out of an all-around collaborative effort. Every musician brought something to the table. "With 'In the Light,' we knew exactly what its construction was going to be," Jimmy said, "but nevertheless, I had no idea at the time that John Paul Jones was going to come up with such an amazing synthesizer intro, plus all the bowed guitars at the beginning as well, to give the overall drone effect."

The intro was a lulu, a tour de force. It stretched on for a minute and forty-five seconds, a sound like the mullahs calling the faithful to prayer. John Paul performed a *Phantom of the Opera*–like overture hunched over a VCS-3 synthesizer, "attempting to get a sort of Indian sound." Jimmy, who chipped in, bowing his guitar, was ecstatic. "It was just unbelievable," he rejoiced.

But not early on, at the drawing board. The track began life as "In the Morning," with a Plant lyric that set out to outdo "The Lemon Song" in its explicit insinuation. An initial version began: "*Sing a song in the morning—come on the one I love.*" Reasonably, the line was altered in other takes to "*Sing a song in the morning, sing a song of the ocean, hear it every day, it's a song of salvation.*" Robert exchanged the refrain "*In the morning, in the morning, in the morning*" for "*In the light, in the light, in the light,*" and gradually the song rambled toward its final shape.

"Trampled Under Foot" underwent a similar genesis. "When we first ran through it," John Bonham recalled, "John Paul and Jimmy started off the riff, and we thought it was a bit soul-y for us. Then we changed it around a bit."

The first six takes of the song, initially entitled "Brandy & Coke," were a stumble through musical wilderness, trying to find the right groove. Bonzo was right, the early attempts were too self-consciously funky. Jonesy and Jimmy conspired to play an opening vamp that referenced Stevie Wonder's peerless "Superstition," and Bonzo, John Paul said, "came in with this glorious stomp that had a great feel," pushing the funk quotient further and giving the song "swagger." But it needed work to refine the structure.

"I immediately thought the drive and the pace of the thing resembled a car," Robert said, "so I started and wrote two verses while the band were running through it." He disappeared into one of the vacant upstairs bedrooms and polished off the rest of the lyrics in half an hour, leaning heavily on a Chuck Berry–style rap scheme that rolled off his tongue. "It's a wordplay," he announced triumphantly. "*Greasy slick damn body, groovy leather trim / Like the way you hold the road, momma it ain't no sin.*"

With the lyrics in tow and eight different takes behind them, Led Zeppelin finally hit pay dirt on the ninth go-round with a definitive version that swung between uptown funk and all-out rocker. Musically, the track exploded. The lurching rhythm—its tension and releases, the thrust of the beat—propelled an ensemble climb into the highest of gears. Occasionally, Jimmy stepped out front to deliver a few stinging asides. His guitar fills were loaded with reverb and backward echo that punctuated each measure with editorial precision. John Paul's elastic solo supercharged the instrumental break, filtering the clavinet's twitchy figures through a wah-wah, thus paying further homage to Stevie Wonder. If anything, "Trampled Under Foot" made a case for how Led Zeppelin could create a danceable beat if they put their backs into it.

"The Wanton Song" was more of a jam, a heavy-metal jam, that gave John Bonham a spotlight in which to shine. His angular jabs and ropy fills provided the song with liftoff and steadied it along its dodgy trajectory. His wrist control throughout was astonishing, like a machine but with soul. As Robert once remarked, "I'd never seen another drummer anywhere as near as dynamic." Bonzo had the shading of a Renaissance artist, so many contrasts and colors. He played on the beat, between the beats, even in the pregnant pauses. "He was a real thrifty player," Robert said. "It was what he *didn't* do that made it work." He was the master of restraint, at least behind his drum kit.

Lyrically, once again Robert couldn't control his adolescent impulses. "*Silent woman, in the night you came,*" he chortled. "*Took my seed from my shakin' frame.*" It was a sop to the young male fans who wanted their music and their fantasies served on the same plate. The combination felt new, yet it was in the tradition of the old blues stylists who dished out the same kind of insinuation in song after song.

"Sick Again," recorded in early 1974, was another song about sex, only this time Robert took aim at the groupie scene during the 1973 tour—"about ourselves and what we see in Los Angeles." His primary target was the "LA queens," the teenagers who serviced the band, held in high regard until their "downhill slide" into adulthood. Robert's girlfriends weren't as young as Jimmy's; many hovered around the age of consent. His bitterness toward the adolescent girls surfaced in lines like "*One day soon you're gonna reach sixteen / Painted lady in the city of lies.*" He didn't feel the need to hide a fascination: "*Said you dug me since you were thirteen / Then you giggled as you heaved and sighed.*"

"The words show I feel a bit sorry for them," he said. "One minute she's twelve and the next minute she's thirteen and over the top."

It's telling of attitudes of the times that cultural commentators didn't call out such sentiments as offensive. Rock 'n roll bands—especially Led Zeppelin, perhaps the most egregious in the behavior department—were given a pass.

There were no such quibbles with "In My Time of Dying," an epic performance adapted from a long line of blues and traditional recordings. The lyrics date back to a 1927 recording by gospel blues evangelist Blind Willie Johnson entitled "Jesus Make Up My Dying Bed" and his identical take the following year on a single, "I Know His

Blood Can Make Me Whole." Charley Patton recorded it in 1929 with the title "Jesus Is A Dying Bed Maker" and Josh White in 1944 as "In My Time of Dying." White was one of Bob Dylan's mentors, so it was no coincidence that Dylan recorded a version on his 1962 debut album. By the time Led Zeppelin got their hands on it in 1974, the song's authorship was credited to "Page, Plant, Jones, Bonham."

Jimmy described the band's version as something "immediate," meaning "it was being put together when we recorded it," and over the course of six takes its evolution was apparent. At the outset, they encountered difficulty coming in and out of Jimmy's sinuous slide-guitar riffs. The split-second timing and syncopation eluded them. But by the third take, the arrangement started to jell.

Jimmy's doleful Danelectro guitar established the mood, drawling out long, heavily accented chords that swooped across stereo channels, creating an air of mystery and unease. His phrasing was detailed and dramatic. Southern accents were evident in his usual nuanced style, contributing to the solitude lying just beneath the surface.

As the title indicates, it's a dying song, a plea to one's maker for mercy, for a fair shake in the afterlife, and Robert was more than convincing in his grizzled supplication. He asked for deliverance with regret and penitence, sounding like a man who knew he had only a fifty-fifty chance. "*Oh, never did, did no harm, did no harm / I've only been that young once*," he implored, and despite evidence to the contrary, one almost believed him. There was an immediacy of feeling, an earnestness he was unable to suppress. The performance, conforming faithfully to the rural blues idiom, was worthy of Robert's vaunted predecessors.

The arrangement, on the other hand, dispensed with formalities. The rhythm section owed more to Lynyrd Skynyrd than to Leadbelly. It tore through the veneer of southern refinement like a summer storm. Bonzo, certainly, showed it no respect. "He just played the guitar riff," Ron Nevison said, "he made it his drum part. Instead of laying down a 4/4 feel with a bass player and letting the riff kind of wander through that, whatever riff Jimmy came up with, he played that riff— and he helped create a very interesting and unique sound."

It was savage, merciless, a barrage of thunder created in the cavernous entrance hall at Headley Grange. The band played right into Bonzo's monster beat. They stretched out, turning the gospel-tinged plaint into a fraught British blues jam that required every reserve of concentration to pull off. A lick or a phrase inserted without warning threatened to capsize the entire thing. There are bass and guitar lines of soaring beauty, but the band got lost as the action snowballed. The song never really drew to a close. "It's jammed at the end, and we didn't have a proper way to stop the thing," Jimmy admitted.

Robert employed every vocal device in an effort to wrap it up— half a dozen *bye, bye*s, an equal number of *I'll touch Jesus*es and *oh, oh, oh, oh*s, an attempt at *go, go, go, take, take, take*, even *go . . . take*—when they finally pulled the plug, someone coughed, and Bonzo announced, "That's gonna be the one, has to be."

Eight new songs in a little under six weeks' time, with plenty of days off in between to check in with families. They even fiddled with an instrumental of Jimmy's called "Swan Song" that got lost in the shuffle, though the title would eventually come in handy. But there was a finality to the work at Headley Grange. By the end of February 1974, the musicians' attention had begun to wane.

Vanessa Gilbert, one of the band's Los Angeles entourage now living in London, recalls that, somewhere toward the end of the sessions, she got a call from BP Fallon, who said, "John Paul wants to see you at Headley Grange." A cab was sent, with Beep and a young female model already seated comfortably in the back. They got lost en route on the maze of country roads, and a roadie named Peppy was sent to recover them. "He was on so many drugs in Bonzo's new BMW, and he hit everything in his path, like bumper cars," Vanessa says.

The scene wasn't much better at Headley Grange. "Everybody was on drugs," she says. "They were sitting around a giant table in the kitchen. Poor John Paul had taken too much Mandrax, and his face

was in a bowl of spaghetti. The guys had to carry him up to a bedroom, and while they were at it, they threw a live sheep into Beep's
room and lit up an orange smoke bomb to go with it."

Yes, definitely time to call it a wrap. There was plenty of material
in the can, and a lot left over from the *Houses of the Holy* sessions. Perhaps enough for a *double* album. Such an option had already entered
the conversation, but there was still much work to be done—overdubs,
a mix or two—and anything could happen.

In the meantime, London was calling. Led Zeppelin had a record
company to run.

## [3]

While Led Zeppelin was recording at Headley Grange, Peter Grant
was laying the groundwork for the band's new record label. He officially opened the office on the King's Road in London but wanted to
establish a presence in New York, where the operation was being combined with Steve Weiss's law office. In any case, G's management responsibilities were steep enough. Neither he nor Zeppelin's principals
had any intention of spending time on the day-to-day drudgery of running a record company. Someone else was needed to do the donkey-
work. Phil Carson would have been a perfect fit; it still smarted that
he'd turned the job down. So, too, had Mark London, with whom G
comanaged Maggie Bell. "I thanked him," London recalled, "but said
I didn't think I could do the job well enough." Clive Coulson, G's
partner on Bad Company, lacked the necessary polish.

In desperation, Peter summoned Danny Goldberg, the band's
publicist, to London. He and the guys had grown fond of Goldberg,
whom they called "Goldilocks," and felt he was plugged in to the
scene in a way that complemented the band's hip quotient. The offer
Grant made Danny was vague. "I'd like you to be my ambassador in
the States," Peter said. "You'll still oversee press but liaise with Atlan-

tic's sales and promotion departments and even handle aspects of the tours." In exchange, Danny talked G into giving him the title of vice president of the label, which still was without a name. Until they came up with something, he'd be employed by a holding company called Culderstead Ltd.

Danny moved into Steve Weiss's suite of offices on Madison Avenue in New York City. Weiss's law practice was in a state of flux. His elderly, old-line partners had left the firm, which was given over almost entirely to a rock 'n roll clientele. In addition to Led Zeppelin, Weiss represented Jeff Beck, Rod Stewart, Herman's Hermits, Dusty Springfield, and an outlier named Jim Henson, who was shopping around an idea he called the Muppets. The former law conference room was reconverted into a music pad, with studio-quality stereo equipment handpicked by John Bonham. The walls, formerly covered in plush rosewood panels, were papered over with purple velvet, and in the center of the room stood a round purple-and-orange couch. Steve had also undergone a makeover of his own. Gone were the pin-striped suits and close-cropped haircuts. He now dressed almost exclusively in sparkly numbers custom made at Nudie's in Texas. At Led Zeppelin's most recent Madison Square Garden concert, Steve had shown up in a lime-green paisley suit over a flowered shirt. He'd let his hair grow long, weirdly long, and he had a girlfriend, Marie Ivey, in tow in place of his wife, Joan, who'd remained behind at their Great Neck estate. He'd even painted his 1957 Rolls-Royce forest green and tan.

According to Danny Goldberg, Steve Weiss took some getting used to. "I never really knew what to make of him," Danny says. "He was a tough guy and quick-tempered, a shady character—Tom Hagen, Zeppelin's consigliere—and gave the impression that he associated with gangsters. He made the people at Atlantic nervous." Steve's swagger and take-no-prisoners attitude suited Peter Grant's way of doing business. "But he worshipped Peter. If Peter said 'Jump,' Steve said, 'How high?'"

The London office was another matter altogether. It remained a pretty bare-bones operation. Grant bought a cottage in Hay's Mews so he could stay in town, close to the business, but he rarely came into the office. He'd become hostage to his growing cocaine habit. Instead, he delegated the daily responsibilities at King's Road to Richard Cole, a man with his own significant drug issues. "There were low-life drug dealers always hanging around the office," says a colleague. In fact, Ricardo had already solidified a reliable contact in the neighborhood, a sleazy character named Byron who dealt out of Granny Takes a Trip, a boutique around the corner.

Mark London moved into the second-floor office, where he ran a music publishing company, Color Me Gone (London cowrote the hit "To Sir with Love," among other songs), and looked after Maggie Bell. Otherwise, the nuts and bolts of Culderstead Ltd. were left to Carole Brown, Peter's long-suffering assistant.

"Most of what I was doing," she says, "was arranging shipment of all the cars—Cords and Pierce-Arrows—he'd bought in America. I had to get in touch with Lord Beaulieu at the Montagu Museum in Hampshire to find out how to get old cars into the country and clear everything with DHL Air Freight at the airport."

Occasionally G focused on getting Led Zeppelin's record label off the ground. Contrary to everyone's wishes, Bad Company would not be the first release. They had a killer single on their album that everyone was convinced would be a smash hit. "Mick Ralphs had written 'Can't Get Enough' for Ian Hunter when they were in Mott the Hoople, but Ian couldn't sing it," says Phil Carlo. Bad Company had turned it into an unforgettable, smoking-hot rocker. Unfortunately, Paul Rodgers and Simon Kirke, both late of Free, were still under contract to Island Records, so the album would be an Island release.

Instead, the still-unnamed label would make its debut with Maggie Bell. Since the tragic end of Stone the Crows, Maggie had fashioned a solo career that paid dividends on her earlier promise. She was a riveting performer, animated, unflinching, able to wring every last ounce of emotion from a song. When she ripped into a feverish blues, it was as though Janis Joplin's ghost were dubbing her voice. Few women artists demonstrated that kind of raw power. But getting it on a record was no easy feat.

She made quick work of an album produced by Felix Cavaliere, the lead singer from the Rascals. "We did a number of Laura Nyro songs. Luther Vandross did the backup vocal," Maggie recalls. There were a ferocious set of soul classics tailor-made for her voice: "Rescue Me," "If You Want to Make a Fool of Somebody," "I Know (You Don't Love Me No More)." There was even a cover that featured a photo of Peter Grant dressed to the nines, sitting in a throne-like chair with a shotgun on his lap. "But the album just disappeared, as in *disappeared*. It never was mastered as far as I know," she said.

In fact, the album was rejected. "It was lousy," says Janine Safer, the new record label's press officer. "The production was an unholy mess, over-produced within an inch of its life. And more backing vocals than you could shake a stick at." Peter Grant decided they shouldn't put it out. So Maggie went back into the studio and cut another album, entitled *Belle Star*, with another Felix—Felix Pappalardi, the bass player and lead vocalist from Mountain. According to Maggie, "It was a nightmare. We'd have a session booked for ten in the morning, and he'd turn up at ten at night. He was out of control. They scrapped the whole thing."

Maggie, admittedly, was "upset, a real mess." Peter Grant provided no comfort. He was "indisposed" or "unavailable" whenever she sought advice from him, and Led Zeppelin had taken a hands-off approach. Her career seemed to be in limbo when she took an unexpected call from Ahmet Ertegun. "Jerry Wexler wants to record you," he said. *Jerry Wexler!* It was like winning the lottery. Wexler had rescued Aretha Franklin's career and produced those incredible soul masterpieces, one after the other. And he took Dusty Springfield to Memphis and delivered the album of a lifetime. Wexler had the golden touch. He invited Maggie to his home in the Hamptons, and the two spent days strolling along the beach, sorting out a game plan. Wexler promised her great songs—he had a knack for uncovering hits and had already put aside some by John Prine and J.J. Cale—and an all-star group of session players, including Cornell Dupree, Hugh McCracken, Richard Tee, and Steve Gadd.

Despite all the setbacks and the odds stacked against her, Maggie Bell would wind up being the first artist released on Led Zeppelin's new record label. But even that distinction had strings attached. She was on the label . . . but *not* on the label. Her album would appear on Atlantic Records, because Led Zeppelin's label still had no name.

## Chapter Fifteen

# FLYING TOO CLOSE
# TO THE SUN

**[1]**

Despite the layoff, Led Zeppelin had plenty on their plates to deal with.

While working on the new album in early 1974, they'd taken a night off to check in with Joe Massot on the progress of their documentary. The director organized a screening to preview a rough cut of the work in progress and, hopefully, to give them reassurance that things were rolling along smoothly. They were a rough bunch to please, never reticent about their feelings. Jimmy acknowledged that "the band was mad at [Massot] all the time." Massot knew there were doubts. The footage, he hoped, would speak for itself.

Unfortunately, it spoke all too vividly. Everyone fidgeted from the moment the lights went down. As actors readily admit, it's a strange experience to see your image on the screen. Flaws and blemishes are too easily magnified, no one is ever satisfied. A few invitees at the screening claimed Jimmy thought his ass looked too big; when he appeared as Father Time in the fantasy sequence, Bonzo burst into hysterics. "They finally came to the 'Stairway to Heaven' sequence," Massot recalled, "and started to fight and yell." Robert had worn extremely tight-fitting jeans during that scene, making his crotch look IMAX-ready. "They thought it was my fault that Robert had such a big cock."

There was plenty of bellyaching to go around. "We found a lot of the things we'd hoped would be there hadn't come out right," Bonzo said.

The biggest knock against Massot, Jimmy said, was "that he didn't get all of 'Whole Lotta Love' on film." There were bits and pieces of it, but not enough to capture the song's dynamism. "At the time, the film didn't seem very meaningful. It actually seemed amateurish and weird."

Peter Grant had seen enough. He summarily sacked Massot and, in typical fashion, sent a team of thugs to the director's flat to repossess the editing equipment. As for the film, the lingering question was whether to continue—to throw good money after bad. G had had some preliminary discussion with Peter Clifton, a young Australian documentary filmmaker, about taking over and sent him to look at Massot's rough cut. Clifton came away unimpressed. Massot, he realized, was out of his depth.

"None of the material he had captured on 16mm or 35mm actually created sequences," Clifton said. "There were a few good shots, but they didn't match up; there was no continuity and no cutaways or matching material to edit or build sequences." Some of the documentary footage was worth salvaging, in his estimation, "but there's nothing that holds together as a film." He also got the impression from Led Zeppelin that "the guys weren't terribly into it." Clifton was all for moving on and forgetting it.

Instead, Peter Grant called him and said, "Jimmy loves your editing, so we'd like you to make the film."

Clifton agreed to work on a script that would include shooting additional concert footage, either at a gig or on a soundstage. In the meantime, he'd evaluate the overall project and come up with a plan on how to proceed.

The most pressing piece of business for Led Zeppelin, however, was naming the damn record label. The clever names had all hit a dead end, either because they were salacious, because they were already taken, or because one of the guys expressed an objection. Somewhere in the exchange, Jimmy flashed on the unfinished instrumental on his studio drawing board. *Swan Song.* Supposedly, a swan song was a beautiful sound that normally silent swans emit in the throes of death. It was apocryphal but sparked some lively discussion. "If you think about it in relation to the original Led Zeppelin idea of a lead balloon, it's carrying on the original idea," Jimmy quipped.

Robert understood the allusion in a way only he could. "The name Led Zeppelin means a failure and Swan Song means a last gasp," he said, "so why not name our record label that?" Consider their roster: Bad Company's Paul Rodgers and Simon Kirke were late of Free and Mick Ralphs ex–Mott the Hoople; Maggie Bell was formerly with Stone the Crows; Robert was flirting with signing the Pretty Things, who had been around the block once or twice. It'd be the Miami Beach of record labels, where old rock 'n roll acts went to die.

*Swan Song*—everyone liked the way it sat on the tongue. Finally! The label had a name.

Lore has it that Jimmy saw a print of *Evening (The Fall of Day)*, a painting by eccentric Romantic painter William Rimmer and adapted it as the Swan Song logo. In fact, Peter Grant commissioned Aubrey Powell, who had designed the artwork for *Houses of the Holy*, to create something that would make a statement.

"I immediately came up with a design for a Formula One racing car with zeppelins on the side and dark blue stars all over it," Po recalls. Close—but the band wanted something that had more poetry to it. "I had four or five illustrators working on it, so lots of ideas came along. Storm [Thorgerson, his partner] and I had been talking about an image of the winged Icarus figure in Milton's *Paradise Lost* who flew too close to the sun. I got Joe Petagno, an American artist, to draw the illustration, and I showed it to the band. Everybody loved it."

Still, there was a rub. "It looks a bit like Robert," Bonzo said.

Sure enough, the figure had a fey, hippie-like aspect. Po insisted Robert had never crossed his mind and was given the go-ahead to put it into production. "But I found it strange," he says. "Nobody said to me, 'Icarus flew too close to the sun . . . and got burnt.'"

———

Swan Song officially opened for business in May, 1974. The King's Road office was a hive of activity, and in the beginning, Jimmy and Robert made a concerted effort to show up there regularly. The two frontmen were determined that the label not depend entirely on the next Led Zeppelin album to drop.

"I didn't want to end up as Led Zeppelin's label with *only* Led Zeppelin on it," Robert reminded anyone who asked.

They were acutely aware that it had taken the Rolling Stones two years to sign the first act to their label—Kracker, an unqualified bust. That was a hard lesson learned by example. No, Swan Song was not "going to be an ego thing," Jimmy insisted. He was clear about how Led Zeppelin would avoid obvious pitfalls. When it came to signing acts, they were interested only in bands who were reasonably self-sufficient. "We didn't really want to get bogged down in having to develop artists. We wanted people who were together enough to handle that type of thing themselves."

They already had a good head start. Peter had opted to manage Bad Company himself and word on their album was heating up in places that mattered. "Atlantic knew they had a smash on their hands," says Phil Carson. The album was a barn burner from start to finish—great performances, four or five potential singles. The group had already been booked on a long Edgar Winter Band tour. "And Jerry Wexler was delirious about his Maggie Bell sessions."

The Pretty Things would be another key addition. The journeyman band had *succès d'estime*—massive critical respect without a popular following. Their 1968 album *S.F. Sorrow* was acknowledged as the first rock opera, recorded eighteen months before *Tommy* (but in U.S. stores three months after The Who's epic), and their follow-up, *Parachute*, was a *Rolling Stone* "Album of the Year." Neither of them, however, found any sort of audience.

Robert bumped into Phil May, the Pretty Things' lead singer and remaining original member, in a club one night in 1974. "I told him how great I thought the band's albums were," he said, adding: "One day, I'd love to come to you and make you an offer and help you move it along a bit."

That day had finally arrived. Jimmy was completely on board. He had played on the Pretty Things' first session in 1965 and thought "Rosalyn," one of their early singles, packed enormous punch. Both he and Robert hoped that a Swan Song makeover would provide the band with a long-overdue breakthrough.

They also made a play for Roy Harper. He continued to captivate them as a shape-shifting artist, to the consternation of others in their entourage. Harper was an acquired taste. He could play—no doubt about that. His fingerpicking wizardry blew the mind of no less a stylist than Jimmy Page, who had played on two tracks of Harper's *Lifemask* album. But the general consensus on Roy was, as one music manager so eloquently put it, "fucking weird, on some strange planet of his own." Talking to him was challenging; he was a master of ornate misdirection. Was he putting you on or a serious space cadet? Jimmy and Robert loved his eccentricity. Roy was unique, they felt. He had a loyal following and was the kind of artist who would give Swan Song class.

Negotiations, however, dragged on forever. According to Richard Cole, "Peter could never make an amicable agreement with his manager."

It wasn't chiefly the manager's fault. Peter had become a hard man to reach. He put in an occasional appearance at the Swan Song office, but mostly he worked from home. It had become a refuge from the craziness of the road. An appointment to see G inevitably meant an

odyssey. First of all, it required a two-hour trek to Horselunges in East
Sussex. If that weren't demanding enough, a scheduled meeting time
had anywhere from a three- to five-hour window to it—*if* luck was
on your side. People had been known to arrive at the planned hour
on a Wednesday morning and not see Peter until Friday afternoon.
Phil Carson, who made the trip regularly, says, "I always packed an
overnight bag and made sure I had enough work to keep me busy."

"Horselunges was a lovely old house," Aubrey Powell says, "especially in those early days, when it was full of joy and family. The interior was especially beautiful." Mixed in with the animal heads and
trophies on the walls was a world-class collection of antiques. A gorgeous medieval billiards table stood regally in a grand salon. Peter had
also built a ballet studio, complete with barre and mirrored walls, for
his daughter Helen and wife, Gloria. "There was a very laid-back atmosphere at Horselunges," says Phil Carlo, who visited often. "All
sorts of people wandered in and out—roadies, drug dealers, musicians. Peter's son had a nasty-looking snake, and there were two dogs
that ran around the place and shit on the floor."

But there were rules, as well. If and when Grant conducted business at home, he'd retire to "the great chamber," a salon off the entrance, and seal it off. "When you saw this piece of leather string go
through the door," his daughter recalled, "it meant it was locked from
the inside, and the message was to 'fuck off.'" G preferred never to set
foot in the London office, but as Swan Song rolled out its roster of
acts, his presence there was imperative.

Maggie Bell's album, *Queen of the Night*, was released in April
1974, and while it had an Atlantic label on it, she was being touted and
recognized as Swan Song's debut artist. The record, despite huge expectations, was an artistic letdown. It was too slick. It sounded like it
was made with studio musicians playing airtight arrangements, but
without soul. As one Swan Song staffer put it: "over-produced within
an inch of its life—an unholy mess." It had no edge. Jerry Wexler

made the kind of studio album he might have constructed for Roberta Flack, "giving the whole thing a clean production," a British review concluded. Maggie sounded neutered, uninspired. "There is rarely more than a momentary flash in which you feel that the voice is un-selfconscious: its elemental quality is transparently stylized." Peter Grant put it in his usual blunt way. "The album lacks balls," he said. "It lacks Maggie Bell."

Still, the game plan was to extoll Maggie as the First Lady of Swan Song, so her presence was ceremonial at three consecutive launch parties for the label—in New York, Los Angeles, and London. The first one, on May 7 at the legendary Four Seasons restaurant in Manhattan, was a particularly lavish affair, with two hundred of New York's toniest scene makers on hand. Predictably, the swan theme was omnipresent. There were swan-shaped cream pastries and a flock of the creatures swimming in the Pool Room's renowned fountain, a body of water through which Bonzo made a sloppy entrance. Danny Goldberg, who arranged for the animals, was a city boy who could differentiate between Bruce Springsteen and Lou Reed, but *swans* and *geese*? Not so much. Peter grant threw a fit. "We all live on fucking farms!" he bellowed. "*Get these geese out of here!*"

Led Zeppelin had flown in from London and sat isolated in a corner, giving off the vibe that anyone approaching their table would be dragged off in leg irons. Bonzo was particularly sullen. He'd drunk throughout the journey from Heathrow to JFK and had pissed himself rather than get up to use the bathroom. At the launch party, he took up where he'd left off, throwing back one glass of wine after the next. Wives and partners had been left off the guest list—judiciously so, as young Lori Mattix had arrived from Los Angeles to resume her relationship with Jimmy Page, and a bevy of groupies gravitated to the St. Regis hotel, where Led Zeppelin had a series of suites.

It wasn't long before things went squiffy. Richard Cole had requisitioned a platter from the Four Seasons' swank buffet, emptied a mound of cocaine onto it, and draped a cloth napkin, waiter style, over his arm. "Hors d'oeuvres, anyone?" he intoned, offering his fare to those at the band's table. "We snorted the drug right off the plate," he recalled, "with Jimmy, Bonzo, and I monopolizing most of it."

At some point in the festivities, Richard and Bonzo, both drunk and intemperately high, began riling up the geese, no mean undertaking, as they had weights strapped to their feet to keep them from leaving the fountain. Cole managed to chase two out onto busy Fifty-second Street, where they were instantaneously killed in traffic.

New York was potentially dangerous for Led Zeppelin, too. The FBI's investigation of the Drake Hotel robbery remained unsolved and ongoing, with agents scouring the St. Regis, conducting new, harder-edged interviews while the band was in town. "It was heavy-duty shit, but Jimmy told me not to worry about it," Lori recalls, "that Richard had taken the money, and everything was fine." Peter Grant wasn't as worried about the FBI's probe so much as he was about their finding an underage girl in Jimmy's suite. "You can't have fucking Lori hanging around here," he declared. He had her put on the next plane out of town.

Jimmy wasn't as sorry to see her go as he might have let on. Lori had arranged to have her friend, twenty-one-year-old model Bebe Buell, stay in an adjoining suite next to Jimmy's. As soon as Lori was out of the picture, Bebe, who had been in a relationship with Todd Rundgren, moved in on Jimmy and accompanied him to Los Angeles.

The flight to LA for the second launch party nearly ended in disaster. A yahoo in the first-class cabin took offense that scruffy-looking characters in jeans—he called them "degenerates"—had the temerity to invade his space. "What do you guys do for a living?" he demanded. The guy was drunk, so they ignored him. Returning sometime later, he descended on Maggie Bell, Lisa Robinson, *New York Times* music columnist Loraine Alterman, and Atlantic's PR flak Annie Ivil, who were giggling and camped out around a seat near the front of the plane.

"This is a boys-only section," he sneered menacingly. He thrust his jaw in the direction of Peter Grant. "Who's this—your pimp?"

G, who had chased a couple Valium with several glasses of champagne, was slow to get up. "Hold on a second," he said, struggling to his feet. "Mind your mouth in front of these ladies."

"The guy was on Peter in a flash," Maggie said, "and he drew a bloody gun."

"Do you know what this is?" the man asked Peter.

There are various accounts of what happened next, but however the argument resolved, the would-be assailant was met by federal agents and led away in handcuffs once the plane touched down.

Ahmet Ertegun had rented the ballroom of the Hotel Bel-Air for Swan Song's Los Angeles launch party on May 10. Danny Goldberg had given him a wish list of guests that flummoxed the Atlantic Records president. "Jane Fonda. Warren Beatty. Cary Grant. How the fuck am I going to get people like that to come?" Ahmet wondered. "Zeppelin sells a lot of records, but they are *not* the Rolling Stones." The Stones were avid socialites; they loved to hobnob with celebrities, and vice versa. The only people movie stars envied more than other movie stars were rock stars; actors loved being seen in their company. But Led Zeppelin didn't encourage those kinds of friendships. They kept to themselves. At parties, they closed ranks in the back of VIP sections. They expressed no interest in cultivating relationships with cultural and artistic figures outside the world of music, nor were they political like other musicians and celebrities, who were engaged with the antiwar and civil rights movements. And the band's reputation preceded them, not just as bad boys—the Stones, of course, were bad boys—but as *bad* bad boys. A suggestion of violence shadowed them and their management. In the end, Ahmet was able to convince the Stones' Bill Wyman to show up, along with Bryan Ferry, another Atlantic artist. As far as Hollywood celebrities went, Lloyd Bridges was the sum total.

Maggie Bell had better luck. "I was told I could invite people, so I invited Groucho Marx," she says. She was "gobsmacked" when the frail, eighty-four-year-old comedian turned up, steered to her table in a fancy wheelchair. When they were introduced, Groucho broke into a croaky rendition of the music-hall ditty "I Belong to Glasgow."

"Groucho," Peter Grant interjected, "Maggie is one of the great singers of all time."

"Fuck that," Groucho said. "All you girls from Scotland have big tits. Let me see them. Let me give them a squeeze."

Whether or not Maggie complied is open to debate. But Groucho did rope Ahmet Ertegun into helping him sing "Hooray for Captain Spaulding" from the Marx Brothers' *Animal Crackers*, reducing Ahmet to barking out *"Hooray, hooray, hooray"* and clapping like a trained seal every time Groucho pointed at him.

At least the swans at the Los Angeles party were true to form— and so was Bonzo, who'd been drinking since he woke up that morning. He accosted a writer from *Sounds* magazine, who was happy to kowtow before the man he considered to be "the greatest drummer in the world." Unmoved, Bonzo grabbed the writer by the lapels and screamed, "I've taken enough shit from you guys in the press, and I'm not taking any more."

While Bonzo was being sorted out, another scene was developing across the room. Jimmy had arrived with Bebe Buell on his arm at around the same time Lori Mattix wandered in, woozy from a Quaalude she had taken and clearly suffering a case of heartache. "I was devastated she stole my boyfriend," Lori recalls. "Bebe and I had it out in the bathroom. I got a bloody nose." When Lori returned to the ballroom, she looked like Carrie at the prom. Her white dress was stained with blood and her mascara had run down her cheeks. "How can you *do* this to me?" she wailed later that night, throwing herself at Jimmy.

Lori envisions the scene vividly forty-five years later. In a voice filled with melancholy, she says, "Bebe was sitting in *my* place at the table. It was the end. I'd just turned fifteen."

## [2]

Over the years, Led Zeppelin openly paid tribute to their mentors. They were never reticent about the debt they owed to musical forefathers like Chuck Berry, Eddie Cochran, Buddy Rich, James Burton, Alexis Korner . . . The list was extensive. But one name loomed above all others: the King, Elvis. His was the voice of rock 'n roll, the sound that had ignited their earliest imaginations. So the guys were thrown off their stride when G told them they'd been invited to see Elvis perform at the LA Forum on May 11, 1974, and to visit with him afterward in his suite at the Beverly Wilshire.

They were more than starstruck. Elvis had always been something of a mythic figure, not quite real. He'd never toured the UK, never hung out with other musicians, never gave in-depth interviews. He lived in his own bubble world. He was larger than life. He was *Elvis*. "I can tell you, we were really nervous," Jimmy recalled of the visit.

It did not get off to an auspicious start, similarly to an awkward Elvis-Beatles get-together in the 1960s. Rock stars, no matter how famous, tended to get tongue-tied in Elvis's presence, and Led Zeppelin was no exception. The guys hemmed and hawed for a few minutes until Bonzo brought up his classic-car collection. Cars were right up Elvis's alley. He had a garage full of them back at Graceland. It was a good icebreaker, because Elvis knew practically nothing about Led Zeppelin's music. He'd heard only "Stairway to Heaven" and that they were notorious roués on the road, which Robert flatly denied, claiming they were all "family men."

Jimmy mentioned that Robert often sang Elvis numbers at their sound checks, especially "Love Me," which Robert promptly improvised. "So when we were leaving, after a most illuminating and funny ninety minutes with the guy," Robert recalled, "I was walking down the corridor. He swung around the door frame, looking quite pleased with himself, and started singing: *'Treat me like a fool . . .'*"

Never shy, Robert answered back: "*Treat me mean and cruel . . . bu-u-u-t love me.*"

It was a thrilling experience, singing a duet with Elvis Presley. But it was also something of a warning, if not a portent. Elvis, for all his exalted godliness, was something of a cultural dinosaur by then, and that same distinction was beginning to breathe down Led Zeppelin's necks.

Since Jimmy Page first picked up a guitar at the age of twelve, the through line of rock 'n roll had wound from rockabilly to garage band, pop, electric blues, folk rock, psychedelic, glam, and heavy metal. Now another stage of evolution was looming.

The moment The Who kicked over their drum kit and destroyed their instruments onstage, the seeds of unhinged musical anarchy were planted. The roots of the sound lay in the petulant impulses of underground and experimental bands like the Velvet Underground and the Stooges, whose songs were unsentimental, often cynical and provocative, occasionally subversive. A handful of chords and stripped-down instrumentation were enough to get the message across.

In 1970, another phase emerged. At the Cincinnati Pop Festival, Iggy Pop, wearing nothing but a pair of ripped jeans and silver lamé gloves, launched into "T.V. Eye," "smashing his palms together in a kind of frantic, childlike clap," according to a keen observer, "that makes almost no psychological sense, but there is nonetheless real poetry to it. . . . He's on the stage, he's off the stage, he's barking, he's curling up." Perhaps with that performance, a new sound was born.

By 1974, the first stirrings of punk could be felt in downtown New York. Inspired by the anarchic New York Dolls, a new generation of bands would soon lead the charge toward a bare-bones version of rock 'n roll that took the garage-rock sound and stripped it to its studs. Television, Mink DeVille, the Ramones, Suicide, Zolar X. "Punk bands started cropping up who were writing their own songs but taking the Yardbirds' sound and reducing it to this kind of goony fuzztone clatter," Lester Bangs famously wrote. It was the antithesis of "Stairway" or "How Many More Times" or "Kashmir"—songs that were developed methodically, with precision, and expanded into long, elaborate riffs or jams. Punk rejected the excesses associated with mainstream rock. Songs were deconstructed—a chord or two sufficed—and were often over before the end of the second verse, collapsing into chaos. They owed nothing to the disciplined studio background of Jimmy Page and John Paul Jones, whose refined professionalism and expert musicianship defined their sound. Punk was the opposite of that. Many musicians couldn't even play their instruments—they merely bashed away with a relentless, forced rhythm, making a noise. The rawness was the point. Anybody could tap into their id and stir up a crowd.

Jimmy couldn't help but appreciate the spectacle. Punk delivered the same kind of anarchic performance he had experienced the night he decided to join the Yardbirds. It would not have been out of the ordinary to drop by the Mercer Arts Center or CBGB in New York, the earliest epicenters of punk rock culture, and encounter a similar undisciplined display. There was an obvious ancestral link between Robert's rendition of "The Lemon Song" and Richard Hell's "Love Comes in Spurts." But they had little else in common. Punk scraped by in seedy clubs; Led Zeppelin ruled the arenaverse. As they continued to ready their new album, a confrontation with punk was nowhere on their radar.

Jimmy especially had his hands full. He'd begun working at Olympic Sound in an attempt to give structure to the unfinished album. The eight songs recorded at Headley Grange ran long, way too long. "We had more material than the required forty-odd minutes for one album," he concluded. All told, it would weigh in at slightly under an hour and a half. Wholesale edits were out of the question; they'd ruin the integrity of the songs.

"We thought, 'Why not put a double album out?'" Robert recalled. There was plenty in the can. "Black Country Woman" and "The Rover" were left over from *Houses of the Holy*. "Down by the

Seaside," "Night Flight," and "Boogie with Stu" had been recorded during sessions for the fourth album. Even "Bron-Yr-Aur," from way back on *LZIII*, was a finished master that might work. And how cheeky would it be if they included "Houses of the Holy," which had never made it onto its namesake album? "We had an album-and-a-half of new material," Jimmy said, "and we figured it was better to stretch out than to leave off."

There was still plenty of work to be done on it. Sequencing was key; with the addition of material from a range of different sessions, the songs had to have relevance, they had to relate to one another, and the flow had to feel unforced. Many of the new songs required overdubs, effects, and mixing. With Ron Nevison lost to the filming of *Tommy*, a new engineer, Keith Harwood, was hired, requiring Jimmy to bring him up to speed.

Jimmy had also gotten himself involved with a character named Kenneth Anger, an underground avant-garde filmmaker of some repute whose work blurred the lines between the occult, erotica, the perverse, and the downright loony. Jimmy had seen Anger's early films, *Scorpio Rising* and *Invocation of My Demon Brother*, at a film festival in Kent and knew of his efforts to restore Aleister Crowley's Abbey of Thelema in Sicily, which made him someone Jimmy was eager to meet.

Anger had a new film in the works—*Lucifer Rising*—which he'd been preparing since 1969. At the time, it featured a gadabout named Bobby Beausoleil in the title role—until he was found guilty of murder in a Manson-related execution. Still, Jimmy was intrigued, so much so that he agreed to provide music for Anger's film. "I had a lot of respect for him," Jimmy said. "As an occultist, he was definitely in the vanguard."

As a filmmaker? That was another matter. "Jimmy asked me to help him with *Lucifer Rising*," recalled Peter Clifton, the director who had taken over what would eventually be called *The Song Remains the Same*. "We projected the film onto a wall, and I didn't like it at all.

Marianne Faithfull was in it, and it was all devil worship and candles, and I didn't want to be around that. I said, 'Jimmy, don't do it, mate.'"

Jimmy couldn't resist. Anger was deeply involved in the Ordo Templi Orientis, or O.T.O., an occult organization modeled on the Freemasons and dedicated to the practice of magick. Aleister Crowley had joined O.T.O. in 1910 and became its "Supreme and Holy King of Ireland, Iona, and all the Britains within the Sanctuary of Gnosis," a title as windy as its premise.

"I could see that Anger was passionate about Crowley," Jimmy said. So he struck a deal with Anger to start composing the soundtrack for *Lucifer Rising* and even agreed to make a cameo appearance in the film, holding the plaster cast of the Stele of Revelation that Po had acquired for him in Egypt.

Meanwhile, Swan Song Records continued to gallop ahead. In June 1974, the label released Bad Company's debut album and watched it soar up the charts. Its success was spectacular. Raves began piling up. *Rolling Stone*, normally cool to hard-rock bands, delivered an uncharacteristically generous review. "This is an uncompromising album, reflecting the wills as much as the talents of the participants," its critic wrote, going on to say, "Bad Company could become a tremendous band." They had no shortage of hit singles. Deejays zeroed in on "Can't Get Enough." Airplay turned it into a number-one hit, and the follow-ups—"Ready For Love," "Rock Steady," and "Don't Let Me Down"—were also strong.

Bad Company's triumph emboldened the new label. Maybe Swan Song had the magic touch? Thinking they might be on a roll, Peter Grant arranged to have the Pretty Things move into Headley Grange to begin work on an album, hoping the Led Zeppelin–Bad Company alchemy would rub off. The band, however, had a history of rotten luck that continued to dog them from the day they arrived. A $35,000 Bösendorfer grand piano fell off a truck and shattered before the first note of music was played. Other damage was self-inflicted. The old manor house was pillaged; a number of antiques disappeared or were destroyed. And the extravagance of hiring the London Philharmonic sent session costs spiraling into the stratosphere. "In the end," Phil May said, "Swan Song paid for everything."

And sometimes the label simply missed the boat. In the late summer of 1974, Harvey Lisberg, who managed Herman's Hermits, approached Peter with the opportunity to get involved with a band on the upswing. "Peter and I were going to manage Queen," he says. They'd put out two albums that made considerable noise and knew a breakout was imminent with *Sheer Heart Attack*, which was already in the can. "We had a meeting in London with all four members and Jim Beach, their lawyer."

"Fellas, I would love to do it," Peter claimed to have told them, "but I haven't got that many hours in the day."

In fact, Lisberg says, "Negotiations stalled when Peter insisted they record for Swan Song. They were categorically opposed to doing that."

Queen had slipped through Swan Song's grasp. Other opportunities came and went as well. "I never wanted to be an empire builder," Grant confessed. And if actions spoke louder than words, he put up convincing evidence. Often he disappeared for days, remaining incommunicado or refusing to engage. Major decisions were neglected, decisions beyond the scope of Jimmy, Robert, John Paul, or John. The guys loved the idea of signing acts, but they wanted no part of the nuts-and-bolts responsibilities of running a label. Peter was a manager, not a label head. If he didn't intend to step up to the job, then who?

Danny Goldberg was a capable enough administrator who was plugged in and very well liked. But Danny was a gentle soul, a "club-soda-and-lime guy" devoted to Eastern philosophy, who meditated and had a spiritual guide. He wasn't enough of a shark, and he lacked front.

Instead, Peter turned to Abe Hoch, who had once worked for Atlantic Records as the director of artist relations in Los Angeles. During a stopover there, G made a pitch: "Do you want to come run our record company?"

Hoch had never run a company, much less been to Europe. "Tell me what it'd entail?" he asked.

"You'll know," G said cryptically. "You'll understand." He offered to double Abe's salary and threw in his mews flat in London as housing, which iced the deal.

At the end of summer in 1974, Hoch flew over to London to get the lay of the land. "I walked into the Swan Song offices on King's Road," he recalls, "and there was nothing going on. *Zero!* Absolutely fucking zero."

As a coworker confirmed, "It was fairly remarkable the amount of nothing that went on there, apart from meeting up with people and going down the pub."

Abe Hoch was dumbfounded. "There was nothing that would give anyone any indication that they had any idea how to buy, sell, promote, create, develop . . . *nothing! There was nothing there!*" He called Peter Grant and said, "There. Is. No. Record. Company."

Peter laughed and said, "I knew you'd know."

Abe realized the record company consisted only of what Danny Goldberg was doing in New York, some paper shuffling, some public relations. Otherwise, no one was running the show. As far as he was concerned, that could be a good thing—or a bad thing. It depended on how much autonomy he had. If he was fortunate, he could sign important acts and shape Swan Song in his own image.

His first order of business was the label's UK launch party, which coincided with the release of the Pretty Things album *Silk Torpedo*. The marching orders were clear: this shindig had to be outrageous and irreverent, something the music crowd would never forget. Even the location required a certain cachet.

"We decided to do it at Chislehurst Caves," says Phil Carson, "not far from the part of southeast London where Peter Grant and I come from." The caves, a labyrinth of crusty tunnels, dated from the midthirteenth century and were created from the mining of flint and chalk.

During World War II, they were used as an air-raid shelter, accommodating as many as fifteen thousand people. "But in the sixties, it was a gig—you'd go play Chislehurst Caves."

It had the perfect ambience—it was a curiosity, offbeat, a bit spooky—and landed on a perfect day: Halloween, All Hallows' Eve. Jimmy loved its nod to witchcraft and the occult. "Do what thou wilt," the invitation warned, "but know by this summons that on the night of the full moon, 31 October 1974, Led Zeppelin requests your presence . . ." Dress was optional—*undress* preferred—but it was recommended that guests arrive in costume.

A display set the tone at the mouth of the torch-lit caves: a naked woman lay in a casket covered in cherry Jell-O. Ian Knight and Benji Le Fevre had used a cobweb-making machine to dress the interior. Roaming about were male and female wrestlers, strippers dressed in nuns' habits with cutaway backsides, and naked "virgins" sacrificed at makeshift altars. "It was like being at a medieval orgy," one of the guests observed. "In all it was a strange and disturbing night." A troupe of fire-eaters, body sculptors, and escape artists entertained at selected stations. Several local bands performed. Models and villains intermingled at the bar. It was perhaps the only party at which Led Zeppelin, Bad Company, and the Pretty Things were not the main attraction.

By rights, the affair should have kicked off a Pretty Things renaissance, but as usual, they were their own worst enemy. Infighting marred a smooth transition to touring, and their attempt to please a broad spectrum of listeners resulted in their alienating their diehard fans. The album, *Silk Torpedo*, was good, if unexciting—*solid*, which in music-industry parlance was code for uncommercial. The knock had always been that outside the UK, the Pretty Things were an unknown entity, and this album wouldn't break new ground. Even British critics weren't particularly enthused.

*New Musical Express*, one of the band's longtime cheerleaders, reached the conclusion that the new album "lacks the inspired vision of *Parachute*," its predecessor, but gave the band "top marks for perseverance," a nod to their status as mainstays, if nothing else. "Next time, if they can match the excellence of the album cover, the world will cease as we know it." A review in *Phonograph Record* echoed the "next time" critique. *Rolling Stone* called the Pretty Things "a marvelous rock 'n roll band," but by that time half a year had passed, and the record had more or less played itself out.

In November 1974, the launch party behind him, Abe Hoch tried to make a go of Swan Song. With Peter out of the country on a Bad Company tour and Led Zeppelin sequestered in a London theater, rehearsing, he seized the opportunity to make some inroads. A label manager was hired—Unity MacLean, a young woman who had paid her dues in the Artist Relations Department of CBS Records, where she looked after the UK careers of Paul Simon, Billy Joel, Bruce Springsteen, Patti LaBelle, and Dr. Hook.

"When I came to Swan Song, I expected it to be run like a record company," she says, "but there was no office procedure, no decision making, no plans whatsoever."

Abe Hoch attempted to expand the artist roster. "I knew a guy in Seattle who sent me a tape of Ann and Nancy Wilson—Heart," he recalls. "With it came a note that said, 'Ann sings like Robert Plant, but with more balls.' She killed the fuck out of the demo. I gave a tape copy to Robert and said, 'You've got to listen to this. This chick really sings rock 'n roll.'"

Robert wasn't having any of it. *Ann? Sings like Robert Plant?* The note about the Wilson sisters had sunk it for him. "He took it and the tape and threw them in the wastebasket," Hoch says. "So I had to pass on Heart."

Abe also passed up another opportunity that came his way through a lawyer acquaintance. "He urged me to listen to a cassette of a band that he insisted on playing in the tape deck of his car. The tape was so awful that you couldn't hear what the fuck they were doing. I told him I couldn't make heads nor tails of it, but I sure wished I had signed Dire Straits."

Hoch realized the A&R aspect of his job was a figment of the imagination. He was never going to sign any act, because neither Led Zeppelin nor Peter Grant would allow it if they weren't involved. *And they weren't involved.* Every once in a while, one of the guys would pop into the office, but only to request that a personal chore be done—or to score drugs. One could always put in an expense for coke, so long as it was disguised as something else. Joan Hudson, the label's stern accountant, "never questioned anything or ran it by Peter," according to Phil Carlo. Her marching orders were to pay whatever voucher came across her desk. "I'd give her a paper that said '£2,000 for supplies'— for 'bits and pieces'—and she'd say, 'Right, Phil, no problem.'" Legend has it that Richard Cole once put in an expense of $50,000 for a *farm tractor* and got reimbursed in full. Benji Le Fevre had a similar experience. "I once turned in a receipt to Joan for £7,000 for fish-and-chips that Robert cosigned," he said.

"Joan always wired Jimmy lots of money," says Unity MacLean.

One night, when Jimmy needed an immediate infusion of cash, he was unable to raise Joan Hudson by phone. Instead, he went into a check-cashing shop and asked them to charge the amount against his American Express card.

"This is Jimmy Page's card," the owl-eyed desk clerk said.

"Yeah, that's right," Jimmy replied.

The man laughed and said, "So *you're* Jimmy Page, are you?"

Jimmy grinned back and said, "Well, yeah, I am."

The man picked up the phone and said, "We'll let the police sort this out."

Even the cops refused to accept that he was Jimmy Page and kept him confined to a chair until someone from Swan Song appeared to identify him.

Peter Grant wasn't around to intervene. He was on the road with Bad Company, giving the band and its manager, Clive Coulson, the benefit of his experience. G's presence paid dividends with promoters, but sometimes he stepped on his own guile.

He'd prevailed on Bill Curbishley, The Who's manager and an old friend, to add Bad Company to a Who gig at The Valley, Charlton Athletic's football ground in South London. It was a massive stadium, holding 83,000 people, a bonanza to introduce the relatively unknown Swan Song band. "As a favor to Peter, I agreed to put Bad Company on between the second band and Lindisfarne, who were pretty big at the time," Curbishley says. "It was a good showcase for them."

The promoter had his hands full from the start. The crowd was overliquored and unruly; they ripped the gates out of the concrete stanchions, which prompted a flurry of fistfights that spread through the stadium. "The next thing I know is: no Bad Company," recalls Curbishley. The band hadn't arrived on time. "I had no choice but to put Lindisfarne on. When Grant and the band showed up a few minutes later, I realized they'd done it deliberately so that Bad Company would come on immediately before The Who. Which is when I informed them they weren't going on."

Curbishley knew trouble lay ahead. He signaled his brother, Alfie, a titled heavyweight boxer, to join him in the office. A minute later, Grant, Richard Cole, and Phil Carson burst through the door.

"What do you mean Bad Company ain't going on?" G demanded.

"I did you a favor," Curbishley said, moving toe to toe with Peter. The two men were equals in the tough-guy department, each with a history of protecting his turf. "You deliberately turned up late to jump the bill. They're not going on."

Grant narrowed his eyes. "Who the fuck do you think you are?"

Curbishley lowered his voice to a near whisper. "Close that door and we'll see who walks out of this fucking room," he said.

G and his henchmen backed right off.

In the end, Paul Rodgers appealed directly to Curbishley and an equitable solution was reached. Bad Company would perform but play a shorter set—and no encores.

Grant was satisfied, but he realized the upshot. He didn't have the leverage with other acts that he had with Led Zeppelin. Hard-knuckle tactics only worked only with an act at the top of the world. He needed to leave Bad Company's day-to-day management to others and devote his energies to the band that paid the bills.

During the layoff, Jimmy had kept up a fairly rigorous routine. He continued to haunt the control booth at Olympic Sound, distilling Led Zeppelin's prodigious output into the fifteen tracks that would form the basis of a double album. Somewhere along the way, he'd come up with a title—*Physical Graffiti*—and approved the concept for the cover based on José Feliciano's 1973 album, *Compartments*, which featured a tenement building whose windows were stamped on a pull-out card. For *Physical Graffiti*, the designers constructed a die-cut window whose illustrations could be interchanged to reveal the building's iconic inhabitants: King Kong, Elizabeth Taylor, Charles Atlas, the Virgin Mary, Jerry Lee Lewis, Laurel and Hardy, Neil Armstrong, Flash Gordon, the cast of *The Wizard of Oz*, Marlene Dietrich, and Peter Grant, as well as a photo of Robert and Richard in drag taken at the Hyatt House in Los Angeles. It wasn't original, but it was eye-catching.

Naturally, the cover was difficult to produce. There were so many moving parts to it; the printing process was complicated, problematic. The album was supposed be released in time to coincide with Led Zeppelin's next tour, beginning in mid-January 1975, but the cover's production would delay it. The best-case scenario was mid-to-late February. That meant that yet again Led Zeppelin would be performing for a month without records in the stores, a tremendous financial setback.

Nevertheless, the show would go on as scheduled. The dates were booked, the arenas sold out months in advance. Besides, the long eighteen-month layoff had made the band antsy. They'd appreciated the downtime, but they were musicians who needed to play and entertainers who needed to perform. Jimmy and Robert had appeared sporadically onstage with Bad Company during their American tour, but it wasn't the same as playing a Led Zeppelin gig. "The time comes," Robert said, "when we know it's time to go out on the road again."

A few days' rehearsal served to take the rust off the rails. On November 24, 1974, the band reconvened at the Liveware Theatre in Ealing to see where they stood and to determine how best to map a new show. "Obviously, we had to rehearse the stuff from the new album to get it into some viable shape," Robert explained. "Kashmir," in particular, was a bitch to play live. So were "When the Levee Breaks," "Custard Pie," "Sick Again," "Trampled Underfoot," and "In My Time of Dying," which they ran through until the arrangements clicked. The sheer amount of new material meant some of the old standbys had to be sacrificed. "Celebration Day," "Misty Mountain Hop," "Since I've Been Loving You," and "The Ocean" were dropped from the standard set list. Even "Dazed and Confused" was retired for the time being.

No expense was spared to make the upcoming tour more spectacular than the previous one. The production included a twenty-foot-high backdrop consisting of several hundred bulbs that spelled out L-E-D Z-E-P-P-E-L-I-N, just in case an unsuspecting ticketholder had stumbled into the wrong arena.

In December, Peter Grant summoned Jack Calmes, the owner of Showco, to the Swan Song office to give him and the band a preview of the production design. Before Calmes made his presentation, G suggested they have some blow first.

"He pulled out a big bowie knife—about a foot long with a three-inch blade on it—and dipped it into this kind of grocery sack of blow," Calmes recalled. "They had to give me five minutes to recover from that."

A powerful stimulant was necessary for what he had in store. The model Jack unveiled was complex and elaborate. Five lighting towers with laser effects were mounted on a truss that required six or seven trucks and a sizable crew to assemble it. The stage looked like something out of a Jules Verne fantasy.

Bonzo threw the production designer a fearsome stare. "How much fucking money is this going to cost us?" he asked.

When Calmes replied, "$15,785 per show," it became so quiet you could hear a penny drop. The band began cutting looks at each other. Even to millionaires like Led Zeppelin, it was an enormous expenditure. Bonzo strode menacingly to the window and threw it open in a swift, dramatic flourish. Calmes braced himself to be launched like a projectile onto King's Road.

Instead, Bonzo grinned and laughed wickedly. "Yeah, go for it," he said. "We're in." The others agreed. They weren't about to let money be a factor. Fifteen grand was a drop in the bucket compared to what they'd net from each show—and in cash.

But in part, that was the cocaine talking. The drug had become so prevalent, so much a part of who Led Zeppelin was, that it took the brakes off any caution. They felt invincible; nothing was too big, too grand, too fast. Over-the-top seemed just right.

Everything was now *go-go-go-go!* It set the tempo for the entire tour.

## Chapter Sixteen

# HOME AWAY FROM HOME

## [1]

The tour got off to a rocky start.

On his way into London, in preparation to leave the country, Jimmy Page disembarked at Victoria Station and jammed the third finger of his left hand in one of the train's automatic doors. He knew right away he was in trouble. The pain was excruciating; he suspected he'd broken the finger.

"I was just totally numb—numb with shock," Jimmy recalled. X-rays revealed only a severe sprain, but the damage was done. "It's the most important finger for any guitarist, the one that does all the leverage and most of the work," he said. "I can't play blues at all, can't bend notes either."

They considered postponing the tour. What was the point if Jimmy Page couldn't play the blues? But rescheduling wasn't the answer. "A postponement would have meant chaos," he acknowledged. They'd sold out thirty-six shows in twenty-four cities—"expected to be the largest grossing undertaking in rock history." Arrangements were already set in stone, promoters on the hook.

There had already been riots in several cities when Led Zeppelin seats went on sale. "In Boston, fans lined up three days early for tickets," *The Village Voice* reported. "The hall's beer supply was seized, bottles thrown, furniture destroyed, and an estimated $50,000 in damages resulted." Needless to say, the city canceled the gig. In Chicago, fans camped out all night in near-zero temperatures, only to have scalpers scarf up vast numbers of tickets, depriving the stalwarts. And in New York, fistfights broke out at a department-store Ticketron outlet.

There was too much at stake to postpone the tour—advance ticket sales totaled roughly $5 million—but the incentives for doing so were attractive. The tune-ups hadn't gone well. As always before a tour, Led Zeppelin played a few warm-up gigs in out-of-the-way places to test new material and work out bugs. An unannounced show on January 11, 1975, at a club in Rotterdam was a clear indication that the band wasn't at anywhere near its peak. They sounded ragged, and Robert, clearly rattled, flubbed the lyrics to "Stairway to Heaven." The next night's gig in Brussels was confused and chaotic. Bonzo, who had been drinking heavily in Holland, was hung over and inconsistent. Jimmy looked wasted. They muddled through, but it was clear to all that the layoff had left its mark. Everyone had to pull it together before they got to the States.

The Fates weren't finished. By the time Led Zeppelin arrived in Minneapolis on January 18, Robert was ill. He'd arrived there in the dead of winter dressed in an open-fronted girl's blouse and no coat. "I'm catching flu and can't sing properly," he complained. By Chicago, two nights later, his cold was full-blown. The second song, "Sick Again," was no joke. "[Plant's flu] had given him an inability to come to grips with most of the high notes he usually takes with ease," noted a review of the show in the *Chicago Tribune*, "and at times he had difficulty getting his voice over Jimmy Page's guitar." Part of the blame could be laid on the sound mix and a wonky PA. But Jimmy was also wonky. His hand hurt. "Codeine tablets and Jack Daniel's deadened the pain," but Jimmy was obviously struggling. Certain songs were too physically demanding. "'Dazed and Confused' and 'Since I've Been Loving You' were indefinitely retired." Jimmy was unable to execute either of them with finesse. The band substituted "When the Levee Breaks" and "How Many More Times," neither a fan favorite.

Bonzo suffered in his own inimitable way. The entire trip from New York to Chicago, he'd been "swigging from a quart bottle of blue-label Smirnoff and muttering disconsolately to himself." Only a day away from England, he was already homesick and rueful of his circumstances. "What the fuck am I doing here?" he grumbled. "I want to be back *home*." He was obviously wasted as they took the stage.

Even the band's attire left something to be desired. Robert was decked out in "a cherry adorned wrap-around number" and "a sort of Sino-Afro print vest that seems six sizes too small," as one observer noted. "He wears tight blue jeans and clearly no underwear." John Paul Jones was in a ludicrous silver lamé waistcoat. He appreciated showmanship but admitted, "it's just that I was never very good at it." Bonzo went completely in another direction. He and his roadie, Mick Hinton, dressed identically in sinister-looking white boiler suits and black derby hats, mimicking the hooligan droogs in *A Clockwork Orange*.

Only Jimmy looked resplendent. He had a suit hand made at great expense by a woman named Coco in Los Angeles. He called it his "dragon outfit" because of the highly stylized pair of colorful Lung dragons, symbolizing benevolent powers, embroidered along each side. "I asked her to personalize the pants with astrological symbols—Capricorn, Scorpio rising, Cancer," he said. They were the most dominant signs in his horoscope, his sun sign, rising sign, and moon sign. His glyph from Led Zeppelin's fourth album—ZoSo—appeared front and center, as did "666," which according to the Book of Revelation was the mark of the beast with seven heads. The trousers were finished with long silver cuffs. When the lights hit Jimmy, he was an eyeful.

"I thought about what I wanted on my stage clothes carefully," he said. Image had always figured prominently in Jimmy Page's priorities. "He was a pretty dapper guy, even way back when," John Spicer recalls. "He loved the outfits, the fancy suits we wore with Neil Christian, always checking himself out in the mirror before we went on." Chris Dreja remembered a more aggressive mode of attire during Jimmy's Yardbirds days. "The Confederate hat and Nazi regalia pinned on the same costume didn't go down too well," he recalled. In the States, it occasionally drew a violent response.

The dragon suit, however, was the ultimate rock 'n roll garb— loud, bold, and over-the-top. He wore it when the spirit moved him, which on the 1975 tour was just about always. But there were nights when his Dr. Jeykll persona warranted something more debonair, more tasteful. "After Coco made the dragon outfit, I had her make my white suit with the poppy on it," he said. The clothes tipped the others off to which Jimmy Page was showing up on a given night.

In Chicago, showing up was about all that went well. No one in the band was at his best. The music was lethargic. Robert kept apologizing from the stage—for the sloppiness, for the sound, for his voice. Jimmy could tell it was an off night, and his playing reflected it.

"This is so damn futile," he grumbled after the show. "I can't fucking play the way I should."

"There was a minute there when I thought we'd lost it after that first Chicago show," Robert said.

After the show, Peter Grant huddled with the band and Richard Cole at the Ambassador Hotel to review the situation. Robert was told in no uncertain terms to stop mentioning from the stage that he had the flu, that it upset the fans who'd waited years to hear Led Zeppelin play. Otherwise, G wasn't overly concerned. An off night was an off night; the kids didn't know any better. The audience reaction was ecstatic. No one had an inkling that Jimmy's hand injury kept him from dazzling on solos. Even the critics were merciful. An indifferent review in *Sounds* noted that, despite the shaky health concerns, Led Zeppelin "still reach heaven."

"The second night in Chicago turned it all around," said Danny Goldberg.

The band hit its stride. Jimmy played with efficiency, especially on some nifty slide-guitar passages, and Robert reined in his vocals on new songs like "Trampled Under Foot" and "Kashmir," which required fewer flights into the high altitudes.

But two nights later, at the Richfield Coliseum near Cleveland, the concert's first hour, according to a newspaper report, was "soggy and spiritless." Jimmy swigged from a bottle of Jack Daniel's between numbers, contributing to the malaise. Robert's singing "demonstrated his vocal pipes are almost shot." The band picked up the pace in the second half of the show, but everyone was happy to get out of town. The weather was lousy; it was cold and snowing, and there was an hour of travel ahead before they could put the night behind them.

The strategy had been to stay at the Ambassador in Chicago and commute to nearby gigs in Cleveland and Indianapolis. It was relatively easy with the *Starship*. However, by the time they reached the airport in Cleveland for their return flight, a full-blown blizzard was in progress. All commercial air traffic was shut down. Fortunately, private planes had the right to fly *if they so chose*, but conditions were dreadful.

"We've got to go," Peter insisted. The pilot was dubious. He'd been listening to radio reports and knew flying was hazardous. Peter was adamant. They had a gig the next night in Indianapolis that couldn't be postponed. "We're going to Chicago!"

Joe Jammer, a musician, who had joined them in the cockpit, recalls, "Peter pulled out a mirror, took a gram of cocaine, laid it down in one line, and stuck it under the pilot's nose. The pilot snorted the whole fucking line."

"Okay, we're ready to go to Chicago!" he announced.

Jammer, whose real name was Joe Wright, sat in the navigator's seat behind the pilot throughout the flight across the lake. "It was a massive blizzard," he said, "you saw *nothing*. The pilot flew entirely on instruments. It's a wonder we got there safe and sound."

Mercifully, there was a three-night layoff after the Indianapolis show. Three nights for the band to recharge. But no one wanted to stay in frozen Chicago. They had a plane that was costing them $2,500 a day—they could go anywhere they wished. Led Zeppelin prided itself on being a democracy; the destination would be a group decision, with Robert remaining in Chicago to recuperate. John Paul Jones voted for the Bahamas, but the plane was licensed to fly only within the continental United States. That also negated Bonzo's desire to fly home to see his family. But, in fact, the vote was a sham. Jimmy always held the deciding vote, and he wanted to spend time with a girl in Los Angeles. Quicker than anyone could say "Hollywood," the *Starship* was routed to LAX.

The flight west started out like a full-blown party in the sky. The plane was licensed to carry forty-two people, but the manifest, which included the band, Ricardo and G, a few security guys, and three journalists, gave the affair a pleasing intimacy. Champagne flowed throughout the two-thousand-mile trip, along with a full larder: canapés, hors d'oeuvres, steak, lobster, anything the heart desired. Videos of *Deep Throat* and *Don't Knock the Rock* alternated in loops on TV screens suspended from the ceiling. So much cocaine was snorted en route that the passengers could have flown to LA under their own power.

For an hour or so, everybody gathered round the bar getting pleasantly pissed. John Paul sat perched behind the electric organ, playing a medley of fossilized pub songs—"Bye-Bye Blackbird," "Any Old Iron," and "I've Got a Lovely Bunch of Coconuts"—to the delight of Peter Grant, who led a group sing-along. Even Susie and Bianca, the two flight attendants, joined in. Only Bonzo was missing, out cold. He'd downed an entire bottle of vodka in the limo on the way to the airport and collapsed as soon as he'd boarded the plane. He was a mess.

"Bonzo drank for *reasons*," John Paul volunteered. "He hated being away from home, and between gigs he found it hard to cope. And he was terrified of flying."

He snorted cocaine for *reasons*, too. "Taking cocaine just enabled

Bonham to drink more," said Nick Kent, who covered Led Zeppelin for *New Musical Express* and was an avid drug taker himself.

Danny Goldberg knew to be on his guard. "The chance for violence was high when John got loaded and drunk." It was important to keep him away from journalists and other civilians.

About an hour out of LA, Bonzo staggered out of the bedroom in full Beast mode, wearing nothing but a red hooded robe, unbelted at the waist. According to Chris Charlesworth, the *Melody Maker* columnist covering the tour, "he grabbed one of the stewardesses from behind, put her in a chokehold, and pulled up her skirt, with every intention of mounting her." Terrified, she was no match for him and began to "scream her bloody head off."

Grant put one of his old wrestling holds on Bonzo about the same time the pilot emerged from the cockpit.

"What the fuck's going on here?" he demanded.

"It's all right, everything's under control," Peter assured him. "Go back to the cockpit."

Grant and Ricardo dragged Bonzo into the bedroom, which effectively broke up the party. Jimmy was delegated to calm the flight attendant, who continued to tremble and cry as a result of the attempted rape.

A few minutes later, Ricardo emerged and leaned forebodingly over Chris Charlesworth's seat. "I don't want a fucking word of this getting into your fucking newspaper," he said.

Charlesworth exchanged glances with Cameron Crowe, the young *Rolling Stone* reporter seated opposite him. "We both recognized the threat," Charlesworth recalls. "Our silence, otherwise we were off the tour."

Playing good cop to Ricardo's bad cop, G invited Charlesworth into the cockpit to enjoy a front-row seat for the flight over the desert. The pilots were enjoying a coffee break, with the plane operating on instruments. "I chat with them and they ask me if I'd like to have a go," he recalled, meaning: take over the controls. In a moment of madness, they disengaged the autopilot and allowed Charlesworth to operate the joystick, lifting the nose of the plane, then dipping it.

"I could envision the headline," he says all these years later. "'Zeppelin's Plane Crashes—Journalist at the Controls.'"

"Enjoy that?" Grant asked him afterward. Charlesworth assured him of the thrill. "That's nothing. Bonzo flew us all the fucking way from Los Angeles to New York on one tour."

Los Angeles reenergized the party spirit, lifting it back into high gear. The entourage made a beeline straight from the airport to the Rainbow Grill, the scene of some of Led Zeppelin's most unsavory encounters. Peter Grant had called ahead from Chicago to make sure the band's favorite table was waiting and champagne was on ice. The groupies were ready; the marquee welcoming the band outside the Continental Hyatt House was like a summons to report for duty. Even G's "concubine," as he referred to her, was present and accounted for, a young woman named Alice who called herself Raven and turned up everywhere in America.

The groupies who showed up weren't in the same league as Miss Pamela or Lori Mattix. They didn't aspire to be girlfriends; they were more transactional: sex for access. Which was fine with the band. That's what certain bands went to the Rainbow for. It wasn't an up-scale scene. It was a place to cavort, to act out, to parade as rock stars. And sometimes the scene got ugly.

That night, one of the customers, who was clearly overstimulated, zeroed in on Jimmy Page. *"You can't fucking play guitar! Fuck you!"* he howled, jabbing a finger in the guitarist's direction.

Jimmy, who was a lover, not a fighter, leaped toward the heckler in an uncharacteristic response. Not uncharacteristically, Peter Grant stepped between them, then hauled the guy outside behind the club and administered a few well-placed kicks.

Jimmy wasn't having the R&R he expected. "Some of the guys had

On good nights, their excitement was palpable.

Zep unplugged: the acoustic set offered a respite from the hysteria.

Maggie Bell and Leslie Harvey turn up the heat.

Led Zeppelin finally gets the front-page press they crave.

Jimmy and Robert scour the columns for any slight.

Do what thou wilt . . .
But know by this summons
That on the night of the Full Moon
of 31st October, 1974

## Led Zeppelin

request your presence
at a
Halloween Party
to celebrate
Swan Song Records'
first U.K. album release
'Silk Torpedo'
by

## The Pretty Things

in
Chislehurst Caves,
Chislehurst, Kent.
Celebrations will commence
at 8.00 p.m. . . .

## Swan Song Records
Distributed by Atlantic Records

Swan Song's "Come As You Are" party. Some guests took it literally.

Karac, Maureen, Robert, and Carmen in Wales, near Bron-Yr-Aur, October 1976

John Paul entertaining his wife, Mo, and their daughters, Jacinda and Tamara, July 1970

A rare shot of the entire band onstage

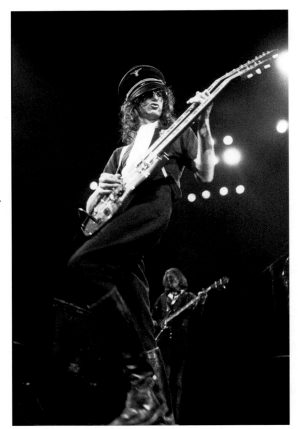

Jimmy in Chicago, 1975.
Robert called him
"the führer of the
Fourth Reich."

Bonzo in the throes of a "Moby Dick" marathon

Jimmy goes neck-and-neck on "Stairway to Heaven."

"I'll see your two necks and raise you one."

The boys from the Midlands

When it was good it was
very, very good.

Some nights, Jimmy was higher than a kite.

The aftermath of havoc wreaked by a crowd waiting to purchase advance tickets to a Led Zeppelin concert in Boston, January 7, 1975

Backstage wasn't always glamorous, but G hit the fashion high notes with his trademark coonskin cap.

"For I was thirsty, and you gave Me something to drink."—Matthew 25:35

"Thanks, but I've got my own."—Jimmy 08:75

Tour doctor, Larry Badgley, shows off his stash. Jimmy admitted to swiping the doctor's Quaaludes.

Robert nurses his bum foot while rhapsodizing in Sweden.

"Get to the limos!" A fast getaway was needed following the premier of *The Song Remains the Same*.

At the premier of *The Song Remains the Same*. Ahmet Ertegun asks Robert: "Who was that guy on the horse?"

Led Zeppelin at a loose rehearsal before the Knebworth gig

Peter Grant and Bill Graham on their way to "make peace" with Jim Matzorkis, Oakland 1979

Led Zeppelin's last U.S. performance, Oakland 1979. The creators of *This Is Spinal Tap* would never forget it.

G and son Warren, whose sticky fingers touched off a backstage brawl, Oakland 1979.

"Ouch!" Jimmy winces his way through their painful Live Aid performance, July 18, 1985.

started a rumor that Jimmy liked to put a fishbowl on girls' heads and then shit on it," says Abe Hoch. "It wasn't true, of course, but it was funny. So they went out and bought the biggest fish bowl they could find and put it next to Jimmy wherever he sat at the Rainbow. He had no idea what was going on, but nobody would come near him all night. He kept looking around, saying, 'What the fuck is going on here?'"

It was almost a relief to head back east. There was no partying on the plane this time. Thankfully, the trip was uneventful; everyone kept his own counsel. Robert was waiting in a limo on the airport tarmac in Greensboro, North Carolina, for a show at the Coliseum on January 29, 1975. There were five limos, in fact, one for each of the guys, including a lead car for Peter Grant; the convoy sped off to the arena with no time to spare.

The Coliseum was a horrible facility for music, cavernous and cold, with terrible acoustics. The band was tired, the sound awful, Robert's voice shaggy. "It was a rotten show," Chris Charlesworth recalls, "one of the worst I ever saw." The audience, for its part, couldn't have cared less. This was Led Zeppelin. "Their 17,500 fans were still cheering," according to the critic for the *Greensboro Daily News*, "happy to get their money's worth from a group that puts on a really entertaining show."

The five hundred fans who showed up without tickets didn't feel the same way. They stormed the arena in an attempt to get inside, "throwing broken bottles, stones, and pieces of scaffolding." In the melee, three of the band's five limos were vandalized. The drivers of the remaining two cars approached Peter Grant midway through the concert to advise him they were removing their vehicles rather than risk further damage to them.

G was livid. No limos meant that Led Zeppelin would be stranded. There was no plan B for leaving the arena. "You can't take your fucking cars away," he shouted. "We need 'em. You'll be fucking sorry, you cunts."

The drivers apologized but said they were responsible for the cars.

"All right," G relented, "then I'll buy them. How much do you want for your fucking cars? What are they worth—twenty grand each? Thirty? I'll fucking buy them from you right now." He opened his holdall, which was stuffed with cash.

"Sir, we can't sell them. They don't belong to us."

"In that case, you fucking cunt, I'm going to take your cars."

"Sir, you can't."

"Don't be fucking stupid," G scoffed. "Of course I can fucking do that. I can do what I fucking want. Can't I? I've got twenty fucking men working for me. There's only two of you. You can't fucking stop me, you fucking cunts."

At the end of the show, after "Stairway to Heaven," the band usually came offstage, had a drink, and then returned for an encore—"Whole Lotta Love" and whatever else suited their fancy. This time, Peter instructed Jimmy, "Do 'Whole Lotta Love,' and don't make it a long one." He'd already taken control of the two limos.

While the fans in the arena were still on their feet, applauding, Ricardo hustled the band, draped in red hooded robes, out the back door and into one of the limousines. Grant was behind the wheel, grinning at his temerity. A roadie was driving the second limo with the rest of the retinue and two ex-cops who handled security. The grim-faced limo drivers stood helplessly on the curb.

G rolled down his window. "We don't have any fucking use for you, you cunts," he said, then gunned the car through the angry crowd, leaning on the horn. "Get out of the way, you fucking cunts! *Out of the way!*"

A police escort parked in front of the lead limo had stalled, so G began bumping the back of it until it moved out of the way.

The ride to the airport was more exciting than the show. Grant drove like a madman. The car reached a speed of seventy on city streets, often driven on the wrong side of the road, running all red lights. "I'd never seen driving like it," said Neal Preston, the band's tour photographer. Carloads of fans in hot rods pulled alongside, keeping pace, trying to get a look at the band. It was like a chase scene out of *Smokey and the Bandit*, but wilder and more reckless.

The *Starship* was idling, ready for takeoff, as the two cars zoomed onto the runway. But Grant wasn't done demonstrating his Grand Prix skills. Instead of pulling up to the plane, he drove around it four times, each time faster than the last, skidding on two wheels, tires screeching, with smoke coming off the car. He was using the hand brake to keep it from overturning. Finally, it buckled to a stop at the foot of the plane's gangplank and Led Zeppelin tumbled out, laughing their heads off.

According to a passenger, "They were placing bets whether he'd crash that limo deliberately into the other one, just for the hell of it, so he could leave both cars smashed."

Next stop was New York, from where they could fly to gigs in Detroit, Pittsburgh, and Boston, and as the *Starship* headed up the East Coast everyone's spirits picked up. Bonzo played bartender, and the drinks never stopped, nor did the cocaine, which G dispensed like Johnny Appleseed. No one gave much thought to the mediocre show. This wasn't simply rock 'n roll anymore. It was crazy excess. The drugs and violence had taken over.

## [2]

And sometimes you reap what you sow. The review of the January 31 show in the *Detroit Free Press* began to put it in perspective. "The landing of the Led Zeppelin is inevitably accompanied by the best hard blues rock in the business and the most violent, unruly crowds ever to inflict themselves upon a concert hall." The two extremes seemed to be inseparable.

Once again, an outbreak of violence raked the arena, "including shoving, punching, shattering bottles on the ground, and rushing the hall." It didn't help that the band seemed uninspired, deflated. A "fairly credible performance" was inexcusable for one of the world's top rock 'n roll bands. "Plant was flat on the opening numbers, not even trying for the high notes," the review noted, "and Page's guitar runs careened way off-track." They appeared tired, and Robert's sad story, delivered between numbers—that his throat was sore and Jimmy had hurt his hand—came off as lame alibis. "Led Zeppelin made nearly $50,000 for two hours of 'work,'" wrote a critic for the *Ann Arbor Sun.* "I mean, it was obvious: to them this was only a job. It could have been a celebration."

There was violence in Pittsburgh the next night as well, and again in Philadelphia on February 8. Security, presided over by a collection of bloodthirsty ex-cops, wasn't helping matters. They seemed to enjoy mixing it up with the fans. One recruit offered Richard Cole advice in Pittsburgh. "Let me loan you a blackjack in case you need to bash in a skull or two tonight," he said, providing a metal baton. He also showed Ricardo how to conceal small weights in gloves, the better to deliver a message to an overzealous fan.

The violence in Philadelphia was beyond the pale.

"I saw this incident happen, and I was almost physically sick," Jimmy explained to Beat writer William S. Burroughs, who interviewed him for an article in *Crawdaddy* a few nights later over dinner in New York. "Somebody came to the front of the stage to take a picture or something and obviously somebody said, 'Be off with you,' and he wouldn't go. And then one chap went over the barrier, and then another and then another, and they all piled on top. You could see the fists coming out . . . on this one solitary person. And they dragged him by his hair, and they were kicking him. It was just sickening."

Burroughs commiserated with Jimmy about the unpredictability of large audiences. "You have to be careful," he said. "It's rather like driving a load of nitroglycerine."

Jimmy would have really been ill had he gotten a look at Richard Cole, who contributed his own method of crowd control. "When dozens of fans began congregating near the front of the auditorium," Ricardo recalled, "I positioned myself underneath the stage and frantically began smashing them on the kneecaps with a hammer."

Punishment was dispensed without regard for safety or consequences. "The undercurrent of unpleasantness was so unnecessary," said Chris Charlesworth. "They were the biggest band in the world. There was nothing like that around The Who, the bad vibes and that hint of menace around Zeppelin. They behaved as if they were a law unto themselves."

*A law unto themselves.*

When confronted about it by a journalist in New York, Robert went on the defensive. "There's no violent energy here," he insisted. "Because we've got a sizeable audience, people may think we'll bring out violence, but it doesn't happen."

The shows were suffering, nevertheless. At times, Jimmy seemed disengaged, in his own world onstage. Guitar solos unspooled one after another, their execution often "sloppy, careless, and unimaginative." "After a while," wrote a reviewer in *The Washington Post*, "Page's solos seemed to sound alike." Pacing was lugubrious. "In My Time of Dying" and "Since I've Been Loving You" put a drag on what should have been a high-spirited set. John Paul's meandering, self-indulgent etude during "No Quarter" seemed to go on forever. It drained all the excitement out of the show. The audiences felt the lack of effort, and reviews called it out.

"In the end there is still something missing," *The New York Times* concluded. "And what is missing is creative significance. They simply didn't reach down deep inside their audiences." *Newsday* complained about Jimmy's and John Paul's "stock riffs" and surveyed the fans, who "seemed disgruntled by the performance" and "felt Led Zeppelin was just having a bad night of it." Robert could tell that he'd lost the audience. "Despite our depleted physical conditions," he announced, "we fully intend to shake this building." In Montreal they were criticized for "not hitting on all cylinders." Philadelphia-based papers used words like "lifeless . . . lackluster . . . unimpressive . . . over-produced" and said "there was something missing. Maybe it's the group, which is getting older and running out of gas." Almost every review took issue with Robert's "half a voice," his inability to hit the high notes and subsequent dive into lower registers.

Led Zeppelin needed a breather. There was a ten-day break after the February 16 show in St. Louis, and it couldn't come soon enough. The band wanted to reclaim its mojo. With a day off between the New York and St. Louis gigs, the *Starship* transported everyone to a new base in New Orleans—geographically unsuitable, but a city where the music, food, and nightlife captivated the musicians and their managers.

They loved the hotel there, the Maison Dupuy, located in a quiet residential section of the French Quarter. A profusion of used record stores along Bourbon Street provided treasures—stacks of vintage 45s and obscure local R&B singles. Fabulous food and great quantities of alcohol were consumed.

The getaway satisfied but didn't adjust the band's attitude. "For the St. Louis show, we left the hotel in New Orleans ten minutes before they were supposed to be onstage," recalls Phil Carson. "It was thirty minutes to the airport and almost a two-hour flight. And of course, the audience rioted and damage was done. It was a low point for me. Jimmy was a mess, but somehow he got away with it, playing-wise."

As soon as the show was over, Bonzo and John Paul jumped on flights home to the UK. Jimmy and Robert decided to forgo the seven-hour trip and puddle-jumped to the Caribbean island of Dominica instead. A few days together away from the hustle and the background noise of others would benefit their relationship immensely. They had never been friends, per se. "They had no connection to each other socially," according to Abe Hoch. They never hung out together except for work, there was little intimacy between them. And their roles had shifted since the early days of Led Zeppelin.

When Robert initially joined the band, Jimmy had called every shot. "He dominated Robert completely," says Danny Goldberg. Jimmy had been playing professionally for nearly ten years, while Robert had desperately attempted—and failed—to crack the big time. Still only nineteen, he'd begun to wonder if rock 'n roll wasn't in the cards. Jimmy gave Robert the break he'd been lusting after, and for two years or so Robert deferred to the older, more experienced musician in all things Led Zeppelin. Jimmy taught him the ropes, and he gave Robert the opportunity to come into his own as a performer—and to grow up—while fronting the band and establishing his career. There was a lot of confidence building in the interim. Robert developed poise on-stage and in the spotlight in general. His personality blossomed. And he discovered that he could write damn good lyrics. In fact, songwriting put him on equal footing with Jimmy as far as new material went. Jimmy *depended* on him. That did a lot for Robert's self-assurance.

"But Led Zeppelin was Jimmy's band," says Janine Safer, one of Swan Song's young press officers, "and Jimmy never let Robert forget it." They never really pursued friendship. It was strictly professional between them.

They were different animals. A deep-rooted, only child, Jimmy kept to himself; he rarely socialized. He was leery of people, especially fans, not inclined to engage. "A loner," was the way he described himself. "Isolation doesn't bother me at all. It gives me a sense of security." He practiced the occult. He enjoyed unusual sexual proclivities, and he more than dabbled in drugs. Heroin had reared its head on the tour, and Jimmy became an enthusiastic user.

Phil Carson blamed the heroin for an incident at the recent gig in St. Louis. Jimmy had worked out an effect with his roadie that involved putting the guitar down and turning a dial in order to produce a weird declining sound. "Robert and I stood at the side of the stage, rolling our eyes, while Jimmy did that for ten minutes, entranced, oblivious to the audience," Carson says.

Robert had tried heroin but usually avoided anything heavier than a line or two of recreational cocaine. And he was upbeat, *always*. "He wasn't a brooding personality," says Abe Hoch. "He was outgoing. He had a smile and charm that were irresistible." Robert courted outsiders, fans, even the press. He was fundamentally optimistic and positive.

Benji Le Fevre puts the relationship in another perspective. "Robert was the Leo extrovert, fantastic front man, and Jimmy was the fucked-up great, *great* guitar player, neither of whom associated with each other. It was a carbon copy of the Rolling Stones."

The vacation in Dominica gave them a chance to reconnect. They checked out a lot of island music together, intermingling with the local Rastafarians, smoking ganja, and "eating hallucinatory boiled jelly-fruit." More important, they discussed taking time off after the tour to travel, to broaden their musical horizons. They'd gone to India together in 1971 and returned the next year to record with the Bombay Symphony Orchestra, but there was so much more to learn about international music. William Burroughs had intrigued Jimmy with his knowledge of the relationship between music and magic. He felt the "hypnotic power" created by Led Zeppelin in concert had "quite a lot in common with Moroccan trance music."

"He then encouraged me to go to Morocco and investigate the music firsthand," Jimmy explained. Burroughs was especially eager for him to tap into the Gnaoua and Joujouka musicians, who "think of music entirely in magical terms."

"I think it's time to travel," Jimmy said, "to start gathering some real right-in-there experiences with street musicians around the world."

Robert was all ears. He had his heart set on Morocco as well, and they made plans to head there—together—right after the tour ended, later that summer.

After eighteen months of continuous work, *Physical Graffiti* finally got its release on February 24, 1975, three days before Led Zeppelin reconvened in Texas for the next leg of the tour. To call the album a sensation would be an understatement. There were advance orders totaling $15 million, deejays played it endlessly, the buzz was enormous. "I never saw an album sell as much as *Graffiti*," Danny Marcus said. "You'd go to stores, and there were lines, and everybody was waiting to buy the same record. A *double album*—it was worth the long wait.

Reviews were somewhat mixed. The British rock press dispensed with critical objectivity. *Melody Maker* described the album as "pure genius" and *NME*'s resident fanboy called the music "absolutely the toughest, most downright brutal I've heard on record in well over a year." The besotted *Let It Rock* compared *Physical Graffiti* to the magnificence of *Blonde on Blonde*, *Beggars Banquet*, and *Revolver*. American critics were somewhat more reserved. *Creem* considered the album "better than the other five offerings . . . more confident, more arrogant, and more consistent," but felt songs like "Kashmir" could be "trimmed," while "Trampled Under Foot" was "rescued from mediocrity by the elaborate punctuation of Page's guitar." And, of course, Jim Miller's *Rolling Stone* review got in a few trademark punches. "Taken as a whole, [*Physical Graffiti*] offers an astonishing variety of music," it conceded, and while "it contains no startling breakthroughs, it does afford an impressive overview of the band's skill." That said, Robert was dismissed as "a singer of limited range and feeling" who succumbed to Jimmy's "preoccupation with sound."

*Stone* was cautiously straddling the fence. The magazine had persisted in bad-mouthing Led Zeppelin since their formation. No reviewers were as contemptuous or disapproving. But Jann Wenner, *Stone*'s demanding publisher, had been chasing the band for a cover story, which Jimmy, up until now, had vehemently opposed. He couldn't forgive the magazine's litany of demeaning comments directed at him and his bandmates over the years. Given the opportunity, he could probably recite the bad reviews verbatim.

Wenner refused to take no for an answer and had finally found an antidote to Jimmy's resistance. *Stone* proposed assigning the article to a seventeen-year-old writer who had caught Led Zeppelin's gimlet eye. Cameron Crowe was talented, and he was a fan. He wrote favorably and incisively about the hard-rock bands the magazine's older editors detested. Jimmy had read some of Crowe's pieces in *Creem* and *Circus* and had agreed to let him dog the band on tour. As it turned out, "he really smoothed out the relationship between *Rolling Stone* and Led Zeppelin," according to Tony Mandich, Atlantic's West Coast artist relations exec. But Jimmy refused to go quietly into *Rolling Stone*'s poison pages. For the cover's photo shoot at New York's Plaza Hotel, he turned up two hours late, clutching several dozen dead roses. The gesture, indicative of Jimmy Page, bore its own magic. When the photographer's negatives were developed, Led Zeppelin's dark, ghostly images were unusable.

The band may have come back rested from the ten-day layoff, but the performances continued to be uneven and to mystify. The headline in the *Houston Chronicle*, long a champion of Led Zeppelin, asked: WHO WOULD HAVE THOUGHT? ZEPPELIN SHOW WAS BORING. "After a couple of songs," the article reported, "the band fell into a tired rut just when it should have been hitting the groove." They fared no better in Baton Rouge the following night. Both the local paper and the university press used the same word to describe the show: "uninspiring."

The shows in Dallas, on March 4 and 5, were also flat, by which time the audience sent the band a message. Only a smattering of applause rippled through the arena. Robert seemed disturbed by the crowd's listless reaction.

"Dallas? Come in? Are you receiving us?" he chided.

It usually fell to Jimmy to regain the momentum. An extended guitar solo by a true master of the art had the potential to wire the house for electricity. His playing was usually a show in itself. But Jimmy couldn't get a rise out of the crowd. "Come *on!*" Robert pleaded. "Why don't you all . . . *wake up!*"

Even John Bonham's half-hour "Moby Dick" solo, a regular crowd-pleaser, failed to do the trick. Bonzo was veering off the rails. His prodigious drinking competed for honors with his drug taking, which had increased. During performances, he positioned a baggie of cocaine between his legs, "reaching in and rubbing handfuls of the drug into his mouth and nostrils as he played." Danny Marcus, Atlantic's artist relations man who was traveling with the band, says, "How he played was how they played. If he was off, they were off."

Bonzo's excess wasn't limited to stimulants. He collected cars the way people collected stamps, from Model Ts to Rolls-Royces, whatever struck his fancy. By Richard Cole's count, he'd purchased twenty-eight cars in the first year and a half after joining Led Zeppelin. Between the shows in Dallas, he had spotted a 1959 red Corvette parked just outside the hotel. As classic cars go, the 'Vette was a beauty, and Bonzo couldn't get it out of his head. He had been assigned a babysitter during the day to keep him out of trouble—Jack Kelly, one of the security detail, an ex–FBI agent who, during the sixties, had "spied on radicals from the Bureau's Boston office." Together they cruised around the city taking in the sights, but talk always came back to the '59 'Vette. Bonzo had to have it, and he instructed Kelly to find the owner and detain him, even having the person arrested if that's what it took.

Bonzo knew the security guys routinely flashed their credentials in extralegal situations. Often, ex-cops who worked the concerts for the band took weed away from kids in the audience and split it up among the musicians and crew. In this case, Jack Kelly used his influence to run the plates on the Corvette so he could track down the owner for Bonzo.

The Corvette wasn't for sale. But when Bonzo offered $18,000 in cash for a car worth about half the price, it was a done deal. Never mind that Bonzo's British license had been revoked and he wasn't permitted to drive in the States. The car was his. He hired someone willing to drive it to Los Angeles, where it was garaged at the Riot House, awaiting his arrival five days later.

## [3]

Everyone was looking forward to Los Angeles, their home away from home, where Led Zeppelin blended into the quotidian circus. The bustling club scene was their milieu. No one batted an eye at the outrageous behavior. Drugs were plentiful and easily obtained, music flowed in the collective bloodstream, and the border between fantasy and reality was semipermeable.

On March 9, 1975, Led Zeppelin and an entourage of handlers, functionaries, groupies, journalists, drug dealers, and assorted hangers-on moved into their maximum-security lair, the eighth, ninth, and eleventh floors of the Continental Hyatt House, all except for Robert Plant, who opted for more discreet accommodations with a girlfriend in Malibu Canyon. Jimmy Page and Peter Grant claimed two suites apiece—one for which they officially registered, the other a hideaway where they slept to avoid Bonzo's nocturnal rampages. A number of other suites remained empty and available, according to Richard Cole, in order to swap out "girls we had rounded up on any given night."

Jimmy's situation resembled a door-slamming bedroom farce. He entertained Krissy Wood, Ronnie Wood's footloose wife, in one suite; Lori Mattix was stashed in a room on a lower floor, with Bebe Buell likely to arrive at any time. Jim Osterberg—Iggy Pop—was another frequent visitor, owing to his access to heroin.

As far as drugs went, the tour now traveled with its own resident doctor, a character named Larry Badgley, who wrote scrips as requested. Danny Marcus, the self-described "enabler," never failed to produce excellent dope. And at Jimmy's behest, Grant invited a neighbor of his, Dave Northover, to pose as John Paul's assistant. "I had once been a physicist," Northover explained, but when G introduced him to the guys in the band, they heard *pharmacist* instead of *physicist*. "Jimmy's ears pricked up, and he said, 'Bring him along!'"

"The amount of drugs was just insane," says Benji Le Fevre. "Because of it, the tour was like the beginning of a nightmare. Everyone was involved in it—the band, G, Ricardo. No one was in control. It was its own entity, slowly going off the rails."

Even simple travel plans flirted with catastrophe. For Led Zeppelin's first West Coast gig, on March 10 in San Diego, the trip took on a nightmarish subplot. Richard Cole organized a convoy of six limos leaving from in front of the Hyatt, with a beggarly cast of groupies competing for precious seats. Instead of driving two hours south on Interstate 5, a sensible choice, Ricardo decided to put the *Starship* into service, despite the threat of a severe weather pattern circling the Southland. Sure enough, a thunderstorm struck as soon as they were in the air. Lightning flashed along the wings, and turbulence bucked the plane around the sky during the entire trip. Pleas to the deity were not uncommon. The twenty-minute white-knuckle flight dragged on like an eternity. Even the landing produced a few errant shrieks.

The last thing Led Zeppelin felt like doing after that was playing music. There were too many frayed nerves. It fell to Peter Grant to lift their spirits. Before the lights went down in the San diego Sports Arena, he marched the band into a washroom for a few lines of blow. As soon as the first chords of "Rock and Roll" were struck, they fell right into the groove.

Jimmy attempted to describe the transformation. "It's like a trance state, you don't think," he explained. "It's just like, you almost have to cleanse yourself of all thought and everything, and then you start playing and it starts to jell with everybody else." There was nothing magical about the process. It was comparable with how jazz combos performed, with loose arrangements that depended on synchronicity and intuition. But it happened only with a group operating on the same wavelength. "There's so much improvisation that goes on and so many times where you'll be playing something and the staccato rhythms will just fit, in total synchronization. . . . You'd look at each other and wink and know that it was never going to come again, but there it was."

John Paul agreed. "Nothing was preplanned about our solos," he said. "We took some chances and sometimes we'd get lost a bit, but when that improvisation worked it was very satisfying."

The audience sensed it right away. In San Diego, they abandoned all soundness of mind and plugged in to that high-voltage trance state. In a flash, fans seated on the floor of the arena leveled the folding chairs and rushed the stage, dancing and bouncing off one another like dervishes. Girls, many of them bare-breasted, were hoisted onto the shoulders of young men. Here and there, kids collapsed from the suffocating heat and were passed, hand over head, to safety at the side of the stage.

Despite the conditions, the show was superb, one of Led Zeppelin's best. "What those eager fans got for their time and money was a virtuoso demonstration of hard rock by the skull-busters extraordinaire," wrote the critic for *The San Diego Union*, "thunderous drums by John Bonham and lightning guitar by Jimmy Page, along with screaming, occasionally Janis Joplin–like vocals of strutting, bare-chested Robert Plant and the steady bass but somewhat unsteady piano of John Paul Jones."

Overall, the tour's pace was frenzied, feverish—and very uneven. Too many variables conspired to affect the outcome. One night, Bonzo struggled with intense stomach issues; another night Jimmy was too wasted to give it his all. In Long Beach, the night after San Diego, Led Zeppelin hit an obvious low. Despite the band's showing up more than an hour late, the energy level in the arena was wildly enthusiastic, and the opening number—"Rock and Roll," an ace in the hole—landed like a blast of nitroglycerin. It is impossible to sit still when that sound bomb discharges. After that, though, the bottom seemed to fall out. "The group ran through songs like 'No Quarter,' 'Kashmir,' 'Over the Hills and Far Away,' 'Stairway to Heaven,' and others with absolutely no concern for what they were doing," observed a respected music journalist. For some unknown reason, the amps buzzed like a swarm of angry hornets. Jimmy's twelve-string was noticeably out of tune and his solos, riddled with flaws, gave another journalist "cause to question his presence on the stage." Robert Hilburn, the *Los Angeles Times*'s esteemed music critic, called the show "a numbing combination of intense, tenacious music and hopelessly limited imagination." The reviewers weren't alone in their assessments. "The audience was . . . bored," said the columnist for the *Long Beach Independent*. You couldn't fool a paying audience. They sat on their hands.

The next night, back at the San Diego Sports Arena, the band turned in an even more sluggish performance. Right off the bat, "Rock and Roll" was "almost unrecognizable," with Robert singing it an octave lower than usual. Solos stretched into mind-numbing experiences. "It was always a toss-up over whose solo would be longest on a given night, Bonzo's or Jimmy's," says Benji Le Fevre, "and whose was going to be most boring, Bonzo's or Jimmy's." Bonzo extended his odyssey on "Moby Dick" to a bloated twenty-five minutes, but Jimmy won hands down for self-indulgence, including a ten-minute stretch conjuring weird, atonal sounds on the theremin during "Whole Lotta Love." Meanwhile, his playing was notably sloppy. During one interlude with the Gibson double-necked guitar, a crew member observed Jimmy strumming the twelve-string neck but chording the six-string neck. Years later, Robert, who'd noticed the gaffe, would describe it as the turning point when he realized that "Jimmy was in the weeds."

It was therapeutic to get out of California for a while. Half a dozen days in the Pacific Northwest did wonders for Led Zeppelin's erratic showmanship. Gigs in Seattle and Vancouver drew the kind of kudos—"spectacular" and "stunning"—that pointed to their enviable strengths. Robert was especially delighted to be performing in Vancouver again. The last time the band had appeared there, on July 18, 1973, they had been forced to cut their show short. Someone had spiked his drink backstage with LSD and he had grown disoriented halfway through the set. Now, nearly two years later, Robert recounted the episode from the stage, saying, "Something strange happened to me that evening. I found the light show to be amazing, and I wondered what the name of the group was." But all was forgiven, with the local critic calling the concert "awesome enough, in delivery and production, to rival almost any concert of its kind." Portland's *Oregonian*, covering one of the shows, concluded, "There is just no other rock band like this one—anywhere."

Led Zeppelin recaptured their focus in the north. Los Angeles, alas, offered too many distractions, and the band's return there for three shows at the Forum—the final engagements of the tour—stirred up a fresh share of high old times. The Continental Hyatt House was awash in drug dealers and groupies with valid passports to Led Zeppelin's floors. Keith Moon, The Who's resident bad boy, turned up to conduct a master class in mischief. According to Richard Cole, Moon and Jimmy treated themselves to a pair of underage girls, one of whose fathers turned up threatening to call the police. It was that kind of atmosphere, heedless hedonism.

Bonzo, particularly, was in rare form. His liquor intake consumed much of the waking day, augmented by unstinting rations of Quaalude and cocaine. "Bonzo was on everything except fresh air," Danny Marcus recalls. For a while, a very short while, he succeeded in staying out of trouble. His new Corvette occupied a reserved space in the Hyatt's underground garage, where he withdrew for hours each day. Unable to drive the car (his license had been revoked), he was content to sit behind the wheel with Mick Ralphs, Bad Company's guitarist, just revving the engine, admiring his purchase. He also bought a souped-up Ford sedan. Unable to resist temptation, he dared to take it out for a spin, "doing about 90mph up and down the Strip," according to John Paul Jones, who watched the action from his Hyatt House balcony. Predictably, Bonzo was pulled over by a pair of LA's finest, who weren't amused when he jumped out to confront them. Somehow, he managed to talk his way out of arrest, even showing off "the bloody size of the engine" and sending the cops on their way with a couple tickets to the next show.

But for most of the three days in LA, Bonzo was a hot mess. "After a certain point, the Beast goes on the prowl, and the only thing that amuses him is pillage," a roadie warned. For a while, he amused himself by heaving half a dozen TV sets out the hotel window onto Sunset Boulevard, eight stories below. Dave Northover insisted he saw an upright piano from Bonzo's room sail past his window, "missing a limo by about ten feet," but that's probably apocryphal. Otherwise Bonzo drank, and as more than ten sources for this book echoed: "Bonzo was a mean drunk." He choked Steve Marriott during an altercation at the Whisky; he provoked fights at the Rainbow, where Deep Purple's Glenn Hughes saw him "take an eight ball of coke out of his pocket," cupping the entire ball "up into his face"; he terrorized *NME* journalist Nick Kent, dousing him with a Bloody Mary; and he cursed the tour doctor, who feared for his life.

The company line about John Bonham's behavior was that he missed his wife and kids so intensely, so painfully, that he acted out. For every person who attested to his drunken rages, an equal number recounted tender moments when Bonzo reminisced about his family grievously, mournfully, often reduced to tears.

He'd soon have a better reason to sing the separation blues. One night, before Led Zeppelin departed for home, Peter Grant called a group meeting and laid out some hard facts. He had good news and bad news. On the one hand, the band had surpassed every expectation he'd ever had for them. *Physical Graffiti* was a runaway hit—it had gone gold and platinum on the day of its release—spurring sales not only of the group's entire backlist but of Swan Song's roster artists as well. Their projected income from record sales and the tour hovered around the $40 million range. That was the also the bad news. Inland Revenue, the British tax vultures, assessed a whopping 87 percent tax bite on England's highest earners.

"Our accountant, Joan Hudson, told us of the massive problems we would have if we didn't go," Grant explained. Go meaning: *into exile.*

Tax exile allowed British high-income earners to hold onto most of their overseas income by living outside the UK for most of the year. The Stones had taken advantage of the economic dodge in 1971, with Mick hibernating in the Republic of Ireland, where, according to Irish Inland Revenue, someone recognized as "producing genuine original work of cultural artistic merit," such as a composer, pays no tax on his earnings. Keith Richards fled to Montreux, Switzerland, and Charlie Watts and Bill Wyman to the South of France, where the tax rate was 60 percent. Peter Frampton had his songwriting royalties paid to companies in Jersey, with a flat tax of 20 percent. Rod Stewart was another energetic tax nomad. But it wasn't as cut-and-dried as simply relocating. One couldn't remain in any one place for more than six months, and living in the United States for more than 181 days required paying U.S. federal taxes, all of which meant you were constantly on the move. To dodge the tax bite, Led Zeppelin couldn't return home until April 1976, almost a year away.

Jimmy and Robert were down with the plan. They'd intended to take some time off and travel anyway. No time like the present, they concluded. John Paul, imperturbable to the bone, would make do, although it meant putting his girls in boarding school for the duration. Only Bonzo balked. Home was his sanctuary. Everyone knew how much he hated being on the road, and uprooting his family seemed wrong to him. Besides, he had no intention of leaving his children anywhere. Peter eventually talked him into the plan, laying out exactly how much Bonzo stood to lose in pounds and pence. Bonzo gasped and decided to join the nomads—but he wasn't going to like it.

Grant raised the possibility of touring in places they'd never played—perhaps in South America or Africa—but no one was in a hurry to consider dates there just yet. In the meantime, he would direct operations from Montreux, leaning on Claude Nobs, the promoter of the Montreux Jazz Festival and a friend of his and the band. Nobs had helped engineer the Stones' year adrift and had contacts across Europe and elsewhere.

Excitement built around the plans, but Led Zeppelin still had one big obligation left to fulfill.

## Chapter Seventeen

---

# THE YEAR OF LIVING DANGEROUSLY

### [1]

There were many loose ends to tie up before Led Zeppelin set off on its rock 'n roll diaspora.

The band remained in Los Angeles for several weeks while Peter Grant navigated a clear course for complying with the strictures of tax exile. It was going to take a group effort to conform to the timetable. Any slip-up could cost a musician millions of dollars.

John Bonham continued to chafe at the situation. His wife, Pat, was expecting their second child any day, and he was determined to be at her side through the birth. The delay in Los Angeles struck him as additional injustice. He was lonely, depressed. His behavior deteriorated further. Onstage, Robert had been jokingly introducing Bonzo as "Mr. Ultraviolence," but it was no longer a joking matter. At the Rainbow, he misinterpreted the smile of a woman he knew who was in the midst of eating dinner and punched her so hard—in the face—that it knocked her off the seat. "Don't ever look at me that way again!" he screamed. A few days later, he assaulted a clerk at Tower Records.

When it came to alcohol and drugs, his self-indulgence was stunning. Danny Goldberg expressed it succinctly: "Bonzo was a huge adult with the emotions of a six-year-old child." Richard Cole was told to keep an extra-vigilant eye on him, which in retrospect seemed counterintuitive. Richard had his own short fuse that frequently led to violence. In early 1975, while still in LA, he pulled a gun on drummer Aynsley Dunbar during an altercation at the Beverly Hilton.

"I've never seen anyone behave worse in my life than Bonham and Cole," said journalist Nick Kent, who was traveling with Led Zeppelin at the time. "I once saw them beat a guy senseless for no reason and then drop money on his face."

At the end of March 1975, Ricardo was given the disagreeable job of shadowing John Bonham at a Swan Song press party for the Pretty Things at the Biltmore Hotel. He must have known it was a fool's errand. During cocktails, Bonzo asked Atlantic's West Coast artist relations manager to get him a cup of coffee, then poured it over the man's natty beige suit. Later that same night, Cameron Crowe reported, Bonzo encountered *Sounds* correspondant Andy McConnell, with whom he had a friendly meeting earlier in the day. For some unknown reason, McConnell shone a flashlight in Bonzo's face and said, "You're an ugly fucker aren't you?" To which "Bonzo responded by knocking McConnell across the room," Crowe said. It took considerable muscle for Richard to extricate an unhinged Bonzo from the melee and hustle him out of the party.

As payback, Bonzo smashed up his suite at the Hyatt House, not an uncommon occurrence. It was almost a blessing when he finally passed out. Almost. It might have passed without incident, had he put out his lit cigarette. But the bed caught fire, activating the sprinkler system and summoning a quorum of firemen, who broke down his door.

It was the final straw. Led Zeppelin was evicted from the Hyatt, not for drugs, not for underage groupies, not for fistfights or motorcycles in the corridors, not even for the destruction of the hotel's furniture, much of which landed in splinters on Sunset Boulevard. It took a cigarette, not even a joint, to ban them once and for all.

The move from West Hollywood to the Hilton in Beverly Hills

wasn't far enough from the action to sidetrack the drummer. He had
no self-discipline. Soon after settling in, he picked a fight with the
bouncer at the Rainbow, a man half his size who happened to be a
black belt in karate and gave Bonzo a taste of his own medicine. A few
knife-like strikes sent him to the hospital with two black eyes and a
broken nose.

It was high time for a change of scenery. Led Zeppelin went back
to London for two months, enough time to get their respective houses
in order and to stage a farewell performance. "We want to find somewhere," Robert indicated, "where we can make it into a bit of an event."

It was settled soon enough—three shows at Earls Court Arena on
May 23 through 25. The place was cavernous, the largest indoor hall
in Britain, which staged the yearly auto show along with boxing events.
It had been two years since the band's last concert in the UK, an eternity, to hear the hometown fans complain. So the show would effectively serve as "hello"—and "goodbye." Was Led Zeppelin still relevant
in Britain? The 51,000 tickets sold out an hour after they went on sale,
forcing the band to agree to two additional shows. Those, in turn, generated more than 100,000 mail-order requests.

First, there was housecleaning to do at Swan Song Records. Bad
Company and Maggie Bell were both releasing sophomore albums in
April 1975. Expectations were high, especially for Bad Company, with
two obvious singles—"Good Lovin' Gone Bad" and "Feel Like Making Love"—each with killer potential. Maggie Bell's follow-up LP, *Suicide Sal*, was harder to nail. Producers seemed intent on polishing her
edges, anesthetizing the badass truck-driver voice. Maggie was a rocker
at heart. She'd fronted bands that knew how to utilize her gritty delivery, but the material producers fed her skewed mainstream pop, making her sound more like a cabaret act. It was going to be difficult
conveying her image to record buyers, even with Jimmy Page handling
guitar on two tracks.

To generate more product, Robert drove over to Rockfield Studios, a few miles from his cottage in Wales, where Dave Edmunds was producer in residence. Edmunds had had a monster hit a few years back with the Smiley Lewis cover "I Hear You Knocking," but as an artist he'd gone cold since. "If you want a record deal, we'll look after you at Swan Song," Robert told Edmunds.

"I seduced Dave Edmunds," Robert admitted, and the singer-producer fell for him in return. He talked it over with his razor-toothed manager, Jake Riviera, and decided that riding Led Zeppelin's coattails might be worth a shot. Robert and Jimmy courted another of Riviera's acts, Dr. Feelgood, a scrappy British R&B pub band whose lead guitarist, Wilko Johnson, played with a stony, unrelenting energy. Jimmy loved his attack, and Robert admired their protean singer, Lee Brilleaux. Dr. Feelgood would have been a perfect fit at Swan Song, but according to Jake Riviera, "Brilleaux didn't like the hierarchy of it all." Ultimately, they decided to stick with their original label, United Artists.

Dave Edmunds would be enough of a challenge. With Led Zeppelin banished to exile for a year, they'd have to leave the label in the hands of their minions. Besides, Peter Grant was sidetracked setting up another U.S. tour, to begin in August 1975.

The Earls Court gigs were also problematic. Led Zeppelin was determined to leave a lasting impression, so they went all in on the production, agreeing to install two gigantic video screens on either side of the stage so fans at the rear of the hall could follow the action. "It cost a lot of bread," said Bonzo, though later he'd admit "it was worth every penny." By Jimmy's calculation, it took such a bite out of profits that the band would "come out of it with only a few hundred pounds over the five days." There were also equipment headaches. One of the road crew had tried to bring a guitar back from the States without declaring it and had been stopped at Heathrow. "So Customs and Excise were on us like a ton of bricks," says Benji Le Fevre. That triggered an investigation into why Led Zeppelin was importing

instruments and speakers from America when they could be purchased in England. All of which required a wad of cash to change
hands in order to make the problem go away.

Despite everything, Led Zeppelin was never more up for a show
than they were for those at Earls Court. There was something about
playing in front of the hometown crowd that was undeniable. Friends
and family made plans to attend, colleagues from the British rock empire, fellow musicians—everyone clamored for tickets. It was more a
homecoming, a celebration, than another gig to play.

For Jimmy Page, it brought back an early, indelible memory. The
last time he was in the exhibition hall he'd been fourteen years old.

"The BBC had a little studio there, where they did live broadcasts—
*The Radio Show*," recalls Dave Williams. "Jimmy and I went to see
what it was all about (and to see if any girls were around). There was
a little trio that played popular songs, and one of the guys had a sunburst Telecaster. Jimmy's eyes almost came out of his head! The only
person who'd had one before was Cliff Gallup. Jimmy had to touch it."

There was a line to get up to the stage and Jimmy waited his turn.
"The kid in front of us was exactly our age—Laurie London, who'd
sung 'He's Got the Whole World in His Hands.'" Jimmy eventually
elbowed past him and reached for the guitar. "It was the first time he'd
laid his hands on a Fender."

Now, sixteen years later, he had a shelf full of them at the side
of the stage, along with his Harmony Sovereign, a number of Les
Pauls, the Danelectro, a Martin D-28, and the inimitable Gibson
double-neck.

The expectation in the hall was enormous, unrestrained. As the
lights came down and a roar rose up, Whispering Bob Harris, the BBC
Radio 1 deejay, bellowed, "We'd all like to welcome back to Britain . . .
*Led Zeppelin!*" The sound the crowd made was inhuman, matched
only by the detonation of "Rock and Roll" and an explosion of lasers,
smoke, and lights.

Robert was especially loose at the mic—"a jolly raconteur," as one observer tagged him—and in superb voice, a welcome relief after his bout with laryngitis in America. Following the first song, he laid out Led Zeppelin's initiative. "We want to take you through the stages of six-and-a-half years of our relationship." That meant a trip through highlights of all the albums, a breathtaking cross section and contrast of styles, including a reprise of the acoustic set in which all four musicians played from chairs at the front of the stage. It was fascinating to hear them give relaxed, if uneven treatments to "Tangerine," "Going to California," "That's the Way," and "Bron-Yr-Aur Stomp" before hammering back with "Trampled Under Foot" and "No Quarter." Three and a half hours of transcendent music.

There was ongoing levity from Robert about the band's tax predicaments, with a shout-out to Denis Healey, the chancellor of the exchequer. It was tasteless and tone-deaf. Most of the audience was suffering the effects of woeful economic stress, the result of ongoing labor strife, power outages, and an OPEC oil embargo that had plagued Britain through an extremely harsh winter and spring. Rich rock 'n rollers who dodged paying their fair share weren't exactly objects of sympathy.

Nevertheless, the British press carried on like a varsity cheerleading squad. An effusive review in *Melody Maker* called Led Zeppelin's show "the definitive rock performance, so much so that it's inconceivable that another band could do as well." Not to be outdone, *Record Mirror* proclaimed the concert "a nocturnal delight, one which should be remembered for eons to come." Even customary fusspots at *The Guardian*, the *Daily Mail*, *The Observer*, and *The Times* waxed rhapsodic, jumping on the bandwagon.

Be that as it may, Led Zeppelin remained thin-skinned in regard to the press, continuing to feel they were owed more respect than they received. *Melody Maker*'s Chris Welch, who had sung the band's praises the way Caruso sang arias, with euphoria and abandon, "arrived at Earl's Court to be told that no review tickets were available to *Melody Maker*, which meant he had to buy a pair from a tout." It seems someone in the band had taken offense at a throwaway remark in his lukewarm review of *Houses of the Holy* and sought to teach him a lesson. No objectivity, no matter how insignificant, was countenanced when it came to reviewing a Led Zeppelin album.

The same punishment was dealt to Charles Shaar Murray, one of the band's longtime champions in the pages of *New Musical Express*, who happened to have reviewed a show when Robert had muffed the words to "Stairway to Heaven." Robert decided it was time to settle old scores. During the May 23 show at Earls Court, just before launching into "Stairway," he grabbed the mic and started having a go at Murray—*from the stage*. "Despite Charles Shaar Murray, we kept going," he told a uniformly indifferent audience. "I believe there's a psychiatrist on his way, Charles. Just hang on. Keep those teeth gritted. But here's one for you in your better moments, Charles."

"The audience didn't know what the fuck he was talking about," says Chris Charlesworth. "But that's how touchy and insecure they were."

Digs and sarcasm aside, the Earls Court concerts reminded fans in the United Kingdom that Led Zeppelin wasn't lost to the temptations of America. They hadn't forgotten where they came from. They'd played their hearts out "for our families and friends and the people who have been close to us through the lot." They left everything they had on that stage, knowing that it was anyone's guess when they'd be back on British soil.

"Thank you for very good health, and keep your fingers crossed for mine," Robert proposed.

He had no idea how that request would resonate. It would be the last public comment he'd make for nearly two years.

## [2]

Led Zeppelin's migration was immediate. On May 26, 1975, the day after the last concert at Earls Court, everyone took off for his respective safe haven. John Paul Jones flew to Switzerland with his wife, Mo, and their daughters, while John and Pat Bonham moved their family into a villa in St.-Paul-de-Vence. Jimmy Page joined Peter Grant in Montreux to go over plans for the summer tour, then headed to Rio de Janeiro to check out the effervescent Brazilian music scene. Robert Plant was raring to explore. He, his wife, and their two young children packed up and traveled to Agadir, a Moroccan beach town at the foot of the Atlas Mountains that might have served as a stand-in for Nice or Miami. From there, they intended to bump around the country, eventually winding up in Marrakesh.

Was the getaway idyllic? Not for everyone. John Paul despised being forced out of his home. "He used to ring me at the office all the time, saying how desperate he was to come back to the UK," recalls Carole Brown, who operated much like an air traffic controller in London's Swan Song office. The novelty soon wore off for Bonzo as well. He was exasperated living in the South of France, where he didn't speak the language. "He couldn't stomach the elaborate French food and insisted on steak and chips all the time," says Sally Williams, the girlfriend of Mick Hinton, whom Bonzo imported as his personal servant. Richard Cole also showed up to splash in the villa's pool with Bonzo and his son, Jason. "When John wasn't drunk, he was like a kid," Williams says. "But after a few drinks or if something hit him the wrong way, things turned violent in an instant." That was exactly what happened one evening in June when the party moved to a casino in Monte Carlo and Bonzo was ejected by the French authorities.

Swan Song's acts also suffered because of the exile. Maggie Bell's second album, *Suicide Sal*, urgently needed a shot in the arm to raise its profile with the public. The release had stalled at radio and with the press, owing to the lack of a meaningful tour. "She was desperate to do some promotion, a few gigs." says Unity MacLean, who was working overtime to drum up support. The album had generated mostly lackluster reviews, but management also had to take responsibility. Abe Hoch, the acting label head—emphasis on *acting*—was impotent when it came to matters of real importance. He had no authority whatsoever. He was beating himself up for taking the job. "Nobody was around to make any decisions, and we could never get ahold of Peter."

Dave Edmunds was another Swan Song casualty. "There was no plan for him," MacLean says. "We brought out 'Here Comes the Weekend,' but there was no one appointed to plug the record or generate airplay or drum up interest at the BBC, no one to help get press interviews. Dave was absolutely furious with the whole thing."

Bonzo had warned MacLean not to expect much support. "We're musicians," he told her before disappearing into exile. "We're not record executives. That wasn't part of the deal."

"What it came down to was: nobody was home," Abe Hoch explains. "If I needed Peter, I would have to call him, and he might—*might*—call me back two or three days later. He'd always be sleeping when I needed him, so I might have to wake him up, and he'd growl unintelligibly over the phone. This is how the record company was being run."

Peter remained in Montreux for most of June, palling around with promoter and fixer Claude Nobs, whose house he had rented as a base of operations. The rest of the band was expected to turn up toward the beginning of July. G wanted to gauge how they were faring away from home and to iron out details for the next major tour.

Robert and Jimmy arrived together. They had met in Marrakesh a month earlier to begin a car trip through Morocco with their families. Jimmy had heeded William Burroughs's advice about digging into the native music scene, so in Marrakesh they spent several nights at a local folk festival that, as Robert noted, "gave us a little peep into the color of Moroccan music and the music of the hill tribes." Afterward, they squeezed into a Range Rover—Robert, Maureen, Karac, and Carmen, along with Jimmy, Charlotte Martin, and their daughter, Scarlet—and headed across the Spanish Sahara toward the port of Tarifa, in Gibraltar, with Bob Marley songs blaring through the tape deck.

They were thwarted by army roadblocks every thirty miles or so, freaked out by having machine guns pointed at their windshield. Hostilities between Spain and Morocco prevented them from crossing the border. "For two months, I'd lived at a Moroccan speed, which is no speed at all," Robert recalled, "and then suddenly I was in Spain being frisked." Reluctantly, they turned back to Tangier before reconvening a week later in Switzerland.

The band was relieved by the news in Montreux. The summer tour Grant set up was modest in scope—only eleven U.S. dates, beginning at the end of August, just long enough to satisfy their tax-exile status but immensely profitable. Mostly stadiums seating upward of 35,000 people, beginning on August 23, 1975, with two shows at the Oakland Coliseum for 90,000 fans and culminating at the Superdome in New Orleans, with a capacity of 76,000. They'd net pretty much the same amount they would have from a marathon through the States. The merchandising alone would keep everyone well endowed—all in cash, as usual, and off the books.

The rest of the exile would encompass a world tour, "playing possibly in South America, Hawaii, Japan, and Asia Minor, and ending up doing dates in Europe, especially Scandinavia," before resuming a normal residency in Great Britain.

Robert and Jimmy hung around Montreux for a while. The jazz festival was in full swing, and the 1975 edition featured an extraordinary lineup of all-stars—Dizzy, Mingus, Ella, the Count, but also Albert King, Etta James, and Rory Gallagher, whom they were eager to see perform. Eventually, Robert came down with a case of wanderlust.

"After a while," he said, "I started pining for the sun again—not just the sun, but the happy, haphazard way of life that goes with it." The dozy pace of Morocco had been a blessing after six tumultuous years of go-go-go. And Greece. "Rhodes seemed like a good idea."

Roger Waters owned a house on the bucolic Greek island, which he'd rented to Phil May, the Pretty Things' lead singer, and his wife, Electra. Robert accepted an invitation to join them and decided to drive to Greece with his wife and kids. Jimmy, Charlotte, and Scarlet followed in another car, with Maureen's sister, Shirley, and her husband.

On August 3, 1975, Jimmy got sidetracked. He heard through the grapevine that Aleister Crowley's Abbey of Thelema in Cefalù, Sicily, might be for sale. To occultists, it was a shrine, the spiritual center where Crowley and his disciples indulged in "sex magick" and drug rituals throughout the early part of the twentieth century. Jimmy decided to detour there, perhaps even buy the place, leaving Robert and the others to go on ahead. If all went according to plan, he'd meet Led Zeppelin in Paris for a week of pretour rehearsals.

For the rest of the party, Rhodes couldn't wait. The island was everything they'd fantasized—perfect climate, a gorgeous coastline with fresh, rosemary-scented salt air, sun-washed pastel villages, and snug harbors, all framed against the Mediterranean Sea. Everyone was so taken with the resplendent scenery that it was all the more of a shock when an Austin Mini sedan Maureen Plant was driving skidded off the road and toppled over a precipice before crashing into a tree. Robert, who'd been riding in the passenger seat, knew he'd been badly injured— but he was alive. He couldn't say the same for his wife.

"I looked over at Maureen," he said, "and thought she was dead. [She] was unconscious and bleeding, and the kids were screaming in the back seat."

Charlotte Martin, who'd run up from the follow car, took one look and "was hysterical."

It was a bad scene. No one could move. Robert figured it was only a matter of time before an ambulance arrived. But Greek speed matched the Moroccan speed he had so adored a week earlier. As far as he could tell, Maureen still had a heartbeat; there was no time to spare. "Finally, the driver of a fruit truck loaded us onto his open flatbed." A small clinic was located nearby.

Robert had suffered a broken ankle and elbow, and the bones in his right leg had shattered in several places. His six-year-old daughter, Carmen, had broken her wrist, and four-year-old son, Karac, had a broken leg. Maureen was more seriously injured. She'd ruptured her pelvis and had a fractured skull, among other issues. Worse, she'd lost a lot of blood and was "near death," Benji Le Fevre was informed in a phone call later that night. "Robert told me she technically did die for a couple minutes and was resuscitated."

She was in dire need of emergency transfusions. The hospital was primitive, woefully understaffed, and lacking crucial supplies, without a reserve of Maureen's rare blood type on hand. Her sister, Shirley, was a match but could provide only so much. The sole doctor on duty was near exhaustion. They needed outside help, a miracle.

Charlotte Martin phoned London, raising Richard Cole. Ricardo, perhaps better than anyone, knew how to grease wheels and spent several hours working the phones. He convinced a British physician who provided medical services to the Greek embassy in London and an orthopedic surgeon to leave immediately for Rhodes, then rustled up a private jet to fly them there. He even managed to find eight pints of Maureen's blood type and stored them in the plane's fridge, much the way he provisioned the *Starship* with champagne.

In the meantime, Robert was stranded in a squalid ward next to a drunken soldier who recognized him. "I was lying there in some pain trying to get cockroaches off the bed," he said, "and he started singing 'The Ocean' from *Houses of the Holy*."

Upon arrival, the British doctors sized up the lamentable situation, ordering the patients transferred to a hospital in London. The Greek authorities, however, refused to cooperate. Police were investigating the accident to determine if alcohol or drugs were involved. Complicating matters, Maureen had sideswiped another car.

"Apparently, under Greek law, if you cause an accident, they can charge you with assaulting whoever was in the other vehicle," says Jeff Hoffman, the lawyer who'd represented Peter Grant during the aftermath of the Drake robbery and was now appointed to represent Maureen Plant. "In this instance, there was a Greek family involved." No one was injured, but once they realized who Robert was, Maureen was charged. Extricating her was a straightforward if slippery process. "You work out a deal, and whatever they deem your sentence to be, there is a daily rate you can pay to make it go away."

Richard Cole wasn't waiting for the outcome. Over the objections of the doctors, he staged a great escape from the hospital that would have impressed Steve McQueen. "I hired a private ambulance and rented two station wagons and had them parked at a side entrance," Richard recalled. "At two in the morning, Charlotte and I wheeled Robert, Maureen, and their children—along with their IV bottles and other medical equipment—down the hospital corridors to the get-away cars."

The police had specified that the Plants couldn't leave the country, but little attention was paid to private jets. Before the authorities could intervene, Robert and his family were in the air and headed to London. Richard had ambulances waiting at Heathrow to transport the patients to Guy's Hospital in the center of the city. It might have gone smoothly, had Led Zeppelin's accountants not realized that by delaying Robert's arrival an hour or two they could add another day he could spend in the country to satisfy the tax-exile mandate. As a result, Cole ordered the pilot to circle outside British airspace until after midnight.

Robert was placed in a body cast that ran from his hip to his toes. "The doctor in London told me I wouldn't walk for at least six months, and he gave me some odds of various possibilities about the future," Robert said. "I didn't know what the implications and the final outcome of the wounds or whatever would turn out to be, but they were of minimal importance at the time." There was an outside chance he might be permanently disabled. "I didn't think about the possible consequences for the band."

One thing was for certain: there would be no summer tour. That was a best-case scenario. Peter Grant feared it "could be the end of the line." Grant felt that Robert was irreplaceable, as was any member of Led Zeppelin. If he was unable to perform, they'd have to pack it in.

Jimmy was more optimistic. "I've always felt," he said, "that no matter what happened, provided [Robert] could still play and sing—and even if we could only make albums—that we'd go on forever."

As Maureen's condition improved, Robert gave some thought to resuming his career. But something had changed; his irrepressible spirit would never be the same. "I know that my kind of vision, or the carefree element I had, disappeared instantly when I had my accident," he said. "That kind of ramshackle 'I'll take the world now' attitude was completely gone."

This wasn't his first serious car crash, either. In February 1970, on his way home from seeing Spirit at Mother's in Birmingham, he had been involved in an accident when he lost control of his Jaguar and collided with a minivan. Both cars were totaled. "It was a horrific scene," Jimmy recalled. "The police came banging at my door with flashlights and asked me if I knew a Mr. Robert Plant." It was the kind of encounter in which grim news is usually conveyed. Robert was lucky. He got off with lacerations above an eye, a dislocated shoulder, and a couple of lost teeth.

Then, as now, Robert faced a lengthy recovery process. "He looked white as a sheet, bewildered, traumatized," says Benji Le Fevre, the band's able crewman, who agreed to assist Robert for as long as he was laid up. "He was in a lot of pain, unable to walk." It meant recuperating somewhere remote, away from the hustle—and getting there fast. The tax exile permitted him to be back in England for only one sixth of the time he'd been away, and that grace period was just about up.

Once again, Richard Cole pulled strings and found temporary quarters nearby, in Jersey, one of the Channel Islands off the coast of Normandy. Locals referred to their island hideaway as "sixty thousand alcoholics clinging to a rock." It was a haven for financial magnates, with pristine, sandy bays, wall-to-wall yachts moored in the harbors, championship golf courses, and, of course, cattle—Jersey cows responsible for a bounty of rich cream and cheeses. A wealthy lawyer with ties to Led Zeppelin offered his estate to Robert and his entourage for as long as was necessary. Despite the proximity, it was an ordeal getting him there. He was immobile, confined to a wheelchair, and the plane was small.

Money, especially the kind of money Led Zeppelin knew how to wield, solved such problems. It's how Peter Grant operated. "I bought the seats in front and then had them removed," G said, shelling out a cool £7,000. "There was a bit of a row, but I got the captain to make sure we could unscrew the seats before we took off. That way, Robert got the space he needed."

Too much space. The trip to Jersey meant leaving Maureen behind in the hospital, which sent Robert into a tailspin. He was depressed, his morale low. It cheered him somewhat when the rest of the gang showed up. G flew in first, with Jonesy, Jimmy, and Bonzo in his vapor trail. They had a big decision to make about continuing the tax exile. The general vibe was: "If Robert can't do it, we won't do it," a generous sacrifice, considering the money at stake. Performing was out of the question, but everyone seemed to agree that they could still make music, using the downtime—however long it might last—to record a new album. G and Jimmy volunteered to find someplace suitable to spend a few months.

In the meantime, the band took some time to enjoy each other's company without any obligations to the wages of rock 'n roll. "There were lots of days with everyone together on sun lounges, jumping in and out of the pool," recalls Benji. There was an ornate snooker table, a first-class wine cellar, a fleet of luxury sports cars at their disposal, the usual cache of cocaine to keep everybody in the groove. "I cooked big Sunday lunches—a roast in the oven, potatoes, a beautiful laid table. Plenty of laughter. Jersey is where they reunited, where they re- alized how much they enjoyed each other's company."

But soon they were on the move. Again. Jimmy had settled on a place to lay down roots for a while, where they could live comfort- ably, rehearse, maybe even record, a place beyond the tax man's greedy reach but where they would feel right at home. It was a place where women have love in their eyes and flowers in their hair and where the mountains and canyons tremble and shake.

No one was surprised. They were heading to LA.

## [3]

Young girls may have been headed to the canyon, as the song implied, but once Led Zeppelin arrived in LA, they rapidly changed course.

The idea was to spend the exile in comfort, so houses were rented in the Malibu Colony, on the beach—five houses, one for each band member and Peter Grant. It was an idyllic setting. Acres of white sand and the hypnotic Pacific Ocean lay right outside the front door. Surfers rode waves in to the shore. California girls frolicked like water nymphs. The occasional whale drifting by sent spouts of water into the air. On a clear day, Catalina Island shimmered in the distance like a mirage. Movie stars strolled by and waved—Leslie Caron right next door, and on the other side, Rod Steiger. Robbie Robertson and Neil Diamond were neighbors. Dylan lived down the beach in Point Dume. Burt Lancaster pushed a cart in the supermarket. Idyllic, Hollywood style.

"They each had their own rhythm in LA," says Abe Hoch, who'd arrived from London to help with arrangements.

Robert scheduled physiotherapy every day. "We drove into Hollywood, where they would work on his ankle, stretch his arm, and give him exercises to do at home," says Benji Le Fevre. "There was so much weed and cocaine around. I had to be strict and say, 'You're not going to have any Charlie until you've done these exercises.' He was still physically compromised, still in a wheelchair, and I had to lift him in and out of the bath." Robert was unmoored. He drew inward, became philosophical. "We talked a lot about the meaning of life and what was important—*really* important. The accident had been a big wake-up call. 'I nearly died! *I could have died!* I'm not invincible, and I'm only twenty-eight years old.'"

They rarely went down the road to Jimmy's house, now referred to as Henry Hall, *Henry* being British slang for heroin. Jimmy wasn't seen during daylight hours. Drapes and blinds were pulled in his windows until eleven o'clock at night, when a light would finally come on. "He was so far gone," says Michael Des Barres, who was hovering, agitating for a record deal.

"Peter pulled me aside one day and said, 'Go see what Pagey's doing,'" Abe Hoch recalls. "His house was dark inside in the middle of the day, and he was passed out, unconscious, naked on the bed. There were strange-looking books strewn across the covers—Crowley books and shit like that. It was a pretty weird scene." When Peter asked Hoch about Jimmy's condition, he said, "I've seen more movement in a Timex."

At night, Jimmy worked on music. The intention was to lay down riffs for new songs and develop them with the rest of the band. But Jimmy was unreliable, not communicating smoothly with Robert, not showing up for scheduled rehearsals. A guitar tech named Ray Thomas was supposedly looking after Jimmy, but Thomas was similarly in heroin's thrall. This put a strain on Jimmy and Robert's relationship at a time when they needed to produce an album's worth of material. But nothing concrete was happening musically.

When Jimmy was lucid, he signed a band to Swan Song led by charismatic Michael Des Barres, who shared his fascination with Aleister Crowley and drugs. The two had first met in 1974, when Des Barres fronted a band called Silverhead and Led Zeppelin happened to check them out at a club in Birmingham. Des Barres was a lightning rod for attention, a natural onstage, cheeky, glam, and in his words, "narcissistic, decadent, and debauched."

"I was different from the others," Des Barres says. His father, a disgraced, opium-smoking marquis who eventually went to prison, gave

Michael an upper-crust education and an endowment that allowed him way too much freedom. "I led the life of a prince. Middle-class Jimmy and working-class Bonzo had to respect the aristocracy because they were trained to do so. It elevated my status."

Jimmy was especially impressed. "I used to meet him at his Plumpton home," Des Barres recalls. "It was what you'd expect: closed drapes and black candles. We got deeply into Jimmy's tarot deck, which had been Crowley's personal deck. But we didn't sit around listening to music. It was drugs. It was drugs all the time."

Des Barres and Silverhead managed to eke out the beginnings of a career. "Our fan base was coke dealers," he said. It seemed inevitable that the band scratched up a gig at the Whisky and found themselves occupying a suite at the Continental Hyatt House. "We pulled up to the hotel fresh off the plane from London, and there was a hearse parked outside with a tiger in the back. Turns out the tiger was the star of a TV show called *Daktari*." Des Barres rented the tiger for a week and walked it around the Hyatt's lobby, attracting his share of groupies. The go-to groupie was Lori Mattix, along with her mother and Sable Starr.

"It was indescribable. All of it. But none of it seemed incredible to me. I was Caligula at the time."

Des Barres had been married only three weeks when he arrived in Los Angeles, but he took up immediately with Pamela Miller as Silverhead also fell by the wayside, and he moved on from that, too. "My managers put me with a teenage guitar player called Michael Monarch who'd been in Steppenwolf and a great drummer named John Hyde who was obsessed with Bonzo—and we became Detective."

The hype machine cranked into full gear. Before a note was played, every major label was knocking at Detective's door. Columbia Records offered $1 million, but Detective was entranced by the Led Zeppelin mystique.

"One of my managers got hold of Peter Grant and gave him a big bag of coke to come to our rehearsal," Des Barres recalls. "Jimmy came too and didn't say much." But the next morning, negotiations began in earnest to sign Detective to Swan Song. "It was green-card rock 'n roll. Peter Grant arranged my divorce, and I married Miss Pamela. Jimmy Page agreed to produce our album. We'd get a support tour with Led Zeppelin. It was a dream come true. But from that moment—and I'm not kidding, *that moment*—I knew the jig was up. You give young guys a million dollars, and what do you think is going to happen? Everybody got strung out."

With Bad Company, Maggie Bell, the Pretty Things, Dave Edmunds, and now Detective, Swan Song had assembled a reasonably enviable roster of artists. Including, of course, Led Zeppelin, the label's mighty anchor. But a label needed a strong leader and a clear-cut business strategy, and in 1975 it had neither. Swan Song's officers—Danny Goldberg in New York and Abe Hoch in London—were figureheads, powerless to make a significant decision. All authority resided with the inaccessible Peter Grant. Even his wife, Gloria, had trouble reaching him.

"She used to call the office and say, 'I need to speak to my husband,'" recalls Unity MacLean. "Our standard answer was, 'He'll call you right back.' But he'd never call back, and it angered her. When she did get through, he'd say, 'Don't give me this fucking grief.' She was trying to keep the family together while he was away. She was lonely, neglected. He'd spent long stretches in Switzerland, Paris, and Jersey. Now, according to Gloria, he'd disappeared into America with his tax problems, living the high life."

The very high life. Peter Grant's cocaine habit remained prodigious, as outsize as he was. He was always in possession of a big pile of blow. "It was a bagful," says Betty Iannaci, an Atlantic Records colleague, "and his coke spoon was the size of a ladle!" He was never without his stash, which was always replenished—easily done in the Los Angeles entertainment arena, where cocaine was ubiquitous. G had become dependent on it, often coked out of his mind. Whether he acknowledged it or not, he was in its powerful grip. "When something like drugs own you, they own you," said Sam Aizer, Swan Song's artist relations manager in the States. "Peter had another master, and it wasn't Led Zeppelin. It was his own hell."

His sense of entitlement grew all out of proportion. One night, on his way home from the Whisky, Peter grew exasperated with the way the car ahead of his was traveling. "Go on," he instructed his limo driver, "drive into him."

The driver hesitated. "Mr. Grant, I can't possibly do that."

G dug into his coat pocket and pushed a wad of bills at his driver. "Here's a thousand dollars," he said. *"Do what you're told!"*

Peter was a pastiche of excessive highs and extreme lows. He was routinely late for appointments, a no-show more often than not. Always unpredictable, he'd become impulsive, erratic.

During the tax exile in LA, Jimmy was becoming ever more drug-addled and undependable. He'd agreed to participate in a signing photo for Detective at the Beverly Hills Hotel that would be distributed to the press and music trade magazines. It was a standard ceremony that all record companies practiced to draw attention to a new, unknown band, though it rarely raised an eyebrow. Having Jimmy in the picture, however, guaranteed plenty of coverage, so everyone involved was looking forward to the event.

Jimmy was late, which wasn't unusual—but he was *fifteen hours late*. And when he showed up, he was anything but present. "He was carried into the photo session, and he was unconscious," Michael Des Barres recalls. "'Tired,' we were told. He was '*really* tired.'"

Danny Goldberg knew from the get-go there was going to be difficulty. He saw Jimmy nod out in the limo on their way to the session. "Michael and I tried repeatedly to wake him, even going to the extreme of throwing cold water on his face, but it was to no avail. Although he was breathing, he was out cold."

In true show-must-go-on tradition, they decided to salvage the session. Danny directed the band to pose around the comatose Jimmy, whom they propped up in *Weekend at Bernie's* fashion, and gave the photographer the go-ahead to shoot it. It wasn't your everyday signing photo, but it wasn't boring.

No matter how fucked up things got, there was always plenty of action in LA. On nights when everyone was conscious and functioning, Led Zeppelin would pull together and hit the town as a band. Even Robert could be wheeled almost anywhere. "We'd all go to Trader Vic's or to the Whisky," says Betty Iannaci. "Uproarious times, but civilized. Not the way they usually acted in LA, which was almost as though they had been let loose in the Wild West."

Sometimes it was a relief to exist as a face in the crowd, out of the glare and turmoil of their ridiculously public lives. How nice it felt to steal unnoticed into an Etta James concert or see George Burns, remaining anonymous in a darkened nightclub. There was a memorable Little Feat show at a club in Venice, Donovan at the Santa Monica Civic Auditorium, and Bob Marley onstage at the Roxy, where Bonzo sat wedged between Keith Moon and Ringo Starr. There were also small, private parties where Led Zeppelin could unwind and be themselves.

As the band arrived at one fabulous bash, at the Greenhouse Restaurant on Sunset Boulevard, they noticed a woman in a beret and smoking a cigarette seated by herself in the corner. Was it a mirage—or actually Joni Mitchell, their idealized muse, the subject of "Going to California"? It took a while for Jimmy to work up the nerve to approach her, but they wound up chatting for a while and exchanging phone numbers.

Abe Hoch recalled a party that Elton John threw in Malibu for director Bryan Forbes. "I brought David Cassidy and Warren Beatty, and Groucho was there," he says. Groucho Marx sang a song called "Father's Day," after which Elton sat down at the piano and played through the entire *Don't Shoot Me, I'm Only the Piano Player* album. He just killed it. Afterward, Elton approached Abe and asked if he could help get Groucho to sign a picture he had of Margaret Dumont, the dowager straight lady of so many Marx Brothers movies. Elton claimed he was too shy to ask Groucho on his own.

"Who's it for?" Groucho asked when Abe put the photo under his nose.

"Elton," Abe said.

"Who the fuck is Elton?"

Abe replied, "Elton is the host of the party."

"Oh," Groucho's face lit up, "the *piano* player. What's his name?"

"Elton John."

Groucho looked confused. "What a stupid fucking name. His last name is where his first name ought to be."

So he autographed the photo: "To Elton John—Marx, Groucho."

The life of a rock star in Los Angeles was always potentially precarious. Returning home one night, Benji Le Fevre noticed the lights on in Robert's Malibu house. Benji was certain he'd turned them off before they'd left. "Just wait here a moment," he suggested to Robert, who was stuck in a wheelchair in the back of an SUV.

Crawling up to a window, Benji peered inside. "Man, it was freaky," he recalls. "There were two girls, with Robert's clothes spread across the floor, and they were doing little rituals in the living room."

Fortunately for Led Zeppelin, there was more of their security detail than coyotes lurking in the outlying Malibu brush, and in a flash the house was swarming with owl-eyed heavies. "It turned out to be a couple of the Manson girls," says Phil Carlo, who helped to remove the perpetrators with a squad of rent-a-cops.

"There was a lot of tension about the period, all holed up in houses we didn't really want to be in," Peter Grant recalled. The main focus was supposed to be on music, coming up with songs for another album. But "it was an uphill struggle," Grant admitted. "It was difficult in the writing and rehearsing stage."

Jimmy and Robert had done their individual parts, but there was little communication between the two creative principals. Most days,

Robert sat alone by his rain-soaked window, scratching out lyrics that were uncharacteristically autobiographical. Snatches of remorse and vitriol appeared in "The Wheelchair Song," describing his car crash and subsequent exile from family and friends. "Tea for One" summed up his resentment about loneliness and being separated from his kids and Maureen, who was still recovering from her injuries. There was a scathing diatribe on the superficial Los Angeles lifestyle called "For Your Life," which Robert described as "a sarcastic dig at one person in particular that I know who was a really good person but got swallowed up with the whole quagmire of the downhill slide," a clear reference to Jimmy. Borrowing from the masters, as usual, he adapted a Blind Willie Johnson spiritual, "It's Nobody's Fault But Mine," from an old Fontana EP he had called *Treasures of North American Negro Music* and inserted a line about having "a monkey on my back."

"I was just sitting in a wheelchair and getting morose," he admitted. "It was like: Is this rock 'n roll thing really anything at all?"

The way out of a funk was to rehearse. There was always true joy when the four men made music together. That had never changed. Jimmy's guitar, John Paul's bass, Bonzo's drums, Robert's vocals created a sound that never failed to produce something good to their ears. The Led Zeppelin magic—it lifted their spirits. But substance abuse had intruded on the enchantment. It affected their personalities, which affected the music. Drugs had Jimmy turned inward. It was never certain that the once-reliable studio musician with the iron work ethic would show up to play.

"We just couldn't find him," Jonesy lamented. Nothing remotely stirred at Henry Hall, which remained shuttered. "I wanted to put up this huge banner across the street, saying, 'Today's the first day of rehearsals.'"

They'd scheduled time at Studio Instrument Rentals, an establishment in Hollywood that had a space in which bands loved to play. John Paul and his roadie drove in from Malibu every night for an eight o'clock session "and waited and waited until finally [after Jimmy joined them] we were all in attendance, by which time it was around two in the morning." Six hours of sitting around idly, watching TV and smoking, drained Robert and Jonesy of whatever creative enthusiasm they had. It was hard to get anything serious going.

For the brief intervals when they did, however, it felt like old times. Robert kicked things off with snippets of "Hoochie Coochie Man" and "Minnie the Moocher." They warmed up with an old favorite, "Stop Me Talking."

"You could see Robert and Jimmy connecting," says Betty Iannaci, who was invited, along with a few friends and roadies, to observe the action from the sidelines. "They seemed to intuit each other, just like when they were onstage, and there was great joy in the process."

Robert, whose mobility remained negligible, welcomed the opportunity to get into a groove. "I was sitting in an armchair singing," he recalled, "and I found myself wiggling inside my cast."

The problem was flow—or the lack thereof. "There just wasn't a lot of continuous rehearsal," John Paul complained, "and it was easy to lose interest."

Nevertheless, they managed to bang a few songs into shape, making enough progress to get them down on tape. But not in Los Angeles, where their allotted number of days was due to expire. They needed to pull up stakes and move on before owing considerable tax to Uncle Sam. There were several good studios available in exile sanctuaries around the globe, one especially that Keith Harwood, their engineer, favored. After some discussion, they packed up and headed to Munich.

## Chapter Eighteen

# THE OTHER SIDE
# OF THE SPECTRUM

## [1]

Eighteen days. That was the extent of time available to Led Zeppelin at Musicland Studios in Munich—eighteen days, from November 3, 1975, until November 21, when the Rolling Stones were booked to finish work on *Black and Blue*. It was asking a lot, especially without a full complement of songs ready to go. "We went in with nothing really," Jimmy acknowledged some time later. "We all agreed that we'd go right back to square one. Start with nothing, just a few basic structures and the minimum of rehearsal." Only the first Led Zeppelin album had been recorded in less time, though Jimmy had worked out much of that one in advance. That wasn't the case this time around. Jimmy was barely communicative. And with so little time to spare, the usual organic process to making a Led Zeppelin album, with everyone pitching in, was abandoned. John Paul, always an unfailing force in the studio, had little to contribute. Besides, his heart wasn't in it.

"When we eventually started recording in Munich," he said, "I just sort of went along with it all."

Robert was understandably contemplative. "If ever there was a time to quit, this was it, because before we went to Musicland, we didn't actually know if we'd ever play together again or, if we did stop, just how long we'd have to wait—and whether or not it would ever be the same show we get back together again."

Commuting wouldn't be a factor. The studio, owned by Giorgio Moroder, was located in the basement of the Arabella Hotel, where each of the guys had a suite. Even Bonzo, perennially late (even to his brother's wedding), couldn't plead traffic delays. But little had changed from the situation in Los Angeles. Jimmy remained locked in his room, a no-show for the first day . . . and the second . . . and the third. "We didn't see him forever," says Abe Hoch, who arrived in Munich to help with details. "He was just *not awake*. He was in a coma."

Robert had looked forward to recording as a means of occupational therapy. He felt that after "sitting in a fucking chair, pushed everywhere for months and months," the prospect of making music was invigorating, "so when we did record I got more enthusiastic and that helped me physically."

But without Jimmy in the mix, Robert lay in bed most of those days, working on lyrics, revising what he had already sketched out in Los Angeles. "The Wheelchair Song" evolved into a paean to his accident.

"What rhymes with 'Achilles'?" he asked Hoch, torturing the poetics.

Peter Grant recalled, "Robert was behind with his lyrics and apologized to Jonesy, who said: 'Personally Robert, I've never bothered to listen to the lyrics on any of our albums.'"

Robert's cast was about come off, though his leg was still tender, fragile. He was in considerable pain, with medication prescribed to see him through the endeavor.

Others self-medicated in alternative ways. According to Richard Cole, "Bonzo, Jimmy, and I used smack during the daytime hours in Munich, and none of us seemed the worse for it." That statement might have carried a scrap of weight, if Jimmy were conscious, Bonzo sober, and Cole benign.

"There were enormous frustrations, especially for those of us who weren't as fucked up as the others," says Benji Le Fevre.

Robert and Jonesy lived on the other side of that spectrum. They kept each other company during the idle days in Munich. They ventured outside to escape the internal group inertia, but the city lay encrusted beneath an icy winterscape. "The band was splitting between people who could turn up on time for recording sessions and people who couldn't," John Paul recalled. "My main memory of that album is pushing Robert around in the wheelchair from beer stand to beer stand." Otherwise, they just bided their time.

Led Zeppelin's days at Musicland Studios were dwindling without any action to show for it. With the first week nearly gone, Jimmy suddenly woke up on November 12, 1975. He appeared unannounced in the studio, looking frail and unsteady. "He hadn't even showered," says Abe Hoch, who was hanging out in the control room with Keith Harwood. "He just shook his hair out, picked up a guitar, and started to play."

Word circulated in the suites upstairs. *"Pagey's in the fucking studio!"*

Jonesy and Bonzo rushed in like firemen to a blaze. Robert was wheeled in a few minutes later. There was no time to waste. Bonzo's drums had been set up in the hotel dining room. Even though guests were in the middle of lunch service, Bonzo sat down and started to play—"loud as fuck-all and aggressive"—which cleared the room. As long as Jimmy was of sound mind and body, the goal was to step on the gas and not let up.

"I'd never seen anything like it," Abe Hoch marvels. "The minute Jimmy started to play, it organically came together. The words all fit to the music—'Nobody's Fault But Mine,' 'Achilles Last Stand.' They made it look like a jam, though it was anything but that. The songs came together as if they had practiced for weeks."

Jimmy was on fire. He never came up for air. Somewhere deep inside he knew he was playing on borrowed time. He had only to look to rock 'n roll for its directory of cocaine and heroin casualties. Still, he maintained cavalierly, "I don't regret it at all," referencing his dependence on the drugs, "because when I needed to be focused, I was really focused." The whole experience, according to Jimmy, was a test of willpower and perseverance. "I mean, that was eighteen hours a day at a real intensity, *every* day," he admitted in retrospect. "You just plunge in, and you don't start thinking about three meals a day." He characterized the breakneck sessions as "pure anxiety and emotion," saying, "we didn't know whether we'd ever be able to play in the same way again."

With "Achilles Last Stand," Jimmy said, "it was straight off into the deep end."

The song was a bildungsroman in which Robert came to terms with his accident and the subsequent emotional growth he experienced as a result—an attempt to forge an identity from muddled feelings. And yet it doesn't come off at all as woebegone—it's one of his most buoyant, optimistic lyrics, "about travels and dreams and wishes and positivism." That would have been conceptual enough, but he embellished it with an account of his travels through Morocco, Greece, Spain, Switzerland, Jersey, and California.

The lyrical texture was spare and elemental, but once Jimmy got his hands on it, a tempest rose out of the guitar, injecting wattage into everything it touched. "I just dove in and built that track piece by piece," he said. There were dramatic surges of brilliance—and undertows of self-indulgent excess. He attempted to "give the piece a totally new identity by *orchestrating* the guitars"—an "epic quality," Jimmy called it. Overdub after overdub was stacked atop the track, each featuring a different effect. "I knew that every guitar overdub had to be very important, very strong within itself to sort of identify each section." There were no landing points, just six ferocious guitar parts battling for supremacy.

"It's got quite a pace to it," Jimmy said, an understatement, to be sure.

The instrumentation facilitated Robert's sense of journey. "Achilles Last Stand" galloped along for more than ten minutes, shape-shifting, the riffs spurred by countertacking from an eight-string bass that Jonesy fairly lacerated with a pick. The drums underscored each passage with an explosive backbeat. It was "prog rock gone mad," Robert enthused, "and it was brilliant . . . the music was stunning."

Robert could hardly wait to put a vocal to it. He rashly insisted on standing, something he hadn't done with any conviction in four months. Halfway through the take, he tripped over a cable, his foot wrenched out from underneath him. "I put all my weight on it," he recalled, and—"went down, bang." The reaction in the studio was swift and immediate. "I've never known Jimmy to move so quickly," Robert said. "He was out of the mixing booth and holding me up, fragile as he might be, within a second." The fear was strong that Robert had refractured his leg.

The prognosis was more favorable. Nothing a little bed rest wouldn't cure. "And where it got to a point where I could lower it again off the bed without touching the ground," he recalled, "I was wheeled to the studio while the others were asleep and did the vocal track all over again, from start to finish."

"Achilles" satisfied Jimmy's desire to make "a guitar album." It was hell-bent, loud, and bombastic, a song that would rattle the bones. Still, it was impossible to resist a good traditional blues. The structure of "Tea for One" had been shaped at SIR in Los Angeles. Jimmy acknowledged it was somewhat derivative—"us looking back at 'Since I've Been Loving You,' being in a very lonely space at the time and reflecting accordingly." There was nothing trailblazing about the song. "It was basically a twelve-bar," he said, "and there were two verses to do as solos on guitar. Suddenly it hit me that everybody has played a blues number, and there are so many musicians whose forte it is, like Eric [Clapton]." A hard act to follow. He felt compelled to avoid the blues clichés, to take it to another level.

Incredibly, he took nine and a half minutes to get there. There was a touch of challenge evident in the execution. The intervals were full of longing, the flourishes graceful and warm, playing off the sentiment of the lyric. "It's so held back," Jimmy said of the restraint he exercised. "Seven minutes long [*sic*], and at no point does it blow out." The extra effort he put into it lifted his solos from the ordinary, even if they didn't break any new ground.

"Tea for One" was as easygoing as things would get. It was time to pivot to thunder and lightning. As Jimmy had planned it, the album would have "no acoustic songs, no mellowness or contrasts or changes to other instruments." Taken as a whole, it would reflect the rootlessness Led Zeppelin felt in their months of tax exile—"a lot of movement and aggression."

"For Your Life" certainly lived up to that standard. Lean and hypnotic, the rhythm section in the opening measures pulsed dolefully, with just enough movement and aggression to evoke the sneering disenchantment Robert felt toward the "people who come and go" in the band's road entourage, "usually of the opposite sex." The funk interlude that punctuated the middle section gave the beat a tart, assertive bite. But the song was held in check until a break before the final verse, when Jimmy played a countermelody to Jonesy's arching bass figures, letting the guitar spew with peels of sinewy phrasing.

The contrast between the slashing texture and the bitter lyric was the opposite of that in "Royal Orleans." The band hearkened back to a frisky funk groove but set it on fire, Led Zeppelin style. The song's rhythmic impulse stuttered in a series of syncopated offbeats against a constant bass line that set the stage for the mischievous tale. Robert rolled out a story that had been tickling the band's funny bone since their trip to New Orleans earlier that winter. In the retelling it had grown all out of proportion, but as John Paul confessed, "It was a mish-mash of several stories all put together."

As legend had it, he had picked up a woman at the New Orleans hotel bar, not realizing she was a transvestite. "'Stephanie' ended up in my room and we rolled a joint or two. I fell asleep and set fire to the hotel room, as you do. And when I woke up, it was full of firemen." Robert changed the name of the protagonist to "John Cameron," a musician who had played with Jonesy on the session circuit back in the day, and pounded away at the inside joke, repeating the word *whiskers* to make his point.

It was hard to take "Royal Orleans" as anything but a parody, considering the thrust of Robert's vocal. Much like "The Crunge," from *Houses of the Holy*, his near-indecipherable delivery was intended as uptown funk but landed more like a slapstick impersonation of James Brown at his earthiest. The song was mostly improvised in the studio, as was "Candy Store Rock," a tribute to rockabilly, but on steroids. The song raced from verse to verse like a train about to jump the tracks. Jimmy's hiccuping licks met Bonzo's incisive, perfectly placed fills head-on, their rhythmic precision rushing everything along with irrepressible force. Robert fired up a sassy, lip-trembling vibrato, aping one of his favorite Elvis impersonators, Ral Donner, exaggerating with great relish. But the overall feel sounded more like novelty and ultimately failed to launch.

"Hots On for Nowhere" was also spontaneous, slapped together in the studio in about an hour one day and fused to peevish lyrics Robert had written earlier in Malibu. A particularly caustic line, about "friends who would give me fuck all," was aimed at Jimmy and Peter Grant, both of whom he felt had deserted the band in California. The overall result was haphazard but surprisingly joyous, as though the band had agreed to let the listener into an informal jam where they just played *to* each other, letting it all hang out. There was an unmistakable delight evident in their offhand approach: Jimmy's slightly unhinged, alternating solos, the scraggly *la-la-la* refrain. A closer listen, however, revealed a strong ensemble at work, perhaps not making a song for the ages but hitting an uncompromising Zeppelinesque groove.

Throughout the weeklong session, everyone had kept an eye on the clock. "We were under incredible pressure to finish the record," Jimmy acknowledged. It was no secret Led Zeppelin would have to pack up and move on November 21, when the Stones were due to arrive. Yet they were *so close* to wrapping everything up. No one wanted to leave with the album unfinished. They needed two days more, maybe three at most. Jimmy swallowed his pride and placed a call to Mick Jagger. "Can I have two days to finish what we're doing?" he pleaded. Mick, in a charitable mood, granted Jimmy's request.

"That was the ultimate test of that whole lifestyle," Jimmy said, alluding to the drugs needed to keep him at the tiller—the tea for the tillerman, so to speak. "The band went away leaving me and Keith Harwood the engineer to do all the overdubs. We had a deal between us: whoever woke up first woke the other up, and we'd continue the studio work." At least until they passed out again.

At the outset, Jimmy figured on needing three days to put everything in order. "I didn't think I'd be able to do it in one night," he admitted. "But I was so into it that my mind was working properly for a change. It sort of crystalized, and everything was just pouring out." At the end of the first night—a brutal fourteen-hour session—the album was complete.

When the Stones arrived at the Arabella on November 24, 1975, Mick Jagger phoned Jimmy to hear how he'd made out.

"I had a copy of what we'd done, took it to his room, and put it on," Jimmy recalled.

"Is that what you managed to do over the three weeks?" Mick asked.

Jimmy shook his head. "No, we've got a whole album."

"You mean the basic tracks," Mick insisted.

"No, we're done, finished. Thanks for the two days."

An entire album in thirteen days flat—it reminded Jimmy and the others of making their first record. It was lean and tenacious, unencumbered by the lassitude of trial and error. Less like a studio band than a group with something to prove.

Even so, they were keen to clear out of Munich. Everyone was chilled to the bone. The weather in Jersey wouldn't be much of an improvement, but their accommodations there were a giant step up.

The band and their associates cleared out quickly, all except for Abe Hoch. "Peter had called and said, 'We want you to take the tapes back to London for us,'" Hoch recalls. The responsibility intimidated him, but he figured: two sixteen-track magnetic tapes—he'd just put them under his arm and get on the plane. Peter assured him they'd have everything all wrapped up for travel. The next morning, there were seventy kilos of tapes in a footlocker waiting for departure.

On Hoch's way back to London, somewhere over Bonn, the pilot announced a minor complication with the plane's mechanics. "Everything is okay, but we're going to land," he said.

This unnerved Abe, a concentration-camp kid. "I was afraid to be in the country in the first place. As far as I was concerned, nothing good ever happened in Germany."

Trouble came a-courting when the plane landed in Bonn and taxied toward the terminal. The pilot announced: "There's another flight to London waiting to take off. We'll just move the luggage to the other aircraft."

*Move the luggage!*

Abe practically tackled the flight attendant coming down the aisle. "I need to see my luggage moved," he stated emphatically.

"No, that's impossible," he was told. "We'll move the luggage."

"I'm sorry, but I have to physically *see* it put on the other plane. I have valuables on board."

"Sir," the male attendant said, with mounting impatience, "everybody's luggage is valuable."

"Not like mine, it isn't," Abe said. "Mine is *very* valuable. It's worth millions of dollars."

That caught the flight attendant's attention. "Oh, go on! What kind of luggage do you have worth millions of dollars?"

"It's the new Led Zeppelin record."

"*Led Zeppelin! I love* Led Zeppelin!" The man's eyes lit up. "Can I have one?"

"Not the album," Abe said. "It's the tapes. I have the tapes of the new Led Zeppelin album. So let's go and watch them move the luggage. Okay?"

As Hoch recalls, "Here is this blond, Aryan German guy walking me onto the tarmac in Bonn. I have no identification, an earring in my ear, a ratty jean jacket on, and I look a mess. A Jewish mess. All of a sudden, lights go on and machine guns are trained at me and Germans are screaming '*Halt!*' My hands are in the air. It was my worst possible nightmare."

Without batting an eye, the flight attendant screamed, "It's okay! He has the new Led Zeppelin album!"

"He'd said the fucking password," Abe recalls. "They dropped their guns and came running over, because they couldn't believe I had the new Led Zeppelin album. And that's how the album got from Germany to London."

## [2]

Recording was a satisfying experience, but Led Zeppelin sorely missed the stage. It was frustrating being a band and not doing what a band does best. Performing was another kind of drug, and a powerful one. On a good night, the high one got from connecting with mates and making music—the surge of sound, the chemistry, and the audience response—delivered an enormous rush.

Jonesy and Bonzo needed that kind of fix. They'd located a club in St. Helier on the island of Jersey where Norman Hale, a local rock 'n roll pianist of some ability, jammed with a pickup band on Wednesday nights. Behan's West Park wasn't much to look at. It was a sleepy little joint in the best English dance-hall tradition, with a makeshift stage, but it gave Jonesy and Bonzo the opportunity to stretch out. An honest-to-goodness gig: forty-five minutes playing rock 'n roll classics. It was liberating! They were invited to return the next week and mentioned they'd be bringing along a few friends.

Robert wasn't so sure he would make it. "Look," he told Bonzo, "I can't even walk for God's sake. Don't embarrass me. I can't hobble across the dance hall and go on to the stage."

Bonzo assured him the logistics would make things effortless. They could enter through a side door and then up the back steps. "Come on, man," he said encouragingly. "Let's plan on going."

Robert was dubious, but he felt the old tingle. "You see the possibility of performing and who can avoid it," he said.

On December 10, 1975, Led Zeppelin appeared in front of an audience for the first time since the Earls Court shows the previous May. It was a minuscule crowd by the band's standards, about 350 people, not one of whom had to clamor for a ticket. "No one really knew who we were," Robert said. As far as anyone knew, the band was another ragtag ensemble of Norman Hale's, perhaps a little on the longhair side, but nothing that would attract undue attention.

Unable to stand, Robert plunked down on a stool wedged inconspicuously between the piano and the drums, with Jimmy out front, a pale-blue Strat slung across his hips in typical rock-god fashion. Even so, no one batted an eye through the warm-up—fifteen minutes of Eddie Cochran and Little Richard songs. Things were nice and loose, everyone hanging together.

"I felt myself edge forward a little bit," Robert recalled. "Then, after the third number, and this is no lie, I found myself sort of wiggling the stool past the drums and further on out. And once we got going, we didn't want to stop." Especially when they eased into a long blues number, with each man stepping out for an overdue solo. "Suddenly, all the stops and dynamics we subconsciously activate on stage came out." They were content to play—all night if allowed, but after the club's standard forty-five minute set, the manager flashed the lights on and off. "Get them offstage now—they've done enough!"

Afterward, they celebrated like an untested band that had just pulled off its first big gig. Playing together had felt great. Better than great. The circumstances were ideal—a little out-of-the-way club, an unsuspecting audience, no promoter, no demands, no groupies, no hairy getaway. No "Whole Lotta Love" or "Stairway to Heaven." What a throwback to the days when they could relate to an audience and just groove on each other and the music they made. It produced an extraordinary high, but nothing they could get used to.

It would be another eighteen months before Led Zeppelin appeared together on a stage again.

———

The band celebrated the New Year in Paris, at the posh George V, where Robert endeavored to walk for the first time. "It was one small step for man," he mused, "and one giant leap for six nights at Madison Square Garden."

That was getting ahead of himself. Robert was in no condition to endure a tour, much less walk from here to there. As a precaution, so as not to tempt him, nothing was scheduled through 1976. Paris was a distraction—the first of many—to take the band's minds off performing. The first night there, their indefatigable host, Benoit "Frenchy" Gautier—the record exec who had nicknamed Bonzo "the Beast"—took everyone to a show at the Casino de Paris: Señor Wences, the Spanish ventriloquist, headlined, along with a chorus line of stark-naked female dancers.

Peter Grant wrested the hosting duties from Gautier, dispensing foot-long lines of cocaine in the bathroom stall between acts. Motioning to Abe Hoch, who had joined the festivities, he said, "Do me a favor. We're expecting an important call. Go back to the hotel and handle it for me."

No sooner was Hoch settled back at the George V than a visitor appeared at the door to his suite—a stunning redhead who announced, "I'm a gift from Mr. Grant. And my girlfriend is on her way up."

*Girlfriend!* Abe was beside himself with pleasure. "The girls and I were just about to get things under way," he recalled, "when the door to the suite burst open—Robert, Peter, Richard, and a cop from Zeppelin's security detail, all wearing gendarme hats and flashing badges, rushed in and surrounded us." Abe futilely tried explaining to the naked women who these men really were, but they were having none of it. They got dressed and stormed out, only to return a few minutes later.

"You forgot to pay me," the redhead said. Abe reminded her that she was a gift from Mr. Grant. "Yes, but he did not pay me."

From Paris, the road show moved to New York, where the entourage moved into suites at the Park Lane Hotel on Central Park South. It was an opportunity to reconnect with old friends and new. Bad Company was in town, as was Maggie Bell, who was encamped next door in the Essex House. Her career was in a tailspin, and Peter had flown in to offer encouragement.

"Rudolf Nureyev was in the room next to me, and Dorothy Tutin, a great English actress, just across the hall," Maggie recalled. "There was a storm, and I had them over for a late New Year's dinner. We were all snorting and watching it snow."

Jimmy, staying alone in a suite, had his own distinct problem with snowfall. Around three in the morning, he picked up the phone and dialed a room downstairs, which was shared by Dave Northover and Benji Le Fevre.

"You've got to get up here *right away!*" Jimmy insisted. "I've had a *disaster!*"

A few minutes later, the two men arrived to find Jimmy "quite agitated." He was seated at a desk, holding a Parker fountain pen over a bottle of Quink ink, next to a big bottle of cocaine streaked with lines of blue.

"Honestly, I was trying to refill my pen and emptied it into the wrong bottle. *Please*—you've got to be able to do something to save this." He gazed beseechingly at Northover. "You're a physicist! Can't you separate the ink from the cocaine?"

"We'll take this away and see if we can do anything with it," Benji said. "But we'll just get you some more, man."

Instead, they left him with an ample supply of Quaalude and an invitation to go ice-skating in Central Park as soon as the Wollman Rink opened.

"That's exactly what we did," Benji says. "We took 'ludes and the Charlie and went skating in the park. And for the next three days we all had blue snot running out of our noses."

Meanwhile, Bonzo was skating on thin ice at Radio City Music Hall, where he had gone to catch a Deep Purple concert. True to form, Bonzo was drunk and pushed his way onto the stage while the band was performing. Grabbing the mic, he announced, "Hi, I'm John Bonham from Led Zeppelin, and we've got a new album coming out soon—and it's fucking great!" It took some effort to steer him into the wings, but not before he gave Deep Purple's guitarist a shout-out: "And as far as Tommy Bolin is concerned, he can't play for shit!"

Bonzo, who consistently grappled with demons, had entered a new phase of dysfunction. "It was clear that he and Jimmy had gone on their own set of rails together," says Benji Le Fevre. "Henry had taken them both away from who they had been and who they really were."

Jimmy's embrace of the drug had turned him inward. Not self-reflective. He'd crawled inside himself, become even more distant than usual. But with Bonzo it had the opposite effect. He became even more unruly. There was another incident when he, Robert, Benji, and Aubrey Powell went to see Mott the Hoople. Bonzo stumbled onstage and insisted on playing the drums with Dale "Buffin" Griffin. "Buffin wanted no part of it and pushed him away," Po recalled, "and a fistfight broke out. It was embarrassing."

Po was in New York on Led Zeppelin's dime, working on the new album cover and artwork for the band's film. Neither had a name as of yet, but they were getting close.

The brain trust at Hipgnosis had put their heads together for an album cover concept while Led Zeppelin was still in Munich. They intended to create an image influenced by their infatuation with Dadaism. A *noncover*, they called it, reminiscent of the one they had done for Pink Floyd's *Wish You Were Here*, in which two businessmen shake hands, one of them on fire.

"We began by asking the question: What is something that everybody needs, something they cannot do without?" Po recalled. "That led to a discussion about something that had to be held, like a talisman. Someone suggested a cat. 'How about a party where everyone walks around stroking a black cat?' Cats often act as placebos in terms of helping people emotionally, but they're also a symbol of black magic, bad luck, and all those things that relate to blues, like the black-cat bone."

Storm Thorgerson said, "Not a cat, but a black object. A black *obsessional* object. Perhaps a battery charger, without which you couldn't exist."

The original object was made out of black felt, and it was square. "It was quite sinister," Po says. "We imagined everybody having to have one, and if you didn't have one you would die."

Storm tied its mysterious quality directly to Led Zeppelin. "The band are a very powerful band, musically and socially," he argued, "and the black object is a definite thing of power."

Po flew to Germany with a mock-up and presented it to Jimmy and Peter Grant. Jimmy took one look at it and said, "That's it! That's it! But . . . what is it?"

"It's a symbol of power," Po said. "That's all I can tell you."

Jimmy was sold. "I get it," he said. "But it's too formal. I'd like to put a twist on it."

Incorporating Jimmy's suggestions, Hipgnosis redesigned the object, making it more phallic. An obelisk—Po suggested to Jimmy they title the album *Obelisk*. But Jimmy recalled an earlier conversation in which the album-cover designers explained how four people—four *musicians*—create an effect, a *presence*. That was it, as far as Jimmy cared. "I held out for *Presence*," he said. "You think about more than just a symbol that way."

Robert agreed. He liked the ambiguity of the title and the mysterious black object. "I'm glad people are wondering what it means," he said. "Everybody should work it out for themselves."

The cover photo featured a 1950s-era family staring at the object, with a photograph from the boat show at Earls Court stripped in behind them. The back cover featured a schoolgirl—Samantha Gates, an older version of the naked child on the cover of *Houses of the Holy*—with the object on the blackboard behind her.

The album was slated for release in February 1976, but problems with printing the sleeve delayed it until the last day in March. Timing would be everything. Swan Song had big promotional plans that coupled split-second timing with enormous hype. Danny Goldberg and Abe Hoch had collaborated on a scheme to release the album at the exact same time worldwide, regardless of time zones or pleas by industry insiders. "Nobody would get it a minute earlier," Hoch recalled. "The idea was to create so much excitement that it would appear at the number-one spot on the charts the week of its release. No album had done that before, except for Elton John's *Captain Fantastic* LP, and the guys were upset that it had never happened for them."

Rock 'n roll's key tastemakers had already been fired up with anticipation. A thousand plastic copies of the black object had been manufactured and sent to journalists and media dignitaries with no explanation provided. Originally, Peter Grant had planned to have them placed outside 10 Downing Street, Buckingham Palace, the Houses of Parliament, and the White House as a publicity stunt, but an incident involving Po and Hipgnosis forced him to cancel that approach.

"I picked up the phone toward the end of March," Po recalls, "and

Peter was screaming furiously, *'Fuck you, you fucking cunt!* You fucking let the fucking picture of the fucking cover out. It was supposed to be a secret.'" He assured Grant he'd done nothing of the kind and that the cover image was under lock and key. "Yeah, well *Melody Maker* has a fucking picture of it."

That night, at three o'clock in the morning, Po was awakened by banging on his door. "In came Richard Cole and a gangster named John Bindon, and both were coked out of their minds," Po says. There were more choruses of "You fucking cunt!" amid accusations that he'd leaked a photo of the object to the press. They roughed Po up pretty well, Bindon holding him against the wall while Ricardo tossed the apartment, oblivious to the fact that Po's wife and child were asleep. Po showed them that the cover was locked securely in his safe, and it wasn't until late the next day that they discovered that the culprit who had leaked it was an assistant at Atlantic Records. But by then, the black-object stunt had lost its allure and was scrapped.

The sideshow antics were unnecessary. *Presence* was a new Led Zeppelin album, which was all the event the fans needed. The record, on the day of its release, was awarded gold status in the UK and platinum in the U.S. None of their previous albums had sold as fast or as well. The reviews in general were encouraging but reserved. Stephen Davis, writing in *Rolling Stone*, said the album "confirms the quartet's status as heavy-metal champions of the known universe." Still, he acknowledged "the results are mixed" but that "there is some fine rock on *Presence*." Robert Christgau, in *The Village Voice*, graded *Presence* a B in his regular "Consumer Guide," saying, "This is one of their better albums, but that's only because it avoids the silly and offers at least one commanding cut, 'Hots On for Nowhere.'"

The British music papers were much more complimentary. Jonh Ingham experienced a divine revelation in *Sounds*. "This album is unadulterated rock 'n roll. It's fantabulous," he gushed, comparing it to Led Zeppelin's first album for its musical diversity. "In terms of urgency and aggression and an all-out attack on rock 'n roll, this is Zeppelin's best album yet." *New Musical Express* called the album "solid, non-stop, copper-bottomed, guitar-bass-and-drums Led Zep rock 'n roll. No mellotrons, no acoustic guitars, no boogies-with-Stu, no hats-off-to-Harper, no funk or reggae piss-takes, just mercilessly methodical two-fisted pounding Led Zep for the entire duration." And Chris Welch carried the band's flag through fields of flattery in *Melody Maker*, as though his words would ward off a much-feared phone call from Peter Grant.

Jimmy acknowledged the divergent opinions. "It's not an easy album for a lot of people to access," he said, reflecting on it some time later. He was convinced, however, "the urgency of it is there if you listen."

In any case, there would be no tour to support *Presence*. Live performances were pushed back to 1977 at the earliest.

Travel might have been severely curtailed, but there was optimism for heading back to England. The tax exile was due to expire in May, at which time life could return to normal, with opportunity for the members of the Led Zeppelin entourage to reconnect with their families. It was long overdue.

## [3]

Peter Grant especially needed to repair his relationship at home. He not only had been exiled for tax reasons but was completely off the grid, holing up in a house in the Hamptons on Long Island with a rotating cast of nefarious characters and an endless stash of cocaine. He could have brought his family along but chose not to. For years, G had called home every night to touch base with his wife, Glo, and their two kids. But the calls had stopped. He'd made himself unreachable.

"Glo called the office day and night trying to reach him," says Unity

MacLean. "She had things to discuss about Helen and Warren, but Peter had forgotten all about his family. He was living the high life in America and had more or less written them off."

Gloria Grant wasn't naive. She'd been a rock 'n roll wife for nearly twenty years; she been through the wars with Don Arden and Mickie Most. Led Zeppelin, as far as she cared, was just another theater of battle. She'd gone along to get along, but she'd never had to cope with drugs before. Cocaine had a firm grip on her husband, and its power was devastating the family.

Maggie Bell recalled a holiday Peter and Gloria had planned, taking the kids away for some time in the country. "Gloria and the kids sat at the Hilton at the airport for two weeks," she said. "Peter never showed up."

Gloria was isolated at Horselunges, raising the kids on her own. They'd worked through long separations before, but the radio silence was inexcusable. She suspected—knew—it was more than drugs. There was another woman, she was sure of it. Mickie Most's wife, Chris, recalls a conversation with Gloria after Led Zeppelin's last tour in the United States. "She used to do all of Peter's mail and opened a letter from Peter's girlfriend. It was all right there on the page." Drugs was one thing, and yes, Glo suspected there were other women on the road, but it had never been put in her face like that. "She was heartbroken," Chris Most says, "and indignant." Gloria Grant had had it.

Peter got wind of the situation and attempted to deal with the consequences, but it was difficult from three thousand miles away. He was also up to his eyeballs in arrangements concerning the Led Zeppelin movie. After two years, two directors, and several hundred thousand dollars invested into the scheme, an end was finally in sight.

The last few months of production had hit a number of snags. Cocaine paranoia led G to suspect that the director, Peter Clifton, had a hidden agenda—that perhaps he was working on another film at their expense. Or that he'd stolen the negatives and was bootlegging them. As a precaution, Peter sent Richard Cole and a security thug to search Clifton's hotel room, which led to an ugly scene. A month later, Richard Cole and Joan Hudson showed up at Clifton's home in London while he was away on holiday, armed with a court order allowing them to search for and remove anything with Led Zeppelin's name on it.

"It was absolute drug paranoia," Clifton said. "I felt humiliated. I felt they had betrayed my trust."

Despite the shenanigans, he delivered a work print of the movie while Jimmy and Peter were in New York. The intention was to sell it to Warner Bros. for distribution, but before that could happen Ahmet Ertegun had to sign off on the deal. Clifton arranged a midnight screening at the MGM Screening Room on West Fifty-fifth Street. Ahmet arrived straight from a party—and fell asleep several times during the movie. It was long, almost two and a half hours long. He woke up at the end, blinked a few times, and asked Peter, "Who was that guy on the horse?" G was so insulted, he got up and, without another word, stormed out of the theater.

Ahmet, bewildered, appealed to Clifton for an explanation. "What have I said?" he wondered.

"Ahmet, that was *Robert* on the horse," he was told.

"Oh, gee, well I nodded off."

Ahmet and Clifton tried to catch up with Peter, but he was a few blocks ahead of them, on his way to the Plaza Hotel. It was three o'clock in the morning, and the city streets were empty. All three men scuttled along the pavement with a convoy of limousines and their chauffeurs following comically behind.

They eventually caught up with Peter at the hotel, and he was in tears. "How could you say that?" he whimpered to Ahmet. "We worked so hard on this thing."

His emotions were fragile; he was losing his grip, his professional composure.

Nevertheless, Ertegun promptly signed off on the film. All that remained to get it released and recoup expenses—money borrowed from National Westminster Bank on personal guarantees by the band—was negotiating a deal with Warner Bros. It was a foregone conclusion they'd distribute the movie, which was now entitled *The Song Remains the Same*. Led Zeppelin had a huge impact on the parent company's bottom line; structuring a deal was merely a formality.

In early February 1976, a meeting with Warner Bros. executives was arranged at the studio in Los Angeles with Frank Wells, the company president, his éminence grise David Geffen, and the entire senior management. It was a daylong event to iron out the terms of the deal, refine technicalities like twenty-four-track quadraphonic sound and color correction of the prints, and plot an advertising strategy for the movie's eventual release. At eleven o'clock in the morning, the scheduled hour to begin, there was no sign of Peter Grant.

"Where is he?" Wells demanded.

Peter Clifton was beside himself. He called the Swan Song office and was told Grant was still in London, sorting out a problem with his wife. In his place, they were sending Richard Cole and Benji Le Fevre.

Wells and Geffen were furious. Grant's input was central to the deal. It didn't help matters when Ricardo barreled in—"coked out . . . completely off his face," according to Clifton—juggling several bottles of liquor. No one was amused by his foul mouth and a litany of uninformed suggestions on how Warner Bros. should handle the release. Were it not for Led Zeppelin's stature, any self-respecting movie executive would have scuttled the deal there and then.

This was the kind of meeting that Peter Grant normally relished. He enjoyed taking on the suits, knowing how his swagger unsettled them. It never failed to turn things to his advantage. But a few days before he was due in LA, G had gotten a taste of his own medicine. Gloria had caught him flat-footed, announcing that she was leaving him. There was more to it than that. She was going to live with their estate manager, Jim Thompsett, with whom she'd been having an affair.

Peter became incensed, erratic. He had no template for how to deal with this situation. It lay outside his mighty authority, which was being challenged and muddied by drugs. Well, he still had his crew. A team of no-nonsense sidekicks was called in to commiserate at Horselunges, where G had repaired with a stockpile of cocaine. He kept a hard crew around him at all times, men who were fearless and radiated menace. A dolorous character named Ray Washburn became G's right-hand man, and five people interviewed for this book used the same exact phrase to describe him: "He was quiet, but you didn't fuck with Ray." Don Murfet, who handled security, was described as "polite, always a gentleman, but," as Unity MacLean recalls, "I was told he could snap your neck with one hand." There was plenty of tough talk, drug-fueled tirades about payback and revenge. "There were all these bad vibes," recalled Dave Northover, another member of G's inner circle, "people talking about how Peter was going to get this bloke, Jim."

Richard Cole admitted to driving to Horselunges with "a shotgun and a few other guns locked in the trunk of the car, while [Peter] decided what he wanted me to do with this guy."

Johnny Bindon was frequently on the scene with G, which was a sign to others that things had gone off the rails.

"Now, he was a very scary person to be around," Jimmy Page said. Bindon's presence, he knew, "was a recipe for disaster."

To polite company, John Bindon was known as a part-time actor who'd appeared in minor TV and film supporting roles, usually typecast as a thug. But his main line of trade was muscle—threatening people, intimidation, meting out physical punishment. "He was a dangerous character, part of a family that terrorized people in Fulham," says Carole Brown, "a nasty piece of work." He'd done jobs for the Krays and other East End villains. "We all knew to keep our distance," Maggie Bell says. "He was scary, always showing his cock."

*His cock*—it was an object of intense fascination. "Johnny Bindon had the biggest cock in rock 'n roll," says Michael Des Barres. "He would wave it around and slap people with it." Princess Margaret, with whom he'd reportedly had an affair, told friends that Bindon was "able to balance three big ale glasses on his cock." Cynthia Sach, who worked as a receptionist at Swan Song, recalled, "He'd wave it around and hang beer mugs off it."

People extolled John Bindon's sense of humor, his gift of gab, his apparent charm in quieter, offhand moments, but he was a psychopath—"beyond scary," Abe Hoch notes. "You watched your Ps and Qs around the guy because there was a level of insanity about him. Ricardo was as nuts as you could get, but Johnny made him look positively stable."

His girlfriend, model Vicki Hodge, became part of the office decor, faithfully perched on Bindon's lap, the way Edgar Bergen perched Charlie McCarthy on his lap. Hodge was a familiar face in London's society circles, the former girlfriend of Prince Andrew and daughter of Sir John Rowland Hodge, the Second Baronet of Chipstead, Kent. People recalled her penchant for wearing leather miniskirts with no underwear. "She and Johnny spent a lot of time getting pissed at the Water Rat, the pub up the street from the office," says Phil Carlo. "Occasionally, to entertain Bindon, she would step into the middle of King's Road, lift her skirt up, and moon people." On other occasions, Bindon would rip away the snaps on her skirt and she would twist about and coo, mock-modestly, like Betty Boop.

Bindon became a fixture at the Swan Song office in London. He never left Peter Grant's side, and Richard tended to them with a steady stream of drugs. "There were now a ton of drugs in the office," says Unity MacLean. "Peter was snorting an awful lot of cocaine. He kept it in a sandwich baggie. He'd take his door key and shove it in the bag. All the rocks would fall out as he brought it up to his nose. When he left, you could get yourself a good gram of cocaine off the desk or carpet."

From time to time, Bindon brought a girl back to the office from the pub so that Peter could watch their activity through the keyhole.

Not much music business was being done. "It wasn't an office where anybody went in at ten a.m.," said Phil Carlo. "It was waifs and strays and heroin dealers and odd people, a bit like the American tours but a scaled-down version."

Other than Bad Company, which had an independent management team looking after them, the other Swan Song acts were basically ignored. "Jimmy never got off his ass to do anything for the Pretty Things," says Unity MacLean. "And when they came into the office to plan their next move, Peter went down the back stairs, making himself scarce."

Maggie Bell had a single, "For Hazel," being released but couldn't get Peter to pay attention. "He had absolutely no time for me," she says. "I took a back seat right about then because I could see the wheels coming off the bus."

As far as Detective cared, the bus had already departed—without them. "One year later, we had nothing going on," says Michael Des Barres. "We hadn't played, we didn't gig, we didn't do shit. We waited." Jimmy had lost interest in producing Detective's album. "Then it was, 'Okay, we'll have Steve Marriott produce you.' Another six months went by waiting for him. We couldn't get hold of Jimmy, or anybody at Swan Song for that matter. We'd been handcuffed. The only thing that happened in that year and a half while we waited was heroin. So we waited and waited, getting more fucked up."

A producer, Jimmy Robinson, was finally dredged up for Detective. "We went into the Record Plant to record and spent more time in the fucking Jacuzzi," says Des Barres. "It took us three months to get a snare-drum sound. It was so indulgent. The sessions cost a million dollars. Then we scrapped what we'd done and did it again. Because we could."

Dave Edmunds fared only somewhat better. He made a good album that got nary a whiff of label support but was given the go-ahead to return to the studio for a follow-up. According to his manager, Jake Riviera, "Dave knew he was trapped in that thing, but he loved Robert Plant telling him how fantastic he was."

"There was nobody really running the record company at all," says Unity MacLean. "Jimmy used to come into the office regularly when we started up, but since they returned [from tax exile], he didn't want anything to do with running Swan Song—and frankly he was too out of it."

Danny Goldberg was a capable administrator, but he got side-tracked promoting a singer-songwriter discovery named Mirabai who, like Danny, was an advocate of Eastern religions and vegetarianism. "I was besotted with her spiritual songs," he admitted. Shelley Kaye, who worked for Swan Song in New York, says, "She was terrible. Nobody thought she was talented." But Danny sweet-talked Peter Grant into signing Mirabai and put out an album that was DOA. Finally an ultimatum was delivered. Danny could manage Mirabai or work for Swan Song, but not both. To everyone's amazement, he quit his job.

Around the same time, Abe Hoch sent word to Peter that he intended to resign. "I'm not happy," he said. "I'm not doing anything, not signing any act, not having any fun. Nothing's going on. It's time for me to go." Before accepting Hoch's resignation, Peter asked him to meet and discuss it.

A few days later, Abe was ushered into Peter's office on the second floor of the King's Road building. "So you want to resign?" G asked, smirking. He reached into his briefcase and took out a pound of cocaine, made a slit in the little bag, and said, "Let's talk."

"That was on a Tuesday," Abe recalls. "*Thursday*, when we finished talking, I was completely out of my head. We talked, we cried. He told me all about his life; I told him about mine. It was cocaine talk, fucking ridiculous—and I agreed to stay on the job."

But not long afterward, when Hoch acknowledges he was "a basket case, having done too much coke and run through my money," G announced that he'd decided to accept Abe's resignation. There'd be no grace period to get his house in order, no severance package. They cut him loose the same day.

It was a rocky period for Swan Song—and Led Zeppelin. *Presence*

had sold decently—three million albums was nothing to sneeze at—
but not as well as the band's previous six albums. It was regarded by
fans as an unsatisfying record, difficult to embrace, as Jimmy had
pointed out. And the movie, while nearing release, was hardly anyone's idea of first-rate cinema. As a documentary, it was far from representative of the band. There was so little music, the concert footage
barely adequate.

In the interim, Led Zeppelin had gone their separate ways. There
was little communication between the musicians. "There was no hanging out. They weren't really friends," says Abe Hoch, a sentiment
joined by at least a half dozen others. Jimmy was mixed up in an ugly
and very public war of words with Kenneth Anger over the soundtrack
for *Lucifer Rising*. Robert continued to nurse his wounds with faint
progress toward total recovery. Bonzo and his family returned to
France, where he pulled a gas blowback gun on his roadie, Mick Hinton, at a Monte Carlo nightclub and spent a night in police custody.
And Jonesy disappeared into the refuge of his family, putting the trail
of chaos and mayhem behind him.

There was no Led Zeppelin for the time being.

## Chapter Nineteen

# THEIR OWN PRIVATE
# SODOM AND GOMORRAH

**[1]**

While Led Zeppelin veered off the radar in mid-1976, a new wave of young British musicians seized the opportunity to claim their piece of the rock. Just as the Yardbirds, The Who, and the Stones had apprenticed in makeshift clubs tucked away in places like Epsom, Richmond, and Ealing, the new scene shifted to provincial pubs, where ragged, garage-type bands lacking finesse—in fact, scoffing at finesse—showcased their songs out of the glare of music-business slicks.

Pubs had long been a wellspring of local up-and-coming bands. "It was the social meeting point of every town in England and offered good paying gigs," says Terry Reid, who began his career years earlier working the UK pub circuit. "They had enormous rooms called saloons that held two to three hundred people. You could develop quite a reputation playing those joints."

Reid maintains that playing pubs gave a band discipline, but discipline was the last thing on the minds of these new groups. They were ungovernable, unrestrained—*punks*. Their music wasn't Top 40 bound. It was loud and aggressive in the best rock 'n roll tradition, down-and-dirty but also anarchic, confrontational, not superannuated hippie idealism, certainly not heavy metal, with its "endless solos that went nowhere" and reverence for virtuosity.

Dr. Feelgood, the Stranglers, the Vibrators, and the 101ers, led by Joe Strummer, were among the bands on the pub-rock circuit making a name for themselves in 1976. They took their cues from stripped-down forebears like the Velvet Underground, the Stooges, and the New York Dolls, but also the pandemonium ignited onstage by The Who, reducing the music to its lowest common denominator. Consider "You Really Got Me," the Kinks' blowtorch of a single, sped up a few rpm, and you hear the bones of the punk-rock movement. Primal, hardcore, no-bullshit rock 'n roll: a couple chords at most, no more than a whiff of an arrangement, lightning-fast tempos, and attitude, plenty of attitude. *Punks*, they often provoked their audiences into physical confrontations. They traded in shock and outrage. Mainstream rock had become too tame. The punks had only contempt for their elders: Billy Joel, Simon & Garfunkel, Elton John, Chicago—nothing but slick lounge acts. Metal bands like Led Zeppelin—dinosaurs, a joke.

At the outset, punk was cold-shouldered by the rock-music establishment. The scene was like liquid mercury; it couldn't be contained. Punk bands weren't interested in record-label deals—at least not at stuffy corporate labels like EMI, Decca, or Polygram, which rode roughshod over their acts. A small group of upstart independent labels like Stiff, Rough Trade, and New Hormones nurtured the punk sound, putting out EPs that were often recorded, mastered, and pressed the same day. *Immediate*—as Andrew Oldham had once envisioned it. No overdubs or layered effects or fancy-ass edits. No arty, conceptual Hipgnosis sleeves. It was fly-by-the-seat-of-your-pants rock 'n roll, back to basics—and smoking hot.

Jimmy Page hit the nail right on the head when, in July 1976, he said, "I am actually out of touch with what's going on today, more than I'd like to be, but I'm pretty optimistic about the future. What seems like a stagnant period may actually be a prelude to a renaissance."

The punk movement was in its incubation stage while Jimmy

carried on in a cocoon, laboring hermetically in two studios—Electric
Lady in New York and Trident in London—over Led Zeppelin's next
record: the soundtrack to *The Song Remains the Same*. If ever a project
required elaborate editing and discretion, this was it. The material
was from three Madison Square Garden shows in July 1973, in fits and
starts in the film version. But the soundtrack could cheat. With songs
that didn't have to be synced to video, Jimmy could pick and choose
the best takes from the three nights, cutting and splicing them like a
master tailor, even chipping in a few studio overdubs. That meant taking the intro, say, for "Rock and Roll," from one night, and stitching
Robert's vocals from two other nights to the master track with brief
guitar bursts recorded at Trident. The same was done for "Celebration Day" and "No Quarter." "Stairway" was pieced together from
all three nights.

"It's an honest soundtrack live album," Jimmy insisted, dancing a
bit around the word *honest*. "It was the live material that went with the
footage, so it had to be used." Yet he admitted preferring to release a
chronological live album culled from tapes in Led Zeppelin's vault, a
temperature-controlled room in the basement of the King's Road office. "We've got some *fabulous* live stuff," he revealed. There was a
master tape from the legendary 1970 Royal Albert Hall concert, as
well as the 1972 Long Beach and LA Forum concerts, that contained
raw and exciting performances, and intimate recordings from the
Back to the Clubs tour. "There's a winning version of 'No Quarter'
from Earls Court," Jimmy said. "The 'How Many More Times' is also
pretty good." Ten years later, he was still salivating over the prospect
of a chronological live Led Zeppelin compilation.

Instead, the soundtrack for *The Song Remains the Same* was a lugubrious rehash of familiar material that froze the band in 1973. "Dazed
and Confused" dragged on for an interminable twenty-six minutes,
and it was anyone's guess why Jimmy chose to include a fifteen-minute
slog through Bonzo's drum marathon, "Moby Dick." Without the
propulsive visual chicanery, the song was stripped of its vital impact.

"Celebration Day" was added to the mix but wasn't featured in the film. There were exciting snatches of "Black Dog," "Since I've Been Loving You," and "Heartbreaker" in the film, but for some reason those songs were excluded from the soundtrack album.

The documentary finally opened in October 1976, with premieres in New York, Los Angeles, London, and Birmingham. To everyone's amazement, it was awarded a PG rating by the MPAA, the movie industry's moral watchdog. The rating seemed overly generous, if not preposterous, considering the chilling backstage sequence filmed at the Baltimore Civic Center in which Peter Grant accosted the promoter, using the words *cunt* and *fuck* no less than eighteen times. Peter Clifton, the director, recognized the financial blow an R rating would have delivered, excluding hundreds of thousands of adolescent fans from theaters. Before screening the film for the MPAA, he used a pen to smudge the offending words on the print so that they were inaudible to the censors. As soon as the PG was secure, he restored the language so it was crystal clear.

The trip from London to the New York premiere was not without incident. A sizable Led Zeppelin entourage had piled into the first-class cabin of a 747. Richard Cole and John Bonham had self-medicated before taking off, bracing themselves throughout the flight with ridiculous quantities of alcohol. Somewhere over the Atlantic, they noticed Telly Savalas, the actor, sitting a few rows in front of them.

"Hey, baldy, what are you doing?" "Hey, you ain't got no fuckin' hair, huh, Kojak?" When Savalas failed to take the bait, food started getting lobbed. Then a knife and a fork. Before it escalated into a full-on fight, a flight attendant intervened.

In New York, the day of the premiere, Jimmy had gone ahead to oversee the technical elements. Creating the right ambience and pacing was crucial to the movie's success. At Led Zeppelin's insistence and at considerable cost, the theaters were wired specially by Showco, the band's sound team for live concerts. "Theaters in those days used three speakers," Jimmy explained, "the center speaker for dialogue, and left- and right-side speakers, which were used for effects. For *The Song Remains the Same* we mixed the sound for five speakers and provided two additional speakers in the rear of the theaters." He wanted to sharpen the dynamics, so that "John Bonham's drum solo came out right over your head," and when Jimmy stroked the violin bow across the guitar strings, "the sound would travel around the auditorium."

The New York premiere on October 20, 1976, at Cinema I was especially important. Major critics from both the rock and mainstream press had promised to cover it, and the house was papered with rock 'n roll nobility. Mick Jagger was in the audience, so were Linda Ronstadt, Rick Derringer, Roberta Flack, Mick Ronson, and Carly Simon. Led Zeppelin hoped to soothe opening-night jitters with bottles of brandy they'd smuggled in under their coats. Before the lights went down, Peter Clifton recalled, Jimmy "told the projectionist to turn the sound up to full volume."

No matter how he enhanced the volume and dynamics, no matter how much booze the band consumed, it couldn't salvage the messy *The Song Remains the Same*. New Yorkers knew the jig was up from the opening scene, which depicts the band landing in Pittsburgh, going through a tunnel, and emerging in New York City. A few minutes later, during the first song, Jimmy and Jonesy are shown wearing different outfits in successive verses, indicating footage from different nights spliced haphazardly together. Vocals didn't sync perfectly, the footage was uneven. Editing gaffes like that made viewers cringe. They rolled their eyes during the fantasy sequences.

"You can look at those as either an attempt to break new barriers," Jimmy argued in retrospect, "or just *Spinal Tap*."

The critics, unfortunately, chose *Spinal Tap*.

"Members of the group put on cloaks, ride around on horses,

stand in the moonlight," wrote *The New York Times*'s third-string movie critic, Richard Eder, who ducked out long before the film ended. "They are pseudodreams, like the unconvinced artwork on rock record jackets. The scenes showing the group performing are more informative though not much more powerful."

The *Daily News* ran its review under the headline FILM-WISE, IT'S DEAD ZEPPELIN, with the rarely awarded rating 0★ (out of a possible five), calling the movie "a hopelessly pretentious piece of trash."

It may have seemed unfair of the *Times* and the *News* to send fusty, old-school critics, but *Rolling Stone*'s review was equally unforgiving. Dave Marsh, who'd written favorably about the band in the past, assessed the film as "a tribute to Led Zeppelin's rapaciousness and inconsideration" and that "(even if their best songs are behind them) their sense of themselves merits only contempt." *Circus* was even more dismissive, concluding the film felt as though it were written, produced, directed, and edited "by junior college students who had just discovered LSD."

None of the members of Led Zeppelin had thought they were making art. Jimmy admitted straight out: "It's not a great film." But the reviews stung. They confirmed to the band what they had felt all along—that the media were disrespectful louts with too much critical power. Journalists, especially the subcategory of music critics, had it out for them. The film was no exception.

"I just don't trust those sort of writers," Jimmy said. "You never know what they were after."

In Los Angeles, Led Zeppelin was back in its element. Lori Mattix worked the lobby at the movie theater in Westwood, matching her "girlfriends" up with guests of the band. The Hyatt House was forsaken in favor of the Beverly Hilton, but there was no less a degree of hedonistic behavior. Groupies spun in and out of the suites. Drug traffic in the halls was bumper to bumper. "Some drug dealer came in who had ripped off John Bonham, and the next thing I knew he was laying on the floor bleeding," recalls Po, who had flown there with the band. "Richard Cole had knocked him clean out."

It took more finesse than Ricardo could muster to help Jimmy out of a similar jam. "He was being shaken down by a drug dealer," says Jeff Hoffman, the New York lawyer, who was flown in to handle the situation. A meet was arranged between the dealer and Jimmy, but Hoffman, no stranger to clandestine arrangements, showed up in Jimmy's place. "It was a preppie kid, a young guy who didn't have the smarts to realize what he was doing. He wanted money to keep his mouth shut—a lot of money."

"I can get them arrested," he threatened Hoffman.

Jeff said, "I hear you. Let me go back and talk to the clients, and we'll have another meeting."

Unbeknownst to the dealer, Hoffman had taped the conversation, aware that he couldn't use it in a court of law. In California, unlike in New York, both parties had to agree to the recording of a conversation. If the lawyer tried to introduce it into evidence, he would have committed a misdemeanor. Still, he waved a tape recorder at the dealer and said, "Just listen to this." It was a bluff, but a good one, and the kid disappeared.

But it was indicative of the behavior that transpired in LA. "It was all power, all madness," Po recalls. "Every night it was a crazy Sunset Strip scene at either the Rainbow Grill, the Roxy, or the Whisky. Rodney Bingenheimer held court with the band. Young girls hung over their chairs in anticipation. Pure hedonism. I'd never experienced anything like it."

Back in London for the premiere at the Warner West End and the ABC Shaftesbury Avenue, everyone was on his best behavior. The WAGs—wives and girlfriends—were in attendance. John Bindon lurked ominously in the shadows. After the screening, there was a party at Floral Hall, one of the old storage warehouses in Covent Garden, former thriving market stalls, one of the first being renovated in what was destined to become a smart upscale neighborhood. Guests were kept segregated. The riffraff were restricted to a hall on the ground floor. Upstairs, in a private room with a window overlooking the crowded hall, the band gathered with their VIPs—Paul and Linda McCartney, songwriter Lionel Bart, Rick Wakeman, and, inexplicably, Joe Strummer, who must have been amused by the trappings of vaingloriousness. "No one was mixing," says Unity MacLean, who was trying to coerce the band to circulate among their downstairs guests, shaking hands and thanking people for coming to the screening.

A pool photographer traipsed up the steep flight of steps to take a few pictures for the morning editions. "Where do you think you're going?" G greeted him on the landing. Instead of waiting for an answer, Peter butted the guy down the stairs using the nuclear mass of his enormous stomach.

Led Zeppelin had lost all sense of what they were—a rock 'n roll band, not the ridiculous fantasies they portrayed on the screen. Their self-importance had taken over their identities. There were groups like the Beatles and The Who who chafed over how they were cut off from the fans; Led Zeppelin welcomed the alienation. They'd become imperious, overweening, "at war with everybody"—the press, the filmmakers, promoters, the record company, even fans. Their MO was to steamroll over anyone who veered into their gilded orbit. They no longer existed as mortals; they had loyal subjects—handlers, retainers, procurers, muscle, and security. They existed behind glass, bulletproof glass. During an interval when they could have shown some humanity and repaired this image, they chose to remain aloof instead.

The music papers pilloried them for it. "This is one dumb movie," Nick Kent reflected in *NME*, "dumb because it's excessive, pretentious, and grossly narcissistic—sometimes all at once—and it ultimately presents the film's subjects, the once formidable Zeppelin, as some kind of corporate, flabby electric behemoth." He was particularly offended by "the repertoire of music that is bloated in every way, from its brutish volume assault to the wired-out adrenaline input that feeds that basic fire below." *Sounds* called the movie "depressing, embarrassing even." Only *Melody Maker* kowtowed to the band with a rave, preserving the paper's all-expenses-paid seat on the *Starship* and easy access to the musicians' suites.

Jimmy, more than the others, understood that the cost of the film was a time suck, too much of a distraction. "It's a horrible medium to work in," he said, "It's so boring! So slow!" Overall, "it was an incredible uphill struggle."

It was time for Led Zeppelin to put moviemaking behind them, to return to the one thing they knew how to do instinctively. It was time to play music.

## [2]

Robert seemed well enough to go back to work. His leg strength was gradually returning. He'd been training with the Wolves—Wolverhampton Wanderers, the Midlands football club he followed as a longtime fan—and fattening up on Maureen's legendary curry. He still couldn't straighten his arm, and his ankle wobbled when he put full weight on it. But his voice sounded in mint condition.

"He wasn't that eager to go back on the road," says Benji Le Fevre, who remained glued to Robert's side throughout his rehab. "But he knew people wanted to see him perform. They wanted him to be Robert Plant."

Jimmy and Peter Grant were already laying the groundwork for a tour. And not just any tour but a whopper of a comeback from the year-and-a-half-long layoff: fifty-one concerts stretched over four and a half months, figuring to put Led Zeppelin in front of 1.3 million fans. It'd be profitable beyond belief but grueling, especially considering the band's fragile makeup—a hobbled vocalist, a guitarist and drummer struggling with alcohol and heroin addiction, a road manager pretty much off his tree, and a manager, the person charged with holding things together, mixing cocaine and violence like a shaky-handed bomb maker. All in all, it was a recipe for ruin.

Rehearsal time was planned. In late November 1976, Led Zeppelin moved into Manticore Studios, a converted cinema in West London owned by Emerson, Lake & Palmer, and imported an engineer from America to monitor the process. They set up equipment on the cinema stage and over three months rehearsed exactly twice. Most of the time was split between Blake's, a luxurious boutique hideaway hotel in Kensington, and the Golden Lion pub just off St. James's Square. "We'd all get fucked up," recalled Benji Le Fevre. "Someone would say, 'Shall we go and rehearse, then?' And they'd say, 'Ah, not today.'"

For reinforcements, they dipped in and out of the Swan Song office and used the staff to run interference with the WAGs. Robert and Bonzo showed up when they needed infusions of cash, and Jimmy came by to get away from home, always arriving incognito, lest anyone put the touch on him for an autograph or a drug debt.

"Charlotte Martin regularly called the office looking for Jimmy," says Unity MacLean. "'Is James there? Well, where is he?' The stock answer was 'I haven't seen him,' even though he was right there in the office." Invariably, Charlotte would hop in the car and make an unannounced visit. 'Oh! Jimmy! I just called and they said you weren't here.'"

Their relationship was long lasting, though anything but solid. *Fraught* was a more apt way to describe it. They led what one person called "separate lives conducted under the same roof." She waged her own struggle with alcohol and drugs, and she gave as good as she got. "Charlotte was a tough character who bossed Jimmy around," says MacLean. "One night, I saw her clock him one. She cut his face open and really bashed him."

Peter Grant never came into the office anymore. Since his wife's abdication, he'd barricaded himself in the master bedroom at Horselunges, surrounded by a security system that rivaled the Situation

Room at the White House. A bank of closed-circuit and commercial TV screens hung from the ceiling, and phones, a good half dozen phones, balanced perilously on the bedcovers. The only object more prominent in the bedroom was a receptacle on the nightstand that held cocaine, a trough the size of a fishbowl, from which G habitually dipped and snorted.

"Peter was completely out of it," says Phil Carson. "He was not paying any attention to detail. The house was collapsing around him. The divorce had hit him hard, but the drugs had kicked in way before that."

He'd become a recluse. Even *New Musical Express* noticed it and ran an article about his condition—how he'd become unresponsive and surly (more surly than usual) and that he was delegating key business duties to assistants.

Carole Brown, G's assistant, hadn't seen him for about six weeks. "He'd just disappeared," she recalls. "I was still taking messages, trying to run the office, but nothing felt right."

One afternoon Peter arrived without notice. "He looked awful," Brown says, "like he'd been sleeping under a bridge. He went into his office and closed the door. I was trying to get as many calls to him as I possibly could." At some point, G's son Warren called. "I told him, 'Your dad's on the phone. Let him get some of these business calls out of the way. As soon as he comes up for air, I'll give him the message that you called.'"

When Brown told Peter that Warren's call hadn't been put through, "he went ballistic," she says. He called her a cunt, said he'd have her head for this. He was so furious, even Richard Cole fled the room. Brown calmly leashed the two dogs she brought to the office with her, grabbed her handbag, and marched out the door. "I can't do this anymore," she said. "I have too much self-respect." Grant let her go without so much as a word. They had worked together intimately for more than ten years. She never heard from him again.

Peter had turned the running of Swan Song over to a friend of Jimmy's named Alan Callan. Callan, competent and personable like Danny Goldberg and Abe Hoch before him, was given no mandate and no real authority. "Call Peter and discuss what it's all about," Jimmy advised him. That was a typical blind alley, during which G and Callan "just talked and laughed about stuff."

Callan's goal was to sign two artists to Swan Song: Vangelis, the progressive-electronic music composer who collaborated on projects with Yes's vocalist, Jon Anderson; and John Lennon, who at the time was bumping around his Dakota apartment compound in New York, supposedly baking bread and tending to his son Sean. Callan and G spent a few days at Horselunges bombarding Lennon with messages—to no avail. Vangelis eventually signed with RCA and Lennon with David Geffen's label.

Callan realized soon enough that Swan Song was all about Led Zeppelin. The other artists on the roster—Bad Company, Maggie Bell, the Pretty Things, Detective, and Dave Edmunds—were window dressing, "signed as a musical adventure," he acknowledged. If they made money, like Bad Company, so much the better, but Led Zeppelin was the motor—and for that matter, the chassis and the wheels—that drove the label. And the new 1977 model, much like its well-admired predecessor, was about to be unveiled on February 27, 1977, in Fort Worth, Texas.

In early December 1976, the band got serious about toning up for the tour. "The first task was to clean off the rust," Jimmy said, "after eighteen months without being on stage." He was concerned about stamina and "the fatigue aspect" of playing three-and-a-half-hour shows on a nightly basis. The schedule, as G had formulated it, allowed for a three-days-on, one-day-off routine in order to keep the endurance level strong throughout.

Mostly, during rehearsals, they concentrated on the repertoire. They had eight albums to draw from—a wide variety of material—and strove to introduce a number of songs from *Presence* while reuniting with favorites from the past. "Achilles Last Stand," "Candy Store Rock," and "Nobody's Fault But Mine" won immediate approval. So did "Ten Years Gone" from *Physical Graffiti*, which they'd never played live before due to the challenge of all the guitar overdubs. To attempt it, John Paul had a special three-neck guitar made so he could synchronize with Jimmy to create the "feel" of the original song. Of course, the epics—"Stairway to Heaven" and "Kashmir"—would be given pride of place. And for nostalgia, they worked on new versions of "The Battle of Evermore" (with Jonesy grudgingly singing the Sandy Denny part) and "Babe, I'm Gonna Leave You" accompanied by pedal steel guitar.

"Trampled Under Foot," "Whole Lotta Love," and "Rock and Roll" were added as insurance to raise the roof at key moments. To appease Bonzo, "Moby Dick" stayed in the set, although it had become something of an albatross by this time.

No concession was made to the rumblings generated by punk or what was being referred to as "new wave," punk's friendlier, more accessible cousin, which would soon establish the Police, Elvis Costello & the Attractions, Squeeze, Blondie, and the Talking Heads in the foreground of popular music. Led Zeppelin had an eagle eye trained on these upstarts.

Robert loved the punk movement. "It was marvelous," he said, "especially if you discounted the lack of originality in most of it." But he appreciated punk's "year zero" mentality, which dismissed everything that came before in rock 'n roll. "I could understand that because it wasn't that much earlier I'd felt exactly the same, especially about English rock 'n roll, which was always so flaccid." Robert knew the score. "To a large degree, the punks were right," he said. "Groups like Deep Purple and Black Sabbath had lost the point, if they ever had it." He was insightful when it came to Led Zeppelin's durable life span—and its inevitable mortality. "You can't be in the youth club forever."

John Paul Jones, on the other hand, couldn't have been less interested. Punk offended his trained-musician sensibility, "it just sounded loud and horrible," and he was unwilling to concede Led Zeppelin's relevance to the revolutionary scene. "For us, it was just a case of carrying on regardless," he said. "We could still turn our hand to that high-energy stuff and have great fun in the process."

BP Fallon, the PR elf who seemed to lock onto every scene of the moment, had landed at Stiff Records, an emerging independent record company concentrating on punk and new wave, and invited Jimmy and Robert to see the Damned, one of the label's rising stars, on a twin bill with Eater. On January 13, 1977, the two Led Zeppelin front men slunk into the Roxy, a converted fruit and vegetable warehouse in Covent Garden, hoping to avoid being recognized.

Glen Matlock, who played bass for the Sex Pistols, encountered Robert and Jimmy at the bar between acts. "Everybody was winding everybody up," he recalled. "'What are those old hippies doing here?'"

"I was aware there was a bit of nudging going on from the audience when they saw us in there," Jimmy admitted, "but we felt very comfortable. And when the Damned kicked off it was absolutely fantastic. You felt this wall of sound pressing down on you."

The band was hyperkinetic—*mad*. They didn't play so much as attack—*bam! bam! bam!*—at a volume that gave Led Zeppelin a run for its money, but without all the fuss. "It was phenomenal," Jimmy declared. "The energy coming off them nailed you to the wall."

Four nights later Robert went back for seconds, this time taking John Bonham along. Beep had called ahead to give the Roxy a heads-up about the VIPs, but the doorman pointed Robert and Bonzo to the back of the queue and insisted they fork over cash for their tickets. It was punk all right, but the point was made. There'd be no limos waiting at the stage door after the show.

According to Brian James, the Damned's guitarist, "[Bonzo] was out of his head, drinking vodka all night." At some point, he jumped onstage and challenged the band's drummer, Chris Miller, who went by the name Rat Scabies, to play longer than the two-and-a-half-minute songs that flew by without solos. At the end of the short set, Bonzo shouted, "Where's the fucking band gone? They've only been playing for fifteen minutes—we play for three fucking hours because we're real men, not a bunch of wimps! Get the band up there without that Mouse Scabies. I'll show him how to play drums!"

A chant of "Fuck off!" emanated from the crowd as Bonzo was ushered roughly off the stage. "Piss off you old hippie!"

Robert had famously referred to *Rolling Stone* as "mainlining Geritol" and its writers as "old farts." Now he was getting a taste of his own medicine.

The punk bands put up a take-no-prisoners front, but they exhibited a sense of humor about themselves. Robert recalled how, one night, John Lydon—the Sex Pistols' notorious Johnny Rotten—"fawned at my feet in mock respect." And when the Damned were invited to visit Led Zeppelin at Manticore Studios, they actually showed up, expressing considerable respect. Rat Scabies even grinned when Bonzo pinned him against the wall and said, "Listen you little fucker, *I* used to be that fast!"

They'd had their fun. They'd endured Switzerland, Jersey, Malibu, France, Munich, Morocco, even Greece. They'd banked their tax savings. They'd made a new album, released a documentary film and a soundtrack. They remained out of the public eye and they'd come out whole on the other end. But to a man, the members of Led Zeppelin knew it was time to get back on the horse. As Robert Plant noted: "After two years off, there's nothing in the world I want to do more than get on that stage."

Jimmy was fired up. "The last day of rehearsal was pure magic," he recalled, "and I thought, 'Right, we're going to have a go. We've got the stamina to play ten hours straight.'"

At long last they were ready. They were going to perform.

## [3]

But not so fast. A week before the tour was set to launch, Robert spent a few days relaxing at the cottage in Wales. "I was in the hills when I woke up one morning with soreness in my throat." He knew right away: laryngitis and a fever. "Oh, good Lord," he thought, "isn't there any end to this?"

He couldn't sing—let alone travel. It meant postponing the tour at least a month and scrambling to reschedule concerts. Jimmy was demoralized, flustered, "pacing around like a caged lion." His guitars had already been shipped overseas, leaving him with only a dulcimer to pluck, strum, or bow. "After the postponement, I didn't touch a guitar for four weeks," he said.

The beloved *Starship* was another casualty. The jet had been grounded at an airport in Long Beach, California, after encountering engine failure in midflight. Its return to service was uncertain. Fortunately, there was a similar jet available—*Caesars Chariot*, owned by Caesars Palace, the Las Vegas casino. It was every bit as posh, up to Led Zeppelin's standards. Richard Cole provisioned it with the usual inventory of liquor and delicacies and had it waiting to transport everyone to the first gig, in Dallas on April 1, 1977.

The entourage that arrived in Texas instilled an ominous note. Some new faces raised an alarm that the nature of the tour had taken an ugly turn. "There were bodyguards *everywhere*," according to Jaan Uhelszki, one of *Creem*'s cofounders, who wrote often about Led Zeppelin. Don Murfet, the fear-inspiring security head, had a crew of itchy goons. Peter had hired Rex King, an ex–rug fitter with a stony, no-nonsense disposition, to keep Bonzo out of trouble—or at least limit his mischief such that it would protect him from himself. Robert had his own new tail, Maggie Bell's former roadie Dennis Sheehan, another no-nonsense minder who didn't suffer fools or indulge hotheads like Ricardo. Two other faces that spelled trouble belonged to

Steve Weiss, Peter Grant's slit-eyed Salieri, and the notorious John Bindon, whom friends called Biffo.

"I couldn't really figure out what Bindon was doing on the tour," said Dave Northover, whose job was tending to John Paul Jones. As far as anyone could tell, Biffo attached himself to Grant as his alter-ego bodyguard, armed to take issue with any irritant that needed trodding on. "Peter liked to think of himself as a gangster," says Phil Carson, "so having Bindon around satisfied that urge." He was also a clown, a court jester with an untapped reserve of funny stories. "But mostly he wasn't funny," says Benji Le Fevre. "He traded in intimidation, and there were times I saw him swing a fist for no apparent reason." The unwritten rule was to stay out of Bindon's way.

There were written rules, too. Anyone from the rock press or print media who was invited to accompany the Led Zeppelin road show received a printed form that laid out ground rules:

1. Never talk to anyone in the band unless they first talk to you.
2. Do not make any sort of eye contact with John Bonham. This is for your own safety.
3. Do not talk to Peter Grant or Richard Cole—for any reason.
4. Keep your cassette player turned off at all times unless conducting an interview.
5. Never ask questions about anything other than music.
6. Most important, understand this—the band will read what is written about them. The band does not like the press, nor do they trust them.

The crew was given the same set of instructions.

Led Zeppelin tuned out the cosmetic changes. In Dallas, they were focused obsessively on getting back into the spotlight—not only performing but reclaiming their old lives. They wanted to play, to see if they still had the power.

"Everyone was excited because the Butter Queen was there," recalls Janine Safer, Led Zeppelin's press officer for the tour. Barbara Cope was a well-known rock 'n roll groupie in the South, a hefty woman with a big personality, so nicknamed for her fond use of a stick of oleo during sex. "Was she the band's friend? No," Safer says. "Would they sleep with her? Yes. But more than the sex, they looked forward to *seeing* her because she was a familiar face. That was the peculiar, insular world they'd constructed for themselves."

The Butter Queen was given VIP status backstage before the Dallas show, but the band was too wrapped up in the moment to pay much attention to anything but the task ahead. Despite being old troopers, their hearts were in their throats. Robert, especially, suffered opening-night jitters. "I was petrified," he recalled. "For the ten minutes before I walked up those stage steps, I was cold with fright." His right foot, which was swollen and tender, was killing him. It felt like an anchor. Supposing he couldn't move properly, was unable to stalk the stage like the virile Robert Plant everyone expected to see? "I was so nervous," he said, "that I almost threw up."

The roar of the crowd and the glare of the lights succeeded in sweeping the jitters aside. From the opening notes of "The Song Remains the Same," the old Led Zeppelin machinery clicked into place. Robert became unglued, "swirling . . . strutting . . . his amplified voice rolling up through the octaves." Jimmy danced from foot to foot like a demented leprechaun—he called it his "psycho strut"—wielding his guitar with gladiatorial panache. The rhythm section, never a chink in the machinery, did its level best to keep the beat, despite a bum PA system that buzzed without mercy.

The sequence of songs gave the band time to find its swing. There was a variable mix of rhythms through "Nobody's Fault But Mine" to "In My Time of Dying" to "Since I've Been Loving You" to "No Quarter." "I could feel tenseness in my throat for the first couple of songs," Robert said. "I kept telling myself to loosen up." Jimmy, too, took time to hit his stride, fumbling a lead here, a solo there in the opening moments. "Since I've Been Loving You" began uncharacteristically out of sync, but the band recovered nicely, building to a fine, dramatic climax.

One could judge the outcome by the expressions on the musicians' faces. As the rust came off, as the butterflies flew away, they acknowledged the triumph, cutting grins at each other. "The whole show possessed an element of emotionalism that I've never known before," Robert confessed. Led Zeppelin was *back*. They were in near-peak form. Three hours later, there was no question about stamina.

The reviews were, for the most part, glowing. *The Dallas Morning News* called the show "amazingly professional—loose, easygoing, but never sloppy." And the *Los Angeles Times*, recognizing the importance of the event, flew Robert Hilburn, the paper's pop music savant, to Texas, where he documented "a stirring performance that reassured both the group and its fans about Zeppelin's ability to continue."

But it wasn't all smooth sailing. A week later, in Chicago, things went sideways. The band moved into Chicago's Ambassador East hotel for a four-night stand in the city and as a base to gigs in Minneapolis, St. Louis, Louisville, and Detroit. "The mood was ugly," recalled Jack Calmes, Showco's sound-and-lighting impresario. Jimmy appeared dressed in storm-trooper regalia, with a braided magenta waistcoat, military jodhpurs, sunglasses, peaked visor cap, knee-high jackboots, the works. Backstage at Chicago Stadium, he was prancing around and goose-stepping.

"We've got a new Jimmy Page," Robert announced snarkily. "He's the leader again, the führer of the Fourth Reich."

No one knew what possessed him to wear the tasteless uniform. Was it the effect of seeing the Damned at the Roxy, a punk statement? There was nothing in his character that pointed to Nazi sympathies. He wasn't political. He was flamboyant, sure, but never outrageous. Everyone in the organization, including the other band members, looked at him with an expression that read: *What the fuck are you wearing?*

It got weirder and uglier. Because of that persistent PA buzz during the first part of the set, Jimmy threw a trash can at one of the technical crew. The next night, during the acoustic interlude, he leaned his guitar against an amp, walked to the side of the stage, and spit in the face of a sound man. The atmosphere turned dark—and tense.

The third night in Chicago, April 9, 1977, was one for the record books. It began badly, with Jimmy playing "Since I've Been Loving You" while the band broke into "In My Time of Dying." In general, his guitar work was sloppy, the syncopation jagged. Forty-five minutes into the concert, Jimmy sat down, clutching his stomach, smack in the middle of "Ten Years Gone."

"Jimmy has got a bout of gastroenteritis," Robert announced, explaining they were going to take a five-minute break. But ten minutes later, Richard Cole grabbed the mic, canceling the rest of show.

Jimmy attributed the ailment to food poisoning, although rumors circulated that it was drug related. "He definitely wasn't Junkie Jim at that point," says Janine Safer, who was backstage during the show. "He was on a weird diet, drinking odd smoothie concoctions which might have been the cause." Since arriving in the States, his meals had been entirely liquid—bananas and vitamins with a daiquiri mix that he whipped up in a blender. Might Jimmy's problem have been caused by the smoothie and a bottle of Jack Daniel's, or the smoothie and a Quaalude, or the smoothie and something stronger? It was anyone's guess.

But the atmosphere of the tour was strangely out of whack. In Minneapolis a few nights later, Led Zeppelin showed up at the Met Center an hour and ten minutes late. After the show, Jimmy got into a shouting match with the tour doctor, Larry Badgley, over Quaaludes that had gone missing from the doctor's black bag. (Later Jimmy admitted, "I really *did* steal the Quaaludes from Dr. Badgley.") They were late getting to St. Louis, too. And to Indianapolis. And to Louisville. And to Cleveland.

Bad behavior was ratcheting up the stakes. In Chicago, Bonzo destroyed his suite at the Ambassador, jettisoning the couch, end tables, air-conditioner, and television set ten stories onto the street below before demolishing an entire pool table by lifting it repeatedly and smashing it to smithereens. The damage added $5,100 to the room charge.

In Cleveland at the end of April, the rampaging reached epic proportions. At Swingos Hotel, an illustrious rock 'n roll pitstop, where every room had a different motif, "Led Zeppelin," according to the *Plain Dealer*, "turned it into their own private Sodom and Gomorrah."

"I was staying in the Bamboo Room," recalls Danny Marcus, who joined the band's entourage through the Midwest swing. "All four of them showed up in my room. They each grabbed a post of the bamboo four-poster bed and pulled them out until the mattress dropped. Bonzo's post broke off, and he used it to whack at the bamboo fan until the blades broke off. They destroyed the entire room." Everything was fair game. According to Jim Swingos, who owned the hotel, "They smashed light fixtures, walls, windows, mirrors—everything." Bonzo then went from room to room, using that bedpost to inflict as much mayhem as was possible. The bill came to $13,000 just for damages.

"It goes as far as it does because it's a laugh," Robert explained. "We only do what we do because it's fun."

But it was hard to overlook the underlying current of anger. For a band that had been on top of the world for eight years and was admired—beloved—by untold numbers of fans, wealthy beyond means, doing a cool, creative job, the anger and hostility were incomprehensible.

Cocaine played a major role. There was so much of it on the tour—"boatloads of it," according to a key member of the entourage, "and the more coke people did, the more paranoid and aggressive they got." The music, too—or at least the tone it set. The fans had bought into the legend of the band's bad behavior and acted accordingly. There were rioting and arrests in St. Paul, Minnesota, when hundreds of ticketless fans stormed the arena, and again in Cincinnati, where local papers reported that "legions of rowdy gatecrashers" battled with police, leading to more than a hundred arrests. In Miami, a thousand fans waiting to buy tickets vandalized the Orange Bowl and were teargassed by police. A second night in Cincinnati was marred by a fan's death after he fell from the third tier in Riverfront Coliseum. Wherever Led Zeppelin went, the legend went with them.

Jimmy's condition had changed; you could see it physically. He was an ethereally beautiful man, always super-skinny, but he'd become wraith-like; he ate less and less. And he started nodding out. He got sloppier onstage. By the time the band rolled into Detroit at the end of April 1977, Jimmy was a full-blown mess.

Led Zeppelin had an important date at the Silverdome, a megaarena in Pontiac that held more than 75,000 people. For convenience, the band had registered at a classic seedy drive-in motel right next door to the facility. Jimmy had agreed to do a phone interview an hour before the concert.

"I went to his door and got no response," recalled Janine Safer. "I knocked louder and louder—no response, nothing." She got someone from the office to unlock the door. "There was a wing chair knocked over in his room, and Jimmy was sprawled on top of it, on the floor, unconscious. I slapped him a few times and got nothing. It was clear he'd OD'd." She struggled him to his feet and dragged him around the floor until he gradually came to. He begged her to let him lie down and sleep. A few minutes later, Richard Cole arrived on the scene. He took one look at the situation and knew exactly how to handle it. Ricardo was dealing with heroin himself.

And so was Bonzo. He'd been nodding off onstage while playing tambourine during the acoustic set of the shows. Alcohol was not enough of a payload for him. His obsessive personality demanded a more potent kick. In Paris, during the tax exile, he'd begun snorting heroin. "We had three junkies on that tour," says Janine Safer, "and a morbidly obese, profoundly unhappy manager snorting way too much cocaine."

Were the concerts suffering as a result? Not if the reviews were any indication. Everywhere Led Zeppelin played, accolades followed. Newspaper headlines swelled with praise. ZEPPELIN'S SHEER POWER, ABILITY, AND SHOW OF INTEGRITY DELIGHT 20,000 FANS IN STADIUM . . . ZEP: NO MESSING . . . ZEPPELIN KEEPS AUDIENCE IN FRENZY . . . ZEPPELIN FLIES HIGH . . . LED ZEPPELIN LANDS TRIUMPHANTLY . . . LED ZEPPELIN THRILLS PACKED HOUSE. About 20 percent of the time the band played brilliantly. About 60 percent of the time they put on a workmanlike show. Benji Le Fevre, who was stationed at the band's soundboard, says, "I don't think any of the shows on that tour were any good." But the audience loved it *100 percent* of the time. "With the kids, it was total infatuation."

Things began to come apart on the second leg of the tour, which began in the South in mid-May. The rhythm of the shows, once a smooth, buoyant sail, had run aground. John Paul's classical intro to "No Quarter" meandered for an excruciating twenty minutes, while Bonzo's nearly half-hour drum solo sent fans winging to the refreshment stands. Jimmy's playing, always a highlight of any show, lapsed into gratuitous displays of pyrotechnics that were often riddled with mistakes. "The tightness and precision of early days is gone," noted one reviewer, "replaced by excess and sloppiness." ( "I wonder if Page, Bonham and Jones realize how crowded the snack bars and rest rooms get every time they start into one of their solo jaunts," the *Los Angeles Times* critic Robert Hilburn wryly noted of a later show.)

It all came down to what state Jimmy was in on any given night. "There were evenings, when it came to his solos, that I cried because he'd played so brilliantly, but there were many more times I cried when he played so badly," recalls Le Fevre. "Twice, during those long, drawn-out spectacles, Robert didn't leave the stage as he usually did. He just stood by the piano, glaring at Jim with a stare that said, *What the fuck are you doing?*"

The reviews started to pick up on the ruptured vibe. In Fort Worth, where Bad Company's Mick Ralphs appeared with the band to juice up the encore, the *Star-Telegram*'s critic asserted, "Their 1977 tour is tedious to a fault." Aubrey Powell—Po—who caught the show from backstage, says, "It was the worst concert I'd ever seen. They weren't together, Jimmy was not on it, and the sound wasn't good—the audience wasn't having it." At the Capital Centre, outside Washington, DC, the reviews were brutal. *The Washington Post*'s reporter called the show "polished but uninspired" and the band "lazy and self-centered." *The Washington Star*, usually a more forgiving authority, observed, "Rarely has a major rock act come through Washington and played as badly, with as little feeling, as Led Zeppelin did last night. The entire evening had all the trappings of a concert by a group that is on the slide but hasn't realized it."

Eyewitnesses pointed to "a very wasted-looking Page." There was no disguising Jimmy's condition. He looked emaciated, frail, at times unkempt and abstracted, his drug problem no longer simply kept under wraps. His playing was so ragged that a reviewer in North Carolina expressed his unqualified disgust. "Jimmy Page ought to be ashamed of himself. Was Page drunk? Was this an off-night?" During "The Song Remains the Same," which he played on his double-neck Gibson, "he'd have the chord shape on the twelve-string, and he'd be strumming the six-string," which had happened other times, while Robert looked on, cringing.

Bonzo's playing was similarly affected by drugs, with missed beats and choppy syncopation. "I didn't realize how bad off Bonzo was," says Phil Carson, who saw him fall asleep on his drum kit one evening. Usually lionized for his technical excellence on the drums, the slipshod execution began catching up with Bonzo. A respected reviewer chastised him as "the clumsiest and most simpleminded percussionist in any major rock group." Another complained, "He can barely keep 4/4 time." Almost every review sought the demise of "Moby Dick."

Robert and Jonesy began pairing off from their mates. On days off, they hung out with Danny Marcus, Atlantic's facilitator, steering clear of Jimmy and Bonzo's escalating drug activities. They also put distance between themselves and Grant, Richard, and Bindon, who were stoking fear and mistrust among the inner circle. "Everybody was nervous," said Sam Aizer, Swan Song's Bad Company liaison, who joined the tour for the Texas gigs. "'Should I stand *here?*' 'Did you see *that?*' 'What's *he* looking at?' It was a constant look-over-your-shoulder."

"Jonesy especially stayed away from the madness," says Michael Des Barres. "He seemed disgusted by the whole seamy business. You could tell the camaraderie was coming apart."

"Robert and Jonesy enjoyed each other's company because it was the only company they had," says Benji Le Fevre. "Their pals were too fucked up. I don't know if the camaraderie had gone, so much as one half of the camaraderie had drowned under the influence of drugs. It was a sad fucking thing to witness."

The atmosphere grew darker on the way to Florida. *Caesars Chariot* flew with a full cabin of passengers. Po, the Hipgnosis designer, had joined the tour, as had John Bindon's girlfriend, Vicki Hodge, who proceeded to do a cartwheel down the aisle of the plane in her miniskirt-and-no-undies getup, amusing the boys in the peanut gallery. G made sure everyone had a line or two of coke to settle flight fear, but nerves in general were jumpy.

Bindon was fulminating about an incident that had occurred in the Speakeasy in London with Steve O'Rourke, the manager of Pink Floyd. "Johnny had stolen money out of the trunk of Steve's car and was seriously planning to kill Steve," said Po, who wondered what "a well-known villain" was doing in Led Zeppelin's entourage. "Peter knew Bindon would follow through on the threat and changed my seat on the plane so I couldn't be construed as an accomplice."

Bindon was increasingly hyper. He was itching for a fight, some kind—*any* kind—of altercation that would allow him to engage in violence. Rage radiated off of him. He scared the hell out of people.

There was an uneasiness on board that flight, courtesy of John Bindon, that cast a pall over the collective spirit.

The weather added to the anxiety. The weather report for Tampa was not encouraging. It was steamy hot in the city, and afternoon thunderstorms were forecast by the National Weather Service. Peter Grant was reasonably comfortable with the situation because Led Zeppelin's contract with the promoter specifically stated that a metal roof would be constructed over the stage. He took extra precautions because he remained freaked out by the memory of Leslie Harvey, Stone the Crow's guitarist, being electrocuted during a concert. But there was an added, unexpected wrinkle.

"We were flying to the gig and Cole showed me the ticket for the gig, which clearly stated: 'Come Rain or Shine,'" Grant recalled. Below that was written: "Good This Date Only." This meant there was no provision for rescheduling the show if weather intervened. "This was a big mistake." If, for any reason, the band couldn't perform, seventy thousand ticket holders would be extremely disappointed—*irate* was more like it.

The signs were discouraging from the get-go. It had rained earlier in the afternoon before the sun returned full strength. Fans had been sitting—*baking*—in Tampa Stadium for three or four hours. "By the time the band was ready to go on," Po said, "you could see it getting darker and darker. Lightning flashed all over the place." And Peter Grant was hopping mad. The roof over the stage was canvas, not metal.

Janine Safer, who had decided to watch the show from the audience instead of her usual backstage perch, had misgivings about the crowd, which was enormous, packed tightly together, and hot, uncomfortably hot. "There was also a massive police presence," she says, "far more than I recall seeing at any other show—and they were in full riot gear. *Huh?*"

The heavens opened up twenty minutes into Led Zeppelin's show, a blistering downpour. Benji Le Fevre, who was monitoring the soundboard, says, "The canvas roof over the stage had been put up in such a way that it had gathered an enormous lake of water in it." The band was in the middle of playing "Nobody's Fault But Mine." According to Peter Grant, "I quickly actioned Robert to wind it up, and we ran off stage."

"Everybody into the dressing room!" Richard barked, commanding the action like a demented general. "Fucking get in there quick!"

G argued ferociously with the promoter, who felt the band could return once the rain had stopped. Peter agreed to comply, but only after he tried sending two fighter jets into the air to determine whether there was a break in the clouds. Clearly, his concept of Led Zeppelin's importance had gotten away from him.

"There were about twenty thousand kids sitting on the grass who started getting really uptight once they sensed the band wasn't coming back," recalls Le Fevre, who had moved to safety at the right of the stage. The police, using megaphones, ordered the sound crew to lie down behind the speaker cabinets, cover their heads, and not get up. "All of a sudden, the riot cops came charging in around the crash barriers in front of the stage—they were just swinging batons, clubbing kids, laying into everybody. It was brutal, frightening."

It was a bloodbath, the kind of carnage Led Zeppelin had witnessed at the Velodromo Vigorelli in Milan in 1971. There was no way the band would return to the stage, not under those conditions. G ordered everyone into the limousines for an immediate getaway. There was panic at first: Jonesy's car was missing; the driver had gotten lost with John Paul's wife and children in it.

Fortunately, the airport was close to the stadium. *Caesars Chariot* had been alerted and was idling on the tarmac, ready to take off as soon as its passengers were buckled in. Everyone piled onto the plane, nervously eyeing the airport perimeter. "The crowd had followed us from the stadium and were trying to break through the fences," Po recalled. "We could see them through the portholes in the plane. They felt Led Zeppelin was deserting them, and they were *pissed*."

The city was of the same frame of mind. Tampa's mayor not only refused to grant permission for a makeup date, he went one step further. "Led Zeppelin will not perform in Tampa again," he decreed. "There will be no future concerts scheduled by that group. We have to protect the health and welfare of the police officers as well as the citizens of Tampa."

Peter Grant wasn't overly concerned. There were myriad places for Led Zeppelin to perform, cities that would welcome the income and prestige derived from their shows. Tampa might have been a bust, but Led Zeppelin was richer for the experience. G invited a few guests into his stateroom at the back of the plane and dumped the contents of his holdall onto the bed. He'd taken a page out of the Chuck Berry playbook, the one that said "Make sure to get paid *before* you go on." He tossed a fistful of the $1 million in cash into the air.

"At least we got the fucking money," he said.

## Chapter Twenty

# A TRANSITION PERIOD

## [1]

Led Zeppelin fixed on America's two coasts in an effort to regroup and pump fresh enthusiasm into their 1977 tour.

New York was an obvious place to hunker down after the catastrophe in Tampa. Manhattan was a psychological pick-me-up for a band on the road. Jimmy Reed said it best: *Bright lights, big city.* There was always something exciting going on, fascinating people, and they could walk on the streets without security shadowing every step. Even better, the band could reconnect with friends and resume their hedonistic lifestyles.

They had three days off before opening a six-show stretch at Madison Square Garden, a place every group loved to play. Robert and Jonesy killed time poking through record shops and bookstores. Robert treated himself to Big Macs at McDonald's, one of his favorite pastimes, and a shiny new Lincoln Mark IV with red-leather interior. Jimmy mostly slept through the days and spent the nights in clubs, cavorting with Ronnie Wood and Keith Richards. "Keith was the last guy Jimmy should have hung out with," says Janine Safer. Bonzo also slipped further into addiction. "I went to visit him one afternoon at the Plaza [Hotel], where the band was staying," Po recalls, "and he was in terrible shape, incoherent and nodding out. It was obvious he'd done some smack in addition to binge-drinking." In his more lucid hours, Bonzo once again overcame boredom by heaving furniture out the hotel window, a stunt that may have been tolerated in Chicago and Cleveland, but not at the courtly Plaza. The band was barred from ever staying there again.

The bullshit was starting to get to Robert. "I see a lot of craziness around us," he complained in an interview from that time. "Somehow, we generate it and we revile it. This is an aspect, since I've been away from it, which made me contemplate whether we are doing more harm than we are good."

It was certainly worthy of his consideration. Tampa had unnerved him. It was one thing to deal with an excitable crowd, another to admit you had helped set off the violence. Would things have been different had they shown up on time—or returned to the stage after the rain had stopped? Could they have helped to calm the volatile situation if Jimmy and Bonzo were together enough to deal with a crowd? Had John Bindon's presence infected the entire atmosphere?

It was imperative that Led Zeppelin change up the tempo, beginning with their performances in New York City. It was the hottest ticket in town—hotter than *Annie* at the Alvin Theatre. The New York Swan Song office was besieged with requests. "Every single celebrity in the entire goddamn world seemed to decide that day they wanted to see Led Zeppelin that night." Key press would attend, major broadcast media, record-company bigwigs, the most important names in rock 'n roll. It was like appearing in front of the Supreme Court. Even Jimmy and Bonzo understood that scoring with the New York audience was vital to the band's reputation. "Before each of the shows, we met in the Oyster Bar or Trader Vic's and hung out for a while before getting into the limos," Janine Safer recalls. "It was clear the guys were looking forward to playing, showing everyone they were still the best damn band in the world."

New York audiences, as everyone knew, weren't as forgiving as those elsewhere. Shows were expected to begin on time, at 8:00 p.m., exactly as advertised. Keep New Yorkers waiting half an hour and they'd likely be into their second drink at Ashley's or Maxwell's Plum.

It said something about Led Zeppelin's stature that at nine fifteen, when the lights finally went down, everyone was still in their seats. And a good thing, too, because the Garden shows were as good as it got—"spellbinding," in the opinion of a hard-nosed critic, delivered with "such an exciting edge." The band was light on its feet, "good-natured and almost puckish." Jimmy, decked out in a white embroidered suit, stretched out his solos as if he were getting paid by the note; otherwise he was on top of his game. His playing "was positively kaleidoscopic," according to *The New York Times*. Robert had never sounded stronger or as fresh, especially during the acoustic set. Jonesy and Bonzo's deep-in-the-pocket rhythm section added a puncture-proof, muscular backbeat. "Kashmir" was a knockout. "Whole Lotta Love" and "Rock and Roll" succeeded in bringing down the house. John Rockwell, the *Times*'s buttoned-down critic, whose tastes ran to artsier fare, felt it "was the best Led Zeppelin show this observer has ever heard . . . a triumphant reassertion" of the band's preeminence.

The shows on the West Coast were as spellbinding—maybe better, "some of the finest concerts in their history," according to a keen observer. "L.A. is our spiritual home," Robert declared from the stage of the Forum, and there wasn't anyone who sought to take issue with that.

Led Zeppelin always seemed to end up in Los Angeles. The city was where their reputation had become legend, and they were not content to let it stand without a good embroidering. Evenings at the Rainbow and the Whisky were typically riotous affairs, attracting a full retinue of slightly older groupies. "They were a mystery to me," says Janine Safer, "but I adopted the band's view that these girls weren't quite human. I certainly never thought of them as sentient."

Lori Mattix was still on Jimmy's dance card. He sent Betty Iannaci, an Atlantic Records receptionist, to pick her up at a motel room in Westwood, where she was now living with her mother. "I felt so conflicted," Iannaci says. "She was a young teenage girl who looked and acted like she was twenty-five, wearing a $300 beaded-crystal dress. It was clear that her mother was grooming her for a night out with Jimmy Page. And I knew he was mixing it up with heroin."

LA meant it was party time. Swan Song and Atlantic rented a fabulous house in one of the canyons and packed it with a guest list of relatively high-profile friends, everyone from Roger McGuinn, Keith Moon, and Rod Stewart to Kareem Abdul-Jabbar. It was a glittery champagne-and-cocaine affair that soon devolved into debauchery. The company pulled out all the stops, somehow sensing this might be a send-off, the last time Led Zeppelin performed in LA.

"I brought along a friend unlike Lori, a thirty-five-year-old, successful woman who knew how to take care of herself," says Betty Iannaci. Later, Peter Grant invited Iannaci's guest to his room. "He had come into a large quantity of cocaine and was feeling very generous." Eventually Betty's friend wound up naked and handcuffed to the pipe under Grant's bathroom sink so that, for an entire weekend, she was at the disposal of anyone who came in. Jimmy came across her almost by accident and, in an uncustomary show of gallantry, found a key to unlock the cuffs and helped her to escape.

The behavior on the West Coast, beyond outrageous, had reached a point of no return. Jimmy functioned admirably once he took to the stage but was pretty well knackered otherwise. Bonzo was so wasted, so starved for attention, that he acted out any chance he got. In one strange misadventure, for no apparent reason he bit a woman's finger so hard it bled. Jonesy wisely adhered to the press guidelines: "Never talk to the band unless they talk to you first. Do not make eye contact with John Bonham." Robert also made sure he kept his distance. On the tour plane, he buried his nose in a book, even if sometimes the book was upside down. The musicians no longer left gigs together. Each man had his own limo and they never rode with one another.

Management wasn't providing any semblance of management. Richard Cole had ceded control of his authority to Quaalude, cocaine, and heroin. He took stupid chances, which he'd never done before. On an Air India flight from Heathrow to New York, he'd been arrested for creating a disturbance. And on July 17, 1977, on his way back to the States from a break in the tour, he was met at the Seattle airport by local police for general drug-induced bad conduct. Mick Hinton, Bonzo's roadie, was a full-blown alcoholic and addict, as was Ray Thomas, Jimmy's assistant. Peter Grant was another sad story. "Peter had lost it by then," says Phil Carson, who was Grant's lifeline to Atlantic Records and an unswerving admirer. "Cocaine had taken such a terrible toll on him that he wasn't capable of dealing as shrewdly anymore." He was tethered to John Bindon "and people still feared him," but having Bindon around also made Grant vulnerable.

The confluence of misbehavior came to a head in Oakland, California, on July 23, 1977. Led Zeppelin was a featured headliner at the "Day on the Green" festival, a two-day extravaganza promoted by Bill Graham at the Oakland Coliseum. The band had arrived directly from a pair of lackluster dates—the Kingdome in Seattle and Arizona State University—where Jimmy's and Bonzo's conditions precluded efficient showmanship. Graham spared no expense at his events. There were plush trailers at the band's disposal, a first-class banquet laid out, not the usual cold cuts curling at the edges. He even provided Led Zeppelin with an elaborate stage backdrop, a cringeworthy replica of Stonehenge. No one made much of it at the time, but it would haunt them ever after when *Spinal Tap* hit movie screens.

The show seemed to drag on forever. Led Zeppelin was late, as usual. The crowd had been waiting all day, then suffered through two pedestrian warm-up acts, Rick Derringer and Judas Priest. Led Zeppelin's performance was a huge step up, and the band was inspired by the reception from their fans to play at peak form, "a rock legend come to life," as *The Oakland Tribune* noted. Jimmy had been unresponsive before the show—"he was so loaded that they had to lead him up on the stage," according to Graham's production manager—but he found his sea legs during "The Song Remains the Same."

While they were winding up the crowd, Peter Grant and John Bindon walked up the ramp toward the backstage area. It was set at a steep incline, and Jim Downey, one of Graham's able stagehands, quipped, "Jeez, it's a long way up that ramp." Peter misinterpreted it as a dig at his girth and took offense. Without any provocation, Bindon threw a punch, knocking Downey out cold.

"Bindon had been spoiling for a fight from the second he got on that tour," says Janine Safer. "He'd been walking around with his hands balled into fists. You could tell he was waiting for something—*anything*—to set him off."

The assault on Downey whetted his appetite for a more violent encounter. It would not be long until he got his wish.

Shortly before the end of Led Zeppelin's show, Grant's eleven-year-old son, Warren, cruised the backstage caravan of Winnebagos that served as dressing rooms for the bands. "Bill Graham used to have these lovely hand-carved wooden dressing-room signs with the band's name attached to the trailer door," says Phil Carson.

"I thought it looked cool," Warren said later. He began pulling Led Zeppelin's sign off its mount.

Jim Matzorkis, one of Graham's colleagues, happened to be walking by. He told Warren they needed the signs for the next day's show. They had to remain on the door until then.

"I'm taking them," Warren insisted.

"No you're not," Matzorkis said, and he took them from the boy.

Warren ran directly to his father and reported the incident, but he enhanced it. In his retelling, Matzorkis had slapped him and knocked him down.

"I had been standing right there," recalls Janine Safer. "Nobody had slapped Warren Grant. I turned to John Bindon, who was whipping Peter up, and said, 'Nothing happened. *Nobody touched him!*'"

Her exhortation fell on deaf ears. Bindon and Peter were pretty coked up and heard what they wanted to hear. "They were like two in-cendiary creatures," Safer says.

Storm clouds had been brewing since they arrived at the site. Grant and Graham had a love-hate relationship, stemming from hard-nosed negotiations at early Fillmore shows—two self-styled tough guys used to having their own way. Steve Weiss, another hothead who had an antagonistic relationship with Graham, was part of Led Zep-pelin's entourage in Oakland. There was only slightly concealed hos-tility between the two factions from the moment they'd encountered each other that afternoon.

In fact, temperatures had begun rising a day before the show. Rich-ard Cole had, on Grant's orders, phoned Graham and demanded $25,000 in advance. *Right now!* And *in cash*. That wasn't part of the deal. They were making hundreds of thousands of dollars for the weekend event. A cash advance late on a Friday afternoon, when the banks were already closed, seemed like an unsporting request, if not heartless. It felt like a shakedown. But Bill knew that if he didn't comply, there was a good chance Led Zeppelin wouldn't show. So he scrounged up the cash, stuffed it in three shoeboxes, and took it himself to the Miyako Hotel, where G was staying.

As soon as Graham walked into Peter's suite, he got the whole pic-ture. There was another man in the room, a character in a cowboy hat, someone Bill recognized as Oakland's biggest drug dealer. "What I should have done was walk right out of there with the money," Gra-ham said, regretting his complicity as the bag man in an obvious drug deal. But he had too much invested in the two-day festival and couldn't risk alienating Peter Grant.

As it was, Led Zeppelin's set the next afternoon was neither their best effort nor their worst. Jimmy took some time to get going. He seemed disoriented, sticky-fingered. His myriad solos sounded too similar, one bleeding into the another. According to the *San Francisco Chronicle*, his playing "frequently did not make the kind of guitar sense that has established him for years as one of rock's greatest stars."

But the rest of the band was in fine form, especially Robert, whose voice hadn't sounded as strong in years. In any case, they covered all bases, playing a full three and a half hours, finishing with a tactical bombardment of hits: "Kashmir," "Achilles Last Stand," "Stairway to Heaven," "Whole Lotta Love," "Rock and Roll," and "Black Dog"— one right after the other. The fans left not knowing what had hit them.

The same could be said of Jim Matzorkis, who was storing equipment in a trailer just behind the stage. As Led Zeppelin walked off, Peter Grant and John Bonham detoured to accost Matzorkis. "You don't talk to *my* kid that way," G fumed, working off a highball of anger that had been building throughout the afternoon. "Nobody does. Who do you think you are? Roughing this kid up. I'll have your job."

"No, you can't have my job," Matzorkis replied.

Before he could turn around, Bonzo strode up a few metal steps and planted a kick squarely in Matzorkis's crotch, causing him to fall back into the trailer. Bonzo was about to go in for seconds when he was held off by his own security detail long enough for Matzorkis to scramble away and take cover in another trailer.

Shortly thereafter, Bill Graham sought out Grant, who was in a murderous, coke-induced rage. "Your man put his hands on *my* people. On my *son*," G seethed. He insisted on meeting Matzorkis—"to make my peace with him and settle this."

That was not a good idea. Graham had gotten a good look at Led Zeppelin's security team and concluded they "were vicious fucking wild animals," thugs who "were just waiting to kill." He was more than familiar with Grant's penchant for violence. He tried talking Peter down, trying to gain some assurance that no one was going to get hurt. "Do I have your word?" Graham asked. When Grant answered, "Yes," they went to find Matzorkis.

Jim Matzorkis had withdrawn to another Winnebago. Graham unlocked the door, ushered Peter inside, and made introductions. Matzorkis reached out to shake Peter's hand. In an instant, Grant pulled the man toward him, then hauled back and punched Matzorkis in the face with a fist covered in bulky metal rings. Graham tried to intercede, but as he recalled later, "he picked me up like I was a fly and handed me to the guy by the steps." That guy was John Bindon, who now joined Grant inside the trailer. Richard Cole stood guard outside, with a length metal pipe as a weapon.

"Bill! Help me! Bill!" Matzorkis cried.

Bindon was wound up and in his element. Invigorated by cocaine, he put Matzorkis in a full nelson from behind while Peter Grant continued to punch him in the face. He knocked Jim's tooth out, then kicked him in the balls. Bindon pummeled Matzorkis to the ground, jumped on him, and went for his eyes. Somehow the bloody, badly beaten man managed to break free and escape, which was when Graham's security team arrived. They had gone to their cars to get guns out of the trunk and were ready to square off with Led Zeppelin's posse. In any case, they intended to avenge their mate.

Graham had a problem. He wanted nothing more than to exact vengeance for what happened, but there was another sold-out concert the next day to think about. If there was a turf war and Led Zeppelin canceled their appearance, sixty thousand kids would exact their own brand of vengeance and the repercussions would be ruinous for Graham. The show had to go on; he ordered his men to back down, promising them he'd turn them loose afterward.

Led Zeppelin had fucked with the wrong guy this time. Bill Graham wasn't about to let them get away with it.

---

Richard Cole hustled the band and the staff into waiting limousines and sped off to the Miyako Hotel. "We all attended a big powwow in Peter's suite, a spin conversation," recalls Janine Safer, the band's press manager. Steve Weiss and Richard Cole were there. So was Steve Rosenberg, the head of Led Zeppelin's security detail. "They were nervous, more than usually so. Peter was paranoid. They feared being busted by local law enforcement."

Myriad charges could be leveled by Graham: Bonham, Grant, and Bindon for inciting assault, Cole for assault with a deadly weapon. Because Peter had been a professional wrestler, his fists were considered deadly weapons as well. Weiss immediately phoned George Fearon, the band's outside counsel at Phillips Nizer. "Do we flee the jurisdiction?" Weiss wanted to know. "Do we turn ourselves in?" Everyone agreed, says Safer: "Let's get out of Dodge." "It's the prudent thing to do."

But Bill Graham had the exits covered. And Led Zeppelin's limo drivers were *his* guys, who had driven for hundreds of *his* shows. They had been instructed to report any movement by the band's people, especially if they tried heading to the airport.

For some unknown reason—perhaps a sense of obligation to fans, perhaps greed—Led Zeppelin decided to remain in Oakland and play the Sunday-afternoon concert. Steve Weiss called Graham to inform him that before showtime, he would have to sign a waiver stating no one could be sued for more than two thousand dollars for the incident at the stadium. And they were demanding Jim Matzorkis's home address, because he was expected to sign a waiver as well. "Please understand," Weiss made clear, "if that document is not signed, there may well be no performance."

A team of civil lawyers was called by the head of Graham's company to determine the validity of such a document. Sign it, they reported back. If it was signed under "economic duress . . . the signature's not worth the paper it's signed on."

A half hour before the show on Sunday, Steve Weiss arrived at Graham's trailer with the waiver. "Look, the boys got a little bit out of hand yesterday. We hope there are no hard feelings." Graham signed it without a word.

Despite his compliance, Led Zeppelin arrived an hour and twenty minutes late. No one spoke to them or made any effort to get them situated. Peter Grant and Richard Cole couldn't have cared less, but the band felt it. They had heard about the altercation and were exasperated by it. "There was a very nasty, heavy energy about the whole day," Jimmy said. "It was getting very ugly behind the stage. . . . It was just abhorrent."

Robert agreed. "It was an absolute shambles," he recalled. He felt sad having to sing "Stairway to Heaven," a song he cared deeply about, "in the shadow of the fact that the artillery that we carried with us was prowling around backstage with a *hell* of an attitude." Robert made an effort to engage Bill Graham, who was too disgusted to respond. He genuinely liked Robert—they had sons the same age and, under normal circumstances, shared stories about them—but it was "good riddance" as far as Graham was concerned. He promised himself he'd never play Led Zeppelin again.

It was an easy promise to keep. It was the last concert Led Zeppelin ever performed in the United States.

———

Getting out of Dodge was not going to be easy. Bill Graham's security team was headed by a retired San Francisco police sergeant who recognized the ex-cops on Led Zeppelin's detail. Monday morning, a trio of cars converged on the Miyako Hotel. Details from the Oakland Police Department, the Alameda County Sheriff's Office, and the California Highway Patrol came roaring in and surrounded the place. There was a face-off in the hotel lobby, with everyone flashing badges. It was explained as a fait accompli that Peter Grant, John Bindon, John Bonham, and Richard Cole were going to be arrested, and no one was leaving the hotel before that happened. It was advised that the four men surrender themselves so as not to require a full-scale police raid. An hour later they were led through the lobby in handcuffs, heads bowed, eyes averted. Graham made sure they were met at the police station by every TV reporter he could scrounge up.

Steve Weiss had Jeff Hoffman waiting for them. Hoffman, "the charismatic, well-connected young fixer," had negotiated Grant's release from jail following the Drake Hotel robbery and disentangled Jimmy from the drug shakedown in LA. This was right up his alley. He arranged for bail. "My instructions were: 'Get rid of the case. We're never coming back to court.'"

Hoffman had to explain that in criminal cases, unlike civil cases, one was required to appear in person in court; otherwise it was considered bail jumping, which in itself was a crime. In the meantime, they were free to go.

Led Zeppelin and Peter Grant went in opposite directions. G, his son Warren, and John Bindon traveled to Long Island, where they met Phil Carson for a day's sharking aboard Jerry Greenberg's sport-fishing boat that was anchored in Montauk. John Paul Jones rented an RV and took his family on a brief holiday to Oregon. The rest of the band and crew flew to New Orleans in preparation for a July 30, 1977 show at the Superdome, practically a city unto itself. Everybody was stressed. Five days in New Orleans was the perfect place to recharge. It was a low-key place where you could get lost in a crowd. They arrived early, around six thirty in the morning, and checked into the Maison Dupuy, a favorite local hotel.

It was still feasible, time-wise, to call London, so Robert checked in with his wife, Maureen. His son, Karac, was sick, he learned, "a mild stomach bug." Then another call: the boy had contracted pneumonia, and Maureen was taking him to the doctor. A short time later, Robert learned Karac's condition was worsening. His temperature had risen.

On Long Island the next day, G's fishing party enjoyed a deep-sea outing, pulling in an impressive share of small sharks. "We got back into the marina and were in high spirits," recalls Jerry Greenberg. "There was an emergency phone call for Peter Grant."

Robert's son was dead. He was five years old.

"If you ever want a quick reminder of what's going on in the real world," Robert realized when the news had sunk in, "one minute you're in New Orleans and the toast of the new world, and you get a phone call without any warning. He'd gone."

The car crash had already challenged Robert's sense of his own invincibility. Karac's death dealt Robert a blow against which he had no defenses.

He had to get home to his family immediately. It was difficult arranging passage out of New Orleans. *Caesars Chariot* couldn't fly; the plane was grounded, a mandatory rest period after its long haul from Oakland. Instead, a chartered flight was arranged to Newark with a British Airways connection overseas. Robert, Bonzo, Richard Cole, and Janine Safer made the trip.

"Robert and I sat across from each other from New Orleans to Newark," Safer recalls. "I had never witnessed human grief like that. Robert just stared into his hands. I don't think he exchanged a word with anyone throughout the entire flight."

Only Bonzo accompanied Robert home to Jennings Farm in Kidderminster and stood by his side throughout a heartrending funeral. Neither John Paul, Jimmy, nor Peter Grant bothered to attend. Colonel Tom Parker sent a wreath in Elvis's name.

G claimed he was busy "trying to sort out the cancellations" for the rest of the tour—and every date for the foreseeable future. It was a vague sort of indeterminable task, not knowing when, or even if, Robert Plant would perform again. For the time being, the future of Led Zeppelin was in limbo. When Grant finished, he picked up the phone and placed a final call—to Bill Graham, of all people.

"I hope you're happy," he snarled into the receiver. "Thanks to you, Robert Plant's kid died today."

For Robert, the tragedy put into perspective his connection to his life's work, his family, his mortality. As months passed, secluded at home with Maureen and their surviving child, eight-year-old Carmen, he would reflect on the shambles that Led Zeppelin had become, the cruelty, the heedlessness, the decline.

"The 1977 tour ended because I lost my boy," he acknowledged, "but it had also ended before [that]. It was just a mess. . . . Everybody was insular, developing their own worlds."

He questioned whether he would even again want a place in them.


## [2]


The Led Zeppelin apparatus, formerly a beast of a machine, ground to a halt. For the rest of 1977 and 1978 the band was effectively *dis*banded. "Robert phoned me," G recalled, "and I just said, 'Let me know the situation when you're ready.' He obviously needed a break."

More than that. He wanted to be left alone. Steve Weiss felt compelled to put a spy in the house of Plant. He called Benji Le Fevre and said, "You'd better get on a plane. Robert needs you."

Benji found a man grappling with anger and guilt. "Mostly, Robert was angry at himself," Le Fevre recalled. "Angry that he wasn't there for his family. Angry that he'd gone on tour when everything with the band—and especially Jimmy—was so fucked up. Angry at his comrades-in-arms, who seemed to have deserted him. Angry at the doctor who had tragically misinterpreted Karac's symptoms. Angry at life in general. He was full of self-recrimination. The whole nightmare that started in the Zeppelin machine had started to tip over and had become his own personal nightmare."

They spent many nights in the Queen's Head pub in nearby Wolverley, downing pint after pint of beer, rehashing the tour, Karac's death. It was all Benji could do to console Robert.

Bonzo and Pat came often. They understood Robert's pain, his Midlands psyche, and were able to put him at ease in their company. No matter how Robert had matured, no matter how worldly he'd become, he and Bonzo spoke the same language, inhabited the same skin. They'd known each other since they were sixteen. There was a lot of mileage on their friendship. Bonzo was a mensch in this time of need. "He was the only guy that actually hugged me, that helped me at all," Robert said.

But Bonzo had his own difficulties. In September 1977, while he was driving home from the Chequers pub in Cutnall Green in his Jensen Interceptor, speeding as usual, shitfaced as usual, his car spun off the road into a ditch and flung him sideways. He managed to disengage from the wreck and get himself home but discovered soon enough that he'd broken two ribs. His drinking continued to dominate him—and the drugs.

"After Karac died, the drugs were in force," says Sally Williams, Mick Hinton's girlfriend at the time. Hinton, Bonzo's factotum, was of little help when it came to cleaning up his act. "Mick was an alcoholic who spent everything he made in the pubs," Williams says. "He and John were two birds of a feather." Hinton was on call to Bonzo twenty-four hours a day. If Bonzo needed something from a store near his farm, something as trivial as a broom or a bar of soap—Mick would have to drive from London to Worcestershire—a two-and-a-half-hour trip—and pick it up for him. "Mick was always having to drive to Bonzo's to take him cocaine. But after the '77 tour, it was all about heroin."

Despite the drugs, Bonzo attempted to carry off a normal day-to-day existence, immersing himself in a family construction business, renovating old farmhouses near his home with a crew of friends. John Paul Jones chose a country-squire existence. "I had just got a farm in Sussex so I did a bit of farming and generally caught up with my family life," he said. The grind and all that came with it had caught up with Jonesy. He felt the need to step off the Led Zeppelin treadmill. "We needed some breathing space."

Jimmy was of a similar mind. Mostly he remained incommunicado, listening to material in the vault for an unrealized live album. He fended off rumors that the band was breaking up or that he'd replace Keith Richards in the Rolling Stones following Keith's arrest for heroin possession and trafficking in Canada. Apart from routine business matters, Jimmy felt little incentive to engage with his bandmates. He took Charlotte Martin and their daughter to Guadeloupe, as far off the beaten track as was humanly possible, in an effort to clean himself up.

"It means about two weeks without heroin, but with plenty of white rum," Jimmy told Richard Cole, who was invited to accompany them. Richard was in similar shape to Jimmy, nursing a habit that had all but devoured him. Going cold turkey was no easy proposition. Heroin, as a veteran user like Keith Richards knew, was "far more seductive than you think, because you can take it or leave it for a while, but every time you leave it, it gets a little harder." Richards turned to booze as a reliable antidote. In Guadeloupe, Jimmy and Richard went on a two-week bender, with little regard for Charlotte, who had her own drinking problem. They managed to get clean—but only until returning home to England, where access to heroin was plentiful and uncomplicated.

Richard spent his homecoming drinking at Horselunges with Peter Grant. For days on end, Grant had shut himself away in a bedroom, where he plotted strategy in his divorce case with Glo that would give him custody of the children, as well as the continuing legal fallout from the assault arrest in Oakland, California. To fortify himself, of course, G relied on cocaine. A cache of it was never far from reach.

"Peter was in bad shape at that time," recalls Bill Curbishley, who would later manage Robert Plant and Jimmy Page individually. "One of the consequences of cocaine addiction is that it creates fear—fear of running out of money." In the throes of this anxiety, G and Steve Weiss made a deal with Ahmet Ertegun to sell Led Zeppelin's record royalties and ownership of the masters to Atlantic and music publishing rights to Warner Chappell. "For their royalties," Curbishley says, "they got a twenty-five-year annuity—£25,000 each per annum—which by today's standards was a pittance." It also meant that, for twenty-five years—a time during which they sold more albums than the Beatles—Led Zeppelin's sales figures were unaccounted for to the band.

"Peter was nonfunctioning," says Shelley Kaye, who was administering Swan Song's New York office for Steve Weiss. "Communication dried up between Steve and Peter. It was impossible to get in touch with him. No key business decisions were being made, so there wasn't a way forward with anything. Steve worried about Led Zeppelin's future a lot. They owed records. Would they live up to their contractual commitments? No one knew."

No one was minding the shop at Swan Song, as usual. Alan Callan, like Abe Hoch before him, had no authority to do anything. Maggie Bell was at the top of his list, but Steve Weiss told him, "Alan, we just can't go there right now."

Maggie attempted to take things into her own hands. She went to Horselunges to discuss with Peter what to do next. "He was upstairs in his bed," she recalls. "I sat there for four hours waiting for him. Joan Hudson, his accountant, was also there; she'd been sitting on a couch, waiting all night to see him." Eventually, Maggie was ushered into the bedroom, where G was watching several movies simultaneously on a bank of overhead televisions. "He was not in good shape," she recalls. "Peter's PA asked me what I'd like for lunch. When the food arrived, Peter picked up one of the TV remote controls and bit into it, thinking it was a sandwich—and broke two of his front teeth. That's when I started thinking, 'I do not want to be involved in this anymore. I deserve better.'"

So did Dave Edmunds, who was struggling to restart his career. "Jake Riviera, Dave's manager, couldn't get anywhere with Peter," recalls Unity MacLean, who bore the brunt of Riviera's venom. "Jake was a vicious guy, but it was understandable. Dave was being completely ignored by Peter. It would get so exasperating you'd want to scream."

"*Get It*, Dave's album, wasn't an expensive record to make," Janine

Safer says, "but we went in there and fought for it." Ultimately, the powers that be decided Dave Edmunds wasn't a priority. The same went for the Pretty Things and Detective. *Silk Torpedo*, the Pretty Things' first Swan Song album, made a little money, but their follow-up, *Savage Eye*, flat-out bombed. And Detective was a total disaster. "Detective *sucked!*" Safer says. "They made a terrible record and they were a terrible band. They also had a big drug problem."

"That's true," Michael Des Barres agrees, "but we made a big, fat, bluesy, Faces-like album. We were rockin', tight, and had great songs. We just got no feedback at all from Swan Song. In the end, I couldn't get hold of Jimmy or Peter. There was nowhere to play, no promotion, nothing being done. The whole thing was so damn frustrating."

As long as Led Zeppelin remained vital, Atlantic considered the vanity label a necessary evil, even if it meant supporting its ancillary acts. Bad Company was an unexpected windfall—and something of a nightmare for Atlantic, which would have preferred to concentrate on its own roster of acts. A vanity label with *two* multiplatinum acts was a force to be reckoned with.

It was in everyone's interest to reunite Led Zeppelin. "I'll admit it," Phil Carson conceded, "nobody wanted to kill the golden goose." But Robert Plant was of no mind to participate. "My mojo for life, for music, for everything just vanished," he said.

Peter Grant entertained a scheme to draw Robert out of his lethargy that might have worked, had fate not intervened. G had heard through the grapevine that Elvis Presley was mulling the prospect of his first-ever European tour. Led Zeppelin's and Elvis's shows were both promoted by Concerts West, and G used this connection to arrange a meeting with Elvis's manager, Colonel Tom Parker. The idea was for Peter to produce the European gigs so that Elvis could be assured of access to painkillers—and knowing full well that Robert idolized Elvis. There was a chance Robert would have turned up to pay homage, maybe even reconnected with his mates, had Elvis not died suddenly on August 16, 1977, the victim of a drug overdose.

Benji Le Fevre felt strongly at the time that Robert might never perform with Led Zeppelin again. "It was such a shocking period," Benji recalls. "Robert still wasn't thirty, and he was questioning the relevance of the band in his life." Considering all that had transpired, there was no incentive to perpetuate the golden-god image, or "the god-head shit," as Robert now referred to it.

"I tried to pick myself up, and as I did so slowly, I realized my family was more important than the luxurious life I'd been living in Zeppelin," he acknowledged. "I'd already lost my boy, and then you think, I really have to decide what to do. I applied to become a teacher in the Rudolf Steiner education system. I was accepted to go to teacher training college. I was really quite keen to just walk.'" Music remained an essential part of his life, but relegated to a back burner. "I tinkered on the village piano and grew so obese drinking beer that nobody knew who I was."

Eventually, he tired of carrying so much extra weight and began training at Molineux, the Wolverhampton Wolves' football ground, running the stadium stairs to get his wind back. And on weekends, Robert and Benji played for the Queen's Head Football Club, Robert a winger with a bum ankle and Benji in goal. In an effort to "re-focus the whole deal," Robert also swore off drugs. "Addiction to powders was the worst way to see yourself," he said, "a waste of your time and everybody's time." It was a baby step toward reclaiming some normalcy. A larger step would require confronting the future of Led Zeppelin, which he was reluctant to do anytime soon.

The first time the band assembled under the same roof was for two days of business meetings at the Royal Garden Hotel in Kensington, beginning on March 14, 1978. In a room overlooking the park, Peter Grant, various lawyers, and the Swan Song accountants gathered to review outstanding issues relevant to the band's financial empire. When the suits cleared out, the discussion turned to Swan Song and upcoming sessions for Bad Company and Maggie Bell.

"What the fuck are you talking about?" G bellowed, interrupting. "You should worry about your own careers."

He'd been urging them to put their heads together and play some music, if only to gauge where things stood, to rediscover themselves, so to speak. G recommended a secluded rehearsal retreat at Clearwell Castle, in Gloucestershire, on the border with Wales. Bad Company had recently used it and gave it top-notch reviews. There was an opening in early May when they could move in for a while. Jimmy, Jonesy, and Bonzo were game, but Robert remained on the fence. "My joy of life had been cudgeled and bashed so hard," he said. Playing with Led Zeppelin, even informally, seemed unimportant, frivolous.

"Robert kept saying he'd do it and then back down," Grant recalled.

Benji tried talking to him about it but was told to mind his own business. "When it came to the band's affairs, there was still a strong divide—band/crew—and I would always be 'crew,'" he said. "The same went for staff. Even Abe Hoch and Alan Callan had no influence."

It was left to Bonzo to convince Robert. "He encouraged rather than coaxed me back," Robert said. "He was very gentle. I really didn't want to go back." Leaving his family seemed unwise, pointless. In the long run, he didn't know if it was worth it. Up until then, Robert revealed, he had been parading around his property with "a shotgun and a bottle of Johnnie Walker," warding off paparazzi. Bonzo "nuanced all the reasons why it was a good idea." There was a good deal of gin involved in the encouragement. "He said, 'Come on, we're all going down to Clearwell Castle to try and do some writing.'"

On May 2, 1978, Led Zeppelin finally plugged in, after nearly a year off from playing together. The castle, a Gothic revival structure located deep in the Forest of Dean, was better set up for rock 'n roll than anyone had realized. There was a state-of-the-art recording studio tucked into a corner of the tower basement where Deep Purple had laid down the tracks for *Burn* and Black Sabbath recorded *Sabbath*

*Bloody Sabbath*. Led Zeppelin had no such substantive agenda. In fact, no one involved really knew where to begin. Jimmy saw it as a chance to limber up, "a period of saying hello to each other musically." But what do you say after hello?

Jonesy was completely indifferent. "I didn't really feel comfortable," he said. "I remember asking, 'Why are we doing this?' We were not in good shape, mentally or health-wise." Nobody, he felt, was strong enough to say no to either Jimmy or Peter, both of whom sought to re-kindle the old flame.

Robert just wanted to jam. To ease him into a groove, they warmed up with a selection of comfortable rock 'n roll standbys that had filled Led Zeppelin's medleys onstage—Elvis, Jerry Lee, and Ricky Nelson were represented handsomely—before working on a new song, "Car-ouselambra," a typical conceptual Led Zeppelin epic that embroidered remnants of psychedelic, progressive, disco, and postpunk into a tap-estry of abstraction. Robert seemed to warm to his element, but at the end of the day, he couldn't cope with more. "I felt quite remote from the whole thing," he said. "I wasn't comfortable in the group at all. I didn't know if it was worth it anymore."

John Paul experienced a similar feeling. "It's not that we didn't have a laugh at Clearwell," he concluded, "it just wasn't going anywhere."

Months passed before there was any more movement in one direc-tion or another. In the meantime, Robert had begun turning up un-announced in public—to sing "Blue Suede Shoes" with a Worcestershire pub band at Wolverley Memorial Hall, and in August 1978 singing "Johnny B. Goode" at a club in Ibiza, where he was vacationing with Phil Carson. He even made a surprise guest appearance on Septem-ber 16, teaming with Dave Edmunds at Birmingham Town Hall for a rockabilly-inspired version of "My Baby Left Me."

Robert seemed reinvigorated, inclined to move forward. Express-ing a degree of optimism, he said, "I started to play again, and I real-ized that I still possessed something that really turned me on."

Proposing anything more concrete, however, was still a touchy subject. Robert's grief remained profound, his armor intact. The others gave him a wide berth. They feared that pressing him to return to work could have the opposite effect.

Finally, in October 1978, making a new album was broached. Jimmy had gotten an offer from Polar Studios in Stockholm, which belonged to the members of ABBA. They were trying to establish the new venture by luring a big established band with three free weeks of studio time and the services of a superb engineer, Leif Mases. *Three free weeks*—that was all penny-wise Jimmy needed to hear. Was Robert up to it? Were Jimmy and Bonzo, for that matter, both still burdened with serious drug issues? Did Led Zeppelin have anything left in the tank, anything to say as a band? Three years had passed since they'd recorded new material.

It seemed like now or never. It was time to take their best shot.

## [3]

Stockholm offered refuge, a good place to get away from it all. The city was enjoying an economic and cultural renaissance, with a youthful vibe that was easy to embrace. Sure, it was cold, colder perhaps than the band had bargained for, but Led Zeppelin's stay would be short and sweet. Jimmy was determined to wrap things up in the three-week allotment granted by the studio owners. Even then, the workweek was streamlined so that everyone could spend more time with their families. The band would arrive in Stockholm on Monday afternoons and return to their homes in the UK on Friday mornings. To accommodate the abbreviated schedule, three weeks of rehearsals were held at a studio in North London, going over material.

Unlike previous rehearsals, Jimmy came virtually empty-handed. There were no cassettes with slow-burning riffs fleshed out, no iconic solos in the making, nothing for Robert to pursue as a road map or to sink his teeth into. New song fragments came courtesy of John Paul Jones, of all people.

Jonesy had gotten his hands on a new toy, a Yamaha GX-1 synthesizer, nicknamed the Dream Machine, a prototype for the ubiquitous consumer synths that would become standard rock 'n roll gear for years to come. This one, however, was a beast of a contraption, a three-keyboard console with twenty-five pedals, weighing in at 660 pounds and a price tag of $60,000. Few GX-1s were in circulation as of 1978. ELP's Keith Emerson had one, and so did Stevie Wonder and Benny Andersson of ABBA. John Paul Jones was an obvious beta tester.

"The sound one could get out of the machine was at the time very inspiring," he said.

"John had it at home and had been working on it," Jimmy recalled, "and lo and behold he'd got these songs together." *Lo and behold*. Songwriting wasn't exactly up Jonesy's alley. He'd contributed in the past, but not in a way one would call world-beating, not even substantive. He wasn't the person you'd turn to for a barn burner or a potential hit. Nevertheless, Jimmy wasn't opposed to taking a back seat. He took Jonesy's enthusiasm in stride. "If he had numbers he'd written on this new state-of-the-art keyboard, let's do an album which focuses on the keyboards and feature it in the forefront."

Jonesy's "songs" at this early stage were more like loose instrumental arrangements that still depended heavily on input from his mates. But they sufficed as good templates for the work ahead in Sweden. "Carouselambra" was one such number that would benefit from Jimmy's and Bonzo's contributions. And Jonesy had bits and pieces of what became "South Bound Suarez," "In the Evening," and something called "The Hook," which served as the foundation for "All My Love."

Unfortunately, Led Zeppelin's welfare in Sweden was left in the addled hands of Richard Cole. Richard had always been a mean son of a bitch but he was devoted to the band and altogether dependable.

No one was better at wrangling musicians on the road or maintaining order when things got hairy. Now his heroin addiction warped his better judgment. In fact, one of his first tasks upon landing in Stockholm was to line up a drug dealer who lived directly across the street from Polar Studios, so that he and Jimmy had access to smack.

Peter Grant was indisposed—a euphemism for drug-addicted and paranoid—and had remained behind at Horselunges. He'd also suffered a mild heart attack earlier in the year, which gave him something else to worry excessively about. Doctors warned him to drastically reduce his weight, which had ballooned to twenty-eight stone (just shy of four hundred pounds), but they'd never mentioned anything about cocaine. According to Unity MacLean, with whom Grant stayed in touch, "He continued sending Dave Northover or Ray Washburn to get drugs for him."

Polar Studios was a gorgeous facility—a former cinema sporting a cutting-edge control room with five angled plate-glass dividers, each angle defining an isolation room, and a nifty thirty-two-track board. "It was sensational," Robert said, "and had just the amount of live sound we like." Benny Andersson and Björn Ulvaeus stopped by to welcome Led Zeppelin and to help them settle in, regretting there was no chance in the schedule for a Led Zeppelin–ABBA jam.

Beginning on November 7, 1978, it was down to business—or so the situation would seem. "For much of the time at those Polar sessions only Robert and I were turning up," Jonesy recalled. Jimmy and Bonzo were more or less indisposed.

"Robert, Jonesy, and I would go out and drink beer at lunchtime," says Benji Le Fevre, "because we'd show up at ten, when the session was supposed to start, and we'd still be waiting for the other two to get it together." In the afternoon, they sat around drinking Pimm's. Waiting . . . and waiting . . . and waiting. Vital time ticking away.

"We'd sit there with the instruments and nobody else would turn up," John Paul recalled.

Jonesy spent much of the downtime grappling with his GX-1.

"We'd very gingerly taken it to Stockholm and reassembled it," Benji recalls, "but it was so complicated that it had lost the raw sound, it wasn't tactile."

Jonesy was undeterred. "I wasn't going to sit around and just look at it," he said. And he wasn't about to stare at four walls, hoping Jimmy and Bonzo would make the scene. "The thing is, when that situation occurs, you either sit around waiting or get down to playing."

Teaming with Robert, who was in the same frame of mind, they began to work on their own. "Jonesy and I, who had never really gravitated toward each other at all, started to get on well," Robert acknowledged. When things grew dark and weird, they turned to each other. The band's straight men. "It was kind of odd, but it gave the whole thing a different feel."

He knew they weren't going to come up with anything that sounded like "Communication Breakdown" or "Rock and Roll," but there were songs that allowed them to explore new territory, melodies that updated Led Zeppelin's sound out from under the riff-laden thunderstorms. The inspired piano figure that announced "Fool in the Rain" only hinted at what would follow, with the bridge overtaking the meter by shifting into a different rhythm. They worked a feverish samba groove into the middle, leaving plenty of room for Bonzo to lay in sharp, precise—disruptive—jabs against the beat. Everything about the track showed how willing they were to be inventive, to torpedo expectations. The same with "South Bound Suarez," which opened with another red-hot piano flourish that burst into a blues-based riff with just the right amount of bite.

They also transformed "The Hook" with yawning synth patterns into "All My Love," a plaintive supplication that darkened into an expression of heartache, and laid down the bones to "I'm Gonna Crawl," a sultry, soul-stirring ballad that veered further from the Led Zeppelin signature than almost anything they'd ever recorded.

When Jimmy and Bonzo finally showed—in the middle of the

night, after Richard had scored drugs for them—a fair amount of work had already been done. "I would have preferred having some input at that point," Jimmy allowed, but he dutifully added guitar parts to the Jones-Plant arrangements. "All My Love" was a different story. It oozed sentimentality. Robert had written the lyric "on the spot," and to most ears it was gut-wrenching, an obvious paean to his departed son.

"I was a little worried about the chorus," Jimmy said, especially since they had sworn off such devices in the past. "I could just imagine people doing the wave and all of that. And I thought, 'That's not us.'"

Still, Jimmy took the work tapes back to England with him each weekend and performed hocus-pocus on them in his Plumpton home studio. "When the stuff came back after the weekend, you wouldn't even recognize it," Richard noted.

The most obvious surgery had been performed on "In the Evening," which began life as one of John Paul's conceptual pieces, now converted into the sole genuine rocker from the session. At first, it seemed as though Jimmy would play along with the Jones-Plant approach. The song opened with almost a minute of technical horseplay—a spooky electronic confection that had less to do with instrumentation than with the turning of knobs and switches. Jimmy saw the GX-1 and raised the ante with a gizmo he'd borrowed from the brain trust behind 10cc called a Gizmotron. He described it as "a hurdy-gurdy type of thing," a motor-driven apparatus that effectively bowed the strings of his guitar, much as he did physically on "Dazed and Confused," producing a weblike chorus of wheezes and whines. Just when it seemed like a Vincent Price voice-over might chime in, the rhythm section erupted with a Bad Company–type three-chord riff that drove the song with a ferocious attack. The beat was daring and direct, relentless. A supercharged rock number was what Jimmy had in mind when he feared Led Zeppelin was getting "a little soft."

The framework of an album was beginning to take shape. When Jimmy and Bonzo had it together, the music they summoned up enthralled. They were the hairline crack in the bowl. Led Zeppelin was a four-man band, each integral to the full equation. But it was a drama of personalities as well as sound. Bonzo, especially, needed to be on his game. There were times through these sessions when he played brilliantly—and times when he phoned it in.

During the best take they made of "Carouselambra," Bonzo was locked in. *Locked. In.* He was flawless. The drums took a beating. In the middle of the number, the fire alarm went off. The band had been warned this might happen. The system was new, faulty, unpredictable. About a minute later, a troop of firemen burst through the studio door. Bonzo looked up, shouted, *"Fuck off!"* and didn't miss a beat.

Good times . . . bad times. There were so many factors weighing on the outcome. It was no longer just about music. Life had intruded. Life and death and too much in between. Jimmy and Bonzo, once superlative craftsmen, were dancing with demons that sapped their skills. Robert, who had always been high-spirited and ebullient, was burdened by sadness. John Paul, never all that simpatico, felt even more alienated, discouraged by the dysfunction of his mates—"people who could turn up at recording sessions on time and people who couldn't," as he put it. "We were beginning, I suppose, to think, 'Well, wait a minute, it may be coming apart more than it should.'"

Robert seconded Jonesy's train of thought. "It was the four of us," he said in retrospect, "but I don't think it was as Led Zeppelin as it might have been for myriad different reasons."

Jimmy was less concerned about the band's disposition. Yes, *Presence* had been a guitar-heavy album, while this newest effort was more keyboard oriented. So be it. "It was a summing up of where we were at that moment in time," he said.

Be that as it may, all of the differences found their way into the music. Instead of using dueling perspectives to fuel a creative tension, the band allowed tentativeness, indecisiveness to creep in. When all was said and done, they'd made a record, a new Led Zeppelin album, and put a bow on it in a fleet three-week marathon session. Jonesy considered it "a transition period . . . a chance to see what else we could do." But underneath the web of synth embellishments and tremors from the Gizmotron, the magic was gone. The riffs were stagnant, the arrangements spiritless. The band had lost its groove.

Whether or not they admitted it publicly, Led Zeppelin knew they'd hit a wall. It was time "to cut the waffle out," as John Paul said, "take note of what's going on, and reinvent ourselves." Nothing invigorated the band like the sound of a half-crazed audience.

"We are what we are when we walk onto the stage and play," Robert agreed.

They needed a stage, a spotlight, and an enormous crowd.

## Chapter Twenty-one

# SWAN SONG

## [1]

Peter Grant was one step ahead of them. From his heavily fortified bunker upstairs at Horselunges, he'd been plotting ways to put Led Zeppelin back into the spotlight and reclaim their rightful glory. A new album would set the table for the band's return; gigs would reassure the fans that no other act was more exciting or deserved to wear the crown. G knew exactly how to play it: a few warm-up dates in an off-the-beaten-track locale, followed by a long tour of U.S. arenas. They'd make a fortune and push into the 1980s with a new head of steam.

That was his plan until Robert Plant got wind of it. There was no way Robert intended to go back to America. Not now, anyway. It held too many memories that touched raw nerves. He couldn't face them, couldn't deal with the pain. And he wanted to stay close to his family. In January 1979, Maureen had given birth to another child, a son they named Logan. Robert resolved to be present for his kids, not traipsing around the United States out of reach, an absentee father.

G knew better than to press him. "I said, 'Fuck doing a tour,'" he recalled. Led Zeppelin could work in England for a change. They hadn't played there in four years. It was time, overdue. "We're the biggest band in the world so we better get out there and show them we still are."

But where? And how? There weren't many purpose-built auditoriums in the UK. And they'd already played the country's largest indoor facility—Earls Court in 1975, the last time they appeared on a hometown stage. "We could have gone back to the Queen's Head pub," Robert said. "We talked about doing something like that." But Jimmy was adamantly opposed to playing small local halls after the disastrous club tour in 1971.

Peter had it figured out. "Knebworth was the gig," he said.

*Knebworth*. To British rock 'n roll fans it was the equivalent of Woodstock, a day-long, open-air rock show in a natural amphitheater that drew audiences in the hundreds of thousands. Led Zeppelin had been asked to headline the first Knebworth extravaganza in 1974 for the unheard-of sum of £225,000 but turned down the invitation. In the meantime, the Allman Brothers, Van Morrison, Pink Floyd, Frank Zappa, the Rolling Stones, Genesis, Lynyrd Skynyrd, and Tom Petty had appeared.

"Knebworth was the gig, and I reckon we could do two dates."

Traditionally, the festival took place on the first and second weekends in August. It would be an ideal way to give the new Led Zeppelin album a second wind. Tentatively titled *Look*, it was slated for release in late February 1979. Sometime after the first of the year, Peter summoned the Hipgnosis team, Po and Storm Thorgerson, to Horselunges for a meeting with Jimmy to spitball ideas for a cover.

"I'd like to go back to the roots in a bluesier way—an acknowledgment of where we were, rather than going outward," Jimmy explained. He told them about a funky old bar he'd seen while on his vacation in Guadeloupe that might provide an excellent backdrop for the cover.

Rather than studying his pictures of it, the band handled the decision in typical Led Zeppelin fashion—by bankrolling a trip to Guadeloupe for Po. "I found the bar," he recalls, "but it wasn't any great shakes aesthetically." Instead, he detoured to New Orleans and spent five days photographing every honky-tonk on Bourbon Street. His idea was to take the best from each to create a fantasy bar and build it from scratch on a movie soundstage. Storm Thorgerson went him one better: he proposed photographing it in the style of a movie—the different views of six people in the bar of each other.

"It's going to be six album covers," Po explained to G and Jimmy. "So if you buy one, you need to get the other five." They *loved* that aspect. Of course, it meant a lengthy development process, which would delay the release of the album. Yet again.

The bar set was built on a soundstage at Shepperton Studios. "It cost an absolute fortune," Po makes clear, "maybe $40,000 by today's standards." The six different scenes were photographed in black-and-white—each depicting a man in a white suit sitting at a bar taken from a different perspective, and each bearing a brushstroke superimposed over the image. "It was like you were looking inside the bar through a dusty window," Thorgerson said, "and the smear was where you'd wiped the pane with your sleeve to peer through." Po took a chemical-reaction detail from children's coloring books, so that the brush-stroke would turn to color when splashed with water, although that wasn't explained to album buyers; you had to discover it by accident.

When all was said and done, he took a mock-up of the cover to Horselunges in order to secure Peter's approval to manufacture it. G and [Bad Company's manager] Clive Coulson were passing a bottle back and forth, drinking absinthe, which Po declined. "Suddenly, they just nodded out," he says. "I sat there for twenty minutes, paranoid as hell. Cigarettes were burning down that I had to take out of their fingers. I thought, 'Fuck, they've both died.' I was just getting ready to call for emergency medics when their eyes snapped open. 'All right, now. Where were we? Carry on!'"

Approval was given to produce the album cover, now retitled *In Through the Out Door*, but not without a gentle reprimand. "Your fucking album cover was so fucking expensive," Peter grumbled. "Seriously, I could sell Led Zeppelin in a brown paper bag."

"What a good idea!" Po replied. "Let's put it in a brown paper bag, a grocer's bag." That way, anyone buying the album wouldn't know which cover they were getting. It was the crowning touch.

Of course, each additional detail delayed the album's release by weeks, then months. It became clear during the spring of 1979 that the date would have to be pushed back further, perhaps to summer, hopefully before Led Zeppelin's appearance at Knebworth. But there were no guarantees.

In the meantime, Peter continued to dicker with Freddy Bannister, the promoter of the two Bath Festivals in Led Zeppelin's past and now the ringmaster of the Knebworth events. G was demanding £1 million for the two performances. Recouping the fee would necessitate selling out both weekend shows, roughly 300,000 people. The Stones held the record with 100,000 ticket sales in 1976, but G argued that Knebworth would be Led Zeppelin's first UK appearance since 1975 and their first appearance anywhere in two years. That alone guaranteed a record-breaking event. Bannister balked but negotiated an agreement that would automatically trigger the second show and, hence, the entire £1 million fee, if the first weekend generated 145,000 ticket sales. No contract was required by Peter Grant. They sealed the deal with his usual handshake.

They also discussed supporting acts. Jimmy had a wishlist. *Melody Maker* quoted him as saying, "The lineup we had hoped for was Fairport, Dire Straits, Little Feat, and Joni Mitchell." Grant threw a few other names into the mix, including Bob Seger, Aerosmith, and Van Morrison. It seems odd that he didn't give preference to Bad Company, the Pretty Things, Maggie Bell, or Dave Edmunds. Nor was consideration given to the fact that England was in the grip of the punk and new-wave movements. The music scene had undergone an enormous shift since Led Zeppelin last appeared on a stage, with a new generation convinced that pre-1977 bands were old hat—and worse. It might have made good business sense to extend an invitation to the Clash, the Sex Pistols, Elvis Costello & the Attractions, Ian Dury, or the Jam. No one thought to acknowledge the new direction rock 'n roll was taking. *New Musical Express*, a torchbearer for everything new, took them to task for the oversight, adding, "The manner in which old superfart Led Zeppelin have consistently presented themselves has made the band's name synonymous with gratuitous excess." When it came to the bigger picture, they were out of touch.

And self-indulgent. In June 1979, two months before Knebworth, Led Zeppelin visited the site for a photo session that would appear on the cover of the festival's official program. It was a beautiful setting— thirty-six acres of verdant English landscape that fed into a bowl where the stage would sit. Knebworth House, one of England's venerable stately homes, shimmered in the distance. It was easy to envision a sea of young bodies grooving to music under a canopy of stars. Hipgnosis prepared for the shoot by hiring two voluptuous strippers to flank the photographer in the expectation that their presence would relax the band and ensure smiles all around. Jimmy promptly unzipped his fly; not to be shown up, Robert slipped his pants down around his ankles, exposing himself.

In the end, no one was satisfied with the outcome. "Jimmy was moaning about his hair because Richard had driven him up in his Austin-Healy with the top open," Peter recalled. "Then Bonzo complained the pictures captured his love handles, and they had to be airbrushed out. And the sky was too dull, and we had to overlay a sky scene from a shot of Texas to give it some color."

Nothing seemed to be working out to everyone's satisfaction. One by one, the leading supporting acts sent their regrets. Bob Seger, Little Feat, Roxy Music, B.B. King, and Van Morrison all said no. Ed Bicknell, who managed Dire Straits, held his band back, telling them they weren't ready to play such a gig, but in truth he didn't want them sharing a stage with Led Zeppelin. "No one," according to Freddy

Banister, the promoter, "wanted to play with Led Zeppelin." As a result, Bannister was forced to settle for a bill of "middle-weights," as *NME* described them: the Marshall Tucker Band, Southside Johnny and the Asbury Jukes, Todd Rundgren's Utopia, and a British pub sing-along duo known as Chas and Dave. Fairport Convention, a group that had just been dropped by its record label and were on the brink of disbanding, agreed to step in at the last minute.

The arrangements seemed feeble, disorganized. "Robert didn't want to do Knebworth, and I could understand why," said John Paul. "But we really *did* want to do it, and we thought he'd enjoy it if he did—if we could just get him back out there."

The rest of the band viewed the gig as a fitting venue at which to make a spectacular comeback, and they weren't leaving anything to chance. If all went according to plan, it would be the largest audience they'd ever played to, with a new album sitting in stores. They intended to rehearse, really rehearse, to shake off the cobwebs: two weeks at Bray Film Studios, next door to Jimmy's house in Windsor, and a few warm-up gigs in Copenhagen.

The Bray rehearsals were like all Led Zeppelin run-throughs, a loose sprint through their old standbys, followed by demanding work on new numbers from the Stockholm sessions that included "In the Evening," "Carouselambra," "Hot Dog," and "Wearing and Tearing," the latter left off *In Through the Out Door* but under consideration for release as a commemorative Knebworth single.

"I was worried whether we could still gel together," Jimmy admitted. "Having felt something special towards this band for so long, I still wanted that to be there." The rehearsal provided him with "a very good feeling." It reassured him there was plenty left in the tank.

The tune-up in Denmark in late July would serve to tighten the screws. Richard Cole flew ahead to Copenhagen, saddled with "money for drugs," he explained, "because Jimmy and Bonzo and I needed the fucking gear." He arranged for a dealer to occupy the hotel room next to his to ensure easy access, laying out this detail in a meeting called by Robert when the band arrived. Jimmy feigned ignorance, lamely denying his dependence on heroin, until Bonzo interrupted. "Don't be so fucking stupid," he said. "If there's no gear, there's no show!"

The first gig, at the Falkoner Theatre on July 23, 1979, was only sparsely attended. The show started two hours late, a delay attributed to production problems. Jimmy had concocted a special laser effect to cast him in a glittery green pyramid during solos with the bow, but the apparatus was too big and powerful for the venue. So was the PA system; during a sound check, the generator kept blowing. Once Led Zeppelin took to the stage, they went through an elaborate tuning process that eventually morphed into "The Song Remains the Same." The band was rusty—and it showed.

"For those of us who'd seen the band at their peak, they were more than just rusty," said journalist Lisa Robinson, whom Swan Song treated to a round-trip ticket on the Concorde to see the performance. "The wit and the wonder weren't really there."

"They appeared sloppy and under-rehearsed, bewildered, and lost," a reporter from *NME* observed. The solos were perfunctory, endless, the sound muddy. "There was so little feeling inherent in the set, it was like watching a fully-automated factory producing an endless string of chords that neither musicians nor audience cared about."

Just in case fans got the wrong idea, *Melody Maker* sent a representative to gin up support for Led Zeppelin, filing a predictably gushy review to shill for Knebworth.

The second show—coincidentally, two years to the day since their last appearance, in Oakland—was somewhat better. "No Quarter" electrified the crowd, and new material like "In the Evening" struck a powerful chord. "Perhaps by Knebworth," sensed a reporter from *Sounds*, "it'll be more than 'okay.'"

The groundwork for Knebworth wasn't any less rocky. The Marshall Tucker Band dropped out a few days before the concert, replaced at the last minute by the Commander Cody Band (the Airmen were long gone). And ticket sales weren't as robust as anticipated. Only

115,000 of the 150,000 advance orders were filled. Bannister suggested canceling the second show, but Grant flat-out refused. "This is the biggest fucking band in the world, and we can do two dates," he insisted. If sales didn't pick up, he'd renegotiate Led Zeppelin's fee, but Freddy would have to take his word for it.

The most discouraging news, however, was that the album, *In Through the Out Door*, would not be ready until sometime after the festival. There were so many elements involved in printing the cover; the process was a manufacturing nightmare. "We had a huge problem with the brown paper bags," recalls Nick Maria, a salesman for WEA, Swan Song's distribution company. "With the test pressings, the bags kept ripping, which drove our accounts nuts. The album wasn't going to be shrink-wrapped, either, so retailers weren't happy." In any event, the album's release was being pushed back. Again. An enormous setback.

Peter wasn't in any shape to handle the recurring problems. The cocaine had taken a serious toll on him. He wasn't thinking as sharply as the Peter Grant of old, who would have been on top of each situation. Jack Calmes, the Showco chief in charge of light and sound, and Freddy Bannister recalled a discussion they had with G at Horselunges in preparation for Knebworth. "Peter kept himself going with long lines of cocaine," Bannister said. Calmes had a similar recollection. "We'd sit there and talk for a while, and then he'd drift off and disappear. Then he finally just drifted off, and I took the car back [to London] the next morning."

Had Peter been in good health, a different spirit might have prevailed. Knebworth was problematic; it needed a good shot of his expertise, his presence of mind, his infectious enthusiasm, his relentless drive. Knebworth was a homecoming as far as Led Zeppelin was concerned. It was an event to celebrate with friends and family, but the run-up to it wasn't a smooth operation.

At two o'clock in the morning the night before the festival, Unity MacLean, Swan Song's artists manager, was awakened by a call from

Patricia Page, Jimmy's mother. It was obvious she'd had a couple drinks and wanted to lodge a complaint: she hadn't received tickets to Knebworth. "She'd called Jimmy two or three times and he was vague about getting them for her," MacLean recalled. "I promised her that I'd sort it out."

An hour later, going on 3:00 a.m., Jimmy was on the phone. "My mother's not to have tickets for Knebworth," he said. When Unity pressed him, he became peevish. "You're not to speak to her. Mind your own business."

At ten minutes past three, Unity's phone rang again. "Jimmy just told me what you did," Peter roared. "You're fucking fired. You're fired! *You're fired!*"

Unbeknownst to MacLean, she'd waded into a Page family feud. "My parents had split up and they both had different families," Jimmy explained. In fact, it was a twitchy divorce, loaded with animosity and recriminations—and only his father had a different family.

Later, after tempers cooled down, Jimmy took Unity MacLean aside and said, "My mum and dad can't be within two hundred feet of each other. I didn't want them upstaging the band at Knebworth, each ranting and raving at the other." To establish détente, he gave his father tickets for the first weekend and entertained his mother on weekend two.

Situations like that were the easy fixes. For Led Zeppelin, the heavy lifting lay ahead. So much was riding on their performance. They had a legend to preserve. The British music press was full of insulting stories predicting the band's imminent demise, saying they were anachronisms, "a behemoth . . . almost a museum piece"—too old, too smug, too passé. Led Zeppelin was out to prove them wrong, to show what they were made of—to take back the mantle as the most exciting band in the world. As Robert Plant was quick to point out, "People may think we're conventional now, but we are still a law unto ourselves."

## [2]

Even laws unto themselves were occasionally gobsmacked. When the band arrived at Knebworth on August 4, they were stunned by the reception.

"We had to come in by helicopter," Jimmy recalled, "and you could see this huge sea of people. It was astonishing."

Observers disagreed about the size of the crowd, but it was enormous, there was no debating that. Robert ventured out onto the grounds in a Jeep and was awestruck by the vibe. The fans were not to be denied. *They* were a law unto themselves. "People pushed the stone pillars down with the metal gates attached, because they wanted to get in early," he observed. "Those gates had been there since 1732, and they just pushed them over. It was a phenomenally powerful [sight]." Somehow, Robert had never witnessed firsthand that aspect of the Led Zeppelin phenomenon, the lawlessness and destruction that followed the band from Boston to Detroit, Tampa, Miami, St. Louis, Pittsburgh, Dallas, Chicago, Philadelphia, Greensboro . . . wherever they'd performed.

Another type of vibe was transpiring backstage. Knebworth was a homecoming, a family reunion. Wives, girlfriends, children, and assorted relatives crammed into the VIP area, where a trailer was parked to accommodate the joyful tribe. Mixed in among them were fellow musicians who had come to pay their respects—Mick Ralphs and Boz Burrell represented Bad Company, Chris Squire from Yes, drummer Cozy Powell, the Pretenders' Chrissie Hynde. And lurking in the shadows like pledges to a fraternity party were Mick Jones and Topper Headon from the Clash, the Sex Pistols' Steve Jones and Paul Cook, and Steve Nieve from the Attractions. Even J. J. Jackson, the American deejay who'd emceed one of the famous Led Zeppelin debuts at the Boston Tea Party in 1969, turned up. There was a general feeling that this was a show not to be missed, that it should be savored for posterity.

Just to prove they hadn't lost their mojo, Led Zeppelin went on late. It had been a long and grueling lead-up to the headliner spot on the bill. On a blistering-hot day, the crowd sat attentively, melting under the Hertfordshire sun as the show dragged on and on. The supporting acts, while not transformative, performed respectable, if unexceptional, sets. Led Zeppelin's appearance turned the festival into an occasion. The reception they received from the crowd was beyond jubilant.

"I was wracked with nerves," Robert admitted. "It was our first British gig in four years." The tension was evident in the music. The first three numbers—"The Song Remains the Same," "Black Dog," and "Nobody's Fault But Mine"—sounded perfunctory, awkward. According to Jonesy, whose bass had been mistakenly turned off throughout the medley, "the sound was initially ropey." Robert had trouble controlling his voice and sang using harmonizer effects, which "changed the vocal delivery too much," producing high-pitched squeals.

"We played too fast and we played too slow," Robert said, "and it was like trying to land a plane with one engine."

On the whole, the performance was solid but uneven. Over the course of three and a half hours, Led Zeppelin showcased moments of single-minded brilliance—and undisciplined excess. "Some of it was breathtaking, some woefully inept." The critic for NME, a paper whose allegiance had shifted to punk and new wave, gave them credit where credit was due. "At times, they were playing rock 'n roll of such stinging insistence and convulsive perseverance," he wrote, "it wouldn't have mattered how old or processed it was."

The classic haymakers—"Achilles Last Stand," "Trampled Under Foot," "Kashmir," "Rock and Roll," "Whole Lotta Love," and "Heartbreaker" were exhilarating, full of ruthless power. "Stairway," naturally, brought down the house. But there were stretches of torpor, where the momentum ground to a halt and self-indulgence took over.

Jimmy's solos, from the *Sounds* critic's point of view, "were ill-conceived wanderings and, what's more, very poorly executed." There were times he galloped ahead of his rhythm section, other times his fingers couldn't keep up. Bonzo didn't swing so much as thrash. And John Paul's rambling, pseudo-artsy introduction to "No Quarter" continued to stymie forward thrust.

Oddly, no consideration was given to the sea change occurring in British music, not even recognition that audiences' attention spans had grown shorter. "In the era of the Jam and Stranglers," wrote journalist David Hepworth, "this looked almost like historical reenactment."

For all the highs and lows, the reviews were mostly upbeat. Only *Rolling Stone* complained that "the group sounded woefully complacent and anachronistic, even obsolete." *Sounds*, whose reporter had been ostracized by Led Zeppelin, said, "I quite like them. . . . They gave value for money" and "honored memories of their great days," owing to the rich cross section of material in the set. *Melody Maker*, of course, couldn't contain its rapture, proclaiming Jimmy's solos "absolutely outstanding," on par with Jonesy's piano piece. Praising and nitpicking aside, *NME* hit the nail on the head, saying, "Jimmy Page, Robert Plant, John Paul Jones, and John Bonham enjoyed themselves and showed it."

Jimmy was ecstatic. "It was fantastic," he concluded. Robert, however, was full of mixed feelings. In retrospect, he considered it "a shit gig." He was hard on himself—"I wasn't as relaxed as I could have been"—and hard on the band. "There was so much expectation there," he said, "the least we could have done was to have been confident enough to kill." He wasn't sure what the outcome really meant over the long term. The band, he felt, "had been on its knees" before Knebworth. "After it was over, I don't know if I was breathing a sigh of relief because we'd got to the end of the show in one piece—or whether we'd actually bought some more time to keep going."

Peter Grant was certain of one thing: the turnout at Knebworth had been better than he'd expected, guaranteeing the second week's performance. On August 7, a few days after the concert, he sent his accountant, Joan Hudson, to collect the balance of Led Zeppelin's fee—in cash. Freddy Bannister said he didn't have it. The official attendance record for the August 4 show was 104,000, with barely 40,000 advance sales for the following weekend. That didn't wash with Peter's numbers. He insisted that 250,000 had showed up and expected the band to be paid on that figure.

Unbeknownst to Bannister, Neal Preston, Led Zeppelin's pet photographer, had been sent up in a helicopter to shoot images of the crowd. G claimed he'd sent Preston's negatives to NASA, in the States, for analysis and that the space agency had confirmed his estimates.

Bannister and his wife, Wendy, arranged to meet with Peter at Horselunges to discuss their differences of opinion. G wouldn't share the data from NASA, nor would he budge off his attendance claim, even though Bannister insisted that the site couldn't handle that many people. Eventually, Peter lost his temper, "jumped up, and began waving his fist in [Wendy Bannister's] face, yelling, 'Don't get smart with me,'" causing the Bannisters to flee.

The next morning, a shady, hollow-eyed character named Herb Atkin arrived unannounced at Bannister's office with a plug of a retired London cop in tow. The promoter knew from appearances they were there to intimidate. John Bindon wasn't available to do G's dirty work. While Led Zeppelin had been in Stockholm recording *In Through the Out Door,* Bindon had gotten into a knife fight at Fulham's Ranelagh Yacht Club and killed his adversary. In the fracas, Bindon was also stabbed in the back and chest, and he had fled the country with Peter Grant's assistance. Herb Atkin was a more sinister version of Bindon, furtive, insidious. He purported to be an ex-CIA operative with strong mob connections in Miami and Chicago. In fact, *The New York Times,* in a 1969 article, had unmasked him as Herbert Itkin, a flamboyant FBI informer involved in the takedown of New York City political boss Carmine DeSapio and the arrest of mob figures and corrupt union officials. Itkin resurfaced from a witness protection program as Herb Atkin and fell in league with Steve Weiss. For over a year, they had been preying on Peter Grant's cocaine paranoia with trumped-up stories about plots to kidnap G's children and Led Zeppelin's giving him the heave-ho as manager. Atkin also warned that a group of villains was plotting to rob the box office during the second weekend of Knebworth, which precipitated hiding loaded sawed-off shotguns in the bags of cash.

Atkin did his number on Bannister, who was frightened out of his skull. The next day, Peter and several heavies paid a late-night visit to Bannister's home and left with £300,000 in cash. G still claimed his band was owed more money and announced that he was taking control of the box office for the second show. He hired cashiers who reported only to him, put them in charge of £30,000 worth of tickets, and stationed his own security team at the festival gates. Bannister had more or less thrown in the towel. "If they want the tickets, they can have the fucking tickets," he told his assistant.

G wasn't done putting his stamp on the event. When Fairport Convention dropped off the second weekend's bill, he insisted Bannister book the New Barbarians, a ragged, poorly rehearsed jam band that Keith Richards and Ronnie Wood had cobbled together. They turned up in Knebworth with a bass player borrowed from Rod Stewart's band at the last minute and a replacement drummer. It was a rather cynical attempt to cash in by the Barbarians, and cash was very much on their minds. Peter Grant advised them not to go on until they'd been paid in full by Freddy Bannister, so the aptly named Barbarians held up the show for two hours, until Richard Cole delivered £18,000 in small bills and sat in the band's trailer, counting it into Woody's hand.

Money wasn't a substantial problem. Throughout the evening, bags were being stuffed full of cash—from ticket receipts and sales of T-shirts, caps, programs, and posters—for easy transport off the site. "Peter and Zeppelin had two hundred grand each in bags," Richard recalled, "thrown into the back of their cars."

Meanwhile, after the two-hour delay, Keith Richards still refused to come out of the Barbarians' trailer. "He was in pretty bad shape," says Maggie Bell, who was a guest of Peter Grant's. She overheard G tell Cole, "Get him out of that fucking caravan, or I'm going to go over there and move him *in* the caravan." When that didn't produce the desired result, G rocked the trailer until the Barbarians tumbled out and headed to the stage.

In the big picture, the music that night was almost incidental. The band played well, more confident and tighter than the previous weekend. But it sounded mechanical, unconvincing. "It wasn't horrendous," Jimmy conceded in a dubious postmortem. And the crowd that turned out—no more than forty thousand people, tops—came away convinced they'd heard some badass rock 'n roll. But the handwriting was on the wall. Led Zeppelin's drawing power wasn't what it had been. Knebworth had been less of a comeback than a comedown to earth. The layoff had come at a heavy price. In the interim, music had moved on, gotten younger, more biting, less slick, while Led Zeppelin played pretty much the same set they'd performed at Earls Court four years earlier. It was unfashionable, nostalgia.

Drugs and money had corrupted the organization. Peter Grant had lost his singular charm, as well as his focus. Once the savviest of managers, his tactics had taken on the nature of a criminal enterprise—lawyers, guns, and money, as the maestro sang. Jimmy and Bonzo were pale vestiges of themselves, their immense talents plundered by substance abuse. Robert and Jonesy seemed adrift. Even Richard Cole, who'd always kept the trains running, was little more than an unhinged lackey. Ricardo was in serious shape. His marriage had fallen apart, he'd lost his enthusiasm for work. His interests, he said, were "caught up in a world where drugs were the most important thing in my life."

It was a sorry situation. Ten years on the road seemed to have taught them little, certainly not how to deal with success or to survive, not even how to get along. Was it the end of the line for Led Zeppelin? Were they now a reflection in rock 'n roll's rearview mirror? As musicians, as performers, the band felt rejuvenated after Knebworth but desperately in need of direction. With a new album set for release, with the guaranteed airplay and reviews, they seemed determined to play off the momentum and kick the old chassis back into gear.

## [3]

But the gears ground slowly.

*In Through the Out Door*—released in its brown paper bag on August 22, 1979, a long week after Knebworth—was a commercial success but a critical disappointment. Competition was fierce, with press attention more fixed on the Clash's *London Calling*, *Reggatta de Blanc* by the Police, Michael Jackson's breakout *Off the Wall*, Joy Division's *Unknown Pleasures*, the Talking Heads' *Fear of Music*, Joe Jackson's *Look Sharp!*, and *The Wall* by Pink Floyd. Led Zeppelin had waded into a crowded field. Only *Record Mirror*, a minor-league voice among the music press, called the album a "grand reunion." *Rolling Stone* bemoaned the lack of memorable songs and said, "With Page's creativity apparently failing and no one able to compensate—even Led Zeppelin is not Led Zeppelin." The *Sounds* critic, who was forced to buy his own review copy as a result of a silly Led Zeppelin vendetta against the magazine, delivered a crushing critique. "I'm sad, disillusioned, downhearted," he wrote. "It's the end of an era. The dinosaur is finally extinct."

The most unexpected and cutting judgment, however, came from *Melody Maker*, which sharpened knives for the occasion. Rather than the review being handed off to faithful Chris Welch, as was the standard drill, it was left to Chris Bohn, a younger postpunk enthusiast, who wasn't hewing to the paper's party line. "The performances are generally dull," he concluded, not pulling any punches. "Zeppelin are totally out of touch. . . . It's time they accepted their fate like men. They squeezed their lemons dry long ago."

Knocks like that hurt, but Led Zeppelin licked their wounds by limiting reading to Atlantic's sales figures. The album racked up the same stellar numbers as their previous efforts and rose straight to the top of the charts on every continent. By the end of September, Atlantic had shipped three million copies. It also spurred sales of their entire back catalog, with all eight of their previous albums elbowing onto *Billboard*'s "Top Albums" chart the week of October 27, an unprecedented coup. They also took heart from *Melody Maker*'s annual Readers Poll Awards. Considering the paper's review of *In Through the Out Door* and the band's general malaise, Led Zeppelin wasn't expecting much in the way of a response. In fact they were named Best Live Act, Band of the Year, Best Album, Best Guitarist, Best Composer, Best Producer, and Best Male Vocalist—seven out of the twenty awards.

The unexpected sweep prompted Jonesy, Robert, and Bonzo to show up to acknowledge the honors at a gala hosted by *Melody Maker* on November 28, 1979, at the Waldorf in London. Bonzo and John Paul arrived in a chauffeur-driven Rolls-Royce, confirmation to the new-wave upstarts, perhaps, that Led Zeppelin lived in their own bubble. Jimmy was conspicuously absent. Excuses were made that he was vacationing in Barbados, when in fact he was appearing in front of a magistrate at an inquest in Sussex.

On October 24, in the wake of a party at Jimmy's Plumpton house, a twenty-four-year-old photographer named Philip Churchill Hale had collapsed and died. "It was the usual thing—drugs and drinking," says Unity MacLean, who got a heads-up at the Swan Song office. Don Murfet, head of Peter's security detail, was dispatched to "clean up" the scene—in other words, get rid of any drugs and make sure there was no evidence implicating Jimmy. "I arrived at the same time as the police," Murfet recalled, so all he could do was to contain the damage to the guest room, where the body was found.

Jimmy managed to clear himself at the inquest, the final verdict ruling it an "accidental death" despite the autopsy revealing lethal doses of alcohol and cocaine, but as soon as it was over, he moved out of Plumpton and put the house on the market, replacing it with a retreat in Windsor he bought from Michael Caine.

The best way to stay out of trouble was to play music. The band agreed. It was time to get out in front of an audience again, if not simply to promote the new album, then to generate excitement in the manner they knew best. "It was a way of getting back to the people," said John Paul. Led Zeppelin was a working band, first and foremost. Even Robert, "in a difficult frame of mind," according to Grant, was on board, albeit somewhat reluctantly. "We desperately needed to come together and create a new directive," Robert admitted. But his participation, he emphasized, depended on any tour being a low-key affair—no laser effects, no smoke bombs, no rear-projection screens, no stadiums, and *no extended solos.*

"I was really keen to stop the self-importance and the guitar solos that lasted an hour," he said. There was a loose promise made that no song would last more than four and a half minutes, a real challenge when it came to "Stairway to Heaven."

They dubbed it the "Cut the Waffle" tour (officially it was called Led Zeppelin Over Europe 1980)—a concise fourteen dates beginning in Germany on June 17, 1980, and ranging into Belgium, Holland, Austria, and Switzerland. Advance ticket sales were sluggish. They were going head-to-head against the European tours of Santana, Bob Marley, Roxy Music, Styx, Devo, and Stephen Stills. But a few killer performances would give Led Zeppelin momentum, should they head to the United States in the fall.

"Robert kept insisting at the time that he wouldn't go back to America," Peter recalled. He'd made his point clear onstage at Knebworth when he announced to the crowd: "We're never going to Texas anymore . . . but we will go to Manchester," casting a sidelong glance to the corner of the stage, where G was watching. Robert also decided he'd had enough of Richard.

"I found it very difficult to be a doting father on the one hand and have to deal with people like Richard Cole on the other," he said.

Richard and Robert, whom he usually addressed as Percy, had always had a difficult relationship. Over the years, they had eyed each other with misgiving bordering on contempt. Richard considered Robert a prima donna. "From the beginning," Ricardo said, "he had an aura of arrogance about him." They'd clashed often, Robert treating Richard like the hired help, Richard dismissing Percy as "rude," too self-involved, "being the center of attention."

Personality conflicts aside, Richard's heroin addiction made him a dangerous liability. He'd once attempted to kick out a window of *Caesars Chariot* while the plane was in midair, screaming, "I'll teach you to fuck with me!"

No, Robert didn't want Richard anywhere around him anymore. "He became progressively unreliable and, sadly, became a millstone around the neck of the group."

In the tradition of Caesar, Robert's knives were out for Richard. "Him and Jonesy were getting pissed off," Richard said. "They'd had their fill of the fucking chaos when they were making *In Through the Out Door*."

Robert left the dirty work up to G, who was now dabbling in heroin himself. Peter told Richard he wasn't going on the tour and suggested instead that he go to Italy to clean himself up. Led Zeppelin would pick up the tab. Richard was floored. He'd been with the band from its first date in Denver in 1969, every day, every damn day. He'd always done everything that was asked of him. He'd put his life on the line for Led Zeppelin.

Nothing doing, he couldn't talk his way out of it. G had already hired a replacement road manager, Phil Carlo, a Bad Company operative who had last worked for Led Zeppelin on the 1971 tour. "G had me to the house and said, 'We're going to strip the tour right down,'" Carlo recalls. "'Robert's had enough of the fucking huge entourage, the fisticuffs, the violence, the unpleasantness. We're going to make it low-key—no smashing stuff up or knocking people around. Let's make it enjoyable so that Robert will agree to an American tour.'"

The European dates were pocket change. Peter's goal was to soften Robert up with a short, intimate tour so that he'd agree to a marathon in North America in the fall of 1980. That's where the real money was, as well as the true-blue Led Zeppelin audience. "I reckoned that once Robert got over there and got into the swing he'd be okay," Grant said. G also realized the competition was becoming fierce. Aerosmith had already benefited considerably from Led Zeppelin's absence in America, and now the next wave of metal bands, like Judas Priest, Iron Maiden, Def Leppard, Kiss, Rush, and Van Halen, were siphoning fans from Led Zeppelin's deep reserves. If the band intended to hold onto their preeminence in the 1980s, they *had* to go back to the States. There was an all-night band meeting at Horselunges a few days before the tour launched when G laid out that scenario in no uncertain terms. According to him, "All the others said it was down to me to get Robert to go back to the States."

First things first: the European tour. There were details yet to be negotiated for several of the dates, but G, never in the Swan Song office, had been lax in nailing things down. Alan Callan had quit as the label's general manager. "There were too many fights going on, and there were too many drugs around," he said. Unity MacLean, now the label's senior executive, couldn't so much as get Peter on the phone. "I would send him tapes of groups, bands I thought he'd really be interested in, and hear nothing, *nothing*, for days," she says. "Then I'd finally get Ray Washburn on the phone and ask if Peter had a chance to listen to anything. 'Oh sure, he's listened. Just keep sending things.' But he never responded, and I'm sure he never listened."

"It was absolute chaos at Swan Song," says Phil Carson. "Nobody would dare do anything without Peter Grant, and Peter had become reclusive. He never came out of his fucking bedroom."

He'd left most of the European tour arrangements to Harvey Goldsmith, England's foremost concert promoters, who had just organized the benefit Concerts for Kampuchea, at which Led Zeppelin—minus Jimmy—had performed. There were still outstanding contracts to be signed with German promoters, and expenses had already been flowing out. Goldsmith needed answers fast, but Peter refused to take his calls. According to Phil Carson, "Jimmy and Robert came to see me and said, 'You've got to fix this.'"

Carson dreaded going to Horselunges. He knew the drill. He'd show up and have to sit in the living room for two days before being ushered into G's bedroom. And even then, he'd have to withstand a rambling, circuitous exchange. "Peter had lost it by then," Phil says. "He wasn't capable of doing anything, but everyone was still afraid of him." Eventually, Carson gained an audience and explained that Harvey Goldsmith's hands were tied. He couldn't finalize the equipment or put tickets on sale until Peter gave him the go-ahead.

"Phyllis," Peter sniggered in his consumptive way, employing his nickname for Carson, "I understand you do quite a good impersonation of me. You call Harvey pretending to be me, and I'll sit here and tell you what to say."

Carson rolled his eyes. It seemed like such a childish stunt to pull at this point. But they placed the call, with Carson standing in for Peter Grant, and spent a half hour wrapping up the tour. "I couldn't resist," Carson says, "I even managed to say, 'Harvey, don't give me any more of your fucking lip!'"

A new tour in a new decade—a new beginning, so to speak—required a new look. When Over Europe 1980 opened in Dortmund, West Germany, on June 17, 1980, Led Zeppelin had undergone a significant makeover. The dragon suits, spangles, and gauzy shirts were gone. To update their image, the clothes were more tailored, trendy. Jimmy wore a plain white suit and skinny tie, Jonesy a white dress shirt and blue jeans (although his red shoes raised a few eyebrows). And everyone, even Robert, had *haircuts*. "Punk kind of woke us up again," Jonesy offered, a concession, if a small one.

The staging was minimalist, with only a black backdrop, no razzledazzle. The opening number was "Train Kept a-Rollin'," a throwback to New Yardbirds days. Jimmy was so loose he even announced a song or two. If the audience had brought coffee and come in pajamas to endure the interminable three-and-a-half-hour concert, they'd miscalculated; the 8:00 p.m. show (which began *on time*) was over before the clock struck ten. "It's just like 1968!" Robert exclaimed during an encore. The security detail, usually twenty strong, was limited to ex–Special Forces commando Dave Moulder and a few colleagues. An unsuspecting concertgoer might have mistaken the act for a Led Zeppelin tribute band.

At the outset, everyone was in a playful mood. "The first night, I was fast asleep when suddenly my door crashed in, a cherry bomb went off, and two buckets of ice water were thrown on me," Phil Carlo, the new road manager, recalls. Through the billowing smoke, he was able to make out Bonzo, who was convulsed in laughter and shouted, "Welcome to the tour!" Before the drummer ran for cover, he told Phil, "By the way, Robert wants to go swimming for his physical therapy at six o'clock in the morning when nobody's in the pool. Sort it out."

The next morning, dutifully at half past five, Carlo, dressed in a Speedo with goggles and a pair of flippers, knocked on Robert Plant's hotel door. "Robert—time to go!" he called. A few minutes later, Robert appeared in an overcoat with a scarf, a woolly cap, and dark glasses. He took one look at Phil and said, "What the fuck are you up to?"

"I've come to take you swimming," he said.

Robert shook his head. "At six o'clock in the morning? Are you mad? Fuck me, Phil, Bonzo's done you up. We'll have to figure out how to get back at him."

It was that kind of frivolity—at the beginning. "Everybody was happy, functioning, even Peter was in great spirits," recalls Shelley Kaye, Steve Weiss's assistant, who had joined the tour in Brussels. In Amsterdam, during a lazy preconcert afternoon, Robert and John Paul rented a boat with her and sailed the canals. The mood was blithe, relaxed. Eventually, however, drugs intervened.

"Jimmy and Bonzo were doing heroin," Carlo recalls. "That changed the mood and the music—the music wasn't as good as before."

Songs were occasionally rushed and sloppy. They weren't fooling anyone. In Rotterdam, at the Ahoy, the audience sat on its hands. After the fourth number, before launching into "The Rain Song," Robert, who'd had trouble rousing the crowd, got snarky. "The main group will be on shortly," he announced. "This song is not guaranteed to wake you up any more than you are now—but there's always a chance." In Hanover, West Germany, three nights later, he lashed out at the acoustics. "Nice echo in here," he said sarcastically. "Many people play here today, or is this just part of the torture? Fucking horrible place." The next night, in Vienna, the audience was rowdy, repeatedly calling out for "Rock and Roll." Jimmy eventually lost his patience. "We haven't been sitting around on our asses for seven years," he carped. "We've got a lot of new songs to play, too." In the middle of "White Summer," he was hit with a firecracker in the midst of a solo, and he bolted from the stage. Emotions were beginning to run high.

Nuremberg, on June 27, brought no relief. Bonzo wasn't well. His drinking had been excessive early in the day, and by showtime he was complaining of stomach pain. Jimmy was also under the weather. "There's two of us tonight that aren't feeling at all well," he blurted into the mic onstage before launching into "In the Evening," the band's fourth number. But before counting off, Bonzo collapsed and was rushed to the hospital.

There was no tour doctor, like in America. "You see, the only reason that we ever had a doctor around in Led Zeppelin was to get some Quaaludes," Robert admitted.

Bonzo's issues were deeper. He was still compensating for his hatred of being away from home by combining alcohol and drugs to excess. Tony Iommi, Black Sabbath's guitarist and a mate from the Midlands said, "I saw John a few times when he'd throw up and then do a line and have another drink." Mick Hinton reported that he'd counted the number of drinks Bonzo put away one night in Germany— "thirty-two vodkas." Benji Le Fevre, who helped road-manage the European tour, says, "Bonzo was drunk almost all the time, and it just caught up with him."

The official explanation was "physical exhaustion," but folks couldn't keep their lame excuses straight. "As he'd eaten something like twenty-seven bananas before the gig, it's not surprising," Grant suggested to an observer, while Robert indicated the drummer lacked sufficient potassium and "had to eat fifty bananas immediately." The truth was closer to Phil Carson's recall: as he drove back to the hotel with Bonzo and G, "John was right out of it, and Peter was furious with him."

Bonzo was more distressed and confrontational than ever, his logic greatly impaired. In Hamburg, during a rare day off, the entourage arrived back at the hotel too late to order room service. "Bonzo sometimes got a little too aggressive, and you had to try and calm him down," said Dennis Sheehan, whose job was to keep John out of trouble. "So I went out in my station wagon and found him some burgers and fries." Bonzo couldn't wait to unwrap the food; he just bit straight through the greasy paper. When Sheehan pointed this out, Bonzo swallowed and said, "Tastes just as good!"

Drug use was now more rampant than ever. There may not have been a tour doctor, as Robert had noted, but G made sure Jimmy and Bonzo had access to whatever they needed. In the midst of the dates, a courier, a cousin of Princess Diana's, was flown in from England in time to replenish their stash. Phil Carlo was sent to pick her up at the airport.

"She was one of those aristocratic people who like hanging about with bands," Carlo says—a tall, slender, very attractive woman who got off the plane wearing gloves up to her elbows and a floppy hat with a veil obscuring her face. "Fucking hell, they've sent the beekeeper!" Carlo chortled, and from that moment on, the nickname stuck. "She and Jimmy used to sit next to each other in the hotel bars, swaying about, barely able to stay sitting up. It was hard to watch."

On the evening of July 3, Jimmy was nowhere to be seen at the Mannheim Hof, where the band was staying. "Everyone was down in the hotel bar, and it was time to leave for the gig," Carlo recalls. "We looked all over for him. It was getting late, when all of a sudden, from the sill of a window placed overhead, there was a rustling of cur-tains and Jimmy fell out onto the table. He'd somehow gotten up there and nodded off, as he was prone to do. That's how bad things were getting."

Later, at the airport, Jimmy was out of it. He sat on the concourse floor, his expression grave but somewhat vacant, and made little piles of six currencies, humming to himself, while passengers walked by star-ing at the bizarre scene. A group of onlookers began to gather. "For fuck's sake, get him up and hidden," Carlo admonished Rick Hobbs, Jimmy's minder, but Hobbs knew how to handle the behavior. "Leave him be," he said. "He'll get up in a minute. Better not to make a scene."

They had played perhaps their best show in Frankfurt on June 30. It was largely an effusive American crowd, owing to the Rhein-Main Air Base, located just outside the city, where Elvis Presley had done his tour of duty. U.S. servicemen managed to get ahold of large blocks of tickets and raised a good deal of hell clapping and stomping to the songs, especially during a rocking version of Elvis Presley's "Frank-furt Special" laced seamlessly into the middle of "Whole Lotta Love." Ahmet Ertegun had flown in to celebrate the success and gain some insight into the future of the band. He must have liked what he'd seen and heard. Afterward, he cornered Peter Grant and broached the pos-sibility of signing a new five-year, five-album deal.

*Five years.* That was wishful thinking. It was all they could do to get from one gig to the next. And the band's objectives weren't aligned. Too many heads were in too many different places. Nobody could agree on what the character of the band should be, not in five months' time or five minutes earlier, let alone five years from now.

Two concerts had been scheduled in Berlin, the last city on the tour, but the band decided to play only one night, on July 7. Everyone was exhausted, ready to head home. Uncharacteristically, the show was long and ragged, the arrangements to several songs "tired and obsolete." As far as short solos went, all promises were off. "Stairway" rambled on for over fourteen minutes, while "Whole Lotta Love," loaded with effects and midsection jams, weighed in at a seemingly endless seventeen minutes. "Munich was the nearest feeling to that of the big American shows," Jimmy said. "There was a lot of energy, and it was really exciting." At the conclusion, the four musicians stepped to the front of the stage, wrapped their arms around each other's shoulders, and bowed to the crowd.

Robert grabbed the mic and said, "Thank you very much, everyone who's worked for us and put up with us and all those sorts of things. And, er . . . good night."

They hugged again and walked off the stage, waving. It was the last show Led Zeppelin ever played.

## Chapter Twenty-two

# CODA

## [1]

The future of Led Zeppelin rested with Robert Plant. His refusal to participate in an American tour threw a wrench into the band's prospects.

"I was developing my own independence, and I didn't feel tied to them anymore," he said. "But I wanted to be there because there was still a lot of love. I just didn't want to do anything a minute longer than was necessary if I didn't like it."

The European tour had given Robert incentive to at least consider another trip through the States. As long as things were kept lean and mean, he was game to carry on and indicated as much to his bandmates.

"We were battling on," John Paul said. For him, playing live with this group of musicians was what he looked forward to most; even touring suited him. As far as he cared, making albums was only the starting point for live performances. "Nobody ever wanted to say it was over. We certainly didn't want to throw that away." He felt they "still had a lot to offer" and just needed to get back on the road.

The recipe was simple: a U.S. tour and a new album. That had worked like a charm for ten years; there was no reason to tinker with the tried and true.

Even so, Peter Grant had avoided raising the issue with Robert. The strategy was to give him a wide berth—let him enjoy performing again—so that he warmed to the idea on his own. Grant had played his cards perfectly. While in Germany, Robert asked Bonzo, "How come Grant hasn't said anything to me about America yet?" Finally, as the band landed at Gatwick and walked across the tarmac to the terminal, Robert sidled up to Peter and gave it his blessing. "Okay, I'll do it," he said, "but only for four weeks."

Four weeks—it was a start. G would book four weeks and then another four weeks behind it, just in case. They'd call the tour "Led Zeppelin, the 1980s: Part One," with every expectation there'd be a Part Two, even a Part Three once Robert got comfortable. Grant immediately put Phil Carlo on call. "I've gotten the go-ahead from Jim and Robert," he said. "We're going to America. You're their man on the road."

Richard Cole wasn't simply out of the picture: he was in jail. He'd gone to Italy, as G instructed, with every intention of cleaning himself up. Before he left, Herb Atkin asked Richard to make contact with an associate at the Excelsior Hotel in Rome, where they both happened to be staying, to discuss Led Zeppelin business. Richard checked in, but for some strange reason Atkin's colleague wasn't registered at the hotel. The next morning, an Italian SWAT team showed up at Richard's room. The day he'd arrived in Italy, the Bologna train station had been blown up. He was arrested on suspicion of terrorism. It didn't help that the police discovered a bag of cocaine as well.

Clearly, he'd been set up by Herb Atkin. The trumped-up terrorism accusations were eventually dropped, but a drug-dealing charge stuck. "After Cole was convicted and sentenced and appeals were gone, I got a call from Steve Weiss: 'You've got to do something,'" recalls Jeff Hoffman, the New York fixer. At the time, Hoffman was the lead counsel for mob boss John Gotti, who was dodging a number of

LED ZEPPELIN

racketeering cases. Hoffman flew to Rome and arranged to see Richard, who was serving time in Rebibbia prison on the outskirts of the city. "It was a real serious situation, but through a series of machinations we got Richard released in six months."

While this drama was playing out, all systems were go for Led Zeppelin, the 1980s: Part One. The bones of a North American tour were falling into place—nineteen dates had been booked, beginning in Montreal on October 17, 1980. It was a solid schedule, with days off built in, all arenas in major East Coast cities, winding up in Chicago on November 15.

"Everything was getting organized," says Shelley Kaye, who was coordinating details out of the Swan Song offices in New York. "The itinerary was in place, we were booking hotels, working on a plane, tour jackets were ordered. All parts of the machinery were functioning. Everyone knew what their job was. Communication even started flowing again."

A new album was also discussed. Jimmy was most eager to get something under way. *Presence*, in his opinion, was "not an easy album to listen to" and *In Through the Out Door* "a little soft," certainly not his best effort. "Bonzo and I had already started discussing plans for a hard-driving rock album after that," he said. "I wanted to get back to that sort of urgent intensity we managed to evoke." Back to the basics: austere, percussive, and Big Bertha chords, "some really intense riffing" Led Zeppelin style. It sounded like a plan.

The band booked Bray Studios in Windsor to rehearse for the tour. Robert and Bonzo drove down together from the Midlands on September 22, 1980. Bonzo was on edge. "The guy was miserable," according to Deep Purple's Glenn Hughes, who had run into the drummer while they both were at home. "There was something eating him so badly." Bonzo, as usual, was dreading the tour and being away from home. He found going to America daunting.

"It's so much easier to play in England," he said. "You get the motor out of the garage and toddle off, and you're so at ease all the time. Whereas if you're in America, you're all day in a hotel somewhere, having arguments with bloody rednecks and everything, and then you've got to go to the gig."

He was agitated during the drive. He ripped off the car's sun visor and threw it out the window. "I don't want to do this," he told Robert. "You play the drums and I'll sing." It was an old song to which Robert knew the words; Bonzo sang it every time they planned to be away. Not giving it more than a passing thought, he dropped Bonzo off to stay with Jimmy at his Old Mill House along the Thames in Windsor and drove on to Blakes Hotel in London, where he and Jonesy were staying.

Only Robert and Jonesy showed up the first day of rehearsal, and they spent a few minutes checking out a model of the tour stage and lighting rig, "a basic design without a lot of special effects," according to the Showco team. "Well, [Jimmy and Bonzo] aren't here, let's fuck off," the other two said and returned to Blakes. The next day, Bonzo arrived at Bray fairly loaded. On the way to the studio, he'd stopped off at a pub and downed a couple vodka–orange juices. "Breakfast," he called it. At rehearsal, he continued drinking vodka straight from the bottle. "He got on the drum stool, fell off it two or three times," Mick Hinton reported. Mercifully, Robert said, "Let's call it a day and sort it out tomorrow."

They rescheduled rehearsal for the next afternoon, September 24, 1980, at two o'clock. On the way to Windsor from Blake's that afternoon, Benji Le Fevre, who was driving Robert and Jonesy, suggested making a detour. "I think we should stop at Jim's," he said, turning off and heading toward the Old Mill House. "There is no point going back to the studio to sit and wait for them. Let's make sure Jimmy and Bonzo are up."

At the house, Jimmy wasn't anywhere to be found. Benji asked Rick Hobbs, Jimmy's guy Friday, where Bonzo was. "Oh, man, he was really out of it last night," Hobbs responded, relating details of an impressive drinking binge—forty shots of vodka. "I put him to sleep a little after midnight. He's upstairs in the guest suite."

Benji volunteered to tip him out of bed and started up the stairs, Jonesy a few steps behind him. "I opened the door and immediately knew that something wasn't right," Benji recalls. "Bonzo was laying on his arm, with his back to the door, but . . . *it wasn't right*. I pushed Jonesy into the hall and said, "'I don't think you'd better come in here, man. Let me just have a look.'" Benji had seen a warning: a pool of vomit on the pillow next to Bonzo's head. "I knew he was dead, but I tried to take his pulse. He was cold, half blue. He'd been dead for a few hours."

Benji and John Paul went downstairs, encountering Jimmy and Robert, who were in the parlor, laughing. "I had to go in and say, 'Hold it!' and tell them what happened," Jonesy said.

Robert reacted with disbelief, mumbled, "Are you sure?" Benji nodded wordlessly. "I've got to go and have a look."

Benji put a gentle hand on Robert's chest, restraining him. "I don't think you should," he cautioned. "You don't want to remember him like that." Instead, Benji placed a call to Horselunges and gave the news to Ray Washburn.

"Ray came up to me and said, 'Come downstairs,'" Peter Grant recalled later. "He sat me down, handed me some Valium, and said, 'Take these.'" At first, G resisted, but Ray eventually told him that Benji had news. "John Bonham's died."

G was in shock. Bonzo . . . Still, he recovered enough to tell Benji to phone for an ambulance, then called Don Murfet to "contain the situation, limit the damage—and that meant keeping the police and the press at bay."

Back at Jimmy's, Robert pulled on Benji's sleeve. "We've got to go," he said. "We've got to get to Pat before she hears it from anybody else."

Benji hustled Robert into the car and then gunned it, doing 120 miles per hour all the way from Windsor up the M1 to the Midlands. Neither man spoke through the entire journey. They found Pat Bonham at home, alone.

"I don't know how to say this . . . ," Robert began.

"He's dead, isn't he?" Pat said.

Robert hung his head and nodded.


Peter Grant and Ray Washburn arrived at Jimmy's house an hour or two later. By that time, word had gotten out about Bonzo's death, and the media circus was already forming in the road. "The three of us discussed all the angles," Murfet recalled, "made contingency plans, and decided how we would box for the next few days."

When he arrived in Windsor, Murfet encountered a scene that summed up the mood. "Jimmy was sitting there by the stairs smoking cigarette after cigarette," Murfet recalled. "He didn't say anything. Not a word. To be honest, he didn't need to. Jimmy just looked . . . lost."

Ray Washburn called the Swan Song office and got Unity Mac-Lean on the phone. "Peter wants everybody out of the office," he insisted. "Turn out the lights. He wants the office locked, and he doesn't want anybody to take any phone calls. Stay at home until you're told to come back."

"What's going on?" Unity asked.

"None of your business," he snapped. "I've told you what to do. Lock up and go home until further notice."

What was Peter up to now? she wondered. Had he been alerted to a drug bust? Had the business gone belly up? Did he want the office to himself for a private assignation? Locking the place up was a new one for her.

When MacLean got home, her husband, Bruce, was waiting and said, "Let's go around to the pub and have a drink."

"It's a little early for that," she protested.

At his insistence they went to the Goat, where he ordered her a large brandy. He explained that before she arrived home, he'd had a call from the *Daily Express* asking for a comment about "the untimely death of John Bonham." Unity nearly fell off her chair.

*Richard*, she thought—*someone has to get word to Ricardo*. Before she could figure out how to reach him, Richard contacted her from his prison cell in Italy.

"The guards told me one of Led Zeppelin had died," he said, certain the victim was Jimmy Page.

"No, it was Bonzo," she told him and could make out a sob on the other end of the line.

Richard was crushed by the news. "Bonzo had been my closest friend and ally in the band," he reflected later.

They were two of a kind, a couple of "wide boys," as both might have acknowledged in jest. They'd burned the candle at both ends and raised hell wherever the spirit took them. Now Bonzo was dead and Richard was in jail. They'd both pressed their luck too far.

John Henry Bonham's funeral was held on October 10, 1980, at St. Michael's Church in Rushock, close to his farm. It was a family affair, and he had a big extended family, from his bandmates to the Swan Song and Atlantic teams and an army of Midlands musicians—Bev Bevan, Jeff Lynne, Roy Wood, Denny Laine, Tony Iommi, all of them, like Bonzo, once scrounging for work on the Midlands circuit and now headed to the Rock & Roll Hall of Fame. The wake afterward was held at Chequers, Bonzo's favorite pub. The amount of alcohol consumed there would have impressed even the deceased as he was toasted repeatedly throughout the day and long into the night—until everyone was just plain toasted.

Nobody knew quite what to do after that. The surviving members of the band fled to Jersey to avoid the media and to mourn. "We went to a hotel," says Benji Le Fevre, "and they tried to come to terms with what had happened. But it was clear that Led Zeppelin was over. Everyone knew it."

"They came back from Jersey, and I booked a suite for afternoon tea at the Savoy," Peter Grant recalled. The powwow was called ostensibly to discuss the band's future, but it was pretty well determined before anyone said a word. Still, they asked for G's opinion. "I said it just couldn't go on because it was the four of them. They were relieved because they had decided the same."

"I couldn't even think how to do this without John," John Paul reflected. Led Zeppelin was a *band*, a performance-based band. For all their differences, the whole was greater than the sum of its parts. He felt it would have been a different band without Bonzo behind the drums. The chemistry would have been all wrong. "No John Bonham, no Led Zeppelin—it's as simple as that."

"We'll be together certainly until one of us punts out," Jimmy had told Lisa Robinson in 1973, and his attitude had never changed. "It would be silly to even think about going on with Zeppelin," Jimmy said. "It would have been a total insult to John."

"For me, there was no debate," Robert said. "The band didn't exist the minute Bonzo had gone. There was no Led anything."

Atlantic Records wasn't so sure. "The record company were absolutely a hundred percent pressuring me into talking the lads into reforming," Peter recalled. Steve Weiss reminded him that Led Zeppelin still had an outstanding commitment to the label for another album and pressed to consider replacing Bonzo with another drummer. He already represented the most likely candidate, Carmine Appice, Vanilla Fudge's heavy hitter, who was currently employed by Rod Stewart. Simon Kirke, Bad Company's drummer, was mentioned, as were Bev Bevan, Aynsley Dunbar, and Carl Palmer, the usual suspects. "Within a day of Bonzo's death, drummers were coming out of the woodwork, calling the house, saying, 'I'm the man for the job,'" recalls Phil Carlo, who was running interference for Peter at Horselunges. When he felt up to it, G would grab the phone out of Phil's hand and say, "How *dare* you fucking ring up? We're not the fucking Who."

His reaction wasn't only about sentiment. Bonzo had extraordinary talent; his drumming was essential to Led Zeppelin's driving sound. Historically, he was one of the most influential drummers in all of rock 'n roll, his legendary foot and wrist control an astonishing feat of dexterity, his sense of rhythm and beat as precise as the tides. Replace Bonzo? Not just unlikely but unimaginable.

Swan Song made it official on December 4, 1980. To end speculation once and for all, the company issued a statement that said, "We wish it to be known that the loss of our dear friend and the deep respect we have for his family, together with the sense of undivided harmony felt by ourselves and our manager, have led us to decide that we could not continue as we were."

Jimmy was devastated. Led Zeppelin was his baby; he had conceived it, fed it, nurtured and educated it—and buried it. The shock left him dazed. "I just felt really insecure," he said in retrospect. "I was terrified. . . . I just didn't know what to do. I lived in a total vacuum. In the end, I went to Bali and just thought about things." He says he didn't touch a guitar again for two years.

Robert wasn't in much better shape. "He was trying to come to terms with what happened," Le Fevre says. He asked Benji to stay in Kidderminster for a while to keep him company but steered clear of anything that reminded him of Led Zeppelin. "We went down the pub, the Queen's Head, we went to football, occasionally we'd arrange a football game in Wales on Sunday. That's all there really was: football and beer." Benji and Rex King positioned a mobile home at the foot of the Plants' driveway and stood sentry there for weeks to keep the paparazzi away.

Jonesy had less of a problem with the press. He was a cipher, the man who, even after a decade of worldwide celebrity, could walk into an arena lobby filled with Led Zeppelin fans and go completely unnoticed. "On the European tour, Jonesy and I had been in town one day and came back to the hotel, with fans clustered around the front door," says Phil Carlo. He told John Paul they'd have to go around the corner and in the back door. "Why, Phil?" Jonesy replied. "Nobody's going to recognize me." And he walked straight through the crowd.

Now Jonesy burrowed in at home, consumed with anger. "It seemed such a waste," he said. Bonzo's death hit him as hard as it did the others. He also struggled with frustration over the recklessness in which they'd all indulged. "After all, it could have happened to any one of us."

Of all of them, Peter Grant had the most difficult time adjusting to the tragedy. "After John's death, Peter just disintegrated," says Po, one of the few friends permitted to visit the manager. "I'd never seen such a powerful man fall apart so quickly." He went into a very dark place—"the beginning of the period of blackness," G called it. "He sunk deeper and deeper into depression and the knowledge that the adventure was over," says Phil Carlo.

Bad Company had also broken up—Paul Rodgers had had a falling out with Boz Burrell—contributing to Peter's melancholy. He was unable to function. The business went completely ignored. "Nothing was getting taken care of," recalls Shelley Kaye. "Steve [Weiss] couldn't get in touch with Peter. He and I ran scenarios: Was Peter okay? What was he thinking? Was he even functioning?"

Steve Weiss's livelihood was at stake and he demanded answers. Unable to reach Peter, he flew to London for a face-to-face, but Grant refused to leave his home to meet him. "They sent a limo for him," says Benji Le Fevre, "then a helicopter. He refused to even acknowledge them." Eventually, Benji was asked to mediate. He drove to Horselunges and was told by Ray Washburn that Peter was out by the moat, that he'd been there for most of three days.

"I found G sitting on a little bench with a loaded shotgun across his knees, staring into the water. He kept repeating: 'I know that fucking pike's in there, Benji, and I'm going to have him.'" Benji asked him about meeting Steve Weiss. "Fuck Weiss," Peter said. "I've got to get this pike."

It had come to that. Horselunges, once an architectural showpiece, had fallen into disrepair, like its owner. There was garbage strewn everywhere, the once-beautiful drapes lay in tatters, cobwebs laced rafters in the corners of rooms, cigarette burns pockmarked the Georgian pool table. Similarly, the Swan Song office on King's Road was abandoned.

"I used to go in and answer phones, trying to keep it going," says Maggie Bell. "I did it for a couple weeks, on and off, but there was nothing there anymore. The only things left were the phones." One day, as she arrived, the front door gaped wide open. The office had been ransacked. "All the beautiful paintings that had belonged to Peter and Mark London—gone. The Chesterfield couches and stereo equipment—gone. The art nouveau and Tiffany lamps—gone. There were villains from the King's Road who knew about Swan Song and just came in and took the lot."

The New York headquarters was hardly in better shape. "Atlantic was paying a certain amount every quarter for us to run the office and pay salaries," says Shelley Kaye. "The uncertainty of it rattled Steve [Weiss], who became an alcoholic. Finally, Swan Song ended for us with no notice. The quarterly checks from Atlantic just stopped coming, and everybody got fired instantly."

Atlantic had run out of patience. "There were no records coming out, so we were no longer supporting the label," says Phil Carson. "Ahmet decided he'd had enough—*everybody* decided they'd had enough."

## [2]

There was to be a final Led Zeppelin album. The band still owed Atlantic a record or two on their existing deal, but that obligation had been mutually terminated with the understanding that there was material in the vault that could be stitched together for one last rodeo. "That was an agreement we struck with Ahmet," Peter said, referring to a separate deal called the Omega contract. "Ahmet was great and paid an advance even knowing that it was sub-standard and we couldn't find enough material for a decent set."

Jimmy was already working on his live-album concept. "When we lost John, I was very keen to do a chronological live album, because I knew we had the tapes that spanned these periods," he said. He felt it would showcase the excitement the band produced onstage, "that Led Zeppelin's live performance was so important to the sum of the parts."

There was a trove of material to work from—a few tapes from the first U.S. tour in 1969, the 1970 debut at the Royal Albert Hall, BBC recordings, great material from the soundboard at early shows—"all that sort of naiveté and the absolute wonder of what we were doing—and the freshness of it," Robert chipped in. Of course, the bootleggers had archives that made Jimmy's head spin. "When I saw all the oceans of live bootlegs about," he said, "I thought fans would prefer the last of the unreleased studio material." Atlantic knew there were unreleased masters of songs, and the record company wanted—insisted on—a *studio* album.

Dutifully, Jimmy Page began sifting through tapes in the storage vault, selecting random cuts before taking them, for a touch-up or new coat of paint, to Sol Studios, a converted two-hundred-year-old water mill he'd bought at a fire sale from producer Gus Dudgeon. There were some interesting chestnuts they'd recorded but, for whatever reason, socked away for posterity. Now Jimmy dusted them off in an effort to dish up a viable compilation.

All told, it was like a sorry potluck from a bad Cantonese restaurant menu: one from column A, two from column B. Eight lackluster tracks mostly in chronological order—reelin' in the years, so to speak—lasting a charitably brief thirty-three minutes. The opener, "We're Gonna Groove," was recorded on the fly in June 1969, in London, during a frantic week when a young Led Zeppelin spun from one event to the next every day, culminating in a Sunday night appearance at the Royal Albert Hall Pop Proms. The song was a Page/Plant "original," lifted from Ben E. King's "Groovin'" and earmarked for a track on *Led Zeppelin II*. "Poor Tom," a laid-back, folksy tune in the mode of "Gallows Pole," came out of the Bron-Yr-Aur trip Robert and Jimmy made in 1970 and was recorded later that June during sessions for *Led Zeppelin III* at Olympic Studios in London. Also credited to "Page/Plant," it was a reworking of two Reverend Robert Wilkins originals, "Poor Tom" and "That's No Way to Get Along."

Earlier in 1970, at the band's Royal Albert Hall concert in January, they warmed up during the soundcheck with "I Can't Quit You Baby," the Willie Dixon classic from their debut album. Jimmy considered this "live" version a suitable example of Led Zeppelin's blues roots, and their spontaneous, catalytic performance was fleshed out with inventive vamps and a stupendous windup at the end.

The basic track for "Walter's Walk" was recorded in 1972 at Stargroves for *Houses of the Holy*. Whether a vocal was added at the time is a matter of dispute. In any event, Robert's vocal for the new album was recorded in 1982 at Sol Studios. And more than any song in the compilation, "Walter's Walk" paid tribute to Led Zeppelin at their heaviest and most action-packed. It was a full-throttle hard-rock extravaganza, with Bonzo flaunting the bass-drum triplets he first showcased in 1969.

"Ozone Baby" and "Darlene" were rejects from the sessions in Stockholm for *In Through the Out Door*, both resembling loose, lighthearted jams more than carefully finessed songs. And "Bonzo's Montreux," a rather unspectacular drum solo enhanced electronically with a harmonizer during the mixing stage, was included, if for no other reason, as a posthumous tribute, while "Wearing and Tearing," also from the Polar Studio sessions, was the album standout.

"We wrote 'Wearing and Tearing' because of the punks," Robert explained, "to say we could make challenging, crashing music just as well as they could."

"Wearing and Tearing" wasn't punk by any stretch of the imagination, but it was aggressive and unruly—manic—just attack-attack-

attack, with Robert screaming, "*Medication!*" as the song approached its mushroom cloud of a conclusion. The plan had been to offer it as a commemorative single at Knebworth. "We wanted to put it out on a different label under the name of a different artist alongside the Damned and the Sex Pistols because it was so vicious and emphatically fresh," Robert said. "And if you hadn't known it was us, it could have been anybody at all who was young and virile and all the things that we were then not supposed to be."

What Led Zeppelin was *not* supposed to be had always been an issue: not heavy metal, not traditional, not progressive, and, yes, not punk. "I don't know what category we fit into," Jimmy said. "It's just music." No critic or magazine had managed to typecast the band in a way that put them snugly in a box. Led Zeppelin refused to be pigeonholed. Jimmy insisted the band, from album to album, was "highly intent on change and ever onward pressing as far through the boundaries as one can possibly go." Perhaps that was true for the collaborative albums, but he was stretching the point with *Coda*.

Aubrey Powell remembers being consulted on the album cover design but says, "Nobody's heart was in any of it. It was difficult getting any input out of Jimmy or Robert." Jimmy had come up with a title, *Early Days and Latter Days*, but Jonesy had come up with a better one: *Coda*, the passage in music that brings the piece to an end. Po suggested something simple and respectful. He created a graphic using an image that mimicked the circular water irrigation systems that could be seen when flying over the Mojave Desert in California. And for the outer sleeve, an introspective look back on the history of Led Zeppelin, with a montage of photographs, thirty in all.

The idea was to release it in the summer of 1982, but it was held until November so as not to interfere with *Pictures at Eleven*, Robert's first solo album, the final issue on the Swan Song label. *Coda* crept in on little cat feet with littler fanfare and even less support. Even case-hardened music critics hadn't the heart to administer a eulogy. Most of the magazines ignored *Coda*. Only *NME*, now the grand master of snark, delivered the coup de grâce. Led Zeppelin's "graveyard status seems assured when you hear this record and realize that there is nothing on it you want to recall," the reviewer concluded, referring to the album as "this sackcloth." The article, lacking any subtlety, held Led Zeppelin "largely responsible for the terrible state of American rock."

A breather. Led Zeppelin, what was left of the band, needed a breather. They couldn't fight the tide; they were all too sensitive. No one felt up to defending the unloved album. It was unwarranted, undignified. Above all, it seemed necessary to get the specter of Led Zeppelin out of their systems.

Jimmy, Robert, and Jonesy were used to layoffs, and each man went to ground in order to recover and reflect. Jimmy kept busy working on a soundtrack for *Death Wish II*, a movie that eventually lived up to its name. But he remained in the grip of drug addiction, and at the 1982 ARMS charity concert at the Royal Albert Hall, he looked to one observer "like a walking skeleton." As far as playing went, he was careful to only put his toe in the water: a jam here, a jam there. In December 1981, he waded in the shallow end with Chris Squire and Alan White, both of Yes, in a venture called XYZ. Robert was invited to sing, but he lasted only one rehearsal, unable to commit in the wake of Bonzo's death.

Robert was better off on his own. "I did nothing for as long as was respectful to Bonzo," he said. "I cut my hair off, and I never played or listened to a Zeppelin record for two years." His solo effort, *Pictures at Eleven*, was received warmly, if with a degree of reserve. In 1984, beginning to feel the old pull, he put out a five-song EP called *The Honeydrippers: Volume One*, a miscellany of Ahmet Ertegun's favorite songs, R&B covers that included "I Got a Woman," "Sea of Love," and "Rockin' at Midnight," with Jeff Beck and Jimmy Page handling guitars.

John Paul Jones had a rougher go of it. "I never worried that I'd have to get a real job, but it was kind of hard in the Eighties," he said. He attempted to branch out, scoring films. "But everybody was saying, 'He's a rock bass player. What does he know about scoring?'" The same thing happened with Jonesy's reentry into the studio. "When I first decided to try and get some work, nobody took me seriously at first. It was like, 'Now wait a minute! I'm a professional musician and an arranger and a producer.'" He'd been central to more sessions than most working musicians. He put in a bid to produce John Hiatt's new album, but the record company disputed his "relevance." It frustrated him; he wanted to get back to work.

The three men, however, hadn't played together in any serious way since the last Led Zeppelin concert in Berlin. They'd made guest appearances for Robert's solo *The Principle of Moments* tour in London and Bristol, but there were no real plans for a reunion of any kind.

Rumblings started in the spring of 1985. Bob Geldof, the lead singer for the Boomtown Rats, was organizing a benefit concert on July 13, 1985, called Live Aid to raise funds for Ethiopian famine relief. He viewed it as a "global jukebox" that would be held simultaneously at Wembley in London and JFK Stadium in Philadelphia, as well as at satellite venues in Canada, the Soviet Union, Japan, Australia, Yugoslavia, and Germany. Robert very quickly offered to appear, as he was on tour in Detroit the night before the benefit and would have no trouble getting to Philadelphia. Jimmy did too, but with a separate band he was forming called the Firm. Geldof wanted something splashier, and what could be splashier than a Led Zeppelin reunion?

"I called Jimmy and said, 'Let's do it,'" Robert recalled, but he instantly regretted it. Getting together with Jimmy, he reasoned, "would be like meeting a former wife and going to bed—and not making love. It's impossible, just not appropriate anymore."

No one had invited John Paul Jones for a threesome. For some reason, they didn't seem to fit him into the picture. It was assumed that Paul Martinez, from Robert's touring band, would handle bass chores at Live Aid. When word got back to Jonesy, he laid down the law. "I had to say to them, 'If it's Zeppelin, and you're going to be doing Zeppelin songs, hi, I'm still here, and I wouldn't mind being part of it.'" The way he saw it, "I had to barge my way into Live Aid."

As far as drummers went, the situation was unique. They invited Tony Thompson, who played with Chic and Power Station, to sit in with the band. But replacing Bonzo required two drummers. No less a candidate than Phil Collins agreed to shore up the percussion. He was appearing with his band on the London stage earlier in the day but would hop on the Concorde and then helicopter to Philadelphia to appear with Led Zeppelin as well.

Everything seemed to be going according to plan when Robert announced that he had no intention of singing "Stairway to Heaven." Jimmy was irate. "I fucking knew this would happen," he fumed. "Isn't it ridiculous? I've got to play this stupid fucking game with him, and of course he'll end up doing it."

"The next day, while Queen was onstage, we got together for rehearsal at the Warehouse Studios in Philadelphia," says Phil Carlo, who was working as Jimmy's road manager at the time. "I remember watching Freddie Mercury on TV with Robert, who turned to me and said, 'Fucking hell, how are we going to top that?'"

There was only one way, and he knew it. "Stairway" became the centerpiece of their set.

Jimmy was visibly nervous. He had been studying the performances of the bands who preceded them earlier in the day—Santana, Tom Petty, Eric Clapton, Crosby, Stills, Nash & Young, Hall and Oates, and Mick Jagger—marveling at the tightness of their sets. "John Paul Jones arrived virtually the same day as the show, and we had about an hour's rehearsal," he said. "That sounds a bit of a kamikaze stunt, really, when you think of how well rehearsed everybody else was."

Phil Collins landed in Philadelphia in the nick of time to play his own short set as the sun set over the open-air stadium. After finishing his signature "In the Air Tonight," he pulled the mic close and said, "I'd like to introduce some friends of mine. Would you welcome Mr. Robert Plant, Mr. Jimmy Page, Mr. John Paul Jones . . ."

The stadium erupted in cheers as a curtain folded back and the remnants of Led Zeppelin bounded onto the stage. The intro to "Rock and Roll" sent a jolt through the overwrought crowd. It should have been a smash to end all smashes. It *should* have been. But Robert's voice was shot—he realized he "had nothing left at all"—and Jimmy's guitar was horribly out of tune, and the monitors were feeding back, causing all sorts of problems. "The whole thing ran away with itself, and it was almost too much of an emotional thing for me," Jimmy said. Emotions aside, he knew they just didn't cut it. "We were awful," Robert said. "Seventeen years, and we still can't get it right."

Worse, perhaps, Phil Collins, flailing away, couldn't keep proper time. He'd been sent a tape of the material but hadn't had the chance to practice it. "After the second number, Jim leaned toward me and said, 'Turn his fucking mic off!'" recalls Phil Carlo.

Somehow, they salvaged the set with a sentimental version of "Stairway to Heaven" that produced the kind of arm-swaying, Bic-lighter tribute that Jimmy had always dreaded. And afterward they played the game, giving interviews that acknowledged how great it felt to play together again. But Robert changed his tune as soon as the lights were turned off.

"What I hated about Led Zeppelin came right back," he said. "It was like some kind of aimless dog trying to bite its tail. . . . It being such a special day, for me to stand there and do probably one of the worst performances I've ever done in my life seemed to contradict my very being, my reason to be, as an entertainer, as a musician." Small wonder that the group refused to allow their performance to appear on the Live Aid DVD package released in 2004.

———

The magic of Led Zeppelin, however, was too strong to deny—or maybe just a fraught relationship that was impossible to end. John Paul Jones was reluctant to put it all behind. He suggested that "it might be nice to have a bit of a blow again."

Six months later, in January 1986, he, Robert, and Jimmy met secretly in a village hall near Bath in an attempt to make new music together. The band toyed with a new configuration. Jonesy moved to keyboards, ceding the bass to Robert, with Tony Thompson of Power Station on drums. And like all fraught relationships, it started off smoothly. "Two or three things were quite promising," Robert admitted, "a sort of cross between David Byrne and Hüsker Dü." But old grievances soon rose to the surface. Everything Jimmy did grated on Robert's nerves, nothing more so than waiting endlessly while he changed the batteries on his wah-wah pedal every other song. It was only a matter of time until things soured.

One evening, after a particularly exasperating rehearsal, the situation came to a head. "What I recall," John Paul said, "is Robert and I getting drunk in the hotel, and Robert questioning what we were doing."

"Nobody wants to hear that old stuff again," he complained.

Jonesy couldn't have agreed less. "Everybody is waiting for it to happen," he insisted.

Fate eventually intervened. On the way home from the next rehearsal, Tony Thompson suffered injuries in an auto accident that confined him to a hospital bed. Without a drummer, and with a nagging lack of enthusiasm, plans for a comeback soon disintegrated. Everyone went his own way.

Over the years, there were other couplings—invitations to play on each other's albums, at various charity events, a guest appearance here, a guest appearance there, a few uninspired duets that resulted in lackluster projects. They reconvened in May 1988 to play at a fortieth-anniversary tribute to Atlantic Records, again at the wedding of Bonzo's son, Jason, in April 1990, and for a third time in September 1995, when Led Zeppelin was inducted into the Rock & Roll Hall of Fame. But unlike The Who, Pink Floyd, the Rolling Stones, Black Sabbath, the Police, even the unfailingly estranged Simon & Garfunkel, all of whom pulled off successful comeback tours, all the king's horses and men couldn't put Led Zeppelin back together again.

"There might have been a couple of occasions where we could have got it back together," Jimmy lamented, "but I just presented scenario after scenario to him and Robert wasn't interested. He just didn't want to know. He said he doesn't want to sing Led Zeppelin numbers."

Their last performance together was on December 10, 2007, at a charity event at London's twenty-thousand-seat O2 Arena honoring Ahmet Ertegun, the undisputed "Record Man" and Led Zeppelin godfather, who had died the previous December. Led Zeppelin volunteered to play their first full solo concert in three decades—their first ever without Peter Grant, who had suffered a fatal heart attack in November 1995 at the age of sixty—to benefit an education fund in Ertegun's name. There were plenty of naysayers who shuddered at the thought. The ghost of Live Aid was still fresh in people's minds, and word from the road wasn't encouraging. There were reports that fifty-nine-year-old Robert's voice was shot, that Jimmy, now sixty-three, was showboating with various bands. Still, twenty million fans from fifty countries applied for tickets in a lottery.

This time they recruited a drummer with incomparable chops. Jason Bonham, at forty, wasn't his father, but he was pretty damn close. He'd learned at the feet of the master. He'd paid his dues, drumming with a half dozen bands, including a demanding stint with Foreigner. And he knew the songs inside and out, even his father's nuances, from listening to umpteen bootlegs.

The concert at the O2 in London was standing room only, with tickets from the touts going for $1,000 a pop. The arena fairly percolated with expectation. When Led Zeppelin appeared—on time and in tune—it was a bit of a shock. The quintessential bad boys appeared to have grown up. Robert's face was drawn with middle age, Jimmy had put on some much-improved weight, and Jonesy, at sixty-one, looked ready for a yacht outing. But looks were deceiving. The sound that ripped across the arena was stunning, vicious, a reminder of the sheer power of the group's by-now-classic work, still selling three decades later. "Good Times, Bad Times," appropriately, the first song on their first album, packed the kind of punch that had shell-shocked unsuspecting fans in the late sixties and seventies. "Heard from the floor, the group sounded hard and coherent," *The New Yorker* reported, "and close to the stage the sound was fierce."

The set was an anthology of well-conceived gems. "Ramble On," "Black Dog," "Nobody's Fault but Mine," "No Quarter" . . . There was no time between numbers to catch one's breath.

"There was a kind of loud serenity about Led Zeppelin's set. It was well-rehearsed," *The New York Times* confirmed. "Some of the top of [Robert's] voice has gone," but "he was authoritative . . . dignified." Jimmy's riffs were "enormous, nasty, glorious." And John Paul was "thoroughly in the pocket . . . keeping that same far-behind-the-beat groove." There were also kind words for Jason Bonham—"an expert in his father's beats, an encyclopedia of all their variations."

The hits, as the saying went, kept on coming. "Dazed and Confused," "Stairway to Heaven," "The Song Remains the Same," "Misty Mountain Hop" . . .

There was none of the communication breakdown that had riddled so many shows. Robert and Jimmy functioned on a common wavelength. They intuited each other, set each other up, fed off each other's energy.

They played assuredly, even gracefully. The historically frosty press saw fit to sing praise. "Plant's voice was rich and strong, and the mingling of Page's guitar with Jones's keyboards was thrilling." There was no place to take cover during the riveting, unsparing wrap-up: "Kashmir," "Whole Lotta Love," and "Rock and Roll," one right after the other.

"If there were skeptics tonight, Led Zeppelin silenced them," *NME* proclaimed, while *Forbes*, hardly a bastion of rock 'n roll advocacy, said, "They delivered the best show that ever was."

The sound was huge, and so was the legacy. Yes, this was a band with some miles on it—a certain heaviness that hearkened back to the blues origins of the music itself, weary, troubled, but defiant. The toll of time—the drugs, the drama, the tragedy, the clash of personalities—fed the music for once instead of hindering it. Pure talent and intensity shone through.

There were other attempts to reunite, none more attractive than a $90 million offer for the band to return to the road. While Jimmy Page and John Paul Jones waited for Robert Plant's decision to participate, they prepared with Jason Bonham on drums and a temporary vocalist—none other than Steven Tyler, who presumably didn't have to hitchhike to rehearsals. But in the end, Robert refused to get involved. He was finished, and so was the band.

The O2 concert was it: one final appraisal to remind the world of a band that left its mark. Led Zeppelin had finally earned the reviews they'd chased for almost forty years.

# Acknowledgments

I am indebted to many individuals who encouraged and assisted me throughout the process of researching and writing this biography. My deepest gratitude, first and foremost, goes to my editor, Scott Moyers, who proposed this project, shepherded it through every stage, exhibited enormous patience and unassuming expertise, and to whom this book is gratefully dedicated. He truly loves rock 'n roll, and I drew on his infectious spirit while writing the manuscript. I am also beholden to Sloan Harris, whose advocacy and candor has kept me focused on what's important throughout our long relationship, and to Ann Godoff for her leap of faith.

I also want to express my debt to Barney Hoskyns and his extraordinary archive, rocksbackpages.com, whose resources are second to none. Barney's oeuvre of stylishly written rock books, including his excellent oral history of Led Zeppelin, *Trampled Under Foot*, provided a wealth of illuminating interviews, and his offer to quote extensively from it was not taken lightly. Additionally, he provided inside dope and contact information for many of the sources in this book.

My appreciation extends to many kind folks, but especially to David Williams, Jimmy Page's boyhood mate and a quintessential blues expert, who answered endless questions and shared fascinating personal details. The same with the unflappable Chris Charlesworth, whose fine music journalism I've read and enjoyed for nearly fifty years. Chris took a machete to the manuscript and worked his ass off, collecting the author's copious errors as though they might somehow endow the Charlesworth Retirement Fund. I owe that guy several fabulous meals. Dave Lewis, who publishes *Tight But Loose* and is the foremost archivist of all things Led Zeppelin, also contributed guidance that is evident throughout this book.

I am especially grateful to the men and women, eyewitnesses to the thrilling Led Zeppelin odyssey, who shared their recollections and insights: Carmine Appice (a double threat: drummer extraordinaire and blessed with a set of awesome pipes), the irrepressible Maggie Bell, Dave Berry, Danny Betesh, Ed Bicknell, Rodney Bingenheimer, Cookie Brusa, Phil Carlo, Phil Carlson, Michal Des Barres, Bill Curbishley, Clive Davis, Bob Emmer, BP Fallon, Mitchell Fox, Kevyn Gammond, Vanessa Gilbert, Danny Goldberg, Colin Golding, Jerry Greenberg, Bill Harry, Abe Hoch, Jeff Hoffman, Elizabeth Iannaci, Glyn Johns, Shelley Kaye, Don Law, Benji LeFevre, Harvey Lisberg, Paul Lockey, Unity MacLean, Danny Marcus, Nick Maria, Lori Mattix, Roger Mayer, Jim McCarty, John Mendelsohn, the fabulous Graham Nash, Dave Pegg, Aubrey Powell, Terry Reid, Alan Rogan, John "Carter" Shakespeare, Henry "the Horse" Smith, John "Jumbo" Spicer, Shel Talmy, Phil Wells at Marshall Amps, Janine (Safer) Whitney, Sally Williams, Carole (Brown) Woods, and Joe "Jammer" Wright.

Additionally, I'd like to thank Michael J. Brennan, Jeanne Busson, Peter Ames Carlin, Jonathon Green, Bob Gruen, Casey Kaplan at Morrison Hotel Gallery, Mark Knopfler, Gered Mankowitz, Robin Mayhew of the Presidents, Paul McCartney for granting me permission to print Linda's lovely photo of Jimmy Page and Jeff Beck, Marc Myers, Jon Pareles, Barry Plummer, Neal Preston, Michael Zagaris, the late, great Peter Simon, and Helen Walker. Several friends read portions of the manuscript and weighed in with opinions and suggestions, among them Jonathan Eig (a wonderful biographer in his own right), Sandy D'Amato, Mark Bittman, John Scheinfeld, Rob Harris, Jon Whitney, and Lynne Kirby.

As always, Mia Council marshalled the publication process, keeping everything on track. When my next book comes due, if she decides to take a hasty, loooooong vacation, I will completely understand. Her colleagues at Penguin Press who contributed enormously to the look, feel, and legitimacy of this book include: Evan Gaffney for a beautifully designed cover; Hilary Roberts for a painstaking and meticulous copyedit (sorry, Hilary, but "blowjob" is one word); Eric Wechter, the fearless production editor; Laura Ogar for a thorough index; and Amelia Zalcman, who gave the manuscript a legal read and earned every penny of her hourly rate. I must also thank the gang of extraordinary photographers whose images appear in the book and who, contrary to their reputations, cut me a considerable break.

Lastly, no one was more supportive than Becky Aikman, the Iron Lady of grammar, who whacked her way through the adverbial weeds and provided insight, wisdom, and love, although not necessarily in that order. She continues to have my back, my front, even my rough sides, in exchange for the promise that I will not play "Stairway to Heaven" again. Ever.

Friends, family, colleagues, sources—to one and all, a whole lotta love.

# Notes

---

The names of Led Zeppelin band members are abbreviated in the notes as follows:

JB (John Bonham)
JP (Jimmy Page)
JPJ (John Paul Jones)
RP (Robert Plant)

Abbreviated forms of books and magazines have been used in these Notes for the following:

MM (Melody Maker)
NME (New Musical Express)
*Trampled* (Barney Hoskyns, *Trampled Under Foot*)
*Trouser Press* interview (Dave Schulps, "Jimmy Page Gives the Interview of His Life"), Part 1 ("Pre-Yardbirds," September 1977); Part 2 ("Paging the Yardbirds: Jimmy Page Gives His Version," October 1977); Part 3 ("The Final Page: Jimmy P. on Led Z.," November 1977)

## Prologue

1 **Alison Steele, NEW's Nightbird:** "The first place I got the record played was New York City, on WNEW on Alison Steele's nighttime show." Mario Medious, quoted in Barney Hoskyns, *Trampled Under Foot* (London: Faber & Faber, 2012), p. 128.

3 **converted Unitarian meeting house:** Music Museum of New England, "The Boston Tea Party," n.d., www.mmone.org/the-boston-tea-party.

3 **"It was a tough neighborhood":** Don Law, interview with the author, November 8, 2018.

4 **"lived up to [their] advance":** Ben Blummenberg, "Jimmy Page: After the Yardbirds . . . Comes Led Zeppelin," *Boston After Dark*, February 5, 1969.

4 **He felt at home:** "It's one of the best places he's ever played," Robert Plant announced from the stage, January 23, 1969.

5 **Law spent a few minutes:** Don Law interview.

5 **"One of the things":** RP, quoted in Chris Welch, "Robert Plant," MM, March 19, 1977.

5 **Just that Thursday afternoon:** Randy Harrison, comment (June 16, 2010) on "January 26, 1969, Boston, MA, Boston Tea Party," Timeline, ledzeppelin.com.

6 **"to whom we all owe":** RP, interview with Terry Gross, Fresh Air, NPR, August 24, 2004.

6 **"were jamming as if they":** Bob Kenney, concert review, Guitar Player, June 1968.

6 **"ranked in the company":** Philip Elwood, "Impressive New Rock Group," San Francisco Examiner, January 11, 1969.

6 **"Several critics, myself included":** Ritchie Yorke, "Led Zeppelin," Toronto Globe & Mail, January 3, 1969.

6 **"After the San Francisco gig":** JP, quoted in Nick Kent, "Session Star: Jimmy Page," NME, September 1, 1973.

6 **"Each member of the group":** Pam Brent, review of concert January 19, 1969, at Grande Ballroom, Detroit, MI, in Creem, March 1969.

7 **"We got better each day":** JP, quoted in Beat Instrumental, April 1969.

7 **"like kings, like conquering heroes":** W. Brennan, comment (December 8, 2008) on "January 26, 1969."

8 **"hit your chest":** Brennan, comment on "January 26, 1969."

8 **"like a runaway freight train":** Harrison, comment on "January 26, 1969."

8 **"You could feel the whole":** Mario Medious, quoted in Hoskyns, Trampled, p. 124.

8 **"getting sound and feedback":** Brennan, comment on "January 26, 1969."

8 **"If you don't want to":** Blummenberg, "Jimmy Page."

9 **After some deliberation:** "We played the act twice." JP, quoted in Mat Snow, "Led Zeppelin," Q, December 1990.

9 **They looked as though they'd:** "The room was a steam bath." Stephen Davis, LZ-'75 (New York: Gotham Books, 2010), p. 22.

9 **"There were kids actually bashing":** JPJ, quoted in Nick Kent, "Led Zeppelin: The Zeppelin Road Test," NME, February 23, 1973.

9 **"Zeppelin was so fucking heavy":** Steven Tyler, quoted in Davis, LZ-'75, p. 23.

10 **"It was in such a state":** JPJ, quoted in Kent, "Led Zeppelin."

10 **As they staggered into:** "Peter hugged us at the end of the gig, picked all four of us up at once." JP, quoted in Snow, "Led Zeppelin."

10 **"was crying, if you can":** JPJ, quoted in Kent, "Led Zeppelin."

10 **"were actually going to":** JP, quoted in Snow, "Led Zeppelin."

10 **"the key Led Zeppelin gig":** JPJ, quoted in Kent, "Led Zeppelin."

11 **"For four consecutive evenings":** Blummenberg, "Jimmy Page."

## Chapter One: A Case of the Blues

15 **"sounded tough, unpolite":** "But with some light and shade in each number." Max Jones, concert review, MM, October 25, 1958.

15 **"reverberate[d] through the annals":** Owen Adams, "Muddy's Blues Didn't Rock Us," Music Blog, theguardian.com, March 17, 2008.

15 **"sometimes ankle-deep in condensation":** Keith Richards with James Fox, Life (New York: Little, Brown, 2010), p. 88.

15 **The night the club opened:** "It was packed from the first night." Alexis Korner, quoted in John Pidgeon, "A Conversation with Alexis Korner," unpublished, November 15, 1971, transcript posted on Rock's Backpages.

15 **"Of course, I knew Lewis":** "He finished his little bit, came over, and we had a chat." David Williams, interview with the author, November 28, 2018.

16 **"Who are you listening to?":** David Williams interview.

16 **"all lips and ears":** Long John Baldry, quoted in John Pidgeon, "Blues Incorporated: How British R&B Trashed Trad," *Rock's Backpages*, September 24, 2009.

18 **"Whatever it was":** Jim McCarty with Dave Thompson, *Nobody Told Me!* (self-published, 2018); Jim McCarty, interview with the author, September 12, 2019.

19 **"This was serious shit!":** David Williams interview.

20 **"I was struggling":** "I saw him play bottleneck guitar." JP, quoted in David Fricke, "Jimmy Page: The Rolling Stone Interview," *Rolling Stone*, December 6, 2012.

21 **Illinois Golden Gloves Heavyweight Championship:** Willie Dixon and Don Snowdon, *I Am the Blues* (New York: Da Capo, 1990), p. 33.

21 **"produced a harmonica and blew":** David Williams, *The First Time We Met the Blues* (York, UK: Music Mentor Books, 2009), p. 85.

22 **"he dropped the guitar":** Williams, *First Time We Met the Blues*, p. 89.

22 **"Their jaws were on their knees":** David Williams interview.

24 **"It was a matter":** Vic Johnson, quoted in Bill Wyman with Ray Coleman, *Stone Alone* (New York: Viking, 1990), pp. 121–22.

25 **"It was a nondescript street":** David Williams interview.

26 **"complete and utter junk":** David Williams interview.

26 **"He liked to listen to records":** Patricia Page, quoted in Ritchie Yorke, *Led Zep* (New York: Two Continents, 1976), p. 25.

26 **"You had to stick":** JP, quoted in Steven Rosen, "Jimmy Page," *Guitar Player*, July 1997.

27 **"like divine intervention":** JP, quoted in Fricke, "Jimmy Page."

27 **"I heard the acoustic guitar":** JP, quoted in Dave Schulps, *Trouser Press* interview, Part 1, p. 12.

27 **"I wanted to play it":** JP, quoted in a *Sunday Times* article, blind-quoted in Chris Salewicz, *Jimmy Page* (New York: Da Capo, 2019), pp. 20–21.

27 **Called skiffle, after African American slang:** Jonathon Green, *Green's Dictionary of Slang* (online edition, 2019), definition provided to the author by Jonathon Green.

28 **Between thirty thousand:** Ronald D. Cohen, *Folk Music: The Basics* (New York: Routledge, 2006), p. 98.

28 **"From the beginning":** David Williams interview.

28 **"I was far too impatient":** JP, quoted in John Tobler and Stuart Grundy, *The Guitar Greats* (London: BBC Publishing, 1983), p. 96.

28 **"You listened to the solo":** JP, quoted in David Fricke, "Q&A: Jimmy Page," *Rolling Stone*, June 12, 2008.

28 **Trouble was, his guitar wasn't:** "The Spanish guitar quickly became obsolete to my needs." JP, quoted in Michael Odell, "The Jimmy Page Interview," *Uncut*, November 2019, p. 64.

28 **"was something you would see":** JP, quoted in Fricke, "Jimmy Page."

28 **"you have to do":** "My dad could see I was making progress." JP, quoted in Odell, "Jimmy Page Interview."

29 **"I did a paper round":** "But obviously, what I always wanted was a proper electric guitar." JP, quoted in Odell, "Jimmy Page Interview."

29 **"When the sound came through":** "I remember playing it through my parents' radio." JP, quoted in Brad Tolinski, *Light & Shade* (New York: Crown, 2012), p. 122.

29 **"I could get together":** JP, quoted in Fricke, "Q&A: Jimmy Page."

30 **"quite nervous":** JP, quoted in Martin Power, *No Quarter: The Three Lives of Jimmy Page* (London: Omnibus, 2016), p. 14.

30 **"There was some blues"**: JP, quoted in Fricke, "Q&A: Jimmy Page."

31 **"It was a crappy film"**: "We went back the next day just to see him again." David Williams interview.

32 **"Solos which affected me"**: JP, quoted in Tobler and Grundy, *Guitar Greats*, p. 96.

32 **"Jimmy was obsessed"**: David Williams interview.

32 **"The only way"**: JP, quoted in *Mojo*, March 2010.

33 **"That was the style"**: Rod Wyatt, quoted in Salewicz, *Jimmy Page*, p. 30.

33 **"We were too young"**: David Williams, interview with the author, May 16, 2019.

33 **"Bobby was so influential"**: John Spicer, interview with the author, May 16, 2019.

33 **"Jimmy *idolized* Bobby Taylor"**: David Williams, interview with the author, November 28, 2018.

34 **"It was a pretty sketchy"**: Anna Williams, interview with the author, May 16, 2019.

35 **"He'd talk to us"**: John Spicer, interview with the author, May 10, 2019.

36 **"were very encouraging"**: "They had enough confidence that I knew what I was doing." From a Q magazine interview, blind-quoted in Salewicz, *Jimmy Page*, p. 32.

36 **Friends say he never called:** "It used to piss me off. His father was very condescending." David Williams interview, May 16, 2019.

36 **"He reassured my parents"**: JP, quoted in Tobler and Grundy, *Guitar Greats*, p. 97.

36 **"If I promise to pay"**: Chris Tidmarsh, quoted in Kieron Tyler, "Jimmy Page: Educating Jimmy," *Mojo*, May 2001.

37 **He was a rugged bloke:** "He would have needed cosmetic surgery to make him look like a pretty boy." John Spicer interview, May 10, 2019.

38 **"We can't keep going on"**: John Spicer interview, May 10, 2019.

38 **"Why don't you start"**: JP, quoted in Tyler, "Jimmy Page."

39 **"arc[ing] over backwards"**: JP, quoted in Tyler, "Jimmy Page."

39 **"We used to build up"**: John Spicer interview, May 16, 2019.

39 **"a smart lad, immaculately dressed"**: John Spicer interview, May 16, 2019.

39 **"We did every cover version"**: Neil Christian, quoted in Tyler, "Jimmy Page."

40 **"Everywhere we played"**: John Spicer interview, May 10, 2019.

40 **"Oh, probably six hours"**: JP, quoted in Nick Kent, "Jimmy Page: Guitars I Have Known," *NME*, October 12, 1974.

40 **"Jerry Lee was his great love"**: David Williams interview, May 16, 2019.

41 **His girlfriend, Anna:** "I went in his place." Anna Williams interview.

## Chapter Two: Getting Down to Business

43 **To cut their losses:** "We used to chat up this girl called June Cutler." David Williams, interview with the author, November 28, 2018.

43 **"There was this great"**: JP, quoted in Howard Mylett, *Jimmy Page: Tangents Within a Framework* (London: Omnibus, 1983), p. 10.

43 **"was a purist"**: JP, quoted in Dave Schulps, *Trouser Press* interview, Part 1, p. 12.

44 **In addition, several club circuits:** Two promoters in particular: Ron King had nine venues and Stanley Dale had six that employed the Crusaders on a regular basis.

45 **"on a Saturday night"**: John Spicer, interview with the author, May 10, 2019.

45 **"if you overlooked the obscenities"**: Spicer interview.

45 **"We acquired a good reputation"**: JP, quoted in Tolinski, *Light & Shade*, p. 14.

46 **"We knew that American"**: JP, blind-quoted in Salewicz, *Jimmy Page*, p. 38.

46 **Jimmy composed original:** "Jimmy composed his own music to back my poems." Royston Ellis interview, forums.ledzeppelin.com/topic/308-zeppelin-mysteries-hosted -by-steve-a-jones/page/102/?tab=comments#comment-369179.

46 **"vaguely provocative verse":** Williams, *First Time We Met the Blues*, p. 44; John Spicer, interview with the author, May 16, 2019.

46 **"Jimmy would study those tapes":** David Williams interview.

47 **He did, however, manage:** "It was amazing. I'd never heard anything like it before." John Spicer interview, May 10, 2019.

47 **"He was also into overdubbing":** Colin Golding, interview with the author, May 15, 2018.

48 **He played it and played it:** "I remember going around to Jim's and playing it dozens of times. All he wanted to know was 'What do you think? What do you think?'" Colin Golding interview.

48 **"traveling to one-nighter gigs":** JP, quoted in Kieron Tyler, "Jimmy Page: Educating Jimmy," *Mojo*, May 2001.

48 **"We lived out":** Neil Christian, quoted in Tyler, "Jimmy Page."

48 **"I remember we were driving":** JP, quoted in Tolinski, *Light & Shade*, p. 14.

48 **To stay wired:** Royston Ellis maintained, "I was shown how to [chew the Benzedrine tab] by . . . a guitarist who used to accompany me in those days, Jimmy Page." Royston Ellis interview, forums.ledzeppelin.com/topic/308-zeppelin-mysteries-hosted-by-steve -a-jones/page/102/?tab=comments#comment-369179.

49 **"The numbers we were doing":** JP, quoted in Schulps, "*Trouser Press* interview, Part 1, p. 12.

49 **"It was just disheartening":** JP, quoted in Nick Kent, "Jimmy Page: Guitars I Have Known," *NME*, October 12, 1974.

49 **"You didn't have to do":** Chris Dreja, quoted in Tolinski, *Light & Shade*, p. 54.

49 **"It was cool being":** John Spicer interview, May 16, 2019.

50 **"a terrible draftsman":** "I was also accepted at Croydon—I don't know how because I was a terrible draftsman." JP, quoted in John Tobler, "Jimmy Page: The Life and Times of a Guitar Prophet," *Musician*, January 1984.

50 **"It had a very relaxed":** Colin Golding interview.

50 **"There were loads of people":** Richards, *Life*, pp. 68–69.

50 **Michael Des Barres recalls:** Michael Des Barres, interview with the author, February 20, 2019.

51 **"We didn't play":** JP, quoted in David Fricke, "Jimmy Page: The Rolling Stone Interview," *Rolling Stone*, December 6, 2012.

51 **"Glyn [Johns] introduced me":** JP, quoted in Tobler and Grundy, *Guitar Greats*, p. 97.

51 **"I was about to do":** Glyn Johns, interview with the author, May 18, 2018.

51 **"sort of impenetrable brotherhood":** JP, quoted in Tobler and Grundy, *Guitar Greats*, p. 97.

51 **"kept telling me that Jimmy Page":** Tony Meehan, quoted in Yorke, *Led Zep*, p. 30.

52 **"they stuck a row of dots":** "I'd never bothered or tried to read music." JP, quoted in Tobler and Grundy, *Guitar Greats*, p. 97.

52 **"I knew right away":** Tony Meehan, quoted in Yorke, *Led Zep*, p. 30.

52 **"Jimmy rang me and said":** Glyn Johns, quoted in Hoskyns, *Trampled*, p. 20.

52 **"Jimmy wasn't any kind":** David Williams, interview with the author, May 16, 2019.

52 **"She kept telling me":** Jeff Beck, quoted in Tobler and Grundy, *Guitar Greats*, p. 83.

53 **Jimmy, for his part:** "He played 'Not Fade Away.' I never forgot it." Jeff Beck, quoted in Hoskyns, *Trampled*, p. 10.

53 **"We would play Ricky Nelson songs"**: Jeff Beck, quoted in Tolinski, *Light & Shade*, p. 31.

54 **"They were playing flat-out R&B"**: Jeff Beck, quoted in Tobler and Grundy, *Guitar Greats*, p. 67.

54 **"We'd had some modest success"**: John Shakespeare, interview with the author, May 14, 2018.

55 **"The old guard used to sit"**: Dave Berry, interview with the author, November 29, 2018.

55 **referred to themselves as "hooligans"**: "Suddenly, you've got these hooligans like myself and Jim who had come in from the rock 'n roll era groups." Clem Cattini, quoted in Hoskyns, *Trampled*, p. 24.

55 **"I was mainly called"**: JP, quoted in Schulps, *Trouser Press* interview, Part 1, p. 13.

55 **"wonderful fingerpicking style"**: John Shakespeare interview.

55 **Jimmy, who was still learning**: "Page always ended up on rhythm guitar because he couldn't read too well." JPJ, quoted in Hoskyns, *Trampled*, p. 24.

56 **"I was more jazz influenced"**: Jim Sullivan, quoted in Tyler, "Jimmy Page."

56 **"Big Jim could play anything"**: Glyn Johns interview.

56 **"total spontaneity"**: Jim Sullivan, quoted in Tyler, "Jimmy Page."

56 **"You had to be a special"**: Jim Sullivan, quoted in Hoskyns, *Trampled*, p. 24.

56 **"The first session"**: Bobby Graham, quoted in Hoskyns, *Trampled*, p. 24.

56 **"You never knew what"**: JP, quoted in Cameron Crowe, "The Durable Led Zeppelin," *Rolling Stone*, March 13, 1975.

57 **"That was a phenomenal session"**: JP, blind-quoted in Power, *No Quarter*, p. 58.

57 **"a shockingly baby-faced"**: Graham Nash, interview with the author, April 23, 2012.

57 **"What was stifling"**: "Session work is frustrating much of the time." JP, quoted in Mick Houghton, "Zeus of Zeppelin: An Interview with Jimmy Page," *Circus*, October 12, 1976.

57 **"It just happened"**: "It was cool!" JP, interview with John Sugar, BBC Radio 4, October 11, 2011.

58 **"You'd be there"**: JP, quoted in Houghton, "Zeus of Zeppelin."

58 **"I don't think he had"**: Glyn Johns interview.

58 **"polite, old-fashioned rock 'n' roll"**: Shel Talmy, interview with the author, January 30, 2019.

59 **"Ray didn't really approve"**: "The Kinks just didn't want me around when they were recording." JP, blind-quoted in Power, *No Quarter*, p. 63.

59 **"I wasn't really needed"**: JP, quoted in Nick Kent, "Session Star: Jimmy Page," *NME*, September 1, 1973.

60 **"a stuck-up prick"**: Billy Harrison, blind-quoted in Salewicz, *Jimmy Page*, p. 51.

60 **"It was very embarrassing"**: JP, quoted in Schulps, *Trouser Press* interview, Part 1, p. 13.

60 **"There was much grumbling"**: Billy Harrison, blind-quoted in Salewicz, *Jimmy Page*, p. 51.

60 **"Their lead vocalist, Van Morrison"**: Bobby Graham, blind-quoted in Salewicz, *Jimmy Page*, p. 51.

60 **"There wasn't anyone"**: Shel Talmy interview.

61 **"Great, let's have him"**: Jackie DeShannon, blind-quoted in Salewicz, *Jimmy Page*, p. 88.

62 **"Furious beat with vocal touches"**: Review of "She Just Satisfies," *Record Mirror*, February 22, 1965.

62 **Wexler, as astute a businessman:** Jerry Wexler and David Ritz, *Rhythm and the Blues* (New York: Knopf, 1993), p. 158.

63 **"What wasn't to love?":** Graham Nash, interview with the author, April 26, 2012.

## Chapter Three: Reinventing the Wheel

65 **"He was a ridiculous figure":** Shel Talmy, interview with the author, January 30, 2019.

65 **"a poor man's Bob Dylan":** "Mickie didn't want to keep him in the direction he was going in." Chris Most, interview with the author, May 14, 2019.

65 **"They made making records easy":** Mickie Most, quoted in Kieron Tyler, "Jimmy Page: Educating Jimmy," *Mojo*, May 2001.

65 **"Mickie had no patience":** Chris Most interview.

65 **Most famously he insisted:** "A pop song is something that takes fifteen minutes to make and two weeks to forget." Mickie Most, quoted in Steve Turner, "The Midas Touch: Mickie Most," *The History of Rock*, 1983.

65 **"wanted the backing track":** Chris Dreja, quoted in Tolinski, *Light & Shade*, p. 63.

65 **donning street gear:** Pete Frame, "Getting to the Bottom of the Page," *ZigZag*, December 1972.

66 **The perfect instrument had come:** "I was one of the first people in England to have one." JP, quoted in Tolinski, *Light & Shade*, p. 53.

66 **"more responsive to the player's":** JP, quoted in Yorke, *Led Zep*, p. 37.

66 **"Jimmy had a Gibson Maestro":** Roger Mayer, interview with the author, November 28, 2018.

67 **Session work had become:** "It's a boring life. You're like a machine." JP, quoted in Dave Schulps, "*Trouser Press* interview, Part 1, p. 14.

67 **"The whole thing wasn't enjoyable":** JP, quoted in Tobler and Grundy, *Guitar Greats*, p. 98.

67 **"The work was stifling":** "It was often like being a computer when you had no involvement with the artist." JP, quoted in Yorke, *Led Zep*, p. 38.

67 **"a hired hand, a phantom":** JP, blind-quoted in Power, *No Quarter*, p. 85.

68 **"I know all the crooks":** JP, quoted in Schulps, *Trouser Press* interview, Part 1, p. 14.

68 **no "old farts":** "We offered [Jimmy] a job as in-house producer because . . . we were so fed up with old farts." Andrew Oldham, quoted in "The Real Jimmy Page," *Uncut*, November 28, 2008.

69 **"I did four tracks altogether":** JP, quoted in Tobler and Grundy, *Guitar Greats*, p. 99.

69 **"He'd never heard feedback":** JP, quoted in Yorke, *Led Zep*, p. 36.

70 **"I'd been going to gigs":** JP, blind-quoted in Power, *No Quarter*, p. 106.

70 **"with awe-stricken disbelief":** McCarty, *Nobody Told Me!*, p. 48.

70 **"It was exactly how":** Jim McCarty, interview with the author, September 12, 2019.

71 **"In a matter of weeks":** Chris Dreja, quoted in Tolinski, *Light & Shade*, p. 55.

71 **"The colors were starting":** Jimmy Page, quoted in David Fricke, "On the Way to Led Zeppelin: Jimmy Page on the Yardbird Years," *Rolling Stone*, November 27, 2012.

71 **"a bit stiff":** "Topham's guitar playing was a bit stiff." Eric Clapton, *Clapton* (New York: Broadway Books, 2007), p. 46.

71 **"A nice kid":** Jim McCarty interview.

72 **"I asked Eric Clapton to join":** Giorgio Gomelsky, quoted in Yorke, *Led Zep*, p. 40.

72 **a technique he learned:** "[King's playing] was absolutely earth-shattering for me, like a new light for me to move toward." Clapton, *Clapton*, p. 41.

72 **"jamming in the middle":** Clapton, *Clapton*, p. 49.

72 **"He was obsessed":** JP, quoted in Dave Schulps, *Trouser Press* interview, Part 2, p. 23.

72 **"I have to play what I believe":** Eric Clapton, quoted in Dawn James, "Eric Clapton: The Yardbird Who Got Left Behind," *Rave*, June 1965.

73 **"I was destroying myself":** Eric Clapton, quoted in James, "Eric Clapton."

73 **To replace him, the Yardbirds:** "I'll tell you who we wanted. Jimmy Page." McCarty, *Nobody Told Me!*, p. 103.

73 **"He used to come around":** Jim McCarty interview.

73 **"it just seemed really distasteful":** JP, quoted in Schulps, *Trouser Press* interview, Part 2, p. 23.

73 **"We were so taken aback":** McCarty, *Nobody Told Me!*, p. 105.

73 **"Musically, he was so versatile":** McCarty, *Nobody Told Me!*, p. 107.

74 **"He was a great experimenter":** Chris Dreja, quoted in Tolinski, *Light & Shade*, pp. 58–59.

74 **"We were using feedback":** Jeff Beck, quoted in Tobler and Grundy, *Guitar Greats*, p. 69.

74 **"They were always talking":** Jeff Beck, quoted in Tobler and Grundy, *Guitar Greats*, p. 33. Remembered somewhat differently: "For fuck's sake, I'm in the band now, so shut up." Jeff Beck, quoted in McCarty, *Nobody Told Me!*, p. 108.

75 **"They could only play":** Jim McCarty interview.

75 **"By bending the notes slightly":** Jeff Beck, quoted in Tolinski, *Light & Shade*, pp. 34–35.

75 **"uncomfortable playing to the elite":** Tolinski, *Light & Shade*, p. 61.

76 **"It was a great crowd":** "I normally don't get fucked up before a show, but this time I did." Graham Nash, interview with the author, November 21, 2018.

76 **"Do you know about karate?":** Jim McCarty interview.

76 **"Keith decided to have":** McCarty, *Nobody Told Me!*, p. 149.

77 **"rolling round the stage":** JP, quoted in Tyler, "Jimmy Page."

77 **"we had to literally tie him":** Chris Dreja, quoted in Tolinski, *Light & Shade*, p. 58.

77 **"just fantastically suitable":** JP, quoted in Frame, "Getting to the Bottom."

77 **"it was a great anarchistic night":** "There was this great argument going on." JP, quoted in Steven Rosen, "Jeff Beck on Jimmy Page," *Guitar World*, July 1986. "It was great, just fantastically suitable for the occasion, I thought." JP, quoted in Yorke, *Led Zep*, p. 44.

77 **"I can't stand this anymore":** Paul Samwell-Smith, quoted in Nick Kent, "Session Star: Jimmy Page," *NME*, September 173.

77 **"Jeff often used to say":** JP, quoted in Frame, "Getting to the Bottom."

78 **"not being able to express":** JP, quoted in Johnny Black, "Your Time Is Gonna Come," *Q Special Edition: Led Zeppelin*, March 2003, p. 10.

78 **"drying up as a guitarist":** JP, blind-quoted in Hoskyns, *Trampled*, p. 60.

78 **"Yeah, I'll play bass":** JP, blind-quoted in Salewicz, *Jimmy Page*, p. 94.

78 **"I was terrified":** JP, quoted in Tobler and Grundy, *Guitar Greats*, p. 99.

78 **"He couldn't play the bass":** Jeff Beck, blind-quoted in Salewicz, *Jimmy Page*, p. 95.

78 **"I tended to play it":** JP, quoted in Jim Delehant, "Yardbird Jimmy Page Says, 'Open Your Mind,'" *Hit Parader*, March 1967 .

78 **"We needed stability":** Jim McCarty interview.

79 **"We'd see him drive":** Jim McCarty interview.

79 **He also had a riff:** "Apparently, he made up the riff to 'Over Under Sideways Down'—he'd sung it to Jeff." JP, quoted in Mick Houghton, "Zeus of Zeppelin: An Interview with Jimmy Page," *Circus*, October 12, 1976.

79 **"I didn't know much":** Simon Napier-Bell, quoted in Hoskyns, *Trampled*, pp. 60–61.

80 **If he picked up:** "If he'd had a bad day, he'd take it out on the audience." JP, quoted in Steven Rosen, "Jimmy Page," *Guitar Player*, July 1977.

80 **"The amp would be crackling":** Jeff Beck, quoted in Tony Hibbert, "Jeff Beck: Rough 'n' Ready," *The History of Rock*, 1983.

80 **"He did have a discipline":** JP, quoted in Rosen, "Jeff Beck on Jimmy Page."

80 **"When he's having a shining":** "I've always said that he's a brilliant musician." JP, quoted in Yorke, *Led Zep*, p. 47.

80 **"To keep me quiet":** Jeff Beck, quoted in Tobler and Grundy, *Guitar Greats*, p. 69.

80 **"He had a twelve-string":** Jeff Beck, quoted in Rosen, "Jeff Beck on Jimmy Page."

80 **"you've got to break away":** Jeff Beck, quoted in Douglas Noble, "Jeff Beck: Beck's Bolero," *Guitar Magazine* 3, no. 4 (June 1993).

81 **"worked out the other beat":** Jeff Beck, quoted in Rosen, "Jeff Beck on Jimmy Page."

81 **"the first heavy metal riff":** Jeff Beck, quoted in Martin Power, *Hot Wired Guitar: The Life of Jeff Beck* (New York: Omnibus, 2012), p. 131.

81 **Jimmy insists he wrote:** "I did the main construction on it—the opening and the riff." Schulps, "Jimmy Page Gives the Interview of His Life," Part 2, p. 27.

81 **"Keith Relf had a melody":** JP, quoted in Schulps, "Jimmy Page Gives the Interview of His Life," Part 2, p. 27.

81 **"Beck's doing the slide bits":** Rosen, "Jimmy Page."

81 **"Even though he said":** Rosen, "Jimmy Page."

81 **"a momentous recording session":** Jeff Beck, quoted in Black, "Your Time Is Gonna Come," p. 10.

81 **"It was at a point":** Pete Townshend, blind-quoted in Salewicz, *Jimmy Page*, p. 92.

81 **"He got out of the cab":** Jeff Beck, quoted in Tobler and Grundy, *Guitar Greats*, p. 71.

82 **"You could feel the excitement":** Jeff Beck, blind-quoted in Salewicz, *Jimmy Page*, p. 90.

82 **"We didn't deliberate":** Jeff Beck, quoted in Black, "Your Time Is Gonna Come," p. 10.

82 **"Keith upped the tempo":** Jeff Beck, quoted in Power, *Hot Wired Guitar*, p. 132.

82 **"Cream was being formed":** Simon Napier-Bell, blind-quoted in Salewicz, *Jimmy Page*, p. 89.

83 **"He told me in a club":** Jeff Beck, quoted in Tobler and Grundy, *Guitar Greats*, p. 71.

83 **"It was going to be me and Beck":** JP, quoted in Tobler and Grundy, *Guitar Greats*, p. 99.

83 **"The first choice":** JP, quoted in Schulps, *Trouser Press* interview, Part 2, p. 27.

83 **"was well known for threatening":** Glyn Johns, *Sound Man* (New York: Blue Rider, 2014), p. 66.

83 **"How would you like":** JP, quoted in Schulps, *Trouser Press* interview, Part 2, p. 27.

84 **"down like a lead zeppelin":** Dave Lewis, *From a Whisper to a Scream* (London: Omnibus, 2012), 19; David Fricke, "Jimmy Page: The Rolling Stone Interview," *Rolling Stone*, December 6, 2012; Mick Wall, *When Giants Walked the Earth* (London: Orion, 2008), 15.

## Chapter Four: Front

85 **"He'd come in on bass":** Chris Dreja, quoted in Gene Santoro, "Of Yardbirds and the Shapes of Things to Come," July 1986.

85 **"Jeff was going to be":** JP, quoted in Tolinski, *Light & Shade*, p. 47.

86 **"Something went wrong"**: Jim McCarty, quoted in Yorke, *Led Zep*, p. 46.

86 **"The power amp had"**: Jeff Beck, quoted in David Sinclair, "Jeff Beck: Just Say No," *Q*, October 1989.

86 **"There was a macho contingent"**: Jeff Beck, quoted in Sinclair, "Jeff Beck."

86 **"It was really nerve-racking"**: JP, quoted in Mylett, *Jimmy Page*, p. 15.

86 **"It'd take your breath away"**: Henry Smith, interview with the author, October 2, 2019.

87 **"playing harmony lines"**: JP, quoted in Tolinsky, *Light & Shade*, pp. 45–46.

87 **"couple of Freddie King solos"**: "Jeff and I have had quite a few workouts round at my place, and they have been pretty successful." JP, blind-quoted in Mylett, *Jimmy Page*, p. 15.

87 **"We rehearsed hard"**: JP, quoted in Pete Frame, "Getting to the Bottom of the Page," *ZigZag*, December 1972.

87 **"There were fucking brainstorms"**: Jeff Beck, quoted in Steven Rosen, "Jeff Beck: In Retrospect," *Los Angeles Free Press*, December 1973.

87 **"a couple of gunslingers"**: Chris Dreja, quoted in Hoskyns, *Trampled*, p. 62.

87 **"It was fascinating to watch"**: McCarty, *Nobody Told Me!*, p. 158.

87 **"I personally don't think"**: Chris Dreja, quoted in Yorke, *Led Zep*, p. 46.

88 **"Jeff was just uncontrollable"**: Chris Dreja, quoted in Hoskyns, *Trampled*, p. 63.

88 **"Beck would often go off"**: JP, quoted in Frame, "Getting to the Bottom."

88 **"If Jimmy played something"**: Jim McCarty, interview with the author, September 12, 2019.

88 **"we were just on opposite sides"**: Jeff Beck, quoted in Nick Kent, "Beck Looks Back," *NME*, November 4, 1972.

88 **"Every night"**: McCarty, *Nobody Told Me!*, p. 156.

89 **"All the American groups"**: Jeff Beck, blind-quoted in Salewicz, *Jimmy Page*, p. 110.

89 **"You had to sleep"**: JP, quoted in Frame, "Getting to the Bottom."

89 **"People just shouted out"**: Jim McCarty interview.

89 **"hyper, nervous, insecure"**: Jim McCarty, quoted in Kieron Tyler, "Jimmy Page: Educating Jimmy," *Mojo*, May 2001.

89 **"You wake up in the middle"**: Jeff Beck, quoted in Charles Shaar Murray, "The Jeff Beck Interview," *Mojo*, April 1999.

89 **"He'd gone fucking crazy!"**: JP, blind-quoted in Power, *No Quarter*, p. 121.

90 **"Six hours in that thing"**: Jeff Beck, blind-quoted in Salewicz, *Jimmy Page*, p. 111.

90 **"I was on this escalator"**: Jeff Beck, quoted in Murray, "Jeff Beck Interview."

90 **"The Yardbirds weren't"**: RP, quoted in Steve Peacock, "Robert Plant," *Sounds*, June 26, 1971.

90 **"They were just totally adamant"**: JP, quoted in Dave Schulps, *Trouser Press* interview, Part 2, p. 25.

90 **"I'd burned all my bridges"**: Jeff Beck, quoted in Murray, "Jeff Beck Interview."

91 **"very difficult to deal with"**: Simon Napier-Bell, quoted in Salewicz, *Jimmy Page*, p. 112.

91 **"an opportunist" who knew nothing**: JP, quoted in Schulps, "Jimmy Page: The Trouser Press Interview."

91 **"Napier-Bell called up"**: JP, quoted in Schulps, "Jimmy Page."

91 **"It was really weird"**: "We were shocked. Nobody told us this was going to happen." Jim McCarty interview.

91 **"I'd known Peter"**: JP, quoted in Hoskyns, *Trampled*, p. 64.

92 **"There used to be great battles"**: Peter Grant, quoted in Michael Watts, "Peter Grant: The Man Who Led Zeppelin," *MM*, June 22, 1974.

92 **"Ingram Road, as it was called"**: "I went to a school for the sons of gentlemen." Phil Carson, interview with the author, July 2, 2019.

92 **"I was fascinated"**: "It seemed pretty glamorous and better than the steel factory." Peter Grant, interview with Malcolm McLaren, 1988.

93 **"besotted with show business"**: Chris Most, interview with the author, May 14, 2019.

93 **"Every new record he heard"**: Brian Gregg, quoted in Pete Frame, *The Restless Generation* (London: Rogan House, 2007), p. 264.

93 **"the English Everly Brothers"**: Mickie Most, quoted in Frame, *Restless Generation*, p. 265.

94 **Grant worked as a timekeeper**: Peter Grant, interview with Malcolm McLaren.

94 **His Royal Highness Count Bruno Alessio**: "That was one of the names he used, and also Count Massimo." Ed Bicknell, interview with the author, November 17, 2018.

94 **"Peter only had one surefire move"**: Ed Bicknell interview.

94 **"Nobody had any money"**: Mickie Most, quoted in Chris Welch, *Peter Grant* (London: Omnibus, 2002), p. 21.

95 **"Make sure that fucker"**: Don Arden with Mick Wall, *Mr. Big* (London: Robson Books, 2004), p. 70.

95 **"If you intend to be"**: Ed Bicknell, interview with the author, November 27, 2018.

96 **"introduce Stigwood to the view"**: Ed Bicknell, interview with the author, May 11, 2019.

96 **"We're in Cal Danger's band"**: Phil Carson interview.

96 **Peter Grant retired**: "Peter left the road and had a room of his own, with a desk and telephone, to work as a booking agent for Arden." Carole Brown Woods, email to the author, November 12, 2019.

97 **"at Jimmy's insistence"**: Jim McCarty interview.

97 **"a bloody nuisance"**: Simon Napier-Bell, quoted in Welch, *Peter Grant*, p. 49.

98 **"The first thing we did"**: JP, quoted in Schulps, *Trouser Press* interview, Part 2, p. 26.

98 **"The future was calling"**: Jim McCarty, quoted in Power, *No Quarter*, p. 128.

100 **"We were conned"**: "I was actually getting at frustration in recording terms which *Little Games* exemplifies." JP, quoted in Mick Houghton, "Zeus of Zeppelin: An Interview with Jimmy Page," *Circus*, October 12, 1976.

100 **"It was just so bloody rushed"**: JP, quoted in Schulps, *Trouser Press* interview, Part 2, p. 26.

100 **"On half the tracks"**: JP, blind-quoted from an article in *ZigZag* in Yorke, *Led Zep*, p. 48.

100 **"The bridge of the guitar"**: JP, quoted in Tolinski, *Light & Shade*, p. 82.

101 **"tone poem"**: Jim McCarty interview.

101 **"When I heard 'Goodnight Sweet Josephine'"**: Jeff Beck, blind-quoted in Salewicz, *Jimmy Page*, p. 122.

102 **"Someone tapped me"**: Terry Reid, interview with the author, February 14, 2018.

103 **"It was kind of hard"**: Jeff Beck, quoted in Rosen, "Jeff Beck."

103 **"He hit me like an earthquake"**: Jeff Beck, quoted in Johnny Black, "Jimi Hendrix and the Birth of Heavy—by the People Who Were There," *Classic Rock*, May 11, 2018.

103 **"just didn't have their hearts"**: JP, quoted in Frame, "Getting to the Bottom."

103 **"I went to see Jefferson Airplane"**: JP, radio interview with Alan Freeman, Capital Radio/DIR, April 1976.

104 **"just didn't seem interested"**: McCarty, *Nobody Told Me!*, p. 198.

104 **"I used to say"**: JP, quoted in Chris Welch, "The Yardbirds: Only Jimmy Left to Form the New Yardbirds," MM, October 12, 1968.

104 **"That was a lot of money"**: Peter Grant, quoted in Dave Lewis, "Peter Grant: The TBL Interview," in Dave Lewis, *Led Zeppelin: The "Tight but Loose" Files—Celebration II* (London: Omnibus, 2003), p. 89.

104 **"I didn't want the Yardbirds":** JP, quoted in Welch, "The Yardbirds."

104 **there was an outside chance:** "Maybe Keith and Jim would change their minds and come back." Frame, "Getting to the Bottom."

105 **"What are you going to do":** Peter Grant, quoted in Lewis, "Peter Grant: The *TBL* Interview," p. 89.

105 **"When the band folded":** JP, blind-quoted in Salewicz, *Jimmy Page*, p. 128.

106 **"I certainly had a good idea":** "It goes back to the band I was going to form with Jeff Beck." JP, quoted in Nigel Williamson, "Forget the Myths," *Uncut*, May 2005, p. 71.

106 **"I knew exactly the style":** JP, quoted in James Johnson, "Jimmy Page, the Mild Barbarian," *NME*, April 21, 1973.

106 **"with the fourth member":** JP, quoted in Williamson, "Forget the Myths," p. 71.

**Chapter Five: The Black Country**

107 **"a really fiery singer":** "I knew what I wanted." JP, quoted in Mat Snow, "Led Zeppelin," *Q*, December 1990.

108 **"I was mainly going after":** JP, quoted in Tobler and Grundy, *Guitar Greats*, p. 101.

108 **"There are only three":** Aretha Franklin, quoted in Keith Duncan, "Terry Reid: Biography," (2007), https://www.terryreid.com/external/biography2.html.

108 **"I was doing bread-and-butter":** Terry Reid, interview with the author, February 14, 2018.

109 **"Terry was controlled":** Carole Brown Woods, interview with the author, November 4, 2019.

109 **"taking the mick":** RP, quoted in Nigel Williamson, "Good Times, Bad Times," *Uncut*, May 2005, p. 53.

110 **"The group was doing":** JP, quoted in Pete Frame, "Getting to the Bottom of the Page," *ZigZag*, December 1972.

110 **"The band overplayed":** RP, quoted in Williamson, "Good Times, Bad Times," p. 53.

111 **"distinctive sexual quality":** JP, quoted in Mylett, *Jimmy Page*, p. 17.

111 **"primeval wail":** Mylett, *Jimmy Page*, p. 17.

111 **"too great to be undiscovered":** JP, quoted in Cameron Crowe, "The Durable Led Zeppelin," *Rolling Stone*, March 13, 1973.

111 **"I immediately thought":** JP, quoted in Dave Schulps, *Trouser Press* interview, Part 2, p. 27.

111 **"We did the whole thing":** Kevyn Gammond, interview with the author, May 7, 2019.

111 **"You know, I think":** JP, radio interview with Alan Freeman, Capital Radio/DIR, 1976.

112 **"It was obvious":** JP, blind-quoted in Mick Wall, *When Giants Walked the Earth* (London: Orion, 2008), p. 50.

112 **"jewel in the crown":** RP, quoted in Williamson, "Good Times, Bad Times," p. 53.

112 **"It's very big":** "I own a launch, but I can't drive it very fast." JP, quoted in Jim Delehant, "Jimmy Page's New Yardbirds," *Hit Parader*, December 1968.

112 **"quite sassy American girlfriend":** "He must have thought, 'This is all right.'" JP, quoted in Hoskyns, *Trampled*, p. 92.

113 **"The way he carried himself":** RP, quoted in Williamson, "Good Times, Bad Times," p. 53.

113 **"I looked through his records":** RP, quoted in Richard Williams, "Robert Plant: Down to the Roots," *MM*, September 12, 1970.

113 **Jimmy laid on a full banquet:** Mat Snow, "Robert Plant's Record Collection," *Q*, May 1990.

113 **"His ideas were fresh"**: "We came together and we had the same likes and dislikes." RP, quoted in Steve Peacock, "Robert Plant," *Sounds*, June 26, 1971.

113 **They had bumped into each other**: According to JPJ, JP assumed it was on a session for Donovan's "Hurdy Gurdy Man," but JP was not on that session. Dave Thompson, "Led Zeppelin: Pre-Flyte," *Goldmine*, July 2007.

113 **"During a break"**: JP, quoted in Yorke, *Led Zep*, p. 54.

113 **"I was making a fortune"**: JPJ, quoted in Dave Lewis, "Anchor Man: The Ultimate John Paul Jones Interview," *The Tight but Loose Files*, December 2003.

114 **"Jimmy told me"**: RP, quoted in Williamson, "Good Times, Bad Times," p. 53.

114 **"We definitely approached"**: "But he went off to Zappa's band." Peter Grant, quoted in Dave Lewis, "Peter Grant: The *TBL* Interview," in Lewis, *Led Zeppelin: Celebration II*, p. 90.

114 **"old news . . . a step backwards"**: Aynsley Dunbar, quoted in Wall, *When Giants Walked the Earth*, p. 13.

114 **"When I saw what a thrasher"**: JP, quoted in Pete Frame, "Getting to the Bottom of the Page," *ZigZag*, December 1972.

114 **"I hitched back from Oxford"**: RP, quoted in Williams, "Robert Plant."

115 **"I'd never seen anyone"**: JP, quoted in Wall, *When Giants Walked the Earth*, p. 37.

115 **"He might as easily"**: Dave Pegg, interview with the author, November 28, 2018.

115 **"coming from the Midlands"**: Robert Shore, "Why the Midlands Is the Best Place in Britain," *Guardian*, March 26, 2014.

116 **"You'd need an interpreter"**: Kevyn Gammond interview.

117 **"You could actually survive"**: Dave Pegg interview.

117 **"There were so many bands"**: Glenn Hughes, quoted in Hoskyns, *Trampled*, p. 34.

117 **"uncommonly devoid of visual pleasure"**: Nikolaus Pevsner, *The Buildings of England: Worcestershire* (London: Penguin, 1968), p. 203.

117 **"Furnaces everywhere, all open"**: Mac Poole, quoted in Hoskyns, *Trampled*, p. 32.

118 **"I used to do Elvis"**: RP, quoted in Snow, "Robert Plant's Record Collection."

118 **"They cut the plug"**: RP, quoted in Williamson, "Good Times, Bad Times," p. 52.

119 **"beyond parental control"**: "[My mother] said I was beyond parental control." RP, quoted in Williamson, "Good Times, Bad Times," p. 52.

119 **"I got in with this crew"**: RP, quoted in Chris Welch, "Robert Plant," MM, September 12, 1970.

119 **"I was sweating with excitement"**: RP, quoted in Snow, "Robert Plant's Record Collection."

120 **"I always got a shiver"**: RP, quoted in Welch, "Robert Plant."

120 **unlistenable "insipid dross"**: "Everything we were being peddled at the time was insipid dross." RP, quoted in Williamson, "Good Times, Bad Times," p. 52.

120 **"All of a sudden"**: Dave Pegg, quoted in Hoskyns, *Trampled*, p. 36.

120 **"With the blues, you could"**: RP, quoted in Hoskyns, *Trampled*, p. 36.

120 **"When I was fifteen"**: RP, quoted in Welch, "Robert Plant."

121 **"Robert was on another level"**: Bill Bonham, quoted in Hoskyns, *Trampled*, p. 45.

121 **"the Rubber Man"**: John Crutchley, quoted in Hoskyns, *Trampled*, p. 45.

121 **"secondhand gangster suits"**: Hoskyns, *Trampled*, p. 45.

122 **"We all started to get"**: Kevyn Gammond interview.

123 **"absurdly talented thirteen-year-old"**: Bev Bevan, quoted in "The Plaza's—Handsworth and Old Hill/The Ritz Ballroom—Kings Heath," Birmingham Music Archive, n.d., www.birminghammusicarchive.com/the-ritz/.

123 **"He'd sleep in the back"**: Kevyn Gammond interview.

123 **"I never really knew where"**: RP, quoted in Williams, "Robert Plant."

124 **"All that music"**: RP, quoted in Williams, "Robert Plant."

125 **"what an audience wants"**: RP, quoted in Welch, "Robert Plant."

125 **"There was a romance"**: RP, quoted in Williamson, "Good Times, Bad Times," p. 53.

125 **Robert already had his ideal**: "We just had one meeting to see if it was going to work." Dave Pegg interview.

125 **"Yer all roit"**: JP, quoted by RP in Barney Hoskyns, "Mountain Man: Robert Plant Goes Back to His Welsh Roots," *Tracks*, Fall 2003, p. 40.

126 **"blue-eyed soul circuit"**: RP, quoted in Hoskyns, "Mountain Man," p. 41

126 **"wanted to fight the world"**: Mick Bonham, quoted in Hoskyns, "Mountain Man," p. 41.

126 **"He could have walked"**: Jim Simpson, quoted in Hoskyns, "Mountain Man," p. 42.

126 **"as if someone had stuck"**: Bill Ford, quoted in Hoskyns, "Mountain Man," p. 41.

126 **"I used to play"**: JB, quoted in Yorke, *Led Zep*, p. 9.

127 **"I never had any drum lessons"**: JB, quoted in Chris Welch, "John Bonham: Over the Hills and Far Away," MM, June 21, 1975.

127 **"We would sit in front"**: Mick Bonham, *John Bonham* (Harpenden, UK: Southbank, 2005), p. 21.

127 **"It was from drummers like them"**: JB, quoted in Roy Carr, A *Talk on the Wild Side* (Hamburg, Germany: earBOOKS, 2010).

128 **"a bricklayer vibe"**: Glenn Hughes, quoted in Hoskyns, *Trampled*, p. 32.

128 **"John used to watch me"**: "I was the loudest drummer in the area." Bev Bevan, quoted in Hoskyns, *Trampled*, p. 42.

129 **"We got banned"**: Jim Simpson, quoted in Hoskyns, *Trampled*, p. 42.

129 **"We used to see"**: Tony Iommi, quoted in Martin Popoff, *Led Zeppelin* (Minneapolis: Voyageur Press, 2017), p. 58.

129 **"boisterous" and "utterly outrageous"**: Jim Simpson, quoted in Hoskyns, *Trampled*, p. 42.

129 **"enjoying a pint or four"**: Author interview with Dave Pegg, November 28, 2018.

129 **"Suddenly the drum kit"**: Dave Pegg interview.

131 **"We played with the amps"**: Paul Lockey, interview with the author, May 18, 2019.

131 **"He'd bang away"**: Kevyn Gammond interview.

131 **"Rob insisted on putting his name"**: Kevyn Gammond interview.

132 **"I was shocked"**: Dave Pegg interview.

132 **Rose was so impressed**: "I eventually found John and offered him the job, paying about £40 a week." Tim Rose, quoted in Bonham, *John Bonham*, p. 61.

## Chapter Six: Don't Tread on Me

133 **"Ultimately, I wanted"**: JP, quoted in Dave Lewis, *Led Zeppelin: From a Whisper to a Scream* (London: Omnibus, 2012), p. 20.

133 **he sent "at least thirty"**: Peter Grant, quoted in Dave Lewis, "Peter Grant: The TBL Interview," in Lewis, *Led Zeppelin: Celebration II*, p. 90.

134 **"Pat was not happy"**: "I went with Robert over to John's flat in Eve Hill." Bill Bonham, quoted in Hoskyns, *Trampled*, p. 92.

134 **"Don't you even think"**: "I worked on him and worked on him." RP, quoted in Wall, *When Giants Walked the Earth*, p. 34.

134 **"I was doing okay."**: JB, quoted in "Me and My Music," *Disc and Music Echo*, June 27, 1970.

134 **Word drifted around**: "Bevan said the fledgling Move originally considered offering the drumming job to Bonham." Wall, *When Giants Walked the Earth*, p. 132.

134 **"basically spelled out"**: JP, interview by Mick Wall, *Mojo*, October 2005.

134 **"Even if we didn't"**: JB, quoted in "John Paul Jones: Interview," *Disc and Music Echo*, June 27, 1970.

135 **In typical John Bonham fashion**: "It was bad enough John doing a runner." Tim Rose, quoted in Bonham, *John Bonham*, p. 66.

135 **"You name it, I've done it"**: JPJ, quoted in Gail Worley, "Getting the Led Out: A John Paul Jones Interview," KNAC-FM, Long Beach, CA, April 1, 2002.

136 **"My dad bought a record player"**: JPJ, quoted in Hoskyns, *Trampled*, p. 11.

136 **"My father had a little"**: JPJ, quoted in Steven Rosen, "John Paul Jones," *Guitar Player*, July 1977.

136 **"neck like a tree trunk"**: JPJ, quoted in Rosen, "John Paul Jones."

137 **"bass player's paradise"**: JPJ, quoted in Ritchie Yorke, "Ask-In with a Led Zeppelin a Week: Bassist John Paul Jones--Motown Bass Deserves a Lot of Credit," *NME*, April 4, 1970.

137 **"John Paul heard about it"**: Tony Meehan, quoted in Yorke, *Led Zep*, p. 13.

138 **"I wanted to make"**: JPJ, quoted in Andrew Loog Oldham, *2Stoned* (London: Secker & Warburg, 2002), p. 134.

138 **"It was quite a session"**: JPJ, quoted in Peter Jones, "John Paul Jones: Bass with Everything," *Record Mirror*, April 25, 1964.

138 **"I just knew that John looked"**: Oldham, *2Stoned*, p. 134.

138 **"I was always in demand"**: JPJ, quoted in Tolinski, *Light & Shade*, p. 100.

138 **"Somebody came up to me"**: JPJ, quoted in Hoskyns, *Trampled*, p. 22.

139 **"I discovered that musical arranging"**: JPJ, quoted in Yorke, *Led Zep*, p. 15.

139 **"I was immediately hired"**: JPJ, quoted in Rosen, "John Paul Jones."

139 **"You walk through that door"**: JPJ, quoted in Worley, "Getting the Led Out."

139 **"twenty-four-hour job"**: JPJ, quoted in Tolinski, *Light & Shade*, p. 100.

139 **"So many sessions"**: JPJ, quoted in Hoskyns, *Trampled*, p. 22.

140 **"Will you stop moping"**: JPJ, quoted in Rosen, "John Paul Jones."

140 **"I'm going up to the Midlands"**: JPJ, interview with Anthony Mason and Charles Osgood, *CBS Sunday Morning*, December 16, 2012.

140 **Peter Grant had answered**: "Rehearsal Rooms, 39 Gerrard Street, W1, Available day and night." MM, August 10, 1968.

141 **"There was a space"**: "There was just wall-to-wall amplifiers, Marshalls . . ." JPJ, quoted in "Led Zeppelin Profiled," radio promo CD, 1990. "The room was really quite small; just about got our gear in." JP, quoted in Wall, *When Giants Walked the Earth*, p. 46.

141 **"I was absolutely convinced"**: JP, quoted in Wall, *When Giants Walked the Earth*, p. 45.

141 **"Well, we're all here"**: JPJ, quoted in Rosen, "John Paul Jones."

141 **"The room just exploded"**: JPJ, interview with Mason and Osgood, *CBS Sunday Morning*.

141 **"Far too loud"**: JP, quoted in Nick Kent, "Bring It On Home," *Q Special Edition: Led Zeppelin*, March 2003, p. 136.

141 **"It just locked together"**: JP, interview with Mason and Osgood, *CBS Sunday Morning*.

141 **"unleashing of energy"**: "It wasn't *supposed* to be a pretty thing." RP, quoted in Joe Smith, *Off the Record* (New York: Warner Books, 1988), p. 339.

142 **"The sound was so great"**: RP, quoted in Richard Williams, "Robert Plant: Down to the Roots," MM, Sept. 12 1970.

142 **"Very, very, very exciting"**: RP, quoted in "Led Zeppelin Profiled."

142 **"Right, we're on"**: JPJ, quoted in Rosen, "John Paul Jones."

142 **"It was there immediately"**: JP, quoted in Wall, *When Giants Walked the Earth*, p. 46.

142 **"I've got some terrible news"**: Chris Most, interview with the author, May 14, 2019.

143 **"He didn't seem to me"**: Glyn Johns, interview with the author, May 18, 2018.

144 **"Mr. Grant, I've got a problem"**: Confidential source, interview with the author, November 27, 2018.

145 **"I loved it immediately"**: Jim McCarty, interview with the author, September 12, 2019.

146 **"we were pretty green"**: RP, quoted in Mat Snow, "Led Zeppelin," *Q*, December 1990.

146 **"We were really scared"**: JP, blind-quoted in Power, *No Quarter*, p. 182.

146 **"you could still hear"**: JP, blind-quoted in Wall, *When Giants Walked the Earth*, p. 50; Barney Hoskyns, *Led Zeppelin IV* (New York: Rodale, 2006), p. 23.

146 **"began to stretch out"**: JP, quoted in Yorke, *Led Zep*, p. 57.

146 **"this incredible chemistry"**: Peter Grant, quoted in Mark Blake, *Bring It On Home* (New York: Da Capo, 2018), p. 68.

146 **"I can't say that all"**: Peter Grant, quoted in Mylett, *Jimmy Page*, p. 20.

147 **"They were so loud"**: Ludvig Rasmusson, "Yardbirds Hurt," *Stockholm Daily News*, September 14, 1968.

147 **"I wanted to play hard"**: JP, quoted in Mylett, *Jimmy Page*, p. 19.

147 **"Whisper to thunder"**: JP, quoted in Davis Guggenheim, *It Might Get Loud* (documentary), 2008.

147 **"My contributions were"**: JPJ, quoted in Dave Lewis, "Anchor Man: The Ultimate John Paul Jones Interview," *The Tight but Loose Files*, December 2003.

148 **John Paul discovered:** "We did a couple of things using that. One was 'Tribute to Burt Berns,' and I recall we also rehearsed 'Chest Fever' by the Band from *Big Pink* [*sic*]." JPJ, quoted in Dave Lewis, "The John Paul Jones Interview," *Tight but Loose*, November 12, 1997.

148 **"We were all into the idea"**: RP, quoted in Jimmy Page, Robert Plant, and John Paul Jones, *Led Zeppelin by Led Zeppelin* (London: Reel Art, 2018), p. 46.

148 **"We'd drive home"**: RP, quoted in Wall, *When Giants Walked the Earth*, p. 84.

148 **"the most versatile room"**: Glyn Johns interview.

149 **"The first album was done"**: JP, quoted in David Fricke, "Jimmy Page: The Rolling Stone Interview," *Rolling Stone*, December 6, 2012.

149 **"I knew exactly what"**: JP, quoted in Tolinski, *Light & Shade*, p. 79.

149 **They'd already been deemed:** "Johnny Haines told him, 'I can't control you. There's too much input coming into the machine.'" Dave Pegg, interview with the author, November 28, 2018.

150 **"one of the biggest"**: Brad Tolinski, quoted in Hoskyns, *Trampled*, p. 101.

150 **"It was a lot of fun"**: JPJ, quoted in Mat Snow, "John Paul Jones: The Quiet One," *Mojo*, December 2007.

150 **"Lots of people can"**: JPJ, blind-quoted in Hoskyns, *Trampled*, p. 102.

150 **"I was a little bit intimidated"**: RP, quoted in Lewis, *Led Zeppelin: From a Whisper to a Scream*, p. 20.

150 **"in a very inspired way"**: "What he did was really fitting in, in terms of where we were going." JP, quoted in "Jimmy Page: Forget the Myths," *Uncut*, May 2005.

150 **"Those guys fed off each other"**: Glyn Johns interview.

151 **"I could overhear the response"**: Ed Bicknell, interview with the author, November 27, 2018.

152 **"I was doodling in the office"**: Peter Grant, quoted in Hoskyns, *Led Zeppelin IV*, p. 27.

152 **"the figure was £17,500"**: "They laughed me out of the office." Peter Grant, quoted in Lewis, "Peter Grant," p. 90.

152 **"I really liked what I heard"**: "It was a handshake deal, but I was dealing with Peter Grant, and so it wasn't a deal until it was really a deal." Chris Blackwell, quoted in Robert Greenfield, *The Last Sultan* (New York: Simon & Schuster, 2011), pp. 217–18.

153 **"I reached out to the manager"**: Mo Ostin, interview with Peter Ames Carlin for *Sonic Boom*, provided to the author by email, April 24, 2020.

153 **"Twice a week"**: Jerry Greenberg, interview with the author, January 10, 2019. "It was a tip from the British singer Dusty Springfield that really encouraged me to go after the group." Jerry Wexler, quoted in Wexler and Ritz, *Rhythm and the Blues*, p. 221.

154 **"We arrived on the scene"**: JP, quoted in Keith Altham, "Jimmy Page, Superstar," *Record Mirror*, February 21, 1970.

154 **"The blinking warning light"**: Phil Carson, interview with the author, July 2, 2019.

155 **"at least one virtuoso"**: "It was a lecture Jerry gave me about signing bands." Phil Carson interview.

155 **"without knowing anything"**: Jerry Wexler, quoted in Max Jones, "The Age of Atlantic: Jerry Wexler," MM, February 15, 1975.

155 **"We signed on the strength"**: Peter Grant, quoted in Lewis, "Peter Grant," p. 90.

155 **"a $75,000 advance"**: Wexler and Ritz, *Rhythm and the Blues*, p. 222.

155 **"And no soundtracks"**: Peter Grant, quoted in Paul Henderson, "If Somebody Had to Be Trod On, They Got Trod On," *Classic Rock*, April 5, 2017.

156 **"Our contracts specified"**: Dick Asher, quoted in Yorke, *Led Zep*, p. 59.

156 **"the Epic sound team"**: JP, blind-quoted in Salewicz, *Jimmy Page*, p. 124.

157 **"I was surprised"**: Clive Davis, interview with the author, March 10, 2020.

157 **"If I'm out at a concert"**: Peter Grant, quoted in Michael Watts, "Peter Grant: The Man Who Led Zeppelin," MM, June 22, 1974.

157 **"He didn't take shit"**: Phil Carlo, interview with the author, May 12, 2019.

157 **"He was a lovely guy"**: Michael Des Barres, interview with the author, February 20, 2019.

157 **"an underlying tension"**: Phil Carson interview.

158 **"Phil was a mob guy"**: Carmine Appice, interview with the author, April 9, 2019.

159 **"During a tour in 1967"**: Henry Smith, interview with the author, October 2, 2019.

159 **"And to get them"**: "I was furious when I heard we'd signed The Who." Frank Barsalona, quoted in Bob Spitz, *The Making of Superstars* (New York: Doubleday, 1978), p. 133.

160 **"They just wouldn't accept"**: JP, quoted in Yorke, *Led Zep*, p. 64.

160 **"FM radio was just beginning"**: JPJ, quoted in Lewis, "John Paul Jones Interview."

160 **"Fuck me, what's this queue?"**: Peter Grant, quoted in Lewis, "Peter Grant," p. 91.

161 **"We used to call him Mort"**: Carmine Appice interview.

161 **"He was a man's man"**: Jim McCarty interview.

161 **"he knew every groupie"**: Stephen Davis, *Hammer of the Gods* (New York: Ballantine, 1986), p. 37.

161 **"Richard was an act"**: Terry Reid, interview with the author, February 14, 2018.

162 **"don't let them get"**: Peter Grant, quoted in Richard Cole with Richard Trubo, *Stairway to Heaven* (New York: HarperCollins, 1992), p. 46.

## Chapter Seven: Breaking Through the Sound Barrier

164 **"There was all this stuff"**: RP, quoted in Nigel Williamson, "Good Times, Bad Times," *Uncut*, May 2005, p. 54.

165 **Barry Fey, the promoter**: "Our managers were friends and we shared the same lawyer. I didn't find out until 2006 that we'd picked up half of Led Zeppelin's fee." Carmine Appice, interview with the author, April 8, 2019.

165 **"We knew Jimmy from gigs":** Carmine Appice interview.

166 **He took a Fender Bassman:** "We took out the American tubes and put in British ones." Phil Wells (Marshall Inc.), interview with the author, May 8, 2019.

166 **"It was so friggin' powerful":** Terry Reid, interview with the author, February 14, 2018.

166 **"It's not just noise":** JP, quoted in Page, Plant, and Jones, *Led Zeppelin by Led Zeppelin*, p. 87.

166 **"Led Zeppelin was frightening":** JP, blind-quoted in Wall, *When Giants Walked the Earth*, pp. 111–12.

167 **"I was very uncomfortable":** RP, quoted in Williamson, "Good Times, Bad Times," p. 52.

167 **His arms, especially:** "I didn't even know what to do with my arms." RP, quoted in Hoskyns, *Trampled*, p. 121.

167 **"Right from the very first":** RP, quoted in Williamson, "Good Times, Bad Times," p. 100.

167 **"Len Zefflin":** *Spokesman-Review* (Spokane, WA), December 23, 1968.

167 **"Jimmy Page's new group":** Jerry Greenberg, email to the author, March 16, 2020.

168 **Jimmy had come down:** "Jimmy and I were both chronically ill." RP, quoted in Eliot Sekuler, "Lion Among Zebras: The Robert Plant Interview," http://evenspotspeaks .blogspot.com/2013/12/1976-aug-24th-circus-cover-content-tour.html. *Circus*, August 24, 1976. "We only did two nights because everyone got the flu." JP, quoted in *Boston After Dark*, February 5, 1969.

168 **had been playing Led Zeppelin's:** "Tim [*sic*] Donohue had been playing the album (two cuts per hour) for days before the group hit town." Dave Lewis and Mike Tremaglio, *Evenings with Led Zeppelin* (London: Omnibus, 2018), p. 56.

169 **"if we didn't crack":** RP, quoted in Lewis and Tremaglio, *Evenings with Led Zeppelin*, p. 55. "Peter had said, 'If you do well in San Francisco, you're made.'" JPJ, quoted in Mat Snow, "Led Zeppelin," *Q*, December 1990.

169 **"The audiences were getting":** RP, quoted in Wall, *When Giants Walked the Earth*, p. 111.

169 **"When we started the show":** JPJ, quoted in Snow, "Led Zeppelin."

169 **Jimmy had switched:** "There was something the matter with the pickups." Peter Grant, quoted in Paul Henderson, "If Somebody Had to Be Trod On, They Got Trod On," *Classic Rock*, April 5, 2017.

169 **"Bonzo and I looked":** RP, blind-quoted in Hoskyns, *Trampled*, p. 122.

170 **"awfully loud":** Philip Elwood, "Impressive New Rock Group," *San Francisco Examiner*, January 11, 1969.

170 **"absolutely refused to let":** "They were halfway up the backstage stairs when the cheers brought them back." Robb Baker, "Vanilla Fudge + Led Zeppelin = Musicianship," *Chicago Tribune*, February 16, 1969.

170 **"It was just a joke":** JP, quoted in Yorke, *Led Zep*, p. 64.

171 **"was one of the best sounding records":** Glyn Johns, interview with the author, May 18, 2018.

171 **"I put this band together":** JP, quoted in Tolinski, *Light & Shade*, p. 86.

171 **"Jimmy decided you didn't":** Glyn Johns interview.

172 **"an artistic breakthrough":** Glyn Johns interview.

172 **John Paul plunked himself down:** "I remember there was a Hammond organ in the studio, which I used and I wrote the riff to 'Good Times, Bad Times.'" JPJ, quoted in Welch, *Peter Grant*, p. 63.

172 **"The most stunning thing":** JP, quoted in Tolinski, *Light & Shade*, p. 80.

172 **"I think everyone was laying bets"**: JP, quoted in Tobler and Grundy, *Guitar Greats*, p. 102.

172 **"He did in fact bring"**: JPJ, quoted in Popoff, *Led Zeppelin*, p. 26.

172 **"His right foot repeated"**: Carmine Appice, interview with the author, April 25, 2019.

173 **"a big live room"**: "It was old-style recording." JPJ, quoted in Welch, *Peter Grant*, p. 63.

173 **"Robert's voice was extremely powerful"**: JP, quoted in Tolinski, *Light & Shade*, p. 79.

173 **Jimmy was loath**: "Once you start cleaning everything up, you lose [the ambience]." JP, quoted in Tolinski, *Light & Shade*, p. 78.

173 **a Gibson J-200 he had borrowed**: "It was a beautiful guitar. I've never found a guitar of that quality anywhere since." JP, quoted in Page, *Guitar Player*, July 1977.

174 **"I wasn't used to this style"**: JPJ, quoted in Lewis, *Led Zeppelin: From a Whisper to a Scream*, p. 24.

174 **"Jimmy, it can't be done"**: JP, quoted in Tolinski, *Light & Shade*, p. 81.

174 **"the way the lyrics hung"**: McCarty, *Nobody Told Me!*, p. 201.

174 **"It was played live"**: JP, quoted in Tolinski, *Light & Shade*, p. 82. "I'd be sort of roaring away on the solo and just hit some staccato chords and lo and behold, everybody's there with you." JP, blind-quoted in Mylett, *Jimmy Page*, p. 22.

175 **"everything but the kitchen sink"**: JP, quoted in Tobler and Grundy, *Guitar Greats*, p. 102.

175 **"an orchestra of otherworldly textures"**: Tolinski, *Light & Shade*, p. 71.

175 **"The problem was singing them"**: JPJ, quoted in Lewis, *Led Zeppelin: From a Whisper to a Scream*, p. 25.

175 **"The idea of 'Communication Breakdown'"**: JP, quoted in Tobler and Grundy, *Guitar Greats*, p. 102.

176 **"I was caught up"**: RP, quoted in Williamson, "Good Times, Bad Times," p. 54.

176 **William Burroughs first used**: Deena Weinstein, "Just So Stories: How Heavy Metal Got Its Name—a Cautionary Tale," *Rock Music Studies* 1, no. 1 (2014): 36–51, www.tandfonline.com/doi/full/10.1080/19401159.2013.846655.

176 **"basically a hard rock group"**: JP, quoted in Yorke, *Led Zep*, p. 64.

176 **"bastard term"**: JP, quoted in Mylett, *Jimmy Page*, p. 22.

176 **described as a "bone-rattling"**: Lester Bangs, "Bring Your Mother to the Gas Chamber," *Creem*, June 4, 1972.

177 **"There are mistakes"**: JP, quoted in Rosen, "Jimmy Page."

177 **"a landmark in rock 'n roll"**: Johns, *Sound Man*, p. 116.

177 **"Jimmy's put this band together"**: Glyn Johns interview.

178 **"It was just amazing"**: Jeff Beck, quoted in Dave Thompson, "Led Zeppelin: Pre-Flyte," *Goldmine*, July 2007.

178 **"OK, now where's the album?"**: "I was mortified when Peter Grant played me the acetate." Jeff Beck, quoted in Vince Garbarini, "Jeff Beck," *Guitar*, April 2001.

178 **That may have been so**: "Peter had told Jimmy, 'Watch Jeff's group, they're really taking off over there.'" Jeff Beck, blind-quoted in Power, *No Quarter*, p. 197.

178 **"It was a total freak accident"**: JP, quoted in Thompson, "Led Zeppelin."

178 **"I didn't know he'd recorded it"**: JP, quoted in Wall, *When Giants Walked the Earth*, p. 58. "I hadn't known he'd done it, and he hadn't known we had." JP, blind-quoted in *Guitar Player*. Also in Power, *No Quarter*, p. 195.

179 **"a much better package"**: Jeff Beck, blind-quoted in Power, *No Quarter*, p. 198.

179 **"No one likes people"**: Chris Charlesworth, interview with the author, May 13, 2019.

179 **"Peter had miscalculated"**: Phil Carson, interview with the author, July 2, 2019.

179 **"The conservatism goes":** RP, quoted in Ritchie Yorke, "Ask-in with a Led Zeppelin a Week: Thinking as a Sex Symbol Can Turn You into a Bad Person—Robert Plant," *NME*, April 11, 1970.

179 **"I got a lift back afterward":** "They had gold taps in the bathroom, gorgeous wood-paneled walls. It was like walking into a different world, even though it was a council flat." Dave Pegg, interview with the author, November 28, 2018.

180 **On March 15, 1969:** John Mendelssohn, "Led Zeppelin," *Rolling Stone*, March 15, 1969.

180 **"That album haunted Jimmy":** Chris Charlesworth interview.

181 **"I put it on":** John Mendelssohn, interview with the author, May 6, 2019.

181 **"It was galling":** JPJ, quoted in Hoskyns, *Trampled*, pp. 128–29.

182 **"That's the way":** Peter Grant, quoted in Welch, *Peter Grant*, p. 87.

182 **"We just couldn't seem":** JP, quoted in Salewicz, *Jimmy Page*, p. 167.

182 **"The rock press did not":** Danny Goldberg, interview with the author, August 28, 2018.

182 **"I suppose my early love":** JP, quoted in Marc Myers, "The Making of Led Zeppelin's 'Whole Lotta Love,'" *Wall Street Journal*, May 29, 2014.

183 **"Just atrocious":** "Tony Secunda stuck us in the Madison Hotel and said, 'You're in the studio tomorrow. We need you to write a few songs.'" Kevyn Gammond, interview with the author, May 7, 2019.

183 **"'Well, what am I going to sing?'":** RP, quoted in Hoskyns, *Trampled*, p. 142.

183 **"He used to be at all":** Steve Marriott, quoted in Paolo Hewitt, *Small Faces* (London: Acid Jazz Books, 1995), p. 131.

184 **"We did, however, take some liberties":** JP, quoted in Tolinski, *Light & Shade*, p. 89.

184 **"developed in the studio":** RP, interview with Terry Gross, *Fresh Air*, WHYY-FM, August 24, 2004.

184 **"Wherever it comes from":** RP, blind-quoted in Salewicz, *Jimmy Page*, p. 171.

184 **"sounded strong enough":** JP, quoted in Myers, "Making of Led Zeppelin's 'Whole Lotta Love.'"

184 **"I had this avant-garde":** JP, quoted in Myers, "Making of Led Zeppelin's 'Whole Lotta Love.'"

185 **"My confidence was building":** RP, interview with Gross, *Fresh Air*.

185 **"It was an oscillator":** JP, quoted in Mylett, *Jimmy Page*, p. 23.

185 **"I detuned it and pulled":** JP, quoted in Myers, "Making of Led Zeppelin's 'Whole Lotta Love.'"

## Chapter Eight: The New Normal

187 **"Never had loudness":** Mark Finch, "Led Zeppelin Lets Listeners Feel the Music," *Chicago Sun-Times*, July 20, 1969.

187 **"Rock 'n roll was meant":** Roger Mayer, interview with the author November 25, 2018.

187 **"The plan was to capture":** JP, quoted in David Fricke, "Jimmy Page: The Rolling Stone Interview," *Rolling Stone*, December 6, 2012.

187 **"on the run between hotel rooms":** RP, quoted in Nigel Williamson, "Good Times, Bad Times," *Uncut*, May 2005, p. 56.

188 **"When we recorded that":** RP, quoted in Steve Peacock, "Robert Plant," *Sounds*, June 26, 1971.

189 **"It's not happening":** Chris Huston, quoted in Steven Rosen, "Chris Huston, Eddie Kramer's Co-engineer on *Led Zeppelin II*," *Guitar World*, July 1986.

189 **"They were thirteen":** Rodney Bingenheimer, interview with the author, January 23, 2019.

189 **"They were mostly latch key kids":** Michael Des Barres, interview with the author, February 20, 2019.

189 **"They all had girlfriends here":** Vanessa Gilbert, interview with the author, January 31, 2019.

190 **"'Hello, what are you doing here?'":** Peter Grant, interview with Malcolm McLaren, 1988.

190 **"Maybe it was a sign":** Cole, *Stairway to Heaven*, pp. 77–78.

190 **"Sex, in heavy metal's discourse":** Deena Weinstein, *Heavy Metal* (New York: Lexington Books, 1991), p. 102.

191 **"let loose an earthquake":** Bob Harvey, "Hot Rock Band Loud, Frenzied," *Edmonton Journal*, May 10, 1969.

191 **"ended up leaving":** Ann Wilson, quoted in Lewis and Tremaglio, *Evenings with Led Zeppelin*, p. 98.

192 **"The PA was [nothing more than]":** RP, interview with Terry Gross, *Fresh Air*, WHYY-FM, August 24, 2004.

192 **"an exhibition of incredible":** John Mendelssohn, "Led Zeppelin, Rose Palace, Pasadena," *Los Angeles Times*, May 6, 1969.

192 **He had guzzled a third:** "He was so drunk, he fell off his stool twice." Cole, *Stairway to Heaven*, p. 81.

193 **"I saw Peter get very":** Bill Harry, interview with the author, May 15, 2018.

193 **"They never knew":** Peter Grant, quoted in Lewis and Tremaglio, *Evenings with Led Zeppelin*, p. 113.

193 **Along one wall:** Dave Pegg, interview with the author, November 28, 2018.

194 **"When Led Zeppelin came on":** Hugh Nolan, "Pop Proms—a Riotous Start," *Disc and Music Echo*, July 5, 1969.

194 **"You didn't notice":** JPJ, quoted in Hoskyns, *Led Zeppelin IV*, p. 51.

194 **"I was hanging on":** RP, quoted in Hoskyns, *Led Zeppelin IV*, p. 51.

194 **"a massive personal triumph":** "The Zeppelin truly deserved the acclaim." Nick Logan, "Zeppelin and Fleetwood Take Off with a Roar," *NME*, July 5, 1969.

194 **"Jimmy was elated":** "He gave me a lift home in a black cab we hailed outside Royal Albert Hall." Carole Brown Woods, interview with the author, November 8, 2019, and Carole Brown Woods, email to the author, November 19, 2019.

195 **"When we did shows":** JP, quoted in Hoskyns, *Trampled*, p. 137.

196 **"Three English groups":** Jeff Beck, quoted in Steven Rosen, "Jeff Beck on Jimmy Page," *Guitar World*, July 1986.

196 **Bonzo was warming up:** "He had been drinking all afternoon and was eager to leave." Cole, *Stairway to Heaven*, p. 94.

196 **"John was a good guy":** Carmine Appice, interview with the author, April 9, 2019.

196 **"Bonzo's got to get a grip":** Cole, *Stairway to Heaven*, p. 95.

197 **"at the side of the stage":** JP, quoted in Henry Smith, interview with the author, October 2, 2019.

197 **"Wake 'im up!":** Joe Wright, interview with the author, November 28, 2018.

198 **"You get hammered":** Joe Wright interview.

198 **Robert Plant put voice to it:** "I was the golden god. . . . I was in a palm tree actually." RP, quoted in Williamson, "Good Times, Bad Times," p. 60.

199 **"We recognized we were done":** Carmine Appice interview.

200 **"It was really sickening":** RP, quoted in Ritchie Yorke, "'Ask-in with a Led Zeppelin a Week: Thinking as a Sex Symbol Can Turn You into a Bad Person—Robert Plant," *NME*, April 11, 1970.

200 **"In fact, we were invited"**: "We were in the room when it happened." Robert Plant, quoted in Blake, *Bring It On Home*, p. 83.

201 **"some cream-filled donuts"**: Ellen Sander, *Trips* (New York: Charles Scribner's Sons, 1973), p. 113.

202 **"The rock business is volatile"**: Sander, *Trips*, p. 110.

202 **"just young guys"**: "The thing people forget when they tut-tut about this stuff is what a laugh we were having." RP, quoted in Wall, *When Giants Walked the Earth*, p. 167.

202 **"There was a certain amount"**: JP, quoted in Hoskyns, *Trampled*, p. 150.

202 **"It was quite insane, really"**: JP, quoted in Yorke, *Led Zep*, pp. 73 and 72.

203 **"was an afterthought"**: "I just fancied doing it." JP, quoted in Tolinski, *Light & Shade*, p. 90.

203 **"We recorded and overdubbed"**: JP, quoted in Tolinski, *Light & Shade*, p. 87.

203 **"to get excitement onto a piece"**: JP, quoted in Yorke, *Led Zep*, pp. 72–73.

203 **"It was more like a nightclub"**: Bebe Buell, quoted in Hoskyns, *Trampled*, p. 267.

204 **"It was the epicenter"**: Michael Des Barres interview.

204 **"It was like one big playground"**: Steven Rosen, "Danny Goldberg's Hideaway," *Guitar World*, July 1986.

205 **"How do you alleviate"**: Benji Le Fevre, interview with the author, May 19, 2019.

205 **In *Stairway to Heaven***: Cole, *Stairway to Heaven*, pp. 105–6.

205 **"Richard invited me and Robert"**: Joe Wright interview.

206 **"I said no to Woodstock"**: Peter Grant, quoted in Lewis, *Led Zeppelin: From a Whisper to a Scream*, p. 29.

206 **"may have overstepped the mark"**: JP, quoted in Yorke, *Led Zep*, p.72.

207 **"we'll all just have to go"**: Peter Grant, quoted by Maggie Bell, interview with the author, May 8, 2019.

207 **"Tom Waterson, the man who ran"**: Maggie Bell interview.

208 **Right up until showtime**: June Harris, "America Calling," *NME*, January 11, 1969.

208 **"every musician that happened"**: MM's Chris Welch, quoted in Wall, *When Giants Walked the Earth*, p. 154.

208 **Some, like *Melody Maker*'s Chris Welch**: "They were nicer to Chris Welch than to anybody else, so they got him inside from the very beginning." Chris Charlesworth, quoted in Hoskyns, *Trampled*, p. 132; Chris Charlesworth, interview with the author, May 13, 2019.

208 **"Chris was considered *all right*"**: Richard Cole, quoted in Blake, *Bring It On Home*, p. 106.

209 **"Turned out they'd arranged"**: Chris Welch, quoted in Hoskyns, *Trampled*, p. 132.

209 **he delivered a rave**: Chris Welch, "Led Zeppelin at Carnegie Hall," MM, October 25, 1969.

209 **"It was the first time"**: Chris Welch, quoted in Wall, *When Giants Walked the Earth*, p. 154.

210 **"tortured voice and Page's guitar"**: "Led Zeppelin II," *Time Out: London*, December 6, 1969.

210 **"[Marcus] was probably hoping"**: John Mendelssohn, interview with the author, May 6, 2019.

210 **"Led Zeppelin was very touchy"**: Chris Charlesworth interview.

210 **"Peter made it abundantly clear"**: Nick Kent, quoted in Blake, *Bring It On Home*, p. 106.

211 **"I don't believe in pussyfooting"**: Peter Grant, quoted in Michael Watts, "The Man Who Led Zeppelin," MM, June 22, 1974.

211 **"You'll take the group off stage"**: Peter Grant, quoted in Billy James, *An American Band* (Middlesex, UK: SAF, 2001), p. 83.

211 **"Four men dragged me upstairs"**: Mac Nelson, quoted in Blake, *Bring It On Home*, p. 99.

212 **"AM radio was not"**: Jerry Greenberg, interview with the author, January 10, 2019.

213 **"Peter was not pleasant"**: Phil Carson, interview with the author, July 2, 2019.

214 **"You don't fucking know enough"**: Peter Grant, quoted in Blake, *Bring It On Home*, p. 85.

214 **"call the fucking record back"**: Ahmet Ertegun, quoted in Phil Carson interview; Jerry Greenberg interview.

214 **"a marketing genius"**: "Peter Grant turned out to be right." Phil Carson interview.

214 **"in excess of $5 million"**: *Financial Times*, blind-quoted in Power, *No Quarter*, p. 215.

214 **"the audience surrendered totally"**: Björn Håkanson, "Zeppelin Triumphed," *Svenska Dagbladet*, February 27, 1970.

215 **Countess Eva von Zeppelin**: "We first heard from her right around the time the New Yardbirds became Led Zeppelin." Carole Brown Woods, email to the author, April 7, 2020.

215 **"I had to run and hide"**: JP, blind-quoted in Power, *No Quarter*, p. 215.

215 **"she wasn't going to have"**: RP, quoted in Yorke, *Led Zep*, p. 89.

215 **"We had a couple"**: Phil Carson, quoted in Yorke, *Led Zep*, p. 91.

### Chapter Nine: Into the Distant Past

217 **"I don't think we can"**: JPJ, quoted in Caroline Boucher, "Zeppelin Shoots at the Gasbags," *Disc*, December 12, 1970.

217 **"It never came off"**: Henry Smith, interview with the author, October 2, 2019.

217 **"We were driven off the road"**: RP, quoted in Nigel Williamson, "Good Times, Bad Times," *Uncut*, March 2003, p. 58.

218 **Two cops in a bathroom**: "They didn't know I was there in a stall and were trying to come up with a way to plant shit on Led Zeppelin." Williamson, "Good Times, Bad Times."

218 **And in Memphis, with a coliseum**: "He actually held Peter at gunpoint, and then pointed the gun at Robert." Terry Manning, quoted in Wall, *When Giants Walked the Earth*, p. 176.

218 **"You see so much"**: RP, quoted in Yorke, *Led Zep*, p. 99.

218 **"It's just like being back"**: JP, quoted in Yorke, *Led Zep*, p. 96.

218 **"You'd go into a venue"**: Henry Smith interview.

219 **"living like an animal"**: JPJ, quoted in Phil Sutcliffe, "Getting It Together at Bron-yr-Aur: The Story of Led Zeppelin," *Mojo*, April 2000.

219 **"baronial life"**: "It's like the New Renaissance of Berkshire, I suppose." JP, quoted in Yorke, *Led Zep*, p. 151.

219 **"fed up with humanity"**: RP, quoted in Yorke, *Led Zep*, p. 155.

219 **Jimmy already had two numbers**: "I had already written 'Immigrant Song' and came up with 'Friends' a day or two before we got together at Robert's house in the West Midlands . . . and I had 'Tangerine' from a number of years beforehand—before Led Zeppelin." JP, blind-quoted but attributed to an article in *The Guardian* in 2004 in Salewicz, *Jimmy Page*, p. 204.

219 **"a work in progress"**: JP, quoted in Tolinski, *Light & Shade*, p. 116.

220 **"We'd been working solidly"**: JP, quoted in Yorke, *Led Zep*, p. 92.

220 **"It would do me a lot"**: JP, quoted in Hoskyns, *Led Zeppelin IV*, p. 53.

220 **"It was a fantastic place"**: RP, quoted in Williamson, "Good Times, Bad Times," p. 56.

220 **There was no road**: "You have to drive across the fields and mountains to get to it." RP, quoted in Yorke, *Led Zep*, p. 93.

221 **"Oh, we're here"**: JP, quoted in Hoskyns, *Led Zeppelin IV*, p. 53.

221 **"to create a pastoral side"**: RP, quoted in Williamson, "Good Times, Bad Times," p. 56.

221 **"When I first heard that LP"**: JP, quoted in Rob Mackie, "Jimmy Page," *Sounds*, April 21, 1973.

221 **"country-soul feeling"**: Robert Christgau, "In Memory of the Dave Clark Five," *Village Voice*, December 11, 1969.

221 **a New Zealander, Clive Coulson:** "Sandy MacGregor was a real gypsy. I never knew his real name. It sure wasn't Sandy MacGregor." Henry Smith, interview with the author, October 25, 2019.

221 **"We collected wood":** "We had candles, and I think there were gaslights." Clive Coulson, quoted in Hoskyns, *Trampled*, p. 155.

222 **"The original plan was to just go"**: JP, quoted in Tolinski, *Light & Shade*, p. 112.

222 **"So, there we were"**: RP, blind-quoted in Salewicz, *Jimmy Page*, p. 205.

222 **"It was a tiring walk"**: JP, blind-quoted in Power, *No Quarter*, p. 221.

222 **"I went out on a balcony"**: JP, quoted in Tolinski, *Light & Shade*, p. 115. Elsewhere he has said it occurred at Bron-Yr-Aur.

222 **"Bron-yr-Aur gave Jimmy and me"**: RP, quoted in Barney Hoskyns, "Mountain Man: RP Goes Back to His Welsh Roots," *Tracks*, Fall 2003.

223 **"When we conceived"**: RP, quoted in Yorke, *Led Zep*, pp. 94–96.

223 **"What would it take"**: Glyn Johns, interview with the author, May 18, 2018.

224 **"We'll be recording"**: JB, quoted, unsourced. Lewis, *Led Zeppelin: From a Whisper to a Scream*, p. 38 .

224 **"We were into Joni Mitchell"**: JPJ, quoted in Popoff, *Led Zeppelin* p. 77.

224 **"As soon as I got"**: Andy Johns, quoted in Popoff, *Led Zeppelin* p. 77.

224 **"It didn't come off"**: "We had attempted to record it before." JP, quoted in Tolinski, *Light & Shade*, p. 118.

225 **"blues with a rock 'n roll"**: JP, quoted in Tolinski, *Light & Shade*, p. 120.

225 **"It was meant to push"**: JP, quoted in Tolinski, *Light & Shade*, p. 119.

225 **"lived every line"**: Richard Digby Smith, quoted in Wall, *When Giants Walked the Earth*, p. 193.

225 **"I don't know where"**: RP, quoted in Hoskyns, *Led Zeppelin IV*, p. 63.

225 **"Let's try the outro"**: "I remember Pagey pushing him." JP, quoted by Richard Digby Smith in Phil Sutcliffe, "Getting It Together at Bron-yr-Aur," *Mojo*, April 2000.

225 **"to calm it down"**: RP, quoted in Hoskyns, *Led Zeppelin IV*, p. 65.

226 **"a lot of insecurity and nerves":** "Gradually, bit by bit, I'm finding myself now." RP, quoted in Yorke, *Led Zep*, p. 96.

226 **"The places that the String Band"**: RP, quoted in Yorke, *Led Zep*, p. 61.

226 **"played the kind of music":** Mike Heron, quoted in Steven Brocklehurst, "An Incredible Journey with the Incredible String Band," BBC Scotland News website, April 2, 2017.

226 **"I couldn't really play"**: JP, quoted in Tolinski, *Light & Shade*, p. 124.

227 **"sort of 'Bali Ha'i' melody line"**: JP, quoted in Tolinski, *Light & Shade*, p. 115.

227 **"It made you think of Vikings"**: RP, quoted in Lewis, *Led Zeppelin: From a Whisper to a Scream*, p. 41.

228 **"We knew it was"**: JP, blind-quoted in Power, *No Quarter*, p. 225.

228 **"I went down to the site"**: Peter Grant, quoted in Lewis, *Led Zeppelin: Celebration II*, p. 92.

228 **"suddenly became a free festival"**: Wendy Bannister, quoted in Wall, *When Giants Walked the Earth*, p. 188.

228 **"I remember standing there"**: RP, quoted in Wall, *When Giants Walked the Earth*, p. 190.

229 **"They were in great spirits"**: Chris Charlesworth, interview with the author, May 13, 2019.

229 **"Take care of those bastards"**: Peter Grant, quoted in Cole, *Stairway to Heaven*, p. 150.

229 **"He told us to go"**: Henry Smith interview.

229 **"Hey, we haven't finished"**: Chris Charlesworth, quoted in Welch, *Peter Grant*, p. 92.

230 **"Those guys blew my mind"**: Chris Charlesworth interview.

230 **"There was no way"**: Roy Harper, quoted in Hoskyns, *Trampled*, p. 162.

230 **a few short months later**: "Zeppelin Topple Beatles," *Winnepeg Free Press*, September 17, 1970.

230 **"I couldn't find Freddie Bannister"**: "I had a hell of a battle at the Bath Festival." Peter Grant, quoted in Paul Henderson, "If Somebody Had to Be Trod On, They Got Trod On," *Classic Rock*, April 5, 2017.

231 **"I didn't know exactly"**: JP, quoted in Tolinski, *Light & Shade*, p. 125.

231 **"You really do need"**: "When it comes to playing in the studio, my bottle goes. It's the studio nerves." JP, quoted in Yorke, *Led Zep*, pp. 107–8.

232 **"How much would that cost?"**: JP, quoted by Andy Johns in Popoff, *Led Zeppelin*, p. 104.

232 **"could find you anything"**: "Headley Grange came through Willow Morel." Carole Brown Woods, email to the author, April 22, 2020.

232 **"I'd been evacuated there"**: Peter Grant, quoted in Lewis, *Led Zeppelin: Celebration II*, p. 92.

232 **"It was a pretty austere place"**: JP, quoted in Hoskyns, *Led Zeppelin IV*, p. 58.

232 **"[It] had very large rooms"**: JPJ, quoted in Popoff, *Led Zeppelin*, p. 104.

233 **"some amazing hard work"**: JP, quoted in Michael Odell, "I Was Insatiable," *Uncut*, November 2019, p. 68.

233 **"It can get a bit impersonal"**: "[The truck] is a bit narrow like a corridor." Andy Johns, quoted in Hoskyns, *Led Zeppelin IV*, p. 78.

233 **"It seemed ideal"**: "It was just so exciting to have all the facilities there." JP, quoted in Hoskyns, *Led Zeppelin IV*, p. 79.

233 **"He would just get drunk"**: JP, blind-quoted in Power, *No Quarter*, p. 228.

233 **"all riffs and rhythm track"**: RP, quoted in Mat Snow, "Led Zeppelin," *Q*, December 1990.

233 **"an old Folkways LP"**: "I used his version as a basis and completely changed the arrangement." JP, quoted in Yorke, *Led Zep*, p. 98.

234 **"going back to the studio days"**: JP, quoted in Steven Rosen, "Jimmy Page," *Guitar Player*, July 1977.

234 **"There was no conscious desire"**: JPJ, quoted in Hoskyns, *Led Zeppelin IV*, p. 60.

234 **"The acoustic stuff"**: RP, quoted in Snow, "Led Zeppelin."

234 **"album's bucolic ambience"**: Attributed to JP in Lois Wilson, "Sleevenotes," *Q Special Edition: Led Zeppelin*, March 2003.

234 **"teenybopperish"**: JP, quoted in Yorke, *Led Zep*, p. 101; Tolinski, *Light & Shade*, p. 125.

234 **"there are different moods"**: RP, quoted in Yorke, *Led Zep*, p. 103.

235 **"a rickety, erratic affair"**: Phil Sutcliffe, "Back to Nature," *Q Special Edition: Led Zeppelin*, March 2003, p. 36.

235 **"I, II, III . . . and Zeppelin Weakens"**: "I, II, III . . . and Zeppelin Weakens," *Disc and Music Echo*, October 10, 1970.

235 **"a definite hatchet job"**: JP, interview with Paul Elliott, *Classic Rock*, n.d.

235  **"it remains to be seen"**: Nick Logan, "Zeppelin Solid Gas, Solid Gold," *NME*, October 10, 1970.

235  **"*Zeppelin III* Is Pure Magic"**: Chris Welch, "*Zeppelin III* Is Pure Magic," MM, October 10, 1970.

235  **He didn't take criticism**: "Jimmy was always touchy about reviews. The guy was thin-skinned." Chris Charlesworth interview.

235  **"I got really brought down"**: JP, quoted in Pete Frame, "Getting to the Bottom of the Page," *ZigZag*, December 1972.

235  **"We were so far ahead"**: JP, quoted in Tolinski, *Light & Shade*, p. 117.

236  **"I felt a lot better"**: JP, quoted in Dave Schulps, *Trouser Press* interview, Part 3, p. 18.

237  **"squirming fans and frustrated musicians"**: Pete Cain, "New Acoustic Material Disappoints Led Zep Freaks," *Rock*, October 11, 1970.

237  **"Some places, it's been a bit"**: JP, quoted in Allan Rinde, "Everything You Always Wanted to Know About Jimmy Page (but Were Afraid to Ask)," *Rock*, October 11, 1970.

237  **"Zep had to plug back in"**: Rinde, "Everything You Always Wanted to Know."

237  **"He was not a guy"**: Janine Safer Whitney, interview with the author, April 2, 2019.

237  **"I'd go abroad on these tours"**: JP, quoted in Nick Kent, "Bring It On Home," *Q Special Edition: Led Zeppelin*, March 2003, p. 139.

237  **"Bonzo was getting drunk"**: Henry Smith interview.

238  **"You do that again"**: Peter Grant, quoted in Henry Smith interview.

239  **"This bloke has invited us"**: JB, quoted in Dave Pegg, interview with the author, November 28, 2018.

## Chapter Ten: Invoking and Being Invocative

243  **by November 1, 1970**: "Top LPs," *Billboard*, October 31, 1970.

243  **"It was a pretty extreme change"**: JP, quoted in Mylett, *Jimmy Page*, p. 24.

244  **"great misunderstood genius"**: John Ingham, *Sounds*, March 13, 1976.

244  **"I read *Magick*"**: "It wasn't for some years till I understood what it was all about." JP, quoted in Mylett, *Jimmy Page*, p. 70.

244  **"The thing is to come"**: Mick Houghton, "Zeus of Zeppelin: An Interview with Jimmy Page," *Circus*, October 12, 1976. "He encouraged people to ask what they really want out of life and encouraged them to do it." JP, quoted in Tolinski, *Light & Shade*, p. 170.

244  **"there would be nothing"**: Aleister Crowley, *The Confessions of Aleister Crowley* (Waccabuc, NY: Appledore Books, 1969), p. 82.

245  **"a male child of perfect innocence"**: Aleister Crowley, *Magick in Theory and Practice by the Master Therion* (Paris: Lecram, 1929), p. 166.

245  **"Jimmy was obsessed"**: Jim McCarty, interview with the author, September 12, 2019.

245  **On early tours with Led Zeppelin**: Joe Wright, interview with the author, November 28, 2018.

246  **"bad vibes . . . suicides"**: JP, quoted in Cameron Crowe, "The Durable Led Zeppelin," *Rolling Stone*, March 13, 1975.

246  **"find black swans"**: Carole Brown Woods, email to the author, November 19, 2019.

246  **"There's really no format"**: JPJ, quoted in Caroline Boucher, "Zeppelin Shoots at the Gasbags," *Disc*, December 12, 1970.

247  **"we were drained"**: "We had done so much in such a short space of time." JB, blind-quoted in Hoskyns, *Trampled*, p. 179.

247  **His weight had ballooned**: "Peter was twenty-seven stone." Hoskyns, *Trampled*, p. 179.

247 **His ungainly size:** Welch, *Peter Grant*, p. 93.

247 **"We were in this luxury estate":** Sherry Coulson, quoted in Blake, *Bring It On Home*, p. 96.

247 **"A London record distributor":** Richard Williams, "Led Zeppelin Hammer Bootlegs," *MM*, October 3, 1970.

247 **"radio transmitters that picked up":** Peter Grant, quoted in *24 Hours*, BBC-TV, August 4, 1971, broadcast, https://www.youtube.com/watch?v=L6EwxH1hrcM.

248 **"the Bootleg King":** *24 Hours*.

248 **"Have you got the Led Zeppelin":** Peter Grant, quoted by Mickie Most in Welch, *Peter Grant*, p. 98.

248 **"threw the records all over":** Peter Grant, quoted in Blake, *Bring It On Home*, p. 93.

248 **"I would step on anyone":** Peter Grant, quoted in Phil Sutcliffe, "Trampled Underfoot," *Q Special Edition: Led Zeppelin*, March 2003, p. 40.

248 **"between $150,000 and $200,000":** Peter Grant, quoted in *24 Hours*.

248 **"In Germany, the situation is terrible":** Chris Charlesworth, "Bootlegs," *MM*, October 1970.

249 **"for inspiration":** Henry Smith, interview with the author, October 25, 2019.

249 **"He was my senior":** RP, quoted in Nigel Williamson, "Good Times, Bad Times," *Uncut*, May 2005, p. 56.

249 **"It was the first time":** JP, quoted in Phil Sutcliffe, "Back to Nature," *Q Special Edition: Led Zeppelin*, March 2003, p. 35.

249 **"We were like a marriage":** JP, quoted in Nigel Williamson, "Forget the Myths," *Uncut*, May 2005, p. 70.

249 **Jimmy had been struggling:** "I'd written the music over a long period, the first part coming at Bron-yr-Aur one night." JP, quoted in Yorke, *Led Zep*, p. 115.

249 **He'd been compiling demos:** "I'd been recording demos on a home unit called a New Vista, the deck from the Pye [Records] mobile." JP, quoted in Lewis, *Led Zeppelin: Celebration II*, p. 25.

250 **"I'd been fooling around":** JP, quoted in Tolinski, *Light & Shade*, p. 146.

250 **"To have a piece":** JP, quoted in Wall, *When Giants Walked the Earth*, p. 237.

250 **"Something that would have drums":** JP, quoted in Tolinski, *Light & Shade*, p. 147.

250 **"this great sort of orgasm":** JP, quoted in Wall, *When Giants Walked the Earth*, p. 237.

250 **just drums, acoustic guitar:** Andy Johns, quoted in Popoff, *Led Zeppelin*, p. 105.

250 **"an immediate imposition":** RP, quoted in Caroline Boucher, "Robert Plant Interview," *Disc*, February 1970.

251 **"We've done a good deal":** JPJ, interviewed in *Disc*, 1970, blind-quoted in Hoskyns, *Led Zeppelin IV*, p. 69.

251 **"It seemed ideal":** JP, blind-quoted in Hoskyns, *Led Zeppelin IV*, p. 79.

251 **"The idea was to create":** JP, quoted in Tolinski, *Light & Shade*, p. 142.

251 **fresh from its sessions:** "I had just done *Sticky Fingers* with the Stones, and we'd used the mobile unit on that." Andy Johns, interviewed in *Guitar World*, July 1986.

251 **"develop material and record it":** JP, quoted in Tolinski, Light & Shade, p. 144.

251 **"It was cold and damp":** JPJ, blind-quoted in Lewis, *Led Zeppelin: Celebration II*, p. 21.

251 **"There was stuffing coming out":** Andy Johns, quoted in Hoskyns, *Trampled*, p. 158.

251 **During an early jam:** Transcript of recorded outtakes, Dave Lewis, *Led Zeppelin: A Celebration* (London: Omnibus Press, 1991), p. 20.

252 **"One track is a long":** "I recall Page and I listening to *Electric Mud* at the time." JPJ, quoted in Dave Lewis, "Anchor Man: The Ultimate John Paul Jones Interview," *Tight but Loose*, December 2003.

252 **"didn't end when you thought"**: JPJ, quoted in Mat Snow, "John Paul Jones: The Quiet One," *Mojo*, December 2007.

252 **"I then suggested that we build"**: JP, quoted in Tolinski, *Light & Shade*, p. 145.

252 **"was actually phrased as three"**: JPJ, quoted in Susan Fast, *In the Houses of the Holy* (New York: Oxford University Press, 2001), p. 123.

252 **"You know, they just played it"**: RP, quoted in Yorke, *Led Zep*, p. 114.

253 **"Bonzo was playing"**: JP, quoted in Tobler and Grundy, *Guitar Greats*, p. 105.

253 **"it didn't come off"**: "We tried approaching it different ways." JP, quoted in Lewis, *Led Zeppelin: From a Whisper to a Scream*, p. 86.

253 **"If the track isn't happening"**: JP, quoted in Tolinski, *Light & Shade*, p. 144.

253 **"playing this right-handed"**: Don Brewer, quoted in Jon Bream, *Whole Lotta Led Zeppelin* (Minneapolis: Voyageur, 2008), p. 103.

253 **"It actually ground to a halt"**: JP, quoted in Dave Schulps, *Trouser Press* interview, Part 3, p. 19.

254 **"the most intuitive player"**: Glyn Johns, interview with the author, May 18, 2018.

254 **"just started improvising"**: JP, quoted in Tolinski, *Light & Shade*, p. 145.

254 **"It wasn't an intellectual thing"**: RP, quoted in Hoskyns, *Trampled*, p. 182.

255 **"If you chaps bring cocaine"**: "I thought cocaine was the drug of the devil." Andy Johns, quoted in Hoskyns, *Trampled*, p. 163.

255 **"led him down that path"**: Glyn Johns interview.

255 **"One night I came downstairs"**: "He always had loads of different instruments lying around." JP, quoted in Wall, *When Giants Walked the Earth*, p. 239; Lewis, *Led Zeppelin: Celebration II*, p. 22.

256 **"started moving my fingers"**: JP, quoted in Schulps, *Trouser Press* interview, Part 3, p. 19.

256 **"a dance around the maypole"**: JP, quoted in Yorke, *Led Zep*, p. 114.

256 **Andy Johns slapped a microphone**: "I put a microphone on him, Robert started singing, and we had this amazing track out of nothing." Andy Johns, interviewed in *Guitar World*, 1993.

256 **"I'd been reading a book"**: RP, quoted in *Guitar World*, 1993.

256 **They'd both listened incessantly**: "That's the music I play at home all the time, Joni Mitchell." JP, quoted in Crowe, "Durable Led Zeppelin."

256 **"When you're in love"**: RP, quoted in Crowe, "Durable Led Zeppelin," pp. 115–16.

257 **"There are so many classics"**: RP, quoted in Chris Charlesworth, "Robert Plant: Recording's No Race for Us," MM, February 8, 1975.

257 **"it sounded really labored"**: "We tried 'Levee' in just an ordinary studio." JP, quoted in Tolinski, *Light & Shade*, p. 205.

257 **"We'd been working on another song"**: JPJ, quoted in Hoskyns, *Led Zeppelin IV*, p. 107.

257 **"Bonzo has to stay behind"**: "You're always moaning about your drum sound." Andy Johns, quoted in Hoskyns, *Trampled*, p. 181.

257 **"Whoa! That's it,"**: JB, quoted in Lewis, *Led Zeppelin: Celebration II*, p. 24.

258 **"let's do 'Levee Breaks'"**: JP, quoted in Wall, *When Giants Walked the Earth*, p. 247. "Hold on! Let's try this one again." JP, quoted in Tolinski, *Light & Shade*, p. 205.

258 **"Page had a few things"**: JPJ, quoted in Popoff, *Led Zeppelin*, p. 104.

258 **"Both Jimmy and I"**: JPJ, quoted in Hoskyns, *Led Zeppelin IV*, p. 94.

259 **"a hysterical trill"**: "There's everything flying at that point." JP, quoted in Salewicz, *Jimmy Page*, p. 234.

259 **"I was sitting with Jimmy"**: RP, quoted in Stephen Demorest, "The *Circus* Magazine Interview—Robert Plant," *Circus*, June 1975.

260 **"I was holding a pencil:"** RP, quoted in Hoskyns, *Led Zeppelin IV*, p. 94.

260 "as if I were being guided": RP, quoted in Davis, *LZ-75*, p. 146.

260 "While we were doing it": JP, quoted in Schulps, *Trouser Press* interview, Part 3, p. 19.

260 "Nobody's quite sure": JPJ, quoted in Popoff, *Led Zeppelin*, p. 104.

260 "The lyrics were a cynical thing": RP, quoted in Chris Welch, *Led Zeppelin: Dazed and Confused* (New York: Thunder Mouth Press, 2001), p. 66.

260 "It's like she can have": RP, quoted in Hoskyns, *Led Zeppelin IV*, p. 96.

260 "Somebody would start something": JPJ, quoted in Popoff, *Led Zeppelin*, p. 104.

261 "We really couldn't have done": JP, quoted in Tolinski, *Light & Shade*, p. 146.

261 "I couldn't get that to work": "We probably would have kicked the track out." JP, quoted in Hoskyns, *Led Zeppelin IV*, p. 112.

261 "He had been to see": JP, quoted in Wall, *When Giants Walked the Earth*, p. 242.

261 Double Diamond pale ale: "He had a Double Diamond, picked up four sticks and we did it again." JP, quoted in Tobler and Grundy, *Guitar Greats*, p. 105.

261 "totally different tone color": JP, quoted in Tolinski, *Light & Shade*, p. 146.

262 "out of all the British girls": RP, quoted in Hoskyns, *Led Zeppelin IV*, p. 113.

262 "there was never a struggle": Andy Johns, quoted in Popoff, *Led Zeppelin*, p. 104.

262 "Even in rehearsals, Jim": Phil Carlo, interview with the author, May 12, 2019.

263 "Sounds wonderful": JB, quoted by Richard Digby-Smith in Hoskyns, *Trampled*, p. 183.

263 "When he finally comes in": Richard Digby-Smith, quoted in Hoskyns, *Led Zeppelin IV*, p. 101.

263 "I had the first phase": JP, quoted in Tolinski, *Light & Shade*, p. 147.

264 "He just leaned up against": Richard Digby-Smith, quoted in Hoskyns, *Led Zeppelin IV*, p. 100.

264 "Robert, it's your turn": Andy Johns, quoted in Popoff, *Led Zeppelin*, p. 105.

264 Not if Jimmy had anything: "The next album won't be called *LZIV*. We'll think of something else." JP, interviewed by Caroline Boucher, *Disc*, February 1971.

265 "a real dingy second-hand shop": JP, quoted in Wall, *When Giants Walked the Earth*, p. 257.

265 "the old being knocked down": JP, quoted in Wall, *When Giants Walked the Earth*, p. 257.

265 "would make the whole thing": JP, quoted in James Jackson, "JP on Led Zeppelin's Good Times, Bad Times and Reunion Rumors," *The Times*, January 8, 2010.

266 "pretty bold": "Things like releasing records with no information and no writing on the cover. I mean, that's pretty bold." Jack White, quoted in Hoskyns, *Led Zeppelin IV*, p. 124.

266 "It actually comes from the idea": JP, quoted in Brad Tolinski, "The Fab IV," *Guitar World*, January 2002.

266 "We wanted to demonstrate": JP, quoted in Tolinski, "Fab IV."

266 "Each of us decided": RP, quoted in Yorke, *Led Zep*, p. 111.

267 "it represents courage": JP quoted in *ZigZag*, Issue 28, February 1973.

267 John Paul and Bonzo selected: Their signs appear on pp. 32 and 33, respectively, of Rudolph Koch, *The Book of Signs* (London: Limited Editions Club, 1930).

267 "It's just a doodle": JP, quoted in Tobler and Grundy, *Guitar Greats*, p. 104.

267 "My symbol was about invoking": JP, quoted, in Wall, *When Giants Walked the Earth*, p. 262.

267 "a graven image of energy": Erik Davis, *Led Zeppelin IV*, (New York: Continuum, 2005), p. 44.

268 "There was a lot of opposition": RP, quoted in Lewis, *Led Zeppelin: Celebration II*, p. 26.

268 **"The record company was in shock":** Phil Carson, interview with the author, July 2, 2019.

268 **"I had to go in personally":** JP, quoted in Wall, *When Giants Walked the Earth*, p. 261.

268 **"the fans were going":** Phil Carson interview.

268 **"It didn't matter what was":** Nick Maria, interview with the author, October 14, 2019.

### Chapter Eleven: Just Boys Having Fun

270 *"Melody Maker* **and all that lot":** Peter Grant, quoted in Lewis, *Led Zeppelin: Celebration II*, p. 92.

271 **"[Jimmy] brought the tapes back":** RP, quoted in Caroline Boucher, "Robert Plant Interview," *Disc*, 1972.

272 **"We're going to restrict prices":** Peter Grant, quoted in Chris Welch, "Zeppelin to Tour," *MM*, January 25, 1971.

272 **"The audiences were becoming bigger":** JP, quoted in Keith Altham, "Jimmy Page: Zep Come to the People," *Record Mirror*, February 27, 1971.

272 **"The situation's gotten very bloody":** JP, quoted in Arthur Levy, "Led Zeppelin's Jimmy Page: A Heavy Blimp That Gives No Quarter," *Zoo World*, July 19, 1973.

272 **"It was frightening":** Henry Smith, interview with the author, October 22, 2019.

272 **"Just hours before our concert":** Cole, *Stairway to Heaven*, p. 168.

273 **"a petrol tanker was hijacked":** Welch, *Led Zeppelin: Dazed and Confused*, p. 63.

273 **But he remembered seeing:** "Earl Hooker played the first one I saw . . . but you just couldn't get them." JP, quoted in Nick Kent, "Jimmy Page: Guitars I Have Known," *NME*, October 12, 1974.

274 **In truth, however, it was:** Janine Safer Whitney, email to the author.

274 **"All you've got to do":** Peter Grant, quoted in Lewis, *Led Zeppelin: Celebration II*, p. 94.

274 **"I quaked in my hotel bedroom":** Welch, *Led Zeppelin: Dazed and Confused*, p. 65. "There was a punch-up between Bonzo and Robert." Phil Carson, interview with the author, July 2, 2019.

274 **"Once you've played":** JP, quoted in Cole, *Stairway to Heaven*, p. 172.

275 **"In a place like the Marquee":** Chris Charlesworth, interview with the author, May 13, 2019.

275 **"We just didn't have time":** JP, quoted in Lewis and Tremaglio, *Evenings with Led Zeppelin*, p. 265.

276 **"knew what a dodgy place":** Peter Grant, quoted in Lewis, *Led Zeppelin: Celebration II*, p. 92.

276 **"We could see the riot police":** JP, quoted in Tobler and Grundy, *Guitar Greats*, p. 104.

276 **"If all concerts were":** Cole, *Stairway to Heaven*, p. 180.

276 **"Then we suddenly twigged":** JP, quoted in Yorke, *Led Zep*, p. 105.

276 **"Blow this!":** JP, quoted in Ritchie Yorke, "Zeppelin Hit by Tear Gas as Troops Charge Crowd," *NME*, July 10, 1971.

277 **"Everyone was running":** "The kids came running over the stage." Rick McGrath, "Robert Plant Interview," *Georgia Straight*, August 27, 1971.

277 **"It was just pandemonium":** JP, quoted in Tobler and Grundy, *Guitar Greats*, p. 105.

277 **"I barricaded the door":** RP, quoted in Nigel Williamson, "Good Times, Bad Times," *Uncut*, May 2005, p. 58.

278 **"It was such a shock":** JP, quoted in Wall, *When Giants Walked the Earth*, p. 253.

278 **"I can't do any more":** "So I bopped him [Bonzo]." RP, quoted in Wall, *When Giants Walked the Earth*, p. 254.

278 **"It was just boys having fun"**: Phil Carson interview.

278 **"For example, there was a night"**: JP, quoted in Tolinski, *Light & Shade*, p. 169.

279 **overnight train to Osaka**: "I just shit in the handbag!" JB, quoted in Cole, *Stairway to Heaven*, p. 192.

280 **"Night after night after night"**: "In retrospect, our Japanese hosts were probably completely horrified, but they were so polite, they just kept bowing to us." JP, quoted in Tolinski, *Light & Shade*, p. 169.

281 **"But even lectures"**: "I cannot let you stay in this hotel ever again." Richard Cole, quoted in Tolinski, *Light & Shade*, p. 192.

281 **"At this point, cocaine started"**: Phil Carson interview.

281 **"were an integral part"**: JP, quoted in Tolinski, *Light & Shade*, p. 169.

281 **"Drugs for the band"**: Cole, *Stairway to Heaven*, p. 6.

281 **"Led Zeppelin was a musician's dream"**: JP, quoted in Blake, *Bring It On Home*, p. 123.

282 **"There was a new aristocracy"**: Michel Des Barres, interview with the author, February 20, 2019.

282 **"messing around with that song"**: JP, quoted in Wall, *When Giants Walked the Earth*, p. 244.

282 **"AM radio was insisting"**: Jerry Greenberg, interview with the author, January 10, 2019.

283 **"On a tour with"**: Peter Grant, quoted in Blake, *Bring It On Home*, pp. 108–9.

283 **Bill Graham prided himself**: Don Law, interview with the author, November 8, 2018.

283 **"We hired a promoter"**: Steve Weiss, blind-quoted in Hoskyns, *Trampled*, p. 194.

283 **"We'd been doing ten-percent"**: Bill Curbishley, interview with the author, May 16, 2018.

284 **"Fuck those promoters!"**: Peter Grant to Sam Aizer, quoted in Blake, *Bring It On Home*, p. 110.

284 **"You don't have to promote"**: Mickie Most, quoting Peter Grant in Welch, *Peter Grant*, p. 84.

284 **"We never liked it"**: Don Law interview.

285 **"I'd take ten percent"**: Peter Grant, quoted in Danny Goldberg, *Bumping into Geniuses* (New York: Gotham Books, 2008), p. 64.

286 **"It was probably more painful"**: JP, quoted in Salewicz, *Jimmy Page*, p. 261.

286 **"My main goal"**: JP, quoted in Tolinski, *Light & Shade*, p. 159.

286 **with Jimmy installing himself**: "Jimmy had Jagger's bedroom." Eddie Kramer, quoted in Mick Wall, "Eddie Kramer's Guide to Led Zeppelin's *Houses of the Holy*," *Classic Rock*, March 28, 2017, www.loudersound.com/features/eddie-kramers-guide-to-led-zeppelins-houses-of-the-holy .

286 **"bits of taped ideas"**: JP, quoted in Tolinski, *Light & Shade*, p. 204.

288 **"It's time that people heard"**: RP, blind-quoted in Wall, "Eddie Kramer's Guide."

288 **"in all four of us"**: JP, quoted in James Johnson, "Jimmy Page, the Mild Barbarian," *NME*, April 21, 1973.

288 **"There is no place"**: RP, quoted in Hoskyns, *Trampled*, p. 190.

288 **"There were Jamaicans all over"**: Kevyn Gammond, interview with the author, May 7, 2019.

289 **"a cross between reggae"**: JP, quoted in Dave Schulps, *Trouser Press* interview, Part 3, p. 20.

289 **"just a giggle"**: JP, quoted in Johnson, "Jimmy Page, the Mild Barbarian."

289 **"like bombs going off"**: Eddie Kramer, quoted in Wall, "Eddie Kramer's Guide."

289 **Robert explained how**: "Bonzo and I were just going to go to the studio and talk Black Country through the whole thing." RP, quoted in Yorke, *Led Zep*, p. 124.

290 **"The rhythm section on that"**: JPJ, quoted in Toby Manning, "Broad Church," *Q Special Edition: Led Zeppelin*, March 2003, p. 60.

290 **"I remember putting a Fender amp"**: Eddie Kramer, quoted in Wall, "Eddie Kramer's Guide."

291 **"The sound in the place"**: JP, quoted in Yorke, *Led Zep*, p. 118.

291 **"Everything would be sorted"**: Phil Carlo, interview with the author, May 12, 2019.

291 **"Everybody was now doing it"**: Phil Carson interview.

292 **Les Harvey grabbed the mic**: Roger St. Pierre, "Stone the Crows: Les Harvey—a Rock Tragedy," *NME*, May 13, 1972.

292 **"Peter went to pieces"**: Maggie Bell, interview with the author, May 8, 2019.

292 **"perhaps a kilo"**: Author interview with Benji LeFevre, May 19, 2019.

292 **"the Bionic Hooter"**: Janine Safer Whitney, interview with the author, April 2, 2019.

292 **"Whether you snort it"**: Pete Townshend, quoted in Connor McKnight and John Tobler, "Chatting with Pete Townshend," *ZigZag*, March 1972.

293 **At Nassau Coliseum it was reported**: Stephen Davis, *Hammer of the Gods* (New York: Ballantine Books, 1985), p. 167; Lewis and Tremaglio, *Evenings with Led Zeppelin*, p. 323 (illustration).

293 **"still hard to take them seriously"**: Robert Hilburn, "Led Zeppelin at the Forum," *Los Angeles Times*, June 27, 1972.

293 **"It's the Stones this"**: JB, quoted in Lewis, *Led Zeppelin: From a Whisper to a Scream*, p. 59.

293 **"they were a long way"**: RP, quoted in Williamson, "Good Times, Bad Times," p. 56.

294 **"Who wants to know"**: JP, blind-quoted from NME in Wall, *When Giants Walked the Earth*, p. 270.

294 **"so authoritative"**: "I mean, if it's not your taste in music, then leave it well alone and let someone else do the reviews." JP, quoted in Pete Frame, "Talking with Jimmy Page," *ZigZag*, December 1972 and February 1973.

294 **"They were too busy"**: JP, quoted in Levy, "Led Zeppelin's Jimmy Page."

294 **"There were all sorts of scenes"**: Eddie Kramer, quoted in Hoskyns, *Trampled*, p. 190.

## Chapter Twelve: A Law unto Themselves

297 **"We happened to be sharing a flat"**: Aubrey Powell, interview with the author, May 15, 2019.

299 **"It's a sort of dawn and dusk"**: JP, quoted in Rob Mackie, "Jimmy Page," *Sounds*, April 21, 1973.

302 **"The sky started to look"**: JP, quoted in Rob Mackie, "Jimmy Page."

302 **"You would not be happy"**: Aubrey Powell interview.

302 **sales of the first four**: Goldberg, *Bumping into Geniuses*, p. 61.

303 **"Maybe you could attack"**: JP, quoted in James Johnson, "Jimmy Page, the Mild Barbarian," *NME*, April 21, 1973.

303 **"There was a lot of imagination"**: RP, quoted in Carlton Fuerte, "My Favorite Led Zeppelin Album," *High Times*, April 1991.

303 **"a limp blimp"**: Gordon Fletcher, "Houses of the Holy," *Rolling Stone*, June 7, 1973.

303 **"a clunker"**: "The most glaring flaw is simply weak material." Steven Rosen, "Led Zeppelin: *Houses of the Holy*," *Music World*, June 1973.

303 **The review in *Phonograph Record***: "The whole problem throughout *Houses of the Holy* is that the music just doesn't go anywhere." Metal Mike Saunders, "Led Zeppelin: *Houses of the Holy*," *Phonograph Record*, May 1973.

303 **"an album of the highest quality"**: Roy Carr, "Led Zeppelin: *Houses of the Holy* (Atlantic)," *NME*, March 31, 1973.

303 **"Unlike the previous Zep albums"**: Jonh Ingham, "Led Zeppelin: *Houses of the Holy*," *Let It Rock*, June 1973.

304 **"People still have"**: JP, blind-quoted in Power, *No Quarter*, p. 291.

304 **"How they should approach"**: JP, quoted in Johnson, "Jimmy Page, the Mild Barbarian."

304 **"'Whole Lotta Love'"**: "They start with a chorus of 'Whole Lotta Love,' 'Whole Lotta Love' before [we're] through with the second number." JP, quoted in Arthur Levy, "Led Zeppelin's Jimmy Page: A Heavy Blimp That Gives No Quarter," *Zoo World*, July 19, 1973.

305 **BP Fallon, last seen masterminding,:** "I never remember him even sitting down with a journalist." Gyl Corrigan-Devlin, quoted in Hoskyns, *Trampled*, p. 200.

305 **"the entertainment manager"**: BP Fallon, quoted in Hoskyns, *Trampled*, p. 200.

305 **"Led Zeppelin was not only not cool"**: Goldberg, *Bumping into Geniuses*, p. 62.

306 **"Yeah, of course, they're big"**: Danny Goldberg, interview with the author, August 28, 2018.

306 **To keep the band entertained:** "Just good clean fun." Davis, *Hammer of the Gods*, p. 186.

307 **house pet Chris Welch:** "I remember Jimmy pissing and moaning about Chris Welch's review [of *Houses of the Holy*] in *Melody Maker*." Lisa Robinson, quoted in Hoskyns, *Trampled*, p. 203.

307 **"Look, we were very young"**: RP, quoted in Goldberg, *Bumping into Geniuses*, p. 66.

308 **"When you put the spotlights"**: RP, quoted in Yorke, *Led Zep*, p. 123.

308 **"It was a big box"**: "It looked pretty cool for that time." Benji Le Fevre, interview with the author, May 19, 2019.

309 **"We decided that the denim trip"**: RP, quoted in Yorke, *Led Zep*, p. 123.

309 **"Sparkly clothes became available"**: JPJ, quoted in Hoskyns, *Trampled*, p. 210.

309 **"Please don't ask me"**: Lillian Roxon, quoted in Danny Goldberg interview.

310 **The band picked up the cost:** "I could fly writers down. Not a problem." Danny Goldberg interview.

311 **"a very well-meant gesture"**: RP, quoted in Barney Hoskyns, "Mountain Man: Robert Plant Goes Back to His Welsh Roots," *Tracks*, Fall 2003.

311 **"We felt quite warm vibes"**: RP, quoted in Lisa Robinson, "Whole Lotta Led in the Deep South," *Disc and Music Echo*, June 9, 1973.

311 **"a teenage boy's jaw literally drop"**: Goldberg, *Bumping into Geniuses*, p. 67.

311 **A headline proclaimed:** Cathy Yarbrough and Barry Henderson, "Stadium Rocks," *Atlanta Constitution*, May 4, 1973, p. 1.

312 **"This is Atlanta"**: Peter Grant, quoted in Danny Goldberg interview.

312 **"The majority of the crowd"**: Rick Norcross, "Led Zeppelin No Lead Balloon in Tampa," *Tampa Times*, May 7, 1973.

312 **Robert could feel it:** "The only thing they could pick up on was the complete vibe of what music was being done." RP, quoted in Mary Campbell, "Led Zeppelin in Tampa: Biggest Crowd Ever," Associated Press, May 6, 1973.

313 **"I had heard that"**: Lisa Robinson, "Led Right from the Start," *Disc*, May 19, 1973.

313 **"his guitar-playing is so"**: Lisa Robinson, "It's Only May, but It's the Year's Best," *Disc*, June 2, 1973.

313 **The *St. Louis Post-Dispatch* considered:** Dick Richmond, "Unusual, Maddening Performance by the Led Zeppelin at Arena," *St. Louis Post-Dispatch*, May 11, 1973.

313 **"the band just isn't inventive enough"**: Lee Moore, "Led Zeppelin Concert Too Heavy for 3 Hours," *Mobile Press-Register*, May 14, 1973.

313 **"has become a showcase"**: Terry Kliewer, "Individualism Seems to Be Invading Zeppelin," *Dallas Morning News*, May 22, 1973.

313 **"a show one could take"**: "In concert, Led Zeppelin is relatively contained—not much showmanship at all." "'Zepplin' [*sic*] Group Hits S.A.," *San Antonio Gazette*, May 23, 1973.

313 **"the thunderous opening notes"**: Cameron Crowe, "Zeppelin Alchemy: Transmuting Led into Gold," *Los Angeles Times*, October 7, 1973.

314 **"like Sodom and Gomorrah"**: "Those really were the days of pure hedonism." JP, quoted in Tolinski, *Light & Shade*, p. 161.

314 **"It was the feeling"**: JP, blind-quoted but attributed to an interview with Steven Rosen of *Guitar World* in Power, *No Quarter*, p. 309.

314 **"Everyone knows what"**: JP, quoted in Sander, *Trips*, p. 114.

314 **"He was like the Pied Piper"**: Michael Des Barres, interview with the author, February 20, 2019.

315 **"wicked sexual side"**: "Jimmy had a wicked sexual side that made him a transcendent lover." Pamela Miller, quoted in *Uncut*, 2009.

315 **"Pamela *loved* Jimmy"**: Michael Des Barres interview.

315 **"It is written that the time"**: "Your Very Own Superfox," *Star*, June 1973.

316 **"We were cutting school"**: Lori Mattix, interview with the author, January 21, 2019.

316 **"Sable's morality was something"**: Michael Des Barres interview.

316 **"Why would I not"**: BP Fallon, quoted in Salewicz, *Jimmy Page*, p. 282.

317 **"She's magnificent"**: JP, quoted in Cole, *Stairway to Heaven*, p. 217.

317 **"outrageously gorgeous, draped over"**: Michael Des Barres interview.

317 **"They came out of the woodwork"**: Vanessa Gilbert, interview with the author, January 31, 2019.

317 **"It was a glitter cathedral"**: Rodney Bingenheimer, interview with the author, January 23, 2019.

318 **"These guys were party animals"**: Rodney Bingenheimer, quoted in Steven Rosen, "Rodney B.'s Endless Party," *Guitar World*, July 1986.

318 **"If you went to a disco"**: Danny Goldberg, quoted in Steven Rosen, "Danny Goldberg's Hideaway," *Guitar World*, July 1986.

319 **"The girls would scratch"**: Rodney Bingenheimer, quoted in Hoskyns, *Trampled*, p. 231.

319 **"we'll have your fucking head"**: "All of a sudden, I was in this limousine by myself in the parking lot of the Rainbow." Richard Cole, quoted in Lori Mattix interview.

320 **She'd even accompanied:** "Lori's mother brought Lori and Sable to my suite." Michael Des Barres interview.

320 **When he was told $150:** Yorke, *Led Zep*, p. 130; incident confirmed in Phil Carson, interview with the author, July 2, 2019.

321 **"He took a picture"**: "Then we all jumped into a limousine and went to a party at Cher's in Silver Lake." Lori Mattix interview.

321 **There was another incident:** "They grabbed my friend Ronnie Romano and held him by his heels over the balcony." Rodney Bingenheimer interview; Rodney Bingenheimer, quoted in Hoskyns, *Trampled*, pp. 233–34.

321 **"He treated Mick badly"**: Benji Le Fevre interview.

322 **"He's twenty-one [*sic*] today"**: RP, quoted in *Bonzo's Birthday Party* (bootleg recording of concert).

322 **"easy to get along with"**: Vanessa Gilbert interview.

322 **The party line was that Jimmy:** "Jimmy didn't get thrown in the pool because he had the coke." Vanessa Gilbert interview.

322 **"It got wedged between two"**: Peter Grant, quoted in Blake, *Bring It On Home*, p. 124.

323 *"I am the golden god"*: "I was at the top of a palm tree on the night of Bonzo's birthday." RP, quoted in Hoskyns, *Trampled*, p. 216.

### Chapter Thirteen: The Land of *Mondo Bizarro*

324 **"There was the intensity"**: JP, quoted in Wall, *When Giants Walked the Earth*, pp. 287–88.

324 **"Everything is done for you"**: JPJ, quoted in Mat Snow, "Led Zeppelin," *Q*, December 1990.

325 **It was a disappointing performance**: "The sound throughout the entire concert was painfully thin and hollow. . . . Plant's voice was almost gone." Steven Rosen, "Steel Driven Led," *Sounds*, June 23, 1973.

325 **"Jimmy called me and said"**: "I think Jimmy knew it couldn't be bought." Aubrey Powell, interview with the author, May 15, 2019.

326 **Peter Grant bragged**: *Financial Times*, blind-quoted in Davis, *Hammer of the Gods*, p. 191.

327 **"This time, I'm going"**: JP, quoted in Lisa Robinson, "Jimmy Page," *NME*, February 1, 1975.

327 **"And no boom boxes"**: "I was always invited in to smoke a joint." Danny Marcus, interview with the author, January 16, 2019.

328 **"Actually, it was a lot"**: JP, quoted in Nick Kent, "Session Star: Jimmy Page," *NME*, September 1, 1973.

328 **"On that small plane"**: Peter Grant, quoted in Paul Henderson, "If Somebody Had to Get Trod On, They Got Trod On," *Classic Rock*, April 5, 2017, www.loudersound.com /features/peter-grant-interview-life-with-led-zeppelin.

328 **"I've had it with these"**: Peter Grant, quoted in Cole, *Stairway to Heaven*, p. 246.

329 **"There was a bedroom"**: Danny Goldberg, interview with the author, August 28, 2018.

329 **"The idea was for Zeppelin"**: Phil Carson, interview with the author, July 2, 2019.

329 **"Our feet never really touched"**: JP, quoted in Wall, *When Giants Walked the Earth*, p. 288.

329 **On off nights**: "I wasn't allowed to fly on the *Starship* because I was underage. They weren't going to take me across state lines." Lori Mattix, interview with the author, January 21, 2019.

330 **"What's with that"**: RP, quoted in Lynn Van Matre, "Overwhelmed, Hot and Heavy at the Stadium," *Chicago Tribune*, July 9, 1973.

331 **Rush remained one of Jimmy's**: "He's one of my favorite guitarists." Arthur Levy, "Led Zeppelin's Jimmy Page: A Heavy Blimp That Gives No Quarter," *Zoo World*, July 19, 1973.

331 **"It was strange"**: Danny Marcus interview.

331 **"This isn't necessary, G"**: Benji Le Fevre, interview with the author, May 19, 2019.

332 **"was sure that cocaine"**: "He told me that so many times." Phil Carson interview.

332 **"Definitely the Zeppelin crowd"**: Danny Goldberg interview.

332 **a friend described his habit**: Vanessa Gilbert, interview with the author, January 31, 2019.

332 **he simply put his nose**: "Sherry Coulson remembers seeing him blithely snorting cocaine from the bag, rather than chopping out a line first." Blake, *Bring It On Home*, p. 123.

332 **"He seemed to have the constitution":** Sherry Coulson, quoted in Blake, *Bring It On Home*, p. 123.

332 **"It turned out someone had put":** "I think he had already started to mix heroin and coke." Gyl Corrigan-Devlin, quoted in Hoskyns, *Trampled*, p. 240.

332 **"Jimmy's guitar playing got sloppy":** Benji Le Fevre interview. "It seemed that Page was sometimes getting his fingers caught in the strings." Barry Taylor, "Zeppelin Havoc," *NME*, August 11, 1973.

332 **Nor was Robert always:** "Singer Plant . . . was not in exceptional voice. . . . He could not reach the higher registers." Marshall Fine, "Led Zeppelin Late, 'Pure and Loud,'" *Minneapolis Star-Tribune*, July 12, 1973. "Plant had either lost his voice somewhere along the tour or he was tired." Taylor, "Zeppelin Havoc." "Plant started weakly, but soon caught fire." Fred Kirby, "Led Zeppelin," *Variety*, August 1, 1973.

333 **"we always start off *shaky*":** JP, quoted in Chris Salewicz, "The *Gig* Interview: Jimmy Page," *Gig*, May 1977.

333 **"Led Zeppelin doesn't give concerts":** Dale Anderson, "Led Zeppelin Kneads Crowd to Silly Putty," *Buffalo News*, July 16, 1973.

333 **"The freaks had come out":** Vanessa Gilbert interview.

334 **The next morning at checkout:** "I was standing right behind Peter, a fly on the wall." Vanessa Gilbert interview.

334 **"Apparently the Methodists":** Peter Grant, quoted in Blake, *Bring It On Home*, p. 124.

334 **"The guy was so frustrated":** Peter Grant, quoted in Lisa Robinson, "Stairway to Excess," *Vanity Fair*, November 2003.

335 **"By 1973, we had moved":** JP, quoted in Tolinski, *Light & Shade*, p. 188.

336 **"You call your boss":** Peter Clifton, quoted in Welch, *Peter Grant*, pp. 166–67.

337 **"a seminal moment":** RP, quoted in Wall, *When Giants Walked the Earth*, p. 294.

338 **"When I think that I":** "Robert took a picture of me and Roy in bed." Morgana Welch, quoted in Hoskyns, *Trampled*, p. 235.

338 **He claimed he hadn't slept:** "I didn't sleep for five days! Everything was so exciting." JP, quoted in Tolinski, *Light & Shade*, p. 171. "It was like the adrenaline tap wouldn't turn off." JP, quoted in Wall, *When Giants Walked the Earth*, p. 316.

338 **"We're all terribly worn out":** JP, quoted in Yorke, *Led Zep*, p. 132.

338 **"We announced the dates":** Peter Grant, quoted in Lewis, *Led Zeppelin: Celebration II*, p. 51.

339 **"I would ask if":** JPJ, quoted in Dave Lewis, "Anchor Man: The Ultimate John Paul Jones Interview," *Tight but Loose*, December 2003.

339 **"They started filming":** Peter Clifton, quoted in Hoskyns, *Trampled*, p. 238.

339 **Richard Cole claimed:** "We had a teenage girl from Brooklyn in our dressing room." Cole, *Stairway to Heaven*, p. 252.

339 **"I went to the locker room":** "I stood on the urinal to look over the top, and this cop—a short, heavyset guy—had his eyes closed with a big smile on his face, and this chick had his dick in her mouth." Henry Smith, interview with the author, October 2, 2019.

340 **"in case we wanted":** Richard Cole, quoted in Davis, *Hammer of the Gods*, p. 207.

340 **in some retellings:** "Jimmy phoned me in the middle of the night because he wanted $600 for a guitar." Richard Cole, quoted in Hoskyns, *Trampled*, p. 236.

340 **even $8,000:** Salewicz, *Jimmy Page*, p. 286.

340 **To safeguard the band's privacy:** "They hid out there for a few hours until the cops left." Shelley Kaye, interview with the author, July 15, 2019.

340 **"Hey, I've got some stuff":** "Well, I want the *great* stuff." Vanessa Gilbert interview.

341 **"was watched by the FBI":** Phil Carson interview.

341 **"Peter told me"**: Michael Des Barres, interview with the author, February 20, 2019.

341 **"Jimmy and I just laughed"**: RP, quoted in Yorke, *Led Zep*, p. 132.

341 **"a new private practice"**: Jeff Hoffman, interview with the author, July 30, 2019.

342 **"I was just totally"**: JP, quoted in William S. Burroughs, "Rock Magic: Jimmy Page, Led Zeppelin and a Search for the Elusive Stairway to Heaven," *Crawdaddy*, June 1975.

342 **"enormous amount of adrenaline"**: JP, quoted in Tolinski, *Light & Shade*, p. 169.

343 **"Nothing's preconceived right now"**: RP, quoted in Lewis and Tremaglio, *Evenings with Led Zeppelin*, p. 415.

## Chapter Fourteen: Led Zeppelin Was Otherwise Engaged

344 **"Jimmy would hop on a train"**: Unity MacLean, interview with the author, October 16, 2019.

345 **"the most beautiful residence"**: "It's just a superb piece of architecture." Aubrey Powell, interview with the author, November 28, 2018.

345 **"It was a very spooky place"**: Carole Brown Woods, email to the author, November 30, 2019.

345 **"The catering team were dressed"**: "Richard spoilt it in a way." Carole Brown Woods, email to the author, June 29, 2020.

346 **"Peter particularly liked it"**: Ed Bicknell, interview with the author, May 11, 2019.

346 **"The perfect office"**: Peter Grant, quoted by Alan Callan in Welch, *Peter Grant*, p. 153.

346 **"He'd been pursuing Peter"**: "You should have seen his cheeky grin when we arrived into work the next day." Carole Brown Woods, email to the author, November 16, 2019.

347 **"If you're going to charge me"**: Peter Grant, quoted in Unity MacLean interview.

347 **"The band was thirty percent"**: Phil Carson, interview with the author, July 2, 2019.

347 **"From time to time"**: Jeff Hoffman, interview with the author, July 30, 2019.

348 **"I had great ambitions"**: RP, quoted in Nigel Williamson, "Good Times, Bad Times," *Uncut*, May 2005, p. 57.

348 **"The deal was a great one"**: Phil Carson interview.

349 **"'Are you *nuts?*'"**: "Ahmet talked me out of it." Phil Carson interview.

349 **"an honest sort of mediocre night"**: JP, quoted in Chris Salewicz, "The *Gig* Interview: Jimmy Page," *Gig*, May 1977.

349 **There was no complete take**: "They filmed three nights at the Garden and never got one complete 'Whole Lotta Love.'" Peter Grant, quoted in Lewis, "Peter Grant: The TBL Interview," in *Led Zeppelin: Celebration II*, p. 95.

349 **"really out of it"**: JP, blind-quoted in Power, *No Quarter*, p. 320.

350 **"It was weird"**: Joe Massot, quoted in Peter Doggett, "Dazed and Confused," *Q Special Edition: Led Zeppelin*, March 2003, p. 85.

350 **"I'm suddenly told"**: JPJ, quoted in Doggett, "Dazed and Confused," p. 85.

350 **"one man and a bunch"**: Joe Massot, quoted in Doggett, "Dazed and Confused," p. 86.

351 **"Jimmy felt he had something"**: Joe Massot, quoted in Yorke, *Led Zep*, p. 162.

351 **"They created several"**: JP, quoted in Tolinski, *Light & Shade*, p. 198.

352 **"the most expensive"**: Peter Grant, quoted in Lewis, *Led Zeppelin: Celebration II*, p. 95.

353 **"Most of the album"**: JP, blind-quoted (referring to an interview he gave to *Circus*) in Barney Hoskyns, "Let's Get Physical: The Story of Led Zeppelin's *Physical Graffiti*," *Classic Rock*, September 2010.

353 **During their last visit:** "Bonzo did hundreds of pounds' worth of damage driving his Range Rover across the lawn and through the garden." Carole Brown Woods, interview with the author, November 8, 2019.

353 **"He turned up at my house":** Peter Grant, quoted in Lewis, "Peter Grant," p. 89.

353 **"I'd had enough of touring":** JPJ, quoted in Dave Lewis, "The John Paul Jones Interview," *Tight but Loose*, May 1997.

353 **"I thought the band":** JPJ, quoted in Mat Snow, "John Paul Jones: The Quiet One," *Mojo*, December 2007.

353 **"Have you told anyone else?":** Peter Grant, quoted in Henderson, "If Somebody Had to Be Trod On, They Got Trod On," *Classic Rock*, April 5, 2017.

354 **"the band spent a week":** "We were just hanging around and messing around." Ron Nevison, quoted in Popoff, *Led Zeppelin*, p. 160.

354 **"We began as always":** RP, quoted in Chris Charlesworth, "Robert Plant: Recording's No Race for Us," MM, February 8, 1975.

354 **"I'd made a commitment to Pete Townshend":** Ron Nevison, quoted in Popoff, *Led Zeppelin*, p. 160.

354 **"We'd been rehearsing like mad":** Paul Rodgers, blind-quoted in Wall, *When Giants Walked the Earth*, pp. 316–17.

355 **"We did eleven tracks":** Boz Burrell, quoted in Steven Rosen, "Bad Company: Four of a Kind," *Circus*, August 1974.

355 **"I think he just decided":** Peter Grant, quoted in Henderson, "If Somebody Had to Be Trod On."

355 **"Unbeknownst to the others":** "Fifteen years ago, I had an operation on my throat and couldn't speak for three weeks." RP, blind-quoted (referring to an interview he gave to the *Scotsman* in 1988) in Lewis, *Led Zeppelin: From a Whisper to a Scream*, p. 65.

355 **"He started the drums":** JP, quoted in Tobler and Grundy, *Guitar Greats*, p. 106.

355 **He'd arrived with Robert:** "He had a bag full of fifteen hundred Mandrax." Benji Le Fevre, interview with the author, May 19, 2019.

355 **"A little later, he said to me":** Benji Le Fevre, quoted in Hoskyns, *Trampled*, p. 248.

356 **"Mandrax?" he posited:** RP, quoted in Earls Court, May 24, 1975.

356 **"I wrote the first verse":** RP, quoted in Stephen Demorest, "The *Circus* Magazine Interview: Robert Plant: 'I've Always Flown the Jolly Roger, but with a Twisted Smile,'" *Circus*, June 1975.

356 **"I had a long piece of music":** JP, blind-quoted (attributed to a 2015 BBC interview with Gavin Esla) in Power, *No Quarter*, p. 355.

356 **"I wondered whether":** JP, quoted in Tolinski, *Light & Shade*, p. 216.

357 **"even more to life":** JP, quoted in Tobler and Grundy, *Guitar Greats*, p. 106.

357 **"I knew what 'Kashmir' was":** "'Kashmir' was really groundbreaking." JP, blind-quoted in Power, *No Quarter*, p. 357.

357 **"the definitive Led Zeppelin song":** RP, blind-quoted (referring to a 1988 interview) in Charles R. Cross and Erik Flannigan, *Led Zeppelin* (New York: Harmony Books, 1991), p. 137.

357 **"This is the best thing":** JP, quoted in Phil Carlo, interview with the author, June 23, 2020.

357 **"'Kashmir'—Come down!":** JB, quoted by Peter Grant in Hoskyns, *Trampled*, p. 248.

358 **"When I got there":** Ron Nevison, quoted in Hoskyns, "Let's Get Physical."

359 **"a lot of camaraderie":** Benji Le Fevre interview.

359 **"Some artists like":** RP, quoted in Hoskyns, "Let's Get Physical."

359 **"You'd just work and break":** Ron Nevison, quoted in Popoff, *Led Zeppelin*, p. 160.

359 **"a pompous ass:"** Author interview with Benji LeFevre.

360 **"'Ten Years Gone' was originally":** "Robert is very much in sympathy with the vibe of my music." JP, quoted in Mick Houghton, "Led Zeppelin: Interview with Jimmy Page," *Sounds,* July 10, 1976.

360 **"I demoed it at home":** JP, blind-quoted in Power, *No Quarter,* p. 349.

361 **"With 'In the Light,' we knew":** JP, quoted in Tobler and Grundy, *Guitar Greats,* p. 106.

361 **"attempting to get a sort":** JPJ, quoted in Dave Lewis, "Anchor Man: The Ultimate John Paul Jones Interview, Part 1," *Tight but Loose,* December 2003.

361 **An initial version began:** "Plant sings an entirely different set of lyrics, opening with . . ." Led Zeppelin rehearsal tape for "In the Light." Lewis, *Led Zeppelin: A Celebration,* p. 21.

361 **"When we first ran through it":** JB, blind-quoted (referring to a 1975 interview) in Lewis, *Led Zeppelin: A Celebration,* p. 21.

362 **"this glorious stomp":** JPJ, blind-quoted in Hoskyns, *Trampled,* p. 250.

362 **"I immediately thought":** "Chuck Berry really was the master of that sort of thing." RP, quoted in Demorest, "The *Circus* magazine Interview."

363 **"I'd never seen another":** RP, quoted in Williamson, "Good Times, Bad Times," p. 53.

363 **"a real thrifty player":** RP, blind-quoted in Hoskyns, "Let's Get Physical."

363 **"ourselves and what we see":** "That's exactly what L.A. stands for." RP, quoted in Charlesworth, "Robert Plant."

363 **"The words show I feel":** RP, quoted in Cameron Crowe, "The Durable Led Zeppelin," *Rolling Stone,* March 13, 1975.

364 **"it was being put together":** JP, quoted in Tolinski, *Light & Shade,* p. 204.

364 **"He just played":** Ron Nevison, quoted in Popoff, *Led Zeppelin,* pp. 158–59.

365 **"It's jammed at the end":** "But I just thought it was so good." JP, quoted in Tolinski, *Light & Shade,* p. 204.

365 **"John Paul wants to see you":** BP Fallon, quoted in Vanessa Gilbert interview with the author, January 31, 2019.

366 **"I thanked him":** Mark London, quoted in Hoskyns, *Trampled,* p. 257. "I said I didn't think it was going to work out." Mark London, quoted in Blake, *Bring It On Home,* p. 156.

366 **"I'd like you to be":** Peter Grant, quoted in Danny Goldberg interview with the author, August 28, 2018.

367 **In addition to Led Zeppelin:** Shelley Kaye, interview with the author, July 15, 2019.

368 **"low-life drug dealers":** Unity MacLean interview.

368 **"Most of what I was doing":** Carole Brown Woods interview.

368 **"Mick Ralphs had written":** Phil Carlo interview.

369 **"We did a number":** Maggie Bell, interview with the author, May 8, 2019.

369 **"It was lousy":** Janine Safer Whitney, email to the author, August 30, 2020.

## Chapter Fifteen: Flying Too Close to the Sun

371 **"the band was mad":** JP, quoted in Tolinski, *Light & Shade,* p. 210.

371 **A few invitees at the screening:** Peter Doggett, "Dazed and Confused," *Q Special Edition: Led Zeppelin,* March 2003, p. 86.

371 **"They finally came":** Joe Massot, blind-quoted in Hoskyns, *Trampled,* p. 238.

372 **"We found a lot of the things":** JB, quoted in Doggett, "Dazed & Confused," p. 86.

372 **"that he didn't get all":** JP, quoted in Tolinski, *Light & Shade,* p. 210.

372 **"None of the material":** Peter Clifton, quoted in Wall, *When Giants Walked the Earth,* p. 312.

372 **"nothing that holds together":** Peter Clifton, quoted in Hoskyns, *Trampled,* p. 239.

372 **"Jimmy loves your editing"**: Peter Grant, quoted in Hoskyns, *Trampled*, p. 239.

373 **"If you think about it"**: JP, quoted in "Jimmy Page Interview," *Mojo*, October 2015.

373 **"The name Led Zeppelin means"**: RP, quoted in Lorraine Alterman, "Led Zeppelin: Swan Song Is a Beginning," *Rolling Stone*, June 20, 1974.

373 **"I immediately came up"**: Aubrey Powell, interview with the author, May 15, 2019.

374 **"I didn't want to end up"**: RP, quoted in Steve Turner, "New Pretty Things Get a Led Zep Uplift," *Rolling Stone*, April 10, 1975.

374 **"going to be an ego thing"**: JP, blind-quoted in Wall, *When Giants Walked the Earth*, p. 313.

374 **"We didn't really want"**: JP, quoted in Dave Schulps, *Trouser Press* interview, Part 3, p. 20.

374 **"knew they had a smash"**: Phil Carson, interview with the author, July 2, 2019.

375 **"I told him how great"**: RP, quoted in Turner, "New Pretty Things."

375 **He had played on**: Bob Brunning, *Blues* (London: Helter Skelter, 2002), p. 65.

375 **"fucking weird"**: Ed Bicknell, interview with the author, May 11, 2019.

375 **"Peter could never make"**: Richard Cole, quoted in Hoskyns, *Trampled*, p. 264.

376 **"packed an overnight bag"**: Phil Carson interview.

376 **"a lovely old house"**: Aubrey Powell interview.

376 **"very laid-back atmosphere"**: Phil Carlo, interview with the author, May 12, 2019.

376 **"When you saw"**: Helen Grant, quoted in Blake, *Bring It On Home*, p. 130.

376 **"over-produced within an inch"**: Janine Safer Whitney, email to the author, August 30, 2020.

377 **"giving the whole thing"**: Michael Gray, "Maggie Bell: *Queen of the Night*," *Let It Rock*, April 1974.

377 **"The album lacks balls"**: Peter Grant, quoted in Michael Watts, "Peter Grant: The Man Who Led Zeppelin," *MM*, June 22, 1974.

377 **a body of water**: "Bonzo walked through the fountain in the restaurant." Danny Marcus, interview with the author, January 16, 2019.

377 **"We all live on fucking farms!"**: Peter Grant, quoted in Davis, *Hammer of the Gods*, p. 218.

378 **"We snorted the drug right off"**: Cole, *Stairway to Heaven*, p. 266.

378 **"It was heavy-duty shit"**: Lori Mattix, interview with the author, January 21, 2019.

379 **"a boys-only section"**: Maggie Bell, interview with the author, May 8, 2019.

379 **"Jane Fonda. Warren Beatty"**: Ahmet Ertegun, quoted in Goldberg, *Bumping into Geniuses*, p. 83.

379 **"I was told I could"**: Maggie Bell interview.

380 **"Maggie is one of the great"**: Peter Grant, quoted in Abe Hoch interview with the author, April 3, 2019.

380 **"I've taken enough shit"**: JB, quoted in Goldberg, *Bumping into Geniuses*, p. 83.

380 **"I was devastated"**: Lori Mattix interview.

381 **"I can tell you"**: JP, blind-quoted in Salewicz, *Jimmy Page*, p. 300.

382 **"smashing his palms together"**: Amanda Petrusich, "Where Punk Begins," *New Yorker*, September 15, 2016.

382 **"Punk bands started"**: Lester Bangs, "Psychotic Reactions and Carburetor Dung," *Creem*, June 1971.

383 **"We had more material"**: JP, quoted in Schulps, *Trouser Press* interview, Part 3, p. 20.

383 **"We thought, 'Why not'"**: RP, quoted in Chris Charlesworth, "Robert Plant: Recording's No Race for Us," *MM*, February 8, 1975.

384 **"I had a lot of respect"**: JP, quoted in Nick Kent, "Jimmy Page: The Roaring Silence," *NME*, November 20, 1976.

384 **"Jimmy asked me"**: Peter Clifton, quoted in Hoskyns, *Trampled*, p. 308.

385 **"Supreme and Holy King"**: Francis King, *The Magical World of Aleister Crowley* (New York: Coward, McCann, 1978), pp. 78–81.

385 **"I could see that Anger"**: JP, quoted in Tolinski, *Light & Shade*, p. 184.

385 **"an uncompromising album"**: Bud Scoppa, "Bad Company," *Rolling Stone*, August 29, 1974.

386 **"In the end"**: Phil May, quoted in Blake, *Bring It On Home*, p. 143.

386 **"Peter and I were going"**: Harvey Lisberg, interview with the author, November 21, 2018.

386 **"Fellas, I would love"**: Peter Grant, quoted in Paul Henderson, "If Somebody Had to Be Trod On, They Got Trod On," *Classic Rock*, April 5, 2017.

386 **"I never wanted"**: Peter Grant, quoted in Henderson, "If Somebody Had to Be Trod On."

386 **"club-soda-and-lime guy"**: Goldberg, *Bumping into Geniuses*, p. 18.

386 **"Do you want to come"**: Abe Hoch interview.

387 **"It was fairly remarkable"**: Benji Le Fevre, interview with the author, May 19, 2019.

387 **"We decided to do it"**: Phil Carson interview.

388 **"Do what thou wilt"**: Blake, *Bring It On Home*, p. 143.

388 **"being at a medieval orgy"**: BBC's Bob Harris, quoted in Hoskyns, *Trampled*, pp. 260–61.

388 **"lacks the inspired vision"**: Jonh Ingham, "*Silk Torpedo*" (review), *NME*, November 23, 1974.

389 **A review in *Phonograph Record***: "It would seem only reasonable to expect the Prettys to emerge with a more confidently adventurous album next time around." Alan Betrock, "*Silk Torpedo*" (review), *Phonograph Record*, January 1975.

389 **"a marvelous rock 'n roll band"**: Bud Scoppa, "*Silk Torpedo*" (review), *Rolling Stone*, May 8, 1975.

389 **"When I came to Swan Song"**: Unity MacLean, interview with the author, October 16, 2019.

389 **"I knew a guy"**: Abe Hoch interview.

390 **"I'd give her a paper"**: Phil Carlo interview.

390 **Legend has it**: "When they were dealing drugs, Richard put in claims for a *farm tractor* to get cash." Carole Brown Woods, interview with the author, November 8, 2019.

390 **"I once turned in"**: Benji Le Fevre interview.

390 **"Joan always wired"**: Unity MacLean interview.

391 **"As a favor to Peter"**: Bill Curbishley, interview with the author, May 16, 2018.

391 **G and his henchmen**: "Peter for sure backed right down." Phil Carson, email to the author, July 29, 2020.

393 **"The time comes"**: RP, quoted in Charlesworth, "Robert Plant."

393 **So were "When the Levee Breaks"**: Nick Kent, "The Graffiti of the Physical . . . and the Exploration of the Metaphysical," *NME*, December 7, 1974.

393 **"Celebration Day," "Misty Mountain Hop"**: Lewis and Tremaglio, *Evenings with Led Zeppelin*, p. 418.

393 **"a big bowie knife"**: "He said, 'Well, let's have a blow first.'" Jack Calmes, quoted in Hoskyns, *Trampled*, p. 274.

394 **"How much fucking money"**: JB, quoted in Hoskyns, *Trampled*, p. 274.

## Chapter Sixteen: Home Away from Home

395 **"I was just totally numb"**: JP, quoted in Lisa Robinson, "Jimmy Page," *NME*, February 1, 1975.

395 **"It's the most important"**: JP, quoted in Chris Charlesworth, "Whole Lotta Zeppelin," MM, February 1, 1975.

395 **"expected to be the largest"**: Cameron Crowe, "The Durable Led Zeppelin," *Rolling Stone*, March 13, 1975.

396 **"In Boston, fans lined up"**: Wayne Robins, "Led Zep Zaps Kidz," *Village Voice*, February 3, 1975.

396 **"open-fronted girl's blouse"**: Chris Charlesworth, "Night Flight," *Q Special Edition: Led Zeppelin*, March 2003, p. 92.

396 **"I'm catching flu"**: RP, quoted in Charlesworth, "Whole Lotta Zeppelin."

396 **"[Plant's flu] had given "**: Lynn Van Matre, "Red Hot Led!" *Chicago Tribune*, January 21, 1975.

396 **"Codeine tablets and Jack Daniel's"**: Crowe, "Durable Led Zeppelin."

397 **"swigging from a quart bottle"**: "Bonzo's main problem is that he is homesick." Charlesworth, "Night Flight," p. 91.

397 **"a cherry adorned wrap-around"**: Lewis and Tremaglio, *Evenings with Led Zeppelin*, p. 419.

397 **"a sort of Sino-Afro"**: Robins, "Led Zep Zaps Kidz."

397 **"I was never very good"**: JPJ, quoted in Alan de Perna, "Steady Rollin' Man," *Guitar World*, January 1991.

397 **"I asked her to personalize"**: JP, quoted in Tolinski, *Light & Shade*, p. 175.

398 **"a pretty dapper guy"**: John Spicer, interview with the author, May 10, 2019.

398 **"The Confederate hat"**: Chris Dreja, quoted in Power, *No Quarter*, p. 264.

398 **"After Coco made the dragon"**: JP, quoted in Tolinski, *Light & Shade*, p. 175.

398 **Jimmy could tell:** "I can tell it's not as good as it usually is." JP, quoted in Charlesworth, "Whole Lotta Zeppelin."

398 **"This is so damn futile"**: JP, quoted in Cameron Crowe, "Led Zep Conquers the States," *Rolling Stone*, May 22, 1975.

398 **"There was a minute there"**: RP, quoted in Danny Goldberg, "Led Zeppelin—Under the Hood: A Chronicle of the Historic 1975 Tour," *Circus*, May 1975.

398 **"still reach heaven"**: Don Heyland, "Limp Zep Still Reach Heaven," *Sounds*, February 1, 1975.

399 **"The second night"**: Danny Goldberg, quoted in Heyland, "Limp Zep Still Reach Heaven."

399 **"soggy and spiritless"**: Bob Von Sternberg, "Zeppelin: Slow to Start, but Hot," *Akron Beacon Journal*, January 25, 1975.

399 **"Peter pulled out a mirror"**: Joe Wright, interview with the author, November 28, 2018.

400 **He'd downed an entire:** "I shared a limo with him and watched him down the entire bottle." Chris Charlesworth, interview with the author, May 13, 2019.

400 **"Bonzo drank for *reasons*"**: JPJ, quoted in Hoskyns, *Trampled*, p. 284.

400 **"Taking cocaine just enabled"**: Nick Kent, quoted in Hoskyns, *Trampled*, p. 283.

401 **"The chance for violence"**: Danny Goldberg, interview with the author, August 23, 2018.

401 **"he grabbed one"**: Chris Charlesworth interview.

401 **"I chat with them"**: Charlesworth, "Night Flight," p. 92.

402 **Even G's "concubine"**: "Raven he referred to as his 'personal concubine.'" Joe Wright interview.

402 **"*You can't fucking play guitar!*"**: Quoted in Davis, *Hammer of the Gods*, p. 235.

402 **"Some of the guys"**: Abe Hoch, interview with the author, April 3, 2019.

403 **"It was a rotten show"**: Chris Charlesworth interview.

403 **"Their 17,500 fans"**: Jerry Kenion, "Led Zeppelin Performs Its Magic to Full House," *Greensboro Daily News*, January 30, 1975.

403 **"throwing broken bottles"**: Charlesworth, "Night Flight," p. 93.

403 **"You can't take"**: Peter Grant, quoted in Chris Charlesworth interview.

404 **"Don't be fucking stupid"**: Peter Grant, quoted in Charlesworth, "Night Flight," p. 93.

404 **"I'd never seen driving"**: Neal Preston, quoted in Blake, *Bring It On Home*, p. 49.

405 **"They were placing bets"**: Chris Charlesworth interview.

405 **"The landing of the Led Zeppelin"**: Christine Brown, "Crowd, Zeppelin Do a Show Together," *Detroit Free Press*, February 2, 1975.

406 **"fairly credible performance"**: Lewis and Tremaglio, *Evenings with Led Zeppelin*, p. 433.

406 **"made nearly $50,000"**: "The boys in the band were tired and bored and apparently couldn't give a fuck about either their fans or their music." Chris McCabe, "Led Zeppelin at Olympia," *Ann Arbor Sun*, February 14, 1975.

406 **"Let me loan you a blackjack"**: Quoted in Cole, *Stairway to Heaven*, p. 293.

406 **"I saw this incident"**: JP, quoted in William S. Burroughs, "Rock Magic: Jimmy Page, Led Zeppelin, and a Search for the Elusive Stairway to Heaven," *Crawdaddy*, June 1975.

406 **"You have to be careful"**: William S. Burroughs, quoted in Burroughs, "Rock Magic."

406 **"dozens of fans began"**: Cole, *Stairway to Heaven*, p. 293.

406 **"The undercurrent of unpleasantness"**: Chris Charlesworth, quoted in Hoskyns, *Trampled*, pp. 282–83.

406 **"There's no violent energy"**: RP, quoted in Robins, "Led Zep Zaps Kidz."

406 **"sloppy, careless, and unimaginative"**: Steven Rosen, "Led Zeppelin" (review), *Sounds*, April 19, 1975.

407 **"Page's solos seemed to sound alike"**: Larry Rohter, "Heavy Zeppelin," *Washington Post*, February 11, 1975.

407 **"In the end there is"**: John Rockwell, "Led Zeppelin Excites Crowd at Garden but Somehow Delirium Wasn't There," *New York Times*, February 4, 1975.

407 **"stock riffs"**: Dave Marsh, "Led Zep Shows Why They Are One of the Great Ones," *Newsday*, February 4, 1975.

407 **"seemed disgruntled"**: Dave Marsh, "Whatever the Reason, Led Zeppelin Is Well-Liked," *Newsday*, February 5, 1975.

407 **"Despite our depleted"**: RP, quoted in Davis, *LZ-'75*, p. 75.

408 **"not hitting on all cylinders"**: Bill Mann, "Concert by Zeppelin Has Ups and Downs," *Montreal Gazette*, February 7, 1975.

408 **"lifeless . . . lackluster . . . unimpressive"**: John Fisher, "Led Zeppelin Doesn't Get Off," *Bucks County Courier Times*, February 10, 1975.

408 **"half a voice"**: "Will someone please tell me why Robert Plant is touring with only half a voice?" Mann, "Concert by Zeppelin Has Ups and Downs."

408 **"For the St. Louis show"**: Phil Carson, interview with the author, July 2, 2019.

408 **"They had no connection"**: Abe Hoch interview. "They had nothing to do with each other. They weren't friends." Janine Safer Whitney, interview with the author, April 2, 2019.

409 **"He dominated Robert"**: Danny Goldberg, interview with the author, August 28, 2018. "Earlier, Jimmy really dominated the relationship completely." Danny Goldberg, quoted in Hoskyns, *Trampled*, p. 288.

409 **"Led Zeppelin was Jimmy's band"**: Janine Safer Whitney interview.

409 **"A loner"**: JP, quoted in Crowe, "Durable Led Zeppelin."

409 **Heroin had reared its head:** "The 1975 trip through America was the first Zeppelin tour in which heroin circulated freely among our entourage." Cole, *Stairway to Heaven*, p. 297.

409 **"Robert and I stood":** Phil Carson interview.

410 **"Robert was the Leo extrovert":** Benji Le Fevre, interview with the author, May 19, 2019.

410 **"hallucinatory boiled jellyfruit":** Davis, *Hammer of the Gods*, p. 240.

410 **"quite a lot in common":** Burroughs, "Rock Magic."

410 **"He then encouraged me":** JP, quoted in Tolinski, *Light & Shade*, p. 205.

410 **"I think it's time":** JP, quoted in Crowe, "Durable Led Zeppelin."

411 **"I never saw an album":** Danny Marcus, quoted in Hoskyns, *Trampled*, p. 252.

411 **"absolutely the toughest":** Nick Kent, "Led Zeppelin: *Physical Graffiti*" (review), *NME*, December 7, 1974.

411 **"better than the other five":** Jaan Uhelszki, "Led Zeppelin: *Physical Graffiti*" (review), *Creem*, May 1975.

411 **"Taken as a whole":** Jim Miller, "Led Zeppelin: *Physical Graffiti*" (review), *Rolling Stone*, March 27, 1975.

412 **"he really smoothed out":** Tony Mandich, quoted in Hoskyns, *Trampled*, p. 292.

412 **headline in the *Houston Chronicle*:** Dale Adamson, "Who Would Have Thought? Zeppelin Show Was Boring," *Houston Chronicle*, February 28, 1975.

412 **"uninspiring":** "The group displayed an uninspiring range of diversity—everything from A to B." Phil LaRose, "Zeppelin Decibel Rate Deafening," *Sunday Advocate* (Baton Rouge), March 2, 1975. "The music was for the most part uninspiring." Jere Longman II, "Led Zeppelin Leads in Volume, Not Quality," *Daily Reveille* (Louisiana State University), March 4, 1975.

413 **"reaching in and rubbing handfuls":** Wall, *When Giants Walked the Earth*, p. 334; Benji Le Fevre interview.

413 **"How he played":** Danny Marcus, interview with the author, January 16, 2019.

413 **By Richard Cole's count:** Cole, *Stairway to Heaven*, p. 310.

413 **"spied on radicals":** Davis, *Hammer of the Gods*, p. 240.

413 **Often, ex-cops who worked:** "These ex-cops would take dope off the kids, give them a warning, then hand the stuff over to us." Phil Carlo, interview with the author, May 12, 2019.

414 **"girls we had rounded up":** Cole, *Stairway to Heaven*, p. 300.

414 **"I had once been":** Dave Northover, quoted in Hoskyns, *Trampled*, p. 274.

415 **"The amount of drugs":** Benji Le Fevre interview.

415 **"It's like a trance state":** JP, quoted from Capitol Radio interview with Alan Freeman in Hank Bordowitz, *Led Zeppelin on Led Zeppelin* (Chicago: Chicago Review Press, 2014), p. 202.

416 **"Nothing was preplanned":** JPJ, quoted in Dave Lewis, "Anchor Man: The Ultimate John Paul Jones Interview," *Tight but Loose*, no. 13, December 2003.

416 **"What those eager fans got":** Robert P. Laurence, "Led Zeppelin Is Really a Blast," *San Diego Union*, March 11, 1975.

416 **"The group ran through":** "The total effect of the band's performance had about as much punch as a soggy noodle." Rosen, "Led Zeppelin" (review).

417 **"cause to question":** Tim Devine, "Led Zeppelin's Future Uncertain After Long Beach Concert, New LP," *Daily Sundial* (California State University, Northridge), March 21, 1975.

417 **"a numbing combination":** "The lyrics are often woeful, the themes unaffecting." Robert Hilburn, "Led Zeppelin, Clichés and All," *Los Angeles Times*, March 13, 1975.

417 **"almost unrecognizable"**: Daniel Lower, "Led Zeppelin Losing Magic of Old," *Daily Aztec* (San Diego State University), March 18, 1975.

417 **"It was always a toss-up"**: Benji Le Fevre interview.

417 **During one interlude**: Confidential source, interview with the author.

417 **"Jimmy was in the weeds"**: "He realized Jimmy no longer knew where he was." RP, quoted in Bill Curbishley, interview with the author, May 16, 2018.

417 **"spectacular"**: "For three solid hours the band churned out their heavy metal rock 'n roll . . . and also provided the most spectacular show any rock group has ever done." Patrick MacDonald, "Led Zeppelin Worth the Wait," *Seattle Times*, March 18, 1975.

417 **"stunning"**: Jeani Read, "Zeppelin Gives 3 Stunning Hours," *Globe and Mail* (Vancouver), March 21, 1975.

418 **"Something strange happened"**: RP, at the Pacific Coliseum, Vancouver, March 20.

418 **"awesome enough, in delivery"**: Read, "Zeppelin Gives 3 Stunning Hours."

418 **"There is just no other"**: John Wendeborn, "Zeppelin Spews Musical Energy," *Oregonian*, March 24, 1975.

418 **According to Richard Cole**: "One night, Jimmy and I brought a couple of underage girls back to our rooms." Cole, *Stairway to Heaven*, p. 300.

418 **"Bonzo was on everything"**: Danny Marcus interview.

418 **"doing about 90mph"**: JPJ, quoted in Bonham, *John Bonham*, p. 131.

419 **"After a certain point, the Beast"**: Quoted in Crowe, "Led Zep Conquers the States."

419 **"missing a limo"**: "They'd tipped the piano over the edge of the balcony." Dave Northover, quoted in Hoskyns, *Trampled*, p. 286.

419 **He choked Steve Marriott**: Pamela Des Barres, *Rock Bottom* (New York: St. Martin's, 1996), p. 70.

419 **"take an eight ball"**: Glenn Hughes, quoted in Hoskyns, *Trampled*, p. 286.

419 **he terrorized NME journalist**: Davis, *Hammer of the Gods*, p. 244.

420 **"Our accountant, Joan Hudson"**: Peter Grant, quoted in Dave Lewis, "The Peter Grant Interview," in Lewis, *Celebration II*, p. 96.

420 **The Stones had taken**: Ed Jones, "Bands on the Run from the Taxman," MM, October 11, 1975.

## Chapter Seventeen: The Year of Living Dangerously

422 **"Don't ever look"**: JB, quoted in Wall, *When Giants Walked the Earth*, p. 349.

422 **A few days later**: Davis, *LZ-'75*, p. 196.

422 **"Bonzo was a huge adult"**: Danny Goldberg, quoted in Davis, *Hammer of the Gods*, p. 259.

423 **In early 1975**: "Led Zeppelin at that point thought they were the kings. They had guns with them and everything else." Aynsley Dunbar, quoted in Wall, *When Giants Walked the Earth*, pp. 335–36.

423 **"I've never seen anyone"**: Nick Kent, quoted in Hoskyns, *Trampled*, p. 285.

423 **During cocktails, Bonzo asked**: "I got him the coffee and he emptied the whole thing on my new suit." Bob Emmer, interview with the author, January 24, 2019.

423 **"You're an ugly fucker"**: Andy McConnell, quoted in Cameron Crowe, "Led Zep Conquers the States, 'Beast' Prowls to the Din of Hordes," Rolling *Stone*, May 22, 1975.

424 **"We want to find somewhere"**: RP, blind-quoted in Power, *No Quarter*, p. 369.

425 **"If you want a record deal"**: RP, quoted in Unity MacLean interview with the author, October 16, 2019.

425 **"I seduced Dave Edmunds"**: RP, quoted in Nigel Williamson, "Good Times, Bad Times," *Uncut*, May 2005, p. 57.

425 **"Brilleaux didn't like"**: "Jimmy loved Wilko's lead-and-rhythm playing." Jake Riviera, quoted in Hoskyns, *Trampled*, p. 292.

425 **"It cost a lot of bread"**: JB, quoted in Chris Welch, "John Bonham: Over the Hills and Far Away," MM, June 21, 1975.

425 **"come out of it"**: JP, blind-quoted from an article in NME in Power, *No Quarter*, p. 373.

425 **"So Customs and Excise were"**: Benji Le Fevre, interview with the author, May 19, 2019.

426 **"The BBC had a little"**: David Williams, interview with the author, May 16, 2019.

426 **"We'd all like to welcome"**: Whispering Bob Harris, quoted in Lewis and Tremaglio, *Evenings with Led Zeppelin*, p. 475.

426 **"a jolly raconteur"**: Jan Iles, "Led Zeppelin: Earls Court" (review), *Record Mirror*, May 31, 1975.

427 **"We want to take you"**: RP in bootleg recording from Earls Court, May 17, 1975.

427 **"the definitive rock performance"**: Michael Oldfield, "The Ultimate Trip," MM, May 24, 1975.

427 **"a nocturnal delight"**: Iles, "Led Zeppelin: Earls Court."

427 **"arrived at Earls Court"**: Chris Charlesworth, *Led Zeppelin: Five Glorious Nights* (review), *Just Backdated* (blog), July 24, 2015.

428 **"Despite Charles Shaar Murray"**: RP in bootleg recording from Earls Court, May 23, 1975.

428 **"The audience didn't know what"**: Chris Charlesworth, interview with the author, May 13, 2019.

428 **"for our families and friends"**: RP in bootleg recording from Earls Court, May 24, 1975.

428 **"Thank you for very good"**: RP in bootleg recording from Earls Court, May 23, 1975.

429 **"He used to ring"**: "John Paul Jones *hated* being a tax exile." Carole Brown Woods, interview with the author, November 8, 2019.

429 **"He couldn't stomach"**: Sally Williams, interview with the author, July 9, 2019.

429 **"She was desperate"**: Unity MacLean interview.

430 **He was beating himself up**: "I thought to myself: 'I'm truly a schmuck.'" Abe Hoch, interview with the author, April 3, 2019.

430 **"gave us a little peep"**: RP, quoted in Chris Charlesworth, "Robert Plant: Plantations," *Creem*, May 1976.

431 **"For two months"**: RP, quoted in Charlesworth, "Robert Plant: Plantations."

431 **The merchandising alone**: "G always made sure we got a packet from the merchandising profits. It was an all-cash business and went unreported." Confidential source, interview with the author.

431 **"playing possibly in South America"**: RP, quoted in Charlesworth, "Robert Plant: Plantations."

431 **"After a while"**: RP, quoted in Charlesworth, "Robert Plant: Plantations."

432 **"I looked over at Maureen"**: RP, quoted in Cole, *Stairway to Heaven*, p. 316.

433 **"near death"**: Benji Le Fevre interview.

433 **"I was lying there"**: RP, quoted in Charlesworth, "Robert Plant: Plantations."

433 **"Apparently, under Greek law"**: Jeff Hoffman, interview with the author, July 30, 2019.

434 **"I hired a private ambulance"**: Cole, *Stairway to Heaven*, pp. 315–16.

434 **"The doctor in London"**: RP, quoted in Charlesworth, "Robert Plant: Plantations."

435 **"I've always felt"**: JP, quoted in Chris Salewicz, "The Gig Interview: Jimmy Page," *Gig*, May 1977.

435 **"I know that my kind":** RP, quoted in Smith, *Off the Record*, p. 339.

435 **"He looked white":** Benji Le Fevre interview.

436 **"I bought the seats":** Peter Grant, quoted in Lewis, *Led Zeppelin: From a Whisper to a Scream*, p. 75.

436 **shelling out a cool £7,000:** Ed Jones, "Bands on the Run from the Taxman," MM, October 11, 1975.

437 **"They each had their own":** Abe Hoch interview.

437 **"We drove into Hollywood":** Benji LeFevre interview.

438 **"He was so far gone":** Michael Des Barres, interview with the author, February 20, 2019. "Jimmy was really out of it." Benji Le Fevre, interview with the author, April 3, 2019.

438 **"Peter pulled me aside":** Abe Hoch interview.

438 **"I've seen more movement":** Abe Hoch, quoted in Hoskyns, *Trampled*, p. 318.

438 **When Jimmy was lucid:** "We had a mutual interest in Crowley and drugs." Michael Des Barres interview.

439 **"Our fan base":** Michael Des Barres, quoted in Salewicz, *Jimmy Page*, p. 313.

439 **"We pulled up":** Michael Des Barres interview.

440 **"She used to call":** Unity MacLean interview.

440 **"It was a bagful":** Elizabeth Iannaci, interview with the author, January 17, 2019.

441 **"When something like drugs":** Sam Aizer, quoted in Hoskyns, *Trampled* p. 329

441 **"drive into him":** Peter Grant, quoted in Benji Le Fevre interview, May 19, 2019.

441 **"He was carried":** Michael Des Barres interview.

441 **"Michael and I tried":** Danny Goldberg, quoted in Hoskyns, *Trampled*, p. 330; Danny Goldberg, interview with the author, August 28, 2018.

442 **"We'd all go":** Elizabeth Iannaci interview. "There were nights the band went out together to the Whisky." Benji Le Fevre interview, May 19, 2019.

442 **As the band arrived:** "We walked in as a group, and there she was." Elizabeth Iannaci interview.

442 **"I brought David Cassidy":** Abe Hoch interview.

443 **"Just wait here":** Benji Le Fevre interview, May 19, 2019.

443 **"It turned out to be":** Phil Carlo, interview with the author, May 12, 2019.

443 **"There was a lot of tension":** Peter Grant, quoted in Dave Lewis, "The Peter Grant Interview," in Lewis, *Led Zeppelin: Celebration II*, p. 96.

444 **"a sarcastic dig":** RP, blind-quoted in Cross, *Led Zeppelin: Heaven and Hell*, p. 142.

444 **Borrowing from the masters:** Mat Snow, "Robert Plant's Record Collection," Q, May 1990.

444 **"We just couldn't find him":** JPJ, quoted in "The John Paul Jones Interview," in Lewis, *Led Zeppelin: Celebration II*, p. 115.

445 **Robert kicked things off:** Lewis, *Led Zeppelin: From a Whisper to a Scream*, p. 75.

445 **"You could see Robert":** Elizabeth Iannaci interview.

445 **"I was sitting":** RP, quoted in Charlesworth, "Robert Plant: Plantations."

445 **"There just wasn't a lot":** JPJ, quoted in Dave Lewis, "The John Paul Jones Interview," in Lewis, *Led Zeppelin: Celebration II*, p. 116.

## Chapter Eighteen: The Other Side of the Spectrum

446 **"We went in with nothing":** JP, quoted in Mick Houghton, "Zeus of Zeppelin: An Interview with Jimmy Page," *Circus*, October 12, 1976.

446 **"We all agreed":** JP, quoted in "Led Zeppelin Fab Pix Hot Poop" (cover story), *NME*, February 27, 1977.

446 **"When we eventually"**: JPJ, quoted in Dave Lewis, "The John Paul Jones Interview," in Lewis, *Led Zeppelin: Celebration II*, p. 120.

446 **"If ever there was"**: RP, quoted in "Led Zeppelin's Fab Pix."

447 **"We didn't see him"**: Abe Hoch, interview with the author, April 3, 2019.

447 **"sitting in a fucking chair"**: RP, quoted in Jaan Uhelszki, "Led Zeppelin: Sodom and Gomorrah in a Suitcase," *Creem*, July 1977.

447 **"What rhymes with 'Achilles'?"**: Abe Hoch interview.

447 **"Robert was behind"**: Peter Grant in interview with Malcolm McLaren.

447 **"Bonzo, Jimmy, and I"**: Cole, *Stairway to Heaven*, p. 322.

448 **"There were enormous"**: Benji Le Fevre, interview with the author, May 19, 2019.

448 **"The band was splitting"**: JPJ, blind-quoted in Hoskyns, *Trampled*, p. 323.

448 **"My main memory"**: JPJ, quoted in Lewis, "The John Paul Jones Interview," p. 120.

448 **"He hadn't even showered"**: Abe Hoch interview.

448 **"loud as fuck-all"**: Abe Hoch interview.

449 **"I don't regret it"**: JP, quoted in Nick Kent, "Bring It On Home," *Q Special Edition: Led Zeppelin*, March 2003, p. 139.

449 **"I mean, that was eighteen"**: JP, quoted in Nick Kent, "Jimmy Page: The Roaring Silence," *NME*, November 20, 1976.

449 **"pure anxiety and emotion"**: JP, quoted in Wesley Strick, "The Tour in Progress: Jimmy Page Files His Report," *Circus*, June 9, 1977.

449 **"it was straight off"**: JP, quoted in Kent, "Jimmy Page: The Roaring Silence."

449 **"about travels and dreams"**: RP, blind-quoted in Cross and Flannigan, *Led Zeppelin: Heaven and Hell*, p. 142.

449 **"I just dove in"**: JP, quoted in Cameron Crowe, "Jimmy Page Beats the Devil," *Rolling Stone*, August 12, 1976.

449 **"give the piece"**: JP, quoted in Dave Schulps, *Trouser Press* interview, Part 3, p. 21.

449 **"I knew that every guitar"**: JP, blind-quoted in Cross and Flannigan, *Led Zeppelin: Heaven and Hell*, p. 142.

449 **"It's got quite a pace"**: JP, quoted in Kent, "Jimmy Page: The Roaring Silence."

450 **"prog rock gone mad"**: RP, blind-quoted in Hoskyns, *Trampled*, p. 324.

450 **"I put all my weight"**: RP, blind-quoted in Cross and Flannigan, *Led Zeppelin: Heaven and Hell*, p. 142.

450 **"I've never known"**: RP, quoted in Chris Charlesworth, "Robert Plant: Plantations," *Creem*, May 1976.

450 **"And where it got"**: RP, blind-quoted in Cross and Flannigan, *Led Zeppelin: Heaven and Hell*, p. 142.

450 **"us looking back"**: JP, quoted in Wall, *When Giants Walked the Earth*, p. 346.

450 **"It was basically a twelve-bar"**: JP, quoted in Tobler and Grundy, *Guitar Greats*, p. 106.

451 **"It's so held back"**: JP, quoted in Jonh Ingham, "Jimmy Page: Technological Gypsy," *Sounds*, March 13, 1976.

451 **"no acoustic songs"**: JP, quoted in Tolinski, *Light & Shade*, p. 205. "All our urgency and pent-up passion is there more than ever. That's why there's no acoustic stuff on the album." JP, quoted in Crowe, "Jimmy Page Beats the Devil."

451 **"a lot of movement"**: JP, quoted in Ingham, "Jimmy Page: Technological Gypsy."

451 **"people who come and go"**: RP, blind-quoted in Cross and Flannigan, *Led Zeppelin: Heaven and Hell*, p. 142.

451 **"It was a mish-mash"**: JPJ, quoted in Mat Snow, "John Paul Jones: The Quiet One," *Mojo*, December 2007.

452 **"We were under"**: JP, quoted in Tolinski, *Light & Shade*, p. 205.

453 **"Can I have two days"**: JP, quoted in David Fricke, "Jimmy Page: The Rolling Stone Interview," December 6, 2012.

453 **"That was the ultimate"**: JP, quoted in Lewis, *Led Zeppelin: From a Whisper to a Scream*, p. 76.

453 **"I didn't think I'd be"**: "I did all the guitar overdubs on that LP in one night." JP, quoted in Steven Rosen, "Jimmy Page," *Guitar Player*, July 1977.

453 **"I had a copy"**: JP, quoted in Fricke, "Jimmy Page: The *Rolling Stone* Interview."

454 **"Peter had called and said"**: Abe Hoch interview.

456 **"I can't even walk"**: RP, quoted in Lisa Robinson, "Surprise Live Act by Zep in Jersey," *Hit Parader*, July 1976.

457 **"It was one small step"**: RP, quoted in Lewis and Tremaglio, *Evenings with Led Zeppelin*, p. 483.

457 **"Do me a favor"**: Peter Grant, quoted in Abe Hoch interview.

458 **"Rudolf Nureyev was in"**: Maggie Bell, interview with the author, May 8, 2019.

458 **"quite agitated"**: Dave Northover, quoted in Hoskyns, *Trampled*, p. 327.

459 **"Honestly, I was trying"**: JP, quoted in Benji Le Fevre interview.

459 **"Hi, I'm John Bonham"**: JB, quoted in Wall, *When Giants Walked the Earth*, p. 352; also, in a truncated form, in Lewis, *Led Zeppelin: From a Whisper to a Scream*, p. 77.

459 **"It was clear that he"**: Benji Le Fevre interview.

459 **"Buffin wanted no part"**: Aubrey Powell, interview with the author, May 15, 2019.

460 **"a very powerful band"**: Storm Thorgerson, quoted in Lewis, *Led Zeppelin: From a Whisper to a Scream*, p. 77.

461 **"I held out for *Presence*"**: JP, quoted in Crowe, "Jimmy Page Beats the Devil."

461 **"I'm glad people"**: RP, quoted in Lewis, *Led Zeppelin: From a Whisper to a Scream*, p. 77.

461 **"Nobody would get it"**: Abe Hoch interview.

461 **"I picked up the phone"**: Aubrey Powell interview.

462 **"confirms the quartet's status"**: Stephen Davis, "*Presence*" (review), *Rolling Stone*, May 20, 1976.

462 **"their better albums"**: Robert Christgau, "Christgau's Consumer Guide," *Village Voice*, July 12, 1976.

462 **"This album is unadulterated"**: "This album is very reminiscent of the first album." Jonh Ingham, "Led Zeppelin: *Presence*" (review), *Sounds*, April 10, 1976.

463 **"solid, non-stop, copper-bottomed"**: Charles Shaar Murray, "Led Zeppelin: *Presence*" (review), *NME*, April 10, 1976.

463 **And Chris Welch carried**: Chris Welch, "Led Zeppelin: *Presence*" (review), MM, April 10, 2976.

463 **"It's not an easy album"**: JP, quoted in Nigel Williamson, "Forget the Myths," *Uncut*, May 2005, p. 72.

463 **"Glo called the office"**: Unity MacLean, interview with the author, October 16, 2019.

464 **"Gloria and the kids"**: Maggie Bell interview.

464 **"She used to do all "**: Chris Most, interview with the author, May 14, 2019.

465 **"It was absolute drug paranoia"**: Peter Clifton, quoted in Hoskyns, *Trampled*, p. 301.

465 **"I felt humiliated"**: Peter Clifton, quoted in Welch, *Peter Grant*, p. 134.

465 **"Who was that guy"**: Ahmet Ertegun, quoted in Welch, *Peter Grant*, p. 132.

465 **"How could you say that?"**: Peter Grant, quoted in Welch, *Peter Grant*, p. 133.

466 **"completely off his face"**: Peter Clifton, quoted in Welch, *Peter Grant*, p. 135.

466 **Gloria had caught him**: "When she left, he never saw it coming." Maggie Bell interview.

467 **"He was quiet"**: Maggie Bell interview; Aubrey Powell interview; Phil Carson, interview with the author, July 2, 2019; Unity MacLean interview. Also: Helen Grant, quoted in Blake, *Bring It On Home*, p. 169.

467 **"polite, always a gentleman"**: Unity MacLean interview.

467 **"all these bad vibes"**: Dave Northover, quoted in Blake, *Bring It On Home*, p. 169.

467 **"a shotgun and a few"**: Richard Cole, quoted in Welch, *Peter Grant*, p. 180.

467 **"very scary person"**: JP, quoted in Kent, "Bring It On Home," p. 139.

467 **"He was a dangerous character"**: Carole Brown Woods, interview with the author, November 8, 2019.

467 **"We all knew"**: Maggie Bell interview.

467 **"Johnny Bindon had the biggest"**: Michael Des Barres, interview with the author, February 20, 2019.

468 **"three big ale glasses"**: Author interview with Unity MacLean, October 16, 2019.

468 **"hang beer mugs off it"**: Cynthia Sach, quoted in Hoskyns, *Trampled*, p. 348.

468 **People extolled John Bindon's**: "He was an extremely funny guy, but truly frightening." Benji Le Fevre interview.

468 **"beyond scary"**: "He ripped a friend's balls right off." Abe Hoch interview.

468 **"She and Johnny spent"**: "Bindon would roar with laughter." Phil Carlo, interview with the author, May 12, 2019.

468 **On other occasions**: "He'd just pull the poppers apart on her skirt so she'd be standing there naked." Unity MacLean interview.

468 **He never left**: "It was all Richard—he arranged the drugs for Peter, Bindon, and Jimmy." Carole Brown Woods interview.

468 **"There were now a ton"**: Unity MacLean interview.

468 **From time to time**: "Peter would look in through the keyhole. It was seamy." Unity MacLean interview.

469 **"Jimmy never got off"**: Unity Maclean interview.

469 **"He had absolutely no time"**: Maggie Bell interview.

469 **"One year later"**: Michael Des Barres interview.

469 **"Dave knew he was trapped"**: Jake Riviera, quoted in Hoskyns, *Trampled*, p. 346.

470 **"I was besotted"**: Goldberg, *Bumping into Geniuses*, p. 89.

470 **"She was terrible"**: Shelley Kaye, interview with the author, July 15, 2019.

470 **"I'm not happy"**: Abe Hoch interview.

471 **"There was no hanging out"**: Abe Hoch interview. Also: Phil Carson interview; Phil Carlo interview; Benji Le Fevre interview; Danny Goldberg, interview with the author, August 28, 2018; Elizabeth Iannaci, interview with the author, January 17, 2019; Janine Safer Whitney, interview with the author, April 2, 2019.

### Chapter Nineteen: Their Own Private Sodom and Gomorrah

472 **"It was the social"**: Terry Reid, interview with the author, February 14, 2018.

473 **"endless solos that went"**: Tommy Ramone, quoted in "Fight Club," *Uncut*, January 2007.

473 **"I am actually out of touch"**: JP, quoted in Mick Houghton, "Interview with Jimmy Page," *Sounds*, July 10, 1976.

474 **"It's an honest soundtrack"**: JP, blind-quoted from a 1977 interview in Lewis, *Led Zeppelin: A Celebration*, p. 41.

474 **"It was the live material"**: JP, quoted in Chris Salewicz, "The Gig Interview: Jimmy Page," *Gig*, May 1977.

474 **"There's a winning version"**: JP, blind-quoted from a 1977 interview in Lewis, *Led Zeppelin: A Celebration*, p. 41.

474 **Ten years later:** "It's all in the tape vaults, but it would take a long time to do it." JP, blind-quoted from a 1988 interview in Lewis, *Led Zeppelin: A Celebration*, p. 41.

475 **"Hey, baldy, what are you":** "The stewardess had to tell them to shut up and behave." Chris Charlesworth, interview with the author, May 17, 2019.

476 **"Theaters in those days":** JP, quoted in Tolinski, *Light & Shade*, p. 200.

476 **"told the projectionist":** Peter Clifton, quoted in Welch, *Peter Grant*, p. 136.

476 **"You can look at those":** JP, quoted in Blake, *Bring It On Home*, p. 166.

476 **"Members of the group":** "For the first two-thirds, which was all this reviewer stayed [for] . . ." Richard Eder, "Zeppelin's Rock Pulverizes Eardrums at Cinema I," *New York Times*, October 21, 1976.

477 **with the rarely awarded rating:** Kathleen Carroll, "Film-wise, It's Dead Zeppelin," *New York Daily News*, October 21, 1976.

477 **"Led Zeppelin's rapaciousness":** Dave Marsh, "They Probably Think This Film Is about Them," *Rolling Stone*, December 2, 1976.

477 **"by junior college students":** Robert Duncan, "*The Song Remains the Same*" (review), *Circus*.

477 **"It's not a great film":** JP, quoted in Nick Kent, "Jimmy Page: Shy Rock Star Almost Unburdens Himself," *Creem*, April 1977.

477 **"I just don't trust":** Kent, "Jimmy Page."

477 **Lori Mattix worked:** "I was met in the lobby by Lori Mattix, who said, 'You're here with Led Zeppelin? I'll send some of my girlfriends up to your room.'" Aubrey Powell, interview with the author, May 15, 2019.

477 **"Some drug dealer came in" :** Aubrey Powell interview.

478 **"He was being shaken down":** Jeff Hoffman, interview with the author, July 30, 2019.

478 **"It was all power":** Aubrey Powell interview.

479 **"No one was mixing":** "I was appalled." Unity MacLean, interview with the author, October 16, 2019.

479 **"at war with everybody":** Wall, *When Giants Walked the Earth*, p. 364.

479 **"This is one dumb movie":** Nick Kent, "*The Song Remains the Same*" (review), *NME*, November 13, 1976.

479 **called the movie "depressing":** Jonh Ingham, "*The Song Remains the Same*" (review), *Sounds*, November 13, 1976.

480 **Only *Melody Maker* kowtowed:** "*The Song Remains the Same* is a classy, and surely enormously successful, film." Chris Charlesworth, "*The Song Remains the Same*" (review), *MM*, October 30, 1976. "Robert called to thank me for my loyalty." Chris Charlesworth interview.

480 **"It's a horrible medium":** JP, quoted in Ingham, "Jimmy Page: Technological Gypsy," *Sounds*, March 13, 1976.

480 **"incredible uphill struggle":** JP, quoted in Dave Schulps, *Trouser Press* interview, Part 3, p. 21.

480 **"He wasn't that eager":** Benji Le Fevre, interview with the author, May 19, 2019.

481 **They set up equipment:** "They flew my engineer friend Donnie over from America to monitor everything, and in three months they rehearsed twice." Benji Le Fevre interview.

481 **"We'd all get fucked up":** Benji Le Fevre, quoted in Hoskyns, *Trampled*, p. 350.

481 **"Charlotte Martin regularly called":** Unity MacLean interview.

481 **"separate lives conducted under":** Carole Brown Woods, interview with the author, November 8, 2019.

482 **"completely out of it":** Phil Carson, interview with the author, July 2, 2019.

482 **"He'd just disappeared":** Carole Brown Woods interview.

483 **"Call Peter and discuss what"**: JP, quoted in Welch, *Peter Grant*, p. 153.

483 **"signed as a musical adventure"**: Alan Callan, quoted in Hoskyns, *Trampled*, p. 329.

483 **"The first task was"**: "There was a stamina aspect involved apart from anything else." JP, quoted in Salewicz, "*Gig* Interview."

484 **Jonesy grudgingly singing:** "They got me to sing on 'Battle of Evermore.' I'll never know how I agreed to that!" JPJ, quoted in Dave Lewis, "The John Paul Jones Interview," in Lewis, *Led Zeppelin: Celebration II*, p. 120.

484 **"It was marvelous"**: RP, quoted in Nigel Williamson, "Good Times, Bad Times," *Uncut*, May 2005, p. 60.

484 **"To a large degree"**: RP, quoted in Thor Christensen, "A Decade Later, Plant Refuses to Relive His Past," *Milwaukee Journal Sentinel*, July 22, 1990.

485 **"it just sounded loud"**: "I must say I didn't like punk at first." JPJ, quoted in Lewis, "John Paul Jones Interview," pp. 120–21.

485 **"Everybody was winding"**: Glen Matlock, blind-quoted in Salewicz, *Jimmy Page*, p. 356.

485 **"What are those old hippies"**: Glen Matlock, quoted in Bonham, *John Bonham*, p. 162.

485 **"I was aware there was"**: JP, quoted in Salewicz, *Jimmy Page*, p. 355.

486 **"out of his head"**: Brian James, quoted in Salewicz, *Jimmy Page*, p. 355.

486 **"Where's the fucking band"**: JB, quoted by Glen Matlock in Bonham, *John Bonham*, p. 162.

486 **"Fuck off!"**: "Jeers of 'Fuck off!' greeted him." Dave Lewis, "The 1977 US Tour—the Beginning of the End," in Lewis, *Led Zeppelin: Celebration II*, p. 45.

486 **"Piss off you old hippie!"**: Glen Matlock, quoted in Bonham, *John Bonham*, p. 163.

486 **"mainlining Geritol"**: RP, quoted in *CBS Sunday Morning*, December 16, 2012.

486 **"fawned at my feet"**: RP, quoted in Williamson, "Good Times, Bad Times," p. 60.

486 **"Listen you little fucker"**: Rat Scabies, quoted in Hoskyns, *Trampled*, p. 350.

486 **"After two years off"**: RP, quoted in Robert Hilburn, "Led Zeppelin Lands Safely in Dallas," *Los Angeles Times*, April 5, 1977.

486 **"The last day of rehearsal"**: JP, quoted in Wesley Strick, "The Tour in Progress: Jimmy Page Files His Report," *Circus*, June 9, 1977.

487 **"I was in the hills"**: RP, quoted in Hilburn, "Led Zeppelin Lands Safely in Dallas."

487 **"After the postponement"**: "It was a bit unnerving." JP, quoted in Strick, "Tour in Progress."

487 **"There were bodyguards"**: Jaan Uhelszki, quoted in Hoskyns, *Trampled*, p. 353.

488 **"I couldn't really figure out"**: Dave Northover, quoted in Hoskyns, *Trampled*, p. 351.

488 **"Peter liked to think"**: Phil Carson interview.

488 **"But mostly he wasn't funny"**: Benji Le Fevre interview.

488 **"Everyone was excited"**: Janine Safer Whitney, interview with the author, April 2, 2019.

489 **Barbara Cope was a well-known:** "Her job was to cover herself in butter and we'd all lick her." Joe Wright, interview with the author, November 28, 2018. "She'd give guys hand jobs or blow jobs with butter." Michael Des Barres, interview with the author, February 20, 2019. Also: Carmine Appice, interview with the author, April 9, 2019.

489 **"I was petrified"**: RP, blind-quoted in Wall, *When Giants Walked the Earth*, p. 369.

489 **"I was so nervous"**: RP, quoted in Hilburn, "Led Zeppelin Lands Safely in Dallas."

489 **"swirling . . . strutting"**: Uncredited review, *Buddy*, May 1977.

489 **"psycho strut"**: "It's so embarrassing, because I've been jumping across the stage." JP, quoted in Strick, "Tour in Progress."

489 **"I could feel tenseness"**: RP, quoted in Hilburn, "Led Zeppelin Lands Safely in Dallas."

490 **"amazingly professional"**: Pete Oppel, "Zeppelin Rises to a Night of Firsts," *Dallas Morning News*, April 3, 1977.

490 **"The mood was ugly"**: Jack Calmes, quoted in Hoskyns, *Trampled*, p. 351.

490 **"We've got a new"**: RP, quoted in Strick, "Tour in Progress."

491 **"He definitely wasn't"**: "The cause may have been aggravated by too much booze or coke." Janine Safer Whitney, email to the author, August 27, 2020.

491 **"I really *did* steal"**: JP, quoted by Jaan Uhelszki in Hoskyns, *Trampled*, p. 367.

492 **The damage added $5,100**: Cole, *Stairway to Heaven*, p. 335.

492 **"turned it into their own"**: John Petkovic, "Cleveland Swingos Hotel: Where Rockers Raged and Legends Were Made in the 1970s," *Plain Dealer*, October 15, 2000.

492 **"I was staying in"**: Danny Marcus, interview with the author, January 16, 2019.

492 **"They smashed light fixtures"**: Jim Swingos, quoted in Petkovic, "Cleveland Swingos Hotel."

492 **"It goes as far"**: RP, quoted in Jaan Uhelszki, "Led Zeppelin: Sodom and Gomorrah in a Suitcase," *Creem*, July 1977.

492 **"boatloads of it"**: Janine Safer Whitney interview.

493 **"legions of rowdy gatecrashers"**: Cliff Radel, "Zeppelin Justifies 29-Hour Wait," *Cincinnati Enquirer*, April 22, 1977.

493 **"I went to his door"**: Janine Safer Whitney interview.

493 **He begged her**: "I was not going to let him lie down." Janine Safer Whitney, interview with the author, August 28, 2020.

493 **In Paris, during**: "I picked up the phone and called a dealer I knew in Paris. Within an hour, he had delivered an ounce of smack to Bonzo's door. We both snorted some of it." Cole, *Stairway to Heaven*, p. 326.

494 **"Zeppelin's Sheer Power"**: *Chicago Tribune*, April 7, 1977; MM, May 14, 1977; *Indianapolis News*, April 18, 1977; *Journal News* (Fairfield, Ohio), April 21, 1977; *Cincinnati Enquirer*, April 20, 1977; *Cleveland Press*, April 28, 1977.

494 **"I don't think any"**: Benji Le Fevre interview.

494 **"The tightness and precision"**: "Page simply wasn't interested." Charlie McCollum, "Led Zeppelin's Terrible Fall," *Washington Star*, May 26, 1977.

494 **"I wonder if Page"**: Robert Hilburn, "Zeppelin Vies for Rock Legacy," *Los Angeles Times*, June 25, 1977.

494 **"There were evenings"**: Hilburn, "Zeppelin Vies for Rock Legacy," Author interview with Benji Lefevre, May 19, 2019.

495 **"Their 1977 tour is tedious"**: Gerry Baker, "14,000 Aboard Zeppelin Flight," *Fort Worth Star-Telegram*, May 23, 1977.

495 **"It was the worst concert"**: Aubrey Powell interview.

495 **"polished but uninspired"**: Larry Rohter, "Led Zeppelin" (review), *Washington Post*, May 26, 1977.

495 **"Rarely has a major"**: McCollum, "Led Zeppelin's Terrible Fall."

495 **"a very wasted-looking Page"**: "Page simply wasn't interested. . . . This lack of musical integrity simply can't be tricked away." McCollum, "Led Zeppelin's Terrible Fall."

495 **"ought to be ashamed"**: Bobby Nowell, "Zeppelin: No Progress, No Rock 'n Roll," *North Carolina Anvil*, June 9, 1977.

495 **"he'd have the chord shape"**: "You could see Robert cringing." Benji Le Fevre, quoted in Hoskyns, *Trampled*, p. 355.

495 **"I didn't realize"**: "The audience never knew anything was awry." Phil Carson interview. "He was nodding off a lot during the acoustic set." Janine Safer Whitney, interview with the author, August 20, 2020.

495 **"the clumsiest and most simpleminded"**: Rohter, "Led Zeppelin."

495 **"He can barely keep"**: McCollum, "Led Zeppelin's Terrible Fall."

496 **"Everybody was nervous"**: Sam Aizer, quoted in Hoskyns, *Trampled*, p. 354.

496 **"Jonesy especially stayed away"**: Michael Des Barres interview.

496 **"Robert and Jonesy enjoyed"**: Benji Le Fevre interview.

496 **"Johnny had stolen money"**: "I knew Johnny had done it." Aubrey Powell interview.

497 **"We were flying"**: Peter Grant, quoted in Dave Lewis, "1977 US Tour," p. 49.

497 **"By the time the band"**: Aubrey Powell interview.

497 **"There was also a massive"**: Janine Safer Whitney, email to the author, August 30, 2020.

497 **"canvas roof over the stage"**: "Everyone was worried it was going to rip." Benji Le Fevre interview.

498 **"I quickly actioned Robert"**: Peter Grant, quoted in Lewis, "1977 US Tour," p. 49.

498 **"Everybody into the dressing room!"**: Richard Cole, quoted in Aubrey Powell interview.

498 **"The crowd had followed us"**: Aubrey Powell interview.

499 **"Led Zeppelin will not perform"**: William Poe (mayor of Tampa, Florida), Official Edict, June 6, 1977.

499 **"At least we got"**: "He told us there was a million dollars in cash in there." Peter Grant, quoted in Aubrey Powell interview.

## Chapter Twenty: A Transition Period

500 **"Keith was the last guy"**: Janine Safer Whitney, interview with the author, April 15, 2020.

500 **"I went to visit him"**: Aubrey Powell, interview with the author, May 15, 2019.

501 **"I see a lot of craziness"**: RP, quoted in Jaan Uhelszki, "Led Zeppelin: Sodom and Gomorrah in a Suitcase," *Creem*, July 1977.

501 **"Before each of the shows"**: Janine Safer Whitney, interview with the author, April 2, 2019.

502 **"spellbinding"**: Carl Arrington, "Lotta Love in the Garden," *New York Post*, June 8, 1977.

502 **"good-natured and almost puckish"**: John Rockwell, "Led Zeppelin Puts Best Sound Forward," *New York Times*, June 8, 1977.

502 **"some of the finest concerts"**: Dave Lewis, "The 1977 US Tour—the Beginning of the End," in Lewis, *Led Zeppelin: Celebration II*, p. 51.

502 **"They were a mystery"**: "I never imbued them with the characteristics of a human being." Janine Safer Whitney, interview with the author, April 2, 2019.

503 **"I felt so conflicted"**: "Lori was well beyond her years. She sure wasn't a child." Elizabeth Iannaci, interview with the author, January 17, 2019.

503 **Bonzo was so wasted**: "He bit my finger so hard it bled." Elizabeth Iannaci interview.

504 **On an Air India flight**: "I had gone to pick them up at Kennedy, and Richard was arrested when they landed." Janine Safer Whitney, interview with the author, August 28, 2020.

504 **"Peter had lost it"**: Phil Carson, interview with the author, July 2, 2019.

504 **"a rock legend"**: George Estrada, "Zeppelin Soars to New Heights," *Oakland Tribune*, July 25, 1977.

504 **"he was so loaded"**: Peter Barsotti, quoted in Bill Graham and Robert Greenfield, *Bill Graham Presents* (New York: Doubleday, 1990), p. 401.

505 **"Jeez, it's a long way"**: Jim Downey, quoted in Graham and Greenfield, *Bill Graham Presents*, p. 402.

505 **"Bindon had been spoiling"**: Janine Safer Whitney interview, April 2, 2019.

505 **"Bill Graham used to have"**: Phil Carson interview.

505 **"I thought it looked cool"**: Warren Grant, quoted in Blake, *Bring It On Home*, p. 191.

505 **"I'm taking them"**: Warren Grant, quoted by Jim Matzorkis in Graham and Greenfield, *Bill Graham Presents*, p. 403.

505 **"I had been standing"**: Janine Safer Whitney interview, August 28, 2020.

506 **"What I should have done"**: "Then it hit me for the first time. This was *drug* money." Bill Graham, in Graham and Greenfield, *Bill Graham Presents*, p. 400.

506 **"frequently did not make"**: "On a brief acoustic set, Page was especially disappointing." Phil Elwood, "Led Zeppelin Comes Back—with a Big but Boring Sound," *San Francisco Chronicle*, July 24, 1977. "Page's guitar work, seeming at times redundant and mindless . . ." Estrada, "Zeppelin Soars to New Heights."

507 **"You don't talk"**: "Bonham came up the little stair where I was standing and he kicked me right in the crotch—a good, unobstructed shot." Jim Matzorkis, quoted in Hoskyns, *Trampled*, p. 372.

507 **"vicious fucking wild animals"**: Bill Graham, quoted in Graham and Greenfield, *Bill Graham Presents*, p. 407.

508 **"he picked me up"**: Graham and Greenfield, *Bill Graham Presents*, p. 405.

508 **"We all attended"**: Janine Safer Whitney interviews, April 2, 2019, and August 28, 2020.

509 **"Please understand"**: Steve Weiss, quoted in Graham and Greenfield, *Bill Graham Presents*, p. 408.

510 **"There was a very nasty"**: JP, quoted in Nick Kent, "Bring It On Home," *Q Special Edition: Led Zeppelin*, March 2003, p. 139.

510 **"It was an absolute"**: RP, quoted in Graham and Greenfield, *Bill Graham Presents*, p. 414.

510 **Monday morning, a trio**: Text message to the author from Michael Zagaris, December 1, 2020.

511 **"charismatic, well-connected"**: Shelley Kaye, interview with the author, July 30, 2019.

511 **"My instructions were"**: Jeff Hoffman, interview with the author, July 30, 2019.

511 **"a mild stomach bug"**: "A Swan Song spokesperson said that Plant's son had become ill with a mild stomach bug." "Plant's Tragedy," *NME*, August 6, 1977.

511 **the boy had contracted**: "Karac had pneumonia going on and got another virus on top of it." Benji Le Fevre, interview with the author, May 19, 2019.

511 **"We got back"**: Jerry Greenberg, interview with the author, January 10, 2019. Also: Phil Carson interview.

512 **"If you ever want"**: RP, quoted in Hoskyns, *Trampled*, p. 376.

512 **"Robert and I sat across"**: Janine Safer Whitney interview, August 28, 2020.

512 **Colonel Tom Parker sent**: "Elvis sent a wreath for the funeral. Colonel Parker rang and wanted to know where to send it." Cynthia Sach, quoted in Hoskyns, *Trampled*, p. 378.

512 **"trying to sort out"**: Peter Grant, quoted in Dave Lewis, "The Peter Grant Interview," in Lewis, *Led Zeppelin: Celebration II*, p. 98.

512 **"I hope you're happy"**: "Those were his exact words." Peter Grant, quoted in Graham and Greenfield, *Bill Graham Presents*, p. 413.

513 **"The 1977 tour ended"**: RP, quoted in Hoskyns, *Trampled*, p. 376.

513 **"Robert phoned me"**: Peter Grant, quoted in Lewis, "Peter Grant Interview," p. 98.

513 **"You'd better get on"**: Steve Weiss, quoted in Benji Le Fevre interview.

514 **"He was the only guy"**: RP, quoted in Hoskyns, *Led Zeppelin IV*, p. 159.

514 **"After Karac died"**: "I didn't realize they were actually shooting up." Sally Williams, interview with the author, July 9, 2019.

514 **"I had just got a farm"**: JPJ, quoted in Dave Lewis, "The John Paul Jones Interview," in Lewis, *Led Zeppelin: Celebration II*, p. 120.

515 **"It means about two weeks"**: JP, quoted in Cole, *Stairway to Heaven*, p. 358.

515 **"far more seductive"**: Richards, *Life*, p. 284.

515 **"Peter was in bad shape"**: "There is a twenty-five-year gap where I couldn't get sales figures." Bill Curbishley, interview with the author, May 16, 2018. Also: Bill Curbishley, email to the author, September 7, 2020.

516 **"Peter was nonfunctioning"**: "He was just doing a ton of drugs." Shelley Kaye, interview with the author, July 15, 2019.

516 **"Alan, we just can't"**: Steve Weiss quoted by Alan Callan in Hoskyns, *Trampled*, p. 342.

516 **"He was upstairs"**: Maggie Bell, interview with the author, May 8, 2019.

516 **"Jake Riviera, Dave's manager"**: "He couldn't get to Peter, so he gave me a hard time." Unity MacLean, interview with the author, October 16, 2019.

516 **"*Get It*, Dave's album"**: Janine Safer Whitney interview, April 2, 2019.

517 **"That's true"**: Michael Des Barres, interview with the author, February 20, 2019.

517 **"I'll admit it"**: Phil Carson, quoted in Blake, *Bring It On Home*, p. 204.

517 **"My mojo for life"**: RP, blind-quoted in Blake, *Bring It On Home*, p. 198.

518 **"It was such a shocking"**: Benji Le Fevre interview. "At that point, [Robert] had no inclination to ever want to do anything again." Dennis Sheehan, quoted in Hoskyns, *Trampled*, p. 380.

518 **"the god-head shit"**: RP, blind-quoted in Lewis, "1977 US Tour," p. 53.

518 **"I tried to pick myself up"**: RP, quoted in Nigel Williamson, "Good Times, Bad Times," *Uncut*, May 2005, p. 60.

518 **"I'd already lost my boy"**: RP, quoted in *Robert Plant By Myself*, BBC2, November 6, 2010.

518 **"I tinkered on the village piano"**: RP, quoted in Jerene Jones, "After Tragedy Left Their Hearts Heavier Than Their Metal, Robert Plant and Led Zeppelin Have Risen Again," *People*, August 27, 1979.

518 **"re-focus the whole deal"**: "I haven't taken a drug since that day [Karac died]. . . . I still drink, and I don't spill much." RP, quoted in Williamson, "Good Times, Bad Times," p. 61.

518 **"Addiction to powders"**: RP, blind-quoted in Wall, *When Giants Walked the Earth*, p. 385.

519 **"What the fuck"**: Peter Grant, quoted in Lewis, "Peter Grant Interview," p. 98.

519 **G recommended a secluded**: "I suggested Clearwell because Bad Company had been." Peter Grant, quoted in Lewis, "Peter Grant Interview," p. 98.

519 **"My joy of life"**: RP, quoted in Williamson, "Good Times, Bad Times," p. 61.

519 **"Robert kept saying"**: Peter Grant, quoted in Lewis, "Peter Grant Interview," p. 98.

519 **"When it came to"**: Benji Le Fevre interview.

519 **"encouraged rather than coaxed"**: RP, quoted in Williamson, "Good Times, Bad Times," p. 61.

519 **"a shotgun and a bottle"**: RP, quoted in *Robert Plant: By Myself*.

519 **"He said, 'Come on'"**: "Bonzo came over and worked on me a few times with the aid of a bottle of gin." RP, quoted in Barney Hoskyns, "Robert Plant & John Paul Jones Interview," *Mojo*, June 2003.

520 **"a period of saying hello"**: JP to journalist Simon Pallett, blind-quoted in John Aizlewood, "Closing Time," *Q Special Edition: Led Zeppelin*, March 2003, p. 94.

520 **"I didn't really feel"**: "Perhaps nobody was strong enough to stop it—including our manager who wasn't that well himself." JPJ, quoted in Lewis, "John Paul Jones Interview," p. 120.

520 **"I felt quite remote"**: RP, quoted in Williamson, "Good Times, Bad Times," p. 61.

520 **"I started to play again"**: RP, blind-quoted in Lewis, *Led Zeppelin: From a Whisper to a Scream*, p. 87.

522 **This one, however:** *Origins of the Yamaha Synthesizer*, https://europe.yamaha.com/en /products/contents/music_production/synth_0th/history/chapter01/index.html.

522 **"The sound one could get"**: JPJ, quoted in Lewis, "John Paul Jones Interview," p. 120.

522 **"John had it at home"**: JP, interviewed on radio.com, 2015.

523 **"He continued sending"**: Unity MacLean interview.

523 **"It was sensational"**: RP, blind-quoted in Cross and Flannigan, *Led Zeppelin*, p. 151.

523 **"For much of the time"**: JPJ, quoted in Lewis, "John Paul Jones Interview," p. 120.

523 **"Robert, Jonesy, and I"**: Benji Le Fevre interview.

523 **"We'd sit there"**: "By the time they did, we'd written most of the songs." JPJ, quoted in Mat Snow, "John Paul Jones: The Quiet One," *Mojo*, December 2007.

524 **"never really gravitated"**: RP, quoted in Hoskyns, *Trampled*, p. 381.

524 **When Jimmy and Bonzo finally:** "The truth of the matter was, we never turned up until the middle of the night until we had scored." Richard Cole, quoted in Welch, *Peter Grant*, p. 212.

525 **"I would have preferred"**: JP, quoted in Tolinski, *Light & Shade*, p. 206.

525 **"I was a little worried"**: "I wasn't really keen on 'All My Love.'" JP, quoted in Tolinski, *Light & Shade*, pp. 206–7.

525 **"When the stuff came back"**: Richard Cole, quoted in Hoskyns, *Trampled*, p. 383.

525 **"a hurdy-gurdy type"**: JP, blind-quoted in Popoff, *Led Zeppelin*, p. 208.

525 **"a little soft"**: JP, quoted in Tolinski, *Light & Shade*, p. 206.

526 **In the middle:** "The engineer had warned us the fire alarm sometimes goes off." Benji Le Fevre interview.

526 **"people who could turn up"**: JPJ, quoted in Hoskyns, *Led Zeppelin IV*, pp. 159–60.

526 **"It was the four of us"**: "I don't think it was really a Led Zeppelin record." RP, quoted in Wall, *When Giants Walked the Earth*, p. 395.

526 **"It was a summing up"**: JP, quoted in Nigel Williamson, "Forget the Myths," *Uncut*, May 2005, p. 72.

527 **"a transition period"**: JPJ, quoted in Lewis, "John Paul Jones Interview," p. 120.

527 **"to cut the waffle out"**: JPJ, quoted in Lewis, "John Paul Jones Interview," p. 121.

527 **"We are what we are"**: RP, interviewed on *Rock On*, Radio One, June 9, 1979.

**Chapter Twenty-one: Swan Song**

528 **There was no way:** "That was a very twitchy time. I was racked with nerves." RP, quoted in Nigel Williamson, "Good Times, Bad Times," *Uncut*, May 2005, p. 61.

528 **"'Fuck doing a tour'"**: Peter Grant, quoted in Dave Lewis, "The Peter Grant Interview," in Lewis, *Led Zeppelin: Celebration II*, p. 98.

529 **"We could have gone"**: RP, quoted in Williamson, "Good Times, Bad Times," p. 61.

529 **"I'd like to go back"**: JP, quoted in Aubrey Powell, interview with the author, May 15, 2019.

529 **"I found the bar"**: Aubrey Powell interview.

530 **"like you were looking"**: Storm Thorgerson, quoted in Lois Wilson, "Sleevenotes," *Q Special Edition: Led Zeppelin*, March 2003, p. 97.

530 **"album cover was so fucking"**: Peter Grant, quoted in Wilson, "Sleevenotes."

531 **"The lineup we had hoped"**: JP, blind-quoted from a MM interview in Dave Lewis, "Led Zeppelin at Knebworth 1979," in Lewis, *Led Zeppelin: Celebration II*, p. 56.

532 **"The manner in which"**: *NME*, blind-quoted in Wall, *When Giants Walked the Earth*, p. 398.

532 **"Jimmy was moaning"**: "The traumas we went through to get one picture correct." Peter Grant, quoted in Lewis, "Peter Grant Interview," p. 98.

532 **Ed Bicknell, who managed:** "I told them they weren't ready for it, and I turned it down." Ed Bicknell, interview with the author, May 11, 2019.

532 **"No one"**: Freddy Bannister, *There Must Be a Better Way* (Cambridge: Bath Books, 2003), p. 146.

533 **"middle-weights"**: Nick Kent, "Led Zeppelin/New Barbarians/Todd Rundgren: Knebworth," *NME*, August 18, 1979.

533 **"Robert didn't want"**: JPJ, quoted in Hoskyns, *Trampled*, p. 384.

533 **"I was worried"**: JP, quoted in MM interview with Chris Salewicz, July 20, 1979.

533 **"money for drugs"**: Richard Cole, quoted in Hoskyns, *Trampled*, p. 384.

534 **"Don't be so fucking stupid"**: JB, quoted in Hoskyns, *Trampled*, p. 384.

534 **"For those of us who'd seen"**: Lisa Robinson, "Stairway to Excess," *Vanity Fair*, November 2003.

534 **"They appeared sloppy"**: Eric Kornfeldt, "Dazed 'n Abused," *NME*, August 4, 1979.

534 **Just in case:** "They proved they can still cut it. . . . For Knebworth, it can only be better yet." Jon Carlsson, "Warming Up in Denmark: Duck-Walks and Lasers," MM, August 4, 1979.

534 **"Perhaps by Knebworth"**: Erik von Lustbaden, "Something Heavy in the State of Denmark," *Sounds*, August 4, 1979.

535 **"the biggest fucking band"**: Peter Grant, quoted in Blake, *Bring It On Home*, p. 211.

535 **"We had a huge problem"**: Nick Maria, interview with the author, October 14, 2019.

535 **"Peter kept himself going"**: Bannister, *There Must Be a Better Way*, p. 153.

535 **"We'd sit there and talk"**: Jack Calmes, quoted in Hoskyns, *Trampled*, p. 384.

536 **"She'd called Jimmy"**: Unity MacLean, interview with the author, October 16, 2019.

536 **"My parents had split up"**: JP, quoted in Barney Hoskyns, "An Interview with Jimmy Page," *Rock's Backpages*, March 2003.

536 **"almost a museum piece"**: "Impressive but something from the past . . ." Kent, "Led Zeppelin/New Barbarians/Todd Rundgren."

536 **"People may think"**: RP, blind-quoted from an interview with journalist Jim Taylor in Dave Lewis, "Led Zeppelin at Knebworth 1979," in Lewis, *Led Zeppelin: Celebration II*, p. 56.

537 **"We had to come in"**: JP, quoted in Hoskyns, "Interview with Jimmy Page."

537 **"People pushed the stone pillars"**: RP, quoted in Tom Hibbert, "Robert Plant: Guilty!" *Q*, March 1988.

538 **"I was wracked with nerves"**: RP, quoted in Williamson, "Good Times, Bad Times," p. 61.

538 **"the sound was initially ropey"**: JPJ, quoted in Lewis, "The John Paul Jones Interview," in Lewis, *Led Zeppelin: Celebration II*, p. 121.

538 **"Some of it was breathtaking"**: Lewis, "Led Zeppelin at Knebworth, 1979," p. 60.

538 **"At times, they were playing"**: Paul Hurley, "Ghosts of Progressive Rock Past: Led Zeppelin et al. at Knebworth," *NME*, August 11, 1979.

539 **"were ill-conceived wanderings"**: "Time and again, his fingers wouldn't obey him the way they used to." Phil Sutcliffe, "Led Zeppelin: Knebworth Park, Hertfordshire," *Sounds*, August 18, 1979.

539 **"In the era of the Jam"**: David Hepworth, *Uncommon People* (New York: Henry Holt, 2017), p. 181.

539 **"the group sounded woefully"**: Mick Brown, "The Songs Remain the Same: Led Zeppelin at Knebworth Park," *Rolling Stone*, October 4, 1979.

539 **"I quite like them"**: Sutcliffe, "Led Zeppelin: Knebworth Park, Hertfordshire."

539 **"absolutely outstanding"**: Steve Gett, "Zeppelin: No Quarter," MM, August 11, 1979.

539 **"Jimmy Page, Robert Plant"**: Hurley, "Ghosts of Progressive Rock Past."

539 **"It was fantastic"**: JP, quoted in Hoskyns, "Interview with Jimmy Page."

539 **"a shit gig"**: RP, quoted in Hoskyns, *Trampled*, p. 389.

539 **"I wasn't as relaxed"**: RP, blind-quoted in Lewis, *Led Zeppelin: From a Whisper to a Scream*, p. 90.

539 **"had been on its knees"**: RP, blind-quoted in Hoskyns, *Led Zeppelin IV*, pp. 162–63.

540 **"jumped up, and began waving"**: Peter Grant, quoted in Wall, *When Giants Walked the Earth*, p. 405.

540 **In the fracas**: "Peter helped get him out of the country. G knew a guy in Ireland who looked after Bindon." Phil Carlo, interview with the author, May 12, 2019.

540 **In fact, *The New York Times***: Martin Arnold, "Herb Itkin, Informer Extraordinaire," *New York Times*, December 15, 1969, p. 1.

541 **"If they want the tickets"**: Freddy Bannister, quoted by Tom Fry in Hoskyns, *Trampled*, p. 390.

541 **Peter Grant advised them**: "I remember sitting in their trailer, counting it out for Ronnie." Richard Cole, quoted in Blake, *Bring It On Home*, p. 219.

541 **"Peter and Zeppelin had two"**: Richard Cole, quoted in Blake, *Bring It On Home*, p. 219.

542 **"He was in pretty bad shape"**: Maggie Bell, interview with the author, May 8, 2019.

542 **"It wasn't horrendous"**: JP, quoted in Wall, *When Giants Walked the Earth*, p. 406.

542 **"caught up in a world"**: Cole, *Stairway to Heaven*, p. 367.

543 **"grand reunion"**: "Led Zeppelin: *In Through the Out Door*" (review), *Record Mirror*, September 1, 1979.

543 **"With Page's creativity"**: Charles M. Young, "*In Through the Out Door*" (review), *Rolling Stone*, October 18, 1979.

543 **"I'm sad, disillusioned"**: Geoff Barton, "Close the Door, Put the Light Out . . . Led Zeppelin: *In Through the Out Door*," *Sounds*, September 1, 1979.

543 **"The performances are"**: Chris Bohn, "Led Zeppelin: *In Through the Out Door*" (review), MM, August 1, 1979.

544 **"It was the usual thing"**: Unity MacLean interview.

544 **"clean up"**: "All I could do was confine their investigation." Don Murfet, quoted in Hoskyns, *Trampled*, p. 393.

545 **"a way of getting back"**: JPJ, quoted in Lewis, "John Paul Jones Interview," p. 121.

545 **"difficult frame of mind"**: Peter Grant, quoted in Lewis, "Peter Grant Interview," p. 98.

545 **"We desperately needed"**: RP, quoted in Williamson, "Good Times, Bad Times," p. 62.

545 **"I was really keen"**: RP, quoted in Wall, *When Giants Walked the Earth*, p. 410.

545 **They dubbed it**: Wall, *When Giants Walked the Earth*, pp. 408–9.

545 **"Robert kept insisting"**: Peter Grant, quoted in Lewis, "Peter Grant Interview," p. 98.

546 **"I found it very difficult"**: RP, blind-quoted in Power, *No Quarter*, p. 455.

546 **"From the beginning"**: Cole, *Stairway to Heaven*, p. 47.

546 **"being the center of attention"**: Cole, *Stairway to Heaven*, pp. 345 and 343.

546 **"I'll teach you"**: Cole, *Stairway to Heaven*, p. 342.

546 **"He became progressively unreliable"**: RP, quoted in Hoskyns, *Trampled*, p. 397.

546 **"Him and Jonesy were getting"**: Richard Cole, quoted in Hoskyns, *Trampled*, p. 397.

546 **G, who was now dabbling**: "What happened was, Peter started dabbling in heroin." Richard Cole, quoted in Welch, *Peter Grant*, p. 211.

547 **"G had me to the house"**: Phil Carlo interview.

547 **"I reckoned that once Robert"**: Peter Grant, quoted in Lewis, "Peter Grant Interview," pp. 98–99.

547 **"There were too many fights"**: Alan Callan, quoted in Hoskyns, *Trampled*, p. 392.

547 **"I would send him tapes"**: Unity MacLean interview.

547 **"It was absolute chaos"**: Phil Carson, interview with the author, July 2, 2019.

548 **"I understand you do quite"**: Peter Grant, quoted in Phil Carson interview.

549 **"Punk kind of woke us"**: JPJ, quoted in Blake, *Bring It On Home*, p. 221.

549 **"It's just like 1968!"**: RP, quoted in Dave Lewis, *Led Zeppelin: Feather in the Wind— Over Europe 1980* (Bedford, UK: Tight but Loose, 2011), p. 211.

549 **"The first night"**: Phil Carlo interview.

550 **"Everybody was happy"**: Shelley Kaye, interview with the author, July 30, 2019.

550 **"The main group"**: RP, quoted in Lewis and Tremaglio, *Evenings with Led Zeppelin*, p. 551.

550 **"Nice echo in here"**: RP, quoted in Lewis, *Led Zeppelin: Feather in the Wind*, p. 56.

550 **"We haven't been sitting around"**: JP, quoted in Lewis, *Led Zeppelin: Feather in the Wind*, p. 59.

550 **"You see, the only reason"**: RP, quoted in Wall, *When Giants Walked the Earth*, p. 409.

551 **"I saw John a few times"**: Tony Iommi, quoted in Hoskyns, *Trampled*, p. 401.

551 **"thirty-two vodkas"**: "Mick Hinton told me he'd counted—thirty-two vodkas." Phil Carlo interview.

551 **"Bonzo was drunk almost all"**: Benji Le Fevre, interview with the author, May 19, 2019.

551 **"As he'd eaten something"**: Peter Grant, quoted in Lewis, "Peter Grant Interview," pp. 98–99.

551 **"had to eat fifty bananas"**: RP, quoted in Wall, *When Giants Walked the Earth*, p. 409.

551 **"John was right out of it"**: Phil Carson, quoted in Lewis, *Led Zeppelin: Feather in the Wind*, p. 158.

551 **"Bonzo sometimes got"**: Dennis Sheehan, quoted in Hoskyns, *Trampled*, p. 399.

551 **"She was one of those"**: Phil Carlo interview.

553 **"tired and obsolete"**: Lewis, "Led Zeppelin Over Europe 1980," in Lewis, *Led Zeppelin: Celebration II*, p. 82.

553 **"Munich was the nearest feeling"**: JP, quoted in Lewis, *Led Zeppelin: Feather in the Wind*, p. 80.

## Chapter Twenty-two: Coda

554 **"I was developing my own"**: RP, quoted in Lewis, *Led Zeppelin: Feather in the Wind*, p. 223.

554 **"We were battling on"**: JPJ, quoted in Lewis, "The John Paul Jones Interview," in Lewis, *Led Zeppelin: Celebration II*, p. 121.

555 **"How come Grant hasn't"**: RP, quoted by Peter Grant in Lewis, "The Peter Grant Interview," in Lewis, *Led Zeppelin: Celebration II*, p. 98.

555 **"I've gotten the go-ahead"**: Peter Grant, quoted in Phil Carlo, interview with the author, May 12, 2019.

555 **"After Cole was convicted"**: Jeff Hoffman, interview with the author, July 30, 2019.

556 **"Everything was getting organized"**: Shelley Kaye, interview with the author, July 30, 2019.

556 **"not an easy album"**: JP, quoted in Tolinski, *Light & Shade*, p. 195.

556 **"a little soft"**: JP, quoted in Tolinski, *Light & Shade*, p. 206.

556 **"I wanted to get back"**: JP, quoted in Nigel Williamson, "Forget the Myths," *Uncut*, May 2005, p. 72.

556 **"The guy was miserable"**: Glenn Hughes, quoted in Hoskyns, *Trampled*, p. 402.

556 **"It's so much easier"**: JB, quoted in Tom Doyle, "When the Levee Breaks," *Q Special Edition: Led Zeppelin*, March 2003, p. 111.

557 **"I don't want to"**: "Bonzo was in one of those periods where he thought he was no good." RP, quoted in Nigel Williamson, "Good Times, Bad Times," *Uncut*, March 2005, p. 62.

557 **"a basic design"**: Rusty Brutsche, quoted in Lewis, *Led Zeppelin: Feather in the Wind*, p. 189.

557 **"Well, [Jimmy and Bonzo] aren't here"**: Benji Le Fevre, interview with the author, May 19, 2019.

557 **"Breakfast"**: JB, quoted in Wall, *When Giants Walked the Earth*, p. 411.

557 **"He got on the drum stool"**: Mick Hinton, quoted in "Mick Hinton Interview," *Tight but Loose*, May 1992.

557 **"I think we should stop"**: Benji Le Fevre interview.

558 **"I had to go in"**: JPJ, quoted in Lewis, "John Paul Jones Interview," p. 121.

558 **"Ray came up to me"**: Peter Grant, quoted in Paul Henderson, "If Somebody Had to Be Trod On, They Got Trod On," *Classic Rock*, September 15, 1990.

558 **"contain the situation"**: Don Murfet, quoted in Hoskyns, *Trampled*, p. 403.

559 **"The three of us discussed"**: Don Murfet, quoted in Hoskyns, *Trampled*, p. 403.

559 **"Jimmy was sitting there"**: Don Murfet, blind-quoted in Power, *No Quarter*, p. 460.

559 **"Peter wants everybody out"**: Unity MacLean, interview with the author, October 16, 2019; Unity MacLean, email to the author, September 24, 2020.

560 **"Bonzo had been my closest"**: Cole, *Stairway to Heaven*, p. 371.

560 **"We went to a hotel"**: Benji Le Fevre interview.

560 **"They came back from Jersey"**: Peter Grant, quoted in Lewis, "Peter Grant Interview," p. 99.

561 **"I couldn't even think"**: JPJ, quoted in Lisa Robinson, "Stairway to Excess," *Vanity Fair*, November 2003.

561 **He felt it would have:** "It would have been another band entirely. And that's not what we wanted to do." JPJ, quoted in "John Paul Jones," *San Diego Union-Tribune*, 2004.

561 **"No John Bonham"**: JPJ, quoted in Gail Worley, "Getting the Led Out: A John Paul Jones Interview," KNAC-FM (Long Beach, CA), April 1, 2002.

561 **"We'll be together certainly"**: JP, quoted in Lisa Robinson, "Whole Lotta Led in the Deep South," *Disc and Music Echo*, June 9, 1973.

561 **"It would be silly"**: JP, quoted in Andy Secher, "Jimmy Page Interview," *Hit Parader*, July 1982.

561 **"For me, there was no"**: RP, quoted in Williamson, "Good Times, Bad Times," p. 61.

561 **"The record company were absolutely"**: Peter Grant, quoted in Doyle, "When the Levee Breaks," p. 111.

561 **Simon Kirke, Bad Company's drummer:** "Having Simon come in was discussed." Shelley Kaye, interview with the author, July 15, 2019.

561 **"Within a day of Bonzo's death"**: Phil Carlo interview.

562 **"We wish it to be known"**: Swan Song Records press release, December 4, 1980.

562 **"I just felt really insecure"**: JP, quoted in Chris Welch, "Jimmy Page On Stage '85," *Creem*, April 1985.

562 **"He was trying to come"**: Benji Le Fevre interview.

563 **"It seemed such a waste"**: "At first, the main emotion for me was anger." JPJ, quoted in Lewis, "John Paul Jones Interview," p. 121.

563 **"After John's death"**: Aubrey Powell, interview with the author, May 15, 2019.

563 **"the beginning of the period"**: Peter Grant, quoted in Lewis, "Peter Grant Interview," p. 99.

563 **"Nothing was getting taken"**: Shelley Kaye interview, July 15, 2019.

563 **"They sent a limo for him"**: Benji Le Fevre interview.

563 **"Fuck Weiss"**: Peter Grant, quoted in Hoskyns, *Trampled*, p. 395.

564 **"I used to go in"**: Maggie Bell, interview with the author, May 8, 2019.

564 **"There were no records"**: Phil Carson, interview with the author, July 2, 2019.

564 **"That was an agreement"**: "In fact, the contract for that was called the Omega contract." Peter Grant, quoted in Lewis, "Peter Grant Interview," p. 99.

565 **"When we lost John"**: JP, quoted in Barney Hoskyns, "The Jimmy Page Interview," *Rock's Backpages*, March 2003.

565 **"all that sort of naiveté"**: RP, quoted in Barney Hoskyns, "Interview with Jimmy Page, John Paul Jones, and Robert Plant," *Mojo*, June 2003.

565 **"When I saw all the oceans"**: JP, quoted in Nick Kent, "Jimmy Page Interview," *Vox*, December 1990.

566 **"We wrote 'Wearing and Tearing'"**: RP, quoted in Thor Christensen, "A Decade Later, Plant Refuses to Relive His Past," *Milwaukee Journal Sentinel*, July 22, 1990.

567 **"We wanted to put it out"**: RP, quoted in Steven Rosen, "Robert Plant: Deference to the Taskmaster," *Guitar World*, July 1986.

567 **"I don't know what category"**: JP, quoted in Dave Schulps, *Trouser Press* interview, Part 3, p. 22.

567 **"highly intent on change"**: JP, interview with Alan Freeman, Capital Radio/DIR, November 4, 1976.

567 **"Nobody's heart was in"**: Aubrey Powell interview.

568 **"graveyard status seems assured"**: Richard Cook, "Led Zeppelin: *Coda*" (review), *NME*, December 11, 1982.

568 **"like a walking skeleton"**: Dave Dickson, quoted in Wall, *When Giants Walked the Earth*, p. 421.

568 **"I did nothing for as long"**: RP, quoted in Tom Hibbert, "Robert Plant: Guilty!" *Q*, March 1988.

568 **"I never worried"**: JPJ, quoted in Steven P. Wheeler, "John Paul Jones: Life After Zeppelin," *Happening*, October 1999.

569 **"I called Jimmy and said"**: RP, quoted in Dave Lewis, "Wearing and Tearing Post 1980," in Lewis, *Led Zeppelin: A Celebration*, p. 79.

569 **"would be like meeting"**: RP, quoted in Sylvie Simmon, "Friends," *Q Special Edition: Led Zeppelin*, March 2003, p. 116.

569 **"I had to say to them"**: JPJ, quoted in interview with Dave Ling, *Classic Rock*, March 2003.

570 **"I fucking knew"**: JP, quoted in Phil Carlo interview.

570 **"John Paul Jones arrived"**: "My main memories were of total panic." JP, quoted in Wall, *When Giants Walked the Earth*, p. 424.

571 **"had nothing left at all"**: "I was hoarse, I'd rehearsed all afternoon, I'd sung three concerts in succession with my own band at the time and when I came to sing that night . . . nothing there." RP, quoted in Danny Fields, "Robert Plant," *Details*, July 1988.

571 **"Seventeen years, and we still"**: RP, quoted in Lewis, "Wearing and Tearing Post 1980," p. 80.

571 **"After the second number"**: Phil Carlo interview.

571 **"What I hated about Led Zeppelin"**: RP, quoted in Fields, "Robert Plant."

572 **Everything Jimmy did grated:** "Handling Jimmy Page's eccentricity was now not so easy." Lewis, "Wearing and Tearing, Post 1980," p. 80.

572 **"What I recall"**: JPJ, quoted in Wheeler, "John Paul Jones: Life After Zeppelin."

573 **"There might have been"**: JP, quoted in Wall, *When Giants Walked the Earth*, p. 431.

574 **"Heard from the floor"**: Sasha Frere-Jones, "Stairway to Here," *New Yorker*, December 24, 2007.

574 **"Some of the top"**: Ben Ratliff, "Led Zeppelin Finds Its Old Power," *New York Times*, December 10, 2007.

574 **"Plant's voice was rich"**: Frere-Jones, "Stairway to Here."

574 **"If there were skeptics tonight"**: Hamish McBain, "Led Zeppelin at O2" (review), *NME*, December 10, 2007.

574 **"They delivered the best show"**: Steve Baltin, "Revisiting Led Zeppelin's 2007 Reunion Show," *Forbes*, May 27, 2020.

575 **Jimmy Page and John Paul Jones waited:** Mark Beaumont, "The Untimely Death of Led Zeppelin," *The Independent*, December 1, 2020.

# Bibliography

## Books

Appice, Carmine, with Ian Gittins. *Stick It! My Life of Sex, Drums, and Rock 'n' Roll*. Chicago: Chicago Review Press, 2016.

Arden, Don, with Mick Wall. *Mr. Big*. London: Robson Books, 2004.

Bannister, Freddy. *There Must Be a Better Way*. Cambridge: Bath Books, 2003.

Blake, Mark. *Bring It On Home: Peter Grant, Led Zeppelin, and Beyond—The Story of Rock's Greatest Manager*. New York: Da Capo, 2018.

Bonham, Mick. *John Bonham: The Powerhouse Behind Led Zeppelin*. Harpenden, UK: Southbank, 2005.

Bordowitz, Hank. *Led Zeppelin on Led Zeppelin: Interviews and Encounters*. Chicago: Chicago Review Press, 2014.

Boyd, Pattie, with Penny Junor. *Wonderful Tonight: George Harrison, Eric Clapton, and Me*. New York: Harmony Books, 2007.

Bream, Jon. *Whole Lotta Led Zeppelin: The Illustrated History of the Heaviest Band of All Time*. Minneapolis: Voyageur, 2008.

Bronson, Harold. *My British Invasion*. Los Angeles: Vireo, 2017.

Brunning, Bob. *Blues: The British Connection*. London: Helter Skelter, 2002.

Calef, Scott, ed. *Led Zeppelin and Philosophy: All Will Be Revealed*. Chicago: Open Court, 2009.

Carr, Roy. *A Talk on the Wild Side*. Hamburg, Germany: earBOOKS, 2010.

Case, George. *Jimmy Page: Magus, Musician, Man*. London: Hal Leonard, 2007.

———. *Led Zeppelin FAQ*. Milwaukee, WI: Backbeat Books, 2011.

Clapton, Eric. *Clapton: The Autobiography*. New York: Broadway Books, 2007.

Clayson, Alan. *The Yardbirds*. New York: Backbeat Books, 2002.

Cohen, Ronald D. *Folk Music: The Basics*. New York: Routledge, 2006.

Cole, Richard, with Richard Trubo. *Stairway to Heaven: Led Zeppelin Uncensored*. New York: Dey St., 1992.

Corcoran, Michael. *All Over the Map: The True Heroes of Texas Music*. Austin: University of Texas Press, 2005.

Cross, Charles R., and Erik Flannigan. *Led Zeppelin: Heaven and Hell*. New York: Harmony Books, 1991.

Crowley, Aleister. *The Book of the Law*. London: Createspace Independent, 2011.

———. *The Confessions of Aleister Crowley: An Autobiography*. Waccabuc, NY: Appledore Books, 1969.

———. *Magick in Theory and Practice by the Master Therion*. Paris: Lecram, 1929.

Davis, Erik. *Led Zeppelin IV*. New York: Continuum, 2005.

Davis, Stephen. *Hammer of the Gods: The Led Zeppelin Saga*. New York: Ballantine Books, 1986.

———. *LZ-'75: The Lost Chronicles of Led Zeppelin's 1975 American Tour*. New York: Gotham Books, 2010.

Des Barres, Pamela. *I'm with the Band: Confessions of a Groupie*. Chicago: Chicago Review Press, 1997.

———. *Rock Bottom: Dark Moments in Music Babylon*. New York: St. Martin's, 1996.

Di Perna, Alan. *Guitar Masters: Intimate Portraits*. Winona, MN: Hal Leonard, 2012.

Dixon, Willie, and Don Snowdon. *I Am the Blues: The Willie Dixon Story*. New York: Da Capo, 1990.

Ellis, Royston. *The Big Beat Scene*. York, UK: Music Mentor Books, 2010.

Fast, Susan. *In the Houses of the Holy: Led Zeppelin and the Power of Rock Music*. New York: Oxford University Press, 2001.

Frame, Pete. *The Restless Generation: How Rock Music Changed the Face of Fifties Britain*. London: Rogan House, 2007.

———. *The Road to Rock: A ZigZag Book of Interviews*. London: Charisma Books, 1974.

Friend, Thomas W. *Fallen Angel: The Untold Story of Jimmy Page and Led Zeppelin*. Encino, CA: Gabriel, 2002.

Godwin, Robert. *Led Zeppelin: The Press Reports*. London: Collector's Guide, 1997.

Goldberg, Danny. *Bumping into Geniuses: My Life Inside the Rock and Roll Business*. New York: Gotham Books, 2008.

Graham, Bill, and Robert Greenfield. *Bill Graham Presents*. New York: Doubleday, 1992.

Green, Jonathon. *Green's Dictionary of Slang*. Online edition, 2019. greensdictofslang.com.

Greenfield, Robert. *The Last Sultan: The Life and Times of Ahmet Ertegun*. New York: Simon & Schuster, 2011.

Hepworth, David. *Never a Dull Moment: 1971, The Year That Rock Exploded*. New York: Henry Holt, 2016.

———. *Uncommon People: The Rise and Fall of the Rock Stars*. New York: Henry Holt, 2017.

Herrington, Patrick, and Bobby Graham. *The Session Man: The Story of Bobby Graham*. Monmouthshire, UK: Broom House, 2004.

Hewitt, Paolo. *Small Faces: The Young Mods' Forgotten Story*. London: Acid Jazz Books, 1995.

Hoskyns, Barney. *Led Zeppelin IV*. New York: Rodale, 2006.

———. *Trampled Under Foot: The Power and Excess of Led Zeppelin*. London: Faber & Faber, 2012.

James, Billy. *An American Band: The Story of Grand Funk Railroad*. Middlesex, UK: SAF, 2001.

James, Catherine. *Dandelion: Memoir of a Free Spirit*. New York: St. Martin's, 2007.

Johns, Glyn. *Sound Man*. New York: Blue Rider, 2014.

Jones, Allan. *Can't Stand Up for Falling Down: Rock 'n Roll War Stories*. London: Bloomsbury, 2017.

King, Francis. *The Magical World of Aleister Crowley*. New York: Coward, McCann, 1978.

Koch, Rudolph. *The Book of Signs*. London: Limited Editions Club, 1930.

Laing, Dave. *One Chord Wonders: Power and Meaning in Punk Rock*. London: PM Press, 2015.

Lewis, Dave. *The Complete Guide to the Music of Led Zeppelin*. London: Omnibus, 1994.

———. *Led Zeppelin: A Celebration*. London: Omnibus, 1991.

———. *Led Zeppelin: The "Tight but Loose" Files—Celebration II*. London: Omnibus, 2003.

———. *Led Zeppelin: The Concert File*. London: Omnibus, 1997.

———. *Led Zeppelin: Feather in the Wind—Over Europe 1980*. Bedford, UK: Tight but Loose, 2011.

———. *Led Zeppelin: From a Whisper to a Scream*. London: Omnibus, 2012

Lewis, Dave, and Mike Tremaglio. *Evenings with Led Zeppelin: The Complete Concert Chronicle*. London: Omnibus, 2018

McCarty, Jim, with Dave Thompson. *Nobody Told Me! My Life with the Yardbirds, Renaissance & Other Stories*. Self-published, 2018.

McLagen, Ian. *All the Rage*. London: Pan, 1998.

McNeil, Legs, and Gillian McCain. *Please Kill Me: The Uncensored Oral History of Punk*. New York: Grove, 2016.

Murfet, Don. *Leave It to Me: A Life in Rock, Pop and Crime*. N.p.: M-Y Books, 2004.

Murray, Charles Shaar. *Crosstown Traffic: Jimi Hendrix and Post-war Pop*. London: Faber and Faber, 1989.

Myers, Paul. *It Ain't Easy: Long John Baldry and the Birth of the British Blues*. British Columbia, Canada: Greystone Books, 2007.

Mylett, Howard. *Jimmy Page: Tangents Within a Framework*. London: Omnibus, 1983.

Napier-Bell, Simon. *You Don't Have to Say You Love Me*. London: Elbury, 2005.

Oldham, Andrew Loog. *2Stoned*. London: Secker & Warburg, 2002.

Page, Jimmy. *Jimmy Page by Jimmy Page*. London: Genesis, 2014.

Page, Jimmy, Robert Plant, and John Paul Jones. *Led Zeppelin by Led Zeppelin*. London: Reel Art, 2018.

Pegg, Dave, with Nigel Schofield. *Off the Pegg*. Self-published, n.d.

Pevsner, Nikolaus. *The Buildings of England: Worcestershire*. London: Penguin, 1968.

Popoff, Martin. *Led Zeppelin: All the Albums, All the Songs*. Minneapolis: Voyageur, 2017.

Power, Martin. *Hot Wired Guitar: The Life of Jeff Beck*. London: Omnibus, 2012.

———. *No Quarter: The Three Lives of Jimmy Page*. London: Omnibus, 2016.

Quisling, Erik, and Austin Williams. *Straight Whisky: A Living History of Sex, Drugs, and Rock 'n' Roll on the Sunset Strip*. Chicago: Bonus Books, 2003.

Rees, Paul. *Robert Plant: A Life*. New York: Harper Collins, 2014.

Richards, Keith, with James Fox. *Life*. New York: Little, Brown, 2010.

Roberty, Marc. *Led Zeppelin: Day by Day*. Milwaukee: Backbeat Books, 2016.

Robinson, Lisa. *There Goes Gravity*. New York: Riverhead, 2014.

Russo, Greg. *Yardbirds: The Ultimate Rave-up*. Floral Park, NY: Crossfire, 1998.

Salewicz, Chris. *Jimmy Page: The Definitive Biography*. New York: Da Capo, 2019.

Sander, Ellen. *Trips: Rock Life in the Sixties*. New York: Charles Scribner's Sons, 1973.

Shadwick, Keith. *Led Zeppelin: The Story of a Band and Their Music*. San Francisco: Backbeat, 2005.

Shapiro, Harry. *Alexis Korner: The Biography*. London: Bloomsbury, 1996.

Smith, Joe. *Off the Record: An Oral History of Popular Music*. New York: Warner Books, 1988.

Spitz, Bob. *The Making of Superstars*. New York: Doubleday, 1978.

Tobler, John, and Stuart Grundy. *The Guitar Greats*. London: BBC Publishing, 1983.

Tolinski, Brad. *Light & Shade: Conversations with Jimmy Page*. New York: Crown, 2012.

Waksman, Steve. *This Ain't the Summer of Love: Conflict and Crossover in Heavy Metal and Punk*. Berkeley: University of California Press, 2009.

Wall, Mick. *When Giants Walked the Earth: A Biography of Led Zeppelin*. London: Orion, 2008.

Walser, Robert. *Running with the Devil: Power, Gender, and Madness in Heavy Metal Music*. Hanover, CT: Wesleyan University Press, 1993.

Weinstein, Deena. *Heavy Metal: A Cultural Sociology*. New York: Lexington Books, 1991.

Welch, Chris. *Led Zeppelin: The Biggest Band of the 1970s*. London: Carlton Books, 2017.

———. *Led Zeppelin: Dazed and Confused*. New York: Thunder Mouth Press, 2001.

———. *Peter Grant: The Man Who Led Zeppelin*. London: Omnibus, 2002.

Welch, Morgana. *Hollywood Diaries*. Self-published, Xlibris, 2017.

Wexler, Jerry, and David Ritz. *Rhythm and the Blues: A Life in American Music*. New York: Knopf, 1993.

White, Timothy. *Rock Lives: Profiles and Interviews*. New York: Henry Holt, 1990.

Whiteley, Sheila, ed. *Sexing the Groove: Popular Music and Gender*. London: Routledge, 1997.

Wiederhorn, Jon. *Louder Than Hell: The Definitive Oral History of Metal*. New York: It Books, 2013.

Williams, David. *The First Time We Met the Blues*. York, UK: Music Mentor Books, 2009.

———. *Into the Blues*. York, UK: Music Mentor Books, 2014.

Wyman, Bill, with Ray Coleman. *Stone Alone*. New York: Viking, 1990.

Yorke, Ritchie. *Led Zep: The Led Zeppelin Biography*. New York: Two Continents, 1976.

## Websites

classicrock.com

classicrockmagazine.com

cyrildavies.com

jimmypage.com

johnpauljones.com

justbackdated.blogspot.co.uk

ledzepconcerts.com

ledzeppelin.com

ledzeppelin-database.com

ledzeppelin-reference.com

rambleonzep.com

rocksbackpages.com

robertplant.com

robertplanthomepage.com

thefamousmarqueeclub.comthegardentapes.co.uk

tightbutloose.co.uk

ukrockfestivals.com

uuweb.led-zeppelin.us

wholelottaled.webs.com

zososymbol.com

## Films

*Celebration Day*, 2012

*How the West Was Won*, 2006

*It Might Get Loud*, 2009

*No Quarter: Jimmy Page & Robert Plant*, 2004

Peter Grant interview w/Malcolm McLaren [unreleased]

*Prog Rock Britannia*, 2009/2010, BBC

*Red, White & Blues*, 2003

*The Song Remains the Same*, 1976

*Still On the Run: The Jeff Beck Story*, 2018

**Fanzines**

*Electric Magic*
*The Ocean*
*Oh Jimmy*
*Proximity*
*Tight but Loose*
*Zoso*

# Photo Credits

**Insert One**

Insert page 1 (top): Courtesy of Jeanne Busson

Insert page 1 (bottom): John Spicer

Insert page 2 (top): tracksimages.com / Alamy Stock Photo

Insert page 2 (bottom): Mark and Colleen Hayward via Getty Images

Insert page 3 (top): photograph by Gered Mankowitz © Bowstir Ltd 2020

Insert page 3 (bottom):

Insert page 4 (top): Michael Putland via Getty Images

Insert page 4 (bottom): Ron Howard via Getty Images

Insert page 5 (top): Michael Ochs Archives via Getty Images

Insert page 5 (bottom): David Redfern via Getty Images

Insert page 6 (top): Michael Putland via Getty Images

Insert page 6 (bottom): Shutterstock

Insert page 7 (top): Trinity Mirror / Mirrorpix / Alamy Stock Photo

Insert page 7 (bottom): Jorgen Angel via Getty Images

Insert page 8 (top): Michael Ochs Archives via Getty Images

Insert page 8 (bottom): Gijsbert Hanekroot / Alamy Stock Photo

Insert page 9: ZUMA Press, Inc. / Alamy Stock Photo

Insert page 10 (bottom): Trinity Mirror / Mirrorpix / Alamy Stock Photo

Insert page 11 (top): Neal Preston Photography

Insert page 11 (bottom): Paul Popper/Popperfoto via Getty Images

Insert page 12: Neal Preston Photography

Insert page 13 (top): Koh Hasene/Shinko Music via Getty Images

Insert page 13 (bottom): Michael Ochs Archives via Getty Images

Insert page 14: Michael Ochs Archives via Getty Images

Insert page 15: Bob Gruen

Insert page 16 (top): Express via Getty Images

Insert page 16 (bottom): Express Newspapers via Getty Images

**Insert Two**

# Index

A&R Studios, 203, 206
ABBA, 521–23
Abbey of Thelema, 432
Abbey Road Studios, 61, 98
Aberystwyth, 311
AC/DC, 349
"Achilles Last Stand," 447–50
Ackers, Graham, 19
Aerosmith, 531, 547
Air India, 504
Aizer, Sam, 441, 496
Albert Hall, 194, 224, 261, 335, 474, 565, 566
album cover art, 296–97, 473
  for *Coda*, 567
  for *Houses of the Holy*, 297–302, 461
  for *In Through the Out Door*, 529–31, 535, 543
  for *Led Zeppelin*, 171
  for *Led Zeppelin II*, 209–10
  for *Led Zeppelin III*, 234
  for *Led Zeppelin IV*, 246, 264–66, 268, 297
  for *Physical Graffiti*, 392
  for *Presence*, 459–62
Allman Brothers, 529
"All My Love," 522, 524, 525
*All Your Own*, 29–30
Altamont, 218
Alterman, Loraine, 378

Ambassador Hotel, 327
*American Gangster*, 342
amplifiers, 165–66
Anderson, Jon, 483
Andersson, Benny, 522, 523
Andrew, Prince, 468
Anger, Kenneth, 384–85, 471
Animals, 65, 96, 121, 122, 160, 181
*Ann Arbor Sun*, 406
Appice, Carmine, 158–59, 161, 165, 167, 172, 196, 199–201, 206–7, 241, 561
Arabella Hotel, 447
Arden, Don, 83, 95–96, 109, 157, 283, 464
ARMS charity concert, 568
art college, 49–50
  Sutton Art College, 49–52
Asher, Dick, 156
Asylum Records, 348
Atco Records, 155
Atkin, Herb, 540–41, 555
Atkins, Chet, 47
*Atlanta Constitution*, 311
Atlanta Stadium, 310–12
Atlantic Records, 92, 153–58, 162, 167, 179, 184, 207, 212, 275, 327, 366–67, 370, 374, 378, 386, 503, 504, 517, 544, 564
  Bonham's death and, 561
  *Coda* and, 565
  *Houses of the Holy* cover and, 302

Atlantic Records (*cont.*)
  Led Zeppelin royalties and masters
    ownership deal with, 515–16
  Led Zeppelin's contract with, 155, 162,
    179, 297, 343, 347
  and Led Zeppelin's fourth album having
    no title, 266, 268, 297
  Led Zeppelin's Swan Song label
    negotiations with, 347–49
  "Stairway to Heaven" and, 282
  tribute to, 572
Auger, Brian, 192

"Babe, I'm Gonna Leave You," 1, 9, 112,
    113, 145, 173
Bad Company, 354–55, 357, 366, 368, 373,
    374, 385, 388, 389, 391–93, 424, 440,
    458, 469, 483, 496, 517–19, 530, 531,
    537, 561, 563
Badgley, Larry, 414, 491
Baez, Joan, 1, 9, 112, 173
Bag O'Nails, 102–3
"Baja," 138
Baker, Ginger, 16, 261
Baldry, Long John, 16, 18
Baldwin, Joe, 135–36
Baldwin (Jones), Maureen "Mo," 140, 164,
    189, 429
Baltimore Civic Center, 336
Band, 148, 221, 231
Band of Joy, 109, 111, 114, 124–26, 131–32,
    145, 177, 183, 288
Bang Records, 62
Bangs, Lester, 176–77, 382
Banks, Darrell, 124
Bannister, Freddie, 228–30, 531–33, 535,
    540, 541
Bannister, Wendy, 540
Barber, Chris, 14, 118
Barney's Beanery, 240–41
Barrett, Syd, 297–98
Barry, John, 57
Barsalona, Frank, 159, 160, 284
Bart, Lionel, 479
Basile, Phil, 158–59
Bassey, Shirley, 57
Bath Festival, 227–30, 531
"Battle of Evermore, The," 256, 262,
    303, 484
BBC, 14, 29, 160, 194, 426

Beatles, 60, 61, 64, 70, 82, 99, 105, 108, 122,
    128, 149, 154, 186, 188, 193, 194, 199,
    206, 208, 213, 223, 230, 236, 250, 270,
    276, 297, 310, 312, 349, 381, 479, 516
  *Abbey Road*, 214
  *Sgt. Pepper's Lonely Hearts Club Band*, 98,
    297, 298
  *White Album*, 181
Beatty, Warren, 442
Beausoleil, Bobby, 384
Beck, Annetta, 52–53
Beck, Bogert & Appice (BBA), 199, 206–8
Beck, Jeff, 2, 5, 24, 50, 52–54, 66, 73–83,
    85–91, 101–3, 114, 142, 144, 156, 160,
    161, 169, 178–79, 181, 196, 367, 568
  *Truth*, 99, 105, 142, 154, 171, 178, 180
"Beck's Bolero," 80–82, 99, 106, 107,
    139, 152
Bee Gees, 154
Behan's West Park, 455–57
Belfast, 272–73, 300
Bell, Maggie, 207, 292, 348, 366, 368–70,
    373, 374, 376–80, 424, 440, 458, 469,
    483, 487, 516, 518, 531, 542, 564
  *Queen of the Night*, 376–77
  *Suicide Sal*, 424, 429
Bellson, Louie, 127
Benjamin, Louie, 152
Bennett, Duster, 346
Berns, Bert, 60, 62, 148, 153
Berry, Chuck, 18, 21, 22, 24, 30, 31, 39, 41,
    96, 140, 160, 194, 253, 362, 381, 499
Berry, Dave, 55, 63
Bevan, Bev, 123, 128, 560, 561
Beverly Hilton, 316, 423, 477
Bicknell, Ed, 94, 95, 151, 346, 532
*Billboard*, 170, 186, 243, 544
Biltmore Hotel, 423
Bindon, John, 462, 467–68, 478, 488,
    496–97, 501, 504–6, 511
  knife fight and flight of, 540
  Matzorkis assault and arrest of, 508–11
Bingenheimer, Rodney, 164, 189, 314, 315,
    318, 319, 321, 322, 478
  English Disco of, 314, 315, 317–18
Birkin, Jane, 335
Birmingham, 116–17, 122, 127
Birmingham Town Hall, 193–94
"Black Country Woman," 383
"Black Dog," 252–53, 261

"Black Mountain Side," 148, 175
Black Sabbath, 129, 176, 194, 288, 484,
    519–20, 572
Blackwell, Chris, 152, 153, 156
Blake, Peter, 297
Blakey, Art, 127
Bland, Bobby "Blue," 331
Blind Faith, 297
Blodwyn Pig, 194
Blondie, 484
Blood Sweat & Tears, 186
Blue Cheer, 236
blues, 5–6, 8, 11, 13–24, 30, 41, 42–44, 46,
    54, 56, 64, 66, 70–73, 75, 78, 119–20,
    123–24, 150, 173–74, 177, 225, 226,
    330, 358, 363, 450, 566
Blues Incorporated, 14–16, 20
Blue Star Trio, 127, 128
Blues Syndicate, 18
Blue Whale, 239
Bogert, Tim, 199, 206–7
Bohn, Chris, 543–44
Bolan, Marc, 298, 305
Boleskine House, 246, 351
Bolin, Tommy, 459
Bonham, Bill, 121, 134
Bonham, Jason, 572–75
Bonham, John
    in bands prior to Led Zeppelin, 114,
        126–32
    "Bonzo" nickname of, 126
    car accident of, 514
    cars collected by, 413, 418–19
    cattle farm of, 325
    collapses on stage at Nuremberg, 550–51
    death of, 558–63, 565, 568
    drinking and drunken behavior of, 129,
        192, 196–98, 237–38, 274, 279, 320–22,
        353, 377, 378, 380, 397, 400–401, 413,
        414, 418–19, 422–24, 429, 459, 475, 485–
        86, 492, 493, 501, 514, 550, 551, 557–58
    drug use of, 355, 378, 413, 418, 422,
        447, 459, 493–96, 500–501, 514, 521,
        524–25, 533–34, 542, 550, 551
    drumming of, 111, 126–29, 132, 149–50,
        172–73, 187, 209, 257–58, 261, 289,
        358, 362–63, 495, 561–62
    in formation of New Yardbirds/Led
        Zeppelin, 110, 111, 114–15, 132,
        133–35, 141

funeral for, 560
homesickness of, 237, 397, 400, 419,
    551, 556
jobs of, 130
marriage of, 130
Matzorkis assault and arrest of, 507,
    510–11
Midlands background of, 6, 115, 116, 148
public indecency incident of, 197
replacements after death considered for,
    561–62
tensions between Plant and, 273–74, 278
twenty-fifth birthday of, 320–22
Bonham, Mick, 126, 127
Bonham, Pat, 130, 134, 188, 189, 200, 219,
    237, 351, 422, 429, 513
    John's death and, 558–59
"Bonzo," see Bonham, John
"Boogie with Stu," 254–55, 258, 384
Book of Signs, The (Koch), 246, 266, 267
bootleg recordings, 230, 247–48, 565
"Born to Be Wild," 176
Boston Garden, 336
Boston Phoenix, 9
Boston Tea Party, 3–5, 7–11, 537
Bowie, David, 64, 316
Branson, Richard, 349
Bray Studios, 533, 556–57
Brewer, Don, 253
Bridges, Lloyd, 379
Brilleaux, Lee, 425
"Bring It On Home," 203
Bron-Yr-Aur, 220–23, 231, 248–49, 251, 289,
    311, 358, 566
"Bron-Yr-Aur," 384
"Bron-Yr-Aur Stomp," 226, 237
Brown, Arthur, 286
Brown, Carole, 109, 194–95, 246, 266, 345,
    346, 368, 429, 467, 482
Brown, James, 289, 452
Brown, "Pop," 124
Bruce, Jack, 16
Budokan, 2778
Buell, Bebe, 203, 378, 380, 414
Buffalo Springfield, 125, 154, 155, 168
Buildings of England, The (Pevsner), 117
Burdon, Eric, 16, 102
Burges, William, 345
Burnette, Johnny, 31, 39, 74, 118, 141
Burrell, Boz, 354–55, 537, 563

Burroughs, William S., 176, 406, 410, 430
Burton, James, 32, 36, 381
Butter Queen (Barbara Cope), 488–89
Byblos, 279
Byrds, 125, 168

*Caesars Chariot*, 487, 496, 498, 512, 546
Caesars Palace, 487
Caine, Michael, 545
Callan, Alan, 483, 516, 519, 547
Calmes, Jack, 393–94, 490, 535
Cameron, John, 451–52
"Candy Store Rock," 452
Cantagiro Cantamondo Festival, 275–76
Capaldi, Jim, 122
Capote, Truman, 294, 307
Cardano, Girolamo, 267
Carlo, Phil, 157, 262, 291, 357, 368, 376,
    390, 443, 468–69, 546–47, 549, 551–52,
    555, 561–63, 570, 571
Carnegie Hall, 208–9, 211
"Carouselambra," 520, 522, 526
Carr, James, 124
Carson, Phil, 92, 96, 154, 157, 179, 213–14,
    215, 268, 278, 280, 281, 291, 329, 330,
    332, 341, 347–49, 366, 374, 376, 387,
    391, 408, 409, 482, 488, 495, 504, 505,
    511, 517, 520, 547–48, 551, 564
Carter-Lewis and the Southerners, 54
Cartoone, 207
Cassidy, David, 442
Cattini, Clem, 55, 114, 121
Cavaliere, Felix, 369
CBGB, 383
Chancery Lane Record Centre, 248
Channel Islands, 435–36
Charles, Ray, 43, 107, 120, 136
Charlesworth, Chris, 179, 210, 229, 230,
    275, 401–3, 407, 428
Chas and Dave, 533
Chateau Marmont, 164, 189, 190, 203,
    205, 317
Chess Records, 17, 21, 26, 43, 174, 348
"Chest Fever," 148
Chicken Shack, 122
Chicago, 473
Chicago, Ill., 330–31, 399–400
Chicago Stadium, 330
*Chicago Sun-Times*, 187
*Chicago Tribune*, 170, 330, 396

*Childhood's End* (Clarke), 298
Chislehurst Caves, 387–88
Chkiantz, George, 184
Christgau, Robert, 462
Christian, Neil, 19, 20, 33, 35–40, 43–46,
    48–49, 51, 78, 398
Chrysalis Agency, 97
Churchward, James, 266–67
Cincinnati Pop Festival, 382
*Circus*, 412, 477
Clapton, Eric, 2, 5, 16, 24, 28, 50, 53n,
    68–70, 72–74, 102, 105, 119, 155, 219,
    450, 570
Clark, Dick, 89, 159
Clarke, Allan, 76
Clarke, Arthur C., 298
Clash, 532, 537, 543
Clay, Otis, 124, 331
Clearwell Castle, 519–20
Cliff, Jimmy, 288
Clifton, Peter, 372, 384–85, 464–66,
    475, 476
Cobo Arena, 292
cocaine, 205, 226, 255, 281, 315, 332, 359,
    378, 394, 399–401, 405, 409, 415, 418,
    448, 457, 458–59, 470, 492, 496, 514, 555
    Grant and, 291–92, 331–32, 440–41, 457,
    463–65, 467, 468, 482, 494, 503–7, 515,
    535, 541
Cochran, Eddie, 31, 34, 40, 41, 55, 61, 118,
    253, 381
Cocker, Joe, 105, 114, 134, 223
*Coda*, 564–68
    cover of, 567
    "Walter's Walk," 566
    "Wearing and Tearing," 566–67
    "We're Gonna Groove," 565–66
Cole, Richard ("Ricardo"), 161–62, 168,
    189, 190, 196, 199, 200, 201, 204–8,
    210, 221, 229, 238, 248, 255, 272–74,
    276, 277, 279–81, 294, 314–15, 317, 319,
    321, 328–30, 333–34, 339–41, 344, 346,
    351, 368, 377–78, 390, 391, 398, 400,
    401, 404, 406–7, 413–15, 418, 423, 429,
    447, 462, 464–68, 475, 478, 482, 487,
    488, 491, 493, 496, 497, 504, 506, 512,
    515, 522–23, 525, 533–34, 541, 542,
    546, 555
    arrest and imprisonment of, 555–56, 560
    Bonham's death and, 560

Matzorkis assault and arrest of, 508–11
Plant and, 546
Plants' car accident and, 433–35
Coliseum, 334
Collins, Jeffrey, 248
Collins, Phil, 570, 571
Columbia Records, 156–57, 207, 439
Commander Cody Band, 534
"Communication Breakdown," 1, 145, 175–76, 259
concert promoters, 283–85
Concerts for Kampuchea, 548
Concerts West, 285, 517
Continental Hyatt House, 203–4, 314–21, 402, 414, 415, 418, 423, 439, 477
Cook, Paul, 537
Cooke, Sam, 95
Cooper, Alice, 168
Cope, Barbara, 488–89
Corrigan-Devlin, Gyl, 317, 330, 332
Costello, Elvis, 484, 532
Coulson, Clive, 221–22, 366, 391, 530
Coulson, Sherry, 247
Country Joe & the Fish, 169
Crawdaddy, 235, 304, 406
Crawdaddy Club, 71–72
Crawling King Snakes, 121–23, 125–26
Cream, 6, 59, 82, 84, 86, 99, 105, 108, 133, 153, 154, 159, 161, 181
Creamer, Richard, 320–21
Creation, 58–59, 100
Creem, 6–7, 235, 304, 411, 412, 487
Crosby, Stills, Nash & Young, 255, 570
Crosby, Stills & Nash, 125, 222, 235
Crowe, Cameron, 401, 412, 423
Crowley, Aleister, 244–46, 267, 314, 315, 325–26, 345, 351, 384, 385, 438, 439
Abbey of Thelema, 432
"Crunge, The," 285, 289, 303, 452
Culderstead Ltd., 367–68
Curbishley, Alfie, 391
Curbishley, Bill, 283, 391–92, 515–16
"Custard Pie," 357–58
Cutler, June, 43

Dadaism, 460
Dallas Morning News, 490
Daltrey, Roger, 219
Damned, 485–86, 490, 567
"Dancing Days," 285, 290

Danger, Cal, 96, 213
Daniels, Charlie, 7
Dautrich, Bill, 328
Davies, Cyril, 14, 18, 23, 51, 54, 69, 71, 111, 120
Davies, Dave, 28, 59, 66
Davies, Ray, 59, 102
Davis, Bette, 138
Davis, Clive, 156, 157
Davis, Miles, 297
Davis, Stephen, 462
Day, Ernest, 349
"Day on the Green" festival, 504
"Dazed and Confused," 1, 145, 147, 174–75, 237, 474, 525
Dean, Smoky, 37–38
Dean Aces, 38
Death Wish II, 568
Decca, 473
Dee, Kiki, 121
Deep Purple, 117, 288, 459, 484, 519
Def Leppard, 547
Defries, Tony, 316
De Groot, Keith, 140
Delta Blues Band, 120
Deltas, 136–37
Deltones, 53
Denny, Sandy, 262, 268, 484
Derringer, Rick, 476, 504
DeSapio, Carmine, 540
Des Barres, Michael, 50, 157, 189, 204, 205, 282, 314–16, 341, 438, 438–41, 467, 469, 496, 517
Des Barres, Pamela Miller, 315, 318–19, 439, 440
DeShannon, Jackie, 61–63, 314
Detective, 439–42, 469, 483, 517
Detroit Free Press, 405
"Diamonds," 52, 137
Diddley, Bo, 18, 21, 43, 95, 119
Digby Smith, Richard, 263, 264
Dire Straits, 390, 531, 532
Disc, 113, 140, 235, 303, 309, 313
Dixon, Willie, 21, 174, 177, 183, 566
Dolan, Mike, 121
Dominica, 408, 410
Donahue, 168
Donegan, Lonnie, 27, 118
Donner, Ral, 452
Donovan, 65, 96, 99, 102, 135, 139

Doors, 99, 104, 168, 199–200
"Down by the Seaside," 251, 258, 383–84
Downey, Jim, 505
Drake Hotel, 338, 340–42, 347, 378, 511
Dreja, Chris, 49, 65, 71, 74, 77, 78, 85–88,
    98, 104, 110, 113, 151, 398
Dr. Feelgood, 425, 473
Driscoll, Julie, 192
"Drop Down Mama," 357
drugs, 204–5, 255, 281, 340–42, 368, 414–
    15, 468, 477, 496, 506, 542, 547, 551
  Bonham and, 355, 378, 413, 418, 422,
    447, 459, 493–96, 500–501, 514, 521,
    524–25, 533–34, 542, 550, 551
  cocaine, see cocaine
  heroin, 332, 340, 359, 409, 414, 438, 447,
    448, 469, 493–94, 503, 514, 515, 523,
    534, 546, 550
  Page and, 332, 409, 438, 439, 441–42,
    444, 447–49, 453, 458–59, 478, 491,
    493, 495, 496, 511, 515, 521, 523–25,
    533–34, 542, 550–52, 568
  Plant and, 518
  Presley and, 517
  Quaalude (Mandrax), 355, 359, 365, 418,
    459, 491, 550
Drummond, Norrie, 88
Dudgeon, Gus, 565
Dumont, Margaret, 443
Dunbar, Aynsley, 99, 114, 239, 241, 423, 561
Dunluce Castle, 301
Dury, Ian, 532
"D'Yer Mak'er," 288–89, 303
Dylan, Bob, 15, 186, 231, 305, 364

Eagles, 125
Eaglin, Snooks, 5
Ealing Club, 14–16, 19, 20
Earls Court Arena, 424–28, 529, 542
Eater, 485
Eddy, Duane, 119
Eder, Richard, 477
Edgewater Inn, 199, 333
Edmunds, Dave, 425, 430, 440, 469, 483,
    516–17, 520, 531
Eel Pie Island, 70, 71
Egyptian Museum, 325–26, 385
Electric Lady Studios, 294–95, 474
Elliot, Cass, 76, 114
Ellis, Royston, 45–46, 48

Emerson, Keith, 522
Emerson, Lake & Palmer, 481
EMI, 298, 473
Entwistle, John, 81, 83
Epic Records, 156–57
Epsom Comrades Club, 34–35
Ertegun, Ahmet, 62, 214, 268, 283, 302,
    333, 338, 347–49, 369, 379, 380, 465,
    552, 564–65, 568
  death of, 573
  Led Zeppelin royalties and masters
    ownership deal made by, 515–16
Ertegun, Nesuhi, 62
Estes, Sleepy John, 357
Everly Brothers, 57, 95, 119, 136
Excelsior Hotel, 555

Faces, 207
Fahey, John, 175, 221
Fairport Convention, 117, 131, 173, 179,
    224, 239, 241, 262, 531, 533, 541
Faithfull, Marianne, 61, 63, 68, 385
Falkoner Theatre, 534
Fallon, BP "Beep," 294, 305, 315, 316, 318,
    322, 330, 365–66, 485
Farlowe, Chris, 33, 47, 68, 70, 114, 134
FBI, 340, 341, 540
Fearon, George, 509
Feliciano, José, 192, 392
Ferry, Bryan, 122, 379
Fey, Barry, 165
Fillmore East, 9, 305
Fillmore West, 169–70
Financial Times, 326
Firm, 569
Flack, Roberta, 476
Fleetwood Mac, 123–24, 194, 252
Flock, 229
"Fool in the Rain," 524
Forbes, 574
Forbes, Bryan, 442
Ford, Bill, 126
Forum, 238–39, 247, 252, 284, 293, 314, 320,
    322, 325, 381, 418, 474, 502
"For Your Life," 451
Foster, Perry, 120
Four Seasons, 377–78
"Four Sticks," 250, 253, 254, 261
Frampton, Peter, 108, 420
Franklin, Aretha, 108, 154, 369

Free, 373
Freed, Alan, 27
Freeman, Bob, 349
Free Trade Hall, 18–19
"Fresh Garbage," 169
"Friends," 219, 222, 243
Fuller, Blind Boy, 357
Fuller, Bobby, 188
Fury, Billy, 118
fuzz boxes, 66–67, 187

G, see Grant, Peter
Gallagher, Rory, 272
"Gallis Pole," 233–34
"Gallows Pole," 256, 262
Gallup, Cliff, 426
Gammond, Kevyn, 111, 116, 122, 123, 125,
    131, 183, 288–89
Garrett, Vernon, 124
Gates, Samantha, 300–301, 461
Gates, Stefan, 300–301
Gautier, Benoit, 321, 457
Geffen, David, 348, 466, 483
Geldof, Bob, 569
Genesis, 529
George V Hotel, 457–58
Gerlach, Fred, 233–34
Giant's Causeway, 298–300
Gibbons, Steve, 122, 125
Gilbert, Vanessa, 189, 317, 322, 330, 334,
    340, 365
Gilmour, David, 298
Girls Together Outrageously (GTOs),
    164, 187
Gizmotron, 525, 527
"Glimpses," 101
"Going to California," 256, 442
Goldberg, Danny, 182, 204, 305–7, 309,
    311, 312, 318, 329, 330, 332, 366–67,
    377, 379, 386, 387, 399, 401, 409,
    422–23, 440–42, 461, 470, 483
Golding, Colin, 47
Goldsmith, Harvey, 548
Gomelsky, Giorgio, 68, 71–73, 79
Goodman, Benny, 127
"Good Times, Bad Times," 147, 172, 175
Gotti, John, 555–56
Gouldman, Graham, 74
Graham, Bill, 169, 283, 504–12
Graham, Bobby, 55, 56, 59, 60, 149

Graham, Davy, 221
Grand Funk Railroad, 211
Grant, Gloria, 345–46, 353, 376, 440,
    463–64
  Peter divorced by, 466–67, 481, 482, 515
Grant, Helen, 376, 464
Grant, Peter ("G"), 5, 10, 91–98, 101, 104,
    105, 109–10, 114, 133–34, 140, 190,
    308, 367, 468, 504, 511–13, 515, 516
  Bad Company managed by, 374, 389,
    391–92
  Beck, Bogert & Appice and, 206–7
  Bell and, 207, 292, 369, 377
  Bindon and, 488, 504–6, 540
  cocaine habit of, 291–92, 331–32, 440–41,
    457, 463–65, 467, 468, 482, 494, 503–7,
    515, 535, 541
  death of, 573
  depression of, 563–64
  Des Barres and, 439, 440
  divorce of, 466–67, 481, 482, 515
  heart attacks of, 523, 573
  Horselunges estate of, 345–46, 376, 464,
    467, 515, 523, 528, 547, 548, 563–64
  Iannaci's guest and, 503
  King's Road office of, 346–48, 366–68, 563
  Matzorkis assault and arrest of, 507–8,
    510–11, 515
  New Yardbirds and, 142–44, 146, 151–52
  Stone the Crows and, 207–8, 292
  tax exile and, 419–20, 422, 463
  weight of, 247, 523
Grant, Peter, as Led Zeppelin manager,
    151–62, 167, 171, 172, 178, 179, 181–82,
    193, 197–98, 202–6, 208, 210–14, 217,
    218, 228–32, 247, 262, 270–72, 275–76,
    279, 282, 291, 306, 312, 313, 319, 322,
    326, 328–35, 338, 357, 379, 380, 381,
    393, 398, 400–405, 414, 415, 429, 436,
    437, 443, 447, 457, 463, 480–83, 488,
    494, 496–99, 510, 517, 528, 542, 546,
    548, 550, 552, 564–65
  Atkin and, 540–41
  Bonham and, 238, 241–42
  Bonham's death and, 558–61, 563
  bootlegs and, 230, 247–48
  cameras and, 211
  and cover of fourth album, 268
  and cover of Houses of the Holy, 298, 299,
    301, 302

Grant, Peter, as Led Zeppelin
    manager, (cont.)
  Drake Hotel robbery and, 341–42, 347,
    378, 511
  and European tour of 1980, 547
  Graham and, 506–10
  In Through the Out Door covers and,
    530–31
  and Jones's break from the band, 353, 355
  Knebworth Festival and, 531, 535, 539–41
  limo incident and, 403–5
  poster seller and, 336–37
  Presence and, 460–63
  promoters and, 283–85, 475
  royalties, masters ownership, and music
    publishing deals made by, 515–16
  The Song Remains the Same and, 335–37,
    351, 352, 372, 464–66, 475, 479
  Swan Song and, 366–68, 375–76, 385–87,
    389, 390, 430, 440, 469, 470, 483,
    518–19, 547–48
  U.S. tour in 1975 planned by, 425, 431, 434
  U.S. tour in 1980 planned by, 547, 554–56
Grant, Warren, 376, 464, 482, 505, 507, 511
Greece, 431–34
Green, Mick, 39
Green, Peter, 70, 207
Greenberg, Jerry, 153, 167, 212–13, 282, 511
Greensboro Daily News, 403
Griffin, Dale "Buffin," 459
Grossman, Albert, 305
groupies and other young girls, 161, 187,
    189–90, 199–201, 204–6, 245, 314–20,
    333–34, 339, 363, 377, 402, 414, 415,
    418, 439, 477, 478, 502
  Barbara "the Butter Queen" Cope, 489
  GTOs, 164, 187
  Lori Mattix, 316–20, 329, 377, 378, 380,
    414, 439, 477, 502–3
  mud shark incident with, 200–201, 333
  Sable Starr, 316, 318–20, 439
GTOs, 164, 187
Guardian, 115
Guitar World, 150
Guthrie, Woody, 234
Guy, Buddy, 21, 119, 120, 121, 197

Hair, 186
Hale, Norman, 455, 456
Hale, Philip Churchill, 544–45

Hall and Oates, 570
Hardie, George, 171
Harper, Roy, 230, 330, 338, 348, 375
Harris, Bob, 426
Harris, Jet, 137
Harris, Richard, 345
Harris, Shaky Jake, 21–23
Harris, Wee Willie, 276
Harrison, Billy, 60
Harrison, George, 28, 74, 177–78, 287,
    322, 335
Harry, Bill, 193, 294
Harvey, Leslie, 207, 292, 497
Harwood, Keith, 384, 445, 448, 453
Hawkins, Screamin' Jay, 42–43, 96
Headley Grange, 232–33, 251–61, 263, 265,
    286, 291, 295, 352–56, 358–60, 365–66,
    383, 385–86
Headon, Topper, 537
Healey, Denis, 427
Heart, 191, 389
"Heartbreaker," 203, 237
heavy metal, 176, 185, 547, 567
Hell, Richard, 383
Hendrix, Jimi, 8, 67, 82, 102–3, 154, 181,
    206, 283, 286
Henson, Jim, 367
Hepworth, David, 539
Herman's Hermits, 65, 96, 99, 139, 158,
    160, 181, 367, 386
heroin, 332, 340, 359, 409, 414, 438, 447,
    448, 469, 493–94, 503, 514, 515, 523,
    534, 546, 550
Heron, Mike, 226
Hiatt, John, 569
Hilburn, Robert, 293, 417, 490, 494
Hill, Henry, 158–59
Hillman, Chris, 315
Hindenburg, 171
Hinton, Mick, 276, 277, 321, 397, 429, 471,
    504, 514, 551, 557
Hipgnosis, 297–301, 460–62, 473, 529, 532
Hiroshima, 279
Hobbs, Rick, 552, 557–58
Hoch, Abe, 386–87, 389–90, 403, 408, 410,
    429–30, 437, 438, 440, 442–43, 447, 448,
    457–58, 461, 468, 470, 471, 483, 516, 519
  Presence master tapes and, 454–55
Hodge, John Rowland, 468
Hodge, Vicki, 468, 496

Hoffman, Jeff, 341–42, 347, 433–34, 478, 511, 555–56
Holder, Noddy, 122
Hollies, 57, 63, 75, 76, 108, 181
Holloway Prison, 45
Holly, Buddy, 32, 41
Holmes, Jake, 145, 174
*Honeydrippers: Volume One, The*, 568
Hooker, Earl, 273
Hooker, John Lee, 20–22, 72, 96, 120
Hopkins, Lightnin', 119
Hopkins, Nicky, 70, 81, 83, 99, 140
Hotel Bel-Air, 379
"Hots On for Nowhere," 452, 462
House, Son, 5
Housego, Dave, 29
Houston Wells & the Marksmen, 213
*Houses of the Holy*, 302–3, 366, 373, 383, 384, 566
   cover of, 297–302, 461
   "The Crunge," 285, 289, 303, 452
   "Dancing Days," 285, 290
   "D'Yer Mak'er," 288–89, 303
   inside photograph of, 301
   "Over the Hills and Far Away," 285, 290, 303
   "The Rain Song," 287–88, 303
   release of, 302
   reviews of, 303, 307, 427–28
   "The Song Remains the Same," 286–87, 303
   Stargroves and, 286, 288, 290, 294–95
   writing and recording of, 285–91, 295
"Houses of the Holy," 384
*Houston Chronicle*, 412
Howlin' Wolf, 19, 21, 24, 112, 120, 145, 177, 188
"How Many More Times," 145, 176, 177
Hudson, Joan, 390, 420, 465, 516, 540
Hughes, Glenn, 117, 137, 419, 556
Humble Pie, 3, 108
Hunter, Ian, 368
Huston, Chris, 189
Hyatt House, 203–4, 314–21, 402, 414, 415, 418, 423, 439, 477
Hyde, John, 439
Hynde, Chrissie, 537

Iannaci, Betty, 440, 442, 445, 502–3
IBC Studios, 51, 58, 80, 81, 111, 131

"I Can't Explain," 59
"I Can't Quit You Baby," 177, 331
"I Feel Fine," 188
Ilsington Farmhouse, 286
"I'm Gonna Crawl," 524
Immediate Records, 68, 69, 73, 91, 138
"Immigrant Song," 219, 226–27, 230, 243, 259
Incredible String Band, 226
Ingham, Jonh, 462
"In My Time of Dying," 363–65
"In the Evening," 525
"In the Light," 361
*In Through the Out Door*, 529, 533, 546, 556, 566
   "All My Love," 522, 524, 525
   "Carouselambra," 520, 522, 526
   covers and packaging of, 529–31, 535, 543
   "Fool in the Rain," 524
   "I'm Gonna Crawl," 524
   "In the Evening," 525
   in record charts, 544
   release of, 531, 535, 543
   reviews of, 543–44
   sales of, 544
   "South Bound Suarez," 524
   writing and recording of, 521–27
Iommi, Tony, 129, 194, 551, 560
Ireland, 272–73, 420
   Giant's Causeway in, 298–300
   Troubles in, 272–73, 300
Iron Butterfly, 154, 160
   *In-A-Gadda-Da-Vida*, 186
Iron Maiden, 176, 547
Island Records, 97, 152, 156, 368
Island Studios, 234, 250–51, 261
Italy, 275–77
Itkin, Herbert (Herb Atkin), 540–41, 555
Ivey, Marie, 367
Ivil, Annie, 378

Jackson, J. J., 6, 537
Jagger, Mick, 11, 15–23, 119, 177, 294, 315, 453, 476, 570
   Stargroves estate of, 231–32, 286, 288, 290, 294–95, 358
Jam, 532, 539
Jamerson, James, 137
James, Brian, 485–86
James, Catherine, 190, 315

James, Elmore, 15, 20
James, Harry, 127
James, Skip, 5
Jammer, Joe, 399
Jansch, Bert, 148, 175, 221
Japan, 277–81
Jefferson Airplane, 99, 103–4
Jeffery, Mike, 96
Jersey, 435–36, 454, 455
Jet Blacks, 137–38, 140
Jethro Tull, 3, 97, 117
Joel, Billy, 473
John, Elton, 57, 442–43, 461, 473
Johnny Kidd & the Pirates, 39
Johns, Andy, 202, 224, 231–33, 251, 255,
    257, 262, 264, 286, 358
Johns, Glyn, 51–52, 56, 58, 83, 143–44,
    148–50, 152, 171–72, 177–78, 184, 210,
    223–24, 233, 254, 255
Johns, Glynis, 210
Johnson, Blind Willie, 210, 363–64, 444
Johnson, Robert, 5–6, 112, 119
Johnson, Wilko, 425
Jo Jo Gunne, 320
Jones, Brian, 15–23, 53, 102, 119
Jones, John Paul
    as arranger, 65, 135, 138–39, 569
    as bass player, 65, 136–37, 143–44, 173,
        174, 187
    Bonham's death and, 563
    disenchantment and break from Led
        Zeppelin, 353–55
    in formation of New Yardbirds/Led
        Zeppelin, 113–14, 134, 140–42
    as keyboard player, 135, 136, 172, 225
    in Live Aid, 569, 570
    name of, 55, 135, 138
    parents of, 135–36
    post-Led Zeppelin career of, 568–73
    pre-Led Zeppelin career of, 6, 55, 65,
        81, 135–40
    as session musician, 6, 138–40, 153,
        383, 569
    unnoticeability of, 562
    Yamaha synthesizer of, 522–25
Jones (Baldwin), Maureen "Mo," 140, 164,
    189, 429
Jones, Mick, 537
Jones, Paul, 16
Jones, Steve, 537

Joplin, Janis, 240–41, 305
Judas Priest, 504, 547
Juggy Sound, 203

Kane, Eden, 45
"Kashmir," 356–57, 411
Katz, Charlie, 57
Kaye, Shelley, 340, 470, 516, 550, 556,
    563, 564
"Keep Moving," 62
Kelly, Jack, 413
Kenner, Chris, 118
Kennington Oval, 270–71
Kent, Nick, 210, 401, 419, 423, 479
Kent State University, 218
Kidderminster, 117–19, 121–22, 562
"Killing Floor," 188
King, B.B., 532
King, Ben E., 289, 566
King, Freddie, 72, 87
King, Rex, 487, 562
Kinks, 2, 59, 62, 122, 154, 181, 473
Kirke, Simon, 368, 373, 561
Kiss, 547
Knebworth Festival, 529, 531–43,
    545–46, 567
Knight, Ian, 307, 388
Knight, Terry, 211
Koch, Rudolf, 246, 266, 267
Korner, Alexis, 14, 15, 18, 23, 120, 381
Kramer, Eddie, 206, 286, 289, 290, 294–95
Kray, Ronnie and Reggie, 93, 143, 467
Krupa, Gene, 127, 209

Ladbrooke Sound, 149
Laine, Denny, 102, 123, 128, 560
Lane, Ronnie, 183, 352
LaVern, Roger, 118
Law, Don, 3, 5, 6, 9, 284–85
Law, Don, Sr., 5
Leadbelly, 27, 233–34
Leander, Mike, 54
Led Zeppelin
    Atlantic contract of, 155, 162, 179, 297,
        343, 347
    Back to the Clubs tour of, 271–75,
        474, 529
    at Bath Festival, 227–30
    Behan's West Park show of, 455–57
    bootleg recordings of, 230, 247–48, 565

Boston Tea Party shows of, 3–5, 7–11, 537

at Carnegie Hall, 208–9, 211

concert promoters and, 283–85

Earls Court shows of, 424–28, 529, 542

end of, 560–62

European tours of, 214–15, 275–77, 545–53

on festival circuit, 195–96, 206

film of, see Song Remains the Same, The

formation of, 105–6, 107–15, 132, 133–35, 140–42, 156; see also New Yardbirds

godlike status of, 198–99, 282

hotel provisions for, 326–27

hotel theft and, 340–42, 378

improvisational jams of, 167, 169, 177, 290, 416

income of, 283, 326, 419, 515–16

at Knebworth Festival, 529, 531–43, 545–46, 567

last show of, 553

last U.S. show of, 510

loudness of, 166, 187, 230

Madison Square Garden shows of, 242, 337–39, 349, 474, 500–502

manager of, see Grant, Peter, as Led Zeppelin manager

Marshall stacks employed by, 166, 187, 188

money viewed as motivation of, 179, 228, 270, 271

name of, 1, 84, 152, 373

O2 Arena show of, with Bonham's son on drums, 573–75

as Page's band, 262, 409, 562

press shunned and distrusted by, 193, 208, 294, 306, 427–28, 479, 488

radio play of, 1, 67–68, 181–82, 186, 212–14, 268, 282, 411

record label of, see Swan Song Records

reviews of shows of, 170, 192, 194, 293, 311–13, 333, 396, 398, 405–8, 412, 416–18, 427, 428, 494, 495, 502, 506, 538–39, 574

Rolling Stones as compared with, 293–94, 304, 307, 379, 410

royalties, masters ownership, and music rights and, 515–16

security concerns for, 328

singles eschewed by, 212–14, 282, 296

stage production for, 307–8, 311–13, 333, 393–94, 425, 534, 549, 557

Starship plane of, 329–30, 332, 337, 399–402, 405, 408, 415, 480, 487

Tampa Stadium show of, 497–99, 500, 501

tax exile of, 419–20, 422, 425, 427–31, 434–37, 441, 445, 451, 463

UK tours of, 193–95, 270–75

U.S. and Canada tours of, 160–63, 164–70, 172, 186–87, 191–92, 195–206, 208–9, 217–19, 228, 229, 231, 236–42, 270, 271, 275, 277–78, 285, 291–94, 307–14, 324, 326, 328–43, 395–99, 402–8, 410, 412–18, 480, 483–84, 386–99, 500–513

U.S. tour in 1975 planned by, 425, 431, 434

U.S. tour in 1980 planned by, 547, 554–56

violence at shows of, 218, 403, 405–8, 492–93, 498, 501

Led Zeppelin, 170–82

"Babe, I'm Gonna Leave You," 1, 9, 112, 113, 145, 173

"Communication Breakdown," 1, 145, 175–76, 259

cover of, 171

"Dazed and Confused," 1, 145, 147, 174–75, 237, 474, 525

production credit on, 171–72, 174

radio play of, 1, 67–68

in record charts, 170, 182, 186

recording of, 143–44, 147–51, 172–74, 446

release of, 3, 160, 170, 172

reviews of, 180–82

sales of, 179–80

test pressings of, 165, 167, 177–78

Truth and, 178, 180

Led Zeppelin II, 184, 215, 224, 235, 286, 566

band's wish that no singles be issued from, 212–14

cover of, 209–10

"The Lemon Song," 188, 361, 383

"Moby Dick," 43, 188–89, 203, 209, 237, 474, 484, 495

in record charts, 214

release of, 208, 209

reviews of, 210

sales of, 209, 214

*Led Zeppelin II* (cont.)
  "Whole Lotta Love," 183–85, 212–14,
    236, 282, 304, 333, 349, 358, 372
  writing and recording of, 184–85,
    188–89, 202–3, 206
*Led Zeppelin III*, 234–36, 243–44, 247, 566
  acoustic stylings of, 221, 224, 234, 237, 290
  Bron-Yr-Aur and, 220–23, 231
  cover and inner sleeve of, 234
  "Friends," 219, 222, 243
  Headley Grange and, 232–33, 251
  "Immigrant Song," 219, 226–27, 230,
    243, 259
  "Out on the Tiles," 233, 243
  in record charts, 243
  release of, 234
  reviews of, 235, 243
  Rolling Stones' mobile recording studio
    and, 231, 233
  sales of, 235, 243
  "Since I've Been Loving You," 219,
    224–26, 237, 244, 450
  "Tangerine," 219, 244
  writing and recording of, 222–27, 231–34
*Led Zeppelin IV*, 296, 297, 302, 303
  "The Battle of Evermore," 256, 262,
    303, 484
  "Black Dog," 252–53, 261
  cover and lack of title of, 246, 264–66,
    268, 297
  "Four Sticks," 250, 253, 254, 261
  "Going to California," 256, 442
  Headley Grange and, 251–61, 263, 265
  inside illustration of, 266
  "Misty Mountain Hop," 257
  mixing of, 271, 275
  naming of ⚝ ⚕ ⊕ ①, 266
  in record charts, 282
  release of, 268, 271
  reviews of, 282
  "Rock and Roll," 254
  sales of, 282
  "Stairway to Heaven," *see* "Stairway to
    Heaven"
  symbols on, 266–68
  "When the Levee Breaks," 257, 258,
    261, 358
  writing and recording of, 248–64, 286, 384
*Led Zeppelin Live on Blueberry Hill*, 247–48
Lee, Albert, 49, 68, 70, 140

Lee, Alvin, 196
Le Fevre, Benji, 205, 308, 321, 331, 332, 355,
    359, 388, 390, 410, 415, 417, 425, 433,
    435–38, 443, 448, 458–59, 466, 480,
    481, 488, 494, 496–98, 513, 518, 519,
    523–24, 551, 557–58, 563
  Bonham's death and, 558, 560, 562
"Lemon Song, The," 188, 361, 383
Lennon, John, 50, 188, 249, 270, 483
Lennon, Sean, 483
*Let It Be*, 177
*Let It Rock*, 303, 411
Lewis, Barbara, 62
Lewis, Jerry Lee, 39–41, 107, 136, 137, 358
Lewis, Ken, 54
Lewis, Red E., 20, 35–38
*Life*, 186, 201, 306
Lindisfarne, 391
Lisberg, Harvey, 386
*Listen*, 121
Little Feat, 531, 532
*Little Games*, 101
Little Richard, 31, 95, 119, 136, 137, 253
Little Walter, 21
Live Aid, 569–71, 573
"Livin' Lovin' Maid (She's a Woman)," 202
Lockey, Paul, 131
Loggins & Messina, 125
London, Laurie, 426
London, Mark, 329, 346, 366, 368, 564
Long Beach, Calif., 415–17, 474
*Long Beach Independent*, 417
*Lord of the Rings, The* (Tolkien), 256
*Los Angeles Times*, 192, 293, 417, 490, 494
*Lost Continent of Mu, The* (Churchward),
    266–67
Love, 124–25
Lucas, Frank, 342
*Lucifer Rising*, 384–85, 471
Lulu, 139
Lydon, John, 486
Lynne, Jeff, 560
Lynyrd Skynyrd, 529

MacGregor, Sandy, 221, 248
MacLean, Bruce, 559–60
MacLean, Unity, 389, 390, 429, 430, 440,
    463–64, 467–70, 479, 481, 516, 523,
    535–36, 544, 547
  Bonham's death and, 559–60

Maddox, Lori, see Mattix, Lori
Madison Square Garden, 242, 337–39, 349, 474, 500–502
Magic Arts in Celtic Britain, The (Spence), 259, 260
Magick in Theory and Practice (Crowley), 244, 245
Malibu Colony, 437
M&Bs, 122–23
Mandich, Tony, 284, 412
Mandrax, see Quaalude
Manfred Mann, 16, 99
Mannheim Hof, 552
Manson Family, 203, 218, 384, 443
Manticore Studios, 481, 486
Marcus, Danny, 327–28, 331, 411, 413, 414, 418, 492, 496
Marcus, Greil, 210
Margaret, Princess, 467–68
Maria, Nick, 268, 535
Marquee Club, 16, 18, 20, 51, 54, 65, 69, 70, 78, 151, 160, 275
Marrakesh, 429, 430
Marriott, Steve, 50, 83, 108, 183, 419, 469
Marsh, Dave, 477
Marshall, Jim, 166
Marshall amplifiers, 166, 187, 188
Marshall Tucker Band, 533, 534
Martell, Vinny, 199
Martin, Charlotte, 219, 221, 222, 246, 275, 315, 320, 325, 335, 430, 432–34, 481, 515
Martinez, Paul, 569
Marvin, Hank, 34, 57
Marx, Groucho, 380, 442–43
Mases, Leif, 521
Mason, Dave, 122
Massell, Sam, 312
Massot, Joe, 335–36, 349–52, 371–72
Matlock, Glen, 485
Mattacks, Dave, 239
Matthews' Southern Comfort, 224
Mattix, Lori, 316–20, 329, 377, 378, 380, 414, 439, 477, 502–3
Matzorkis, Jim, 505, 507–9
Max's Kansas City, 305
May, Phil, 50, 375, 386, 431
Mayall, John, 18, 68, 69, 102, 114
May Ball, 75–77
Mayer, Mike, 268
Mayer, Roger, 66–67, 187

McCallum, David, Sr., 100
McCartney, Linda, 479
McCartney, Paul, 83, 102, 249, 479
McCarty, Jim, 18, 70–71, 73, 75–79, 86–89, 91, 97, 98, 100, 101, 103, 104, 145, 161, 174, 245
McConnell, Andy, 423
McCoy, Joe, 257
McCullough, Jimmy, 208
McGhee, Brownie, 357
McLaughlin, John, 137, 161
Meehan, Tony, 137
Meek, Joe, 119
Melody Maker, 140, 179, 193, 208, 210, 224, 229, 230, 235, 247, 270, 274, 303, 307, 401, 411, 427, 462, 463, 480, 531, 534, 539, 543–44
gala hosted by, 544
Memphis Minnie, 257
Mendelssohn, John, 180–81, 192, 210, 307
Mercer Arts Center, 383
Mercury, Freddie, 570
Mersey Beat, 193
Metallica, 176
Michaels, Lee, 225
Midlands, 115–17, 122, 123, 560
Birmingham, 116–17, 122, 127
Bonham as from, 6, 115, 116, 148
Kidderminster, 117–19, 121–22, 562
Plant as from, 6, 115–19, 125, 148
Midwich Cuckoos, The (Wyndham), 299–300
Miller, Chris (Rat Scabies), 486
Miller, Jim, 411
Miller (later Des Barres), Pamela, 315, 318–19, 439, 440
Miller, Steve, 223
Mimms, Garnet, 145
Mirabai, 470
Mirror Sound, 203
"Misty Mountain Hop," 257
Moohan, Tony, 51–52
Mitchell, Joni, 125, 224, 256, 442, 531
Mitchell, Mitch, 50, 102
Miyako Hotel, 506, 508, 510
mob, 158–59, 540, 555–56
"Moby Dick," 43, 188–89, 203, 209, 237, 474, 484, 495
Moby Grape, 124, 225
"Mockingbird," 169
Monarch, Michael, 439

Montreal Forum, 292
Moody Blues, 116, 122–23, 181, 288
Moon, Keith, 81–84, 99, 152, 171, 418, 503
Morel, Willow, 232
Morgan Studios, 202
Morocco, 410, 429–31
Moroder, Giorgio, 447
Morrison, Jim, 199–200, 240, 315
Morrison, Van, 60, 154, 529, 531, 532
Moseley, Roy, 138
Most, Chris, 65, 142–43, 464
Most, Mickie, 64–65, 91, 93–94, 96–101,
    108, 109, 119, 139, 142–43, 174, 213,
    248, 284, 336, 346, 464
Mothers of Invention, 270
Mötley Crüe, 176
Motown, 137, 138
Mott the Hoople, 368, 373, 459
Moulder, Dave, 549
Move, 116, 134
Muni, Scott, 1, 338
Munich, 445, 446–48, 453–54
Muppets, 367
Murfet, Don, 467, 487, 544–45, 558
Murray, Charles Shaar, 428
Musicland Studios, 446–53
*Music World*, 303
Mystic Sound, 188

Napier-Bell, Simon, 79–80, 82, 85, 89, 91, 97
NASA, 540
Nash, Graham, 57, 63, 76, 108
Nashville Teens, 96
Nassau Coliseum, 292, 293
Neil Christian & the Crusaders, 19, 20, 33,
    38–40, 43–46, 48–49, 51, 78
Nelson, Mac, 211
Nelson, Ricky, 32, 53
"Never," 225
Nevison, Ron, 352, 354, 358–60, 364–65, 384
New Barbarians, 541–42
New Hormones, 473
Newman, Tony, 196
*New Musical Express, see* NME
New Orleans, La., 408, 451, 511–12, 530
*Newsday,* 407
new wave, 484, 485, 531
New Yardbirds, 3, 5, 10, 170, 214, 272, 549
    cease and desist order for name of,
        151–52

formation of, 105–6, 107–15, 132,
    133–35, 140–42
Grant and, 142–44, 146, 151–52
Most and, 142–43
renamed Led Zeppelin, 152
Scandinavian tour of, 133–35, 143–47,
    151–52
UK tour of, 151
New York, N.Y., 458–59, 500–502
    Madison Square Garden, 242, 337–39,
        349, 474, 500–502
*New York Daily News,* 309, 477
New York Dolls, 382, 473
*New Yorker,* 574
*New York Post,* 341, 342
*New York Times,* 378, 407, 477, 502, 540, 574
Nico, 68, 297
Nieve, Steve, 537
"Night Flight," 258, 384
Night Timers, 161
Nilsson, Harry, 99
Nitzsche, Jack, 138
*NME (New Musical Express),* 88, 193, 194,
    210, 235, 303, 388–89, 401, 411, 428,
    463, 479, 482, 532–34, 538, 539,
    567–68, 574
"Nobody's Fault But Mine," 448
Nobs, 215
Nobs, Claude, 215, 420–21, 430
"No Place to Go," 177
"No Quarter," 252, 295, 303, 308
Northover, Dave, 414, 419, 458–59, 467,
    488, 523
Nuremberg, 550–551
Nureyev, Rudolf, 458

O2 Arena, 573–75
Oakland Coliseum, 504–7, 509–10
*Oakland Tribune,* 504
Oats, Bobby, 35
Oats, Bruce, 122
Obs-Tweedle, 110, 134, 145
"Ocean, The," 285, 290, 308
Ogden Security, 328
Oldham, Andrew Loog, 68, 138, 473
Old Mill House, 557
Olympia Stadium, 211
Olympic Sound Studios, 57, 98, 140,
    147–49, 173, 177–78, 184, 203, 223, 271,
    291, 383, 392, 566

101ers, 473
Ordo Templi Orientis (O.T.O.), 385
Organisation Unlimited, 232
O'Rourke, Steve, 496
Osaka, 279–80
Osbourne, Ozzy, 194
Ostin, Mo, 152–53, 155
"Out on the Tiles," 233, 243
"Over the Hills and Far Away," 285,
    290, 303

Paar, Jack, 158
Page, James, Sr., 24–25, 28, 36–37, 536
Page, Jimmy
    Anger and, 384–85, 471
    in art college, 49–52
    banjo played by, 234, 256
    Bonham's death and, 559, 561, 562
    bookshop opened by, 345
    childhood of, 24–27
    clothing of, 145–46, 309, 397–98, 490,
        548–49
    Crowley as influence on, 244–46, 314,
        315, 325–26, 345, 384–85, 438, 439
    Crowley's Abbey of Thelema and, 432
    double-necked guitar played by, 273,
        417, 495
    dragon suit of, 397, 398
    drug use of, 332, 409, 438, 439, 441–42,
        444, 447–49, 453, 458–59, 478, 491,
        493, 495, 496, 511, 515, 521, 523–25,
        533–34, 542, 550–52, 568
    echo and backward effects employed by,
        174, 185, 308–9
    finger sprained by, 395–98, 406
    in the Firm, 569
    formation of New Yardbirds/Led
        Zeppelin) by, 105–6, 107–15, 132,
        133–35, 140–42, 156
    fuzz box used by, 66–67
    gastroenteritis bout of, 491
    Gizmotron used by, 525, 527
    guitars of, 27–29, 33–34, 38, 40, 66, 169,
        185, 217, 273, 426
    guitar solos of, 167, 177, 187, 189, 285,
        407, 416, 417, 494, 502, 539, 545
    Hale's death at home of, 544–45
    interviews of, 294
    as leader of Led Zeppelin, 262, 409, 562
    in Live Aid, 569–71

    as loner, 409
    mandolin played by, 255–56
    mononucleosis of, 48–49
    music reading and, 52, 55
    in Neil Christian & the Crusaders, 19,
        20, 38–40, 43–46, 48–49, 51, 78
    occult interests of, 244–46, 325–26, 345,
        384–85, 409, 439
    parents' divorce and animosity and, 536
    pedal steel played by, 226
    penny-pinching of, 232
    Plant's partnership with, 249, 360, 408–
        10, 438, 445
    Plumpton Place manor of, 246, 286, 325,
        344, 355, 439, 544–45
    post-Led Zeppelin career of, 568–73
    as producer, 47–48, 68–70, 77, 139,
        171–72, 174
    in Red E. Lewis & the Red Caps, 20,
        35–38
    relationships of, see Buell, Bebe;
        DeShannon, Jackie; James, Catherine;
        Martin, Charlotte; Mattix, Lori;
        Miller, Pamela
    security concerns for, 328
    as session musician, 2, 6, 51–52, 54–60,
        64, 67–68, 77, 104–5, 137, 139–40, 383
    sexual proclivities of, 245, 314, 315, 409
    skiffle group of, 29–30
    sound explorations of, 47, 66–67, 69, 70,
        100, 101, 174, 175, 185, 411
    stage presence of, 191
    Stele of Revelation and, 325–26, 385
    theremin played by, 185, 417
    Tower House home of, 344–45
    violin bow used by, 8, 9, 100, 145, 175
    in Yardbirds, 2, 5, 24, 73, 77–80, 85–90,
        97–101, 103, 104, 175–76, 178, 219–20,
        226, 398
Page, Patricia, 24–27, 29, 36, 535–36
Page, Scarlet, 275, 315, 320, 325, 430,
    432, 515
Palmer, Carl, 561
Pappalardi, Felix, 369
Paramor, Norrie, 51
Paramounts, 35
Paris, 457–58
Parker, Bobby, 43, 188
Parker, Colonel Tom, 512, 517
Parnes, Larry, 118

Patton, Charley, 119, 364
Paul Butterfield Blues Band, 197
Pegg, Dave, 117, 120, 125, 126, 130–32, 179, 239–41
Pentangle, 173
Perry, Joe, 11
Petagno, Joe, 373
Petty, Tom, 529, 570
Pevsner, Nikolaus, 117
Phillips, Eddie, 58, 100
Phillips, Esther, 63
*Phonograph Record*, 303, 389
*Physical Graffiti*, 383–84, 392
    cover of, 392
    "Custard Pie," 357–58
    Headley Grange and, 352–56, 358–60, 365–66, 383
    "In My Time of Dying," 363–65
    "In the Light," 361
    "Kashmir," 356–57, 411
    release of, 410–11, 419
    reviews of, 411
    "The Rover," 358, 383
    sales of, 411, 419
    "Sick Again," 363
    "Ten Years Gone," 360–61, 484
    "Trampled Under Foot," 361–62, 411
    "The Wanton Song," 362–63
    writing and recording of, 352–66
Pickett, Kenny, 58
Pickett, Wilson, 154
*Pictures at Eleven*, 567, 568
Pink Floyd, 181, 230, 288, 296, 298, 325, 460, 529, 543, 572
Plant, Carmen, 219, 221, 429, 430, 432, 512
Plant, Karac, 291, 429, 430, 432–33
    death of, 511–14, 518, 521, 525
Plant, Logan, 528
Plant, Maureen, 189, 200, 221, 291, 429, 430, 480, 511, 512, 528
    car accident of, 423–36, 444
    marriage to Robert, 144, 162
Plant, Robert
    Bonham's death and, 558–59, 561, 562, 568
    car accident in 1970, 435
    car accident in 1975 and recovery, 432–38, 444, 445, 447–50, 456, 457, 471, 480, 512
    clothing of, 146, 309, 334, 396, 397

Cole and, 546
drugs and, 518
farms of, 219, 325
flu contracted by, 396, 398
in formation of New Yardbirds/Led Zeppelin, 110–13, 132, 134, 141–42
*The Honeydrippers: Volume One*, 568
in Live Aid, 569–71
Manson Family incident and, 443
marriage of, 144, 162
Midlands background of, 6, 115–19, 125, 148
Page's partnership with, 249, 360, 408–10, 438, 445
parents of, 118–19, 123, 220, 307
*Pictures at Eleven*, 567, 568
post-Led Zeppelin career of, 568–73
pre-Led Zeppelin career of, 109–11, 120–26, 131–32, 145, 177, 183
*The Principle of Moments* tour of, 569
singing of, 111, 120, 121, 124, 146, 150, 173, 176, 185, 187, 225–26, 289, 308, 332, 355, 358, 406, 408, 411, 480, 487, 507, 538, 571, 573, 574
son's death and, 511–14, 518, 521, 525
stage presence of, 191
temperament of, 409–10, 435, 526
tensions between Bonham and, 273–74, 278
unannounced public appearances of, 520
and U.S. tour plans in 1980, 545–47, 554–55
vocal cord operation of, 355, 358
*Playboy*, 337
Plaza Hotel, 501
Poco, 125, 224
Polar Studios, 521–23
Police, 484, 543, 572
Polydor Records, 156
Polygram, 152, 473
Pontiac Silverdome, 493
Poole, Mac, 117
Pop, Iggy, 316, 338, 382, 414
Pop Proms, 194, 565
Powell, Aubrey ("Po"), 297–302, 325–26, 373–74, 376, 385, 459–62, 495–97, 501, 529–31, 563, 567
Powell, Cozy, 241, 537
Power, 207
Premier Talent Agency, 159, 283–85

Presley, Elvis, 27, 31, 41, 118, 320, 354, 512, 517, 552
  death of, 517
  Led Zeppelin's meeting of, 381–82
Pretenders, 537
Pretty Things, 298, 373–75, 385–89, 423, 440, 469, 483, 517, 531
Proby, P.J., 63, 144
Procol Harum, 223
progressive rock, 137, 567
Promenade Concerts, 194, 565
promoters, 283–85
*Presence*, 484, 526, 556
  "Achilles Last Stand," 447–50
  "Candy Store Rock," 452
  cover of, 459–62
  "For Your Life," 451
  "Hots On for Nowhere," 452, 462
  master tapes of, 454–55
  "Nobody's Fault But Mine," 448
  release of, 461, 462
  reviews of, 462–63
  "Royal Orleans," 451–52
  sales of, 462, 470–71
  "Tea for One," 450–51
  title of, 461
  writing and recording of, 438, 443–45, 446–53
Preston, Neal, 404, 540
pub circuit, 472–73
punk, 382–83, 473–74, 484–86, 490, 531, 549, 566, 567
Pye Records, 152

Q, 235
Quaalude (Mandrax), 355, 359, 365, 418, 459, 491, 550
Queen, 386, 570
Queen's Head Football Club, 518
Queen's Head pub, 513, 529, 562

Rachman, Peter, 94–95
Radio City Music Hall, 459
*Radio Show, The*, 426
*Raiders of the Lost Ark*, 300
Rainbow Grill, 402–3, 422, 424, 502
"Rain Song, The," 287–88, 303
RAK, 96, 97, 108, 109, 142–43, 152, 156, 215, 248, 298
Ralphs, Mick, 368, 373, 418, 495, 537

"Ramble On," 203
R&B, 24, 26, 43, 44, 62, 66, 70, 72, 119, 121, 124, 154, 155, 256
R&B All-Stars, 18
R&D Studios, 203
Rascals, 153–55, 158, 169
Rattles, 119
RCA, 483
*Record Mirror*, 62, 427, 543
Redding, Noel, 102
Redding, Otis, 315
Red E. Lewis & the Red Caps, 20, 35–38
Reed, Jimmy, 23, 24, 33, 46, 96, 120, 500
Regan, Mary "Ma," 122–23
reggae, 288–89
Reid, Terry, 102–3, 108–11, 132, 140, 156, 161–62, 166, 472
Relf, Keith, 71, 75–78, 80, 81, 103, 104
Reykjavik, 227
Rhein-Main Air Base, 552
Rhodes, Greece, 431–34
Ricardo, *see* Cole, Richard
Rich, Buddy, 127, 209, 381
Richard, Cliff, 34, 45, 57, 93, 137
Richards, Keith, 15, 17, 19, 20, 22, 23, 28, 50, 108, 119, 149, 255, 294, 420, 500, 515
  in New Barbarians, 541–42
Riverfront Coliseum, 493
Riviera, Jake, 425, 469, 516
"Road to Love, The," 51
Roberts, Elliot, 348
Robinson, Jimmy, 469
Robinson, Lisa, 309, 312, 313, 327, 378, 534, 561
Robinson, Pete "Plug," 125
Robinson, Smokey, 119
Rockfield Studios, 424–25
rock 'n roll, 24, 26, 30–31, 41, 58–61, 63, 64, 82, 93, 99, 105, 118–19, 154, 181, 381, 382, 473, 532
  amps in, 165–66
  art college and, 50
  heavy metal, 176, 185, 547, 567
  loudness of, 187
  progressive, 137, 567
  punk, 382–83, 473–74, 484–86, 490, 531, 549, 566, 567
"Rock and Roll," 254
*Rock and Roll Circus*, 177

Rock & Roll Hall of Fame, 572
Rockwell, John, 502
Roden, Jess, 122
Rodgers, Paul, 348, 354, 368, 373, 392, 563
*Rolling Stone* (magazine), 169, 180–81, 192,
    210, 235, 303, 304, 385, 389, 401,
    411–12, 462, 477, 486, 539, 543
Rolling Stones, 6, 17–18, 21–24, 47, 60,
    64, 68, 70–72, 108, 119, 121, 122, 139,
    149, 154, 177, 208, 223, 230, 255, 297,
    298, 348, 357, 374, 446, 453, 472, 515,
    529, 572
    *Exile on Main Street*, 293
    Led Zeppelin as compared with, 293–94,
        304, 307, 379, 410
    press and, 294, 307
    *Sticky Fingers*, 282, 286, 297
    taxes and, 420, 421
Rolling Stones Mobile Studio, 231, 233
Ronson, Mick, 476
Ronstadt, Linda, 125, 476
Roosters, 53
Ros, Edmundo, 127
Rose, Tim, 109, 114, 132, 133–35, 239
Rosenberg, Steve, 508–9
Rose Palace, 192
Rough Trade, 473
"Rover, The," 358, 383
Roxon, Lillian, 309
Roxy Music, 532, 545
Royal Albert Hall, 194, 224, 261, 335, 474,
    565, 566
Royal Garden Hotel, 518
"Royal Orleans," 451–52
Rundgren, Todd, 378, 533
Rush, 547
Rush, Otis, 21, 145, 177, 330–31

Sach, Cynthia, 468
Sade, Marquis de, 245
Safer, Janine, 237, 369, 409, 489, 491, 493,
    494, 497, 500–502, 505, 508–9, 512,
    516–17
Sales, Mick, 19
Samwell-Smith, Paul, 70–71, 75, 77, 78, 98
Sander, Ellen, 201–2, 306
*San Diego Union*, 416
San Francisco Bay Area, 168–70
*San Francisco Chronicle*, 506
*San Francisco Examiner*, 170

Santana, 545, 570
Savalas, Telly, 475
Savoy Brown, 239, 240
Scabies, Rat (Chris Miller), 486
*Scarecrow of Romney Marsh, The*, 350
Searchers, 161, 181
Seattle Pop Festival, 199
Secunda, Tony, 110
Seeger, Pete, 234
Seger, Bob, 531, 532
session work, 54–56
    of Jones, 6, 138–40, 153, 383, 569
    of Page, 2, 6, 51–52, 54–60, 64, 67–68, 77,
        104–5, 137, 139–40, 383
Sex Pistols, 485, 486, 532, 537, 567
Shadows, 45, 51, 120, 137
"Shake," 169
Shakedown Sound, 122
"Shake 'Em On Down," 357
Shakespeare, John, 54, 55
Sheehan, Dennis, 487, 551
Sheeley, Sharon, 61
"She Just Satisfies," 62
Shepperton Studios, 307–8, 530
Sheridan, Tony, 34
Sherman, Bobby, 329
"She Squeezed My Lemon," 188
Showco, 308, 393, 476, 490, 535, 557
"Sick Again," 363
Silverdome, 493
Silverhead, 316, 320, 438, 439
Simmons, Stan, 96
Simon, Carly, 476
Simon & Garfunkel, 473, 572
Simpson, Jim, 126, 129
"Since I've Been Loving You," 219, 224–26,
    237, 244, 450
Singer Bowl Music Festival, 196–97
Sir Lord Baltimore, 288
skiffle, 27–30, 93, 117–18
Slim, Memphis, 20–21, 120
Small Faces, 68, 83, 95–96, 108, 154, 183
Smith, Henry, 2, 4, 87, 159, 196, 197, 217,
    218, 229, 237, 238, 248, 249, 339
Smith, Jimmy, 136
Smith, Tom, 300
*Soft Machines, The* (Burroughs), 176
Sol Studios, 565, 566
Solters, Lee, 305–7
Solters/Sabinson/Roskin, 305

*Song Remains the Same, The,* 335–39, 349–52, 371–72, 384, 464–66, 471, 475–80
  premieres of, 475–79
  reviews of, 476–77, 479–0
  soundtrack for, 474–75
"Song Remains the Same, The," 286–87, 303
*Sounds,* 380, 398, 423, 462, 479–80, 534, 539, 543
"South Bound Suarez," 524
Southside Johnny and the Asbury Jukes, 533
Spann, Otis, 330
Spare, Austin Osman, 267
Speakeasy, 496
Spector, Phil, 69
Spectrum, 292
Spence, Lewis, 259, 260
Spencer Davis Group, 83, 107, 116
Spicer, John, 33, 35–40, 45, 49, 398
*Spinal Tap,* 476, 504
Spirit, 165, 169
Spooky Tooth, 223
Springfield, Dusty, 153–54, 213, 367, 369
Springfield, Tom, 213
Squeeze, 484
Squire, Chris, 155, 537, 568
"Stairway to Heaven," 288, 303, 333, 357, 510, 545
  Atlantic's plea for single of, 282
  first performance of, 273
  Live Aid performance of, 570, 571
  recording of, 261–64
  writing of, 249–50, 258–61
*Stairway to Heaven* (Cole), 205
Staple Singers, 19
*Star,* 315–16
Stargroves, 231–32, 286, 288, 290, 294–95, 358
Starr, Sable, 316, 318–20, 439
*Starship,* 329–30, 332, 337, 399–402, 405, 408, 415, 480, 487
Station Hotel, 24
Steele, Alison, 1
Steele, Tommy, 93
Stele of Revelation, 325–26, 385
Steppenwolf, 176
Stevens, Cat, 135
Stewart, Don, 45
Stewart, Ian ("Stu"), 15, 23, 100, 233, 254

Stewart, Rod, 5, 16, 18, 99, 105, 122, 196, 207, 334, 358, 367, 420, 503, 561
Stiff Records, 473, 485
Stigwood, Robert, 95–96
Stills, Stephen, 2, 155, 222, 545
Stockholm, 146, 214, 521–23
*Stockholm Daily News,* 147
Stone the Crows, 207–8, 292, 346, 348, 368, 373, 497
Stooges, 382, 473
"Stormy Monday," 225
Stranglers, 473, 539
Strummer, Joe, 473, 479
Studio Instrument Rentals, 444
"Sugar Mama," 202–3
Sullivan, Big Jim, 55–56, 140, 173
Sumlin, Hubert, 46
Sun Records, 26, 41, 43, 348
Sunset Sound, 271
Sunshine, Monty, 118
Superdome, 511
Superhype Music, 155
Surrey County Cricket Club, 270–71
Sutton Art College, 49–52
"Swan Song," 365
Swan Song Records, 366–70, 385–90, 429, 440, 461, 468–70, 481, 501, 502, 516, 547–48, 567
  acts passed up by, 386, 389–90
  acts signed to, 354–55, 368–70, 373–77, 385–86, 419, 423–25, 429–30, 438–41, 469, 483, 516–18
  Atlantic Records and, 347–49
  Bonham's death and, 559, 562
  Callan at, 483, 516, 547
  end of, 564
  Grant and, 366–68, 375–76, 385–87, 389, 390, 430, 440, 469, 470, 483, 518–19, 547–48
  Hoch at, 386–87, 389–90, 429–30, 440, 470, 483, 516
  King's Road offices of, 366–68, 374, 387
  launch parties for, 377–80, 387–89
  logo of, 373–74
  naming of, 349, 365, 367, 370, 373
  tax exile and, 429
Swingos, Jim, 492
Swingos Hotel, 492
Sykes, Roosevelt, 188
Sylvester, Ward, 329

Taj Mahal, 169
Talking Heads, 484, 543
Talmy, Shel, 58–59, 65, 69
Tampa, Fla., 312, 497–99, 500, 501
*Tampa Times*, 312
"Tangerine," 219, 244
Tate, Sharon, 203
tax exile, 419–20, 422, 425, 427–31, 434–37,
    441, 445, 451, 463
Taylor, Bobby, 33, 34, 48
"Tea for One," 450–51
Tea Party, 3–5, 7–11
10cc, 525
"Ten Little Indians," 174
Tennessee Teens, 121
Ten Years After, 3, 97, 131, 196
"Ten Years Gone," 360–61, 484
Terry, Sonny, 357
Texas International Pop Festival, 206
"Thank You," 202
Tharpe, Rosetta, 33
"That's the Way," 222, 226, 237
theremin, 185, 417
Them, 2, 60, 62
Thomas, Ray, 438, 504
Thompsett, Jim, 466
Thompson, Tony, 570, 472
Thorgerson, Storm, 297–301, 460,
    529, 530
Thrower, Percy, 274
Tidmarsh, Chris, *see* Christian, Neil
Tolinski, Brad, 149–50
"Tom Cat," 252
*Tommy*, 354, 359, 375, 384
Topham, Tony "Top," 71
Townshend, Pete, 28, 50, 59, 60, 81, 102,
    166, 292, 354, 359
Traffic, 108, 181, 223
"Train Kept a-Rollin'," 7, 11, 74, 141
"Trampled Under Foot," 361–62, 411
Trapeze, 117
Tremeloes, 181
"Tribute to Bert Berns," 148
Tridents, 54
Trident Studios, 474
Troggs, 102
Tropicana, 241
Troubadour, 239, 241
*Truth*, 99, 105, 142, 154, 171, 178, 180
Tutin, Dorothy, 458

2i's Coffee Bar, 93
Tyler, Steven, 11, 575

Uhelszki, Jaan, 487
Ulster Hall, 272–73
Ulvaeus, Björn, 523
United Artists, 425
University of Ohio, 192

Valens, Ritchie, 188, 255
Vangelis, 483
Van Halen, 547
Vanilla Fudge, 153, 154, 158, 160, 161, 165,
    196, 199–201, 206–7, 236, 561
Vaughan, Larry, 337
Velodromo Vigorelli, 276–77, 498
Velvet Underground, 297, 382, 473
Vibrators, 473
Vietnam War, 218
*Village Voice*, 396, 462
Vincent, Gene, 31, 34, 39, 40, 41, 55, 95, 96,
    118, 140
Virgin Records, 349

Wakeman, Rick, 479
Walker, T-Bone, 21–22
"Walter's Walk," 566
"Wanton Song, The," 362–63
Ward, Clifford T., 122
Warhol, Andy, 241, 297
Warner Bros., 152–53, 181, 465–66
Warner Chappell Music, 515–16
Washburn, Ray, 467, 523, 547, 558, 559, 563
*Washington Post*, 407, 495
*Washington Star*, 495
"Watch Your Step," 43, 188
Waterloo Station, 270–71
Waters, Muddy, 5, 14–15, 21, 46, 119, 120,
    174, 183–84, 252
Waters, Roger, 298, 431
Waterson, Tom, 207
Watts, Charlie, 15, 16, 23–24, 420
Wayne, Bruce, 200, 201
Way of Life, 125, 126, 129–31, 239
WEA, 535
"Wearing and Tearing," 566–67
Webb, Terry, 128
Weedon, Bert, 28
Weinstein, Deena, 190
Weiss, Joan, 367

Weiss, Steve, 153–54, 156, 158–59, 162, 165, 171, 197, 211, 283–84, 302, 305, 329, 330, 336, 337, 340–42, 347, 348, 366, 367, 488, 506, 508, 509, 511, 513, 516, 541, 555, 563, 564
    Bonham's death and, 561
    Led Zeppelin royalties, masters ownership, and music publishing deals made by, 515–16
Welch, Chris, 208–10, 235, 274, 307, 427–28, 463, 543
Wells, Frank, 466
Wenner, Jann, 411–12
"We're Gonna Groove," 565–66
West Park Pavilion, 455–57
Wexler, Jerry, 62, 153–56, 369–70, 374, 376–77
Wharton, Alex, 93
"What Is and What Should Never Be," 203
"What the World Needs Now Is Love," 63
Wheldon, Huw, 30
"When the Levee Breaks," 257, 258, 261, 358
Whisky a Go Go, 168, 189, 315, 439, 502
White, Alan, 568
White, Bukka, 357
White, Josh, 15, 364
"White Summer," 175
Who, 2, 6, 59–60, 81–83, 121, 122, 159, 161, 181, 194, 210, 214, 230, 249, 283–84, 352, 382, 391, 407, 472, 473, 479, 572
    Tommy, 354, 359, 375, 384
"Whole Lotta Love," 183–85, 212–14, 236, 282, 304, 333, 349, 358, 372
Wickham, Andy "Wipeout," 153
Wilde, Marty, 118
"Wild Thing," 102
Wilkins, Robert, 566
Williams, Anna, 35, 41
Williams, Big Joe, 119
Williams, Dave, 15, 17, 22, 23, 26, 28, 30–35, 41, 42–44, 46–47, 52, 426
Williams, Sally, 429, 514
Williamson, Sonny Boy, 21, 72, 119, 120, 273
Wilson, B. J., 114

Wilson, Ann and Nancy, 191, 389
Wilson, Shirley, 144
Winwood, Muff, 83
Wishbone Ash, 297
Witherspoon, Jimmy, 21, 119
Winwood, Steve, 83, 107–8, 111, 122
Wolverhampton Wanderers (Wolves), 480, 518
Wolverly Memorial Hall, 520
Wonder, Stevie, 67, 123, 362, 522
Wonderwall, 335
Wood, Krissy, 414
Wood, Ronnie, 5, 50, 99, 294, 414, 500, 541
Wood, Roy, 560
Woodstock Music Festival, 195, 206, 227, 228
Wray, Link, 47, 119
Wren, Andy, 65
Wright, Joe, 197–98, 205–6
Wyatt, Rod, 32–33, 47
Wyman, Bill, 23, 102, 282, 379, 420
Wynn, Peter, 118

XYZ, 568

Yardbirds, 2, 7, 18, 71–80, 82, 85–91, 97–105, 108, 114, 115, 120, 122, 135, 142, 145, 156–60, 165, 167, 174, 177, 178, 256, 297, 357, 382, 383, 472
    Page in, 2, 5, 24, 73, 77–80, 85–90, 97–101, 103, 104, 175–76, 178, 219–20, 226, 398
    see also New Yardbirds
Yes, 155, 181, 483, 537, 568
"You Need Love," 21, 183
"You Need Loving," 183
Youngbloods, 199
"Your Time Is Gonna Come," 147, 175
"You Shook Me," 1, 174, 178

Zappa, Frank, 114, 201, 529
Zeppelin, Eva von, 215
Zeppelin, Ferdinand von, 171, 215
Zeppelins, 209
    Hindenburg, 171